REMAKING RELAPSE PREVENTION WITH SEX OFFENDERS

REMAKING RELAPSE PREVENTION WITH SEX OFFENDERS

A Sourcebook

D. Richard Laws
Stephen M. Hudson
Tony Ward

Editors

Sage Publications, Inc.
International Educational and Professional Publisher
Thousand Oaks ▪ London ▪ New Delhi

For information:

Sage Publications, Inc.
2455 Teller Road
Thousand Oaks, California 91320
E-mail: order@sagepub.com

Sage Publications Ltd.
6 Bonhill Street
London EC2A 4PU
United Kingdom

Sage Publications India Pvt. Ltd.
M-32 Market
Greater Kailash I
New Delhi 110 048 India

Printed in the United States of America

Library of Congress Cataloging-in-Publication Data

Laws, Richard.
    Remaking relapse prevention with sex offenders: A sourcebook / edited by D. Richard Laws, Stephen M. Hudson, and Tony Ward.
        p.   cm.
    Includes bibliographical references and index.
    ISBN 0-7619-1887-6 (cloth: alk. Paper)
    1. Sex offenders—Rehabilitation. 2. Sex crimes—Prevention. I. Laws, D. Richard. II. Ward, Tony. III. Hudson, Stephen M.
RC560.S47 R46 2000
616.85'83—dc21   00-008365

This book is printed on acid-free paper.

00   01   02   03   04   05   06   7   6   5   4   3   2   1

Acquisition Editor:	C. Terry Hendrix
Editorial Assistant:	Anna Howland
Production Editor:	Sanford Robinson
Editorial Assistant:	Cindy Bear
Typesetter:	Tina Hill
Indexer:	Will Ragsdale
Cover Designer:	Michelle Lee

Contents

PART VI. PROGRAMS: MAJOR INTERVENTIONS USING RELAPSE PREVENTION

PART VII. RELAPSE PREVENTION APPLIED TO SPECIAL POPULATIONS

PART VIII. THE BOTTOM LINE

PART IX. THE WAY FORWARD

Foreword

This book contains a wealth of information about the current status of relapse prevention (RP) in the treatment of sex offenders. More than 10 years have passed since the publication of Richard Laws's first edited book on this topic in 1989. Almost 20 years have gone by since the RP model was initially formulated as a cognitive-behavioral treatment approach for individuals with alcohol or drug problems. It was not until the early 1980s that several of us met at Atascadero State Hospital in California to discuss the potential application of RP to the treatment of sex offenders. At that meeting, Bill George and Janice Marques, two former students (now colleagues) of mine, met with Richard Laws, Bill Pithers, and other professional staff at the hospital and began to develop the foundation of applying RP to the problem of sex offending. As the chapters in this volume clearly attest, we have come a long way from this early work in investigating the parallels and differences between addiction treatment and developing successful interventions for illicit and harmful sexual behavior. It is also clear that we have a long way to go. As stated by many authors, modifications are needed in both the theoretical understanding of the determinants of sexual offending and the development of more effective treatment modalities that are linked to this conceptual underpinning.

The same process of reformulating and extending the original RP model in the treatment of addictive behaviors is currently under way. Reviews of RP outcome studies (including a recent comprehensive meta-analysis) in the alcohol, smoking, and other drug treatment literature have revealed a mixed picture. Most studies do not demonstrate that RP programs are associated with higher rates of abstinence as compared to other treatment approaches. For example, the results of "Project Match," a large controlled trial comparing three approaches in the treatment of alcohol dependence (motivational enhancement therapy, Alcoholics Anonymous/12-step facilitation, or cognitive-behavioral treatment based largely on RP), revealed that the three treatment conditions did not differ significantly in terms of overall abstinence rates at the 1- or 2-year follow-up assessments. These results are similar to those obtained in other drug treatment studies (e.g., for smoking or cocaine addiction) that have evaluated RP. Although these studies show that abstinence rates are not usually significantly reduced by participation in RP treatment, results often show a significant reduction in relapse rates for those who engage in any substance use following completion of treatment (e.g., increased temporal delay prior to an initial lapse, reduced magnitude or extent of relapse episodes). As such, RP programs appear to be more effective in relapse management than in preventing any relapse from occurring. These findings support the hypothesis that RP may be more effective as a harm reduction approach than as an intervention designed to inculcate total abstinence in drug dependency treatment.

The other finding noted by reviewers of the RP drug treatment literature is that these programs frequently show a "delayed emergent effect" for positive treatment outcomes. Studies comparing pharmacotherapy with RP in the treatment of cocaine dependency have shown that, although both treatment approaches appear to have equivalent effects early in the posttreatment period, more delayed follow-up assessments (1 year or longer) tend to show that RP is associated with greater consolidation of treatment gains compared to control conditions. The finding that RP treatment effects may emerge later in time is consistent with a learning-based model in which new coping skills and improved self-regulation are acquired and improve over time with practice, particularly if it is gradually reinforced by the benefits of abstinence or less harmful drug use.

Since the publication of our RP book, much new work has evolved in the addiction treatment field. Two developments have had major impacts. The first is the "stages of change" model originally developed by Prochaska and DiClemente to describe the various stages that people go through in their attempts to quit smoking: precontemplation and contemplation for change, preparation and action in intiating change, and long-term maintenance or relapse. In the early movement from "precontemplation" to "contemplation," the major focus is on motivation—considering the "pros and cons" of smoking or quitting, enhancing motivation for change, getting prepared to take action, and so on. The second influential development has been the emergence of "motivational interviewing" or what Miller and Rollnick have called motivational enhancement therapy (MET). Numerous studies have shown that MET can enhance commitment to treatment or self-initiated change in the "action" stage. Professional treatment matching or consumer choice among various treatment options is also promoted to enhance commitment to the action stage. The model postulates maintenance as a critical final stage in which individuals either successfully maintain treatment gains (such as long-term abstinence) or become involved in the relapse process. Most addiction clients are unsuccessful in maintaining total abstinence in any one quit attempt, although many are successful in the long run through participation in formal treatment or self-initiated trials over time.

It is in the maintenance stage that RP appears to have its greatest impact. We originally described RP as a maintenance stage intervention rather than as a complete "stand-alone" program that would embrace both the contemplation and action stages of the behavior change process. As such, RP can be considered as one component of a broad-spectrum cognitive-behavioral approach that also includes relevant interventions for the other stages of change, including MET for clients who are not yet ready or willing to make a firm commitment to abstinence in the action stage. Detailed assessment of the client's problem may reveal important individual differences that may dictate differential treatment plans (treatment matching or informed consumer choice among treatment options).

Motivation and skill acquisition are both essential ingredients of behavior change. As the old saying indicates, "Where there's a will, there's a way"—there needs to be both the "will" (motivated commitment to change) and a "way" (practicing more adaptive coping skills) to change. Whereas motivation addresses the issue of *why* to change in the initial commitment to action, RP can provide the means of *how* to change.

RP is best described as a self-management approach to behavior change. Therapists who are presenting RP to clients sometimes describe it as similar to driver-training programs. Driving is a unique behavior in that it involves both personal freedom and responsibility: One is free to explore the open road, but one must do so in a responsible manner. No matter what happens on the trip, the driver is always ultimately responsible for his or her actions. This model of *auto-regulation* (one of the older terms used to describe self-management) fits well as an analogue to the stages-of-change model that posits various components of the "journey" of behavior change. Of course, students who sign up for "driver's ed" or other driving training programs are already motivated to learn how to drive. These programs have an additional goal of harm reduction in that they attempt to teach novice drivers to acquire and maintain safe driving skills designed to protect both the driver and others who may be affected by the driver's behavior. As such, RP teaches skills that assist the driver how to proceed safely on his or her journey, with a focus on how to proceed in the ever-changing travel environment by encouraging both enhanced awareness and the learning of appropriate driving skills.

In terms of enhanced awareness, drivers are encouraged to keep their hands on the wheel and their eyes on the road ahead (as well as keeping an eye on the road behind in the rearview mirror)—to watch for warning signals, possible sudden detours or dead-ends, and other hazards of the road (especially the behavior of other drivers and pedestrians). In the terminology of RP, drivers need to be aware of "seemingly unimportant decisions" that may lead them into a "slippery slope" where they could end up in the ditch or stuck in "downtown Reno." To facilitate appropriate and safe driving skills, enhanced awareness facilitates better coping strategies on the road, including both cognitive strategies (consulting road maps and planning ahead to avoid high-risk situations) and behavioral skills (e.g., knowing how to steer properly, when to put on the brakes, when and how to pass safely, and when it is time to pull over at a rest stop). What is the parallel motivation for engaging in safe and responsible behavior for sex offenders? For those who are incarcerated, it is the desire to be free, to drive again on the open road, and to pursue one's own destination goals with the dignity that comes from being "back on track" and with the intention of not harming oneself or others. Although driving is not allowed in prison, one can still learn to walk a new path of personal change. Walking is better than stalking.

From a clinical perspective, RP is an individualized approach that varies from driver to driver. Although some "core" components of RP can be taught in groups based on standardized treatment manuals, an individualized approach can help tailor the core elements to meet the individual differences of participants. The heart of driver training is individualized training with the driver behind the wheel. Here the role of the therapist is like that of a "copilot," as is the case with some driver training programs in which the car is equipped with two steering wheels, one for the driver and the other for the trainer. This is a good strategy to employ in RP programs for either addiction or sexual offending problems. Often, the best clinical results occur when there is an active mutual collaboration between the client (driver) and therapist (trainer): Both are mutually responsible for tailoring the treatment to the client's unique characteristics (e.g., different styles of offending). To the extent that the therapist and client can work together as partners in developing an individualized treatment plan, the client is likely to assume a greater stakeholder role in the treatment process. As noted by several authors, RP can also provide a common language for the client and therapist to discuss offending behavior. It also provides a flexible biopsychosocial model of the etiology of the problem, one that fosters both an attitude of acceptance (in which it is hoped that the client comes to accept responsibility for causing harm and to accept responsibility for change) and optimism for the potential of successful change. As one sex offender we talked to during the early Atascadero visit (after discussing possible parallels between recovery from addiction and recovery from offending behavior) said, "You mean I could be like an alcoholic? Alcoholics can recover from their addiction to alcohol, so why can't sex offenders?" Most of us believe that sex offenders are made, not born that way. Most developed their affliction by some combination of Freudian, Pavlovian, and Skinnerian conditioning. Despite the forces of conditioning, it is possible for offenders to "remake" their lives by changing their behavior.

One problem with an individualized RP treatment approach is that it creates problems for treatment outcome researchers who often prefer a standardized treatment protocol that can be manualized and followed in a systematic step-by-step fashion. Participants can then be randomly assigned to receive RP or some other comparison condition. There is merit to this argument, and it appears that RP means a lot of different things to different treatment providers. To many, RP has taken on the meaning of a treatment goal rather than a specific cognitive-behavioral treatment method. In the addiction treatment literature, many different programs have taken on the goal of RP, including pharmacotherapy, various forms of psychotherapy and behavior therapy, and even incarceration itself. From this broad perspective, anything that prevents relapse could be considered an effective intervention. Here, the use of RP as a goal rather than a treatment model reflects the growing awareness that interventions geared to the maintenance stage of behavior change are necessary. Even within the cognitive-behavioral model of RP, a wide variety of cognitive and behavioral assessment and treatment approaches are described, based on social learning theory and its application to the modification of addictive behaviors. As a result, there is no standard definition of RP, and treatment protocols often integrate several RP treatment approaches into a single package, making it difficult for researchers to tease out effective or ineffective components. Despite these methodological problems, many authors in this book have put forth testable hypotheses about what works and what does not in RP. Future revisions of the model will benefit from this important and needed research.

The discussion of the potential overlap between RP and harm reduction (HR) approaches discussed in this book is both stimulating and controversial. Whereas RP is usually described as an individual treatment approach, HR programs are typically more comprehensive in scope, extending the treatment model by including both environmental changes and public policy approaches. To return to the example of driver training as an individualized approach, HR also focuses on a wider approach to reducing harm, including the provision of a safer environment (safer cars and highways) as well as establishing policies designed to protect both the driver and the larger community (e.g., speed limits, low blood-alcohol limits for driving, mandated use of seat belts, etc.). A similar comprehensive approach in working with sex offenders is recommended by several authors in this book. RP programs need to be integrated into the larger context associated with posttreatment supervision and a safe return to the community. Another advantage of the HR model is that it facilitates both primary and secondary prevention goals and may provide access to active offenders by increased outreach and intervention.

Overall, this book is a rich source of information on the application of RP with sex offenders. It presents readers promising directions for change and areas that need revision based on new research findings and the integration of emerging theoretical models that show considerable promise in this field (especially harm reduction and behavioral economics, both of which are covered in different chapters). All of this is valuable "grist for the mill" as we enter the new millennium and strive to develop more effective treatment programs. I like to think of the original statement of the RP model in the 1985 book as a prototype, a vehicle (the 1985 RP model) that was designed to introduce a cognitive-behavioral approach to the addiction treatment field that was previously dominated by a biological disease model of etiology and a strict adherence to 12-step groups such as Alcoholics Anonymous as the only acceptable approach to treatment. Although there have been essentially no changes in the 12-step approach since its origins more than 50 years ago, RP continues to evolve and change based on research findings and clinical experience. This material in this book should help us construct a better, safer vehicle for the treatment of sex offenders in the new millennium.

G. Alan Marlatt
University of Washington

PART I

RELAPSE PREVENTION IN HISTORICAL PERSPECTIVE

CHAPTER 1

The Original Model of Relapse Prevention With Sex Offenders

Promises Unfulfilled

D. RICHARD LAWS
Forensic Psychiatric Services Commission, British Columbia

STEPHEN M. HUDSON
University of Canterbury, New Zealand

TONY WARD
University of Melbourne, Australia

Historical Background

In 1978, Janice Marques, then a psychology intern from the University of Washington in Seattle, showed the senior author a prepublication manuscript by G. Alan Marlatt titled "Determinants of Relapse." Marlatt and his colleagues had developed a cognitive-behavioral intervention, which they had named "relapse prevention," and Marques believed that this could be extended to the treatment of sex offenders. This monograph (Marlatt, 1980) contained some of the early conceptualizations of the formal statement of the treatment that Marlatt and Gordon (1985) would eventually publish. Relapse prevention (RP) has its roots in the drug and alcohol field. Workers had routinely observed that a

AUTHORS' NOTE: Portions of this chapter previously appeared in Laws, D. R. (1999). Relapse prevention: The state of the art. *Journal of Interpersonal Violence, 14,* 285-302, and Ward, T., & Hudson, S. M. (1996). Relapse prevention: A critical analysis. *Sexual Abuse: A Journal of Research and Treatment, 8,* 177-200.

variety of interventions could terminate or moderate addiction to heroin, alcohol, or tobacco. It was at the end of the cessation-oriented treatment that the problems began. Hunt, Barnett, and Branch (1971) observed that with no further intervention past the point of cessation, relapse rates approached 80% over the following 12 months. The vast majority of relapses occurred within the first 3 months following the end of the treatment. Marlatt and his colleagues made a simple conclusion. They reasoned that given the alarming failure rate following apparently successful treatment for addiction, it should be possible to devise a strategy that would *maintain* the effects of treatment. So the original RP for addictions was conceptualized as a *maintenance strategy* and not a formal treatment (Marlatt & Gordon, 1985). Following treatment, the thinking went, the client would inevitably find himself or herself in risky situations or in the presence of factors associated with various risks. If the client learned self-management strategies to deal with these threats to abstinence, then the effects of the cessation-oriented treatment should be maintained. So, although it may still be used in the classical sense as only a maintenance program, today RP would more likely be a package of self-management procedures and a variety of other self-empowering interventions such as anger management, social skills training, assertion training, and so on. In this latter-day incarnation, RP becomes both the cessation-oriented treatment and the maintenance strategy. The underlying notion of RP—that there is no reason to expect treatment effects to persist very long after the end of formal treatment—seemed especially true of classical addictive behaviors such as alcohol and drug abuse, and the original efforts were applied in those areas. More recently, Laws (1995) has suggested that RP might be applied equally effectively to virtually any disorder of impulse control such as compulsive sexual behavior, compulsive gambling, some forms of sexual deviance, problem drinking, compulsive spending, shoplifting, or interpersonal violence.

At the same time that original RP was under development, cognitive-behavioral treatment of sex offenders was also emerging. This integrated effort began to be recognized around 1975 and was spearheaded primarily by Abel and his colleagues (Abel, Becker, Cunningham-Rathner, Rouleau, Kaplan, & Reich, 1984; Abel, Blanchard, & Becker, 1978). The continued development of integrated programs continued for the next 25 years. Following the appearance of the Marlatt (1980) monograph, Pithers, Marques, Gibat, and Marlatt (1983) published the first statement describing the application of RP to sex offenders. That paper has set the standard for much of what has followed. Within the first 10 years, variations of that model appeared (Marques, Day, Nelson, & Miner, 1989; Pithers, 1990, 1991; Pithers, Martin, & Cumming, 1989). Today, 16 years later, virtually any sex offender treatment program that uses RP will use at least some elements of these earlier program descriptions. The classical RP model proposed by Marlatt (1980, 1985) has changed very little in the past 20 years, and this is equally true of the sex offender variation. RP or some variation of it has become the treatment of choice for sex offenders. Its very popularity, however, has been its undoing.

When *Relapse Prevention With Sex Offenders* was published (Laws, 1989), the editor cautioned the readers with the following prefatory remarks:

> Simply because we have gathered together a great variety of apparently face-valid procedures in a book, offered some statistical analyses, and come to optimistic, if tentative conclusions, that in no way *proves* that RP is an effective treatment for sex offenders. There is *no* definitive evidence, here or anywhere else, that RP or any other treatment is effective over the long haul with this difficult clientele. Although sex offenders have been treated for decades it has only been in very recent years that treatment has begun to be carefully documented and follow-up carefully monitored. Sadly, too few have been carefully treated, and even fewer carefully followed for long periods, to warrant excessive optimism. (p. ix)

Regrettably, it seems that few people paid attention. Although it was not a program statement or a treatment manual, the book was embraced as received wisdom by many. Ten years later, local modifications have been made to the model, but the basic structure has stayed the same. This broad acceptance, the ease of implementation, and striking face validity have served to preclude empirical evaluation. Selective reviews such as that of Marshall, Jones, Ward, Johnston, and Barbaree (1991) have bolstered this effect with their enthusiastic nomination of cognitive-behavior therapy as the treatment of choice for sex offenders. Reviews such as Marshall et al.'s, concluding that treatment of sex offenders works, are widely viewed as a vigorous riposte to the widely misunderstood and unappreciated review of Furby, Weinrott, and Blackshaw (1989).

The Original Model of RP

The original theoretical framework of RP may be seen in Marlatt (1985). In an analysis of the model, Laws (1995) divided RP theory into two parts: (a) how people get into high-risk situations (originally, covert antecedents of relapse) and (b) how people can manage high-risk situations (originally, determinants of relapse).

Marlatt (1985) suggested that lifestyle imbalance (more *shoulds* than *wants*) could create a desire for some sort of indulgence or immediate gratification (alcohol, drugs, sexual indulgence). These desires encourage positive expectancies about engaging in the prohibited behavior. Coupled with these urges and craving are a series of small decisions (now called *seemingly irrelevant decisions* or SIDs), which lead the individual closer and closer to a lapse that is facilitated by rationalization and denial. All of this eventually leads the individual into a high-risk situation. It is at this point that relapse prevention is implemented.

Whether the individual can manage the threat of a high-risk situation depends on the availability of effective coping responses and the will to use them. If the coping response is used, self-efficacy will increase, and the probability of relapse will decrease. If effective coping responses are not available, self-efficacy will decrease. This state may encourage the individual to believe that engaging in the prohibited behavior will produce a positive outcome, and a lapse may then follow. The lapse may then lead to the abstinence violation effect (AVE), the recognition that a self-imposed rule has been violated. This, in turn, may produce dissonance, a self-attribution of failure, and a perception of loss of control. These elements in combination are believed to promote relapse. The job of relapse prevention, then, is to teach recognition of risk and build self-management skills.

Criticisms of the Original RP Model

The original RP model suffers from a number of conceptual and empirical problems (Ward & Hudson, 1996). What follows is a consideration of the more significant of these.

Interactions and Decision Making

Although Marlatt (1985) stresses the importance of the interactions between the multiple factors leading both to the establishment of addictive disorders and relapse, his RP model does not adequately reflect these relationships. He does not convincingly address the relationships between lapses, high-risk situations, apparently irrelevant decisions, and so on. Individuals with addictive disorders, who are committed to abstinence, do not tend to relapse in a dichotomous fashion. Frequently, a number of feedback loops or interactions between the various components eventually may lead to a relapse (Hall, 1989; Kirkley & Fisher, 1988; Saunders & Allsop, 1987). For example, an individual might move back and forth from lifestyle stresses to high-risk situations several times before finally relapsing.

A related issue is the difficulty determining when a lapse becomes a relapse. Differences in defining a lapse lead to different definitions of relapse because these are logically related. For example, is a relapse a return to an individual's previous level of drug taking, or simply use that leads to problems? If the former is used to distinguish between a lapse and a relapse, then someone whose drug taking at less than previous levels was still adversely affecting his or her job and relationships would not be seen as relapsing. However, he or she would still

require treatment. If the latter criterion was used, then there remains the difficult issue of deciding what level of life problems suggests that a relapse has
occurred.

Marlatt (1985) consistently emphasizes the covert route to relapse—
specifically, the role of apparently irrelevant decisions and maladaptive decision making in creating high-risk situations and ultimately relapse. He also
suggests that stress reduces cognitive capacity and results in simplistic and concrete thinking. Furthermore, he argues that covert planning reflects the desire to
avoid self-criticism and social disapproval.

The major problem with this pathway and his explanation is that it is not clear
how such planning occurs and what underlying mechanisms are involved. It
seems to require unconscious thinking and defense mechanisms that involve
complex cognitive processes inaccessible to consciousness. This has the effect
of raising more questions than it answers. For example, it does not explain how
an individual whose thinking is adversely affected by stress manages to carefully plan to set up lapse and relapse opportunities. What is the relationship
between the surface cognitive distortions and the underlying covert plans and
goals? Marlatt (1985) places a large burden on the cognitive capacity of individuals who are struggling to comply with their abstinence rules. Certainly,
many clinicians have noted the importance of planning regarding relapse and
the person's reported lack of awareness of this. However, Marlatt has arguably
merely described this phenomenon, not explained it. In a later chapter, we outline a self-regulation model of the relapse process and offer an account of cognitive mechanisms capable of generating these kinds of unconscious decisions
(Ward & Hudson, 2000 [this volume]).

A related criticism is that Marlatt (1985) appears to support the existence of
unconscious desires. He argues that apparently irrelevant decisions are preceded by a desire for indulgence—for example, "I owe myself a drink." This is
said to be part of the process that leads to the setting up of high-risk situations by
the way of apparently irrelevant decisions. The problem concerns the relationship between this desire for indulgence and the subsequent covert planning. If
the individual is aware of the desire to indulge, the link between this conscious
desire and subsequent events would be obvious. This challenges the irrelevance
of apparently irrelevant decisions because the goal of satisfying the individual's desire would be clear.

Therefore, if the individual is in fact planning covertly, then the desire for
indulgence must also be unconscious. Although the existence of unconscious
desires may not be objectionable to some therapists and may in fact follow from
a comprehensive theory of the relapse process, it is not usually associated with
a social learning perspective. One of the major assumptions of mainstream
cognitive-behavioral approaches is that there is no need for the concept of a
dynamic unconscious to explain human behavior (Salkovskis, 1996). The pos-
tulation of unconscious desires for indulgence does appear to suggest such a

view (see Bargh & Barndollar, 1996, for a plausible explanation of uncon-sciously motivated behavior).

Marlatt (1985) needs a mechanism that explains how these processes can operate. We used the concept of cognitive deconstruction to account for cogni-tive and affective deficits in sex offenders (Ward, Hudson, & Marshall, 1995), which may provide what is needed. From this perspective, a desire for in-dulgence may be initially conscious and precipitate the processes resulting in cognitive deconstruction. The client may therefore fail to appreciate the rela-tionship between this desire and subsequent planning because of the effects of deconstruction, impaired self-awareness, and metacognitive functioning.

High-Risk Situations

In a recent article, Saunders and Houghton (1996) argue that Marlatt's (1985) typology of high-risk situations fails to capture the complexity of pre-cursors to relapse. Research using Marlatt's typology reveals that it suffers from poor reliability, and therefore its clinical applicability is questionable (Saunders & Houghton, 1996). They state that clinical descriptions of relapse are typically hard to classify and that relapse can be caused by a multitude of factors and occur in a variety of settings. In addition, substance-related cues appear to play a more important role in precipitating the resumption of addic-tive behavior than Marlatt indicates (see below).

We suggest that it is not clear why individuals who are committed to absti-nence fail to cope effectively in high-risk situations. Marlatt (1985) makes the assumption that they lack adequate coping skills. However, there is some doubt about this, and a major puzzle in the addiction area is why people often report lapsing in situations in which they would normally cope (Rohsenow, Niaura, Childress, Abrams, & Monti, 1991; Saunders & Allsop, 1987; Saunders & Houghton, 1996). Why do they fail to use their coping skills in these high-risk situations on some occasions? If individuals possess the necessary coping skills but fail to implement them for some reason, then a major therapeutic task is to focus on skill access rather than development. Allsop and Saunders emphasize the addicted individual's decision to quit drugs as an integral part of recovering from addiction; the decision to remain abstinent involves a weigh-ing up of the values associated with drug taking versus those of a drug-free life (Saunders & Allsop, 1987; Saunders & Houghton, 1996). Similarly, relapse involves a rational decision to resume drug taking because of its perceived benefits.

Another criticism concerns Marlatt's (1985) definition of high-risk situa-tion, at least vis-à-vis the alternative pathways. It appears that different types of high-risk situations play different roles in relapse and are associated with dif-ferent mechanisms. For example, someone who is in a situation containing addictive stimuli (e.g., a bar) may relapse because of a lack of effective coping skills. However, for a person who is alone and depressed but without any access to addictive substance, further steps are needed that ultimately involve either entering such an environment (i.e., an additional high-risk situation) or purchasing alcohol.

A related problem results from defining high-risk situations in phenomenological terms, that is, when a person's sense of control over behavior related to his or her addiction is threatened. This fails to account for a number of alternatives. First, if cognitive distortions are present, individuals may not recognize high-risk situations as threats to behavioral control. However, it would still make sense to speak of the situation in these terms when taking into account their addiction history. Second, alternatively, a person may feel his or her control is threatened when there is realistically little possibility of relapse. As a result, he or she may be excessively anxious and therefore hypervigilant. We suggest that it would be helpful to restrict the use of the term *high-risk situation* to external situations in which the appropriate addictive stimuli are present, for example, the presence of a drink or potential victim. Internal factors such as negative mood states would then become risk factors or high-risk elements, which may lead to high-risk situations by the way of apparently irrelevant decisions or other mechanisms.

Marlatt (1985) has suggested at least six possible mechanisms facilitating the move from a high-risk situation to a lapse. First, it is possible that individuals could lapse in a high-risk situation simply because they lack the skills to cope effectively. This is the kind of scenario that he frequently cites in his discussion of the relapse process. For example, a person who lacks the assertiveness skills to refuse his boss's offer of a drink might very quickly find himself losing control over his alcohol intake. This lapse could result in an intense AVE and subsequent relapse. Alternatively, the individual may excuse his "mistake" by blaming his employer.

Second, the negative affect created by lifestyle imbalance could result in a failure to employ assertiveness skills in the individual's repertoire when needed. The individual remains passive, frequently seeing himself or herself as deserving the indulgences anyway, and does not actively attempt to cope with the high-risk situation. The experience of negative affect could create a sense of hopelessness and relentless self-criticism. These factors could lead directly to a lapse. Third, negative affect created by lifestyle imbalance (e.g., a high-risk situation) could lead to the direct activation of old (addictive) coping strategies and result in a lapse. In this situation, there is an active decision to use a particular coping strategy (rather than a passive failure to resist)—for example, drinking alcohol—to escape from negative affect. This represents a misregulation strategy (see below).

Fourth, the negative affect created by lowered self-efficacy with respect to restraint, loss of control, and helplessness could lead to the use of addictive substances or behaviors to cope. This is a different type of negative affect than that mentioned earlier because it emerges as a result of a failure to manage early aspects of a high-risk situation, rather than from precursors to the high-risk situation such as lifestyle imbalance. Fifth, the failure to cope and lowered levels of self-efficacy could be mediated by attributions that lead to the perception of diminished control. This is a purely cognitive pathway. Finally, the exclusive focus on the immediate and pleasurable consequences in a high-risk situation and the consequent narrowing of attention and therefore of problem-solving options could result in a lapse. This is what Marlatt (1985) terms the *problem of immediate gratification.*

These multiple and competing mechanisms result from the heterogeneity of high-risk situations, each involving different transitional mechanisms. For example, in a situationally defined high-risk situation, such as being in a bar, the presence of alcohol could result in a lapse in association with a lack of coping skills. However, in internal high-risk situations, such as depression, a lack of coping skills is not enough to lead directly to a lapse; the presence of alcohol is required with an active decision to drink.

Conditioning Factors

A related criticism involves the important role of motivation invoked by Marlatt (1985) in explaining the shift from a high-risk situation to a lapse. The perceived attraction of the addictive substance or activity is viewed as outweighing the longer-term negative consequences. Marlatt effectively collapses two different motivational processes that can function independently. First, he argues that the urges and cravings elicited by stimuli in high-risk situations function to push or drive the individual to indulge—a conditioning perspective. Alternatively, he emphasizes the importance of expectations in facilitating the transition from a high-risk situation to a lapse—a cognitive perspective. These processes can function quite independently, and it is confusing to combine them in this manner; lapses can occur because of low efficacy concerning restraint or overwhelming urges to indulge. Perhaps each has a role to play in different high-risk situations, or, in addition, each may be differentially important in different addictive disorders or in different individuals.

Another issue concerns the relationship between conditioned craving and a lapse or a relapse. Why a person who is committed to abstinence focuses only on the immediate consequences in high-risk situations and "forgets" or ignores what he or she has experienced in the past needs explanation. Why do appetitive processes (problem of immediate gratification) exercise such influence, and what are the mechanisms underlying this process?

Marlatt (1985) appeals partly to conditioning theory to account for urges and cravings. He stresses that classical conditioning processes are likely to exert an influence through positive outcome expectancies (a cognitive factor) and notes that most cravings occur in the absence of drug-related cues. For Marlatt, the likelihood that an individual will return to drug use depends on a lack of skills to cope with a high-risk situation. Decreased self-efficacy follows a failure to effectively manage high-risk situations and leads to a strong desire for the effect of a drug or addictive behavior. Therefore, cognitive factors are causally superordinate over conditioning processes.

There have been three influential behavioral theories of relapse in the addictions area: the withdrawal, compensatory, and appetitive models (Niaura et al., 1988). Contrary to Marlatt's (1985) claim, none requires that drug-related cues be present for craving to occur. The failure to cope with a high-risk situation could result in feelings of inadequacy or another negative emotion. These emotions may have been associated with drug taking in the past and therefore elicit a strong desire to take the drug. Alternatively, the association of cues with the positive affective state generated by a drug could lead directly to craving. In either case, the crucial mechanism underlying drug-seeking behavior is a conditioned response; positive outcome expectancies are the product of conditioning and not hypothesized to be causally related to relapse.

Second, these conditioning models of relapse do not assume that a lack of coping skills (as opposed to a failure to implement skills already in an individual's repertoire) is necessary for conditioning processes to exert an influence on relapse or to increase the attractiveness of using drugs (or engaging in the addictive behavior) as a means of dealing with a situation. Third, cognitive factors are not thought to be primary causes of addictive behavior. Relapse occurs because behavioral control is undermined by a strong desire for the effect of the drug or addictive behavior.

Although Marlatt's (1985) attempt to subordinate conditioning processes to cognitive ones is consistent with his social learning approach, it does not exclude the viability of a conditioning explanation. The available research data suggest that conditioning factors do play an important part in causing relapse in the addiction area, and at this point, the data tend to support the appetitive theory (Niaura et al., 1988; Rohsenow et al., 1991). Therefore, it is quite conceivable that cognitive processes play a relatively unimportant role in the generation of desires for drug effects.

The Abstinence Violation Effect

There are also a number of problems with Marlatt's (1985) formulation of the abstinence violation effect. Marlatt uses a variety of conceptual sources in his formulation of the AVE. We have argued that the integration of such diverse theories has made his analysis somewhat cumbersome and has led to inadequacies (Hudson, Ward, & Marshall, 1992). This has resulted in a narrowing of the range of application of the abstinence violation effect (and related attributional processes) and in the failure to accommodate the full number of attributional pathways to relapse or sexual offending. Because of this, Marlatt has failed to include in his model of the relapse process a number of important behavioral possibilities that are relevant to the conceptualization of relapse and critical to intervention.

The essence of the problem with the abstinence violation effect as currently conceptualized is the reliance on Weiner's (1972) earlier work, which means that causes are defined on an a priori basis (e.g., luck, effort, ability). The use of this older version is important for two reasons. This narrow view of attribution has meant Marlatt (1985) needed to broaden the theoretical base to include constructs such as objective self-awareness to account for the abstinence violation effect phenomena. This is cumbersome. Second, this reliance on Weiner's version leads to a narrower view of the possibilities involved in the relapse processes than is desirable.

Both of these problems are avoided by using the more recent and broader attributional theory proposed by Weiner in 1986. The use of Weiner's (1972) earlier theory ignores that attributions represent naive causal explanations and are therefore best construed as lying along dimensions such as locus, stability, and controllability (Weiner, 1986) rather than representing categorical choices between discrete alternative explanations. An illustration of Marlatt's (1985) confusion between the type of causes and causal dimensions is his translation of Weiner's earlier "basic causes," such as ability (a stable internal factor) to coping skills (unstable internal factor). This is not necessary if a person is rating an attribution directly onto attributional dimensions.

Marlatt (1985) also fails to distinguish between different kinds of affect or emotions and their possible differential impact on behavior. In his recent revision of attributional theory, Weiner (1986) explicitly argues that different emotions occur as a consequence of different causal inferences (via dimensional loading). These emotions, in turn, have different effects on behavior because of their different information value.

The examples of shame and guilt illustrate the relationship between causal dimensions and emotions. Shame arises when the cause of some negative event is attributed to internal, uncontrollable factors such as a lack of ability, whereas guilt arises from attributions to internal but controllable factors such as a lack of effort. As a consequence, these two emotions are likely to have quite different motivational consequences, both when these emotions arise and in terms of avoiding future risks. For example, if an alcohol-dependent individual committed to abstinence blames himself for not having made a big enough effort to avoid a recent lapse, then the consequent guilt may prompt him to escape from the high-risk situation and thereby avoid relapse. On the other hand, if he attributes the cause to his "deficient personality" (a stable, internal, and uncontrollable cause), he will feel ashamed and see further effort as hopeless. This would most likely lead to relapse. Marlatt (1985), however, speaks of these emotions as if they are equivalent.

In terms of theoretical simplicity, Marlatt's (1985) reliance on a diverse range of theories has resulted in confusion in which different, often conflicting, mechanisms are causally linked to the AVE. For example, a discrepancy between ideal and actual behavior is hypothesized to result in negative affect independently of an attribution (which is also thought to create negative affect). Therefore, two types of negative affect are generated by quite different mechanisms. Second, attributions concerning the cause of the lapse are understood to drive ongoing addictive behavior either by negative affect (a drive/energy pathway) or as a consequence of low self-efficacy expectations (a cognitive pathway) or possibly by both. The use of Weiner's (1986) attribution theory does not have this limitation and can be used to reformulate the AVE.

Marlatt's (1985) claim that the emotional impact following violation of abstinence rules is greater when ascribed to internal rather than external factors is mistaken from a broader attributional perspective. It is not a question of being greater but rather different; different affective or emotional consequences follow from different attributional dimensions (Weiner, 1986).

Some evidence suggests that the abstinence violation effect is not a stable phenomenon (Collins & Lapp, 1991; Hall, 1989; Ward, Hudson, & Marshall, 1994), with Marlatt (1985) himself arguing that an individual may only experience it briefly. A significant puzzle is to account for this instability. Certainly, taking into account the biphasic effect of addictive substances, it is clear that for Marlatt, the initial effect of taking drugs or indulging in an addictive behavior is positive. What is the relationship between the abstinence violation effect and the (arguably) appetitive processes associated with this positive effect? Does this lead to some attenuation of the abstinence violation effect, and do mechanisms such as redefining the self as an addict or justifying the lapse also lessen its intensity? Marlatt does not fully explain its instability or clarify the relationship between the various mechanisms involved that affect its intensity.

Finally, Marlatt's (1985) formulation of the abstinence violation effect and associated relapse process is not able to accommodate the full range of attribution/relapse links that are implied by current theorizing and that have different treatment implications. The abstinence violation effect, as defined by Marlatt, probably only represents a few of the possible relationships between attributions and lapse or relapse.

The Biphasic Effect

Another example of confusion resulting from several competing or independent mechanisms being proposed is illustrated within Marlatt's (1985) discussion of the biphasic concept. He argues that the initial effect of taking drugs is positive and that negative or dysphoric effects occur later. However, if this is the case, then the relationship between the abstinence violation effect and the biphasic effect is unclear because both processes are said to occur after a lapse. If they do both follow a lapse, then the AVE must occur later in the process once the positive effects of the drugs or addictive behavior have receded. It is not clear how long this might take or whether it applies to addictive problems such as gambling that do not involve drugs.

A related difficulty is the assumed delayed negative effect of biphasic responses. If the initial responses to a lapse are positive, then it appears to clash with the impact of the abstinence violation effect. This effect is hypothesized to cause negative affect (e.g., guilt), and it seems odd to state that an individual who has broken his abstinence rules is, on one hand, feeling excited and stimulated (initial excitatory effect of the biphasic response) but, on the other hand, is feeling guilty and dysphoric (effect of the AVE). It is possible that the AVE is the dysphoric phase of the biphasic response. However, this is unlikely because in Marlatt's (1985) model the AVE is a cognitive affective construct, whereas the biphasic effect is essentially biological in nature.

Another issue concerns the possible redundancy of the abstinence violation effect in Marlatt's (1985) model of the relapse process. If the biphasic response involves negative affect, is the abstinence violation effect redundant? It also appears to be unnecessary if there is already a link between negative affect and addictive "coping responses," which Marlatt maintains. If one of the functions of addictive behavior is to escape from or reduce negative affect, then either of these two processes will help to escalate the addictive cycle. It is not necessary to include both in a model of the relapse process.

In summary, the major problem is that in Marlatt's (1985) RP model there are multiple pathways to continued addictive behavior. It is not clear whether the mechanisms underlying these are related or whether they can even be theoretically integrated. In the case of the AVE and the biphasic effect, it is not clear how they could be meaningfully integrated.

The Sex Offender Model of RP

The sex offender variation of RP, which most closely resembled Marlatt's (1985) version, was originally advanced by Pithers et al. (1983) and has changed very little over the intervening years. The downward course from abstinence to relapse is the same but has been slightly altered to fit the facts of sexual offending. In the original model, a lapse involved actual reindulgence in the problem behavior (taking a drink, smoking a joint, doing a line of coke). In the sex offender model, lapse is defined as offense precursor activities such as deviant fantasizing, purchase of pornography, or cruising for potential victims. In the original model, a lapse is a momentary indulgence but not a relapse; in the sex offender model, commission of a sexual offense is a relapse. In the latter model, then, considerable attention is paid to behaviors that might lead to a sex offense but fall short of one. With this single exception, the models are strikingly similar.

Following treatment, the individual should be in a state of abstinence, be confident of not reoffending, and have an expectation of continued success. He may eventually make a SID (consciously have a deviant fantasy, cruise likely victim haunts, accidentally pass a playground, etc.). The decisions to do these things may seem harmless, irrelevant, and not dangerous, but each SID places the individual a step closer to relapse. If the offender recognizes the SID and pulls back, continued abstinence will be maintained, self-efficacy will increase, and probability of relapse will decrease. If he fails to cope with the SID, he may place himself in a high-risk situation that threatens his sense of self-control.

If he makes an adaptive coping response, he can maintain abstinence. If he fails to make the adaptive coping response or makes a maladaptive one, then a lapse could occur (e.g., consciously masturbating to a deviant fantasy). It is here that he may experience the AVE, the recognition that he is violating his pledge of abstinence. The model argues that how the AVE is managed will determine if a relapse will occur. If the AVE is viewed as caused by external, controllable factors (e.g., admission of a mistake but a belief that continued coping will be successful), the effect should be minimal and the likelihood of relapse low. If, however, it is viewed as due to internal, unavoidable factors (e.g., personal weakness, lack of willpower), the effect will be negative and the likelihood of relapse increased. However, the model argues that even at this dangerous point, if the individual can summon an adaptive coping response, he can return to a state of abstinence. If he cannot, a relapse to sexual offending is likely.

The evidentiary status of classical RP with sex offenders is not particularly impressive. Possibly because it has been so uncritically accepted, it has almost entirely escaped evaluation. Pithers and Marques, joint authors of the original version of the sex offender model (Pithers et al., 1983), individually developed large-scale treatment programs. Pithers (1991) and his colleagues (Pithers et al., 1989) have reported highly positive results for their program, but they did not empirically compare the RP-based program with a more standard treatment model. Marques's program, which did use an appropriate control group, reported only a slight effect in favor of treatment (Marques & Barbaree, 1995). More recent evaluative work on RP is reported later in this chapter.

Limits of the Model

It was suggested earlier that RP should probably be limited to traditional addictive behaviors such as alcoholism, drug dependency, and smoking, as well as to disorders of impulse control, including sexual deviation. Perhaps one of the mistakes in the sex-offending variation has been to apply it too broadly. It makes more sense to limit the treatment to problems that it is likely to affect, such as pedophilia, exhibitionism, voyeurism, fetishism, or obscene telephone calling. If it is limited in this way, the focus will be exclusively on compulsive habit patterns that produce immediate gratification and are followed by delayed negative consequences. This approach most closely resembles the original Marlatt (1985) model.

Another serious problem has been in the use of the words *relapse prevention*. In the past 15 years, those words have served as an umbrella under which a huge variety of clinical interventions that had little or nothing to do with the original notions of RP could be found. The volume edited by Wilson (1992) shows many egregious examples of this problem. Virtually any kind of posttreatment intervention has been called relapse prevention. In terms of program outcome, then, it is hardly surprising that programs containing very few RP-like elements have not been shown to be more effective than those with a more traditional cognitive-behavioral approach.

In our judgment, one of the major deficiencies of RP has been its assumption that clients participating in this intervention are highly motivated to change their behavior. The road to abstinence is depicted as a "journey" in which client and therapist participate. Because there is so little evidence favoring the actual *prevention* of relapse, this seems to us a highly questionable assumption. Other explanatory frameworks are in play for improving our understanding of addictive behavior and sexual offending. In recent years, Marlatt (1998) has modified his views of relapse prevention. He has advanced the notion of harm reduction, which views abstinence as a highly desirable goal but acknowledges that efforts to reduce the harm that an individual can do to himself or to others may be an acceptable outcome. Damaging behavior is viewed as distributed on a continuum from total indulgence through moderation to total abstinence. The effort is always to move the client away from indulgence and toward abstinence. Hence the slogan of harm reduction: Any steps that reduce harm are steps in the right direction. Laws (1996, 1999) has suggested that harm reduction more accurately describes what sex offender therapists actually do. Not all treatment is successful, but it can seriously affect and modify deviant sexual behavior (see Ward & Hudson, 2000). This commonsense notion has been greeted with horror (Pare, 1998) as well as scorn (Maletzky, 1998). Nonetheless, harm reduction appears to be an idea whose time has come.

Related to harm reduction, Laws (1998) has suggested that we should stop viewing sex offending as a problem that can be ameliorated by law, psychology, or medicine. Rather, we should view it as a public health problem that is everybody's business and everybody's responsibility. Public health approaches have made enormous advances in automotive safety, reduction of smoking, and increase in safe-sex practices, to name only a few. Laws argues that too much of our time is devoted to tertiary prevention (i.e., attempting to prevent the recurrence of deeply entrenched deviant sexual practices). This is the level at which our efforts are least likely to succeed. Instead, he argues, we should be devoting our efforts to secondary prevention, stopping behaviors that have begun but are not entrenched, and primary prevention, stopping deviant behavior before it ever gets started. We are strongly supportive of the public health approach.

Problems With the Sex Offender RP Model

In addition to the contextual difficulties mentioned in the previous section, there are a number of specific problems with the model itself. In this section, we refer to the adaptation of the RP model to sex offenders as the Pithers's model, for ease of exposition. However, we wish to acknowledge that this model was the work of a number of researchers (see earlier reference).

Because Pithers relies so heavily on Marlatt's theory, his adaptation is also vulnerable to many of its problems. We briefly summarize these criticisms before considering in detail difficulties specific to his version of the relapse process in sex offenders. A general point is that Pithers, like Marlatt, postulates the existence of a number of mechanisms associated with the relapse process that appear to either conflict with each other or are not clearly related. In addition, Pithers does not convincingly address the interactions between the major constructs such as high-risk situations, lapses, apparently irrelevant decisions, and so on. An offender frequently experiences a number of lapses before ultimately relapsing (Hall, 1989). He also runs the risk of evoking unconscious decision making (by the way of apparently irrelevant decisions) without accounting for the mechanisms involved. Finally, Pithers overemphasizes the role of skill deficits in relapse compared to decision making (Rohsenow, et al., 1991). The problems specific to the sex offender adaptation are discussed next.

Negative Affect as a High-Risk Situation

Pithers confuses his discussion of high-risk situations by including negative affect as an example of a high-risk situation without further clarification. Negative emotional states are related to high-risk situations in two ways. Such states could constitute high-risk situations in their own right and lead to relapse if individuals fail to cope effectively with them, perhaps because offenders rely on old coping strategies, such as sexual fantasies and so on. Second, such states may lead to high-risk situations by the way of apparently irrelevant decisions. In this pathway, negative affect is a risk factor possibly related to lifestyle imbalance. If a person habitually copes with sadness and anxiety by fantasizing about having sex with children, then he or she may enter a high-risk situation by the way of apparently irrelevant decisions. Pithers does not acknowledge that factors such as negative affect and interpersonal conflict can lead to high-risk situations by different pathways. Therefore, apparently irrelevant decisions are only likely to be involved in setting up some types of high-risk situations.

Also problematic is the relationship between apparently irrelevant decisions and negative affective states. In Pithers's model, covert planning (apparently irrelevant decisions) constitutes the only pathway to high-risk situations. Although this is plausible for external situations, such as being with potential victims, it cannot apply to internal states such as negative affect. It seems odd to speak of offenders creating negative emotional states to provide an excuse for a lapse. Negative affect is arguably not the end state people can seek even if they wanted to; it is a nonvolitional state and not able to be the object of planning in this sense. Any attempt to resolve this difficulty by arguing that reports of negative affect by offenders are simply means of justifying a lapse creates further problems. On one hand, to suggest that offenders set out to make themselves depressed to provide an excuse for lapsing is to face the same problem stated earlier. On the other hand, because the offender was essentially lying, negative affective states would not really be high-risk situations; they would be fabrications.

The specification of only one covert pathway to high-risk situations is unnecessarily restrictive and fails to accommodate the research evidence concerning relapse (Marlatt & Gordon, 1985; Ward, Louden, Hudson, & Marshall, 1995). It lacks Marlatt's (1985) additional direct links to high-risk situations from lifestyle imbalance, in which negative emotional states constitute high-risk situations in their own right and unexpected situations such as being left with children. The covert route will only be associated with some types of high-risk situations, usually external situations.

These criticisms suggest that it is important to distinguish between high-risk situations that refer to external situations and those that refer to nonvolitional states such as negative affect. It is clear that apparently irrelevant decisions can only create some offending situations and not internal states. The introduction of additional pathways from distal factors such as lifestyle imbalance would help clarify the relationship between risk factors and different types of high-risk situations. Another possibility is to restrict the term to external situations and refer to internal states as risk factors. Risk factors tend to be associated with lifestyle factors and precede the offender's exposure to high-risk situations and eventual relapse.

The Abstinence Violation Effect

Pithers's reliance on Marlatt's (1985) earlier formulation of the abstinence violation effect is a weakness of his model. It is logically and empirically possible that the mechanisms comprising this version of the abstinence violation effect—cognitive dissonance and the formulation of attributions—may operate independently. The former is a motivational drive mechanism in which negative affect created by dissonance "drives" individuals to reduce it by redefining their self-image. The latter involves the perception of uncontrollability and therefore the expectation that any future attempt at coping is futile.

An additional problem in opting for this version of the AVE is that it does not place as much emphasis on the affective consequences of violating an abstinence rule. In Marlatt's (1985) reformulation, an important consequence of making a causal attribution after a lapse is the experience of guilt or another negative affective state. In his model, this is thought to trigger the onset of further addictive behavior to escape or reduce negative emotions. In cognitive dissonance, the major causal element is conflict between behavior and identity, between the self as abstinent and the sexually abusive behavior. The available empirical evidence supports the inclusion of negative affect as a key component of the abstinence violation effect (e.g., Collins & Lapp, 1991), suggesting that Marlatt was correct in reformulating it in cognitive and affective terms.

Another major problem concerns the roles of positive, appetitive motivation, on one hand, and the more negative, attributionally based abstinence violation effect, on the other (see Ward, Hudson, & Siegert, 1995). Specifically, Pithers asserts that the problem of immediate gratification, the focus on the immediate pleasurable features, operates after the lapse as part of the abstinence violation effect. This appears problematic because it contrasts markedly with Marlatt's (1985) view that the problem of immediate gratification occurs before the abstinence violation effect and functions primarily to mediate the transition from a high-risk situation to a lapse. For Marlatt, this process constitutes an appetitive motivational factor and leads to positive outcome expectations concerning the addictive behavior. However, in Pithers's revised model, the problem of immediate gratification occurs simultaneously with the abstinence violation effect and therefore would appear to undermine its effect; there is a clash of mechanisms.

The problem of immediate gratification occurs when an offender focuses selectively on the positive, usually short-term consequences of sexual assault and ignores the negative ones that are usually longer term. It involves positive affect and facilitates the transition to a lapse because of its focus on the immediate pleasurable consequences of lapsing. In contrast, the abstinence violation effect involves negative affect as a result of quite distressing perceptions of cause. It leads to relapse because of the impact that these perceptions of cause and the resulting negative affect have on expectations, motivation, and coping skills.

Thus, in Pithers's reformulation, the sex offender experiencing an AVE is considered to be, on one hand, in a state of high sexual arousal and positive expectations regarding abusive sex with little regard for consequences (i.e., the problem of immediate gratification). On the other hand, he is distraught about the occurrence of a lapse, pessimistic about coping, and struggling with his identity as a reformed sex offender (i.e., the abstinence violation effect). This picture of the reaction of an abstinent sex offender to a lapse seems unnecessarily complex theoretically and at variance with the limited data available (Ward et al., 1994).

It appears that the changes made in the relapse prevention model for sex offenders have created this problem. The conceptual movement, in Pithers's model, of the lapse to a point further back in the behavior chain means that the problem of immediate gratification now becomes part of mediating the lapse-relapse transition rather than from high-risk situation to lapse. In addition, the available empirical data suggest that sex offenders are more likely to experience an AVE following a relapse rather than after a lapse (Ward et al., 1994).

Pithers's use of Marlatt's (1985) earlier version of the abstinence violation effect probably has also contributed to this problem. The earlier version stresses the cognitive dissonance an offender experiences once he lapses and downplays the impact of negative affective processes. The coexistence of positive and negative affective states would not have been as obvious because of the less central role of affect in Pithers's formulation of the abstinence violation effect.

Lapse and Relapse Distinctions

Consistent with all RP approaches, Pithers draws a distinction between a lapse and relapse. However, he does not draw a further distinction between the first instance of a sexual offense and a return to pretreatment levels of offending or increased severity of offending. On the face of it, this appears inconsistent with the RP approach and in fact serves to undercut the RP model. Surely there is an important difference between committing one offense and committing many or, as may be more common, increasing the severity of offending during a single assault. An offender treated, according to Pithers's model, may experience a very strong abstinence violation effect after the first offense and therefore is likely to continue (or exacerbate) his sexually aggressive behavior. Perhaps we need to make a further distinction based on the severity or frequency of offending. For example, a single instance of sexually aggressive behavior could be labeled Relapse 1, and multiple offenses or increased severity could be labeled Relapse 2. Arguably, the social costs of the latter are greater than the former. It is a sensible and ethically appropriate strategy to continue to apply RP principles following the first sexual offense. Of course in therapy, it is important to teach offenders to regard relapse as something to avoid.

Offender Type

A final criticism concerns the general scope or applicability of Pithers's RP approach. This model of the relapse process emphasizes the role of negative affective states in both triggering the relapse cycle and constituting high-risk situations. Individuals, whose offending behavior is accompanied by firmly entrenched cognitive distortions concerning the legitimacy and beneficial nature of child-adult sexual contact, are not easily accommodated within the model. Because of the essentially positive views these men have concerning the legitimacy of sexual contact with children, they tend to experience higher levels of positive emotion within the offense cycle (Ward, Louden, et al., 1995). Such individuals may, however, still be motivated to stop sexual offending and therefore exhibit a relapse process that reflects their particular characteristics. Furthermore, as discussed in our earlier criticism of Pithers's incorporation of the problem of immediate gratification in the AVE, the majority of child molesters reported high levels of positive affective states during both lapses and high-risk situations.

Conclusions

Relapse prevention has certainly become the treatment of choice for sex offenders. However, as we have noted already in this chapter, this popularity has partially been responsible for its undoing, insofar as its broad acceptance, apparent ease of implementation, and face validity have made critical comments far from numerous. Moreover, what critical review of the model has occurred has often resulted in negative responses from the professional community, reflecting the "received wisdom" status we noted earlier.

It is not entirely clear what underlies the popularity of relapse prevention as a model. It does not seem to be as simple as clear evidence existing for efficacy because this issue is still being robustly debated. Rather, it seems that relapse prevention offered a model and a language that reduced treatment providers' anxieties with respect to what they were attempting to do. That is, it may be that it reduced anxiety by articulating optimism.

The early efforts to assist men who had behaved in sexually offensive ways came from a behavioral or, more recently, cognitive-behavioral perspective. What relapse prevention offered to these endeavors was assistance with respect to maintaining change generated by treatment. In other words, it focused on the problem of long-term recidivism, long a source of concern to treatment providers, but in a way that provided an apparent solution. Thus, although the focus of the model had the potential to raise anxiety, it also provided some relief—a combination that leads to attachment.

The second or collateral benefit that came with the relapse prevention model, a means to structure treatment, has flowed from the other central tenet—that relapse can very usefully be seen as a series of small behavioral steps that are comprehensible. This aspect of the model is still not clearly embraced by many programs that nevertheless still self-describe as being relapse prevention based. The notion here is that if we (and that most particularly includes the client) understand the offense process, then the skills that need to be acquired or accessed under the appropriate circumstances to interrupt the process become obvious. This approach has the potential to increase the personal specificity of treatment, assisting the heterogeneity of clients' problems and increasing the face validity of the self-management regime.

Thus, in broad terms, relapse prevention at least implicitly promised a means of dealing with the devastating problem of failure posttreatment and a means of structuring treatment in a rational fashion that was compatible with aftercare, raising the expectation that the intervention would be seamless. Less clear were the promises that are reasonable to expect of any theory, be it relevant to treatment or etiology. Propositions should be coherent and comprehensive. As Hanson (1996) noted, a theory should describe and organize existing knowledge—in this case, what offenders actually do—and it should tell us what we need to do to treat these men. Thus, what relapse prevention promised was to map the territory involved in what offenders do and the processes involved, as well as tell us what to do about that in a way that significantly reduced the rate at which these men reoffended. The central question is "Has it done this?"

We believe that the answer to this question has to be only a qualified maybe. The main promise was to reduce recidivism. This is still contentious but in a fashion that should not be taken as an excuse to stop trying. It seems to us that to be critical of how well we are doing is a spur to do better, and no one would seriously argue that that is not possible. Chapter 3 by Marshall and Anderson (2000 [this volume]) addresses this issue in considerable depth, and we pick up this theme again in our final chapter.

The second "promise" was to describe existing knowledge; that is, it should tell us what offenders actually do. We believe it has not done that anywhere near well enough. The issue of scope, or the lack of it, is a fundamental criticism of the model. For too long we have pretended, while knowing otherwise, that all offenders reflected one offense process or pathway. This must affect how well treatment needs were determined and met, which in turn may well have affected efficacy. We deal with this theme in Chapter 2. Finally, the model is contradictory with respect to the mechanisms proposed. Sometimes, phenomena are simply being described; at other times, incompatible mechanisms are proposed; and finally, mechanisms are proposed that are more complex than required. These issues have been discussed earlier and are also addressed in Chapter 2.

What we have done in the remainder of this volume is to bring together the considerable expertise that exists within the sex offender treatment area to focus on what needs to happen in the future. No one ought to complain about the optimism and resulting resources that have flowed from relapse prevention being adopted as the model for sex offender treatment. But we should be less complacent about whether we have finished the job.

References

Abel, G. G., Becker, J. V., Cunningham-Rathner, J., Rouleau, J. -L., Kaplan, M., & Reich, J. (1984). *The treatment of child molesters: A manual.* (Available from SBC-Tm, 722 West 168th Street, Box 17, New York, NY 10032)

Abel, G. G., Blanchard, E. B., & Becker, J. V. (1978). An integrated treatment program for rapists. In R. T. Rada (Ed.), *Clinical aspects of the rapist* (pp. 161-214). New York: Grune & Stratton.

Bargh, J. A., & Barndollar, K. (1996). Automaticity in action: The unconscious as repository of chronic goals and motives. In P. M. Gollwitzer & J. A. Bargh (Eds.), *The psychology of action: Linking cognition and motivation to behavior* (pp. 457-481). New York: Guilford.

Collins, R. L., & Lapp, W. M. (1991). Restraint and attributions: Evidence of the abstinence violation effect in alcohol consumption. *Cognitive Therapy and Research, 15,* 69-84.

Furby, L., Weinrott, M. R., & Blackshaw, L. (1989). Sex offender recidivism: A review. *Psychological Bulletin, 105,* 2-30.

Hall, R. L. (1989). Relapse rehearsal. In D. R. Laws (Ed.), *Relapse prevention with sex offenders* (pp. 197-206). New York: Guilford.

Hanson, R. K. (1996). Evaluating the contribution of relapse prevention theory to the treatment of sexual offenders. *Sexual Abuse: A Journal of Research and Treatment, 8,* 201-208.

Hudson, S. M., Ward, T., & Marshall, W. L. (1992). The abstinence violation effect in sex offenders: A reformulation. *Behavior, Research and Therapy, 30,* 435-441.

Hunt, W. A., Barnctt, L. W., & Branch, L. G. (1971). Relapse rates in addiction programs. *Journal of Clinical Psychology, 27,* 455-456.

Kirkley, B. G., & Fisher, E. B. (1988). Relapse as a model of nonadherence to dietary treatment of diabetes. *Health Psychology, 7,* 221-230.

Laws, D. R. (Ed.). (1989). *Relapse prevention with sex offenders.* New York: Guilford.

Laws, D. R. (1995). A theory of relapse prevention. In W. O'Donohue & L. Krasner (Eds.), *Theories of behavior therapy* (pp. 445-473). Washington, DC: American Psychological Association.

Laws, D. R. (1996). Relapse prevention or harm reduction? *Sexual Abuse: A Journal of Research and Treatment, 8,* 243-247.

Laws, D. R. (1998, October). *Sexual offending as a public health problem.* Paper presented at the meeting of the Association for the Treatment of Sexual Abusers, Vancouver, British Columbia.

Laws, D. R. (1999). Harm reduction or harm facilitation? A reply to Maletzky. *Sexual Abuse: A Journal of Research and Treatment, 11,* 233-240.

Maletzky, B. M. (1998). Harm facilitation. *Sexual Abuse: A Journal of Research and Treatment, 10,* 77-80.

Marlatt, G. A. (1980). *Relapse prevention: A self-control program for the treatment of addictive behaviors.* Unpublished manuscript, University of Washington, Department of Psychology, Seattle.

Marlatt, G. A. (1985). Relapse prevention: Theoretical rationale and overview of the model. In G. A. Marlatt & J. R. Gordon (Eds.), *Relapse prevention* (pp. 3-70). New York: Guilford.

Marlatt, G. A. (1998). *Harm reduction: Pragmatic strategies for managing high-risk behaviors.* New York: Guilford.

Marlatt, G. A., & Gordon, J. R. (Eds.). (1985). *Relapse prevention.* New York: Guilford.

Marques, J. K., & Barbaree, H. E. (1995, October). *Future directions for sex offender treatment.* Plenary presented at the meeting of the Association for the Treatment of Sexual Abusers, New Orleans, LA.

Marques, J. K., Day, D. M., Nelson, C., & Miner, M. H. (1989). The Sex Offender Treatment and Evaluation Project: California's relapse prevention program. In D. R. Laws (Ed.), *Relapse prevention with sex offenders* (pp. 247-267). New York: Guilford.

Marshall, W. L., & Anderson, D. (2000). Do relapse prevention components enhance treatment effectiveness? In R. D. Laws, S. M. Hudson, & T. Ward (Eds.), *Remaking relapse prevention with sex offenders: A sourcebook* (pp. 39-55). Thousand Oaks, CA: Sage.

Marshall, W. L., Jones, R. L., Ward, T., Johnston, R., & Barbaree, H. E. (1991). Treatment outcome with sex offenders. *Clinical Psychology Review, 11,* 465-485.

Niaura, R. S., Rohsenow, D. J., Binkoff, J. A., Monti, P. M., Pedraza, M., & Adams, D. B. (1988). Relevance of cue reactivity to understanding and smoking relapse. *Journal of Abnormal Psychology, 97,* 133-152.

Pare, R. (1998, Fall). Making a case for relapse prevention: Holding the line in an age of compromise. *The Forum,* pp. 2-3.

Pithers, W. D. (1990). Relapse prevention with sexual aggressors: A method for maintaining therapeutic gain and enhancing external supervision. In W. L. Marshall, D. R. Laws, & H. E. Barbaree (Eds.), *Handbook of sexual assault* (pp. 343-361). New York: Plenum.

Pithers, W. D. (1991). Relapse prevention with sexual aggressors. *Forum on Corrections Research, 3,* 20-23.

Pithers, W. D., Marques, J. K., Gibat, C. C., & Marlatt, G. A. (1983). Relapse prevention with sexual aggressives: A self-control model of treatment and the maintenance of change. In J. G. Greer & I. R. Stuart (Eds.), *The sexual aggressor* (pp. 214-234). New York: Van Nostrand Reinhold.

Pithers, W. D., Martin, G. R., & Cumming, G. F. (1989). Vermont Treatment Program for Sexual Aggressors. In D. R. Laws (Ed.), *Relapse prevention with sex offenders* (pp. 292-310). New York: Guilford.

Rohsenow, D. J., Niaura, R. S., Childress, A. R., Abrams, D. B., & Monti, P. M. (1991). Cue reactivity in addictive behaviors: Theoretical and treatment implications. *International Journal of Addictions, 25,* 957-993.

Salkovskis, P. M. (Ed.). (1996). *Frontiers of cognitive therapy.* New York: Guilford.

Saunders, W. A., & Allsop, S. (1987). Relapse: A psychological perspective. *British Journal of Addiction, 82,* 417-429.

Saunders, W. A., & Houghton, M. (1996). Relapse revisited: A critique of current concepts and clinical practice in the management of alcohol problems. *Addictive Behaviors, 21,* 843-855.

Ward, T., & Hudson, S. M. (1996). Relapse prevention: A critical analysis. *Sexual Abuse: A Journal of Research and Treatment, 8,* 177-200.

Ward, T., & Hudson, S. M. (2000). A self-regulation model of relapse prevention. In R. D. Laws, S. M. Hudson, & T. Ward (Eds.), *Remaking relapse prevention with sex offenders: A sourcebook* (pp. 79-101). Thousand Oaks, CA: Sage.

Ward, T., Hudson, S. M., & Marshall, W. L. (1994). The abstinence violation effect in child molesters. *Behaviour Research and Therapy, 32,* 431-437.

Ward, T., Hudson, S. M., & Marshall, W. L. (1995). Cognitive distortions and affective deficits in sex offenders: A cognitive deconstructionist interpretation. *Sexual Abuse: A Journal of Research and Treatment, 7,* 67-84.

Ward, T., Hudson, S. M., & Siegert, R. J. (1995). A critical comment on Pithers' relapse prevention model. *Sexual Abuse: A Journal of Research and Treatment, 7,* 167-175.

Ward, T., Louden, K., Hudson, S. M., & Marshall, W. L. (1995). A descriptive model of the offense chain for child molesters. *Journal of Interpersonal Violence, 10,* 453-473.

Weiner, B. (1972). *Theories of motivation: From mechanism to cognition.* Chicago: Rand McNally.

Weiner, B. (1986). *An attributional theory of motivation and emotion.* New York: Springer.

Wilson, P. H. (1992). *Principles and practice of relapse prevention.* New York: Guilford.

PART II

A REVISIONIST CRITIQUE

CHAPTER 2

What Is So Special About Relapse Prevention?

R. KARL HANSON
Department of the Solicitor General of Canada

Therapists need some theory to guide intervention. The theory can be explicit, involving detailed program manuals, academic references, and direct links to empirically validated treatment procedures. More typically, the theory is implicit: Decisions are made according to what seems right and possible at the time. Although treatment can be conducted without reflection, explicitly examining assumptions transforms treatment from a personal art into a social science. Like the clients that they treat, therapists who examine their expectations have the potential to change maladaptive behavioral patterns. By articulating their beliefs, sex offender treatment providers can learn from each other. To quote Dennett (1995), "Science is not just a matter of making mistakes, but of making mistakes in public" (p. 380).

In this chapter, I examine the dominant theoretical approach to treating sexual offenders—namely, relapse prevention (RP) (Laws, 1989, 1995, 1999). The basic principles of relapse prevention are not new but are firmly rooted in the cognitive-behavioral/social learning tradition (Bandura, 1986; Beck, Rush, Shaw, & Emery, 1979; Meichenbaum, 1977). Concepts such as dysfunctional behavior as learned habits, attributional biases, self-efficacy, situational influences, and decision chains are standard features of cognitive-behavioral therapies (Rimm & Masters, 1979; Thoresen & Mahoney, 1974; Wilson & O'Leary, 1980). Within the broad social learning tradition, however, RP has its own distinctive flavor. Some of the distinctive features of RP have been of considerable benefit to those treating sexual offenders. Other implications of RP have been less than helpful and, I argue, have generated pointless distractions for both therapists and offenders.

Planning for Relapse

As its name suggests, the emphasis of relapse prevention is not on stopping a problematic behavior but on preventing its recurrence. RP makes a strong statement that lapses are to be expected. Rather than viewing lapses as treatment failure, RP views them as the problem to be addressed.

Such a perspective struck a responsive chord among sex offender treatment providers in the 1980s. The existing versions of cognitive-behavioral treatment never claimed a permanent cure. Nevertheless, RP's explicit acceptance of lapses as expected and workable was inspirational to therapists already too familiar with tenacious offense cycles. The unacceptably high rates of recidivism among "well-treated" sex offenders provoked an interest in long-term supervision. To quote Laws's summary comments at the 1987 New York Academy of Sciences Conference, "It is what happens *after* the delivery of the treatment package that is critical" (Laws, 1988, p. 203). One of the great strengths of RP was that it provided a framework for close collaboration between therapists and the criminal justice system. Furthermore, the future orientation of RP was consistent with the need to treat sex offenders who, in most cases, were not currently problematic.

The widespread adoption of RP as the dominant treatment philosophy was not without its drawbacks. One implication of this approach was that all sex offenders were considered high risk. Like its arch rivals—the 12-step programs—relapse prevention did not provide a mechanism for someone who has committed a sex offense to stop being a sex offender. Offenders who claimed to be no longer at risk were considered defensive and uncooperative. Therapists had already heard too many excuses.

It is difficult to estimate the actual recidivism rate for sexual offenders because many offenses are never detected. Nevertheless, the observed recidivism rate is much lower than is commonly believed, approximately 15% after 5 years (Hanson, 1997; Hanson & Bussière, 1998). Even with long follow-up periods, the rates are rarely more than 40%. Low detection rates suggest that the observed rates are underestimates, but it is hard to argue that all sexual offenders inevitably reoffend.

Even if RP treats all sex offenders as likely recidivists, what is the problem with being overly cautious? Like a vaccination, should not every sex offender be treated just in case? If we ignore the costs of unnecessary treatment, there remains the possibility that treatment could actually make offenders worse. Research on general criminals has frequently found that even good treatment applied to low-risk offenders has the potential to increase their recidivism rate (see review by Andrews & Bonta, 1998, p. 243). The research on sex offenders is not well developed, but the same pattern is evident. Nicholaichuk (1996) found that the sex offense recidivism rate (11%) of low-risk incest offenders who received relapse prevention treatment was higher than the rate for a matched group of untreated offenders (3%). In contrast, the high-risk offenders who received a similar treatment program recidivated significantly less often than their untreated comparison group (6% vs. 15%). The evidence is not strong enough to justify banning low-risk offenders from RP treatment, but the possibility of iatrogenic effects cannot be dismissed.

The mechanisms contributing to deterioration are unclear, but some offenders may experience group treatment as an opportunity to meet other sex offenders, learn useful information about how to commit sex crimes, and ruminate about reoffending. Among nonsexual criminals, the association with other offenders is one of the strongest predictors of recidivism (Gendreau, Little, & Goggin, 1996). For men who are genuinely low risk to reoffend, it is hard to understand how constantly telling them that they are dangerous should help with anything.

One group for whom RP seems particularly inappropriate is historical incest offenders. Although incestuous abuse is among the most psychologically damaging (Friedrich, Urquiza, & Beilke, 1986; Herman, Russell, & Trocki, 1986), incest offenders typically stop once the child reaches a certain age. In many cases, these men show no signs of misbehavior (sexual or otherwise) until they are reported many years later by their then adult children. The recidivism rate of incest offenders is among the lowest of all sexual offenders (<7%) (Hanson, 1997), and it would be expected to be significantly lower for those men who have spent many years offense free in the community. Nevertheless, it is not uncommon to find aging incest offenders dutifully creating relapse plans for circumstances that transpired 20 years ago and are unlikely to ever be repeated. Such a preoccupation with sexual recidivism has the potential of distracting therapists' attention from more pressing problems. Preventing reoffense is not the only way to protect society. Incest offenders often have much to learn about how their current behavior (e.g., accepting responsibility) can help to minimize the damage they have inflicted on their victims and other family members.

RP's concern is with the repetitive offender. Its wholesale acceptance by sex offender treatment providers has limited consideration of other potentially valuable approaches to addressing the problem of sexual victimization. In particular, RP is poorly suited to addressing issues of primary prevention. Questionnaire surveys typically find that 25% to 35% of men admit to at least one sexual offense, mostly date rape (Dickie, 1998; Hanson & Scott, 1995; Templeman & Stinnett, 1991). The number of sex offenses committed by each of these undetected community offenders is unknown but is likely to be small. Between 20% and 40% of women report being sexually victimized, most typically by a known male (Finkelhor, Hotaling, Lewis, & Smith, 1990; Johnson & Sacco, 1995; see also review by Koss, 1993). Assuming that males and females are both reporting on the same types of events and that sexual offending is not highly concentrated within a subset of the population, then the average sex offender would be expected to have fewer than two victims. Such statistics suggest that primary prevention has considerable potential for addressing the burden of sexual victimization.

RP, unfortunately, has very little to say about primary prevention. Those interested in primary prevention need to consider other theoretical approaches, such as feminist theory (Sanday, 1981) or general versions of social learning theory (e.g., Bandura, 1986). Such theories provide an opportunity to examine the larger social context in which men learn to be sexual offenders, with attention to factors such as community tolerance of sexual assault and power differentials between offenders and victims (Baron & Straus, 1989).

RP's focus on relapse has also diverted attention away from understanding the majority of men whose sexual aggression stops without any formal intervention. The reasons that offenders stop are unknown, but it seems that the natural consequences of sexual assault are sufficient in most cases. Such consequences could include heterosexual failure, peer rejection, and unfulfilled intimacy needs.

Even the persistent sexual offenders found in the criminal justice system tend to desist with age. Like other criminals, sexual offenders (particularly rapists) "burn out." There are few rapists older than 40, and the recidivism rates of both rapists and child molesters decrease with age (Hanson, 1998). We know very little about why any sex offenders desist from sexual offending or whether the undetected community sex offenders resemble the more persistent sexual offenders typically seen in criminal justice settings. Given the widespread assumption that sex offenders remain forever at risk, attempts to study nonrecidivists are frequently dismissed as naive: The nonrecidivists are simply viewed as those offenders who have not yet been caught.

Although RP has made a valuable contribution by providing a framework for addressing relapse, the assumption of relapse potential in all sex offenders does not necessarily contribute to community protection. RP draws attention away from the most common forms of sex offending, fails to understand why most sex offenders desist, and could even encourage some offenders to attend treatment that is poorly matched to their needs. Nevertheless, RP's charge to anticipate recidivism has been of significant value to treatment providers struggling to intervene with the most persistent sexual offenders.

Orderly Offense Cycles

Another important assumption of RP is that sexual offenses do not "just happen"; instead, they follow a predictable process in which covert planning and a series of seemingly irrelevant decisions set up high-risk situations (George & Marlatt, 1989; Laws, 1995). The steps outlined by RP provide a useful framework for therapists and offenders to begin talking about offense behavior. The assumption of a gradual, orderly offense cycle provides many opportunities to intervene. Although the concepts and language of RP are initially foreign to most sexual offenders, some offenders adopt it as a revelation. Others, however, never quite appreciate how it might apply to them.

Resistance to RP's description of covert planning is typically attributed to a lack of insight or failure to accept responsibility. Given high rates of denial among sex offenders, such assumptions often have merit. It is also possible that some of these reluctant clients may be right. To the extent that RP explicitly describes the features of offense cycles, it risks being wrong. There is no requirement that all offenders follow the same pattern or that the patterns described by RP are necessarily correct for any offender. RP proposes a model of the offense process that, like other scientific models, needs to be subjected to an empirical test.

Given that many stages of RP's offense cycle presume covert processes, the most direct source of information about offense cycles comes from the accounts of cooperative offenders. Some offenders provide accounts reasonably consistent with the standard RP model, but offenders provide other plausible accounts (Ward, Louden, Hudson, & Marshall, 1995). Ward et al. (1995), for example, report a direct, explicit path to offending. Some child molesters actively seek out opportunities for sex with children. Their offense cycles do not begin with negative affect threatening self-control but with the cheerful anticipation of sexual contact with a particular victim (see also Ward, Hudson, & Keenan, 1998). These offenders experience no postrelapse self-blame because they see little wrong with their behavior. Similarly, it is easy to find accounts of rapists who claim to have acted impulsively. These rapists describe first considering the sexual assault only after the opportunity arose (e.g., during a break-and-enter).

The extent to which offender accounts should be believed is debatable, given the obvious social pressures to deflect responsibility. Nevertheless, the explicit path to sexual offending seems highly plausible given that these offenders are admitting to intentions for which they can expect severe censure (Hanson & Slater, 1993). But when, if ever, should we believe impulsive accounts? Although relapse prevention theory says "never," there are reasons to believe that some sexual offending may really be impulsive. Impulsiveness is so closely linked to general criminal behavior that Gottfredson and Hirschi (1990) identified low self-control as the defining characteristic of offenders. Many sexual assaults appear chaotic and disorganized (e.g., efforts to avoid detection are minimal or absent). Also, there is evidence that treatment aimed at reducing impulsiveness in general offenders reduces their rate of sexual recidivism (Robinson, 1995).

If there are alternate routes to sex offending, then therapists' insistence on the standard RP model could lead some offenders to generate plausible nonsense. Therapists need to consider a range of offense cycles to avoid a serious mismatch between the offenders' actual offense cycle and the presumed model. A standard menu of offense cycles has yet to be developed, but the initial work of Ward and Hudson shows promise (Ward et al., 1995, 1998).

It remains an open question, however, whether the linear structure of the offense cycle or chain is the most useful model. Another plausible approach is to consider the accumulative effect of individual risk factors on the probability of offending. Offenders may have specific factors consistently associated with offending, but the temporal order of these risk factors may be of relatively little importance (e.g., a pedophile who drinks and then goes to the park vs. going to the park and then drinking). Instead of looking for cycles or chains, it may be just as effective to monitor the density of risk factors.

Beware of High-Risk Situations

Consistent with RP's behavioral roots, RP attributes considerable power to external situations. RP never adopts a fully determinist position; nevertheless, RP emphasizes the need to avoid high-risk situations. There is little question that situations influence behavior, and willful efforts to change environments are a standard method of behavioral self-control (Thoresen & Mahoney, 1974). RP makes the important statement that offenders can avoid temptation by managing the activities of daily living. Similarly, therapists and community supervision officers can evaluate offenders' commitment to change by monitoring the offenders' willingness to make the necessary changes (particularly when they entail sacrifice).

RP's attribution of causal agency to situations invokes a central problem inherent in behaviorism—namely, the difficulty of distinguishing between external events and the subjective interpretation of these events. The confusion between external and the internal situations is particularly acute in RP given that "negative emotional states" are considered "high-risk situations." Even if there is an empirical association between negative mood and recidivism, RP's conception of the causal link between situations and behavior may not be the most constructive.

Cognitive-behavioral theories tend to be highly critical of disease models (e.g., Alcoholics Anonymous) because, by attributing the addiction to a "disease," transgressors relinquish personal responsibility (George & Marlatt, 1989). Nevertheless, the same relapse prevention theorists are quite comfortable attributing responsibility to situations. For example, George and Marlatt (1989) recommend that lapses should not be blamed on personal weakness: "Instead, responsibility should be distributed across both external situational forces that prevail in the HRS [high-risk situations] and internal deficits in coping skills" (p. 24). George and Marlatt (1989) emphasize the power of situations as a compassionate alternative to the self-blame expected following a lapse (abstinence violation effect [AVE]). Even if the AVE was a serious problem among sex offenders (which I doubt), the attribution of blame to situations appears to be another, perhaps subtler, version of the same attribution shuffle promoted by disease theorists.

Rather than coping with self-blame through deflecting responsibility, a more constructive path would be for offenders to take full responsibility—for their urges, their lapses, their psychological situations, and for their abstinence violation effects. An urge to sexually offend is not an immutable feature of nature, nor, for that matter, is self-blame. It is a personal choice, constructed as one option among many. Offenders may perceive themselves to be compelled by external forces, but they are not. And therapists should do what they can to teach offenders that, in reality, they have the capacity to be free from their destructive schema.

At first it is very difficult to take full responsibility. Gradual steps are needed. For highly entrenched drinkers, the admission of helplessness in the face of "alcoholism" can itself be perceived as liberating. The admission of helplessness paradoxically provides a concrete method for increased self-control (no drinking now). Similarly, RP's attribution of responsibility to external situations implies clear steps to increase self-control (avoid high-risk situations).

Therapists, however, should not confuse heuristics with the final goal. Some situations are best avoided, but, ultimately, offenders should learn not to be seduced by habitual thinking patterns, even in the most provocative of situations. Although RP's blanket recommendation to avoid high-risk situations is understandable, some controlled exposure to high-risk situations may help offenders manage their deviant schema in the difficult situations that they will inevitably encounter (Hanson, 1999).

Develop Good Coping Skills

As previously mentioned, RP theory attributes lapses to failure to cope with high-risk situations. Consequently, RP treatment encourages offenders to avoid high-risk situations and develop good coping skills. The recommendation to teach coping skills to sexual offenders has strong intuitive appeal, given that offenders often have deficits in many areas. RP's conception of coping skills, however, has the potential of focusing attention on problems that have little relationship to offending.

An initial problem with RP theory is that the goals of coping are poorly articulated. If coping is defined as avoiding offending, then the definition is a tautology. If offenders relapsed, they did not cope. Instead of referring to a completely empty conception, RP theorists typically consider the goals of coping to include avoiding negative affect, increasing self-esteem, and improving social competence (George & Marlatt, 1989; Laws, 1995). The obvious problem with emphasizing social competence is that it is only relevant for those offenders who follow the negative affect/covert path. For offenders who deliberately seek victims, there is no reason to believe that social skills training should decrease their recidivism rate.

A more insidious problem with RP's emphasis on negative affect is that it can justify almost any form of treatment. Anything that promotes the well-being of the offender can be interpreted as relapse prevention treatment. In our 1988 review of Canadian sex offender treatment programs (Wormith & Hanson, 1992), almost all programs stated that they did relapse prevention. Reviews of their treatment manuals, however, found very little influence of the core RP concepts. In many cases, the existing regimes, be they self-help groups or horticulture therapy, were simply rechristened relapse prevention without any change in practice.

RP makes the specific point that there is an association between acute negative affect and relapse potential, which has generally been supported by research (Hanson & Harris, 2000; McKibben, Proulx, & Lusignan, 1994; Proulx, McKibben, & Lusignan, 1996). Compared to other types of offenders, sexual offenders are those most likely to invoke sexual fantasies (deviant or otherwise) when confronted with stressful situations (Cortoni, 1998). Nevertheless, RP's lack of conceptual clarity allows programs to drift into treatments aimed at general psychological issues at the expense of addressing the specific links to sexual offending.

Research has never found measures of general psychological adjustment, such as self-esteem, depression, or social competence, to be related to sexual offense recidivism (Hanson & Bussière, 1998). Furthermore, treatment programs that improve general psychological adjustment do not result in reduced recidivism rates (Hanson, Steffy, & Gauthier, 1993; Nicholaichuk, 1996). The distressed offenders are at no greater recidivism risk than the happy offenders, but both types of offenders are at increased risk when their mood deteriorates. These results suggest that therapy should focus on weakening the association between negative affect and sex offending rather than on generally improving the offenders' psychological adjustment.

Abstinence Violation Effect

One of the most distinctive concepts of RP is the AVE. The AVE describes how self-blame following a lapse can increase the probability of relapse. RP was constructed for addressing behavior that became a problem when enacted frequently. A single drink (lapse) was not problem drinking (relapse). Consequently, RP aimed to identify and address psychological mechanisms that turned lapses into relapses.

The application of RP theory to sex offenders required new definitions of *lapse* and *relapse*. Because any sexual offending was considered unacceptable, lapses were defined as any high-risk behavior that could lead to new offenses (relapse). It is not clear, however, that the concept of the AVE survived these new definitions. The AVE assumes a strong motivation to change, which is often lacking in sex offenders. Furthermore, strong self-blame requires that the offenders make clear links between high-risk behavior and relapse potential. Most sexual offenders are not so farsighted. Although offenders may feel badly after the offense (particularly when they expect to be punished), they often experience positive emotions following high-risk behavior, such as deviant sexual fantasies (Ward, Hudson, & Marshall, 1994). Offenders frequently display insufficient rather than excessive self-blame.

Like other aspects of RP theory, the abstinence violation effect makes the most sense in the context of a gradual, passive erosion of self-control. Although it is possible to find cases that fit the description of the AVE, these may not be the norm. The route to relapse is often quite direct, even among the original target populations for which RP was developed. Drinkers who relapse often experience a desire to "get drunk," rather than a covert slippage from the first drink to problem drinking (Saunders & Houghton, 1996). The AVE also has the curious implication that the stronger the motivation to abstinence, the greater the likelihood that lapses will lead to relapse. In fact, high motivation is associated with increased abstinence among problem drinkers (Saunders & Houghton, 1996). There is no reason to believe that motivation to change should not also be associated with positive changes among sexual offenders.

The assumption of high levels of motivation to avoid relapse is a serious weakness in the application of the RP model to the sexual offender. George and Marlatt (1989) consider motivation an "important precondition for applying RP interventions," but many (most?) sex offenders have low motivation to change. Given that RP "offers little promise for the unmotivated offender and cannot induce motivation" (George & Marlatt, 1989), there has been surprising little attention to other methods of motivating offenders. Motivation is not a permanent condition. It waxes and wanes like other personal attributes. If RP is going to be applied as a standard model of sexual offender treatment, then considerable effort should be devoted to maintaining client motivation, both during and following treatment (see Mann, 2000 [this volume]).

Conclusion

Since its inception in the early 1980s, RP has spread to become the most popular approach to the treatment of sexual offenders. This immense popularity is somewhat puzzling considering that the fundamental principles are not new and that many distinctive features of RP appear to have limited applicability to sexual offenders. The concepts drawn from traditional behavioral therapy, such as high-risk situations and behavioral chains, have generally withstood scrutiny. It is not clear, however, that RP's more innovative concepts, such as the abstinence violation effect or the lapse/relapse distinction, accurately describe the problems faced by sex offenders. Sex offenders often lack the motivation that is the prerequisite for RP's interventions. Furthermore, offenders whose crime patterns do not match the assumption of RP theory (i.e., negative affect, covert planning, etc.) are unlikely to derive benefit from attempts to force their accounts into a standard RP mold. RP's inability to conceive of untreated, low-risk offenders has diverted attention away from the majority of offenders who naturally desist and has contributed to some sex offenders receiving interventions poorly suited to their needs.

So what, if anything, is special about relapse prevention? RP has a number of useful treatment techniques (e.g., identify and avoid high-risk situations). The RP language provides a medium through which therapists and offenders can talk about offense behavior. Importantly, the RP model is able to integrate the major goals of treatment providers and the criminal justice system. Yet I believe that the reason for RP's popularity lies in an even more significant achievement. RP performed a deep alchemy through which clinicians could look at rapidly declining survival curves and see mission, not despair.

References

Andrews, D. A., & Bonta, J. (1998). *The psychology of criminal conduct* (2nd ed.). Cincinnati, OH: Anderson.

Bandura, A. (1986). *Social foundations for thought and action: A social cognitive theory.* Englewood Cliffs, NJ: Prentice Hall.

Baron, L., & Straus, M. A. (1989). *Four theories of rape in American society: A state-level analysis.* New Haven, CT: Yale University Press.

Beck, A. T., Rush, A. J., Shaw, B. R., & Emery, G. (1979). *Cognitive therapy of depression.* New York: Guilford.

Cortoni, F. (1998). *The relationship between attachment styles, coping, the use of sex as a coping strategy, and juvenile sexual history in sexual offenders.* Unpublished doctoral dissertation, Queen's University, Kingston, Ontario.

Dennett, D. C. (1995). *Darwin's dangerous idea: Evolution and the meanings of life.* New York: Simon & Schuster.

Dickie, I. (1998). *An information processing approach to understanding sympathy deficits in sexual offenders.* M.A. thesis, Psychology Department, Carleton University.

Finkelhor, D., Hotaling, G., Lewis, I. A., & Smith, C. (1990). Sexual abuse in a national survey of adult men and women: Prevalence, characteristics, and risk factors. *Child Abuse and Neglect, 14,* 19-28.

Friedrich, W. N., Urquiza, A. J., & Beilke, R. L. (1986). Behavioral problems in sexually abused young children. *Journal of Pediatric Psychology, 11,* 47-57.

Gendreau, P., Little, T., & Goggin, C. (1996). A meta-analysis of the predictors of adult offender recidivism: What works! *Criminology, 34,* 575-607.

George, W. H., & Marlatt, G. A. (1989). Introduction. In D. R. Laws (Ed.), *Relapse prevention with sex offenders* (pp. 1-31). New York: Guilford.

Gottfredson, M. R., & Hirschi, T. (1990). *A general theory of crime.* Stanford, CA: Stanford University Press.

Hanson, R. K. (1997). *The development of a brief actuarial risk scale for sexual offense recidivism* (User Report No. 1997-04). Ottawa: Department of the Solicitor General of Canada.

Hanson, R. K. (1998, November). *Predicting sexual offense recidivism: A comparison of rapists and child molesters.* Paper presented at the American Society of Criminology, Washington, DC.

Hanson, R. K. (1999). Working with sex offenders: A personal view. *Journal of Sexual Aggression, 4,* 81-93.

Hanson, R. K., & Bussière, M. T. (1998). Predicting relapse: A meta-analysis of sexual offender recidivism studies. *Journal of Consulting and Clinical Psychology, 66*(2), 348-362.

Hanson, R. K., & Harris, A. J. R. (2000). Where should we intervene? Dynamic predictors of sex offense recidivism. *Criminal Justice and Behavior, 27,* 6-35.

Hanson, R. K., & Scott, H. (1995). Assessing perspective-taking among sexual offenders, nonsexual criminals, and nonoffenders. *Sexual Abuse: A Journal of Research and Treatment, 7,* 259-277.

Hanson, R. K., & Slater, S. (1993). Reactions to motivational accounts of child molesters. *Journal of Child Sexual Abuse, 2*(4), 43-59.

Hanson, R. K., Steffy, R. A., & Gauthier, R. (1993). Long-term recidivism of child molesters. *Journal of Consulting and Clinical Psychology, 61,* 646-652.

Herman, J., Russell, D., & Trocki, K. (1986). Long-term effects of incestuous abuse in childhood. *American Journal of Psychiatry, 143,* 1293-1296.

Johnson, H., & Sacco, V. F. (1995). Researching violence against women: Statistics Canada's national survey. *Canadian Journal of Criminology, 37,* 281-304.

Koss, M. P. (1993). Detecting the scope of rape: A review of prevalence research methods. *Journal of Interpersonal Violence, 8,* 198-222.

Laws, D. R. (1988). Introductory comments. In R. A. Prentky & V. L. Quinsey (Eds.), *Human sexual aggression: Current perspectives* (pp. 203-204). New York: New York Academy of Science.

Laws, D. R. (Ed.). (1989). *Relapse prevention with sex offenders.* New York: Guilford.

Laws, D. R. (1995). Central elements in relapse prevention procedures with sex offenders. *Psychology, Crime & Law, 2,* 41-53.

Laws, D. R. (1999). Relapse prevention: The state of the art. *Journal of Interpersonal Violence, 14,* 279-296.

Mann, R. E. (2000). Managing resistance and rebellion in relapse prevention intervention. In D. R. Laws, S. M. Hudson, & T. Ward (Eds.), *Remaking relapse prevention with sex offenders: A sourcebook* (pp. 187-200). Thousand Oaks, CA: Sage.

McKibben, A., Proulx, J., & Lusignan, R. (1994). Relationships between conflict, affect and deviant sexual behaviors in rapists and child molesters. *Behaviour Research and Therapy, 32,* 571-575.

Meichenbaum, D. (1977). *Cognitive-behavior modification.* New York: Plenum.

Nicholaichuk, T. P. (1996). Sex offender treatment priority: An illustration of the risk/need principle. *Forum on Corrections Research, 8,* 30-32.

Proulx, J., McKibben, A., & Lusignan, R. (1996). Relationships between affective components and sexual behaviors in sexual aggressors. *Sexual Abuse: A Journal of Research and Treatment, 8,* 794-813.

Rimm, D. C., & Masters, J. C. (1979). *Behavior therapy: Techniques and empirical findings* (2nd ed.). New York: Academic Press.

Robinson, D. (1995). *The impact of cognitive skills training on post-release recidivism among Canadian federal offenders* (Research Report No. R-41). Ottawa: Correctional Service of Canada.

Sanday, P. R. (1981). The socio-cultural context of rape: A cross-cultural study. *Journal of Social Issues, 37,* 5-27.

Saunders, B., & Houghton, M. (1996). Relapse revisited: A critique of current concepts and clinical practice in the management of alcohol problems. *Addictive Behaviors, 21,* 843-855.

Templeman, T. L., & Stinnett, R. D. (1991). Patterns of sexual arousal and history in a "normal" sample of young men. *Archives of Sexual Behavior, 20,* 137-150.

Thoresen, C. E., & Mahoney, M. J. (1974). *Behavioral self-control.* New York: Holt, Rinehart & Winston.

Ward, T., Hudson, S. M., & Keenan, T. (1998). A self-regulation model of the sexual offense process. *Sexual Abuse: A Journal of Research and Treatment, 10,* 141-157.

Ward, T., Hudson, S. M., & Marshall, W. L. (1994). The abstinence violation effect in child molesters. *Behaviour Research and Therapy, 32,* 431-437.

Ward, T., Louden, K., Hudson, S. M., & Marshall, W. L. (1995). A descriptive model of the offense chain for child molesters. *Journal of Interpersonal Violence, 10,* 452-472.

Wilson, G. T., & O'Leary, K. D. (1980). *Principles of behavior therapy.* Englewood Cliffs, NJ: Prentice Hall.

Wormith, J. S., & Hanson, R. K. (1992). The treatment of sexual offenders in Canada: An update. *Canadian Psychology/Psychologie Canadienne, 33,* 180-198.

CHAPTER 3

Do Relapse Prevention Components Enhance Treatment Effectiveness?

W. L. MARSHALL
DANA ANDERSON
Queen's University, Ontario

The application of the principles of relapse prevention (RP) to the treatment of sexual offenders was first derived by Marques (1982) from the work of Marlatt and his colleagues (Marlatt, 1982; Marlatt & George, 1984; Marlatt & Gordon, 1985). Shortly thereafter, Pithers, Marques, Gibat, and Marlatt (1983) provided a detailed description of how RP principles could be applied within the context of a comprehensive treatment program for sexual offenders. Because RP is a derivation of social learning theory, it was readily assimilated into the cognitive-behavioral treatments current at the time and was, as a result, enthusiastically taken up by many North American practitioners working with sexual offenders. Since then, RP has become a feature of most treatment programs in the United States, Canada, Britain, Australia, and New Zealand and has begun to make inroads in Europe, particularly the Netherlands.

This enthusiastic acceptance of RP principles and procedures was and continues to be based on the commonsense appeal of this approach rather than on a growing body of evidence substantiating its value. Indeed, even the limited number of published criticisms of RP (Hudson, Ward, & Marshall, 1992; Mann, 1998; Ward & Hudson, 1996; Ward, Hudson, & Siegert, 1995) has relied on logical analyses rather than data. Because RP has now been incorporated, to a greater or lesser extent, into most cognitive-behavioral interventions for sexual offenders, it is an opportune time to attempt an evaluation of its effectiveness. However, problems with such an evaluation are immediately evident when the reviewer examines the varied content and extensiveness of the RP components in different treatment programs. Furthermore, very few programs have provided an analysis of outcome data, and even fewer have attempted to demonstrate that the goals of an RP component have been achieved. Notwithstanding these limitations, we are set the task of completing such an evaluation.

Achievement of Within-Treatment Goals

The RP component of cognitive-behavioral programs aims to (a) instill in the clients the capacity to recognize the factors and situations that serve to initiate their offense chain; (b) help clients identify the steps involved in their offense chain and the associated thoughts, feelings, and behaviors; (c) provide clients with the coping skills necessary to deal with future problems or circumstances that may put them at risk; and (d) have each client generate a set of plans that will reduce the likelihood of him being in a risky state or situation and that will allow him to deal with such circumstances should they inadvertently arise. The first step in an appropriate evaluation of the effectiveness of RP programs, then, should be the determination of how well these goals have been achieved. To do that, we must first develop procedures to assess these skills.

Nelson and Jackson (1989) note that the RP model assumes that if sexual offenders are to avoid lapsing or relapsing, they must be able to "recognize and take responsibility for the sequence of their cognitions and behaviors" (p. 167) that end in the commission of a sexual offense. Without this understanding, so Nelson and Jackson claim, the offender could not "plan, practice, and eventually implement adequate coping responses" (p. 167). On the basis of these assumptions, the therapist assists the client in identifying his offense chain, which is then evaluated by his primary therapist at the end of each quarter of the program (Marques, Day, Nelson, & Miner, 1989). Marques et al. (1989) report that at initial testing, only 39% of their participants' offense chains met satisfactory criteria, although by a third repetition of the evaluation all were deemed to have satisfactorily generated an adequate offense chain.

Miner, Day, and Nafpaktitis (1989) developed the Situational Competency Test to measure clients' ability to employ appropriate coping skills in response to difficult internal states or environmental circumstances that might constitute a threat to their ability to maintain abstinence from offending. However, although Marques et al. indicate that this test has been used to evaluate changes with treatment, they do not report the observed results.

Marques et al. (1989) also employ the Test of Basic Relapse Prevention Concepts, which is meant to assess the participants' understanding of RP concepts and language. It is assumed "that participants must be grounded in the model's lexicon before they can apply it" (Marques et al., 1989, p. 259). It does not seem obvious that this is true. In any case, only 34% of clients were judged by their therapist to have met the criterion of satisfactory mastery at the initial test (end of the first quarter of treatment), although all clients were evaluated as satisfactory at the third assessment.

A common feature of RP programs is the generation of a decision matrix (Jenkins-Hall, 1989). This matrix outlines the client's understanding of the immediate and delayed consequences of either offending or abstaining. Marques et al. (1989) evaluated the adequacy of their clients' matrices by having the primary therapist rate them. They found that, on average, the therapists assigned to these matrices rated them 4.1 on a 7-point scale, which they considered indicated the matrices to be "less than complete." Almost two thirds of the clients were judged to have omitted important consequences. Reliance on the primary therapist's ability to rate the clients' products seems less than satisfactory, although Pithers, Martin, and Cumming (1989) use the same rating strategy for various aspects of their RP program. Aside from the more general subjectivity of such ratings, it seems unlikely that the therapists could be objective. Having spent several months working to get offenders to produce these documents, a therapist would seem more likely to discern positive features in the products than might be observed by either a more removed judge or by a more objective assessment procedure. In addition, of course, there is the possibility that the clients simply learned what the therapist expected them to produce and that the therapist unwittingly provided them with an offense chain that he or she thought was suitable. These are problems with all treatment processes, and it is hard to see how they can be overcome.

Beckett (1998), in discussing an evaluation of seven community-based treatment programs for sexual offenders in England (Beckett, Beech, Fisher, & Fordham, 1994), noted that a significant deficit in these programs was their inability to instill RP knowledge and skills. On an RP questionnaire, Beckett notes that only 27% of clients demonstrated mastery of RP strategies at the end of treatment. Even when they did recognize factors that might put them at risk, treated offenders did not show an understanding of how they might cope with these problems. However, each of the programs evaluated by Beckett and his colleagues offered quite brief treatment, and Mann (1996) has suggested that this might account for the observed failure to achieve the RP goals.

Mann (1996) examined the efficacy of the more extensive prison-based programs in England and compared them to two prison programs that did not have RP components. Mann, who was not a therapist in any of these programs, evaluated the offenders using structured interviews that were conducted prior to, during, and at the end of treatment. She rated the participants on six dimensions: (a) the client's awareness of the thoughts that led to offending, (b) his willingness to admit planning, (c) his recognition of high-risk factors, (d) his motivation for offending, (e) the coping strategies he identified to deal with risks, and (f) his ability to identify for others when he might be at risk. Mann's findings clearly support the value of the RP component of these prison programs in achieving the goals she identified. Compared with the non-RP programs, those having an RP component were markedly more effective in enhancing each of the specific skills. Most important, there were no changes in RP skills throughout treatment until after the RP component was introduced. Mann's results offer the only really satisfactory support presently available for the claim that RP training produces the changes that are expected. Whether these changes are related to postdischarge reductions in reoffending rates remains to be seen.

One obvious obstacle to evaluating RP components in prison-based treatment programs is the setting itself. The chain of events leading to sexual offenses occurs outside prison settings. Therefore, the client is not able to test his new coping strategies in a similar context to that in which the offense originally occurred. Consequently, the therapist cannot evaluate the extent to which the client can successfully avoid a "relapse" following a "lapse."

Issues in Evaluating Treatment

Before proceeding, several things need to be said about the evaluation of the long-term effects of treatment.

Indices of Reoffending

Researchers most often use recidivism (i.e., the percentage of clients who are identified as having committed at least one reoffense) as the index of outcome. This can be derived from a variety of sources—for example, official police records, parole or probation data, or information extracted from the files of various agencies revealing accusations that did not lead to charges. The latter served as the basis for our early examination of the benefits of our outpatient program (Marshall & Barbaree, 1988), but it is so labor intensive to access such information that these data are unlikely to be commonly pursued.

The primary data source for most studies has been official police records, with a few reports also extracting data from parole or probation files. Official police records are not always as complete as we would like, although in Canada, legal requirements demand that all information on charges and convictions must be entered into the national police computer system. In Canada, at least, these records are an exhaustive compilation of all crimes from across the country, so it does not matter where an ex-client decides to live; Royal Canadian Mounted Police records will track him if he is ever charged with an offense again. This may not be true in other jurisdictions, and accurate national data are certainly far more difficult to access in the United States, which can present problems in the interpretation of American outcome studies. Even the best official data will represent an underestimate of the rate of reoffending, although it is not clear how much of an underestimate the official records represent. It is estimated that the incidence of rape reported in the Uniform Crime Reports of the FBI represents only one seventh to one third of the actual rate of rape, depending on which study is examined (see Koss & Harvey, 1991, for a review). However, this consistent underestimate should not differentially affect treated versus untreated sexual offenders, although a low base rate will influence the researcher's capacity to discern statistically significant differences in recidivism rates (see Barbaree, 1997, for a discussion of this issue).

In addition to examining the percentage of clients who reoffend as an index of treatment efficacy, we could also use the number of reoffenses as our outcome data. It might be that treatment has the effect of limiting the number of victims abused by each client, even when the percentage of reoffenders does not discriminate treated from untreated subjects. Similarly, treatment may delay the onset of reoffending, and this may be seen as advantageous. For example, presume a client has, on average, committed one offense per month in the years prior to treatment. If treatment was not effective, we would expect him to reoffend within the first month or two after release. If, after treatment, he did not reoffend for 4 or more years, this would surely represent a positive effect for treatment but would be lost in an index of recidivism and may not be apparent in the number of reoffenses.

Finally, treatment benefits can be evaluated in terms of the financial savings to society. Both Prentky and Burgess (1990) and Marshall (1992) have provided estimates of the cost to society when a sexual offender is identified and prosecuted to conviction. When the effects of treatment are calculated in terms of these costs, a reduction in recidivism that might be obscured by other methods can result in substantial savings.

Duration of Follow-Up

The duration of the follow-up period is critical to discerning treatment effects. As noted, the base rate of the untreated group has to be high enough to allow us to statistically demonstrate lowered recidivism in the treated subjects. Recidivism rates have been shown to increase over the years after release from custody or after discharge from a community program. Apparently, as long as we follow sexual offenders, we continually detect new offenses, even as much as 20 or more years later (Hanson, Scott, & Steffy, 1995; Soothill & Gibbens, 1978). This, however, does not mean we are obliged to follow all clients for 20 years to discern treatment effects, unless it can be shown that the survival curves for treated and untreated subjects converge over time. At the moment, this remains a somewhat open question, but again, if treated subjects take longer to reach the same recidivism rate as untreated subjects, then this should be taken as indicating benefits for treatment.

In any case, for most programs, it appears that a minimum follow-up of 4 to 6 years should be sufficient to demonstrate treatment effects if, indeed, there are any. In the following review of outcome studies, we will assume that this period is satisfactory.

Ideal Versus Practical Design

Both Quinsey (1998; Quinsey, Harris, Rice, & Lalumière, 1993) and Miner (1997) essentially claim that the only methodologically acceptable study of sexual offender treatment outcome so far reported is California's ongoing Treatment and Evaluation Project (Marques et al., 1989). The data generated to date by this study have not been impressive (Marques, Day, Nelson, & West, 1994).

The feature of this study that appeals most to Quinsey and Miner is that subjects who volunteer for treatment are randomly assigned to either receive treatment or not. Elsewhere, we (Marshall, 1993; Marshall, Jones, Ward, Johnston, & Barbaree, 1991; Marshall & Pithers, 1994) have challenged this claim, although we have never denied the methodological advantages of such a design. It is the practical and ethical restrictions that we believe limit the applicability of such a study.

When researchers want to evaluate the efficacy of treatment for disorders such as anxiety, depression, sexual dysfunctions, and substance abuse, the following restrictions represent the minimum requirements demanded by most Canadian ethics committees: (a) participants must be free to give their consent, (b) those who refuse must be offered treatment immediately, and (c) volunteers who are assigned to no treatment must be offered treatment at the earliest possible date. With the possible exception of the first condition, the California project does not meet these ethical requirements. On the issue of freedom to agree to participate, can sexual offenders, who are typically under some judicial constraint, be said to be in a position to freely give consent? The answer to this question is not obvious, and it should trouble those who advocate the random assignment approach. If those who refuse to participate are offered immediate treatment, then they cannot serve as untreated controls, and this provision will indicate to potential volunteers that the sure way to get treatment is to refuse to participate in the study. When receiving treatment is a requirement for being granted parole, as it is in Canada, we can expect most sexual offenders to be eager to enter treatment. The requirement that the no-treatment subjects be offered treatment at the earliest possible moment presents an apparently insurmountable problem. To evaluate treatment for disorders, where the problem is manifest on a daily (e.g., anxiety, depression, substance abuse) or weekly basis (e.g., sexual dysfunctions), then treatment need only be withheld from the comparison group for a limited few months to discern treatment effects. Not so with sexual offending, where the frequency of the problematic behavior is so low that we must wait at least 4 to 5 years before the rate of reoffending in the untreated subjects reaches a level that allows us to discern treatment effects.

Over and above these important issues, there is, or ought to be, a concern about who should be asked to participate in such a study. When people with any of the disorders we identified earlier (i.e., anxiety, etc.) are untreated, they are the primary, if not the only, ones who suffer. Thus, they are the appropriate people to ask to participate in a study because they are taking a risk for themselves alone. When sexual offenders reoffend, they hurt, often quite seriously, innocent people. Because potential victims of sexual abuse are involved in the implications of the random design study and not just the offenders, surely an ethical researcher should take this into account. Although it is likely impossible to manage to ask all potential victims, we could survey a stratified sample. Our guess is they would not consent, but it is not up to us to produce these data; it is the responsibility of those who advocate the use of the design in question. Interestingly, although Miner (1997) takes great pains to deal with and finally dismiss most of the objections we have raised over the random design strategy, neither he nor Quinsey (1998) have offered a rebuttal of this latter ethical objection.

Given our reservations about the random design, we consider the use of convenience groups to be satisfactory so long as efforts are made to ensure they are reasonably well matched to treated subjects on demographic and offense history variables and are drawn from the same setting. Previously, we (Marshall et al., 1991) suggested that the recidivism rates for treated subjects could be compared to the rates of similar untreated offenders from other settings. We have quite rightly been criticized for this suggestion (Miner, 1997; Quinsey et al., 1993), and we now retract that proposal. Our intention, then, in the following review, is to restrict our consideration to those studies that provide reasonably well-matched untreated comparison groups, whether these groups are the product of a random allocation of volunteers or simply convenience samples.

Features to Be Evaluated

We will attempt to evaluate the effects of adding RP components to standard cognitive-behavioral treatment programs. Of course, no one has actually

systematically manipulated the various features of RP within an otherwise comprehensive cognitive-behavioral program. Because the advocates of
methodological purity appear willing to settle for a study that compares one
treatment with another, we encourage researchers to implement a rigorous evaluation comparing the addition and subtraction of one or more aspects of RP. This
seems to us to represent an ethical and desirable study that could readily be done
in the right setting. Until then, our estimate of the value of RP will have to rely
on what limited data are available from programs that have included or
excluded some or all of RP's components. We have chosen to focus only on cognitive-behavioral programs because they are the most popular and because
nonbehavioral programs do not appear to be effective (Frisbie & Dondis, 1965;
Meyers & Romero, 1980; Peters & Roether, 1971; Sturgeon & Taylor, 1980).

Components of RP

Relapse prevention serves as an integrating concept for the participants in
treatment so that they can recognize the value and meaning of each of the other
components. In this way, RP serves to coordinate the overall approach to treatment. Without RP as an overall concept, cognitive-behavioral therapists would
either have to provide some other integrating process (e.g., social learning theory) or leave the participants to do the integration themselves. The latter alternative is not attractive, so the use of an RP framework, whether or not the specific components of RP add effectiveness to treatment, seems to offer some
value.

In addition, and this is the focus of our concern, RP has two components that
are thought to add directly to the effectiveness of treatment. Pithers (1990) has
called these the internal self-management dimension and the external supervisory dimension. The internal self-management component can embrace any
or all of the following: (a) training in the language of RP, (b) identifying risk factors, (c) identifying the features of offense chains, and (d) helping offenders
develop RP plans. The external supervisory component may involve extensive
postdischarge supervision, and it may or may not involve further treatment.

The language of RP is complex, and this complexity may be beyond the
grasp of some clients. Although acronyms such as the PIG, the AVE, AIDS, and
SUDS, as well as notions such as decision matrices, high-risk situations, and
the strained distinction between lapses and relapses, may appeal to professionals, the identification of their meaning and the requirement to remember them
all are burdensome for most clients. Requiring clients to learn this language
needs to be shown to have some value, but until this is done, we consider this
requirement likely to divert clients from the real task at hand. Indeed, Pithers
(1990) noted that learning the lexicon of RP can increase a client's tendency to

intellectualize and thereby avoid dealing with important issues. Assessing the clients' acquisition of this language, which we observed in the last section has been done by some programs, would seem to not only entrench an intellectualized approach but also encourage in both the clients and therapists the idea that treatment is really educational training rather than a therapeutic process. In any case, to date, no one has shown the value of training clients in this language.

The identification of background factors (e.g., psychological, emotional, interpersonal, vocational, financial) and particular circumstances (e.g., being alone with a child, aimlessly cruising in a car) that appear to precipitate offending is such a reasonable goal of treatment that the wonder is that we needed an RP framework to have this introduced as a target of our interventions. However, reasonableness alone is not sufficient; we need evidence of the utility of doing this. In particular, we need to know how comprehensive the range of risk factors needs to be. Here we will introduce a theme that will characterize much of what we say throughout the rest of this chapter. Is the goal of therapy to exhaustively account for every factor that, in the past, contributed or may contribute to the likelihood of offending, or should we use some of the more obvious risks as illustrative of a way of approaching this issue? An exhaustive identification would not only consume a considerable amount of therapy time, but it may also overwhelm the client and convey to him that unless he is aware of every possible risk in advance, he will not be able to avoid offending. This seems to us to increase rather than decrease the likelihood of future failure. We believe that what is required is to provide our clients with a general approach to monitoring their future risks, along with the identification of a limited set of factors that persistently precipitated offending in the past.

Similarly, in helping clients identify their offense chains, different therapists have set themselves variably complex tasks. Some chose one or two offenses from which to derive these chains, and others seem bent on examining every single offense. For example, Salter (1998) indicated that the procedures she was suggesting to overcome denial were essential because it was necessary to know about every offense to develop, among other things, comprehensive offense chains. Is this really necessary? In the context of examining other programs, we have found that not only do some therapists consider a large variety of incidents for each offender, but they also tease out remarkably detailed accounts of each step in each offense, including the client's behaviors, thoughts, and feelings at each of these steps. Our guess is that elucidating the details of several offenses as they unfolded will only serve to confuse and overwhelm most clients. We try to generate a single, prototypical, and essentially simple offense chain that can serve as a model for the sort of manipulative strategies the offender typically uses and the thoughts and feelings that accompany the unfolding chain. We do not see our task as assisting the offender to understand every act, thought, and feeling he has ever had during an offense sequence, but rather to have him understand the generic factors and processes involved so that he can best arm himself against unpredictable future circumstances. We want our clients to learn general strategies rather than how to deal with specific circumstances.

Similar problems beset the generation of plans to avoid the risk of relapsing. These RP plans and their associated warning signs can be comprehensive, covering every possible contingency, or they can be restricted to just those risks associated with a prototypical chain so that a generic approach to reducing risk can be adopted. We aim for the latter, but apparently many, if not most, therapists aim for some version of the former.

One of the problems with examining the comprehensiveness or otherwise of the approaches various programs take in identifying risk factors and offense chains is that very few reports make clear the approach they take. All too often, researchers and clinicians assume that simply describing what they do as an RP program is sufficient. As we have seen, however, an RP approach can involve a considerable range of therapeutic options, and it behooves those who describe their program to be more specific.

On the issue of the external dimension, approaches also differ, although, again, it is not always easy to know exactly the degree of external supervision and treatment that is involved. Clients released after treatment from Canadian penitentiaries are supervised by parole officers and may enter a community treatment program. However, community treatment is only available in major cities and is usually offered only to high-risk offenders. Similarly, supervision is variable, with intensive supervision being provided again only to the high-risk offenders, and then only for a relatively brief period, after which it is significantly reduced. Moderate- or low-risk offenders released from Canadian penitentiaries are less likely to get community treatment, and they will receive minimal supervision. On the other hand, both the Vermont Prisons' Program (Pithers et al., 1989) and California's Treatment and Evaluation Program (Marques et al., 1989) require all discharged offenders to enter treatment for a one-year minimum and sometimes longer and to be extensively and intensively supervised by specially trained staff for at least the same amount of time.

Although we cannot perfectly rate programs along this continuum of post-discharge supervision and treatment, we believe we can categorize them into those that have no external dimension, those that have a minimal external dimension, and those that have extensive postdischarge supervision and treatment. The following evaluation categorizes programs accordingly. In addition, some of the earlier behavioral or cognitive-behavioral programs had little or no internal or external RP components. We therefore compare treatment outcome data across these admittedly somewhat vague categorizations of programs.

TABLE 3.1 Recidivism Data for Programs With Varying Degrees of RP Components

	Treated[a]	Untreated[a]
Programs without RP		
Rice et al. (1991)	38	31
Hanson et al. (1993)	44	38
Marshall and Barbaree (1998)	15[b]	43[b]
Looman et al. (1998)—pre-1989	28	52
Programs with internal self-management		
Steele (1995)		
Rapists	15	27
Child molesters	9	21
Nicholaichuk et al. (1998)		
Rapists	14	42
Child molesters	18	62
Looman et al. (1998)—post-1989	7	25
Bakker et al. (1998)	8	21
Proulx et al. (1998)		
Rapists	39	71
Child molesters	6	33
Worling and Curwen (1998)	5	18
Programs with extensive external dimension		
Marques (1988)		
Rapists	11	18
Child molesters	11	13

a. All recidivism data are rounded to nearest whole numbers.
b. These data include unofficial indicators of relapses.

Outcome Evaluations

Table 3.1 identifies those reports of treatment outcome providing sufficient information for us to classify them according to variations in the level of RP concepts and procedures employed.

Programs Without RP

Two of the studies identified as having no RP elements in their treatment program (Hanson, Steffy, & Gauthier, 1993; Rice, Harris, & Quinsey, 1991) represent early behavioral approaches. Hanson et al.'s report describes a program for men who had received a short prison term (less than 2 years), and Rice et al. describe a program for men incarcerated in a maximum-security psychiatric hospital. These two programs had, as a primary focus, the modification of deviant sexual preferences, although some of the clients in the Rice et al. program also received sex education and social skills training. Both of these programs found no effects for treatment. The value of these two reports is that they justify the move over the past 20 years to more comprehensive programs that target a broad range of problems. Marshall and Barbaree (1988) evaluated a reasonably comprehensive outpatient program that had evolved over its 12 years (1973-1985) of operation. RP elements were added to this program after 1985, although for the last 10 men treated, some discussion of offense cycles was included. The outcome data from the treated men in this program were compared to those who sought treatment at the clinic but who could not attend regularly because they lived too far away. The results of the statistical evaluation revealed clear advantages for the treated men in terms of significantly lower recidivism rates.

Looman, Abracen, and Nicholaichuk (1998) reported on the effectiveness of a program for high-risk sexual offenders in an Ontario prison. The report includes two groups, with the one considered here involving those who were treated up to 1989. Although this program evolved over the course of its operation (from 1973), it targeted a broad range of issues, including sexual preferences, social skills, relationship issues, cognitive distortions, antisocial attitudes, and sex education. All treated subjects were carefully matched with contemporaneous untreated sexual offenders. Significantly fewer of the treated than the untreated subjects reoffended during the lengthy follow-up period. The results from Looman et al.'s study and those from Marshall and Barbaree's (1988) report, when compared with the findings of Hanson et al. (1993) and Rice et al. (1991), offer support for the move to comprehensive programs, albeit without any clear RP components.

Programs With Internal Self-Management

In our earlier evaluation (Marshall & Anderson, 1996), we incorrectly identified the program Steele (1995) evaluated as having no RP components. Steele (personal communication, November 1997) subsequently kindly informed us that there were some but not extensive RP elements and a limited external dimension. She reported very positive effects for this quite comprehensive prison program.

Nicholaichuk, Gordon, Andre, Gu, and Wong (1998), Looman et al. (1998), and Bakker, Hudson, Wales, and Riley (1998) also provide evaluations of prison-based programs. Each of these studies reports significant benefits for treatment by comparing the treated subjects with carefully matched untreated sexual offenders. Nicholaichuk et al.'s program had a comprehensive set of treatment targets, including an internal self-management RP component. Like other Correctional Services of Canada programs, Nicholaichuk et al.'s sexual offenders received some supervision on release, but, as we have seen for Canadian prison programs, this was far less extensive or intensive than the advocates of RP would require. The second part of the Looman et al. report on sexual offenders treated after 1989 is quite similar to Nicholaichuk et al.'s program, and again the data reveal a positive effect for treatment.

Bakker et al. (1998) conducted an analysis of the effects of New Zealand's first prison program for child molesters. The Kia Marama program has been described in detail elsewhere (Hudson, Marshall, Johnston, Ward, & Jones, 1995) and is quite comprehensive, both in terms of the targets and its duration, and it includes an internal RP component. Again, however, there is minimal postrelease supervision, although an attempt was made early in the operation of the program to establish a supervisory support group of friends and family. Unfortunately, these efforts were, for the most part, unsuccessful, in that the support groups seemed to rapidly lose interest. Treated subjects had significantly lower recidivism rates than did matched untreated clients.

In contrast to Rice et al.'s (1991) treatment program described earlier, Proulx et al.'s (1998) evaluation of an approach to similarly dangerous offenders housed in a maximum-security psychiatric institution produced positive results. The treated sexual offenders did significantly better than the untreated subjects over the 4- to 5-year follow-up. This program addressed RP issues in treatment but does not have an extensive external dimension.

Finally, for this group of programs, Worling and Curwen (1998) examined the long-term recidivism rates of treated and untreated adolescent sexual offenders seen at a community treatment center. This program also has an internal management component among its other very comprehensive features but again has little in the way of postdischarge supervision or booster treatment. Once again, clearly positive benefits for treatment were apparent.

It is clear that those comprehensive cognitive-behavioral programs that include the internal self-management component of RP are quite effective. It is important to note, however, that these programs varied in the extent to which they addressed the internal management features of the RP model, and few of them described this aspect of their program in sufficient detail for us to determine just how extensive this was. None, however, had more than a limited external dimension.

Each of the six programs reviewed here had satisfactory follow-up periods, and treated subjects were compared to a convenience sample of matched, contemporaneous, untreated clients from the same setting. In fact, the data seem to us so overwhelmingly convincing that those who claim treatment has not been shown to work would seem to have little grounds for their skepticism. No doubt they will fall back on their objection that a truly randomized design has not yet demonstrated a treatment effect. Indeed, that is true, but the studies reviewed here, we believe, would methodologically satisfy all but the most ardent enthusiasts of methodological elegance. One random design study, however, has been done, and although the final follow-up data are not yet in, the results are disappointing.

An Extensive External Dimension Program

The elaborate study of treatment effects with sexual offenders funded by the state of California (Marques, 1988) involves a truly random design. Volunteers for this program are recruited from California's prisons and then randomly allocated to treatment or no treatment. These two groups are compared both with each other and with nonvolunteers. Treated subjects not only complete a comprehensive internal self-management RP component (which, as noted earlier, includes learning the lexicon of RP), but they are also extensively and intensively supervised after release for up to 2 years. During this period of postrelease supervision, treated clients are required to participate in community treatment. As can be seen from Table 3.1, the data provided by Marques (personal communication, March 1998) do not reveal clear treatment effects. Their chapter in this volume (Marques, Day, Nelson, & Alarcon, 2000) reveals similar data, and although the treated groups have lower recidivism rates, these apparent advantages do not reflect reliable benefits for treatment.

Marshall, Anderson, and Fernandez (1999) suggested that the intensity of the postrelease supervision and the requirement of community treatment in this Californian program may have inadvertently conveyed to the treatment subjects a clear but unfortunate message. It may have convinced the offenders that the program staff did not believe they could manage on their own to avoid relapsing. The treated subjects may have been (again inadvertently) prepared to make this inference as a result of their prior involvement in the elaborate treatment program itself—most particularly, the detailed features of the internal self-management component. If our guess about the message conveyed to these treated subjects is correct, then the prediction would be that as soon as the external dimension is withdrawn, treatment failures should dramatically increase. This is precisely what Marques's recent data indicate. Certainly, the failure of this program, when compared with the successes of the less elaborate programs reviewed in the previous section, calls for an explanation. We suggest that treatment providers be cautious about making their programs too elaborate and too lengthy for fear they may convey to clients that their problems are essentially beyond their capacity to manage on their own.

Conclusions

We believe this review offers strong support for the idea that sexual offenders can be effectively treated. Although it appears that the early strictly behavioral programs were not effective, those that included more elaborate elements were successful. Comprehensive cognitive-behavioral programs having an internal self-management RP component that is not too elaborate appear to be the most successful. However, the presumed success of the increasing comprehensiveness of cognitive-behavioral programs and the apparent appeal of the detailed RP approach appear to have encouraged some treatment providers (e.g., Marques et al., 1989; Pithers, 1990) to expand the comprehensiveness of their programs, perhaps beyond the limits of utility. Treatment providers need to consider not only what they tell their clients but also the inferences the clients inevitably make about the meaning contained in the structure, content, and extent of the programs. When programs become too comprehensive, in terms of the length of treatment and its content and the postdischarge component, they may inadvertently convince clients that they cannot manage on their own. We suggest that excessively elaborate programs may not be the best approach to treating these or any other clients. What is needed to address these possibilities are studies that manipulate the presence or absence of the various aspects of the RP model. These studies, it seems to us, are both ethical and practical and should provide answers that will allow us to make informed decisions about the necessary and sufficient content and extent of our programs.

References

Bakker, L., Hudson, S. M., Wales, D., & Riley, D. (1998). *And there was light: Evaluating the Kia Marama Treatment Programme for New Zealand Sex Offenders against Children.* Christchurch: Psychological Services, New Zealand Department of Corrections.

Barbaree, H. E. (1997). Evaluating treatment efficacy with sexual offenders: The insensitivity of recidivism studies to treatment effect. *Sexual Abuse: A Journal of Research and Treatment, 9,* 111-129.

Beckett, R. (1998). Community treatment in the United Kingdom. In W. L. Marshall, Y. M. Fernandez, S. M. Hudson, & T. Ward (Eds.), *Sourcebook of treatment programs for sexual offenders* (pp. 133-152). New York: Plenum.

Beckett, R., Beech, A., Fisher, D., & Fordham, A. S. (1994). *Community-based treatment of sex offenders: An evaluation of seven treatment programmes.* London: Home Office.

Frisbie, L. V., & Dondis, E. H. (1965). *Recidivism among treated sex offenders* (Research Monograph No. 5). Sacramento: California Department of Mental Hygiene.

Hanson, R. K., Scott, H., & Steffy, R. A. (1995). A comparison of child molesters and nonsexual criminals: Risk predictors and long-term recidivism. *Journal of Research in Crime and Delinquency, 32,* 325-337.

Hanson, R. K., Steffy, R. A., & Gauthier, R. (1993). Long-term recidivism of child molesters. *Journal of Consulting and Clinical Psychology, 61,* 646-652.

Hudson, S. M., Marshall, W. L., Johnston, P., Ward, T., & Jones, R. (1995). Kia Marama: New Zealand Justice Department's programme for incarcerated child molesters. *Behaviour Change, 12,* 69-80.

Hudson, S. M., Ward, T., & Marshall, W. L. (1992). The abstinence violation effect in sex offenders: A reformulation. *Behaviour Research and Therapy, 30,* 435-441.

Jenkins-Hall, K. D. (1989). The decision matrix. In D. R. Laws (Ed.), *Relapse prevention with sex offenders* (pp. 153-166). New York: Guilford.

Koss, M. P., & Harvey, M. R. (1991). *The rape victim: Clinical and community interventions* (2nd ed.). Newbury Park, CA: Sage.

Looman, J., Abracen, J., & Nicholaichuk, T. (1998). *Recidivism among treated sexual offenders and matched controls: Data from the Regional Treatment Centre (Ontario).* Submitted for publication.

Mann, R. (1996, November). *Measuring the effectiveness of relapse prevention intervention with sex offenders.* Paper presented at the 15th Annual Research and Treatment Conference of the Association for the Treatment of Sexual Abusers, Chicago.

Mann, R. E. (1998, October). *Relapse prevention? Is that the bit where they told me all the things I couldn't do anymore?* Paper presented at the 17th Annual Research and Treatment Conference of the Association for the Treatment of Sexual Abusers, Vancouver, British Columbia.

Marlatt, G. A. (1982). Relapse prevention: A self-control program for the treatment of addictive behaviours. In R. B. Stuart (Ed.), *Adherence, compliance and generalization in behavioral medicine* (pp. 329-378). New York: Brunner/Mazel.

Marlatt, G. A., & George, W. H. (1984). Relapse prevention: Introduction and overview of the model. *British Journal of Addiction, 79,* 261-273.

Marlatt, G. A., & Gordon, J. R. (Eds.). (1985). *Relapse prevention: Maintenance strategies in the treatment of addictive behaviors.* New York: Guilford.

Marques, J. K. (1982, March). *Relapse prevention: A self-control model for the treatment of sex offenders.* Paper presented at the 7th Annual Forensic Mental Health Conference, Asilomar, CA.

Marques, J. K. (1988). The Sex Offender Treatment and Evaluation Project: California's new outcome study. *Annals of the New York Academy of Science, 528,* 205-214.

Marques, J. K., Day, D. M., Nelson, C., & Alarcon, J.-M. (2000). Preventing relapse in sex offenders: What we learned from SOTEP's experimental treatment program. In D. R. Laws, S. M. Hudson, & T. Ward (Eds.), *Remaking relapse prevention with sex offenders: A sourcebook* (pp. 321-340). Thousand Oaks, CA: Sage.

Marques, J. K., Day, D. M., Nelson, C., & Miner, M. H. (1989). The Sex Offender Treatment and Evaluation Project: California's relapse prevention program. In D. R. Laws (Ed.), *Relapse prevention with sex offenders* (pp. 247-267). New York: Guilford.

Marques, J. K., Day, D. M., Nelson, C., & West, M. A. (1994). Effects of cognitive-behavioral treatment on sex offender recidivism: Preliminary results of a longitudinal study. *Criminal Justice and Behavior, 21,* 28-54.

Marshall, W. L. (1992). The social value of treatment for sexual offenders. *Canadian Journal of Human Sexuality, 1,* 109-114.

Marshall, W. L. (1993). The treatment of sex offenders: What does the outcome data tell us? A reply to Quinsey et al. *Journal of Interpersonal Violence, 8,* 524-530.

Marshall, W. L., & Anderson, D. (1996). An evaluation of the benefits of relapse prevention programs with sexual offenders. *Sexual Abuse: A Journal of Research and Treatment, 8,* 209-221.

Marshall, W. L., Anderson, D., & Fernandez, Y. M. (1999). *Cognitive behavioural treatment of sexual offenders.* London: Wiley.

Marshall, W. L., & Barbaree, H. E. (1988). The long-term evaluation of a behavioral treatment program for child molesters. *Behaviour Research and Therapy, 26,* 499-511.

Marshall, W. L., Jones, R., Ward, T., Johnston, P., & Barbaree, H. E. (1991). Treatment outcome with sex offenders. *Clinical Psychology Review, 11,* 465-485.

Marshall, W. L., & Pithers, W. D. (1994). A reconsideration of treatment outcome with sex offenders. *Criminal Justice and Behavior, 21,* 10-27.

Meyers, L. C., & Romero, J. J. (1980). *A ten-year follow-up of sex offender recidivism.* Philadelphia, PA: J. J. Peters Institute.

Miner, M. H. (1997). How can we conduct treatment outcome research? *Sexual Abuse: A Journal of Research and Treatment, 9,* 95-110.

Miner, M. H., Day, D. M., & Nafpaktitis, M. K. (1989). Assessment of coping skills: Development of a Situational Competency Test. In D. R. Laws (Ed.), *Relapse prevention with sex offenders* (pp. 127-136). New York: Guilford.

Nelson, C., & Jackson, P. (1989). High-risk recognition: The cognitive-behavioral chain. In D. R. Laws (Ed.), *Relapse prevention with sex offenders* (pp. 167-177). New York: Guilford.

Nicholaichuk, T., Gordon, A., Andre, G., Gu, D., & Wong, S. (1998). *Outcome of the Clearwater Sex Offender Treatment Program: A matched comparison between treated and untreated offenders.* Submitted for publication.

Peters, J. J., & Roether, H. A. (1971). *Success and failure of sex offenders.* Philadelphia, PA: American Association for the Advancement of Science.

Pithers, W. D. (1990). Relapse prevention with sexual aggressors: A method for maintaining therapeutic change and enhancing external supervision. In W. L. Marshall, D. R. Laws, & H. E. Barbaree (Eds.), *The handbook of sexual assault: Issues, theories and treatment of the offender* (pp. 363-385). New York: Plenum.

Pithers, W. D., Marques, J. K., Gibat, C. C., & Marlatt, G. A. (1983). Relapse prevention with sexual aggressives: A self-control model of treatment and maintenance of change. In J. G. Greer & I. R. Stuart (Eds.), *The sexual aggressor: Current perspectives on treatment* (pp. 214-239). New York: Van Nostrand Reinhold.

Pithers, W. D., Martin, G. R., & Cumming, G. F. (1989). Vermont Treatment Program for Sexual Aggressors. In D. R. Laws (Ed.), *Relapse prevention with sex offenders* (pp. 292-310). New York: Guilford.

Prentky, R. A., & Burgess, A. W. (1990). Rehabilitation of child molesters: A cost-benefit analysis. *American Journal of Orthopsychiatry, 60,* 80-117.

Proulx, J., Ouimet, M., Pellerin, B., Paradis, Y., McKibben, A., & Aubut, J. (1998). *Posttreatment recidivism in sexual aggressors.* Submitted for publication.

Quinsey, V. L. (1998). Comment on Marshall's "Monster, victim, or everyman." *Sexual Abuse: A Journal of Research and Treatment, 10,* 65-69.

Quinsey, V. L., Harris, G. T., Rice, M. E., & Lalumière, M. L. (1993). Assessing treatment efficacy in outcome studies of sex offenders. *Journal of Interpersonal Violence, 8,* 512-523.

Rice, M. E., Harris, G. T., & Quinsey, V. L. (1991). Sexual recidivism among child molesters released from a maximum security psychiatric institution. *Journal of Consulting and Clinical Psychology, 59,* 381-386.

Salter, A. (1998, October). *Deception and denial in sex offenders.* Paper presented at the 17th Annual Research and Treatment Conference of the Association for the Treatment of Sexual Abusers, Vancouver, British Columbia.

Soothill, K. L., & Gibbens, T. C. N. (1978). Recidivism of sexual offenders: A reappraisal. *British Journal of Criminology, 18,* 267-276.

Steele, N. (1995). Cost effectiveness of treatment. In B. K. Schwartz & H. R. Cellini (Eds.), *The sex offender: Corrections, treatment and legal practice* (pp. 4.1-4.19). Kingston, NJ: Civic Research Institute.

Sturgeon, V. H., & Taylor, A. (1980). Report of a five-year follow-up study of mentally disordered sex offenders released from Atascadero State Hospital in 1973. *Criminal Justice Journal, 4,* 31-63.

Ward, T., & Hudson, S. M. (1996). Relapse prevention: A critical analysis. *Sexual Abuse: A Journal of Research and Treatment, 8,* 177-200.

Ward, T., Hudson, S. M., & Siegert, R. J. (1995). A critical comment on Pithers' relapse prevention model. *Sexual Abuse: A Journal of Research and Treatment, 7,* 167-175.

Worling, J., & Curwen, T. (1998). *The adolescent sexual offender project: A 10-year follow-up study* (Report on the SAFE-T Program, Thistletown Regional Centre for Children and Adolescents). Toronto: Ontario Ministry of Community and Social Services.

CHAPTER 4

Relapse Prevention and Harm Reduction

Areas of Overlap

SUSAN A. STONER
WILLIAM H. GEORGE
University of Washington

The successful application of relapse prevention (RP) to sex offender treatment has demonstrated the utility of adapting cognitive-behavioral approaches used in the addictions field to this area. Regardless of whether one believes sexual offending is indeed addictive behavior, the pragmatic strategies prescribed by RP have proven useful despite the fact that they were developed for dealing with addictions. In the interest of doing what works, looking again at what our colleagues in the addictions field are doing may provide additional tools or approaches to enhance treatment of sex offenders even further. Insofar as recent advancements in the treatment of addictions may be adapted to sex offender treatment and hold promise, as RP did, they merit consideration. Harm reduction is one such advancement. Although its application has generated significant controversy, it has been presented as a revolutionary philosophy, and its advocates are passionate about the potential it holds to improve the public health and quality of life (Marlatt, 1998).

In this chapter, we consider the applicability of harm reduction to sex offender treatment paradigms. After defining harm reduction, we explore how it is used to treat addictions and how it may be used to enhance sex offender treatment in a way that is beneficial to the public health. In so doing, it will be important to address the interface of harm reduction with RP, a more widely accepted and demonstrably successful approach, and the overlap between them. In the addictions field, harm reduction has been presented not as a substitute to RP but as a companion to it. With regard to the sex offender treatment arena, we will discuss how the issues of lapse and relapse, the cognitive-behavioral offense chain, and the abstinence violation effect—concepts that are central to RP—are also central to an understanding of how a harm reduction philosophy might be beneficial to the field.

Understanding Harm Reduction Through Its Application in the Addictions Field

Defining Harm Reduction

On a basic level, harm reduction seeks to do precisely that: reduce harm. As a philosophy, harm reduction sees the inherent value in any reduction in harm and thus endorses a broad range of potential outcomes. Such a philosophy has shaken the foundation of the traditional addictions treatment arena, where absolute abstinence has historically been the only acceptable outcome. Treatment of addiction, viewed as an incurable, degenerative disease, has traditionally mandated abstinence because ingestion of the addictive substance was believed to result in a progression of the disease. Failure to maintain abstinence was called "relapse" because it presumably meant a return to disease progression. Essentially, "relapse prevention" was conceived to prevent this from happening. Cognitive-behavioral conceptions of addiction began to replace medical or disease conceptions as the notion of addiction as disease became increasingly suspect. Most (but not all—e.g., Gorski, 1989) RP models for understanding and treating addiction are grounded in social learning theory and use cognitive-behavioral approaches (Annis & Davis, 1989; Marlatt & Gordon, 1985). Nevertheless, RP models are often applied in ways that either explicitly or implicitly continue to treat addiction as a disease (even if its practitioners do not endorse the disease concept), as if abstinence is the only acceptable outcome and as if relapse *must* be prevented. Recently, many clinicians who subscribe to a cognitive-behavioral view of addictions have come to view addiction primarily as a chronic-relapsing problem (i.e., the tendency to relapse is inherent to addiction). Thus, attention has come to be placed on what can be done to minimize the harm that comes from relapse and to minimize the harm among those addicts who cannot or will not accept total abstinence as the only acceptable goal.

As a public health alternative to the moral and the medical or disease models of addictions, the harm reduction philosophy suggests a more pragmatic focus on the consequences or effects of the addictive behavior rather than on the behavior itself (Marlatt, 1996). As mentioned, traditionally, the medical or disease model held that addiction was a treatable—but perhaps not curable— disease. From this perspective, addicts were viewed as deserving of medical care and rehabilitation, but even with the most competent care, their best hope might be to turn their diseases over to a "higher power." On the other hand, the moral model of addictive behavior held that such behavior was immoral and that those who do it should be punished with incarceration. The "higher power" of the moral model is generally the criminal justice system. In sharp contrast, the primary purpose of any harm reduction intervention is to reduce the harmful consequences of behavior for the person engaging in the behavior and for the community in which the person lives. Its concern is the public health. Behavior is considered primarily in terms of its helpful or harmful impact on the actor and on society, rather in terms of its morality or intractability (Marlatt, 1996).

From the harm reduction perspective, any degree of harm reduced is considered worthwhile, even if harm is not eliminated entirely. Along these lines, abstinence is not considered the *only* acceptable goal. As the ultimate harm reduction, abstinence may be the ultimate goal, but there may be several intermediate goals or steps along the way. In some cases, however, abstinence may not be feasible even as an ultimate goal, but this is not considered reason to abandon treatment. Abstinence is certainly desirous, but it is not a requirement, and it is certainly not a condition of treatment as it often has been for chemical dependency treatment. Advocates of harm reduction support a "stepping down" approach to the treatment of addictive behavior. Each progressive reduction of harm is viewed as inherently valuable.

Harm Reduction and Treating Addiction

One consequence of the harm reduction philosophy is that many interventions and policies that were previously considered unrelated have come to be seen as having common, harm-reducing goals (Marlatt & Tapert, 1993). Although 12-step programs and needle exchange programs may seem strange bedfellows, they both reduce harm. On the surface, they appear to have mutually exclusive aims. Adherents and advocates of 12-step approaches may take issue with needle exchange programs because they allow a user to continue to use. Taking the 12-step perspective to an extreme, needle exchange programs can be considered as "enabling" users because they remove a potential negative consequence of IV drug use (namely, contracting HIV). If users do not have such a serious risk hanging over their heads, they may be less motivated to seek "recovery." A harm reduction advocate may refer a client to either of these programs. Through very different means, both programs may be effective at reducing harm. Wanting to reduce as much harm as possible, the clinician will make a referral to a program that "meets the client where he or she is." A 12-step program is an option for a client who is so inclined, but for another client with no intention to abstain, a supply of clean needles is a definite improvement over having to share dirty ones.

Harm reduction encompasses a vast range of strategies that can be used to reduce harm. For example, in the addictions treatment field, any of the following may reduce harm on some level: achieving and maintaining abstinence, adopting a safer route or site of drug administration (e.g., snorting or smoking instead of shooting, finding a safer place on the body to inject), acquiring drugs of known purity by prescription, not having to resort to prostitution to support a drug habit, using clean needles, using a relatively safer drug such as marijuana instead of heroin, decriminalizing drug use or possession, implementing drug education programs in the schools, using drugs in a safe or familiar place, getting one's life together enough to go back to work, providing support to family members of drug users, or providing outreach to isolated addicts.

From the above list of examples of harm reduction, it should be apparent that harm may be reduced on as many levels on which harm occurs: at the individual level, the community level, and the societal level. Most obviously, on the individual level, services to addicts can help the harm that comes to oneself through using drugs. Here, reducing harm may mean reducing the risk of overdose, reducing the damage to the body, reducing the likelihood of further trauma due to incarceration, or reducing the necessity to steal or prostitute for drugs. On a community level, harm may be reduced by helping families of drug users, reducing the spread of HIV, preventing kids from getting involved with drugs, taking power away from brutal drug syndicates, or getting addicts in touch with one another for support. On a societal level, harm may be reduced by lessening the burden on the criminal justice system, freeing up space in the prisons to house more dangerous individuals, raising productivity and tax revenues by getting addicts back to work, or reallocating moneys from unsuccessful policies and programs such as the "war on drugs" to more successful programs. To apply a harm reduction approach, we must first identify where the harm is in a particular behavior, on individual, community, and societal levels, so that we can design interventions to reduce it. How to prioritize the reduction of harm on these different levels, however, is a difficult question, but priorities are generally drawn based on the occupations of those who intervene. Typically, clinicians focus on the individual level, community leaders focus on the community level, and policymakers and legislators focus on the societal level.

Scanning the list of possible interventions listed above reveals a variety of unconventional and perhaps even morally repugnant methods. For example, prescribing drugs to drug addicts may seem dangerous or unethical. Having divorced itself from the moral model of addiction and turned its attention to reducing the harmful consequences of behavior, harm reduction does not reject any sensible intervention out of hand because it is morally questionable. If an intervention effectively reduces harm, it is valuable. As long as sound theory

supports a proposed intervention, it is worthy of consideration in the harm reduction arena. Before any intervention is implemented on a large scale, however, it must be supported by empirical data. It cannot be stressed enough that,
like public health, harm reduction is grounded in research. This is possible
because harm can be objectively observed and measured. Thus, harm reduction
lends itself nicely to evaluation of outcomes. Although moral considerations
are of importance, the moral model provides no empirical yardstick by which to
measure success. If we operate under the medical model, making the assumption that addiction is a disease, we have no objective test such as a biopsy to
measure whether it is in metastasis or remission.

In addition to supporting intervention on different levels of a problem (individual, community, or societal), harm reduction also supports intervention at
different stages of a problem. Those familiar with public health or health psychology will recall the definitions of different types of prevention. Primary prevention is intervention across the board before a problem starts. For example, in
the addictions field, primary prevention might take the form of educating
schoolchildren about the harmful effects of drugs. Secondary prevention interventions target those who are at increased risk for developing a problem to prevent the problem from happening. For example, interventions have been
designed to help college binge drinkers achieve a healthier style of alcohol consumption to prevent alcohol dependence and alcohol-related problems.
Smokers are urged to stop smoking before developing lung cancer. Tertiary prevention means preventing a problem from getting worse. Injection drug users
are taught to inject in a way to avoid skin abscesses and to bleach their needles to
avoid HIV infection. All of these represent harm reduction. Each of these interventions is inherently valuable because it was designed to reduce harm at some
stage of a problem, even if harm cannot be eliminated entirely.

Like relapse prevention, harm reduction appeals to cognitive-behavioral clinicians because it is consistent with cognitive-behavioral approaches to mental
health problems in general. Cognitive-behavioral clinicians commonly offer
interventions in a series of steps, making treatment more manageable for the
client. Rarely if ever do we expect our clients to get better all at once. With systematic desensitization, there is progress through hierarchies of feared stimuli.
Treatment for depression takes steps toward increasing behavioral activation
and cognitive restructuring. Decreases in the frequency of panic attacks are
welcomed. Irrespective of the diagnosis at hand, each step clients take in the
right direction is considered inherently valuable as they struggle to overcome
dysfunction. In this spirit, today, cognitive-behavioral clinicians are increasingly embracing harm reduction philosophy (Marlatt, 1998). Many cognitive-
behaviorists in the addictions field, dissatisfied with the zero-tolerance, absti-
nent-now-or-you're-out-of-treatment attitude characteristic of traditional
chemical dependency treatment, have begun to consider how to help clients

who do not respond to such an attitude. Harm reduction philosophy is consistent with the step-by-step approach of cognitive-behavioral treatment.

In the addictions field, cognitive-behavioral approaches such as RP have coincided with a movement away from the essentially medical concept of "addiction" to a focus on the more general and pragmatic question of what can be done to improve dysfunctional or problematic behavior. Because RP has been and continues to be adapted successfully to sex offender treatment, and cognitive-behavioral treatments in general are the treatments of choice with sex offenders, perhaps the field can again profit from looking toward pioneering work in the addictions arena. Perhaps, like RP, harm reduction philosophy can be successfully adapted to sex offender treatment.

Formulating a Working Harm Reduction Philosophy for the Field of Sex Offender Treatment

What would adopting a harm reduction philosophy mean to the sex offender treatment field? It is important to bear in mind that harm reduction is a philosophy or a perspective rather than a static set of interventions. If a harm reduction philosophy were adopted in the sex offender treatment field, appropriate interventions would have to be designed in the context of the field rather than translated unaltered from the addictions field. Existing interventions may look different, viewed with harm reduction lenses. RP, for example, would essentially be applied in the same way, but it could be expanded to consider varying degrees of harm reduction, consistent with different definitions of prevention used in public health (see Table 4.1). As it is commonly applied, RP is essentially secondary prevention of relapse; interventions are used to prevent relapse from ever occurring among those who are at high risk for relapse, sex offenders. As tertiary prevention generally refers to preventing a disease from getting worse, the concept and methods of RP could be expanded to include tertiary prevention of relapse; once relapse has occurred and absolute prevention of relapse has failed, interventions could be implemented for "damage control," that is, to reduce the magnitude of relapse (see the "Reconciling RP with Harm Reduction" section). As quaternary prevention generally refers to slowing the progression of a disease, quaternary prevention of relapse could represent reducing the frequency with which relapse occurs, which would also make an appreciable difference from a harm reduction perspective.

If a harm reduction perspective were adopted by the field, outcomes would be considered in terms of whether harm is reduced and, if so, by how much. Imagine a study of treatment outcomes for RP. At one-year follow-up, all 50 offenders in the control (untreated) group reoffended with 5 victims each, for a total of 250 victims. In Scenario A, of 50 offenders in the treatment group, all

TABLE 4.1   Levels of Prevention as Commonly Applied to Sexual Offending and as
Extended to Relapse Prevention (RP)

Level	Prevention of Sexual Offending	Relapse Prevention
Primary	Preventing sexual victimization across the board	Not applicable
Secondary	Preventing those at risk for sexual offending from ever offending	Preventing those at risk for relapse from ever relapsing (Classic RP)
Tertiary	Minimizing the number of victims during a single offense spree	Minimizing the number of victims during a single relapse episode
Quaternary	Not applicable	Reducing the frequency of relapse episodes

NOTE: All levels serve to reduce harm to some extent.

reoffended with 1 victim each, for a total of 50 victims. Will you call the treatment a failure? In Scenario B, of 50 offenders in the treatment group, 49 offenders remained abstinent for the year, but one offender created 50 victims. Will you call the treatment a success? If the philosophy is RP (i.e., "We must prevent relapse"), in Scenario A, the treatment is clearly a failure; 100% of the subjects relapsed. However, the treatment in Scenario B is a phenomenal success because 98% of the subjects remained abstinent. A harm reduction philosophy would assert that Scenario A and Scenario B are equivalent, with treatment reducing the number of new victims by 80% in each case, compared to the control group.

Using a harm reduction philosophy, new interventions could be designed that take more into account than the likelihood of relapse. "Safety nets" could be installed to catch offenders as they fall from the abstinence tightrope. So far, the primary safety net out there has been the "dragnet"; offenders who relapse may or may not be caught by law enforcement, and once caught, they may have had quite a number of victims and wrecked a number of lives. Going back to prison may be so aversive that after relapse, the behavior is driven so far underground that it can go on for a long time before it is detected. If offenders had fewer aversive alternatives once they have relapsed, relapses may be less severe. Perhaps the legal system could provide leniency to those who turn themselves in, making a return to treatment occur sooner and encouraging offenders "get back on the wagon" and back into treatment as soon as possible.

Another possibility with harm reduction is that potential interventions that might otherwise have been rejected out of hand because they are morally repugnant might be tested and found effective. As mentioned before, from a harm reduction perspective, as long as an intervention reduces harm, it is considered potentially valuable. For example, although in the original adaptation of RP to the treatment of sex offenders, deliberate fantasizing about sexually abusive behavior (short of planning its consummation) was considered a lapse and a danger zone. If it could be conclusively demonstrated that fantasy actually *reduced* the likelihood of relapse, it could be prescribed. Similarly, if it could be conclusively demonstrated that masturbating to child pornography actually *reduced* the desire to go out and molest a child and *did not promote* the desire to go out and victimize more children by producing more child pornography and *did not promote* the child pornography production business, child pornography could be prescribed under carefully controlled conditions. Of course those are big ifs, and perhaps these questions could never be adequately tested. In any event, the point is that with harm reduction, there is a bottom line: "Does this help?"

Reconciling Relapse Prevention With Harm Reduction

With regard to sexual offending, Laws (1997) has described harm reduction both as an alternative and an adjunct to RP. We believe harm reduction is best considered a philosophy, the context in which RP and other treatment techniques are applied. Thus, a harm reduction philosophy would be an alternative to an RP philosophy, but harm reduction techniques would encompass and be an adjunct to strictly RP techniques.

Reducing Harm by Reducing the Magnitude of Relapse

In addressing the question of how RP fits in with the harm reduction approach, Marlatt and Tapert (1993) explained,

> In the treatment of alcohol dependence, in programs with an abstinence goal, RP can be applied as a maintenance-stage strategy to prevent relapse (e.g. training clients to cope with high risk situations). If relapse occurs, RP methods can be used to interrupt the relapse process (e.g. taking steps to prevent the escalation of an initial lapse or slip into a full blown relapse). With ongoing relapse problems, RP programs are designed for relapse management: to reduce the frequency and intensity of relapse episodes, to keep the client involved in the treatment process, and to motivate renewed efforts toward behavior change. Applied to relapse management, RP represents a tertiary prevention approach to harm reduction, designed to reduce the magnitude of relapse. (p. 267)

Defining Lapse and Relapse

The issue of defining relapse in sex offender treatment is at the heart of the relapse prevention versus harm reduction debate. When RP was originally adapted from the treatment of addictive behaviors to the treatment of sex offenders, the designations of *lapse* and *relapse* were carefully considered. In traditional RP with addictive behaviors, a lapse refers to a single violation of the abstinence vow by indulgence in the forbidden behavior. Relapse, by contrast, refers to a full-scale reestablishment of the forbidden behavior. Thus, having a single cigarette would be considered a lapse, but returning to smoking two packs per day would be considered a relapse. In the interest of public safety, adapting RP to sex offender treatment required a redefinition of the terms *lapse* and *relapse*. In 1989, George and Marlatt defined the terms as follows:

> With sex offenders, the term *relapse* will refer to any occurrence of a sexual offense, thus connoting full scale re-establishment of the problematic behavior. The term *lapse* will refer to any occurrence of willful and elaborate fantasizing about sexual offending or any return to sources of stimulation associated with the sexual offense pattern, but short of performance of the offense behavior. (p. 6)

Figure 4.1 shows an abridged version of the sequence of events originally thought to typify the relapse process in general (George & Marlatt, 1989). The heavy dashed line in the figure represents the presumed effect of this redefinition: to abandon RP after the occurrence of a single sexual offense, essentially turning intervention over to the criminal justice system after that point.

The need to redefine the terms *lapse* and *relapse* is certainly understandable. Any single occurrence of a sexual offense is a serious crime, and all available resources must be directed at preventing that from happening. However, it must be acknowledged that there is a big difference between a single sexual offense and full-scale reestablishment of the problematic behavior. Interrupting treatment after a single offense and leaving the matter to the criminal justice system essentially sends the message that 1 victim may as well be 20 victims. Of course, this is not true; each of the following 19 victims is just as important as the first. The problem with leaving the offender to the criminal justice system is that 1 victim may give way to 20 victims by the time the criminal justice system learns of the offense and takes the perpetrator off the streets. Keeping the offender in treatment may interrupt the relapse process, so that the offender stops after one new victim, as opposed to continuing to victimize until being caught.

Espousing a harm reduction philosophy requires a multilevel understanding of the terms *lapse* and *relapse*. Marshall, Hudson, and Ward (1992) suggested that the term *lapse*

> be expanded to include considering plans to offend and entering a high-risk situation as well as deviant fantasizing. In addition. . . it is important to have the client understand that a single offense after treatment does not necessarily have to lead to a full

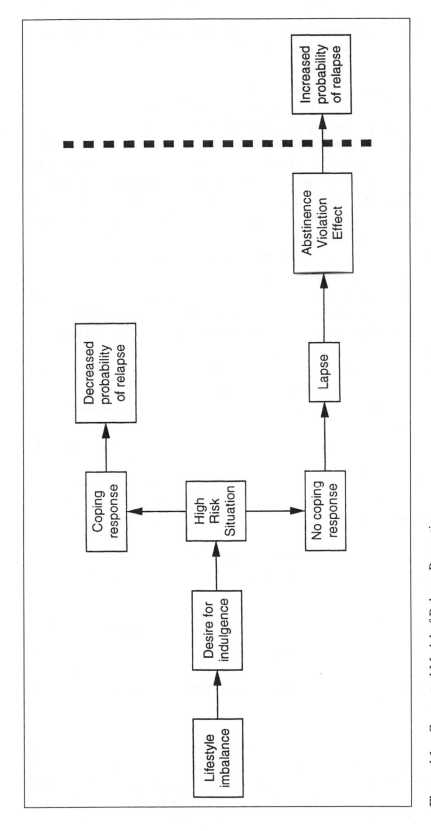

Figure 4.1. Conceptual Model of Relapse Prevention

SOURCE: Adapted from George and Marlatt (1989).

NOTE: The heavy dashed line suggests the boundary of relapse prevention as it is typically applied to sex offender treatment.

return to prior rates of offending, while at the same time emphasizing the importance of avoiding even a single offense. (p. 241)

Thus, the authors explicitly redefined *lapse* and implicitly redefined *relapse,* specifying a continuum rather than the previously implied threshold. Understanding relapse as a continuum is a crucial point in harm reduction, and clients need to realize relapse is a continuum as well. The suggestion of Marshall et al. (1992) shows how to do that without sending the wrong message that even one victim is acceptable. Marshall et al. emphasized, "We do not want clients to view reoffending as an all-or-none phenomenon. If they do reoffend, we want them to stop the process there and not let it escalate to more victims and perhaps more aggressive and intrusive behaviors" (p. 242). Such statements inherently reflect the value of harm reduction: reducing the number of victims and reducing the extent of trauma to each victim.

The client's understanding of the terms *lapse* and *relapse* and of their nature are of critical importance. If we return to a terminology more consistent with RP as it is applied in the addictions field, where a lapse would represent a single new sex offense and a relapse would represent a return to serial victimization, an important empirical question is how clients would interpret this terminology. Indeed, how clients interpret the language we use is an important empirical question in general. If we were to call a single reoffense a lapse rather than a relapse, it is possible that clients would find it easier to rationalize a reoffense: "Oh, it was *just a lapse.*" However, it is also possible that clients could perceive that it is easier to "get back on the wagon" after a first reoffense if it is called a lapse rather than a relapse. Calling the first reoffense a relapse may imply, or clients may infer, that they may as well give up, that one victim may as well be 20. In other words, calling a first reoffense a relapse might fuel the abstinence violation effect.

One major criticism of harm reduction has been that it "sends the wrong message" (MacCoun, 1998, p. 1202), that addicts or sex offenders might take it as tacit approval of drug taking or victimization. This is an important empirical question for which no data exist. Perhaps calling a first reoffense a lapse would be heard by offenders as tacit approval—or at least not strong enough disapproval. We believe the term could be presented with enough gravity so that offenders get the "right" message (i.e., that it should never happen, but if it does, they must get back on track immediately so that it never happens again). As MacCoun (1998) pointed out,

> Braithwaite's (1989) research on reintegrative shaming indicates that it is possible simultaneously to send a social message that certain acts are socially unacceptable while still helping the actors to repair their lives. Braithwaite suggests that this approach is integral to Japanese culture, but it is also reflected in the Christian tradition of "hating the sin but loving the sinner." (p. 1203)

A study on how offenders interpret the language of their treatment providers would be an important contribution to the field.

Describing and Extending the Cognitive-Behavioral Offense Chain

A harm reduction philosophy requires a thorough assessment and understanding of the cognitive-behavioral chain culminating in a sexual offense. Important work by Ward, Louden, Hudson, and Marshall (1995) provided a preliminary description of the offense chain for child molesters. Ward et al. found that there was a large gap between what was originally defined as a lapse, willful fantasy, and the ultimate commission of a sexual offense. Intervening between fantasy and offense was distal planning, contact with a victim, cognitive distortion, and proximal planning, which took on varying forms depending on each offender's style. In a recent revision and elaboration of their model, Ward and Hudson (1997) ascribed a different definition to the term *lapse*. Lapse was defined as "the immediate precursors to the sexual offense, involving behaviors such as getting into bed with a child" (p. 8). Thus, a lapse would demonstrate that an offender is intending to engage in an offense. In this model, a lapse immediately precedes an offense, and three phases intervene between desiring illicit sex and committing a lapse: making approach or avoidance goals for sexual offending, selecting a strategy consistent with the goal, and entering a high-risk situation. Within a single offense chain, offenders should be made aware that they can and *ought* to stop themselves at any point. Doing so will minimize the harm.

If we accept Ward and Hudson's (1997) self-regulation model of the relapse process, it should be clear that this model does not describe a "full-blown relapse" or "a return to previous rates of offending." Rather, the model represents the chain culminating in a single reoffense, defined as a relapse. A full-blown relapse does not stop there. If we understand relapse as a continuum, it should be clear that a full-blown relapse involves a series of these chains, each culminating in victimization. Beyond a single offense chain, along the continuum of relapse, offenders should be made aware that they can and ought to stop themselves at any point. It is best to stop before a single victim, but if that does not happen, stopping before a second victim is important, and if that does not happen, stopping before a third victim is important, and so on. Although a single offense may "connote" full-scale reestablishment of forbidden behavior, it is far from that. Figure 4.2 abbreviates but extends Ward and Hudson's (1997) model beyond a single victim. Indeed, as Marshall et al. (1992) noted, offenders who relapse typically reoffend against more than one victim. Thus, initiating the offense chain after a period of abstinence puts the offender on a "slippery slope," which Figure 4.2 intends to represent. Once on the slippery slope, the tendency will be to continue downward, facilitated by cognitive distortions

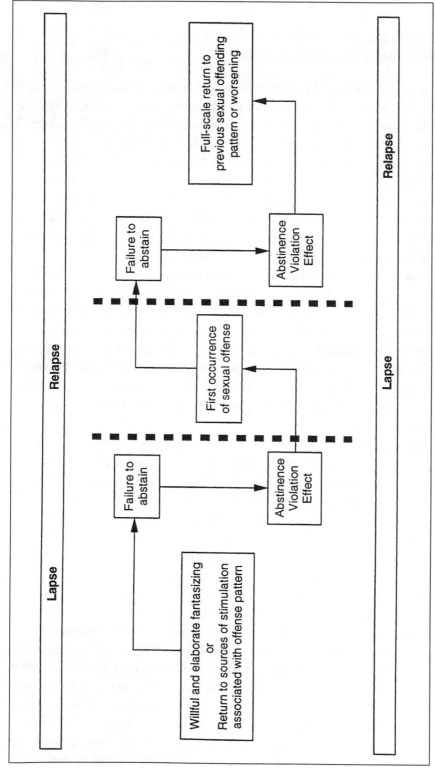

Figure 4.2. The "Slippery Slope" of Relapse, Extending the Cognitive-Behavioral Offense Chain Beyond a Single Offense

along the way. It should be emphasized to the offender that at any point, but *sooner rather than later,* he can and must dig in his heels and climb back up that hill. Ideally, the therapist will be available at the top of the hill to throw him a rope.

The Critical Role of the Abstinence Violation Effect

In the traditional RP model, the transition between lapse and relapse was hypothesized to be mediated by the abstinence violation effect (AVE). The AVE was originally conceived as the cognitive and affective responses to a slip or lapse after a vow of abstinence (Marlatt & Gordon, 1980, 1985), containing two components that could jointly or independently facilitate relapse. The cognitive dissonance component referred to a conflict between one's self-image as an abstainer and one's discrepant behavior (in the lapse), accompanied by feelings of guilt and discomfort. This component was hypothesized to facilitate relapse as the person sought to realign his self-image with the discrepant behavior (from abstainer to nonabstainer) to counteract cognitive dissonance (George & Marlatt, 1989). The personal attribution component referred to the tendency to attribute the cause of the lapse to immutable factors characteristic of the self (e.g., a lack of willpower). This component was hypothesized to facilitate relapse by setting up a self-fulfilling prophecy for continued failure (George & Marlatt, 1989). The potency of the AVE was hypothesized to vary with the person's strength and duration of commitment to abstinence rules. More recently, Hudson, Ward, and Marshall (1992) reformulated the AVE, bringing the concept more in line with current attribution theory. Under this revision, the AVE could be characterized as internal versus external and controllable versus uncontrollable. Offenders who perceived the cause of their lapse as external and controllable would presumably be at a lesser risk of relapse than those who perceived the cause as internal and uncontrollable. In terms of harm reduction, the AVE is critical because it occurs at a potential turning point, between lapse and relapse or between a single reoffense and multiple reoffenses. If the AVE is successfully dealt with, relapse can be averted or halted, and harm can be reduced. If, on the other hand, the AVE is not dealt with successfully, the offender may continue down the path of serial victimization.

Consistent with our continuum notions of lapse and relapse, we believe that the AVE is not a static event. Rather, we believe that the AVE may occur at several points along the offense chain. Given that the AVE was originally hypothesized to vary with the strength and duration of the person's commitment to abstinence, its location may also vary based on from what the person committed to abstain. If the person committed to abstain from willful fantasy, an AVE may be expected to occur after willful fantasy occurs. We would expect some variation between persons in whether this is the case. Russell, Sturgeon, Miner, and Nelson (1989) presented three case histories, designed to illustrate the AVE. In two cases, offenders experienced guilt, feelings of failure, or depression after fantasizing about deviant sex. In the third, however, no AVE was observed in conjunction with such fantasies. This client had verbalized a commitment to abstinence, but he viewed fantasies as permissible as long as he did not act on them. From these examples, it is clear that it is important to understand from what the person has committed to abstain. The first two clients had agreed to abstain from fantasy, and their violation of that commitment led to an AVE. The third client had not committed to abstain from fantasy; consequently, no AVE was evoked.

Thus, it is clear that one potential site of an AVE is after willful fantasy. Another potential site of an AVE, one that we believe carries with it much greater risk, is after relapse (see Figure 4.3). All clients in treatment, we hope, will have committed to abstinence from victimization. If that commitment is breached by the commission of a sexual offense, the AVE could mean the difference between 1 victim and 10 victims. After that first victim, the AVE may effectively drive the offender far enough underground that he is not caught by the authorities until several persons have been victimized, and by that time, the forbidden behavior is that much more entrenched and perhaps less responsive to further treatment. Research by Ward, Hudson, and Marshall (1994) supports two potential sites of an AVE. In their study, 26 incarcerated child molesters listened to an audiotaped description of their most typical offense chain. Although only 7 offenders experienced an AVE at the point of lapse, 18 offenders experienced an AVE after relapse. Such research is crucial because from a harm reduction perspective, minimizing the influence of the AVE means minimizing the likelihood that the offender will go on to create more victims.

Objections to Early Calls for Harm Reduction With Sex Offenders

Previous calls for a harm reduction perspective on sex offender treatment (e.g., Laws, 1998a, 1998b) have met with reactions ranging from resistance to outrage. This is understandable and expectable given the distinct differences between sex offending and substance addiction. Due to these differences, harm reduction, like RP, must be carefully considered and adapted to the needs of the field. We will explore some of the reasonable and expected objections to the adaptation of harm reduction to the sex offender treatment.

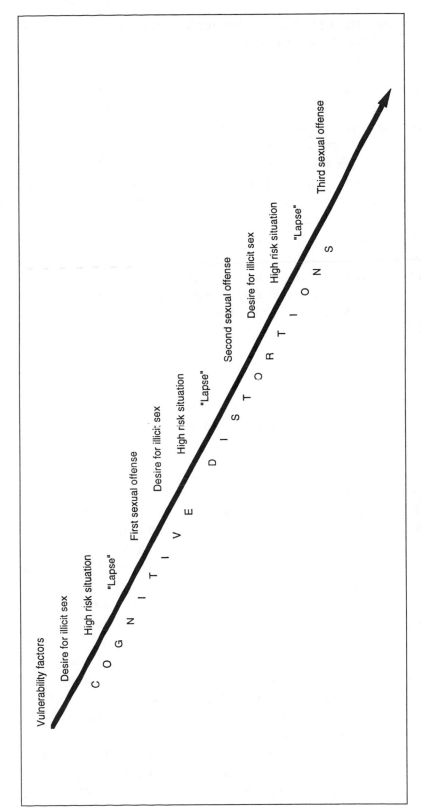

Figure 4.3. Multiple Locations of the Abstinence Violation Effect, Which May Occur After Any Abstinence Vow Is Broken

71

Strategies for Harm Reduction in the Addictions Field
Simply Do Not Translate to Sex Offender Treatment

Although some advocates of harm reduction in the addictions field would call for drug legalization (to reduce crime, to increase safety by controlling purity, to discourage other criminal behavior by controlling cost and access, etc.), no one would argue for the legalization of child pornography or pedophilia, for example, because this would do little to reduce harm. Nor would one suggest, as some in the addictions field advocate the medical provision of heroin, that we provide sex offenders with victims—or even imply that victimization in any form or amount is acceptable. There cannot be a one-to-one correspondence between approaches used in the addictions field and approaches used in the field of sexual deviance. Harm reduction must be considered in the context of sex offender treatment. One can adopt harm reduction as a philosophy without attempting to translate a set of strategies from one field to another with very different characteristics. Sex offender treatment must invent its own strategies but ask the same question, "What can we do to reduce harm where harm occurs?"

Adopting Anything Other Than a Strict Zero-Tolerance
Policy to Sex Offending Would Be Immoral

Harm reduction advocates in the addictions field strive to divorce themselves from a moral perspective because, in that field, moralizing is considered inherently harmful. With regard to sexual deviance, moralizing would be compatible with a harm reduction standpoint if moralizing were effective at protecting the public health. Perhaps it is. Consistent with the harm reduction emphasis on outcomes, it is worthwhile to investigate whether this is the case. If telling sex offenders that offending is wrong keeps them from offending, then it would be worthwhile to do. Regardless, treatment providers with strong moral perspectives on sex offending can maintain them within a harm reduction framework. A moral high ground is not necessarily incompatible with harm reduction. One does not have to say "a little bit of sex offending is okay." It is not. Victimization is devastating, and because each victim is potentially devastated, the purpose is to reduce the number of victims, reduce the number of lives that are devastated. As Maletzsky (1998) states, "Even one victim is one too many" (p. 79), but conversely, *one victim less* is an appreciable improvement. That makes one less person whose life is damaged, and that life is important. Harm reduction does not inherently mean *tolerating* any more than zero, but it does mean seeing the value in at least one victim less, if not complete eradication.

Harm Reduction Implies Abandoning Abstinence as the Absolute Goal

Actually, abstinence is the *ultimate* harm reduction. In the addictions field, the goal used to be abstinence or nothing. If an addict relapsed, the addict was kicked out of treatment, and this practice was inherently harmful. Thus, in the addictions field, harm reduction has meant acceptance of alternate goals. With sex offending, because one victim is indeed one too many, there may be no other acceptable goals. It would be unacceptable to tell a sex offender "Okay, now this month try to reduce your offending to biweekly instead of weekly," which might be an acceptable goal if we were talking about reducing harm from substance use. Of course, victims are not substances. As the ultimate harm reduction, abstinence must always be the ultimate goal. Without abandoning abstinence as a goal, one can put mechanisms in place that reduce harm without embracing nonabstinence goals. An example might be encouraging an offender to turn himself in or to return to treatment after a single victim. This does not imply that one victim is okay. Instead, it seeks to curtail sex-offending behavior, recognizing that 1 victim is less disastrous than 2 or 5 or 20. Another example might be to teach the offender that even if he starts down the road culminating in a sex offense, he can turn back at any time; offending is not to be considered inevitable at any point on the chain of behavior. If the pedophile goes to the playground, it is possible to turn around before targeting a child. If he touches a child, it is possible to stop before he molests her. That does not mean touching a child sexually is okay—it is absolutely *not* okay—but if he found himself doing it, it would be harm reduction if he *stopped right there* instead of going on to complete the molestation. In RP terms, both of these examples seek to break the abstinence violation effect.

Conclusion

Harm reduction has emerged as an innovative yet controversial approach to conceptualizing treatment, prevention, and public policy in the addictions field. Like RP, its migratory predecessor from addictions, harm reduction holds promise for expanding and enriching sex offender treatment. But also like RP, it poses important and vexing translational challenges. In this chapter, we considered the merits of applying harm reduction to sex offender treatment. In so doing, we defined and described harm reduction, we reviewed and updated key RP constructs to foster better reconciling with harm reduction, and we addressed several of the challenges involved with translating harm reduction to sex offender work. We are optimistic that harm reduction may be profitably applied to sex offender treatment protocols. Because harm reduction is still a relative newcomer—even in its parent field of addictions—we recognize a well-founded reluctance to gamble with such high stakes. However, as with RP, success at realizing effective harm reduction applications with sex offenders will ultimately depend on the willingness of clinicians and researchers to engage new ideas and theories, to debate their soundness and rigor, to formulate fair operationalizations, and to evaluate the empirical outcomes. It is worth recalling that RP initially met with some skepticism and that despite formidable translational challenges, it has become one of most prominent intervention strategies for treating sex offenders. This did not occur overnight. Only through years of experimentation, evaluation, and refining did RP become so mainstream. Perhaps harm reduction could follow a similar course.

Using an Olympic analogy, Laws (1999) stated, "On the bottom line [harm reduction] represents an acknowledgment that it may sometimes be better to go for a probable silver than a possible gold" (p. 16). We assert that espousing harm reduction as a philosophy should not be considered giving up on the gold medal of abstinence. Indeed, abstinence is the ultimate harm reduction, and any spirited competitor always goes for the gold. As a philosophy, harm reduction recognizes the value in the silver and also in the bronze. Furthermore, it supports the notion that fourth place is better than fifth, and fifth is better than sixth, and so on. The bottom line is better stated as "Do not drop out of the race if you cannot come in first place." Approximations of perfection are not equivalent to failure.

References

Annis, H. M., & Davis, C. S. (1989). Relapse prevention training: A cognitive-behavioral approach based on self-efficacy theory. *Journal of Chemical Dependency Treatment, 2,* 81-103.

Braithwaite, J. (1989). *Crime, shame, and reintegration.* Cambridge, UK: Cambridge University Press.

George, W. H., & Marlatt, G. A. (1989). Introduction. In D. R. Laws (Ed.), *Relapse prevention with sex offenders* (pp. 1-31). New York: Guilford.

Gorski, T. T. (1989). The CENAPS model of relapse prevention planning. *Journal of Chemical Dependency Treatment, 2,* 153-169.

Hudson, S. M., Ward, T., & Marshall, W. L. (1992). The abstinence violation effect in sex offenders: A reformulation. *Behaviour Research & Therapy, 30,* 435-441.

Laws, D. R. (1997, October). *The harm reduction alternative to relapse prevention.* Paper presented at the meeting of the Association for the Treatment of Sexual Abusers, Victoria, British Columbia.

Laws, D. R. (1998a, February). *Going for the silver: Harm reduction and sex offender management at the millenium.* Paper presented at Forensic Psychology: 2000 Beyond, Liverpool, England.

Laws, D. R. (1998b, October). *Preventing relapse, minimizing harm: Some issues in considering sexual offending as a public health problem.* Paper presented at the meeting of the Association for the Treatment of Sexual Abusers, Victoria, British Columbia.

Laws, D. R. (1999). Harm reduction or harm facilitation: A reply to Maletzky. *Sexual Abuse: A Journal of Research & Treatment, 11,* 233-240.

MacCoun, R. J. (1998). Toward a psychology of harm reduction. *American Psychologist, 53,* 1199-1208.

Maletzky, B. M. (1998). Harm facilitation. *Sexual Abuse: A Journal of Research & Treatment, 10,* 77-79.

Marlatt, G. A. (1996). Harm reduction: Come as you are. *Addictive Behaviors, 21,* 779-788.

Marlatt, G. A. (1998). *Harm reduction: Pragmatic strategies for managing high-risk behaviors.* New York: Guilford.

Marlatt, G. A., & Gordon, J. R. (1980). Determinants of relapse: Implications for the maintenance of be-
    havior change. In P. Davidson & S. Davidson (Eds.), *Behavioral medicine: Changing health lifestyles*
    (pp. 410-452). New York: Brunner/Mazel.
Marlatt, G. A., & Gordon, J. R. (Eds.). (1985). *Relapse prevention: Maintenance strategies in the treatment of
    addictive behaviors.* New York: Guilford.
Marlatt, G. A., & Tapert, S. F. (1993). Harm reduction: Reducing the risks of addictive behaviors. In J. S. Baer,
    G. A. Marlatt, & R. McMahon (Eds.), *Addictive behaviors across the lifespan* (pp. 243-273). Newbury
    Park, CA: Sage.
Marshall, W. L., Hudson, S. M., & Ward, T. (1992). Sexual deviance. In P. H. Wilson (Ed.), *Principles and
    practice of relapse prevention* (pp. 235-254). New York: Guilford.
Russell, K., Sturgeon, V. H., Miner, M. H., & Nelson, C. (1989). Determinants of the abstinence violation
    effect in sexual fantasies. In D. R. Laws (Ed.), *Relapse prevention with sex offenders* (pp. 63-72). New
    York: Guilford.
Ward, T., & Hudson, S. M. (1997, October). *Relapse prevention: Conceptual innovations.* Paper presented at
    the meeting of the Association for the Treatment of Sexual Abusers, Arlington, VA.
Ward, T., Hudson, S. M., & Marshall, W. L. (1994). The abstinence violation effect in child molesters. *Behav-
    ior Research and Therapy, 32,* 431-437.
Ward, T., Louden, K., Hudson, S. M., & Marshall, W. L. (1995). A descriptive model of the offense chain for
    child molesters. *Journal of Interpersonal Violence, 10,* 452-472.

PART III

CONCEPTUAL AND CLINICAL REVISIONS

CHAPTER 5

A Self-Regulation Model of Relapse Prevention

TONY WARD
University of Melbourne, Australia

STEPHEN M. HUDSON
University of Canterbury, New Zealand

Historically, the assumption that relapse constitutes a process or chain of behavior occurring across time has led to the adoption of relapse prevention as a treatment model in the sexual offending area (Pithers, 1990; Pithers, Marques, Gibat, & Marlatt, 1983). Pithers's influential relapse prevention model focuses on factors proximal to offending, describing the process as an affective/cognitive/behavioral chain that culminates in the recurrence of sexually aggressive behavior (Pithers et al., 1983). Despite their enormous value in guiding treatment and research, both Pithers's and Marlatt's (Marlatt & Gordon, 1985) original relapse prevention models suffer from a number of conceptual and empirical problems. Both have been constructed from very diverse and arguably incompatible theoretical elements. This has led to conceptual confusion, as well as significant redundancy. However, from a clinical perspective, the most serious shortcoming of the Pithers's framework is that it does not cover all the possible pathways or processes involved in reoffending. His model emphasizes skill deficits as the major mediators of relapse and fails to cover situations in which individuals consciously decide to use drugs or engage in sexually abusive behavior (for a systematic critique of both Marlatt's and Pithers's perspectives, see Ward & Hudson, 1996).

Drawing on our empirical and theoretical work, we suggest that a comprehensive model of the relapse process needs to contain a number of pathways, preferably taking into account different types of goals (e.g., approach vs. avoidance goals), varying affective states (both initial and ongoing), and different types of planning (see Ward & Hudson, 1998). Second, it should provide mechanisms to integrate cognitive, affective, and behavioral factors as they relate to the offense process. Third, it should include an explicit temporal emphasis and be able to account for the dynamic nature of the offense process. Fourth, it needs to be able to account for the various phases or milestones of the offense process, at least as they are currently understood. This includes the influence of background factors, distal vulnerability factors, decisions that lead to high-risk situations, the initial lapse, the sexual offense, and the impact of the offense on subsequent offending. In addition, the psychological mechanisms that drive and inhibit the relapse process should be identified and described.

In this chapter, a self-regulation model of the relapse process is described that we suggest addresses the problems that have been identified in Pithers's work. This model also has the potential to provide a more comprehensive guide for clinicians. First, we briefly review relevant research and theory on self-regulation to provide a conceptual basis for the model. Second, we present our model of the relapse process, which contains nine phases and four pathways. Finally, we briefly discuss the research and clinical implications of this model. This chapter draws heavily from a number of our recent publications on relapse prevention and sexual offenders (Ward & Hudson, 1998, in press; Ward & Keenan, 1999).

Self-Regulation and Sexual Offending

Self-Regulation Theory

Self-regulation consists of the internal and external processes that allow an individual to engage in goal-directed actions over time and in different contexts (Baumeister & Heatherton, 1996; Karoly, 1993). This includes the initial selection of goals, planning, monitoring, evaluation, and modification of behavior to accomplish one's goals in an optimal or satisfactory manner (Heckhausen & Schulz, 1998; Thompson, 1994). Therefore, it is clear that self-regulation is not solely concerned with inhibiting or suppressing behavior but can include the enhancement, maintenance, or elicitation of behavior as well. On some occasions, the enhancement of emotional states (e.g., when steeling oneself to tackle a difficult situation such as writing an exam) and precipitation of activity are legitimate goals. Also, the maintenance of behavior might be warranted when it has proved effective in achieving desired goals.

Goals are key constructs in theories of self-regulation and function to guide the planning, implementation, and evaluation of behavior. In essence, goals are desired states or situations that individuals strive to achieve or to avoid and as such are important components of personality (Austin & Vancouver, 1996; Emmons, 1996). Arguably, they have their origin in basic human needs for autonomy, competence, and relatedness (Ryan, 1998). Although goals vary according to their degree of abstractness, they can also serve different functions. Cochran and Tesser (1996) make a useful distinction between acquisitional (approach) and inhibitory (avoidance) goals. Acquisitional goals concern gaining or increasing a skill or situation and essentially involve approach behavior. Failure to achieve such goals tends to be a graded occurrence and may function to increase a person's effort to succeed. Attention is focused on information indicating success, and therefore positive memories and cognitions are more likely to be experienced. By way of contrast, inhibitory goals are concerned with the decrease or inhibition of a behavior or situation and involve avoidance behavior. Failure is usually construed in an all-or-nothing manner, and attention is focused on information signaling failure rather than success. Therefore, failure-related memories or cognitions are more commonly experienced by individuals whose behavior is guided by inhibitory goals.

Inhibitory or negative goals are always more difficult to achieve because a person can fail to prevent an event or state from occurring in many ways (Wegner, 1994). Such a task demands considerable cognitive resources because it is necessary to monitor the environment for all types of potential threats. Therefore, when an individual is stressed or experiencing strong emotional states, self-regulation can be impaired relatively easily. In contrast, there may only be a single route to a positive goal, and the major drain on cognitive resources concerns the planning and implementation of the actions necessary to obtain the desired outcome (Emmons, 1996). From a self-regulatory perspective, such a task is more straightforward. The evidence suggests that individuals with avoidance goals experience higher levels of psychological distress than those with approach goals (Emmons, 1996).

In their control theory of self-regulation, Carver and Scheier (1981, 1990) argue that goals are cognitive structures stored in memory in the form of behavioral scripts or knowledge. These cognitive representations contain information that enables individuals to interpret the actions of others and also guide their own actions. Goals and the accompanying behavioral scripts are hierarchically organized and vary according to their degree of abstraction. For example, shoveling snow off the sidewalk, helping one's neighbors, or, at a very abstract level, trying to be a thoughtful and caring individual are all descriptions of related goals. The more abstract or higher-level goals are translated into lower-level behaviors and associated subgoals and ultimately physical actions.

Goals are also related to affective states, with achievement being associated with positive emotions and failure with negative emotions (Carver & Scheier, 1990). Negative affective states typically result in more extensive processing than positive states, probably because they indicate failure to achieve a valued goal (Carver & Scheier, 1990). Some goals can be directly activated by environmental factors and can result in automatic goal-directed behavior without the need for conscious decision making (Bargh & Barndollar, 1996). Once such goals are activated, they exert a direct influence on the processing of information and subsequent generation of behavior.

The self-regulation of behavior typically involves conscious or controlled cognitive processing (Carver & Scheier, 1990). A key question for research concerns how goals become manifest in behavior or, more generally, generate action. When a goal is salient or is activated, it functions as a reference value or standard of comparison, and subsequent information concerning an individual's behavior (and its consequences) is compared to this standard. The relevant cues can be internal (e.g., emotions) or external factors (e.g., the responses of other people). If there is a discrepancy between the perceived information and the internal standard or goal, then the individual attempts to change his or her behavior to match the desired outcome. The system associated with monitoring the relationship between a goal and current behavior is called a feedback loop, and the reduction of a discrepancy between a goal and behavior is referred to as a negative feedback process. Anticipatory processes also influence behavior in complex organisms and take the form of expectations concerning the probable outcomes of specific actions (Ford, 1987; Kanfer & Schefft, 1988). The obstruction of attempts to realize a goal or a failure to achieve it results in attention being directed to the self and the appropriate reference value. The resulting self-focus leads to a comparison between the current situation and the salient goal. Reductions in self-awareness are associated with impaired self-regulation of behavior, presumably because of the loss of goal salience. We have argued in a previous paper that such cognitively deconstructed states are associated with relapse in some sexual offenders (Ward, Hudson, & Marshall, 1995).

Some interesting research has examined the effect of mental simulation on subsequent goal-directed behavior. According to Taylor and Pham (1996), when individuals think about possible outcomes in a concrete and systematic manner, they are much more likely to perform such actions in the future. Simply thinking about the processes needed to reach a particular goal enhances individuals' motivation to behave in certain ways and leads to effective self-regulatory strategies. They suggest that mental simulation makes the occurrence of events seem more likely, helps to establish and refine plans, evokes affective responses, and confirms that certain steps are essential to obtain a desired outcome. For example, individuals who imagined that they had cable television were much more likely to subsequently purchase it (Taylor & Pham, 1996).

This research suggests that sexually deviant fantasies and aggressive ruminations may increase the chances of offenders ultimately assaulting or abusing victims. In a recent paper (Ward & Hudson, in press), we argued that at least two different types of automatic goal-dependent action plans are evident in offenders' implicit decision making: offense scripts (see below) and mental simulations. Although the potential for sexual fantasies to help form and refine plans for offending has frequently been noted (e.g., Pithers, 1990), there has been little theoretical speculation on the possible mechanisms generating this behavior (but see Gagnon & Simon's 1987 paper on sexual scripts). We suggest that the self-regulatory mechanisms associated with mental simulation can provide plausible explanatory constructs. The process of selecting a primary goal such as establishing intimacy, imagining the circumstances in which such a goal might be achieved (e.g., sex with a child), and planning what to do and how to do it can result in automatic decision making when an individual encounters the relevant environmental cues ("When I encounter X, I will perform behavior Y").

This type of automatic goal-dependent action plan will not be mentally represented as an offense script because there is no history of extensive pairing of certain situations and offending behavior. What is required is a prior commitment to certain goals; the occurrence of procedural planning in which the when, where, and how of offending behavior is imagined; and the actual ability to execute the required actions. This represents a simulation pathway in which the mental representation and planning of a sexual offense can result in the automatic activation of a plan once in a particular environment. We suggest that sexual fantasies and ruminations may provide a means through which this type of automatic plan is acquired and refined. For example, in response to lifestyle imbalance, an offender may start fantasizing about abusing a child in a park. He might run through the how, where, when, and what of the possible offense. Once in a particular mood and in an environment similar to that specified in his fantasy, he may automatically start the sequence of offending behavior. He might automatically walk to the pornography section of a video store or attempt to make contact with a vulnerable child by smiling at the child. He has made a number of seemingly irrelevant decisions that placed him in high-risk situations and thereby increased his chances of relapsing.

The important point is that with this type of automaticity, there is no requirement that an offender has *previously* engaged in sexually offensive behavior. Once individuals have consciously decided to perform a sexually abusive action (e.g., in a deviant fantasy), then when the relevant internal or external cures are encountered, they are more likely to effortlessly engage in goal-directed behavior. That is, their plans will unfold automatically without much conscious awareness, and without realizing it, they may make decisions that lead to a high-risk situation. For example, a man may fantasize about raping a woman but never act out this scenario. However, the occurrence of a particularly stressful life event may leave him feeling demoralized and depressed. The presence of a powerful negative mood may make it more difficult to consciously monitor his decision-making behavior, and once in a suitable environment, he may start to act out his abusive fantasies without initially realizing the significance of his actions.

If someone who is attempting to abstain from reoffending fantasizes about certain sexually abusive situations and is confronted with cues that mirror those contained in his fantasies, he may automatically make offense-supportive decisions and run the risk of relapse despite his good intentions. This is more likely to occur if he mistakenly believes that his sexual fantasizing provides an acceptable means of regulating his deviant urges or rationalizes these away as functionally irrelevant to the possibility of relapse. In this situation, the individual has made an explicit attempt to deal with the threat to his intention to abstain from further sexual offending. The problem is that the selected strategy (masturbating to deviant fantasies) is not appropriate and, paradoxically, only increases the probability of an offense occurring.

Self-Regulation Styles

There are three styles of dysfunctional self-regulation (Baumeister & Heatherton, 1996; Carver & Scheier, 1990). First, individuals can fail to control their behavior or emotions and behave in a disinhibited manner. This type of self-regulatory failure can be associated with either positive or negative emotions. This type of self-regulation failure is usually associated with negative emotional states. Second, the use of ineffective strategies to achieve goals can backfire and ultimately result in a loss of control—a misregulation pattern. An example of this pattern would be a person who used alcohol or sexual fantasies to modulate negative mood states or thought suppression to eradicate intrusive thoughts. The paradox is that the faulty use of strategies to achieve certain goals can backfire and lead to the emergence or reemergence of problematic behaviors and emotions.

The third pattern has been somewhat neglected in sexual aggression and paradoxically involves effective self-regulation. The major problem resides in the choice of goals, rather than a breakdown in the components of self-regulation. For example, the setting of goals and their subsequent planning and implementation by a preferential child molester may be impeccable. The difficulty resides in his initial goals and associated values and beliefs. The emotional state associated with this type of problematic self-regulation is likely to be positive;

the person is achieving his goals and does not regard his lifestyle as particularly problematic, at least in any ego-dystonic fashion.

A Self-Regulation Model of the Relapse Process

The self-regulatory model of the relapse process outlined below (see Figure 5.1) builds on our earlier descriptive model of the offense process (Ward & Hudson, in press; Ward, Louden, Hudson, & Marshall, 1995), theoretical and empirical research on self-regulation, and our ongoing research on the offense process in sexual offenders. The model consists of nine different steps, or more accurately, phases as the process is fluid and indeed may appear seamless to the individual. It is important to note that an offender can exit the relapse process at any time by implementing appropriate coping strategies. In addition, the actual relapse process may take place over a considerable period of time. Individuals may also move back and forth between different points in the offense chain or may remain at specific phases for a relatively long time before moving on to the next phase. In other words, although the process is a dynamic one, the time sequences involved can be quite variable.

The minus and plus signs (i.e., – and +) in the bottom right-hand side of each box in Figure 5.1 indicate the primary affective state hypothesized to be present during a particular phase. If both signs are present, it does not mean that offenders experience *both* affective states at the same time but rather that *some* men experience positive emotions and *some* negative. On the rare occasions when offenders are thought to experience a combination of positive and negative affect, it is made explicit in the text.

Phase 1: Life Event

In this first phase, some kind of life event occurs and is appraised by an individual who is attempting to remain "abstinent." The event might be a major life transition (e.g., a divorce) or a daily hassle such as an argument. The initial appraisal of these life events is hypothesized to be relatively automatic and directly precipitated by external events. Their meaning is established in light of preexisting implicit theories, needs, and abstract goals and the interpersonal context in which it occurs. These higher-level goals are closely related to an individual's self-concept and correspond to system goals associated with needs for autonomy, relatedness, and competence (Carver & Scheier, 1981, 1998; Emmons, 1996). They influence what information is attended to, recalled, and processed. For example, if a man with long-standing resentment and distrust of women argues with his partner, he may feel humiliated and angry. These feelings could lead to the activation of salient goals and behavioral scripts designed

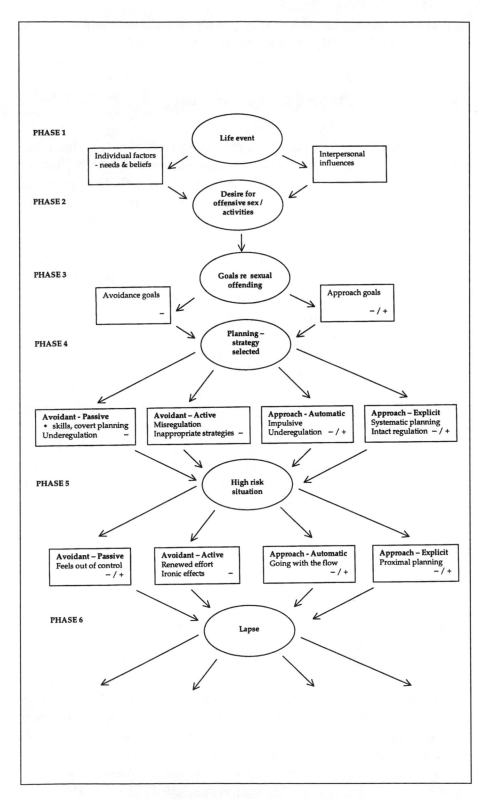

Figure 5.1a. A Self-Regulation Model of the Relapse Process

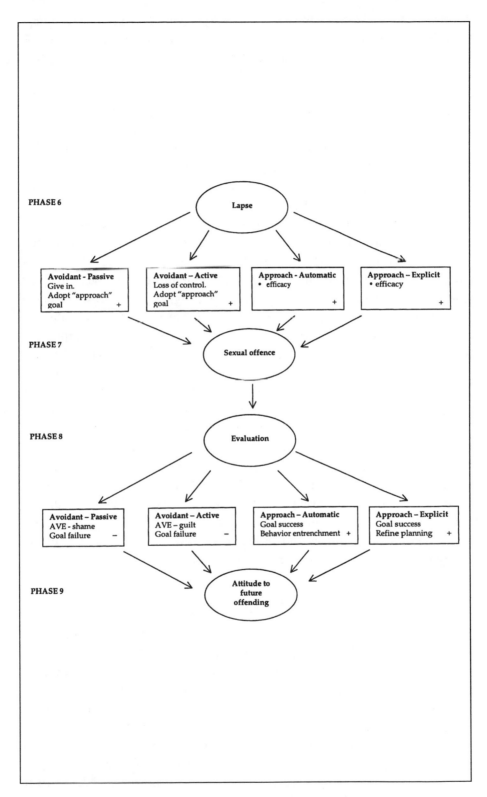

Figure 5.1.b   A Self-Regulation Model of the Relapse Process

to enhance his self-esteem; this may eventually involve a sexual assault. Alternatively, a child molester's chance contact with children might lead to memories of his past offending and positive emotions and evoke goals that ultimately culminate in a reoffense.

In a recent paper, we argued that child molesters' cognitive distortions emerged from underlying causal theories about the nature of their victims, the world, and themselves (Ward & Keenan, 1999). These implicit theories function like scientific theories and are used to explain empirical regularities (e.g., other people's actions) and to make predictions about the world. They are relatively coherent and constituted by a number of interlocking ideas and their component concepts and categories. Implicit theories dictate what counts as evidence and how it is to be interpreted. If there is a discrepancy between an offender's implicit theory and evidence, the evidence may be reinterpreted or rejected, or, rarely, the theory may be modified. For example, a woman's friendly behavior toward an offender could be interpreted to mean that she wants sex or that she is simply being friendly. We suggest that a rapist is likely to interpret this behavior (i.e., "evidence") in sexual terms; his interpretation of the relevant evidence is theory laden. Any revisions are likely to comprise ad hoc hypotheses initially and only result in a replacement theory when the weight of the counterevidence is too hard to ignore (Ward & Keenan, 1999). Offenders also select environments (other child molesters, men with similar attitudes and beliefs, etc.) that support their lifestyles and implicit theories.

The essential point is that experiences of these kinds are thought to automatically activate implicit theories related to an individual's salient goals and needs. These factors, in turn, are hypothesized to trigger specific patterns of thoughts, emotions, and intentions. It is reasonable to assume that such processes have been associated with the event or similar events in the past. For example, an argument might trigger memories of similar incidents, a child's playful antics elicit a yearning for intimacy, and the loss of a job precipitates feelings of inadequacy and a desire to retaliate against the world.

Phase 2: Desire for Deviant Sex or Activity

The life event and its subsequent appraisal results in the emergence of a desire for offensive sex or maladaptive activities and emotions associated with these desires. Sexual and aggressive fantasies frequently coexist with these desires and could function as mental simulations (see above), increasing the possibility of abusive behavior occurring. For example, an offender may desire to have sex with a woman or child, engage in peeping behavior, or sexually expose himself to others. Alternatively, he might want to retaliate against someone and engage in violent and intimidatory behavior. We suggest that the processes necessary to reach these goals may be covertly rehearsed, which in turn may lower an offender's inhibitions against indulging the fantasies. The accompanying affective states might be happiness, curiosity, sexual arousal, anxiety, and anger.

These desires are hypothesized to be directly triggered by the person's associations to the event and may well be outside of his awareness. The activation of memories associated with past offending functions to prime or increase the accessibility of core dysfunctional beliefs and attitudes. These implicit theories are hypothesized to contain goals related to offending and trigger the desire to sexually offend or to engage in some kind of aggressive action (see Bargh & Barndollar, 1996). They may also contain offense scripts (see below). It is likely that links between certain internal and external cues and the desire to offend reflect inappropriate learning experiences (e.g., sexual abuse as a child) and the belief that abusive actions can help the offender to achieve valued goals (e.g., a sense of personal adequacy).

There is likely to be a relationship between the length of offending and the development of offense scripts (Ward & Hudson, in press). Over time, cues associated with sexual offending elicit offense scripts in the absence of awareness. Research supports the idea that familiar, goal-dependent actions are represented in long-term memory in the form of cognitive scripts or action plans (Ward & Hudson, in press). These cognitive representations contain information that guides offending behavior. They specify the conditions under which an offense plan can be enacted, which includes creating access to possible victims and the use of strategies to groom and subdue them. The underlying offense scripts can be enacted without any conscious intention to do so and with minimal awareness of the overall goal. Thus, offense scripts can be activated and implemented in the absence of awareness, can be executed effortlessly, and are coherent and consistent sequences of action tied to the achievement of a specific goal. The relevant cues that activate offense scripts can be internal (e.g., negative mood) or external (e.g., old haunts, previous associates).

Experienced offenders such as serial rapists or preferential child molesters will have a number of coherent, interconnected scripts representing different offense situations and types of victims. This will often include typical offense sequences and, most important, contexts. Such offenders' decision making may be primarily conscious and systematic, but even if they are committed to avoid offending, for whatever reason, the likelihood of covert planning may be involved in setting up an opportunity to offend, and the high-risk situation is greater. Controlling these types of behaviors is difficult, particularly when there is a close fit between the stimulus conditions specified in the script and an offender's current environment. The unfolding of an offense script will also result in sexual arousal and other physiological responses associated with sexually abusive behavior. The decisions and actions contained in these scripts are likely to appear to an offender as irrelevant and unrelated to his subsequent encounter with a high-risk situation. The tendency for these action plans or scripts to be activated in response to negative emotional states or to be difficult to inhibit when in a negative mood is consistent with relapse prevention theory and research (Ward & Hudson, 1998).

The experience of early developmental difficulties or violence may adversely affect the development of self-regulation skills (Cole & Putnam, 1992). Such individuals should exhibit a number of impulsive behaviors and be dominated by the need for immediate gratification. On the other hand, some men may have powerful needs to be intimate with someone but lack the necessary skills to achieve this. Sex may become a means of achieving this goal and establishing a sense of power and importance. Indulging in sex and sexual fantasies may also function as powerful mood regulators and, under particularly unfavorable or stressful circumstances, result in sexual abuse. Some men's sexual aggression or deviant behavior may be related to a generalized difficulty in regulating behavior or mood, but for others it may not.

Phase 3: Offense-Related Goals Established

The desire to engage in deviant sex or a maladaptive activity results in the establishment of an offense-related goal. At this point, an offender considers the acceptability of his maladaptive desire and what, if anything, he should do about it. In addition, the ability (or inability) to tolerate the accompanying affective state will also be considered and may also become a target for self-regulation. For example, some offenders might experience difficulties handling strong negative emotions and engage in escape or avoidance behaviors whenever they are present or anticipated (Thompson, 1994). Alternatively, some sex offenders may crave excitement and seek to enhance or sustain positive affective states such as sexual arousal; we would expect their subsequent goals and related strategies to reflect these preferences.

We suggest that there are two broad classes of relevant goals: avoidance and approach. The former is associated with the desire to avoid sexually reoffending and is essentially negative in nature. That is, the goal is to *not achieve* rather than to achieve a particular state of affairs. As noted earlier, these types of goals are more effortful and difficult to implement because a person can fail to prevent something from happening in a number of ways, whereas a positive goal may be associated with just one pathway (Wegner, 1994). The affective state associated with this category of goals is likely to be negative; a person is fearful or anxious about the possibility of an unwanted event or action occurring and typically experiences higher levels of psychological distress than individuals with approach goals (Emmons, 1996).

In contrast, approach goals reflect the determination to sexually offend, whether in the service of other needs such as aggression or as an end in itself (e.g., believing that one is entitled to sex). This type of goal may be related to positive or negative affective states, depending on the actual aims of the offender. If the aim is to gratify an appetitive process, then it is likely to be positive (e.g., desire for sexual gratification). However, if the intention is to humiliate a person or to execute an aggressive behavior, then strong negative emotions may also be involved.

Phase 4: Strategy Selected

The selection of strategies designed to achieve a goal occurs at this point. It is important to stress that this may not be an explicit decision. Goals and their accompanying strategies can be selected automatically as the result of the activation of offense scripts, that is, action sequences for well-learned and habitual behaviors (Ward & Hudson, in press). Four offense pathways (avoidant-passive, avoidant-active, approach-automatic, and approach-explicit) in our proposed self-regulation model are related to the two broad classes of goals concerning sexual offending. Two relapse pathways are associated with avoidance or inhibitory goals, in which the aim is to *not* sexually offend. There are also two pathways associated with approach or acquisitional goals. Each of these relapse routes is distinguished by the use of distinct strategies in relation to sexually offensive contact and can be further divided into implicit and explicit subpathways. Because the implicit pathways are characterized by disinhibition, they may be traversed more quickly than the explicit ones.

The *avoidant-passive* pathway is characterized by both the desire to avoid sexual offending and the failure to actively attempt to prevent this from happening. It involves the inability to control sexually deviant intentions and is an underregulation or disinhibition pathway. Powerful negative affective states may function as disinhibitors or else lead to behaviors that in turn result in a loss of control. More precisely, behavior is under the control of a more basic-level feedback system. Individuals who follow this relapse pathway are likely to lack coping skills, be more impulsive, have low efficacy expectations, and use covert planning. This type of planning involves what Marlatt and Pithers have referred to as seemingly irrelevant decisions, which are choices that appear superficially reasonable and unrelated to addiction but that collectively help set up high-risk situations (Marlatt & Gordon, 1985; Pithers, 1990).

Individuals attempt to manage the desire for abusive sex and the associated negative emotions through denial or simple and ineffective attempts to distract themselves. The predominant affective state is likely to be negative because of the anxiety associated with the possibility of relapse (i.e., sexual offending). To forestall the chances of relapse occurring, individuals need to constantly monitor the environment for potential threats to abstinence. This goal can fail to be accomplished in a number if ways, and therefore there are numerous possible threats to behavioral restraint. The lack of effective coping skills means that these men, on one hand, are anxious about dealing with threats to control their sexual preferences and, on the other, lack the means to cope with them if they do appear.

The *avoidant-active* or misregulation pathway involves an active attempt to avoid sexual offending. It represents a direct attempt to control deviant thoughts, fantasies, or affective states that threaten to lead to a loss of control. The major difference between this relapse route and the avoidant-passive one is that there is an explicit attempt to deal with the threat to restraint. The problem is that the selected strategies are not appropriate and, paradoxically, increase the probability of an offense occurring. For example, an offender might mistakenly believe that the use of alcohol or drugs might suppress the desire for offensive sex or that indulging in pornography might exhaust his sexual desires. In addition, he might seek to relieve feelings of rejection or anxiety by masturbation. Such men may have high efficacy expectations and possess the ability to plan, monitor, and evaluate their behavior, but they lack knowledge concerning the likely effectiveness of the coping response selected. Unfortunately, the use of alcohol and pornography can increase the risk of disinhibition by potentially strengthening the desire for deviant sex and by decreasing regulatory control. The predominant affective state is also likely to be negative.

Two relapse pathways are associated with approach or acquisitional goals. The third pathway, *approach-automatic,* involves following overlearned behavioral scripts designed to lead to the commission of a sexual offense. Such behavior is relatively impulsive and only planned in a rudimentary way; it appears to occur "out of the blue" and often unfolds in a relatively short time. It is basically a mirror image of the avoidant-passive relapse process in that the goals and the associated strategies are unlikely to be under attentional control and are activated by situational features. It is also essentially an underregulation or disinhibition pathway but differs from the avoidant-passive route to relapse by virtue of its association with an approach goal and appetitive processes. In a sense, it represents a planned impulsiveness (Pithers, 1990). These offenders may vary in their primary affective state, with some experiencing predominantly positive emotions and others predominantly negative ones (see below). The attempt to modulate or heighten positive emotionality, if bound up inappropriately with sexuality, is hypothesized to be related to the relapse process of some of these offenders. The presence of positive emotions is due to the anticipated consequences of indulging deviant sexual or aggressive needs. Positive affect does not reliably result in systematic thinking because it serves as a cue that a person is making satisfactory progress in his or her pursuit of valued goals and therefore does not need to reassess the current strategy (Carver & Scheier, 1990). In addition, the behavioral systems associated with appetitive behavior facilitate rapid action, require relatively few cognitive resources, and are easily activated by relevant environmental cues (Gray, 1990).

Finally, the fourth pathway, *approach-explicit,* involves conscious, explicit planning and well-crafted strategies that result in a sexual offense. Thus, there is intact self-regulation but inappropriate, harmful goals as, for example, when there are inappropriate standards concerning sex with children or attitudes toward women. In Carver and Scheier's (1990) terminology, these are likely to be goals at the principle or program level and represent maladaptive ways of meeting system-level goals, such as the need to be intimate with someone or to establish a sense of personal power or control. Therefore, higher-level goals have become mistakenly linked to sexually abusive behavior. We suggest that these associations reflect early learning experiences (e.g., sexual abuse as a child) and the resultant belief that aggressive or sexually exploitative behavior is an acceptable means to valued ends. These offenders may have excellent strategic and self-regulation skills but use them for socially pernicious ends. The notion of disinhibition does not apply to such individuals; they do not lose control and do not use sex to escape from or reduce powerful negative mood states. Rather, the reverse might very well be true; these offenders may have the goal of maintaining or heightening positive emotions through the offending act. The predominant affective state is likely to be positive or negative.

As indicated earlier, we suggest that each of these four pathways is associated with specific affective states that relate to the type of goal a person is attempting to achieve. Initially, the two avoidance pathways are tagged to negative affective states as the individual is striving to avoid or inhibit an unwanted state or behavior. In contrast, the approach or acquisitional pathways may be characterized by positive or negative affect depending on the nature of the relevant goal. For example, if the goal is to establish a "loving" relationship with a child, then the offender may experience pleasurable anticipation and strong positive affective states. However, if the aim is to intimidate or retaliate against someone (e.g., a woman), powerful, negative emotions such as anger are likely to be present. However, we suggest that as the relapse process unfolds, all types of offenders will experience increasingly positive emotions due to the influence of increased sexual arousal and the perception that important goals are likely to be achieved. In turn, following an offense, the emotional states should be negative for the two pathways associated with avoidance goals (i.e., they have "failed") and positive for those offenders with approach goals (i.e., they have "succeeded").

Phase 5: High-Risk Situation Entered

In the next stage, contact with the victim comes about as a consequence of the earlier implicit or explicit planning or counterproductive strategies. Appraisal processes are thought to occur at this point because of contact or the opportunity for contact with a potential victim. This represents an important event and reflects the offender's initial goals. For those attempting to control or inhibit their behavior, it signifies failure, and for offenders whose goals are acquisitional ones, it signals the likelihood of success. Generally speaking, the affective consequences will be negative for the former and primarily positive for the latter. As an aside, we note that some offenders may be placed unexpectedly in a high-risk situation and enter the relapse process at this phase. However, we suggest that the type of abstinence-related goal they hold (i.e., whether an approach or avoidance goal) will still partly determine the way they interpret and respond to the high-risk situation.

Offenders who are following the avoidant-passive pathway will be struggling with conflicting goals at this point. The contact or anticipated contact with a victim will activate goals linked to offending behavior, and they are likely to be experiencing increasing sexual arousal. The offender may attempt to disguise his real intentions, probably through a narrowing of attention or a movement down to a lower level of behavioral control, probably the program level. The result of control at this more concrete level is that behavior is more automatic and "mindless" and likely to reflect well-rehearsed or habitual sequences of action. The functional autonomy of control at this level means that self-evaluative processes are effectively disengaged. The resulting state is what we have described using Baumeister's construct of cognitive deconstruction (Baumeister, 1990; Ward, Hudson, & Marshall, 1995).

Alternatively, those individuals who are using counterproductive strategies (avoidant-active) will also be finding it increasingly difficult to control their behavior. The presence of a victim will increase the salience of offending-related goals and behavioral strategies and possibly involve more automated and stereotyped responses. Ineffective control strategies such as attempting to suppress unwanted cognitions through the use of drugs may result in ironic rebound effects and a dramatic increase in deviant sexual thoughts or feelings (Johnston, Ward, & Hudson, 1997). Signs that control is failing and subsequent comparisons of the current situation with goals of control and abstinence may result in catastrophic cognitions and a renewed effort to actively manage the situation. The perception that behaviors or thoughts have failed to be inhibited will lead to a sense of personal inadequacy and strong negative affect. The affective states of offenders with avoidant goals are likely to be predominantly negative and their self-efficacy low with respect to restraint.

Offenders following the approach-automatic pathway will be responding to the situational cues in a rapid and automatic manner. They will be focused on the prospect of immediate gratification (what has been called the problem of immediate gratification, or PIG) (Pithers, 1990) and be concerned about their chances of achieving sexual pleasure or related goals. Those offenders consciously planning to achieve their goal of sex with children or the assault of women (approach-explicit) are likely to experience increasingly positive emotions. They will be focused on proximal planning (e.g., considering how to sexually seduce a child or subdue a woman). The sense of efficacy of both approach subtypes is expected to be high at this point. It is important to stress that depending on the exact nature of their intentions, some men with approach goals may still be experiencing negative emotions.

Phase 6: Lapse

The next phase in our model concerns the immediate precursors to the sexual offense, involving behaviors such as getting into bed with a child. In relapse prevention terms, the offender has lapsed and is intending to engage in an offense. We suggest that at this point, individuals following the avoidant-passive pathway will replace their avoidance goals with an approach goal. This may only be temporary and reflects the impact of disinhibition and regulation at a lower level of control. They are hypothesized to give up attempting to control their behavior and become preoccupied with the prospect of sexual gratification. This may be preceded by the experience of a loss of control and an abstinence violation effect. However, the initial self-depreciating attributions and associated negative emotions are hypothesized to be replaced by pleasurable anticipation once the offender decides to sexually abuse his victim. The tendency to focus on immediate gratification signals the dominance of appetitive processes in the lead-up to a sexual offense (i.e., the influence of the PIG). This affective shift may be facilitated by a desire to escape self-evaluation and a subsequent state of cognitive deconstruction (Ward, Hudson, & Marshall, 1995). Similarly, the avoidant-active individual will also judge the attempt to actively control his deviant sexual desires as a failure and, as a consequence, adopt an approach or acquisitional goal. Again, this might only be a temporary transition, and following the offense, many of these individuals will again commit themselves to avoidance goals.

Those offenders with approach goals will continue to strive toward goal satisfaction. Offenders whose offending is driven by automatic processes may exhibit aggressive behavior reflecting their impulsivity. Their behavior is regulated by lower-level goals and associated habitual responses. As such, this behavior is more easily captured by situational cues and likely to be impulsive. Those individuals with explicit approach strategies should demonstrate careful planning and management of the situation and any potential obstacles. Any aggression should be a function of their explicit goals—for example, to inflict pain on a victim (sadism) rather than reflect impulsivity. Because of the impact of increased sexual arousal or pleasurable anticipation, the affective state of *all* offenders is hypothesized to be primarily positive at this phase of the relapse process. The existence of high levels of arousal may cause offenders to reduce the victim to a functionary status; their purpose is serve as an outlet for the offender's sexual and aggressive needs (Ward, Louden, et al., 1995).

Phase 7: Sexual Offense

In our earlier descriptive model, three subcategories concerning the offender's perception of his victims were distinguishable at the time of the actual sexual assault (Ward, Louden, et al., 1995) and were related to different clusters of goals. These were a self-focus, in which the offender's needs are paramount; victim focus, in which offending is justified in terms of "caring" for the victim; and a mutual focus, in which the offense is characterized as a "relationship" with a willing partner. Each of these was associated with different offense styles. A self-focus was associated with short duration but high intrusiveness, and a mutual focus showed typically longer duration, more perceived reciprocity, and typically less intrusiveness (Ward, Louden, et al., 1995). A victim focus at this point in the offense process was not clearly associated with either pattern.

It is not clear whether a particular self-regulation pattern is likely to be associated with each of these different foci. However, the undercontrolled or misregulated individual (left pathways) is likely to be more self-focused, presumably related to the fact that he has become disinhibited and intent on meeting his own needs. Because of the loss of control, the sexual offense may be extremely intrusive and associated with greater levels of violence. However, a man who is self-regulating in an explicit, effective, although maladaptive manner (approach-explicit) may be more concerned with a victim's responses and construe the sexual encounter in mutual terms or attempt to please the victim. Equally, some men self-regulate explicitly but with the intention of humiliating or degrading the victim rather than establishing a mutual relationship. Alternatively, a man who is following the approach-automatic pathway may be impulsive and deliberately intimidating and demeaning, indicating a focus on his own needs.

It is important to note that chronically accessible goals and interpersonal themes will partly determine the manner in which offending is manifested and accomplished. For example, offenders with long-standing negative attitudes toward women are expected to relish the opportunity to express these feelings in their offending behavior. They may exhibit more violence than is necessary or intensify their efforts to humiliate and intimidate their victims. Reflecting the existence of approach goals, the affective state of all individuals is hypothesized to be primarily positive at this phase in the relapse process. However, men whose intention is to intimidate or inflict psychological distress on their victims might experience a combination of negative and positive emotional states.

Phase 8: Postoffense Evaluation

Following the sexual offense, an evaluative process is likely to occur. Offenders following the avoidant pathways are hypothesized to evaluate themselves negatively and feel guilt or shame (a classic abstinence violation effect;

see Ward, Hudson, & Marshall, 1994). In this situation, the comparison of current behavior with the goal of behavioral inhibition (abstinence) reveals a discrepancy and therefore results in the perception that the person has failed. Because an important goal has not been achieved, the offender is likely to experience negative affect (Carver & Scheier, 1990). If an individual attributes the cause of his offending to uncontrollable and stable internal factors, the experience of an abstinence violation effect may lead to more intrusive and prolonged offending (i.e., Relapse 2). Because of the expectation that little could be done to control or change the relevant causal factor, there would be no attempt to inhibit or curtail the deviant behavior. Men who continue to cognitively deconstruct or function at relatively basic levels of behavior control may not evaluate their actions until some later time. Offenders who have approach goals should experience positive affect because they have achieved their goals.

Phase 9: Attitude Toward Future Offending

The final stage of the model concerns the impact of sexual offending on future intentions and expectations. We suggest that those men whose goals are inhibitory may resolve to not offend in the future and attempt to reassert control or return to the use of misregulation strategies. However, it is possible that they may reevaluate their goals and decide that they lack the ability to refrain from further sexual abuse and therefore continue offending. Alternatively, some individuals may be persuaded that sexual offending represents a positive option and change their goals to approach or acquisitory ones.

Individuals characterized by the approach-automatic offense route are likely to have the lower-level behavioral scripts associated with their sexual offending reinforced and strengthened because of their "success." Relatedly, those men following the approach-explicit pathway should continue to refine and develop their abuse-related strategies; they are expected to learn from their experiences and to adjust their modus operandi accordingly. Because of the successful achievement of their approach goals, men following the two acquisitional relapse routes are expected to continue pursuing their goals of sexually assaulting women or children and are unlikely to attempt future restraint.

Generally speaking, whatever offenders learn in a particular offense episode is hypothesized to be assimilated into their existing implicit theories and influence the way future salient life events are interpreted. In addition, self-regulatory styles will also affect how such events are appraised and managed. If a man lacks the capacity to set and implement personally meaningful goals, he will struggle to manage high-risk situations in an adaptive manner. Therefore, if an offender decides to refrain from future sexual offending and adopt an avoidance goal, the existence of self-regulatory deficits suggests that he will struggle to effectively cope with life stresses and high-risk situations. He may simply move from an approach-automatic to an avoidant-passive pathway and still lack the ability to explicitly regulate his behavior. The key point is that enduring deficits in self-regulation and personality style constitute vulnerability factors that will predispose an offender to relapsing.

Conclusions

In this chapter, we have presented a self-regulation model of the relapse process that has several theoretical advantages over the Pithers model. For example, it provides a clearer description of phenomena, such as the abstinence violation effect, without the problems plaguing most versions of this construct (Ward et al., 1994; Ward & Hudson, 1996). It specifies when this phenomenon is likely to occur and formulates it entirely in terms of self-regulation constructs. For example, in our model, it can occur at any point in the offense process, provided that individuals have inhibitory goals. This model can also incorporate previously unrelated theoretically relevant work such as our use of cognitive deconstruction (Ward, Hudson, & Marshall, 1995), Wegner's theory of ironic processes (Johnston & Ward, 1996; Wegner, 1994), and attachment and emotional regulation theory (Ward, Fon, Hudson, & McCormack, 1998). It is also possible to integrate work in other domains of psychology that use a self-regulation perspective (e.g., viewing attachment style and internal working models as representing emotional regulation strategies) (Cole, Michel, & Teti, 1994; Ward, Hudson, & Marshall, 1996).

The integration of goals and self-regulatory style is elegant and simple without being simplistic. The model allows for the addition of other pathways should the data indicate that these are required. It also allows for the incorporation of new theoretical developments as they arise. In addition, it allows for multiple levels of detail where required. For example, a clinician needs a broad-level outline when encouraging an offender's initial disclosure, whereas a researcher may well be interested in the more specific issue of affect regulation in an underregulated participant when entering a high-risk situation.

A number of clinical implications follow from a self-regulation model of the relapse process. A general point is that it provides a coherent conceptual basis for the self-management focus of cognitive-behavioral therapy. The motivational properties of goals means that therapists should assess the kinds of goals individuals possess and whether they are acquisitory or inhibitory. For example, preferential child offenders are more likely to have distorted or maladaptive goals and attempt to establish sexual contact with a child, rather than try to control their behavior. However, a situational or incest offender may be struggling with conflicting goals and experience considerable difficulty in regulating his behavior. Relatedly, it is clinically useful to identify the particular kind of self-regulatory deficits offenders may have. The treatment needs of offenders who are characterized by undercontrol or misregulation are markedly different from those with intact self-regulation skills (see following chapter). For example, issues of impulse control, mood management, and dealing with an unexpected high-risk situation are likely to be common in offenders generally characterized by self-regulatory deficiencies. However, these issues are less likely to be central foci of interventions for a classic pedophile with entrenched beliefs about the rightness of adult-child sexual contact in the context of competent self-regulatory processes. Appreciating the harm to victims and related cognitive distortions is much more likely to be the foci of intervention with a man generally showing this pattern, that is, issues related to core schema.

In brief, the avoidant-passive pathway represents an approximation to the traditional relapse prevention offense process. As such, increased level of skills around relationships, problem solving, and mood management is likely to be required. Another focus of intervention is likely to be with respect to decreasing passivity by addressing core schema about personal efficacy. Finally, these men need assistance in developing more explicit metacognitive control, that is, in selecting, monitoring, and evaluating ongoing behavior. The avoidant-active pathway also requires skill acquisition, especially with respect to metacognitive control. Changing coping styles, especially increasing knowledge about contingencies and ironic effects of some strategies, is likely to be of considerable value for these men. The approach-automatic pathway requires increased awareness to reduce dependence on "scripts" and strengthening of metacognitive control, especially with respect to ongoing monitoring. Goals are also a problem for these men, potentially less so than for the approach-explicit men, such that perspective taking and cognitive restructuring are likely to be important. Finally, the approach-explicit pathway, as noted earlier, is fundamentally about goals, not skills. Core schema (self, intimacy, sexuality, sense of being wronged and blamed) are the primary focus of the intervention, at least in the first instance. These men may also need reconditioning of appetitive processes. A final point is that reoffending may look different from past offenses because any change in goals and knowledge structures may shift men from approach to avoidance goals and in the process may expose previously unseen regulatory and skill deficits.

In conclusion, a model of the relapse process attempts to describe the factors associated with sexual abuse as it unfolds over time. Historically, Pithers's relapse prevention model has provided clinicians with a conceptual map of the factors associated with offenders' sexually deviant behavior and guided clinical decision making. We suggest that our self-regulation model can provide a more comprehensive understanding of the factors associated with relapse and consequently help clinicians to tailor treatment to individual offenders. There are clear clinical and theoretical benefits in continuing to investigate this some-what neglected but central area, and we hope that the self-regulation model out-lined in this chapter can make a contribution to this process.

References

Austin, J. T., & Vancouver, J. B. (1996). Goal constructs in psychology: Structure, process, and content. *Psychological Bulletin, 120,* 338-375.

Bargh, J. A., & Barndollar, K. (1996). Automaticity in action: The unconscious as repository of chronic goals and motives. In P. M. Gollwitzer & J. A. Bargh (Eds.), *The psychology of action: Linking cognition and motivation to behavior* (pp. 457-481). New York: Guilford.

Baumeister, R. F. (1990). *Escaping the self.* New York: Basic Books.

Baumeister, R. F., & Heatherton, T. F. (1996). Self-regulation failure: An overview. *Psychological Inquiry, 7,* 1-15.

Carver, C. S., & Scheier, M. F. (1981). *Attention and self-regulation: A control theory approach to human behavior.* New York: Springer-Verlag.

Carver, C. S., & Scheier, M. F. (1990). Principles of self-regulation: Action and emotion. In E. T. Higgins & R. M. Sorrentino (Eds.), *Handbook of motivation and social behavior* (pp. 3-52). New York: Guilford.

Cochran, W., & Tesser, A. (1996). The "what the hell" effect: Some effects of goal proximity and goal framing on performance. In L. L. Martin & A. Tesser (Eds.), *Striving and feeling: Interactions among goals, affect, and self-regulation* (pp. 99-120). Hillsdale, NJ: Lawrence Erlbaum.

Cole, P. M., Michel, M. K., & Teti, L. O. (1994). The development of emotion regulation and dysregulation: A clinical perspective. *Monographs of the Society for Research in Child Development, 59*(2-3), 73-100.

Cole, P. M., & Putnam, F. W. (1992). The effect of incest on self and social functioning: A developmental psychopathological perspective. *Journal of Consulting and Clinical Psychology, 60,* 174-184.

Emmons, R. A. (1996). Striving and feeling: Personal goals and subjective well-being. In P. M. Gollwitzer & J. A. Bargh (Eds.), *The psychology of action: Linking cognition and motivation to behavior* (pp. 313-337). New York: Guilford.

Ford, D. H. (1987). *Humans as self-constructing living systems: A developmental perspective on behavior and personality.* Hillsdale, NJ: Lawrence Erlbaum.

Gagnon, J. H., & Simon, W. (1987). The sexual scripting of oral genital contacts. *Archives of Sexual Behavior, 1,* 1-25.

Gray, J. A. (1990). Brain systems that mediate both emotion and cognition. *Cognition and Emotion, 4,* 269-288.

Heckhausen, J., & Schulz, R. (1998). Developmental regulation in adulthood: Selection and compensation via primary and secondary control. In J. Heckhausen & C. S. Dweck (Eds.), *Motivation and self-regulation across the lifespan* (pp. 50-77). New York: Cambridge University Press.

Johnston, L., & Ward, T. (1996). Social cognition and sexual offending: A theoretical framework. *Sexual Abuse: A Journal of Research and Treatment, 8,* 55-80.

Johnston, L., Ward, T., & Hudson, S. M. (1997). Suppressing sex: Mental control and the treatment of sexual offenders. *Journal of Sex Research, 34,* 121-130.

Kanfer, F. H., & Schefft, B. K. (1988). *Guiding the process of therapeutic change.* Champaign, IL: Research Press.

Karoly, P. (1993). Mechanisms of self-regulation: A systems view. *Annual Review of Psychology, 44,* 23-52.

Marlatt, G. A., & Gordon, J. R. (Eds.). (1985). *Relapse prevention: Maintenance strategies in the treatment of addictive behaviors.* New York: Guilford.

Pithers, W. D. (1990). Relapse prevention with sexual aggressors: A method for maintaining therapeutic gain and enhancing external supervision. In W. L. Marshall, D. R. Laws, & H. E. Barbaree (Eds.), *Handbook of sexual assault: Issues theories and treatment of the offender* (pp. 343-361). New York: Plenum.

Pithers, W. D., Marques, J. K., Gibat, C. C., & Marlatt, G. A. (1983). Relapse prevention with sexual aggressives: A self-control model of treatment and maintenance of change. In J. G. Greer & I. R. Stuart (Eds.), *The sexual aggressor: Current perspectives on treatment* (pp. 214-234). New York: Van Nostrand Reinhold.

Ryan, R. M. (1998). Commentary: Human psychological needs and the issues of volition, control, and outcome focus. In J. Heckhausen & C. S. Dweck (Eds.), *Motivation and self-regulation across the lifespan* (pp. 114-133). New York: Cambridge University Press.

Taylor, S. E., & Pham, L. B. (1996). Mental simulation, motivation, and action. In P. M. Gollwitzer & J. A. Bargh (Eds.), *The psychology of action: Linking cognition and motivation to behavior* (pp. 219-235). New York: Guilford.

Thompson, R. A. (1994). Emotional regulation: A theme in search of definition. *Monographs of the Society for Research in Child Development, 59*(2-3), 25-52.

Ward, T., Fon, C., Hudson, S. M., & McCormack, J. (1998). A descriptive model of dysfunctional cognitions in child molesters. *Journal of Interpersonal Violence, 13,* 129-155.

Ward, T., & Hudson, S. M. (1996). Relapse prevention: A critical analysis. *Sexual Abuse: A Journal of Research and Treatment, 8,* 177-200.

Ward, T., & Hudson, S. M. (1998). A model of the relapse process in sexual offenders. *Journal of Interpersonal Violence, 13,* 400-425.

Ward, T., & Hudson, S. M. (in press). Sexual offenders implicit planning: A conceptual model. *Sexual Abuse: A Journal of Research and Treatment.*

Ward, T., Hudson, S. M., & Marshall, W. L. (1994). The abstinence violation effect in child molesters. *Behaviour Research and Therapy, 32,* 431-437.

Ward, T., Hudson, S. M., & Marshall, W. L. (1995). Cognitive distortions and affective deficits in sex offenders: A cognitive deconstructionist interpretation. *Sexual Abuse: A Journal of Research and Treatment, 7,* 67-84.

Ward, T., Hudson, S. M., & Marshall, W. L. (1996). Attachment style in sex offenders: A preliminary study. *Journal of Sex Research, 33,* 17-26.

Ward, T., & Keenan, T. (1999). Child molesters: Implicit theories. *Journal of Interpersonal Violence, 14,* 821-838.

Ward, T., Louden, K., Hudson, S. M., & Marshall, W. L. (1995). A descriptive model of the offense chain for child molesters. *Journal of Interpersonal Violence, 10,* 453-473.

Wegner, D. M. (1994). Ironic processes of mental control. *Psychological Bulletin, 101,* 34-52.

CHAPTER 6

Relapse Prevention

Assessment and Treatment Implications

STEPHEN M. HUDSON
University of Canterbury, New Zealand

TONY WARD
University of Melbourne, Australia

The previous chapter covered in detail the problems that we have identified with the relapse prevention model as it is currently applied to men who have offended sexually (see also Hudson & Ward, 1996; Ward & Hudson, 1996a). Before traversing those issues briefly, and to set the scene for the present discussion, the therapeutic optimism generated by relapse prevention in both clients and treatment providers has to be acknowledged. As we have noted previously, the source of this optimism remains unclear because there is not yet unequivocal evidence for its success, certainly over and above the excellent work that has come from a more mainstream cognitive-behavioral perspective. The highlighting of maintaining treatment gains (preventing relapse) as a major problem while offering a face-valid solution may go partway toward explaining the broad, uncritical adoption of the model. The resources that have accrued from the adoption of the model have been well deserved, and despite some statistical reservations, these resources have been parlayed into very tangible benefits for the community. However, much work remains to be done.

The adaptation of treatment strategies from the addiction area (Marlatt & Gordon, 1985), with the emphasis on relapse as an explicable process or chain of behavior occurring across time (Pithers, Marques, Gibat, & Marlatt, 1983), led to the adoption of relapse prevention as a model of treatment, primarily to enhance the client's self-management skills with respect to maintaining the changes induced by treatment. That is, it was initially conceived of as an "add-on" to deal with the "problem of relapse"—hence the negatively languaged term *relapse prevention*. However, this model has also legitimately become a device to guide or inform treatment. This aspect of relapse prevention has not always been explicit, nor has it been well articulated, nor indeed even well used. Not that a viable, alternative, grounded device for planning treatment is immediately obvious, well described, or invoked by those describing the rationale for their treatment procedures.

At these broad levels, the explicit notion that these offensive processes are understandable and therefore may be controllable, at least under the right conditions, has led to considerable resources being devoted to reducing the probability of these men reoffending. This has served to reduce the amount of damage inflicted on women and children within the community. We need to acknowledge that fact while still being courageous enough to challenge what we do and profit from new developments.

Relapse prevention, as a model of treatment and maintenance, has a number of problems that have been identified (Hanson, 1996; Ward & Hudson, 1996a). First, both Marlatt's original relapse prevention theory (Marlatt & Gordon, 1985) and Pithers et al.'s (1983) adaptation for sex offenders rely on diverse theoretical sources that are not well integrated. This has created some conceptual confusion, particularly with some of the mediating mechanisms (e.g., the abstinence violation effect and the problem of immediate gratification). We believe that good theory knitting and reference to current theoretical sources (Hudson, Ward, & Marshall, 1992; Ward & Hudson, 1998b; Ward, Hudson, & Marshall, 1994) can reduce these problems.

Second, the original model does not cover all the possible pathways to a reoffense. The three pathways to high-risk situations all reflect skill deficits and ignore situations in which individuals deliberately "use or abuse," that is, appetitively driven behavior. Third, the adaptation of the model for sex offenders (Pithers et al., 1983) makes this problem of scope worse because it focuses predominantly on the covert route. Finally, moving the lapse and relapse points back to points earlier in the offense chain has created significant problems. Defining a lapse as equivalent to the "first puff" of a cigarette by a person giving up smoking is clearly not acceptable with sexual offending because this means another offense has been committed with yet another victim. Rather, a lapse for a sex offender has been seen as the occurrence of a voluntarily induced risk behavior, such as deviant sexual fantasizing (Pithers, 1990) or, more concretely, the first sign of intention to offend within a high-risk situation (Hudson

& Ward, 1996). This is earlier in the problematic process than in the original model. Similarly, a relapse is now seen as the occurrence of any sexual offense rather than simply a return to previously high levels of the addictive behavior as in Marlatt's original model. This creates problems—for example, the inherent incompatibility between the problem of immediate gratification and the abstinence violation effect as transitional mediators, both said to be active at the same time in Pithers's model.

Another confusion, probably engendered by the title *relapse prevention,* is whether the model even applies to men who are untreated (see Ryan, 1996; Ward & Hudson, 1996b). That is, some people take the position that men who have not been treated simply offend; they do not relapse. The implication is that the model does not need to cope with these men. We disagree with this because the issue of scope is fundamental, most particularly when relapse prevention is used to structure treatment, although the confusion around this point is probably partially responsible for the debate. Moreover, relapse prevention-based treatment typically examines the most recent or typical offense process in considerable detail, either within the disclosure module or in the context of the relapse prevention plan. For the offense process being used in these sections of an intervention not to be within the model makes little sense to us, and it probably does not to the clients either.

We have suggested that it is likely to be most profitable to focus on the core process underlying both the offending and relapse process—what we have termed the *problem behavior process* (Hudson & Ward, 1996). This has the capacity to avoid the debate as to whether the model applies. We have to acknowledge the need for scope and create a model that is broad enough to cover what offenders actually do, rather than essentially tell them how they behaved and expect them to agree. The rationale for this has several components. Some men seem unaffected by treatment, at least in terms of high levels of restraint, so *relapse* is an inappropriate term. Similarly, some men, possibly most given the explicit social constraints on sexual activity with children, are likely to be attempting to limit their offending in some manner. Even restraint has problems as a solution to the dilemma with respect to any difference between relapse and reoffending. Restraint is not a dichotomous variable; moreover, it is unstable (Prochaska, DeClemente, & Norcross, 1992). It is usually detected by self-report, which is at best unreliable in men who offend sexually. Next we have been struck by the considerable similarities between the factors that are thought to underlie both cause and relapse (see Hudson & Ward, 1996, for details). Finally, as we noted earlier, clinicians use a detailed analysis of an individual's past offending to identify the typical offense chain. If future offensive behavior is going to be different from this, then treatment planning, particularly postrelease management plans, need a broad-ranging model that enables accurate prediction of these differences. We give some illustrations of how this might be the case later, but the central empirical question concerning how an offender's offense process changes as a function of treatment remains to be clarified.

Therefore, it has seemed to us that to focus on the problem behavior process directly (the offense process in this case) is likely to be the most profitable. The major strength of the relapse prevention model has been its ability to focus our attention on the idea that behavior occurs in small steps over time rather than in an all-or-none fashion, despite the beliefs of some men in our treatment programs that "it just happened." This puts more pressure on the model with respect to scope. We know from clinical experience and from our data (Hudson & Ward, 1998; Hudson, Ward, & McCormack, 1999) that a number of men have offended sexually with quite different offending patterns. Viewing these problematic patterns as alternative pathways to offending means that we are able to deal with the issue of scope. The self-regulatory model presented elsewhere in this volume (see previous chapter) has developed out of our previous work on modeling offending processes. Our original descriptive model of the offense chain allows for different offense patterns, planned and unplanned sexually deviant behavior, and positive and negative affective pathways, and it incorporates offenders' perceptions of relationships (Ward, Louden, Hudson, & Marshall, 1995). The self-regulation model (Ward & Hudson, 1998a; Ward, Hudson, & Keenan, 1998) both broadens the scope further and provides a metalevel set of mechanisms.

This self-regulatory model has been presented extensively in the previous chapter, but it is recapped briefly to ground the rest of the discussion. Self-regulation is about an individual engaging in goal-directed actions over time and in different contexts and involves selecting, monitoring, and evaluating ongoing monitoring of behavior over time in relation to these goals. Self-regulation does not just include inhibiting behavior, affect, or cognitive activity, but it can also include enhancement of these aspects of functioning (e.g., when anxiety about a future event, such as an examination, can be used to motivate studying). Goals, desired states, or situations are central to self-regulation theories and can vary in abstractness (from very abstract or principle level to process level) and type such as avoidance versus approach (Cochran & Tesser, 1996). Goals are also related to affect insofar as the ongoing monitoring is about evaluating progress with respect to whatever goal is currently salient, with positive affective states being the result of anticipated goal attainment and vice versa (Carver & Scheier, 1990).

The Model

Before examining what the assessment and treatment agenda might look like for each of the pathways or offending patterns associated with the major goals (avoidance vs. approach) and predominant strategy (passive vs. active), we present a brief summary of the model. The avoidant-passive pathway most closely resembles the sex offender adaptation of the relapse prevention picture, that is, the covert route (Pithers, 1990). Life circumstances create negative affect and overload inadequate coping skills, which lead to deviant desire, but the awareness of harm or significant fear of consequences generates restraint. Covert planning, such as apparently irrelevant decisions, together with a deficient level of skills, leads to a high-risk situation arising (i.e., the presence of a potential victim). A lapse (gives in and adopts an approach goal—the problem of immediate gratification) and subsequent relapse follow (with the abstinence violation effect in response to negative postoffense evaluations). Note the separation of the problem of immediate gratification and the abstinence violation effect, with the latter occurring after relapse, which is consistent with what little data address this issue (Ward et al., 1994), rather than lapse as is predicted by the model (Pithers, 1990).

The avoidant-active pathway partially resembles Marlatt's second route to relapse contained within the original model (Marlatt & Gordon, 1985). Life events (*lifestyle,* in Marlatt's terms) directly rather than covertly lead to the development of a high-risk situation ("I am owed . . ."). In our terms, however, the influence of flawed self-regulation strategies (misregulation) drives this process. Misplaced short-term emphasis on affect regulation and paradoxical strategies with ironic effects lead to misregulation despite efforts on the part of the man (Baumeister & Heatherton, 1996). There is still a commitment to restraint because the overall goal is one of avoidance. However, paradoxically, the strategies used to restrain serve to actually enhance the possibility that once in a high-risk situation, the man will experience a loss of control and therefore adopt a short-term approach goal—in other words, a lapse. This reflects misregulation.

The change in goal from one of restraint (avoidance) to behaving sexually (approach), which characterizes both the avoidance pathways, is possibly a function of increased sexual arousal and cognitive deconstruction (Ward, Hudson, & Marshall, 1995b) as the process unfolds over time. Many men who have offended sexually describe "losing it" at this point, reflecting this change in goals. Offending follows these "decisions" but is subsequently evaluated negatively; in other words, an abstinence violation effect occurs at this point (see also Ward et al., 1994). This, as we have noted before (Ward & Hudson, 1996a), has the potential to drive offending to greater levels of frequency or intrusiveness (Relapse 2).

The approach-automatic pathway reflects approach goals and, to a limited extent, resembles Marlatt's final pathway in which high-risk situations are encountered by genuine chance as opposed to covert planning. Goals and the associated strategies are unlikely to be under direct attentional control, at least initially, with only rudimentary planning being evident. The notion of planned impulsivity (Pithers, 1990) captures the essence of this pathway; that is, the desire for offensive sex is acknowledged at a quite general level, but the relevant overlearned scripts are only enacted when opportunity presents itself. Thus, the offense often appears as if "out of the blue" and also occurs over what is often a remarkably short time frame. This reflects underregulation. Postoffense evaluations are typically positive, with the negative attitudes toward women and a sense of sexual entitlement being reinforced. Thus, the probability of future offending is usually strengthened.

Finally, the approach-explicit pathway involves intact self-regulation and explicit goals with respect to sexual offending; that is, the behaviors involved are not really seen by the offender as being offensive. If any restraint is evident, it is likely to be at the level of grooming to avoid "rejection," which is quite similar to the restraint exercised by adults in their appropriate dating behaviors or the avoidance of social sanctions (e.g., getting caught). System-level goals (higher-level or more abstract goals), such as being emotionally intimate with someone, have become linked with abusive or offensive sexual behaviors. As such, the initiating events are as likely to be positive as they are negative. If negative, then this may reflect explicit needs such as wanting to be close or "in love" and being aware that is not yet the case—that is, goal and/or current situation discrepancy. Or the explicit goal may well be to punish and humiliate, in the context of system-level goals regarding the role of women as sexual objects. The initiating events in this case are likely to be negative—for example, anger in the face of interpersonal rejection.

Alternatively, the initiating events may simply be positive anticipation, particularly in the context of extensive prior grooming of the victim and an ongoing relationship with him or her. As the process advances, the associated emotional state becomes increasingly positive as goals are being more closely approximated. There is no great likelihood of an abstinence violation effect because, generally speaking, there is no commitment to restraint. Postoffense evaluations, outside any awareness of the risk of social sanctions, are likely to be positive.

We believe the self-regulatory model overcomes a significant number of the problems. In brief, the model allows for multiple pathways, which attends to the concerns about scope, the issue for whom the model is designed for, and the flexibility to structure treatment according to predictions about what future offending might look like (treatment-induced change in the offense process). Second, it helps clarify where and when the processes that mediate the transition points in the offense chain might occur. Third, it knits together some of the diverse theoretical sources involved in relapse prevention and rationally adds some new material. Finally, the model is open-ended because it has the capacity to be modified in light of both data and theoretical developments.

Assessment

From a clinical perspective, the self-regulatory model has the potential to provide a coherent conceptual basis for the self-management focus of cognitive-behavioral interventions, which is what relapse prevention is about. For clinicians to function effectively, they need to know a fair amount about following the "how" aspects of the man's offending. For convenience, we have associated each of the assessment issues or concerns with the relevant phase(s) of the model.

Phase 1

The first assessment issue, at the most general-level assessment, concerns the explicit identification of vulnerability factors that are a function of the man's developmental history. We have argued before that the critical aspects of developmental adversity are their current consequences (Hudson & Ward, 1996). Indeed, this is what fundamentally distinguishes Level 3 models (Ward & Hudson, 1998b) from single-factor etiological models (Level 2) or the overarching causal frameworks (Level 1). Specifically, by this we mean that areas such as models of relationships and the associated goals, needs, attachment issues, and conflict resolution styles need to be assessed. Closely related are social competency issues—most particularly in the areas of intimacy skills, empathy, and its subcomponents—and beliefs that are supportive of offending (i.e., cognitive distortions). Finally, we suggest that the type of regulatory failure, including the possibility of intact self-regulation, is also of significance to the clinician. We do not yet know whether the type of self-regulation failure, variously associated with the three relevant pathways, is broadly typical across other domains. Similarly, we do not yet know if the apparently intact self-regulatory style, the expert nature of the offending process (Ward, in press) for men exhibiting an approach-explicit pathway, is typical of other important aspects of their lives, such as employment.

The major implication of these clinical decisions at this broad level is how specific the intervention needs to be. This can range from a primary focus on changing core beliefs concerning child-adult sexual contact in someone with intact regulatory skills with inappropriate goals (e.g., issues of victim harm and cognitive distortions) to the acquisition of quite specific skills (e.g., affect modulation) to assist dealing with misregulation pathways. These are remarkably different therapeutic endeavors, with the latter reflecting a more typical traditional relapse prevention intervention. An individual with the requisite skills but who fails to access them under the appropriate circumstances reflects the third broad possibility. In this situation, a self-regulatory perspective emphasizes the need for increased metacognitive control (Alford & Beck, 1997;

Baumeister & Heatherton, 1996) rather than skill acquisition, as typifies the traditional relapse prevention approach.

The specific guidelines we are currently using for a semistructured interview to determine which pathway is evident (Hudson & Ward, 1998) are as follows. We select the most recent or most typical offense and focus the interview with the man with respect to that. If his offending career is extensive, then a representative offense from very early in the person's career needs also to be done. As we have stressed before, being as well informed about what has happened as is possible prior to the interview is essential. We recommend that reviewing any collateral information is of considerable value—for example, police reports, any victim statements or reports concerning him or her, arrest reports, previous psychological or medical reports, and any prior documentation from other interviews or treatment.

We first establish the general self-regulatory context or offense-related issues in which the offense-specific material may be traversed. We focus on occupational, educational, and relationship history, gathering just brief details with respect to these areas. The essence is to determine self-regulatory style (underregulation, misregulation, or intact regulation). There is a need to look for reactions to various significant transitions, such as school or job or living circumstances, major disappointments, frustrations, or traumatic events. As a device, we use "What was the worst or best thing that happened during . . . ?" Thus, job or career changes, relationship changes, educational goals, and achievements are all "grist for the mill."

Phases 2 and 3

We need to know about the man's goals, implicit or explicit, and the associated needs. This is salient not only because of the obvious direct connection with the broad pathway distinctions (approach vs. avoidance) but also because of the close relationship between behavioral strategies and emotional states. Not achieving important goals creates a gap between the reality of the man's situation and his expectations. This state of affairs is likely to be appraised negatively and lead to negative emotional states. This, in turn, leads to behavior designed to rectify the situation or reduce the perceived gap. Some goals or motives are chronically accessible and therefore color much of the person's behavior. For example, an offender with a preoccupied attachment style may spend a considerable proportion of his personal resources attempting to avoid loneliness. In contrast, another offender with a dismissive style of relating is likely to have ready access to potential threats to his independence (Ward, Hudson, & Marshall, 1995a).

The related and fundamental issue is the relationship between these goals with respect to offending and what triggered (or "provided the excuse for") the desire for offensive sexual activities prior to the goal being formed. These issues serve conceptually to link the background factors briefly overviewed earlier (in the main, these are the current consequences of developmental adversity) to the initiation of the offending process. These issues are what have been discussed in the traditional relapse prevention model as high-risk factors (i.e., threats to self-control) but can be either broadly compensatory or appetitive in nature.

Thus, the second level of assessment occurs at the level of goals because these have significant motivational properties and therefore a central role in determining treatment needs. In terms of the pathways, determining whether these goals are inhibitory (avoidant) or acquisitory (approach) is the first step, and the passivity or activeness of the style is second. The issue is one of discriminating between structural goals that deal with sex, intimacy, identity, and self-worth and process-level issues. If the goals are at the system or principle level, as with goals such as wanting a long-term intimate relationship with a pubescent boy or extracting revenge from women for past wrongs, then treatment needs are likely to be quite different when compared with someone who is lonely and isolated, has offended when drunk, and is attempting to avoid this happening again.

We suggest that the major markers for this aspect of the assessment are emotional tone (generally positive or generally negative) and the degree of detail when the offender provides a description of what he has done. Good, fine-grained, emotionally textured descriptions using reasonably sophisticated language are indicative of high-level system goals (i.e., approach path), whereas a reluctance to talk and a lack of detail suggest low-level control (i.e., avoidant goals). A second aspect of this is the explicit point that offenders do not necessarily start with negative affect; positive affect constitutes an appetitive marker, which reflects approach goals.

Our semistructured interview suggests that offense-specific factors primarily involve getting a detailed stepwise picture of the offense process, with quite specific emphasis on the critical transitions as per the model (see Figure 5.1 in Chapter 5). The specific questions we use are the following: What triggered the desire for illicit sex? What was the response to this desire—essentially, was the goal either approach (appetitively driven) or avoidance (restraint evident)? We need just broad categorizations of the goals involved at this stage, and these may well need to be inferred. We also need to get some information with respect to the affective tones at the critical junctures because these will be indirect markers for the goals involved. What remains unclear is how to code affects such as anger because these so-called energizing emotions are still generally conceived as negative but may be tightly associated with approach or appetitive goals. We represent this as "–" on the depiction of the model but acknowledge that this may not reflect the phenomenological experience of the man himself. This is important information.

Phases 4 and 5

At an even more proximal level, clinicians need to know about the degree of planning involved—the "how, what, and when." We need to know whether the offending was situational or ongoing, whether there is evidence of escalation in frequency or intrusiveness of the offending, and the strategies used to groom the victim(s), particularly the amount and type of coercion involved. What constitutes the typical high-risk situation(s) and how they develop or are set up is important to know, as are details about the cognitive and affective processes the man experiences as he progresses through his offending processes; these drive the process. At this level, it is also important to be clear about whether the primary issue is one of skill deficit or skill access because again these imply remarkably different intervention strategies.

Although it is obvious that the degree of planning (or strategy employed) needs to be assessed, the issue of denial is likely to be critical with respect to this. We may need to be more guided by issues of affective tone and the broader evidence with respect to self-regulatory style in the collateral domains mentioned earlier. For example, an offender (say, an intruder rapist) who reports little explicit planning and rapid behavioral execution may well be telling it as it is, at least for him. This approach-automatic pathway may also be evident for a man who molests children who has set up circumstances in which he has structured access to many potential victims. From his perspective, the decision to have sex with a child may in fact need little planning under these circumstances. Similarly, there is a reluctance to allocate men to the avoidance pathways (covert rather than explicit planning) for fear of appearing to collude with their denial. We need to be careful with respect to this. It is in how the man has gone about these aspects of planning his offense that his self-regulatory style is going to be most evident and most centrally relevant.

What happens once the man is in a high-risk situation—that is, the physical surroundings where there is a potential victim or at least the very high likelihood that one will be along soon? In other words, the offender's expectations are positive. "How does he react?" "What does he feel?" "What is his self-talk?" and "How does he evaluate his responses while in the high-risk situation?" are all questions that we have found useful.

We also routinely ask about how he has stopped himself from continuing along the offense path at other times. We are interested in this both at this stage of the high-risk situation and earlier in the process (e.g., at the point of first experiencing the desire for deviant or offensive sexual activity). This serves two purposes. It subtly introduces the notion of controllability while giving the man a chance to describe a positive aspect of his behavior with respect to offending. It is highly unlikely that he will have acted on the deviant sexual urge every time it was experienced, and we believe this is worthy of emphasis. The primary purpose for us, however, is to discriminate avoidant-passive for avoidant-active pathways because these processes have differential treatment needs associated with them.

Phase 6

Once he has begun to lapse—that is, the first overt behavior associated with offending or "moving in"—what happens? As for the high-risk situation, what happens to his goals? They typically become approach oriented and are associated with positive affects because he is getting what he wants at this point in the process. This step is not that critical from a differentiation of the pathway perspective because the picture is likely to be relatively uniform across pathways, but for validity checking of the model we need good data. We cannot fall into the old trap of assuming we know everything the offender is capable of doing; any models we use ought to be open-ended. The shift from avoidance goals for some men to approach goals, along with the relevant affect, also needs to be assessed and made explicit.

Phase 7

We need some details with respect to what actually happened in the offense, but again, although there will be a lot of variation, this is not yet seen as a critical discriminatory step. What we do need is information about the degree of intrusiveness, the type of relationship established with the victim (if any), the type and intensity of coercion, and the behaviors carried out designed to reduce the probability of detection.

Phases 8 and 9

Finally, we need information about how he evaluates what he has done both in terms of cognitive and emotional aspects. This involves assessing his self-talk, the beliefs he has about what he has done, and the "role" he sees the victim as having played, as well as his report of both the victim's and his own affective state. Does he see himself as having achieved or failed at the goals he set, either explicitly or implicitly? To end this part of the interview process, we assess his attitude toward future offending.

Intervention

We briefly review the intervention elements that are likely to be associated with the four pathways that currently comprise the self-regulatory model.

Avoidant-Passive

In this left pathway in the model, the interventions closely resemble those typically associated with a traditional relapse prevention approach. The primary problem area for men with this offense style is inadequate coping skills together with low awareness of the offense process. These skill deficits are likely to be reflected in Phase 1 of the model (i.e., the vulnerability factors that generate the current issues relevant to this offense process). For example, issues such as relationship problems, poor mood and affect regulation skills, and low problem-solving ability are frequently common. The developmental adversity associated with low social competencies is likely to be also common. There are also likely to be companion problems that reflect the passivity or under-regulation that characterizes the offense process generalizing to other life domains (e.g., occupational issues). Phase 2 issues—that is, the circumstances or events that trigger the desire for offensive activity—most likely reflect unfilled legitimate needs such as for closeness and intimacy (Baumeister & Leary, 1995) interacting with low levels of appropriate skills. There is, by definition, a commitment to restraint, although with this offense process, this is unlikely to be well articulated (Phase 3). Interventions most suited to this offense process resemble the now-classic relapse prevention strategies embodied in the core modules of "understanding your offending," "mood management," "relationship skills," and "relapse prevention." These men frequently report that the offense "just happened"—"I was just sitting on the couch with her and . . . ." Making explicit the steps that constitute the offending "chain" that forms the core of the "understanding your offending module" is likely to be critical. Taking a typical offending episode and "unpacking" how he was feeling prior to the first sense of desire (Phase 1), initial reactions (Phases 2 and 3), and the covert steps involved in getting access to the victim are essential. Noting the shift from avoidance to approach goals and emphasizing the positive aspects of appreciating potential harm issues, if this is the case, are also important. The need to stop the process prior to the problem of immediate gratification being strongly involved can also be illustrated, thereby setting the scene for discussion of these issues in the later relapse prevention module.

Although all of these intervention steps are typical of the current relapse prevention model, the general passivity (underregulation) and related core schema about personal efficacy are frequently more implicit than is desirable but are, in any event, in need of direct modification. Beliefs about the personal agency and the possession of the skills required for adequate self-management should not be treated as just another set of dysfunction cognitions but should be treated explicitly and consistently rather than left to chance. Empathy deficits are likely to be constrained to victims—that is, effectively restricted to Phases 5 and 6 of the model—and may respond to modules covering victim harm as well as explication of the offense process and the dysfunctional cognitions that assist it.

Attention to self-regulation—that is, metacognitive control—is the core relapse prevention issue (self-management, in essence) and is important to these men because this pathway represents underregulation. Awareness of the processes involved, as well as when to use the skills that need to be acquired, is an important aspect of any intervention. Although self-management is typically emphasized in the relapse prevention module in the traditional model, again we suggest that this is a more overarching concern and that any opportunity to model, rehearse, and reinforce appropriate self-regulation is worth taking. For example, most men feel anxious prior to doing the disclosure session and are likely to use their usual strategies with respect to short-term affect regulation such as denial, increase in sexual activity, and other types of avoidance. These strategies, reflecting an overemphasis on affect regulation, are a frequent cause of self-regulatory failure (Baumeister & Heatherton, 1996). Predicting these and providing realistic support for affect tolerance (see Linehan, 1993, for a discussion of the use of this) may be very helpful. Success at this stage in the intervention may also be very helpful in beginning to generate the level of self-confidence that Marshall (1999) suggests is a needed prerequisite for significant behavior change. It is clear that issues of motivation are critical—for example, the significant role that victim harm modules play is in terms of motivation to use the relapse plan when needed (Beech, Fisher, & Beckett, 1999) or even to see its relevance (Pithers, 1990).

In summary, this pathway most closely resembles the traditional relapse prevention model, and, as such, the conventional components of any intervention need to include the usual awareness of the relapse process and skill acquisition modules. These modules typically look at issues such as identifying offense precursors, dealing with issues of stimulus control or disinhibition (e.g., pornography or alcohol), specific relapse issues such as programmed escape and coping with urges (essentially decision grids with associated cognitive strategies), and general-level skills such as anger management, stress tolerance, and problem solving (Pithers, 1990). However, in addition to these essential processes, a self-regulatory perspective highlights the need to explicitly target the underregulation that characterizes this pathway. For example, a man with this pathway needs to be acquiring new skills at the metacognitive level (explicit self-regulatory strategies) such as developing affect tolerance, taking time to reflect on his life circumstances, and perhaps keeping a journal to highlight where self-regulation failures occur. These interventions are in addition to the core relapse prevention issues. The self-regulatory issues also have the potential to help sharpen the focus of these traditional modules.

Avoidant-Active

This other avoidant pathway is essentially a misregulation process and therefore requires the man to acquire regulatory skills, especially with respect to strong negative emotion, and strengthening at the metacognitive level of control (Alford & Beck, 1997; Flavell, 1984; Sternberg, 1994). Similar types of background issues (Phases 1 and 2) are likely to be present for men exhibiting this pathway, as was the case for the avoidant-passive group. As such, interventions addressing the skills relevant to relationships, problem solving, and communication (typical relapse prevention again) are almost certainly relevant. However, because planning is explicit rather than covert or passive, there is likely to be less need for significant work to be done in bringing the offending process into awareness. Drawing out all the links in the offending process still needs to occur, but this is likely to be a much easier task than is the case for the other avoidant group given their relative lack of awareness. The major focus for a man with this pathway will likely be convincing him that the strategies he uses, which typically have collateral, short-term positive benefits (such as relaxation with alcohol or sexual arousal with pornography), are paradoxically and ironically harmful. Baumeister and Heatherton (1996) suggest that there are three classes of causes of misregulation: (a) misunderstood contingencies, (b) quixotic efforts to control the uncontrollable, and (c) giving too much priority to affect regulation. Again, some of the interventions derived from this perspective are familiar within a traditional relapse prevention framework. For example, the commonsense notion that the strategy is more likely to be successful if it is used earlier in the chain also derives from the observation that moods and sexual arousal are not usually easily influenced directly—avoidance is better than management. Thought suppression is also an example of attempting control in a manner that is ironically likely to increase the problem (Wegner, 1994).

Prescriptions to avoid masturbating to deviant fantasies also occur within a traditional relapse prevention framework, usually under arousal reconditioning. However, the misregulation perspective highlights the paradoxical nature of this aspect of effort in the client and provides a reason to the client as to why it is not a helpful thing to do. Similarly, the use of various drugs to manage short-term negative effect has the same paradoxical effect. Overoptimistic self-views, particularly about being "in control," are yet another type of false belief about the contingencies operating in the real world that can lead to self-regulatory failure. Once awareness about the nature of these relationships is established, then the task of developing alternative ways of adequately self-managing can begin.

The most positive aspect of the offense process is the effort involved. Although convincing the client—or, rather, setting up the situation such that he convinces himself—that the strategies he has been using are not working is difficult, once that has happened, the motivation to "do things differently" is likely to be substantial. For example, in Phase 8, the abstinence violation effect experienced is likely to be associated with guilt rather than shame (i.e., with internal and controllable rather than uncontrollable causes) (Weiner, 1986). By virtue of being construed as controllable ("I did not try hard enough" or, after the intervention, "I need to do different things"), there is likely to be motivation and the needed self-confidence for changing behavior. The explicit avoidance goal that is a core feature also is likely to assist this process.

In summary, the basic interventions associated with the traditional relapse prevention apply, at least in part. There needs to be less focus on bringing the offending process into awareness because this is not a covert planning pathway; hence, focus at this level is likely to be a relative waste of treatment time. There is still a need for appropriate skill acquisition both in the traditional manner (e.g., problem solving, escape planning) and at the level of metacontrol or self-regulation. Some of the traditional interventions are of obvious continued relevance—for example, persuading men that pornography and alcohol are stimulus control issues with respect to relapse (Pithers, 1990). These issues need to be presented in a broader self-regulation context and need to be tied to the overarching concerns about the strategies that men with this pathway use in their attempts to avoid "succumbing to their deviant impulses." This serves to at least acknowledge that the man is trying, even if he is "getting it wrong."

Approach-Automatic

For this next pathway, the first of the approach goals, awareness is the major issue, with the dependence on overlearned scripts and the absence of metacognitive control (i.e., explicit attention) being the major problems. The primary intervention for a man exhibiting this offense pathway is again to teach appropriate self-regulation strategies because this process reflects similar underregulation, as was the case for the avoidant-passive pathway. This, in practice, means that the traditional relapse prevention "understanding your offending process" module is the key initial task. The beliefs that offending just happened reflect the man's experience. Making explicit the background "plan" represented by deviant fantasy, especially when it is paired with a sexual response, is important, as is the notion that "mental simulation" increases the probability of the behavior occurring. There is also the strong possibility that this underregulatory style is exhibited in other domains, and therefore problems in these areas also exist, for example, in broader social relationships such as friendships, the use of leisure, accommodation, and occupational domains.

The second set of key tasks with respect to adequate self-regulation is primarily an awareness of goals. These approach goals involved sexually abusive behavior and are clearly inappropriate. The associated strategies that require increased monitoring to bring about the needed awareness of the stepwise nature of behavior are also flawed. Overall goals are typically a much greater issue than compared to the avoidant-passive pathway but potentially less so compared to the approach-explicit pathway (see below).

It is predicted that these approach goals will reflect themes either of entitlement or retribution. It is highly likely that this offense pathway will be associated with negative attitudes to others, together with a significant sense of entitlement with respect to him getting his needs met, especially sexual needs. It is when the man perceives that he has been "short-changed" in some way (Phase 1) that the specific desire to behave offensively develops. As such, the usual interventions (e.g., cognitive restructuring for dysfunctional cognitions), along with the techniques designed to ameliorate the likely empathy deficits (e.g., emotional recognition skills and perspective taking), will likely be needed. Finally, given the motivational qualities, as far as fueling the offense process is concerned, some skills for regulating negative affect will almost certainly be needed.

In summary, this pathway again reflects an underregulation style, and therefore the traditional relapse prevention interventions designed to increase awareness of the offending process are highly relevant. The highly scripted, rapid enactment aspect of this pathway makes these processes even more important. The possibility of highly structured access to victims, a state of effectively permanent high risk, also needs to be addressed. The differences in intervention induced by taking a self-regulatory perspective are mainly to do with this pathway reflecting approach goals. The desire to behave offensively either reflects high-level principle goals, such as intimacy (positive affect as for the approach-explicit pathway) or compensatory/redressing harm-to-self issues, associated with negative affects such as anger.

Approach-Explicit

For this final pathway, the man's goals, which are often structural (i.e., related to core beliefs) and affectively laden, are the central issue for the intervention and moreover are likely to be difficult to change. Despite this, these goals and the related needs and beliefs are the central problem because this pathway is not a direct reflection of self-regulatory deficiencies. As such, an appropriate intervention is likely to be dissimilar to one based on the traditional relapse prevention model. Skill deficiencies are not likely, at least in the sense of short-term coping, and planning is definitively explicit and active rather than covert and passive. It may well be the case that some background vulnerabilities reflect skill deficits with respect to managing adult-adult relationship issues such as conflict resolution, but it is unlikely that acquiring these skills alone would prevent a recurrence of the offensive behavior.

The core beliefs that underlie offending with this process are typically about self and intimacy, especially with the positive affect version, as well as a sense of being wronged and blamed, which is more typically going to be associated with the negative (anger) version. With the positive affect version, it is very likely that the man has experienced abuse as a child but is construing it positively—"He was the only person that truly loved me." Modifying these beliefs is challenging for the man, especially because acknowledging victim harm means both accepting that he himself has been harmed (dysfunctional beliefs about victim harm issues at the very least) and reconstruing what is frequently the only "positive" adult figure in his life. The work of Young on early maladaptive schema (Young & Swift, 1988) is likely to be of considerable value in this regard, as is Beck's work on changing core schema (Beck, Emery, & Greenberg, 1985). Reconditioning appetitive sexual processes for both pedophiles and some rapists is probably also required.

For men exhibiting this pathway, another potential issue is what type of goals and strategies emerge if the man is able to make these fundamental changes concerning the appropriateness of his sexual behavior, that is, change his goals. Does the previous intact regulatory style the man has demonstrated in his pursuit of deviant goals become less than obvious as he struggles to restrain his now-acknowledged deviant sexual desires in the face of loneliness and other aversive emotional states? Although from a different perspective, there is some evidence that treatment does change risk prediction variables (Studer & Reddon, 1998), which lends some support to this concern. Specific research needs to address whether the offense process represented in the reoffense is the same or dissimilar to the original offense.

An additional issue here is the essential negativity associated with the explicit goals articulated by relapse prevention. Others have suggested that these avoidance goals are harder to achieve and are more likely to be associated with negative affect (Emmons, 1996; Wegner, 1994), which is paradoxically associated with triggering the desire for deviant activities anyway. Relanguaging the intervention in terms of approach goals associated with an offense-free lifestyle has considerable potential (see Mann, 1998).

Finally, all men who offend sexually, but most particularly those with this approach-explicit pathway, are most likely to be "to and fro" in their commitment to change—that is, spend most of their time in the "precontemplation" stage of change (Prochaska et al., 1992). This raises motivational issues, particularly those relating to therapeutic climate. The "come as you are" notion from the harm reduction literature rather than the "we want you to be" notion goes to the core of this problem in that the latter message is unlikely to be attractive to all men with the explicit offense pattern. For example, we have found that few differences between men incarcerated for sexual offenses against children who volunteer for treatment and those who do not relate exclusively to indicators of regret, such as negative moods (Hudson, Gee, & Ward, 1999). The other details of their offending are very similar. This argument may also inform the low rate of rapists participating in intervention programs (Hudson & Ward, 1997). Beck's notions of collaborative empiricism are congruent with the style of intervention advocated in recent literature (Beech & Fordham, 1997; Kear-Colwell & Pollack, 1997; Marshall, 1996a, 1996b) and with our suggestions about avoiding a cognitively deconstructed state during intervention (Ward et al., 1995b).

In summary, the treatment needs for men who demonstrate this approach-explicit pathway are the most dissimilar from that embodied in the traditional relapse prevention model. This is not too surprising because this pathway, driven by clear approach goals and explicit planning, is not represented within its limited scope. There is likely to be limited need for efforts to bring the offense process into awareness; if the man is not reporting the steps he took, it is very unlikely to be a function of a lack of awareness. As such, techniques such as Socratic questioning and the like are inappropriate because the man is simply choosing not to report something he knows or is reporting something different—lying, in essence. The intervention task then becomes making the therapeutic climate safe enough for the man to disclose and enhancing his motivation to do so. Similarly, there are unlikely to be major deficits in social competency-related skills, although there may well be issues around adult relationships. The major intervention challenge is with respect to changing these explicit goals; this is very different from traditional relapse prevention approaches, reflecting, in part, the focus on posttreatment issues.

Conclusion

The fundamental point we are making is that unless we understand the processes involved for an individual offender, how can we credibly identify areas for clinical intervention (Kaufman, Hilliker, Lanthrop, Daleiden, & Rudy, 1996; Ward & Hudson, 2000 [this volume])? This is even more profound when we consider that treatment might affect how relapse occurs at some time in the future; that is, the offending process might change. Even if relapse prevention is seen as only a method to help maintain treatment-induced change rather than as a way of structuring the intervention, problems still need to be addressed. Relapse prevention plans need to reflect the reality of what might happen and not be arbitrarily constrained by an inadequate model.

We must resist the temptation to simply apply "grapeshot" management strategies for the problem of sexual aggression in the hope that this will somehow reduce the rate at which these men reoffend. Treatment programs typically try to be "all things to all men," and so they should when the consequences of reoffending are considered. What we need are assessment and intervention strategies that reflect the heterogeneity in the offending process that we all know is present. We are arguing not for a completely individualized intervention regime, which is potentially flawed and very time-consuming (Ward, Nathan, Drake, Lee, & Pathé, 1999), but, rather, that the four pathways provide a potentially economical means of partialing the variance in treatment needs. The model provides a possible offense process-driven taxonomy.

Finally, we need to be clearer about the type of offense process exhibited by various offenders (i.e., an adequate taxonomy) to differentially evaluate intervention outcomes. The global strategy, as is generally now the case, of whether treatment works is inadequate because we predict that some types of the offending process are likely to be more difficult to change and maintain. Being able to differentiate would help both sharpen strategies that we are not doing so well and decide who is most likely to benefit from intervention or is most in need.

References

Alford, B. A., & Beck, A. T. (1997). *The integrative power of cognitive therapy.* New York; Guilford.

Baumeister, R. F., & Heatherton, T. F. (1996). Self-regulatory failure: An overview. *Psychological Inquiry, 7,* 1-15.

Baumeister, R. F., & Leary, M. R. (1995). The need to belong: Desire for interpersonal attachments as a fundamental human motivation. *Psychological Bulletin, 117,* 497-529.

Beck, A. T., Emery, G., & Greenberg, R. L. (1985). *Anxiety disorders and phobias: A cognitive perspective.* New York: Basic Books.

Beech, A., Fisher, D., & Beckett, R. (1999, September). *Putting back relapse prevention back where it belongs: As a necessary adjunct to successful treatment.* Paper presented at the 18th Annual Research and Treatment Conference of the Association for the Treatment of Sexual Abusers, Orlando, FL.

Beech, A., & Fordham, A. S. (1997). Therapeutic climate of sexual offender treatment programs. *Sexual Abuse: A Journal of Research and Treatment, 9,* 219-236.

Carver, C. S., & Scheier, M. F. (1990). Principles of self-regulation: Action and emotion. In E. T. Higgins & R. M. Sorrentino (Eds.), *Handbook of motivation and social behavior* (pp. 3-52). New York: Guilford.

Cochran, W., & Tesser, A. (1996). The "what the hell" effect: Some effects of goal proximity and goal framing on performance. In L. L. Martin & A. Tesser (Eds.), *Striving and feeling: Interactions among goals, affect, and self-regulation* (pp. 99-120). Hillsdale, NJ: Lawrence Erlbaum.

Emmons, R. A. (1996). Striving and feeling: Personal goals and subjective well-being. In P. M. Gollwitzer & J. A. Bargh (Eds.), *The psychology of action: Linking cognition and motivation to behavior* (pp. 313-337). New York: Guilford.

Flavell, J. H., (1984). Cognitive devlopment during the infancy years. In H. W. Stevenson & J. Qicheng (Eds.), *Issues in cognition: Proceedings of a joint conference in psychology* (pp. 1-17). Washington, DC: National Academy of Sciences/American Psychological Association.

Hanson, R. K. (1996). Evaluating the contribution of relapse prevention theory to the treatment of sexual offenders. *Sexual Abuse: A Journal of Research and Treatment, 8,* 201-208.

Hudson, S. M., Gee, D., & Ward, T. (1999). *Incarcerated child molesters volunteering for treatment and those who do not: A demographic, offense and psychological comparison.* Manuscript in preparation.

Hudson, S. M., & Ward, T. (1996). Relapse prevention: Future directions. *Sexual Abuse: A Journal of Research and Treatment, 8,* 249-256.

Hudson, S. M., & Ward, T. (1997). Rape: Psychopathology and theory. In D. R. Laws & W. T. O'Donohue (Eds.), *Handbook of sexual deviance: Theory and application* (pp. 332-355). New York: Guilford.

Hudson, S. M., & Ward, T. (1998, October). *The self-regulatory model of the relapse process: Empirical validity.* Paper presented at the 17th Annual Research and Treatment Conference of the Association for the Treatment of Sexual Abusers, Vancouver, British Columbia.

Hudson, S. M., Ward, T., & Marshall, W. L. (1992). The abstinence violation effect in sex offenders: A reformulation. *Behaviour Research and Therapy, 30,* 435-441.

Hudson, S. M., Ward, T., & McCormack, J. C. (1999). Offense pathways in sexual offenders. *Journal of Interpersonal Violence, 8,* 779-798.

Kaufman, K. L., Hilliker, D. R., Lanthrop, P., Daleiden, E. L., & Rudy, L. (1996). Sexual offender's modus operandi: A comparison of structured interview and questionnaire approaches. *Journal of Interpersonal Violence, 11,* 19-34.

Kear-Colwell, J., & Pollack, P. (1997). Motivation and confrontation: Which approach to the child sex offender? *Criminal Justice and Behavior, 24,* 20-33.

Linehan, M. (1993). *Cognitive-behavioral treatment of borderline personality disorder.* New York: Guilford.

Mann, R. (1998, October). *Relapse prevention: Is that the bit where they told me all the things I couldn't do anymore?* Paper presented at the 17th Annual Research and Treatment Conference of the Association for the Treatment of Sexual Abusers, Vancouver, British Columbia.

Marlatt, G. A., & Gordon, J. A. (1985). *Relapse prevention: Maintenance strategies in the treatment of addictive behaviors.* New York: Guilford.

Marshall, W. L. (1996a). Assessment, treatment, and theorizing about sex offenders: Developments during the past twenty years and future directions. *Criminal Justice & Behaviour, 23,* 162-199.

Marshall, W. L. (1996b). The sexual offender: Monster, victim, or everyman? *Sexual Abuse: A Journal of Research and Treatment, 8,* 317-335.

Marshall, W. L. (1999). Current status of North American assessment and treatment programs for sexual offenders. *Journal of Interpersonal Violence, 14,* 221-239.

Pithers, W. D. (1990). Relapse prevention with sexual aggressors: A method for maintaining therapeutic gain and enhancing external supervision. In W. L. Marshall, D. R. Laws, & H. E. Barbaree (Eds.), *Handbook of sexual assault: Issues theories and treatment of the offender* (pp. 343-361). New York: Plenum.

Pithers, W. D., Marques, J. K., Gibat, C. C., & Marlatt, G. A. (1983). Relapse prevention with sexual aggressives: A self-control model of treatment and maintenance of change. In J. G. Greer & I. R. Stuart (Eds.), *The sexual aggressor: Current perspectives on treatment* (pp. 214-234). New York: Van Nostrand Reinhold.

Prochaska, J. O., DeClemente, C. C., & Norcross, J. C. (1992). In search of how people change: Applications to addictive behavior. *American Psychologist, 47,* 1102-1114.

Ryan, G. (1996). A response to the critical comment on Pithers' relapse prevention model. *Sexual Abuse: A Journal of Research and Treatment, 8,* 161-162.

Sternberg, R. J. (1994). PRSVL: An integrative framework for understanding the mind in context. In R. J. Sternberg (Ed.), *Mind in context: Interactionist perspectives on human intelligence* (pp. 218-232). New York: Cambridge University Press.

Studer, L. H., & Reddon, J. R. (1998). Treatment may change risk prediction for sexual offenders. *Sexual Abuse: A Journal of Research and Treatment, 10,* 175-182.

Ward, T. (in press). Competency and deficit models in the understanding and treatment of sexual offenders. *Journal of Sex Research.*

Ward, T., & Hudson, S. M. (1996a). Pithers' relapse prevention model: A response to Gail Ryan. *Sexual Abuse: A Journal of Research and Treatment, 8,* 162-166.

Ward, T., & Hudson, S. M. (1996b). Relapse prevention: A critical analysis. *Sexual Abuse: A Journal of Research and Treatment, 8,* 177-200.

Ward, T., & Hudson, S. (1998a). A model of the relapse process in sexual offenders. *Journal of Interpersonal Violence, 13,* 700-725.

Ward, T., & Hudson, S. M. (1998b). The construction and development of theory in the sexual offending area: A metatheoretical framework. *Sexual abuse: A Journal of Research and Treatment, 10,* 47-63.

Ward, T., & Hudson, S. M. (2000). A self-regulation model of relapse prevention. In D. R. Laws, S. M. Hudson, & T. Ward (Eds.), *Remaking relapse prevention with sex offenders: A sourcebook* (pp. 79-101). Thousand Oaks, CA: Sage.

Ward, T., Hudson, S. M., & Keenan, T. (1998). A self-regulation model of the sexual offense process. *Sexual Abuse: A Journal of Research and Treatment, 10,* 141-157.

Ward, T., Hudson, S. M., & Marshall, W. L. (1994). The abstinence violation effect in child molesters. *Behaviour Research and Therapy, 32,* 431-437.

Ward, T., Hudson, S. M., & Marshall, W. L. (1995a). Attachment style and intimacy deficits in sexual offenders: A theoretical framework. *Sexual Abuse: A Journal of Research and Treatment, 7,* 317-335.

Ward, T., Hudson, S. M., & Marshall, W. L. (1995b). Cognitive distortions and affective deficits in sex offenders: A cognitive deconstructionist interpretation. *Sexual Abuse: A Journal of Research and Treatment, 7,* 67-84.

Ward, T., Louden, K., Hudson, S. M., & Marshall, W. L. (1995). A descriptive model of the offense chain in child molesters. *Journal of Interpersonal Violence, 10,* 453-473.

Ward, T., Nathan, P., Drake, C. R., Lee, J. K. P., & Pathé, M. (1999). *The role of formulation based treatment in sexual offenders.* Paper submitted for publication.

Wegner, D. M. (1994). Ironic processes of mental control. *Psychological Bulletin, 101,* 34-52.

Weiner, B. (1986). *An attribution theory of motivation and emotion.* New York: Springer-Verlag.

Young, J., & Swift, W. (1988). Schema-focused cognitive therapy for personality disorders: Part I. *International Cognitive Therapy Newsletter, 4,* 13-14.

CHAPTER 7

Behavioral Economics

Understanding Sexual Behavior, Preference, and Self-Control

WILLIAM O'DONOHUE
TAMARA PENIX
ERIN OKSOL
University of Nevada—Reno

In this chapter, we argue that behavioral economics provides a useful conceptual structure to understand human sexual behavior, including sexual behavior that is judged to be change worthy. In particular, we claim that it provides a more coherent framework than relapse prevention for understanding sexual preferences, sexual choices, and sexual self-control. Many of the techniques of traditional relapse prevention and harm reduction are consistent with behavioral economics, but we will argue that behavioral economics provides a more thorough analysis of the processes by which these pragmatically useful techniques have their effects. Importantly, behavioral economics also provides new assessment and treatment possibilities.

Behavioral economics begins with the same premise as economics: that scarcity is a fundamental fact of life. That is, shortages and insufficiencies of various resources relative to needs and desires influence behavior in important ways. Two examples: Imagine you are considering where to vacation during your 2-week winter break. You are deciding either a 2-week skiing vacation in Lake Tahoe or a 2-week beach vacation in Maui. Time is a scarce resource: You cannot be in both places at once, so you must choose. Economists note that choices have *opportunity costs* (i.e., they preclude spending the same time, energy, and other resources on some competing possibility). Second example: Imagine an attractive person A who has five suitors interested in having A as a monogamous mate. A is also interested in being monogamous, so there is a shortage of mating opportunities relative to the suitors' desires. Darwin called such female choice of mates "sexual selection" and thought that sexual selection augmented the selective pressures of natural selection. One important aspect to note is that behavioral economics and an evolutionary account are highly related. Both are concerned with scarcity, competition, cost-benefit, and maximizing value.

Scarcity breeds competition. Potential mates compete, vacation sites compete, beverages compete, sleep competes with work, work competes with TV, cake competes with a trimmer waist, and sexual indulgence competes with sexual abstinence. The important question becomes, Which behaviors "win" in this competition and why?

Individuals vary in the choices they make in these competitions. Individuals also vary in their abilities to maximize value in these domains. Evolution continues to select out individuals who are poor competitors in key arenas. For example, there is a subfield in behavioral psychology called optimal foraging theory that studies the relative payoff of animals' energy expenditures used to find and acquire food versus the caloric value of the actual food acquired. If an animal consistently expends 400 calories to consume food that provides 200 total calories, then the animal is at risk of dying of starvation. If another animal in the same niche spends 20 calories to acquire 400 calories of food, that animal is doing a much better job of maximizing the value of its energy output.

Sex is a particularly important domain of choices. Sex, from an evolutionary perspective, is essentially unequaled in importance. Sex has a special prominence for several reasons. Sex is the cornerstone of evolution. It is not survival that is ultimately important but, rather, surviving so that one can reproduce fecund offspring that maintain or increase genetic representation in the gene pool. Sex is also important because it is a powerful primary reinforcer. Ancestors who did not find sex reinforcing or only mildly reinforcing (and capacity for reinforcement was heritable) would, ceteris paribus, place less of their genes in the gene pool than a competing group that found sex highly reinforcing. Sex has evolved to become a highly reinforcing set of behaviors that can evoke a lot of behavior that is only indirectly related to sex (e.g., acquisitiveness, attraction-enhancing activities, etc.).

Trivers (1972) has suggested that males and females have different reproductive strategies because of differing evolutionary pressures on their reproductive roles. Although both sexes are interested in reproducing, because females have a much higher parental investment than males, their orientation toward sex and reproduction has evolved to be different. Because of menopause, significant gestation periods, and increased care of the neonate (e.g., breast-feeding), a female can have only a small number of offspring. Females thus have become highly selective in their choice of mates (as mating may tie up a significant percentage of their limited reproductive possibilities) and highly concerned about the care of their offspring and enlisting male resources for this. Males, in contrast, have a much lower parental investment in their offspring. In reproduction, males expend only a short amount of time and a small amount of easily replenishible sperm. Males are also physically able to have nearly an unlimited number of offspring and are fertile from puberty throughout the life span. Females have a shorter window of opportunity for reproduction.

Thus, evolution produces diversity and variance regarding sex. That is, there are genetically produced variable proclivities to find certain stimuli and responses sexually reinforcing. These vary across individuals and across genders. To say that there are these biological proclivities does not negate the importance of the environment. Environment and inherited proclivities interact to produce behavior.

Biology and Ecology

Although evolution has produced young females that are biologically prepared to be sexually scarce and young males that are sexually available, the environment has interacted with these dispositions to create the diversity of sexual expression. Evolution is a slow-moving process. Humans have had very similar biological drives for centuries, drives that evolved before industrialization, birth control, and an era of greater economic equality between the sexes. Though some contemporary women are less sexually selective and may be more similar to men in the number of their encounters, they are still restrained in those encounters by the biological and social realities of childbearing (i.e., in economic terms—higher costs). At that point, despite the independence provided by industrialization, females seek quality sperm and the protection and assistance of the male's economic resources so that their children will survive and propagate. They become sexually scarce while males retain a high sexual drive into middle age and beyond. Social proscriptions also make female sex less available than male sex. In many cultures, female abstinence is valued, but this is not often the case with males.

Male sexual behavior has also been influenced by environmental changes, particularly industrialization. Social norms have evolved that make sex with desirable females costly for men. Males must sacrifice their resources and often relinquish promiscuity to obtain the most valuable females. They have had to make more difficult choices about sex and to become more concerned with relationship variables as they make those choices. As they work to make choices that would most benefit themselves, they encounter scarcity of sex. Females do not find the same scarcity when they seek sexual release or sexual reproduction. This may begin to explain the discrepancy between the sexes in the paraphilias.

Why Behavioral Economics?

Behavioral economics is a theoretical and empirical tool that entered the behavior analysis scene in 1975 and gained more popularity in the early 1990s (Bickel, Green, & Vuchinich, 1995). It is the application of economic principles to human and animal behavior. One strength of behavioral economics is that it sprang from a field with a much longer history than that to which it is being applied. Although economic theory is by no means static, concepts and mathematical relationships are well established and available for use in other realms. Behavioral economics provides new independent and dependent variables, quantitative techniques, research methods, and theory that permit a more fine-grained analysis of any set of behaviors that involves the principles of reinforcement. Human sexual behavior is no exception.

Relapse prevention (RP) is the most effective conceptualization that has been applied to sexual offending thus far (Ward & Hudson, 1996). It has been most successful in the treatment techniques that have developed from its simple and useful conceptualization of self-control and offending. RP views sexual offending as a process that involves many steps. As a process with many interchangeable and substitutable steps, it is impossible to eliminate every possible variant. Sexual offending cannot be cured; it can only be controlled through increasing awareness of the steps, increasing motivation not to reoffend, learning skills to stop the process at each point, and developing the ability to implement those procedures. This part of RP is pragmatically clear and provides a workable framework for intervening in the process. RP is, however, not a full theoretical framework that can explain the etiology, maintenance, and treatment of the various types of sexual deviancy. As discussed by Ward and Hudson (1996), there are conceptual problems within the theory as well, such as identifying the processes by which RP constructs work. Relapse prevention has provided the field with indications that sexual deviancy is a problem that can be understood and even changed, yet it is an imperfect model on which stronger theory and practice may be built. Behavioral economics is a tool that can strengthen the foundation.

Behavioral Economics: The Basics

Skinner claimed that we manage our own behavior when we deliberately alter the variables of which that behavior is a function, and he called self-control or self-management "man's only hope" (Epstein, 1997). The idea that is inherent in his analysis is that we control ourselves by modifying our world to influence us in desirable ways. The logical extension of that premise is that to control our world we must understand how the principles of reinforcement are influencing our behavior in that world. Behavioral economics promotes this understanding. Behavioral economics is the study of the allocation of behavior within a system of constraint—that is, a system in which choices dictate the distribution of limited resources for maximum benefit. The system of interest in this chapter is sex.

To understand how behavioral economics may be useful in studying sexual deviancy, it is important to review how some economic concepts have been applied toward understanding operant behavior. In the limited space available in this chapter, we provide a brief overview of how economic concepts and terms help us better understand sexual behavior and sexual choices. The scenario that we used to illustrate this throughout the rest of the chapter is that of infidelity. Specifically, imagine a middle-aged, married male (Mr. X) who hires a prostitute for an evening of sexual gratification. Mr. X's wife freely and willingly engages in sex with Mr. X. Mr. X has two children and is the manager of a financially lucrative business. Mr. X feels a lot of guilt and regret due to his use of prostitutes. He knows that if Mrs. X ever discovered his infidelity, she would probably divorce him, take the children, and own at least half of his business, which would likely fail as a result of the split. This scenario is chosen simply for illustrative purposes and the ease by which behavioral economic terms can be applied and explained through an analysis of Mr. X's economic decisions and sexual choices.

All behavior occurs in a context. In sexual offending, the context comprises environmental variables (e.g., availability of sexual partners), perpetrator variables (e.g., person's learning history), victim variables (e.g., willingness to engage in sexual behavior), and variables concerning competing choices. The goal in behavioral economics, as in RP, is to identify variables that may be altered for the purpose of managing harmful sexual behavior chains. Behavioral economics helps us in the identification and analysis of those variables.

People are consumers in a sexual marketplace. Sexual behavior is constrained (i.e., there is an *economy* that is the environment in which behavior occurs). By soliciting and hiring a prostitute, Mr. X is making economic choices regarding how to allocate his economic resources (e.g., his scarce time, money, and sexual behaviors). Behavioral economics has identified two types of economies, open and closed. An *open economy* is one in which total daily consumption is controlled by someone or something other than the consumer. For example, a man cannot go into a bar, choose any woman, and have sex with her. His consumption is controlled by the choice of the females and other inter-acting variables. In a *closed economy,* total consumption is only determined by the consumer's interaction with schedules of reinforcement. Outside of solitary confinement, it is almost impossible for one to operate within a closed econ-omy. In our example, Mr. X is behaving in an open economy because his sexual choices are determined by the availability of the goods he wishes to purchase (e.g., price of prostitute, availability of prostitutes, distance he needs to travel to reach prostitute).

Another part of the economic context is the presence of a *budget.* A con-sumer has only so much income to spend and must allocate that income among different products within the economy. He must make choices about what to purchase and at what price. Mr. X may be willing to spend $200 for a couple of hours with the prostitute. Alternatively, Mr. X could choose to purchase several porn magazines or spend the money taking his wife out to dinner. This implies the concept of *value*—what is a product worth to a particular individual? To Mr. X, the secrecy, excitement, and novelty of a prostitute may be worth $200, although surely his wife would think otherwise. The value of a product can change for an individual over time. Value can be discounted by various pro-cesses, including a delay of reinforcement. Related to the value of items is knowing how much they *cost,* not only in terms of price but also in everything that must enter into the deal of buying a product. Cost is the total amount of combined resources that must be spent to obtain a unit of a given product. In our example, the costs include Mr. X's time, money, the probability of getting a dis-ease, the probability of getting caught, the probability of arrest, and the proba-bility of having a ruined reputation.

Demand is the primary dependent variable in behavioral economics. It is the amount of commodity (reinforcement) that is purchased at a given price (e.g., how many hours with the prostitute and what type(s) of services rendered). *Price* is the overt amount of resources that must be spent to purchase a given commodity. If the price of one prostitute at one street corner is $1,000 per night and the price of another prostitute on another street corner is $500 per night, twice as many nights may be purchased with the same money. This does not mean that everyone will choose the less-expensive prostitute. The concept of unit price begins to capture this phenomenon. *Unit price* is the interaction of multiple variables that comprise the true cost of a product. It incorporates how often one can access the product and its intensity in making a determination of the final cost of a product. For example, if Mr. X wants the more attractive, clean, and safe prostitute, he is considering three variables in the unit price of the purchase.

It is possible to plot the consumption of a reinforcer as a function of its unit price on a *demand curve*. Demand curves allow for the qualitative aspects of reinforcers to be quantified, aspects such as type of reinforcer and the influence of alternative reinforcers in the system. Mr. X may solicit a prostitute in Nevada where the business is legal. His demand may be greater when the potential cost of arrest is eliminated. However, when the government makes prostitution illegal in other states such as California (the new home of Mr. X), a demand curve permits a visual analysis of Mr. X's purchase of the prostitutes in California decreasing in frequency or amount and his trips to solicit prostitutes in Nevada increasing.

This brings in the concept of *elasticity*, the change in consumption due to price. Some goods, such as the purchase of cheese, may be very *elastic*. That is, I can use a substitute or change my menu altogether if I determine that the price of cheese is too high. However, there are other goods for which demand is *inelastic*. If oxygen went from being free to costing a penny a breath, the demand for oxygen would remain the same despite the price. The purchase of some reinforcers is stringently defended, but the purchase of other reinforcers is not at all defended. How highly the reinforcer is defended indicates whether it is a luxury or a necessity for the person in question. The *substitutability* of reinforcers must be considered in an analysis of elasticity. Substitutable reinforcers are functionally and qualitatively similar such as two equally attractive prostitutes standing on the same corner. Complementary reinforcers are not similar. For example, soliciting a prostitute and watching a porn film may both be reinforcing for an individual, but they are not functionally and qualitatively similar. Sometimes, the more one purchases of one of a complementary reinforcer, the more he purchases the other, as in the case of salty peanuts and beer. Though both are reinforcers, they do not substitute for one another. Elasticity and substitutability are features of reinforcers (commodities).

Income is the limit on overall intake or rate of reinforcement. Income can vary and is influenced by the constraints of the economic system. Mr. X only has so much money available to solicit a prostitute and at the same time pay his mortgage, feed his family, and so on. He has only so much sexual energy as well. *Consumption* is the purchase of a reinforcer (e.g., solicitation of prostitute). *Intensity of demand* is the amount of consumption, and *responding* controls consumption. *Responses* are the medium of exchange (money) in behavioral economics. Responses can be quantified in terms of rate, magnitude, frequency, opportunity costs, and effort per response. Responding is affected by states of deprivation (wanting more sex than available), satiation (bored with existent sexual partner), and arousal (novelty of prostitute, thrill of secrecy).

The question behavioral economists want to answer is how the contingencies of reinforcement influence behavior. What variables are controlling sexual behavior? It appears as though consumers are demanding sexual responses and often engage (with or without complete awareness) in *cost-benefit analyses* for the products they would like to purchase. These analyses may involve any or all of the concepts described earlier, depending on the requirements of the situation and the resources of the consumer. How skilled is the consumer whose economic behavior is of interest in making cost-benefit analyses, and are these analyses and the related purchases predictable? These questions may be answerable using the quantitative methods of behavioral economics.

Behavioral Economics and Sex

The application of behavioral economic principles to sexual behavior seems a natural extension of early animal studies and applications in complex human behaviors such as drug abuse. Sexual activity is a reinforcer that is unequally distributed and scarce. Most of us for a lot of the time experience some sexual deprivation. That is, sexual consumers are not always able to engage in their preferred behaviors at a free operant level. They are not maintaining their bliss points with regard to sexual reinforcement. A bliss point reflects the person's optimal distribution of behaviors in the absence of any constraints (Staddon, 1979). If the bliss point is not attained (e.g., the person is not dating anyone at the time, not enough money to pay a prostitute), he or she will then respond to attain this optimal level and will work at some less-desired task to engage in this target behavior at its optimal level (work mundane job for money, hang out at nightclubs to try and get a date).

Men are not equal in their ability to make the economic exchange for sex. Some men will not have the capital to purchase the goods or all of the goods that they want. At this point, the economic choices get interesting. Men who can purchase what they want when they want it are uninteresting in the scheme of sexual exchange. Men must make complex choices about how to compete, how to maximize reinforcement with limited resources, and sometimes how to bypass the economic system altogether. Sexual choices involve analyzing the contingencies of reinforcement and working within a budget to either distribute responses across reinforcer alternatives so as to match the reinforcers across alternatives or to distribute responses across alternatives so as to maximize total reinforcement (Bickel et al., 1995). In early behavioral economics experiments, some subjects have matched whereas others have maximized reinforcement (Miller, Heiner, & Manning, 1990; Rachlin, Battalio, Kagel, & Green, 1981). Whether maximizing or matching is the rule, how the behavior operates and under what conditions is a subject that is under investigation at this time and is a topic that will be interesting to examine for sexually deviant behaviors.

Cost-Benefit Analyses

Sex is a choice behavior that involves the cost-benefit analysis of many variables. Consumers must judge how much income they have and what their sexual bliss points are. They must learn about what they can afford in terms of quality of the partners and desired activities and the frequency of sexual contacts. How does risk enter into the analysis? Risk plays a part in any economic investment. For some, the experience of risk itself is part of the reinforcement. It is always possible to make an investment that does not pay off in the expected manner. Returning to our illustrative example, Mr. X may weigh whether to have sex with a prostitute (an investment of time and money) or to have sex with his wife, who is more sexually available. *Delay of reinforcement* must always enter into the unit price. Although his wife may be available now, the prostitute might be a more coveted sexual partner, one with higher worth. How is the delay entered into the cost of sex?

If we can begin to understand how people enter all of the variables into the cost-benefit equation and how they act on their analyses over time, it is possible for us to predict their sexual choices. It is also possible to alter the controlling variables to produce different outcomes. The ability to control one's sexual behavior is on a continuum. There are those who are perfectly able to control their sexual behavior even in the face of temptation, but at the other end, people have no control. This does not just pertain to criminal sexual behavior but also to infidelity in committed relationships or promiscuous behavior if there is a desire to control it. A behavioral economic analysis may be applied to any of the sets of behavior on the continuum and at both the macro and micro levels of observation. It is not our intention to suggest that the following analyses are calculated, conscious processes on behalf of the consumer. The process seems to be more one of entering new variables into a tried but flexible cost-benefit analysis through repeated trial and error (behaving and contacting the contingencies of reinforcement). That is, individuals develop an idea of how the sexual economy works and how they fit into it as a consumer. The idea is shaped over time through experience, but an evolving analysis remains that may be used as a heuristic when a sexual situation arises. The following sets of sexual behaviors and choices are presented merely for illustrative purposes of applying behavioral economics terms to scenarios involving poor sexual self-control.

Frotteurism. A young man with low resources is repeatedly unsuccessful in dating women. He does not know how to approach them and becomes very anxious (a cost) when he does. As a result of his failures, he has no self-confidence. He has an average income and does not have high career aspirations. He makes a cost-benefit analysis of trying to engage an adult female sexual partner and determines that it is unlikely that he will get a woman to sleep with him. He gets an erection one day on a crowded elevator when he is pressed up against a beautiful woman. He has an orgasm later while masturbating to the memory of the experience. He decides that he could make these arousing experiences happen with very little investment. He could bypass the limits of his income and the high price of sex with a female (e.g., money, rejection, time) by finding situations in which he could rub up against women. He also learns that the possibility of getting caught strengthens his arousal. He gets human contact and sexual gratification with only the slightest possibility of censure. He lowers the risk of his investment even more by rubbing up against adolescent girls he believes are more unlikely than women to tell anyone about it.

Rape. A young and attractive male makes a cost-benefit analysis and determines that he has a high income and should be able to purchase a lot of sex with valuable partners (young, beautiful, apparently sexually available). He estimates little risk of losing his investment of time and money with potential partners and the opportunity cost of not pursuing others because he has obtained the sex he wanted in the past by making a similar investment. He begins dating a girl who appears sexually available but who does not want to have sex with him. They go on several dates (he invests repeatedly) while he waits for the sexual payoff that never comes. One time they are kissing, and the cost of stopping when she refuses sex seems too high for him, so he rapes her. He determines that he has invested enough and "steals" the sex that he feels he is owed. The aggression involved feels just like sexual arousal, and holding a woman down against her will during sex is reinforced by the orgasm. He looks for more women who might not respect his investment to make the economic decision to bypass the free economic exchange and to take the sex that he purchased in advance.

The scenarios above demonstrate how losses of sexual self-control may be conceptualized using a behavioral economics model. Beyond simple conceptualizations, these behaviors may be analyzed at the microeconomics level through the use of demand curve analyses. Remember that demand curves illustrate the consumption of a reinforcer based on its price. Within this analysis, reinforcers may be quantified by type, available alternatives and their relative prices, substitutability of the reinforcers, and the elasticity of demand for a particular situation or for a number of incidents. Patterns may emerge in the data that may indicate possible areas for intervention to improve self-control. Perhaps the problem is in accurately estimating the cost of preferred sexual encounters or in the magnitude of other essential variables such as income. It is also possible that the variable magnitudes are accurately represented, but they are not properly entered into the cost-benefit ratio. Maybe the problem is using dated economic analyses for current situations or not having the necessary income to make the desired purchases. There may be many possible routes to topographically similar outcomes. Behavioral economics can provide indications of the variables and contingencies of reinforcement that are pertinent to the analysis, can provide ways to quantify and compare the reinforcers, and may then indicate the most logical point of intervention for any individual.

Behavioral economics does not depart from relapse prevention in that it recognizes how cognitive distortions, lack of victim empathy, deviant sexual arousal, preplanning, negative emotional states, and other factors contribute to the development and maintenance of deviant sexual behavior and losses of self-control. It uses analyses of states of deprivation, satiation, and arousal as contextual variables for the economic state of an individual. A behavioral economics approach would also incorporate the apparently effective techniques of RP such as increasing victim empathy (learning about "downstream costs" such as the quality of life of the prostitute) and learning to identify dangerous behavioral chains in the treatment of individuals who cannot control their sexual behavior.

Behavioral economics builds on the RP foundation in that it subsumes RP. By providing new independent and dependent variables, behavioral economics encompasses RP under a broader canopy within a much more fertile context. The major steps that RP has taken in recent years are now to be seen as special cases of a wider, more powerful theory—that of behavioral economics. Behavioral economics provides new assessment strategies and points of intervention that have the potential to help clinicians more effectively design treatment of the sexual offender.

RP in Economic Terms: Assessment Techniques. Behavioral economics provides new ways of assessing RP constructs and variables of interest. It can provide new strategies that guide the clinician to effective points of intervention. Through the use of analogue laboratory studies, the following independent and dependent variables can be assessed and manipulated within the context of sexual misconduct.

Elasticity. The demand for the commodity of interest (sex) is assessed to determine if demand is elastic or inelastic. A consumer is said to obey the "law of demand" when changes in consumption are inversely related to changes in price. How elastic is the sexual offender's demand for sexual gratification for sex in general and for particular kinds of sex? Bliss points may be revealed through clinical interviews, psychological inventories, and plethysmography. In an elastic economy, the sexual offender would offend less frequently as the price of offending increased. In our example, soliciting a prostitute would be less likely the greater the negative consequences (illegal, arrest). In an inelastic system, small decreases in consumption would accompany large price increases. For example, a man who favors a certain prostitute may continue to have sex with her at the same frequency even if she doubles her prices.

Discount Functions. It is being asserted here that persons with poor sexual self-control discount behavioral consequences inaccurately. Some discount future positives (engaging in consensual sex) by perpetrating a date rape. Others discount future negatives too heavily. The unfaithful spouse (Mr. X) discounts being caught by his wife or the police, contracting the HIV virus or a sexually transmitted disease, and losing the respect and trust of his children. Still others entirely discount the possibility of achieving optimal sexual gratification according to the constraints of the economic system. They may then resort to strategies that bypass fair economic exchange. A point of intervention could center on the discounting functions held by the client. Educating the client to prevent discounting the future negative consequences to his or her actions seems likely to be an effective point of intervention.

One criticism of RP is the role of motivation in explaining the sexual offender's shift from a high-risk situation (HRS) to a lapse. Why a person who is committed to abstinence focuses only on the immediate consequences in HRS needs to be explained. In economic theory, we contend that the mechanism underlying this process is exactly that of *discounting*.

Unit Price. A unit price can be varied by different combinations of cost and benefit factors. Unit price may serve to be a powerful means by which to understand sexual choices. In an analogue experiment, subjects' behavior could be studied at different unit prices. For example, the number of negative consequences to Mr. X as a result of his choice to solicit a prostitute could range anywhere from one (being caught by his wife) to many (contracting HIV and SDS, losing respect of colleagues at work, etc.). The purpose of the experiment would be to determine if Mr. X's proclivity to have sex with a prostitute is equivalent at different prices and how altering costs or perceptions of costs would alter his sexual misbehavior.

Substitutability. Substitutable reinforcers (commodities) are generally those that are functionally similar. When treating a pedophile, the goal of treatment, then, is to identify a commodity that is equally or almost as equally as reinforcing as the child. Just as Coke and Pepsi may be substitutable to the average soda drinker, one would hope that for a child molester, an adult sexual partner would substitute for a child. In this example, the difficult task is to increase the reinforcing value and hence the substitutability of appropriate sexual partners.

Cost-Benefit Analysis. One technique that may help people to increase self-control is to increase their awareness of the existence of the larger, more delayed outcome. This involves teaching people how to think about self-control situations in terms of cost-benefit rules. Teaching clients to weigh carefully the relative net value of each outcome before making a decision seems crucial. Combining one outcome with another positive outcome may increase the net value of the self-control alternative, thereby maximizing reinforcement across alternatives instead of relying on one powerful but prohibited reinforcer. In the case of Mr. X, this might be accomplished through his recognizing that having sex with his wife can be sexually gratifying and, at the same time, allows him to experience other positive outcomes that are of value to him, such as his children's respect and trust, getting sex for free (in economic terms), and keeping his job.

RP in Economic Terms: Treatment and Interventions

We next attempt to explicate the relevance of important terms and concepts of RP to a behavioral economic conceptualization of clinical intervention. The hope is that through this paradigm shift, new ideas for the treatment of sex offenders and persons with poor sexual self-control strategies will emerge. We consider both specific skills training elements and more global interventions to problems facing sex offenders through each major tenet of RP theory.

Decision Matrix. The decision matrix is one of the cornerstones of relapse prevention. It is here that the sexual offender weighs the pros and cons of his choices. The decision matrix is used as a tool in RP that is based on the utility rule—the client is taught to consider both short- and long-term consequences of abstinence versus relapse (Jenkins-Hall, 1989). Sexual offenders have flaws in their decision making in that they have difficulty foreseeing long-term consequences (positive or negative).

In behavioral economic terms, the decision matrix is synonymous with a *cost-benefit analysis.* The offender must assess how much he can attain with how much he is willing to invest. Relapse is conceptualized as "stealing the goods" in that the offender has inaccurately estimated (a) his resources and (b) how much the goods cost (for himself or others involved in the transaction). When weighing the alternative decisions, the offender must determine what and who are lower-price alternatives. Here the construct of *substitutability* plays a role. For example, a man may want to date a famous, beautiful woman such as Cindy Crawford. The difficult role for the clinician is helping the client accurately calculate the amount of goods he can purchase with the amount of income available to him—in other words, helping the client recognize that even if he cannot date Cindy Crawford, he can potentially date someone who is beautiful but just not famous. *Discounting* is also relevant to decision matrices. It is the accuracy with which costs and benefits are assessed at any point in the cognitive-behavioral chain that is crucial to favorable outcomes.

High-Risk Recognition: The Cognitive-Behavioral Chain. In RP theory, sexual offenses are seen as a culmination of a long series or chain of events. Offenders are taught to identify high-risk behaviors or variables that precipitate reoffenses by identifying their past failures in controlling their own sexual behavior. In an economic context, when offenders find themselves in a high-risk situation, they have inaccurately weighed the cost of reoffending and the small but cumulative investments they are making toward those ends. *Discounting functions* play a role in that the offender has discounted (saying things cost less than they actually do) past events. Discounting is highly related to the cost-benefit analysis. The clinician's task is to help the client formulate accurate perceptions of both the immediate and long-term costs of relapse and to find real, substitutable alternatives.

Developing Coping Strategies for High-Risk Situations. In RP theory, the first phase of developing coping strategies is for the offender to identify the variety of options available to him for how he may choose to behave. The economic concept of *substitutability* is essential to coping. It is the offender's task to identify other, more acceptable sexual behaviors and choices that are equally as reinforcing as those that are deviant or illegal. *Demand* is also of importance in this scenario—what does the offender desire? The clinician must help the client reasonably estimate what and how much he can buy sexually. Admittedly, this is a very difficult task for the clinician and especially for the client, who is being asked to basically face his limitations in securing a sexual partner.

Coping With Urges and Cravings. In RP terms, an urge is defined as an "impulse or behavioral intention toward a consummatory activity or goal," and a craving is defined as the "subjective desire for the gratification anticipated from the indulgent behavior" (Carey & McGrath, 1989, p. 188). In economic terms, both concepts are simply examples of consumer behavior. One may have the urge to purchase Nike shoes when what he can afford are generic brands. Clients experience a sort of *consumer fantasy* when they go beyond their means (their available *income*). An unfaithful husband has the choice to stay with his wife and try to resolve problems in the marriage to build a richer, more satisfying relationship. Alternatively, he may have an affair and risk losing his wife along with other precious commodities such as children, family support, and friendships. When a client has an urge, the key is to move that client to accept that he does not have the income necessary to purchase the commodity he desires. A craving, on the other hand, is essentially a false belief that the goods will give back more than they are worth. For example, a client may have the false belief that the perfect woman will necessarily provide perfect sexual gratification.

Cognitive Restructuring. Cognitive restructuring is the process of modifying thinking, both its premises and its assumptions (Meichenbaum, 1977). In understanding how sexually deviant behavior is maintained, one must necessarily examine the cognitions of the sex offender. A behavioral economic approach to this process would entail educating the client on how *budgets* work, the goal being for the client to embrace the reality of the economy that he lives in. The client can be led to see that he can get sex at a reasonable cost if, and only if, he assesses his economy correctly. The client is taught how to accurately assess both the resources he has as an individual and how much certain commodities are worth.

Increasing Victim Empathy. Being aware of the deleterious consequences to the victim of a sexual offense is another cornerstone of the theory underlying treatment of sexual offenders. Economically speaking, the offender must acknowledge that nonconsenting sex is synonymous with *stealing* goods from another person. The victims of sexual assault have not consented to pay what they are paying. The clinician must also work with the offender toward an acknowledgment of the downstream costs to victims or other parties that are touched by the offender's behavior. For instance, Mr. X may learn that by buying the services of a prostitute he is creating a demand that keeps her from pursuing a career that is safer and more satisfying.

Abstinence Violation Effect (AVE). Essentially, a client's attributions and emotional reactions to a lapse are collectively termed an AVE (Marlatt & Gordon, 1980, 1985). The AVE is said to occur whenever the client lapses in the face of a commitment to abstinence. The result of an AVE is often the offender relinquishing attempts at control after a lapse, believing that because he has lapsed there is no hope for continued abstinence or treatment gains. Here, behavioral economics would turn to the idea of a *discount function*. The "giving up" behavior is thus conceptualized as a discounting of future positive outcomes. The client also fails to recognize that future losses (reoffense) will only compound present losses.

Problem of Immediate Gratification. The problem of immediate gratification, or the PIG effect, is the culmination of strong sexual cravings and the urges to relieve these cravings (Marlatt & Gordon, 1985). A behavioral economics translation would assert that this is another area in which an accurate cost-benefit analysis of the situation would be advantageous. The sex offender must weigh the immediate gratification involved in a sexual offense or the long-term consequences available to a long-term relationship in which having sex available almost any time is an option. In the case of a preferential child molester, it may be impossible to change sexual preference to an adult. However, delaying sexual gratification may function to decrease the client's anticipation of being caught and put in jail.

Conclusions

We have attempted to explain the basic tenets of behavioral economics and how this model may be used toward better understanding the etiology, maintenance, and treatment of uncontrolled sexual behaviors. Sex involves a complex set of internal and external behaviors, the analysis of which is multifaceted and difficult. As everyone in the field knows, there are no simple solutions to the problem of sexual misconduct, though the demand for quick fixes is high. Relapse prevention was an initial attempt to tackle the problem in all of its complexity. Although this approach provided some inroads to the treatment of sexual offending, it failed to explain the behaviors in such a way that valid predictions about the process could be made and tested. We believe that behavioral economics provides a logical framework for more thorough conceptualizations of the process and components of sexual self-control. Behavioral economics also has the potential to broaden the array of useful assessment and treatment strategies through the use of long-observed economic principles. Its worth will be determined by its utility in guiding future theory development, research, and practice.

References

Bickel, W. K., Green, L., & Vuchinich, R. E. (1995). Behavioral economics. *Journal of the Experimental Analysis of Behavior, 64,* 257-262.

Carey, C. H., & McGrath, R. J. (1989). Coping with urges and cravings. In R. Laws (Ed.), *Relapse prevention with sex offenders* (pp. 188-196). New York: Guilford.

Epstein, R. (1997). Skinner as self-manager. *Journal of Applied Behavior Analysis, 30,* 545-568.

Jenkins-Hall, K. D. (1989). The decision matrix. In R. Laws (Ed.), *Relapse prevention with sex offenders* (pp. 159-166). New York: Guilford.

Marlatt, G. A., & Gordon, J. R. (1980). Determinants of relapse: Implications for the maintenance of behavior change. In P. Davidson & S. Davidson (Eds.), *Behavioral medicine: Changing health lifestyles* (pp. 410-452). New York: Guilford.

Marlatt, G. A., & Gordon, J. R. (Eds.). (1985). *Relapse prevention: Maintenance strategies in the treatment of addictive behaviors.* New York: Guilford.

Meichenbaum, D. M. (1977). *Cognitive-behavior modification: An integrative approach.* New York: Plenum.

Miller, H. L., Jr., Heiner, R. A., & Manning, S. W. (1990). Experimental approaches to the matching/maximizing controversy. In L. Green & J. H. Kagel (Eds.), *Advances in behavioral economics* (Vol. 2, pp. 253-287). Norwood, NJ: Ablex.

Rachlin, H., Battalio, R., Kagel, J., & Green, L. (1981). Maximization theory in behavioral psychology. *Behavioral and Brain Sciences, 4,* 371-417.

Staddon, J. E. R. (1979). Operant behavior as adaptation to constraint. *Journal of Experimental Psychology: General, 108,* 48-67.

Trivers, R. L. (1972). Parental investment and sexual selection. In B. Campbell (Ed.), *Sexual selection and the descent of man.* Chicago: Aldine.

Ward, T., & Hudson, S. M. (1996). Relapse prevention: A critical analysis. *Sexual Abuse: A Journal of Research and Treatment, 8,* 177-200.

PART IV

CLINICAL INNOVATIONS: ASSESSMENT AND TREATMENT

Empathy Inhibition, Intimacy Deficits, and Attachment Difficulties in Sex Offenders

KURT M. BUMBY
Missouri Division of Youth Services and
University of Missouri–Columbia School of Medicine

Among the recognized strengths of the relapse prevention framework, as applied to sexual offenders nearly two decades ago, was the necessary departure from outdated and inadequate single-factor theories attempting to explain deviant sexual behavior and a movement toward recognition of more comprehensive and multifactorial models. The identification of multiple determinants associated with sexual offending was a particularly appealing aspect. Another attractive feature of relapse prevention was the assumption that sexual offending is the result of a complex chain of decisions and behaviors rather than something that "just happens." Indeed, one of the essential and most basic tenets of relapse prevention approaches centers on the identification of the various individual, environmental, and lifestyle factors that precede, contribute to, and maintain sexual offending behaviors, with the ultimate goal of developing adequate coping responses to cope with these high-risk factors.

In the seminal 1989 volume *Relapse Prevention With Sex Offenders* (Laws, 1989), it was emphasized that risk factors (i.e., threats to the offender's self-efficacy, which increase the likelihood of lapse or relapse) need not be limited to physical or environmental variables but should also take into account individual and internal elements such as negative affect, cognitive distortions, personality traits, and deviant arousal (see Marques & Nelson, 1989; Nelson & Jackson, 1989; Pithers, Beal, Armstrong, & Petty, 1989). The underlying premise was that the interaction of the various global and specific risk factors is reliably predictive of sexual offending behavior or future relapse. Several chapters in the volume were devoted to the identification and assessment of risk factors, with Pithers et al. (1989) distinguishing between immediate or proximal precursors (i.e., occurring within 6 months prior to the commission of the offense) and early or distal determinants (i.e., present at least 6 months prior to the offense).

Among the identified immediate elements proximal to offending included dynamic, changeable factors such as negative affect (e.g., anger, frustration, rejection, depression, and loneliness) and cognitive variables such as disinhibiting thought patterns and negative attitudes toward women and children. In addition, skills-related deficits in areas such as social competency, as well as global traits such as empathy deficits, were considered to be among the various high-risk factors to be addressed and modified (Long, Wuesthoff, & Pithers, 1989; Pithers et al., 1989). Some of the posited early antecedents were static and unchangeable factors such as a history of familial chaos, maternal or paternal absence or neglect, and physical or sexual victimization as a child, all of which are suggestive of insecure attachments.

Problematic within the relapse prevention model for sexual offenders as outlined in the early years was the clear presumption, albeit understandable, that these various identified antecedents were indeed specific to sexual offenders and distinctly associated with the onset or maintenance of sexually offending behaviors—hence the term *high-risk factors*. Yet at that time there was inconsistent and equivocal empirical support for the significance of the various risk factors reported by the authors. A clear articulation and validation of the specific nature and extent of such factors had been left virtually unexplored. The prevailing assumption appeared to be that repeated observation of such factors in clinical practice with sexual offenders was sufficient to consider them representative of, and perhaps distinct to, sexual offenders. Indirectly implied was a causal relationship between these variables and sexual offending behaviors.

Therefore, it may have been somewhat surprising to professionals in the field when one decade later, Hanson and Bussière (1996, 1998) reported the findings of a meta-analysis of recidivism predictors that revealed no significant statistical relationship between many of these reported antecedents or risk factors (i.e., negative affect, empathy deficits, social skills deficits) and sexual reoffending. Having appeared obvious from a clinical perspective, it had generally been *assumed* that the commonly observed antecedents would be directly linked to reoffending. The previously unchallenged assumption surrounding the importance of various precursors, although intuitively sensible and often clinically and anecdotally supported, had lacked both critical empirical examination and a theoretical framework within which to understand these specific risk factors and their purported relationship to sexual offending. Descriptive statistics reflecting the presence of such factors within sexual offender samples and comparative analyses demonstrating relative deficits in these areas among sexual offenders were simply insufficient to conclude that such factors reliably predict offending.

It is important to note that Hanson and Bussière (1996) did not rule out the possibility of an association between such factors and sexual reoffending. Rather, the authors hypothesized that the failure of the meta-analysis to demonstrate predictive utility of the dynamic elements was twofold. First, the design of most recidivism studies tends to limit the feasibility of adequately including and measuring dynamic predictors. Because of their changeable nature, to truly explore a potential relationship between dynamic factors and recidivism, elements such as empathy and interpersonal difficulties would have to be regularly assessed and, most important, would need to have been measured immediately prior to the reoffense. Because base rates of recidivism are relatively low and recidivism studies require long follow-up periods, the point at which an individual reoffends is often quite distant from the time of assessment of many dynamic elements (Hanson & Bussière, 1996, 1998). Hence, the likelihood of these outdated measurements remaining reliable and accurate for the time immediately preceding reoffense is low. This inherent difficulty with dynamic predictors is contrasted with static factors that, once identified as present, are constant and need not be reassessed.

Beyond the lack of repeated assessment in the traditional recidivism studies, Hanson and Bussière (1996) argued that the lack of predictive accuracy of dynamic elements may also have been a function of inadequate definitions and a lack of underlying theory. Operationally defining constructs, standardizing methods of assessing such concepts, and having a sound theoretical foundation within which to explore such constructs have not been consistent with respect to many dynamic predictors. Without a clear theoretical foundation for understanding these potentially significant and promising relationships between dynamic predictors and reoffending, empirical investigations into recidivism will remain of limited and perhaps misleading value. Ward and Hudson (1998) have similarly argued for the need for more integrated frameworks and theories to guide research into sexual offending, suggesting that middle-level theories focusing on single factors to be incorporated into the comprehensive models are essential.

In recent years, more effort has been directed toward the development of theoretical frameworks attempting to explain the relationship between dynamic elements such as empathy (Marshall, Hudson, Jones, & Fernandez, 1995), intimacy and attachment (Marshall, 1989; Ward, Hudson, Marshall, & Siegert, 1995), and future reoffending. Such models, if validated, may serve to increase the potential for the predictive value of such factors in recidivism-related research, as well as provide a rationale for the inclusion of related measures and interventions in the assessment and management process (Hanson & Bussière, 1996). The remainder of this chapter provides an overview of some of the more recent theoretical and empirical developments with respect to specific dynamic factors (i.e., empathy, intimacy, and attachment) believed to play a role in offending behavior and that have generally been considered an important focus in the assessment and management of sexual offenders.

Empathy

It has long been argued that empathy is an essential ingredient in the prevention and management of sexually offending behaviors and that without empathy, sexual offenders remain likely to reoffend. The interested reader would be hard-pressed to find an article articulating a comprehensive approach to sexual offender management that does not include empathy as a necessary component of treatment. Clearly, empathy-related issues are believed to be a critical and essential target of the sexual offender assessment and management process.

In describing the importance of empathy training for sexual offenders, Hildebran and Pithers (1989) argued that offenders should be required to develop victim empathy skills prior to being exposed to the cognitive management techniques of relapse prevention. This rationale was based on the belief that focusing first on the high-risk situations and intervening coping responses simply resulted in a purely intellectual understanding of the relapse process and interfered with the emotional recognition of the impact of one's behaviors on the victim and others. The authors claimed that the behavioral management techniques of relapse prevention, without the development of empathy, may be inadequate for motivating an offender to avoid relapse. Moreover, Hildebran and Pithers suggested that the emotional connection (i.e., empathy) may provide the requisite inhibitor for future offending, in that empathy can restrain an offender even when he has failed to recognize or has ignored the predictable chain of events leading to relapse. The antithesis, put simply, implies that nonsexual offenders do not offend in part because they possess empathy as a form of restraint.

It is of interest to note that the readily adopted stance that sexual offenders are generally deficient in empathy skills remained virtually unchallenged until Marshall, Hudson, et al. (1995) became among the first to critically contest this long-standing assumption. Revealed in their review of the literature on empathy and sexual offenders was an actual *lack* of empirical support for the existence of general empathic deficits. Equivocal findings regarding the nature and extent of empathic deficits among sexual offenders were noted as well, including the failure to identify significant differences between sexual offenders and nonoffenders (e.g., Hayashino, Wurtele, & Klebe, 1995; Marshall, Hudson, et al., 1995). Furthermore, in those studies that revealed relative empathic deficits among sexual offenders, it appeared that the statistically significant differences were "clinically" insignificant, with the researchers failing to report that the means of the sexual offenders on the empathy measures were actually within "normal" limits. The authors also noted that across studies there existed unclear conceptualizations of the construct of empathy, which led to inconsistent findings in the research (Marshall, Hudson, et al., 1995).

Therefore, it has been suggested that, thus far, the use of nonspecific and general measures of empathy may have resulted in the failure to meaningfully answer the question of interest (i.e., whether sexual offenders lack empathy toward victims) (see Hayashino et al., 1995; Marshall, Hudson, et al., 1995). As noted by Marshall, Hudson, et al. (1995), some of the more commonly used measures of empathy are psychometrically unacceptable and lack specificity, failing to reference individuals in any particular target group and therefore implying that individual and situational characteristics are inconsequential. Continuing to view empathy as a trait that is unaffected by situation or context has fostered the belief that empathy is a relatively stable and singular trait or characteristic that is either absent or present in specific individuals.

Empathy as a Complex and Staged Process

As noted earlier, it had become common practice to consider empathy as a singular trait that was either absent or present among sexual offenders. Approaching empathy from a different standpoint, Hanson and Scott (1995) defined empathy as a multidimensional construct involving three factors. The first component, reflective of a cognitive process, was referred to as perspective taking or the capacity to recognize the emotional state of the victim and to perceive how the victim may respond in a given situation. The second factor of empathy, an affect-driven component, was identified as an "emotional response to others," in which the offender experiences and reflects affect similar to the emotional experience observed in the victim. Third, Hanson and Scott (1995) emphasized the element of caring, an often neglected aspect of empathic responding. Recognized was the reality that offenders may fail to respond empathically because of a lack of concern or interest in the distressed victim. The authors suggested that sexual offenders may be deficient in one or more of the three components of empathy; that the deficits may be generalized, class specific, or victim specific; and that these empathy deficits may be stable or situationally determined.

Similarly appreciating the complex nature of empathy, Marshall, Hudson, et al. (1995) conceptualized empathy as a multifaceted and staged process rather than simply as a trait, individual product, or singular experience. Specifically, the empathic process was theorized to include four discriminable stages, thus providing more specificity and differentiation to the process than had been offered by Hanson and Scott (1995). The first level involves emotional recognition, whereby the offender recognizes the emotional state of the victim and presumably has the ability to recognize and label his own emotional experiences. The importance of this first stage is clear, in that a failure to recognize that one is causing emotional distress to another results in a decreased likelihood that the individual will cease the harmful behavior, having perceived no ill effects on the victim.

Perspective taking is the second stage of the empathic process posited by Marshall, Hudson, et al. (1995), following the emotional recognition phase. This stage has traditionally been referred to as "empathy" in more simplistic definitions. Perspective taking refers to the ability of the offender to identify with, or put himself in the place of, the victim and assume the perspective of the victim. The assumption underlying the perspective-taking stage is that if one is able to take the perspective of another individual, he or she is more likely to be able to recognize the inflicted emotional distress. Hanson and Scott (1995) failed to consider the emotional recognition stage as distinct from the perspective-taking phase and instead combined the two. Certainly, the ability to recognize emotions of others, as well as the ability to take another's perspective, is a separate prerequisite to the next stage, that of emotional replication.

According to Marshall, Hudson, et al. (1995), in the emotional replication stage the offender experiences an appropriate emotional response to the harmed or distressed other. This ability to reproduce or closely approximate the emotional experience of the other person in turn requires the possession of an adequate emotional repertoire. The final stage of the empathic process is referred to as response decision, akin to the "caring" phase in Hanson and Scott's (1995) operational definition. Put simply, it is not sufficient that an offender takes notice of the victim's distress, considers the perspective of the victim, and experiences parallel negative affect. Rather, the offender must still make a decision as to whether he will respond appropriately (e.g., cease the offending behavior), if choosing to respond at all. There has been some limited and indirect empirical support for the staged process model of empathy in sex offenders (for reviews, see Fernandez et al., 1999; Marshall, Hudson, et al., 1995).

Victim-Specific Empathy

Based on the belief that individual, situational, and temporal elements may differentially affect the capacity for experiencing empathy, it has been suggested that empathy measures be reformulated to include more specificity (Hayashino et al., 1995; Marshall, Hudson, et al., 1995).

In response, Fernandez, Marshall, Lightbody, and O'Sullivan (1999) developed and evaluated a context-specific measure for assessing the first three stages of the empathic process as proposed by Marshall, Hudson, et al. (1995). The measure was specifically designed to address empathy toward child victims in three contexts: children in general, nonspecific victims of child sexual abuse, and the offender's own child victim. Assessed by the context-specific measure is the ability to identify types of distress, associated degree of emotional suffering and problematic experiences in the identified target, and emotional reaction of the respondent to the victim's distress. This context-specific measure was found to be psychometrically sound, as evidenced by internal consistency, temporal stability, discriminant validity, and utility in assessing within-treatment changes following empathy enhancement training.

Fernandez et al. (1999) found that the child molesters were less empathic than the nonoffenders toward the nonspecific victim of sexual abuse and were less empathic toward their own victims than toward the general victims of sexual abuse. However, the child molesters and nonoffenders were equally empathic toward the accident victim. Furthermore, the levels of empathy exhibited by molesters for both the general victim of abuse and the accident victim were similarly high. The finding that the child molesters were significantly more empathic toward the accident victim and the nonspecific sexual abuse victim than toward their own victim led the authors to suggest that the molesters may have learned to inhibit empathic responses toward their own victims. Consequently, this selective empathic inhibition would serve the function of allowing the offender to continue to engage in the victimizing behaviors without the negative self-referential evaluation (i.e., guilt or shame) that often accompanies transgressions, much like the process of cognitive distortion.

Cognitive Distortion and Victim-Specific Empathy

Clearly implicated with respect to empathic responding is the role of cognitive distortion. Cognitive distortions such as denial, minimization, justification, rationalization, and victim blaming are believed to mitigate the anxiety, guilt, or shame that accompanies these behaviors (see, generally, Abel et al., 1989; Murphy, 1990; Stermac & Segal, 1989). Although it has been suggested that cognitive distortions are a consequence of sexual offending, it is perhaps more reasonable to consider the existence of such distortions as preceding, during, and following the actual offensive behavior. Ward, Fon, Hudson, and McCormack (1998) have emphasized the importance of cognitive processes at various points throughout the offense cycle, arguing that a more thorough examination of these processes may provide valuable insight into preexisting attitudes and beliefs, initial planning, interpretations of victims' behaviors, and postoffense evaluations and expectations.

Consider, for illustrative purposes, an individual who intentionally exceeds the posted speed limit. This individual has an awareness of the wrongfulness of his behavior and must engage in cognitive maneuvering to allow himself to violate the law prior to engaging in the law-violating behavior. Furthermore, he continues to justify, rationalize, and minimize the transgressing behavior during and following the act. Most would agree that sexual offenders also are cognizant of the wrongfulness of their behaviors, lest they would have no need to engage in a similar process of cognitive distortion. In addition, the experience of guilt or shame suggests that the offender possesses at least some degree of awareness of wrongfulness of the behavior or that the offensive behavior affects the victim in some manner. Hence, one might actually consider victim empathy deficits to be a manifestation of the process of cognitive distortion, which is intentionally used to avoid or ameliorate shame, guilt, or empathic processing.

Indeed, cognitive distortions, which excuse or minimize specific transgressing behaviors or situations, and victim-specific empathic deficits appear to represent the same or a very similar process. This would be consistent with the hypothesis that sexual offenders do not lack empathy in general but, rather, appear to exhibit empathic deficits only when the offender considers his own actions. Again, these so-called empathic deficits may actually reflect a conscious (and after much practice and repetition), learned, and ultimately automatic cognitive response (i.e., selective empathy inhibition) to avoid shame and guilt and heighten the positive affect immediately following the offending experience. The distinction between cognitive distortions and empathic deficits therefore becomes unclear and indeed may be inseparable from this perspective. This point was also recently raised by Fernandez et al. (1999) on the basis of the finding that sexual offenders suffered from empathy deficits primarily with respect to the offenders' own victims. It was subsequently suggested that the conceptual distinction between cognitive distortions and empathy deficits may not be particularly useful (Fernandez et al., 1999).

Other preliminary support for this viewpoint was revealed in a study involving measures of cognitive distortion specific to the offender's case versus the general measures of cognitive distortion often used in studies of sexual offenders (Bumby & Schlank, 1997). In this investigation, sexual offenders who failed to endorse items generally supportive of sexually offending behaviors (e.g., general tendencies toward victim blaming, minimization, and justification) actually tended to endorse numerous types of distortions specific to their own offenses. Therefore, it was not that the sexual offenders justified or minimized the impact or harm to victims of sexual abuse *in general,* but they did so only when the offenses in question were their own. Practitioners are reminded of this phenomenon with clinical observations of sexual offenders in group settings, whereby offenders readily identify and challenge the distortions used by peers but continue to exhibit distorted processing when dealing with their own disclosures and offenses, thus reflecting individualized and context-specific empathic deficits.

A related conceptualization of the association between cognitive distortions and empathic deficits can be found in the Ward, Hudson, and Marshall (1995) article on cognitive deconstruction and sexual offenders. Specifically, it was suggested that to reduce personal discomfort that is induced by self-awareness, the offender focuses on a level of meaning that is concrete and superficial. Disinhibition occurs when the individual cognitively deconstructs and therefore is able to ignore immediate and long-term negative or harmful consequences of the offensive behavior (i.e., emotional recognition, perspective taking). The behavior and responses of the victim are either ignored or attended to only at a superficial level. Consequently, the offending experience becomes egoistic for the sexual offenders, facilitating more immediate personal gratification.

Cognitive distortion and deconstruction used by sexual offenders suggest that they possess the ability to identify emotions, perspective-take, and emotionally replicate, for without such abilities they would have little need to justify and rationalize the offending behaviors or minimize the impact of these behaviors on the victims prior to, during, and following the offense. Moreover, the avoidance of shame and guilt appears to reflect an acute awareness of harm having been caused. Again, this suggests a conscious and selective inhibition of the recognition of harm to the victim, rather than a true empathic *deficit*. The reader is referred to the chapter on cognitive distortions by Langton and Marshall (2000 [this volume]) for a more comprehensive discussion of the role of cognitive distortions, and a proposed relationship between shame, guilt, and empathy follows below.

Shame, Guilt, and the Empathic Process

As briefly outlined in the preceding section, the process of selective empathic responding and employment of cognitive distortions suggests a common mechanism—namely, the avoidance of shame and guilt as a means to initiate or continue offending behavior. Indeed, it has been theorized that the empathic processing of sexual offenders may be differentially affected by the experiences of negative affect such as shame and guilt (see Bumby, Marshall, & Langton, 1999). Specifically, based on a review of the more general literature on shame and guilt (see, generally, Tangney, 1995, 1996; Tangney, Burggraf, & Wagner, 1995), Bumby et al. (1999) theorized that the distinct phenomenological experiences of shame and guilt play a disparate role in sexual offenders' empathic responsiveness and, conversely, proneness to cognitive distortion such as minimization and victim blaming. Both shame and guilt are negative affective experiences that are presumed to have an inhibiting effect on transgressions (much like empathy) and are considered to be self-referential processes involving internal attributions that occur following a transgression (i.e., during the abstinence violation effect). However, the set of *differences* between shame and guilt is believed to be critical to empathic responsiveness and increased likelihood for relapse (see Bumby et al., 1999; Hudson, Ward, & Marshall, 1992).

Early relapse prevention theorists failed to make the distinction between shame and guilt at the point of the abstinence violation effect and instead suggested that these affective experiences equivalently increased the likelihood of relapse. Hudson et al. (1992) argued, however, in their reformulation of the abstinence violation effect in sexual offenders, that shame and guilt are the result of differing causal attributions and therefore have different motivational consequences. For example, the offender who makes internal but controllable attributions regarding the lapse or relapse is expected to experience guilt, which is believed to motivate the offender to maintain a commitment to abstinence (Hudson et al., 1992). However, if attributing the offense-related transgression to internal and uncontrollable factors, the individual is believed to experience shame and decreased self-efficacy. Subsequently, the sex offender is less committed to the avoidance of relapse and is therefore at greater risk to reoffend.

With respect to the impact of negative affect on empathic processing, Bumby et al. (1999) similarly considered the distinction between shame and guilt at the point of the abstinence violation effect. More specifically, the authors theorized that the self-focused nature of the shame experience has particular implications for the empathic inhibition of sexual offenders. As outlined by Tangney (1995, 1996; Tangney et al., 1995), the sequelae of the shame experience involves painful and global self-scrutiny, self-consciousness, and perceptions of negative evaluation, all of which create self-oriented distress. The creation of self-oriented distress obviously impedes other-oriented emotional recognition, perspective taking, and emotional replication—respectively, the first three stages of Marshall, Hudson, et al.'s (1995) model of empathy. The shame-experiencing sex offender is therefore believed to perceive himself as unable to change and is therefore less able to identify and use adaptive coping responses, resulting in decreased self-efficacy, feelings of worthlessness, and feelings of powerlessness. Moreover, due to the perceived negative evaluation by others as well as the self-oriented distress, the offender is more prone toward defensive externalization (see Tangney, 1995, 1996; Tangney et al., 1995) such as victim blaming and additional cognitive distortions about the offense that are clearly counter to empathizing with the victim in the situation (i.e., victim-specific empathy deficits). Ultimately, this is believed to establish a negative emotional state with empathic deficits and dysfunctional cognitions, all of which influence the risk for reoffense (Bumby et al., 1999; Hudson et al., 1992).

In the guilt experience, resulting from the sex offender attributing the lapse or relapse to internal but controllable factors, intense scrutiny occurs regarding the specific offense behavior rather than global self-devaluation. Because critical evaluation of a specific behavior is less painful or threatening to the offender, it may therefore be easier for the offender to examine the impact of such behaviors (Tangney, 1995, 1996). Therefore, as Bumby et al. (1999)

posit, when an offender critically examines his thoughts or behaviors (vs. him-self as a whole), the tendency toward exploring and identifying the impact on the victim (i.e., emotional recognition and perspective taking) is increased. Assuming that the offender is able to identify his own emotions and the emo-tional expressions of others, the offender may therefore experience a parallel discomfort and tension due to the recognition of the harm to the victim (i.e., emotional replication). In turn, the discomfort experienced during the perspec-tive-taking and emotional replication stages may be associated with remorse and a desire to cease the harmful behavior (Tangney, 1995, 1996; Tangney et al., 1995). This is, of course, the final stage in Marshall's proposed empathy pro-cess (i.e., response decision). Recognizing that the offense was within his con-trol, the offender is believed to be more apt to explore the potential options and identify adaptive coping responses, which in turn are believed to be associated with an increased sense of self-efficacy.

Some preliminary support for the differential association between shame and guilt and the empathic process among sexual offenders has been reported (Bumby, Levine, & Cunningham, 1996). Using a sample of sexual offenders in outpatient treatment, the investigators revealed a significant positive associa-tion between shame-proneness and measures of personal distress and external-ization. In other words, as the sexual offenders' proneness to experience shame increased, so did the tendency to experience self-oriented personal distress, feel self-conscious, and externalize responsibility, which is clearly counter to the empathic process. Conversely, as sexual offenders' proneness to experience guilt increased, so did their level of empathic concern and perspective-taking ability. The hypothesized relationship between shame, guilt, and empathy among sexual offenders has clear implications for treatment. Simply put, engaging offenders in a therapeutic approach designed to elicit the guilt experi-ence, versus the shame experience, is likely to enhance empathic responsive-ness by the offenders (see Bumby et al., 1999; Jenkins, 1990, 1998; Marshall, 1996; Pithers, 1997).

Empathy Training

There is no question that empathy training components have long been a crit-ical aspect of most sexual offender management programs. Common approaches and interventions described include the use of role-plays and role reversals, hypothetical letters written by the offenders from their victims' per-spectives, educational and other resources depicting actual victims' experi-ences, abuse survivors as guest speakers, the challenging of abuse-supportive cognitive distortions and myths about victims, and processing of offenders' own victimization (e.g., Hildebran & Pithers, 1989; Pithers, 1994). Interest-ingly, the clear majority of these interventions do not address the generalized empathic deficits that had been assumed to exist but instead target victim-specific (or at least class-specific) empathy deficits. Despite the common use of such interventions, few clinicians or researchers (e.g., Pithers, 1994) have actually reported evaluations of the efficacy of such components.

At present, there remains insufficient empirical information to definitively answer whether sexual offenders lack empathy in general, are unempathic toward sexual abuse victims only, or selectively inhibit empathic responsiveness with respect to their own victims (Hayashino et al., 1995; Marshall, Hudson, et al., 1995). In actuality, it may be unimportant whether sexual offenders have greater empathic deficits than other offenders; rather, it is perhaps more significant to target the specific deficits that exist and promote continued offending. Further research is essential in determining the nature and extent of these deficits, based on clearer definitions and conceptualizations. The aforementioned literature on empathy and sexual offenders reflects recent attempts to clarify some of these issues. Such developments may indeed prove significant in empirically validating the importance of empathy deficits or empathic inhibition as a risk factor to offending. The next sections focus on a review of recent developments with respect to other antecedents and risk factors—namely, those of intimacy deficits and attachment difficulties.

Intimacy and Attachment

Much like the case with the literature on empathy deficits of sexual offenders, it has been assumed, based on years of observation and clinical experience, that sexual offenders lack social competence, manifest difficulties in interpersonal relationships, and come from homes in which the modeling of aggression increases the likelihood of interpersonal difficulties later in life. Returning to the influential *Relapse Prevention With Sex Offenders* text (Laws, 1989), it was reported by several authors (e.g., Hildebran & Pithers, 1989; Jenkins-Hall & Marlatt, 1989; Long et al., 1989; Marques & Nelson, 1989; Pithers et al., 1989) that social skills deficits, interpersonal difficulties, and histories of maltreatment were indeed significant risk factors and antecedents to sexual offending behaviors. Indeed, early sexual offender research on social competence and interpersonal relationships was based on the hypothesis that sexual offenders had deficits in skills necessary for healthy and effective sexual and social relationships, perhaps reflective of social learning processes (see Marshall, Barbaree, & Fernandez, 1995).

Unfortunately, the manner in which social functioning was defined by researchers has been inconsistent and widely varied, with the measurement of factors such as assertiveness, heterosocial skills, social self-esteem, social anxiety, self-consciousness, and social intimacy deficits. The subsequent findings of these studies have therefore been equivocal. However, the continued observation and speculation in clinical practice of such apparent risk factors remained unmistakable. As noted by Ward, McCormack, and Hudson (1997), the failure to find consistent empirical support in this area of inquiry has suggested either methodological or measurement weaknesses or a failure to ask the right questions concerning the relationship between social and interpersonal functioning and sexually offending behaviors. Again, the lack of a clear theory operationally defining these deficits and their relationship to offending behaviors may have resulted in the failure of researchers to demonstrate that such social deficits were an important etiological or maintaining factor for sexual offenders. This, coupled with the inherent inability to have measurements of such constructs immediately prior to reoffending, perhaps led to a lack of predictive utility (Hanson & Bussière, 1996, 1998).

It was not until Marshall (1989, 1993) proposed a framework involving insecure attachments and intimacy deficits that some of the socially related deficits were specifically conceptualized in terms of the development and maintenance of sexually offending behaviors. This model and the subsequent refinements by Ward, Hudson, and colleagues (Ward, Hudson & Marshall, 1996; Ward, Hudson, Marshall, & Siegert, 1995) provided the impetus to reexamine the role of various aspects of deficient interpersonal skills and relationships long considered to be etiologically significant for sexual offenders. The focus on intimacy deficits and attachment difficulties has since become an important contribution to the sexual offender literature.

Intimacy

Akin to the challenge of conceptualizing the construct of empathy, operationally defining intimacy has proved to be an arduous venture, with theorists providing a variety of definitions of intimacy as a state, as a process, and as a combination of both (see Acitelli & Duck, 1987; Perlman & Fehr, 1987; Reis, 1990). As a state, intimacy has been described as an end product or goal that, once achieved, is objectively measurable (Acitelli & Duck, 1987). Still others have suggested that the state of intimacy lies on a continuum, with deep intimacy on one end and emotional alienation on the other (see Marshall, 1989). Conversely, as a process, intimacy has been assumed to include facets of cognitive, affective, and behavioral elements that develop, fluctuate, and change over time (see Acitelli & Duck, 1987; Reis & Shaver, 1988), including significant self-disclose, empathic responding, and feelings of support, understanding, caring, and validation. Although it is possible to consider intimacy as reflecting either a state or a process, it may be more appropriate to combine both perspectives in a manner that outlines intimacy as a process that is subject to change but attains relatively stable defining features (Acitelli & Duck, 1987).

Attachment

Although a variety of theoretical perspectives have included aspects of intimacy, attachment theories appear to provide the most specificity with respect to operationally defining intimacy (Ainsworth, 1989; Ainsworth, Blehar, Waters, & Walls, 1978; Bowlby, 1969, 1973, 1988; Reis, 1990). Because it is beyond the scope of this chapter to provide a thorough review of the general attachment literature, it may be most parsimonious to report the general agreement among attachment theorists that positive and negative internal working models of the self and of others determine an individual's particular attachment style. To illustrate, children who perceive themselves as worthy of love and support (i.e., positive internal model of self) and who view others as trustworthy and available (i.e., positive internal model of others) will be securely attached (Bowlby, 1969, 1973) and therefore more likely to achieve intimacy. A state of emotional detachment and isolation describes the lack of intimacy characteristic of avoidantly attached children, the result of either a negative internal working model of the self or others or both (Ainsworth, 1989; Ainsworth et al., 1978).

Recognizing the parallel processes involved in the attachments of children and adults, Bartholomew and her colleagues (Bartholomew, 1990; Bartholomew & Horowitz, 1991) delineated and empirically tested a four-category model of adult attachment. The four categories derived from the various combinations of the internal models of the self and of others were referred to as secure, preoccupied, fearful-avoidant, and dismissive-avoidant (Bartholomew, 1990; Bartholomew & Horowitz, 1991). According to the framework, securely attached individuals are comfortable with intimacy, maintain high self-esteem, and tend to have few serious interpersonal difficulties (Bartholomew, 1990; Bartholomew & Horowitz, 1991). At the other end of the spectrum, adults with a fearful-avoidant attachment style (i.e., negative view of self and others) perceive themselves as unworthy and unlovable and expect others to be rejecting, untrustworthy, unreliable, and unavailable. Although such individuals desire intimacy and have a strong need for closeness with others to feel worthy, they have a pervasive fear of intimacy. Thus, they ultimately avoid intimacy to protect and defend themselves from the anticipated rejection and pain (Bartholomew, 1990; Bartholomew & Horowitz, 1991).

Intimacy, Attachment, and Sexual Offending

As indicated earlier, Marshall (1989, 1993) developed the first theoretical framework involving intimacy deficits and sexual offending. Specifically, it was hypothesized that poor-quality attachments that develop during childhood are associated with a failure to develop the requisite esteem, self-assurance, trust, and interpersonal skills to establish and maintain healthy intimate relationships in adulthood. According to Marshall (1989, 1993), attachment difficulties and subsequent intimacy deficits are believed to result in emotional loneliness, a painful affective experience distinct from social loneliness. It was further suggested that sexual offenders, who often equate intimacy with sex, may repeatedly pursue the fulfillment of unmet intimacy needs and the mitigation of emotional loneliness through impersonal sexual contacts, even if these sexual contacts are with inappropriate partners (i.e., children) or are nonconsensual in nature. Certainly, the immediate gratification associated with this style of sexual encounter is self-oriented and therefore incompatible with a tendency to focus on the victim (i.e., other-oriented empathy).

Offering support for the significance of these social-related factors as outlined in Marshall's (1989, 1993) model, investigators have revealed the existence of intimacy deficits and emotional loneliness among samples of sexual offenders (Bumby & Hansen, 1997; Bumby & Marshall, 1994; Seidman, Marshall, Hudson, & Robertson, 1994; Ward et al., 1997). In addition, specific anxieties about close, intimate relationships (i.e., fear of intimacy) have been revealed among individuals who molest children (Bumby & Hansen, 1997; Bumby & Marshall, 1994).

Using an interview methodology, Ward et al. (1997) categorized offenders' responses to questions regarding perceptions of and involvement in intimate relationships. Included among these categories were commitment, expression of affection, support received and support given, trust, mutual empathy, sexual satisfaction, and sensitivity to rejection. Interestingly, no significant differences emerged between the sexual offenders and nonsexual offenders in terms of the intimacy-related variables, which suggested that these areas may be more predisposing to criminal behavior in general, rather than distinct to sexual offenders. It was noted, however, that the sexual offenders appeared to have a variety of deficits that may have a detrimental impact of intimacy, such as low self-disclosure, hesitancy to express affection, decreased empathic responsiveness, and poor conflict resolution skills. Furthermore, the child molesters were found to be more sensitive to rejection, reflective of the fear of intimacy held by child molesters in the Bumby and Hansen (1997) study. Child molesters reported less sexual satisfaction in their romantic relationships than did the other groups. Rapists and violent offenders expressed a belief that they received less support from their partners and further reported more negative evaluations of their partners, as well as less commitment to the relationships. According to the authors, the categories identified through the investigation were reflective of interpersonal strategies, internal working models of the self and others, and behaviors associated with the development or maintenance of intimate relationships. The findings suggested that child molesters tended to have more negative perceptions of themselves, whereas rapists held more negative internal schemas of others. The importance of these internal working models became particularly salient in the subsequent expansion of Marshall's (1989) theory.

A More Comprehensive Intimacy-Attachment Framework

When considering Marshall's original model of intimacy and attachment, Ward et al. (1995, 1996) noted that the inclusion of the internal models of the self and others that determine the particular attachment type had been neglected. In addition, the initial model failed to address offender type, which is important given the heterogeneity of sexual offenders and the likelihood that they may possess different types of attachment. Furthermore, the original model solely described the influence of insecure attachment in general, rather than specifically addressing the three types of insecure attachment (preoccupied, fearful-avoidant, dismissive-avoidant). In response to these limitations, the intimacy and attachment model was expanded and reformulated to address the internal working models, offender type, and the differential influence of each of the insecure categories (i.e., preoccupied, fearful-avoidant, dismissive-avoidant) on offending.

Incorporating Bartholomew's (1990) adult attachment model, Ward, Hudson, and Marshall (1995, 1996) argued that the internal schemata of the self and others bridge early attachment difficulties and subsequent intimacy deficits and relationship problems of sexual offenders. These distinct attachment types and the associated intimacy deficits and interpersonal strategies, coupled with disinhibiting factors (e.g., cognitive distortions, victim-specific empathy deficits), were theorized to differentially affect victim selection, strategies, and offense behaviors. Specifically, it was suggested that sexual offenders with preoccupied attachment styles tend to rely on others for approval and attempt to fulfill intimacy needs through sexual experiences. Ultimately, these encounters leave the offender continuing to feel unfulfilled and emotionally lonely. When the preoccupied offender directs his attention toward a child, he will likely engage in grooming behaviors and perceives the relationship as a mutually enjoyable dating encounter. Therefore, the preoccupied offender is unlikely to act aggressively, forcefully, or coercively because he is operating from the perspective of involvement in a romantic relationship. Fearful-avoidant individuals desire but fear intimacy in relationships and therefore tend to avoid venturing beyond the superficial level. The fear and avoidance of intimacy lead these offenders to engage in impersonal sexual encounters as a means to fulfill intimacy needs. However, associated with impersonal encounters is a lack of concern about the partner, who is simply viewed as an object of a sexual experience. Hence, fearful-avoidant sexual offenders are likely to be self-focused and unempathic toward their victims and may therefore be unconcerned and indifferent about whether force or coercion must be used to meet their sexual needs (Ward, Hudson, & Marshall, 1995, 1996).

With the dismissive-avoidant individual, a different picture exists altogether. Because these individuals deny the importance of close relationships and prefer to remain autonomous and therefore protected from hurt or rejection, they may be more likely to be interpersonally hostile. Consequently, impersonal encounters are likely, with an added component of hostility, because they have negative views of others and blame others for their lack of intimacy (see Bartholomew, 1990; Bartholomew & Horowitz, 1991). Last, dismissive-avoidant sexual offenders are more prone to act out aggressively, particularly toward the gender of their preferred adult partners, who are often blamed for the offenders' interpersonal difficulties (Ward, Hudson, & Marshall, 1995, 1996). This is reflective of an increased tendency toward forcible rape versus the covert grooming behaviors used by offenders with a preoccupied attachment style or the indifference to the strategy used to achieve sexual gratification manifested by individuals with fearful-avoidant attachments.

Providing some support for the general trends hypothesized in the expanded model, Ward et al. (1996) found a high prevalence of insecure attachments among their sample of sexual offenders. Consistent with the model's predictions, rapists were more likely than child molesters to have dismissive-avoidant attachments, with child molesters found to be more likely to be preoccupied or fearfully attached. The violent offender and nonviolent offender groups used for comparison in the study also exhibited a high prevalence of insecure attachments, however, which suggested that insecure attachment may be better considered as a vulnerability or predisposing factor to general criminal behavior, rather than specific to sexual offending behaviors (Ward et al., 1996).

In another study, Hudson and Ward (1997) found support for various aspects of the expanded model through an examination of various interpersonal variables, offense type, and attachment style. As expected, preoccupied and fearful-avoidant individuals reported more loneliness than those with secure or dismissive attachment types, who, according to the model, would likely be satisfied with their respective levels of intimacy due to their interpersonal strategies and desires. Further consistent with the model, fearfully attached and dismissively attached persons reported greater fears of intimacy. Of particular interest was the failure to find significant differences between offender groups (i.e., child molesters, rapists, violent nonsexual offenders, and nonviolent nonsexual offenders) on the measures of loneliness and fear of intimacy, hostility toward women, or rape myth acceptance. Again, the authors suggested that attachment style, more than offender type, appeared to be related to the types of interpersonal difficulties such as loneliness, fears of intimacy, and intimacy deficits. It was therefore suggested that attachment style may be more appropriate to use as a categorizing variable than offense type.

Attachment, Intimacy, and Empathic Processing

The prevalence of insecure attachment types among sexual and other violent offenders, coupled with the respective interpersonal strategies and intimacy deficits associated with each attachment style, suggests that sexual and other offenders do not lack empathic *capacity* per se. Rather, it appears that empathic processing and responding may be more a function of conscious or unconscious interpersonal strategies and choices based on their internal schema and attachment style. Specifically, insecure attachments and the various combinations of negative views of the self and others are likely to lead to interpersonal strategies that decrease the likelihood of establishing truly intimate relationships. The resulting negative affect (e.g., anger, hostility, depression, loneliness, fear, anxiety) causes discomfort, which can be temporarily mitigated by the immediate positive affect resulting from sexual contact. However, such superficial and impersonal sexual experiences, which are designed purely to meet intimacy needs, reinforce the problem of immediate gratification and an obvious focus on the self. By doing so, the focus is diverted from the harmed other (i.e., victim-specific empathic inhibition).

Consider the case of the fearfully attached sexual offender. Fearful individuals desire intimacy with others but avoid truly intimate relationships due to fear of rejection and mistrust of others. Based on prior experience, such an individual has become all too familiar with negative emotional experiences such as hurt, rejection, and fear. It is unlikely, then, that the fearful-avoidant offender has true deficiencies with respect to emotional recognition. Indeed, the very experience of negative affect such as rejection and hurt has in part resulted in the offender's perceived unworthiness and unlovability as well as his perceptions of others as negative. As Ward, Hudson, and Marshall (1995, 1996) suggested, the negative view of others leads the fearfully attached offender to be exclusively self-focused on immediate gratification and indifferent with respect to whether he causes harm when striving to meet his needs for intimacy. This indifference clearly suggests an *unwillingness* rather than an *inability* to perspective-take. Given the unwillingness to perspective-take, the process of emotional replication and response decision will be thwarted. Hence, the failure of the fearful-avoidant sexual offender to respond empathically may, in large part, be a function of his attachment style. Nonetheless, he is likely aware of the wrongfulness and harmfulness of his behaviors but resorts to cognitive distortion pre-, during, and postoffense to avoid the negative affect that either accompanies self-awareness or recognition of victim harm.

What is clear is the need to identify attachment style and intimacy deficits among sexual offenders and intervene accordingly. Although not necessarily specific to sexual offenders, just as victim- or situation-specific empathy deficits are not exclusively characteristic of sexual offenders, the importance of targeting these areas is nonetheless important. These elements represent just a few pieces of the puzzle as argued by Marques and Nelson (1989), who added, "The appropriate pieces must first be selected and then joined together in the correct position in order for a complete picture to emerge" (p. 37).

Clinical Implications

On the basis of the indications of the significance of empathy inhibition, intimacy deficits, and attachment difficulties among sexual offenders, several clinical implications are evident from a relapse prevention perspective. Certainly, a crucial component of relapse prevention planning involves the identification of various precursors and individual risk factors for which adaptive coping responses must be developed and implemented. A specific goal of this process is to teach offenders appropriate strategies for coping with experiences of emotional loneliness and to enable them to modify the deficits in their adult relationships. Optimally, this would lead to a reduction in attempts to obtain intimacy through inappropriate and unhealthy sexual contact. Indeed, clarifying these specific relationship deficits, including empathic inhibition, may promote more effective direction for and expansion of the various treatment modules currently in place in sexual offender management programs.

In general, group therapy, cognitively based approaches, and long-term interventions have been identified as particularly suited for treating intimacy deficits, problematic attachment styles, and other related interpersonal problems (Horowitz, Rosenberg, & Bartholomew, 1993). Such difficulties are unlikely to be resolved in brief forms of treatment because individuals who manifest difficulties with intimacy may have similar problems in relating to a therapist, which may in turn impede the treatment process. Furthermore, intimacy difficulties may be more difficult to treat than other types of interpersonal problems (e.g., social skills, assertiveness), in part because such difficulties may be entrenched and threatening to the individual's sense of identity and autonomy.

Ward, Hudson, and Marshall (1995) have stressed the importance of assisting sexual offenders in understanding the close relationship between emotions, behaviors, and internal working models in intimate relationships. By doing so, the offenders may be able to identify cognitive and behavioral patterns associated with their intimate relationships, develop specific interventions to modify these problematic patterns, and ultimately practice adaptive interpersonal goals and strategies as part of relapse prevention planning.

Important for facilitating the development and maintenance of intimate relationships is the targeting of various aspects of interpersonal functioning, specifically focusing on skills necessary for enhancing or achieving intimacy. Included among these areas of emphasis are empathy, reciprocity in relationships, self-disclosure, physical affection, and the development of effective communication, problem solving, and conflict resolution skills (Marshall, Bryce, Hudson, Ward, & Moth, 1996; Marshall, O'Sullivan, & Fernandez, 1996; Ward et al., 1997). Overall, the goal is to identify and practice specific behavioral responses that have a positive impact on intimacy while modifying those that detrimentally influence intimacy in relationships.

Also of particular clinical significance is the enhancement of self-esteem among sex offenders. Sexual offenders and individuals with esteem deficits appear to share a variety of common difficulties (see Marshall, Anderson, & Champagne, 1996), with such deficits associated with distorted and self-serving perceptions, a lack of empathic concern, deficits in social interactions, intimacy difficulties, emotional distress, and negative affect. Because each of these elements has been implicated as immediate and distal precursors to sexually offending behaviors, inclusion of such factors in relapse prevention planning is necessary. Indeed, the importance of self-esteem and self-efficacy alone is critical in the offender's commitment to relapse prevention, for without a sense of self-efficacy, the offender may perceive himself as hopeless, and efforts directed toward the development and adherence to a relapse prevention plan are futile.

The need to address self-esteem is further highlighted by the reflection of self-esteem in the internal working models (i.e., positive vs. negative view of self) associated with the various attachment styles. Specifically, a secure attachment (i.e., positive view of self and others) reflects healthy self-esteem and self-confidence, whereas negative self-concept and negative perceptions of others characterize insecurely attached individuals. Ward, Hudson, and Marshall (1995, 1997) have therefore suggested that the different levels of self-esteem respectively associated with the insecure attachment styles may have differing implications for the initial targets of treatment. For example, the negative view of the self (i.e., low self-concept), which characterizes individuals with fearful-avoidant and preoccupied attachment styles, suggests the importance of an initial treatment emphasis on the enhancement of self-esteem, with a subsequent focus on specific intimacy enhancement skills (Ward et al., 1997). Conversely, for those offenders whose internal working models reflect a negative view of others (i.e., fearful-avoidant, dismissive-avoidant), it may be more beneficial to direct initial treatment efforts toward the development of more healthy and positive perceptions of partners and significant others (Ward et al., 1997).

At present, there is initial evidence supporting the efficacy of specific interventions designed to increase intimacy, empathic responsiveness, and self-esteem. Specifically, Marshall, Bryce, et al. (1996) outlined a specific treatment component for sexual offenders targeting the facilitation of intimacy skills and alleviation of loneliness. The psychoeducational interventions involved instruction about the nature and development of intimacy and other relationship skills, an operational definition of healthy relationships, an understanding of sexual satisfaction differences between partners, education about the phenomenon of jealousy, and the development of effective and adaptive coping responses to manage loneliness. Following the implementation of this treatment component, sexual offenders have been found to report a significant increase in intimacy and a reduction in loneliness (Marshall, Bryce, et al., 1996).

Recently, Marshall, O'Sullivan, and Fernandez (1996) described a comprehensive method for enhancing victim empathy via a three-phase approach. In brief, the first segment involves emotional expression, in which offenders are encouraged to appropriately identify and express their emotions and identify and respond to the emotional experiences of others in the group. The victim harm segment involves each offender discussing immediate and long-term effects of sexual abuse on victims in general as well as their own victims, and the offenders participate in perspective-taking exercises. In the final segment, the offenders are exposed to victim impact information and are required to develop a hypothetical sexual assault scenario involving a loved one or significant other who was not a victim of their own sexually offensive behaviors and then describe the impact on his victim as well as his own emotional reaction.

Prior to exposure to the interventions outlined by Marshall, O'Sullivan, and Fernandez (1996), the sexual offenders exhibited significantly less empathy toward their own victims in comparison to sexual abuse victims in general. Following the victim empathy component, however, the molesters displayed a significantly improved capacity to empathize with their own victims in terms of the identification of their victims' distress (i.e., emotional recognition and perspective taking) and the experiencing of similar distress about their victims (i.e., emotional replication). An increase approaching statistical significance was revealed in terms of empathy regarding nonspecific victims of sexual abuse, with this difference best accounted for by the enhancement of the offender's feelings about the victim but not the ability to identify the child's feelings. In general, that study, and Pithers's (1994) evaluation of empathy training, provide support for the ability to enhance the empathic capacity of sexual offenders.

Similar to the promising approaches to intimacy and empathy enhancement among sexual offenders, Marshall, Champagne, Sturgeon, and Bryce (1997) have delineated a successful approach for the enhancement of esteem among sexual offenders. As part of this approach, therapists modeled empathy, warmness, genuineness, acceptance, and encouragement; clients were expected to parallel these behaviors to promote and facilitate a positive group atmosphere. In addition, the offenders were taught the importance of distinguishing between one's behaviors and the self as a whole (i.e., the guilt-shame distinction). Further addressed were the improvement of appearance and self-presentation, development of vocational and educational skills, participation in health-promising activities, involvement in social activities, and the identification and review positive self-statements. Overall, these interventions were associated with a positive impact on sexual offenders' self-esteem, with the changes in esteem also related to increased intimacy and a reduction in loneliness (Marshall et al., 1997).

Conclusion

The recognized need for assessment and treatment targeting empathy deficits and other aspects of interpersonal functioning has not changed dramatically since such elements were suggested as significant risk factors in Laws's (1989) *Relapse Prevention With Sex Offenders*. What *has* changed is the level of understanding about why such elements are important, as well as an added specificity to the focus of the associated interventions. However, although the nature and extent of these apparent risk factors have been more clearly elucidated, we are far from a comprehensive and unequivocal understanding of the role that such factors play in the offense process. Encouraging is the tenuous confirmation of clinical intuition that empathic and interpersonal functioning may still be relevant risk factors to consider. It remains a matter of asking the right questions and, more important, a willingness to critically examine our theories and methods. The development of clearer and empirically validated theories may continue to facilitate the effective targeting of intimacy and attachment difficulties, as well as victim- and offense-specific empathy deficits or the inhibition of empathic processing. We are grateful to the persistent and diligent scientist-practitioners who refused to abandon the often-observed antecedents that had been only inconsistently empirically supported but have since been reformulated in such a manner as to increase the likelihood that such precursors may be more effectively identified and managed. Indeed, we look forward to the new developments to be included in the next volume.

References

Abel, G. G., Gore, D. K., Holland, C. L., Camp, N., Becker, J. V., & Rathner, J. (1989). The measurement of the cognitive distortions of child molesters. *Annals of Sex Research, 2,* 135-153.

Acitelli, L. K., & Duck, S. (1987). Postscript: Intimacy as the proverbial elephant. In D. Perlman & S. Duck (Eds.), *Intimate relationships: Development, dynamics, and deterioration* (pp. 297-308). Beverly Hills, CA: Sage.

Ainsworth, M. D. S. (1989). Attachments beyond infancy. *American Psychologist, 44,* 709-716.

Ainsworth, M. D. S., Blehar, M. C., Waters, E., & Walls, S. (1978). *Patterns of attachment: A psychological study of the strange situation.* Hillsdale, NJ: Lawrence Erlbaum.

Bartholomew, K. (1990). Avoidance of intimacy: An attachment perspective. *Journal of Social and Personal Relationships, 7,* 147-178.

Bartholomew, K., & Horowitz, L. M. (1991). Attachment styles among adults: A test of a four category model. *Journal of Personality and Social Psychology, 61,* 226-244.

Bowlby, J. (1969). *Attachment and loss: Vol. 1. Attachment.* New York: Basic Books.

Bowlby, J. (1973). *Attachment and loss: Vol. 2. Separation.* New York: Basic Books.

Bowlby, J. (1988). *A secure base.* New York: Basic Books.

Bumby, K. M., & Hansen, D. J. (1997). Intimacy deficits, fear of intimacy, and emotional loneliness among sexual offenders. *Criminal Justice and Behavior, 24,* 315-331.

Bumby, K. M., Levine, H., & Cunningham, D. (1996, November). *Empathy deficits, shame, guilt, and self-consciousness.* Paper presented at the 15th Annual Association for the Treatment of Sexual Abusers, Chicago.

Bumby, K. M., & Marshall, W. L. (1994, October). *Loneliness and intimacy deficits among incarcerated rapists and child molesters.* Paper presented at the 13th Annual Research and Treatment Conference of the Association for the Treatment of Sexual Abusers, San Francisco.

Bumby, K. M., Marshall, W. L., & Langton, C. M. (1999). A theoretical formulation of the influences of shame and guilt on sexual offending. In B. Schwartz & H. Cellini (Eds.), *The sex offender* (Vol. 3). Kingston, NJ: Civic Research Institute.

Bumby, K. M., & Schlank, A. (1997, October). *Issues in the assessment of sexual offenders' cognitive distortions.* Paper presented at the 16th Annual Research and Treatment Conference of the Association for the Treatment of Sexual Abusers, Arlington, VA.

Fernandez, Y. M., Marshall, W. L., Lightbody, S., & O'Sullivan, C. (1999). The child molester empathy measure: Description and examination of its reliability and validity. *Sexual Abuse: A Journal of Research and Treatment, 11,* 17-31.

Hanson, R. K., & Bussière, M. T. (1996). *Predictors of sexual offender recidivism: A meta-analysis* (User Report No. 1996-04). Ottawa: Department of the Solicitor General of Canada.

Hanson, R. K., & Bussière, M. T. (1998). Predicting relapse: A meta-analysis of sexual offender recidivism studies. *Journal of Consulting and Clinical Psychology, 66,* 348-362.

Hanson, R. K., & Scott, H. (1995). Assessing perspective taking among sexual offenders, nonsexual criminals, and nonoffenders. *Sexual Abuse: A Journal of Research and Treatment, 7,* 259-277.

Hayashino, D. S., Wurtele, S. K., & Klebe, K. J. (1995). Child molesters: An examination of cognitive factors. *Journal of Interpersonal Violence, 10,* 106-116.

Hildebran, D., & Pithers, W. D. (1989). Enhancing offender empathy for sexual abuse victims. In D. R. Laws (Ed.), *Relapse prevention with sex offenders* (pp. 236-243). New York: Guilford.

Horowitz, L. M., Rosenberg, S. E., & Bartholomew, K. (1993). Interpersonal problems, attachment styles, and outcome in brief dynamic psychotherapy. *Journal of Consulting and Clinical Psychology, 61,* 549-560.

Hudson, S. M., & Ward, T. (1997). Intimacy, loneliness, and attachment style in sexual offenders. *Journal of Interpersonal Violence, 12,* 323-339.

Hudson, S. M., Ward, T., & Marshall, W. L. (1992). The abstinence violation effect in sex offenders: A reformulation. *Behaviour Research and Therapy, 30,* 435-441.

Jenkins, A. (1990). *Invitations to responsibility: The therapeutic engagement of men who are violent and abusive.* Adelaide, Australia: Dulwich Centre.

Jenkins, A. (1998). Invitations to responsibility: Engaging adolescent and young men who have sexually abused. In W. L. Marshall, Y. M. Fernandez, S. M. Hudson, & T. Ward (Eds.), *Sourcebook of treatment programs for sexual offenders* (pp. 163-189). New York: Plenum.

Jenkins-Hall, K. D., & Marlatt, G. A. (1989). Apparently irrelevant decisions in the relapse process. In D. R. Laws (Ed.), *Relapse prevention with sex offenders* (pp. 47-55). New York: Guilford.

Langton, C. M., & Marshall, W. L. (2000). The role of cognitive distortions in relapse prevention programs. In D. R. Laws, S. M. Hudson, & T. Ward (Eds.), *Remaking relapse prevention with sex offenders: A sourcebook* (pp. 167-186). Thousand Oaks, CA: Sage.

Laws, D. R. (Ed.). (1989). *Relapse prevention with sex offenders.* New York: Guilford.

Long, J. D., Wuesthoff, A., & Pithers, W. D. (1989). Use of autobiographies in the assessment and treatment of sex offenders. In D. R. Laws (Ed.), *Relapse prevention with sex offenders* (pp. 88-95). New York: Guilford.

Marques, J. K., & Nelson, C. (1989). Elements of high risk situations for sex offenders. In D. R. Laws (Ed.), *Relapse prevention with sex offenders* (pp. 35-46). New York: Guilford.

Marshall, W. L. (1989). Intimacy, loneliness and sexual offenders. *Behavior Research and Therapy, 27,* 491-503.

Marshall, W. L. (1993). The role of attachment, intimacy, and loneliness in the etiology and maintenance of sexual offending. *Sexual and Marital Therapy, 8,* 109-121.

Marshall, W. L. (1996). The sexual offender: Monster, victim, or everyman? *Sexual Abuse: A Journal of Research and Treatment, 8,* 317-335.

Marshall, W. L., Anderson, D., & Champagne, F. (1996). Self-esteem and its relationship to sexual offending. *Psychology, Crime, and Law, 3,* 81-106.

Marshall, W. L., Barbaree, H. E., & Fernandez, Y. M. (1995). Some aspects of social competence in sexual offenders. *Sexual Abuse: A Journal of Research and Treatment, 7,* 113-127.

Marshall, W. L., Bryce, P., Hudson, S. M., Ward, T., & Moth, B. (1996). The enhancement of intimacy and the reduction of loneliness among child molesters. *Journal of Family Violence, 11,* 219-235.

Marshall, W. L., Champagne, F., Sturgeon, C., & Bryce, P. (1997). Increasing the self-esteem of child molesters. *Sexual Abuse: A Journal of Research and Treatment, 9,* 321-333.

Marshall, W. L., Hudson, S. M., Jones, R., & Fernandez, Y. M. (1995). Empathy in sex offenders. *Clinical Psychology Review, 15,* 99-113.

Marshall, W. L., O'Sullivan, C., & Fernandez, Y. M. (1996). The enhancement of victim empathy among incarcerated child molesters. *Legal and Criminological Psychology, 1,* 95-102.

Murphy, W. D. (1990). Assessment and modification of cognitive distortions in sex offenders. In W. L. Marshall, D. R. Laws, & H. E. Barbaree (Eds.), *Handbook of sexual assault: Issues, theories, and treatment of the offender* (pp. 331-342). New York: Plenum.

Nelson, C., & Jackson, P. (1989). High risk recognition: The cognitive-behavioral chain. In D. R. Laws (Ed.), *Relapse prevention with sex offenders* (pp. 167-177). New York: Guilford.

Perlman, L. A., & Fehr, B. (1987). The development of intimate relationships. In D. Perlman & S. Duck (Eds.), *Intimate relationships: Development, dynamics, and deterioration* (pp. 13-42). Newbury Park, CA: Sage.

Pithers, W. D. (1994). Process evaluation of a group therapy component designed to enhance sex offenders' empathy for sexual abuse survivors. *Behavior Research and Therapy, 32,* 565-570.

Pithers, W. D. (1997). Maintaining treatment integrity with sexual abusers. *Criminal Justice and Behavior, 24,* 34-51.

Pithers, W. D., Beal, L. S., Armstrong, J., & Petty, J. (1989). Identification of risk factors through clinical interviews and analysis of records. In D. R. Laws (Ed.), *Relapse prevention with sex offenders* (pp. 77-87). New York: Guilford.

Reis, H. T. (1990). The role of intimacy in interpersonal relations. *Journal of Social and Clinical Psychology, 9,* 15-30.

Reis, H. T., & Shaver, P. (1988). Intimacy as an interpersonal process. In S. Duck (Ed.), *Handbook of personal relationships* (pp. 367-389). Chichester, UK: Wiley.

Seidman, B. T., Marshall, W. L., Hudson, S. M., & Robertson, P. J. (1994). An examination of intimacy and loneliness in sex offenders. *Journal of Interpersonal Violence, 9,* 518-535.

Stermac, L., & Segal, Z. V. (1989). Adult sexual contact with children: An examination of cognitive factors. *Behavior Therapy, 20,* 573-584.

Tangney, J. P. (1995). Shame and guilt in interpersonal relationships. In J. P. Tangney & K. W. Fischer (Eds.), *Self-conscious emotions: Shame, guilt, embarrassment, and pride* (pp. 114-139). New York: Guilford.

Tangney, J. P. (1996). Conceptual and methodological issues in the assessment of shame and guilt. *Behavior Research and Therapy, 34,* 741-754.

Tangney, J. P., Burggraf, S. A., & Wagner, P. E. (1995). Shame-proneness, guilt-proneness, and psychological symptoms. In J. P. Tangney & K. W. Fischer (Eds.), *Self-conscious emotions: Shame, guilt, embarrassment, and pride* (pp. 343-367). New York: Guilford.

Ward, T., Fon, C., Hudson, S. M., & McCormack, J. (1998). A descriptive model of dysfunctional cognitions in child molesters. *Journal of Interpersonal Violence, 13,* 129-155.

Ward, T., & Hudson, S. M. (1998). A model of the relapse process in sexual offenders. *Journal of Interpersonal Violence, 13,* 400-425.

Ward, T., Hudson, S. M., & Marshall, W. L. (1995). Cognitive distortions and affective deficits in sex offenders: A cognitive deconstructionist interpretation. *Sexual Abuse: A Journal of Research and Treatment, 7,* 67-83.

Ward, T., Hudson, S. M., & Marshall, W. L. (1996). Attachment style in sex offenders: A preliminary study. *Journal of Sex Research, 33,* 17-26.

Ward, T., Hudson, S. M., Marshall, W. L., & Siegert, R. (1995). Attachment style and intimacy deficits in sex offenders: A theoretical framework. *Sexual Abuse: A Journal of Research and Treatment, 7,* 313-335.

Ward, T., McCormack, J., & Hudson, S. M. (1997). Sexual offenders' perceptions of their intimate relationships. *Sexual Abuse: A Journal of Research and Treatment, 9,* 57-74.

CHAPTER 9

The Role of Cognitive Distortions in Relapse Prevention Programs

CALVIN M. LANGTON
University of Toronto, Ontario

W. L. MARSHALL
Queen's University, Ontario

In addressing the etiology and maintenance of sexually assaultive behavior, a central focus for treatment providers and researchers alike has been the postulated role of cognitive factors. The term *cognitive* is used here to refer to an individual's perceptions and internal thought processes and reflects the construction, representation, and use of knowledge (Hastorf & Isen, 1982; Sherman, Judd, & Park, 1989). Of particular concern with sexual offenders are *cognitive distortions*. However, a problem in addressing the issue of cognitive distortions among sexual offenders concerns just what researchers and clinicians mean when they discuss this topic. Among the numerous facets of distortions that have been identified are attitudes and beliefs, distorted perceptions, forms of denial and minimization, justifications, a sense of entitlement (Hanson, Gizzarelli, & Scott, 1994), and a feeling of emotional congruence with children (Araji & Finkelhor, 1985). Some researchers have also considered the failure by offenders to recognize the harm they have done to their victims as a cognitive distortion (Fernandez, Marshall, Lightbody, & O'Sullivan, 1999), whereas others see this as part of a more general failure to experience empathy.

In this chapter, we examine some of these cognitive distortions in sexual offenders within a social cognition framework (Johnston & Ward, 1996). We aim to illustrate how distinctions between structures, processes, and products (Ward, Hudson, Johnston, & Marshall, 1997) can clarify our understanding of these distortions and inform our interventions. We include a brief consideration of measures currently used to assess cognitions in sexual offenders and outline a number of techniques to modify cognitive distortions that can be used within the comprehensive relapse prevention treatment model.

Aspects of Cognition

Ingram and Kendall (1986) describe a taxonomic system of cognitions comprising four components that are interrelated but conceptually distinct. These components include structures, propositions, operations, and products. Each of these components is understood to be a general classification of particular cognitive variables. *Cognitive structure* refers to the architecture of stored knowledge that an individual possesses. Cantor and her colleagues (Cantor, Mischel, & Schwartz, 1982) have identified basic categories, such as prototypes and stereotypes, consisting of person and situation dimensions, that serve as core units in an organized knowledge structure. A differing but compatible approach has been adopted by Abelson (1981), who outlines the importance of "scripts" in comprehending social scenarios. Schank and Abelson (1977) refer to scripts as spatially and temporally arranged frames that organize sequences of actions around central themes or goals. As such, scripts can be understood as cognitive structures that guide individuals' social behaviors in interpersonal interactions as well as enabling them to understand others' behaviors in terms of social roles.

The *schema* concept has proved useful in understanding the organization of conceptual knowledge. A schema represents a prototypical abstraction of a given concept, consisting of related generic knowledge and memories of associated past experiences (Thorndyke & Hayes-Roth, 1979). Incorporated into this schema are facts and assumptions about the concept that the individual has internalized through social learning processes (Bandura, 1986) and the associated emotions that have accompanied these life experiences (Turk & Salovey, 1985). Theoretically, there has been some difficulty in drawing a distinction between organized knowledge structures and the content of these structures, particularly in understanding the functional roles involved. Cantor et al. (1982) suggest that

> many different structures (e.g., category prototypes, scripts, bipolar dimensions) may simultaneously or equivalently fulfill the same cognitive needs of the perceiver.

> Just as we have multiple, overlapping knowledge in different social domains (con-
> structive alternativism), the same knowledge may be internally represented in dif-
> ferent structures simultaneously (structural alternativism). (p. 48)

This is consistent with the general notion of associative networks of knowledge
that characterizes recent approaches to social cognition (Fiske & Taylor, 1991).

In terms of function, schemas are considered to influence attention, perception, and interpretation of external stimuli through both their structural associations and semantic, episodic, and affective content (Segal, 1988). Ingram and
Kendall (1986) refer to this content as *cognitive propositions*. The structural
associations of related knowledge content about definable concepts, such as
oneself, females, and prototypical situations (Bem, 1981; Segal, 1988), enable
the individual to generate theories or hypotheses about environmental events.
From an interpersonal perspective, these theories or hypotheses can be understood as implicit understandings or readily available interpretations of interactions. The content of schemas and theories produces expectancies in the individual and consequently exerts a direct influence on the individual's attention
and perceptions, as well as influencing the organization of new information
(Segal, 1988). Importantly, schemas are thought to provide "default values" in
circumstances in which there is insufficient information available, thus facilitating the inference of aspects in the stimuli that are in fact absent (Hollon &
Garber, 1988).

The processes by which information present in external stimuli are perceived and interpreted are referred to as *cognitive operations*. These operations
mediate between the environment and the individual's various schemas.
Because not all stimuli in the world can be attended to, perception is selective.
Tversky and Kahneman (1974) have found that under conditions of uncertainty, people adopt heuristic strategies (i.e., shortcuts) to process information
and make judgments. In fact, as Johnston and Ward (1996) point out, people
characteristically adopt various heuristic strategies to reduce information load
(e.g., overgeneralization, selective abstraction). It is under such conditions that
an individual's scripts, theories, and situational or state-dependent processes
are maximally activated (Hollon & Kriss, 1984). One of these heuristics that
has been suggested to play a role in sexual offending is cognitive deconstruction (Ward, Hudson, & Marshall, 1995). In this strategy, the person shuts down
consideration of abstract issues (e.g., right and wrong, a concern for others) and
possible long-term consequences to themselves and others and focuses instead
on the procedural steps involved in meeting their current desires. It is here that
scripts and situational or state-dependent processes are maximally activated.
This simplifies processing by narrowing attention to only those aspects that are
directly relevant to achieving the goal. Thus, goals and desires can be said to
exert a direct influence on the processing of social information.

170

CLINICAL INNOVATIONS

An evaluation of a client's processing must therefore incorporate the particular circumstances, motivations, and emotional state of the individual over the episode of interest. In the case of sexual offenders, this time scale can be considered in terms of the offense chain, and we will discuss this further on.

Cognitive products are the thoughts and imagery that an individual generates by perceiving external stimuli and referencing his perceptions against his memories, that is, the knowledge stored within his various schemas. Some general examples of cognitive products include causal judgments, social inferences, specific person or situation appraisals, and perceptions of agency and locus of control (Hollon & Garber, 1988; Ward, Hudson, & Marshall, 1994). Although they derive from the individual's schemas, information-processing products reflect current awareness of features in the immediate environmental situation. These products have been the main focus of clinical research (Nasby & Kihlstrom, 1986; Ward et al., 1997), yet they represent only "the tip of the iceberg" (Hollon & Kriss, 1984, p. 39) and provide limited insight into a person's cognitions. Importantly, self-reported products are subject to various response biases, most particularly the tendency of the respondent to present oneself in a socially desirable manner.

Cognitions in Sexual Offenders

A meta-theory outlined by Johnston and Ward (1996) represents a social information-processing model of sexual offenders' cognitions. This is valuable because, as Nasby and Kihlstrom (1986) point out, we

> can trace most of the cognitive problems of most clients to a specific domain of content—namely, social information. Most clients misconstrue particular individuals or facets of the self, distort recollections of personal experiences and social events, [and] adopt inadequate or inappropriate strategies of interacting socially. (pp. 218-219)

In their paper, Johnston and Ward (1996) consider all social perceivers to be limited in their general processing capacity. It follows that social perceivers will seek to restrict the amount of cognitive work required for adequate functioning by using a number of heuristic strategies. The determination of what is attended to and what is neglected is directly influenced by cognitive schemas (which provide selection criteria in the form of goal-directed expectancies and confirmatory biases) and is related to underlying motivations for the behavior. In this view, all individuals are said to be unaware of the systematic distortions that result from their information processing and to process information in a personally biased, selective, and therefore, to some degree, inaccurate manner (Hollon & Kriss, 1984).

According to Johnston and Ward (1996), it is not that sexual offenders are deliberately restrictive in the cognitive resources they use, but rather that their social cognitive functioning is actually deficient or dysfunctional in one or more of the cognitive components. This conceptualization suggests that research should address differences between sexual offenders and other social perceivers in specific aspects of their cognitive functioning (i.e., structures, propositions, operations, and products) rather than merely attempting to distinguish sexual offenders by their expressed attitudes or beliefs (i.e., only in terms of their cognitive products). A comprehensive review that integrates the existing literature on sexual offenders' cognitions within the social cognition framework has already been provided by Ward et al. (1997) and therefore is not repeated here. However, the temporal dimension of the model is integral to a meaningful conceptualization of the dynamic and interrelated nature of sexual offenders' distortions and resulting offenses, and we therefore consider it further.

Ward and his colleagues have identified distinct cognitive distortions at particular stages in the offense chain (Ward, Fon, Hudson, & McCormack, 1998; Ward, Louden, Hudson, & Marshall, 1995) and have argued that the nature of these cognitions is intimately linked to their function at each particular stage. It is worth noting that within this staged approach, the various components of relapse prevention theory can be identified (Laws, 1995; Ward, Hudson, & Keenan, 1998). Throughout the rest of this chapter, we treat the terms *offending* and *relapse* synonymously (Hudson & Ward, 1996).

Preoffense cognitive distortions consist of highly developed belief systems, stereotypes, and attitudes (i.e., schemas) and resulting decision processes. Sexual offenders' beliefs and attitudes undermine the autonomy of victims and objectify them, as well as validating the offenders' sexually aggressive behavior (e.g., Abel, Becker, & Cunningham-Rathner, 1984; Darke, 1990; Scully & Marolla, 1984). Researchers have found that adversarial sexual beliefs, male-dominant ideology, acceptance of interpersonal violence, and endorsement of rape myths are related to negative attitudes toward women (Burt, 1983), rape tolerance (Malamuth, 1981), self-reported history of sexually aggressive behavior (Malamuth, 1986), and self-reported likelihood of being sexually aggressive (Check & Malamuth, 1983). It has been suggested that these distortions may be instrumental in disinhibiting sexually aggressive behavior (Malamuth & Brown, 1994), and Segal and Stermac (1990) proposed that such distortions may moderate sexual arousal. However, attempts to differentiate rapists' attitudes toward women from those of comparison groups of non-offending males have been inconclusive (Feild, 1978; Segal & Stermac, 1984), and it has been suggested that the potential to rape varies from situation to situation rather than reflecting a traitlike characteristic (Schewe & O'Donohue, 1998). Perhaps distorted beliefs and negative attitudes toward females might best be construed as lying on a continuum on which all males are located rather than as a distinctive characteristic of rapists.

Research into the nature and content of child molesters' beliefs about children and about sexual involvement with children has been more conclusive. In particular, child molesters have been shown to construe children as sexually attractive, willing, and motivated (Hanson et al., 1994) and as submissive and nonthreatening when compared to adults (Howells, 1978). Stermac and Segal (1989) reported that child molesters were more likely to consider children responsible for the assaults and to construe sexual abuse as beneficial to the victim. What is not clear from the existing literature is whether these less equivocal findings on identifiable attitudes with child molesters reflect a difference in the role that beliefs about others play in the etiology of sexual offending against children compared with sexual assault on adult females. Although many of the studies on attitudes toward others do not clearly differentiate convicted sexual offenders from comparison groups (Segal & Stermac, 1990; Stermac, Segal, & Gillis, 1990), the evidence suggests there is a close association between an individual's propensity for sexual aggression and his or her distorted conceptions of others (Malamuth, Sockloskie, Koss, & Tanaka, 1991).

As we have noted, these preoffense cognitive distortions, along with the expectancies they engender, directly influence the processing of external cues. In the presence of stimuli that activate schemas with sexually assaultive components, such distortions threaten the offender's personal control and compound the affective and situational elements that constitute a high-risk situation for the offender (Marques & Nelson, 1989). Importantly, when deviant situational or interpersonal scripts are so entrenched and rehearsed that they distort appraisals of the unfolding situation, the likelihood of apparently irrelevant decisions increases (Jenkins-Hall & Marlatt, 1989). These covert processes, involving rationalization and projection, constitute a series of distortions that, without his awareness, facilitate the offender's progression through a sequence of lapses toward offending while precluding negative self-appraisal. Furthermore, a sense of deprivation or unmanageable stress may promote a general desire for self-gratification and initiate an apparently irrelevant decision sequence.

Indeed, emotions exert a pervasive influence on motivation and appraisal both at this preoffense stage and throughout the unfolding offense chain (Ward et al., 1997). Emotions contribute to dynamic cognitive and behavioral adaptations as components in an ongoing process of self-regulation (Ward, Hudson, & Keenan, 1998). Therefore, both trait measures of affective dispositions and the identification of affective states during the offense are important in understanding sexual offenders' cognitions. In situations precipitating strong affective states (either positive or negative), such as those that characterize stages in a sexual offense cycle, the increasing demands on cognitive resources lead to the adoption of heuristic strategies. As we have already noted, these mental short-cuts result in cognitive distortions that facilitate offending behavior.

Positive emotional states, particularly those induced by the short-term immediate satisfaction derived from sexually deviant behavior (e.g., lapses, such as using pornography, or full relapse), confirm the expectancies and appraisals derived from existing schemas and tend to entrench the dispositions to activate these rather than other nonassaultive schemas in similar future circumstances. The problem of immediate gratification (Marlatt, 1989) has been shown to characterize lapses for child molesters (Ward et al., 1994) and may be particularly evident in the case of rapists, who often demonstrate cognitive distortions reflecting their sense of entitlement and superoptimism (Hall, 1989). Sexual offenders who hold core beliefs within their schemas that legitimate their deviant sexual behavior will be unlikely to construe their assaults negatively or experience aversive emotions at any stage in the offense cycle (Ward & Hudson, 1996). Ward, Hudson, and Keenan (1998) consider this pathway to sexual offending to result from intact self-regulation that is oriented toward the unacceptable goal of sexually deviant behavior.

Negative affective states may also feature in the various stages of an offense chain. Segal and Stermac (1990) identify three contextual stressors that, particularly in interaction with each other, are thought to contribute to offending behavior: intrapersonal stress, interpersonal stress, and the social environment. The experience of shame, guilt, and other self-conscious emotions may result from intrapersonal stress, whereas frustration and anger are possible outcomes of interpersonal stress in social contexts that are characterized by conflict or isolation.

Pithers (1990; MacDonald & Pithers, 1989) argues that negative affective states constitute a primary pathway to relapse, and it seems likely that the cognitive distortions that result from emotional stress facilitate the progression. Consistent with these observations of a connection between aversive emotional states and offending, Proulx, McKibben, and Lusignan (1996) have found that sexual offenders experience loneliness, humiliation, and anger following interpersonal conflict. Furthermore, the presence of conflicts and negative moods precipitates deviant sexual fantasizing in child molesters and both deviant sexual fantasizing and increased masturbatory activity in rapists (McKibben, Proulx, & Lusignan, 1994).

The abstinence violation effect (AVE) is directly relevant here. Russell, Sturgeon, Miner, and Nelson (1989) refer to the AVE as a particular pattern of reactions to a lapse (i.e., the occurrence of a voluntarily induced risk behavior such as deviant fantasizing) that leads to full-blown relapse. The AVE mediates progression from lapses and high-risk situations to relapse through an attribution process, in which the offender construes a lapse as an indication of stable, internal factors that are beyond his control. This attribution exerts its effect by strengthening the offender's negative self-schema, confirming the beliefs he has about his abilities (i.e., his low sense of self-efficacy), and focusing his attention on his failings. Within their self-regulatory model, Ward, Hudson, and Keenan (1998) consider this negative affect pathway to sexual offending to result from the offender's underregulation of his emotions and behaviors.

Cognitive distortions arising *during the offense* result from the offender's selective and biased processing of social information (i.e., operations). The sum effect of these biases is the facilitation of the offense by minimizing awareness of inhibiting features such as distress and physical resistance from the victim. The sexual offender actively seeks information from the social interaction that is consistent with his preexisting beliefs. By selectively exposing himself only to certain features of the situation, he can maintain his distorted conceptions without experiencing cognitive dissonance. There is empirical support for the idea that rapists fail to accurately interpret women's negative responses (Lipton, McDonel, & McFall, 1987), that they misinterpret friendliness as seduction (Murphy, Coleman, & Haynes, 1986), and that they discount the veracity of a female's communications (Malamuth & Brown, 1994). As we have already noted, child molesters tend to perceive children as sexually attractive and sexually motivated (Hanson et al., 1994).

It is not clear from the literature, however, whether only certain subtypes of sexual offenders misperceive social and emotional cues (Hudson et al., 1993; Langton & Marshall, in press) or whether such distortions characterize their perceptions only while they are perpetrating an assault (cf. Ward, Hudson, & Marshall, 1995). It seems likely, given the heterogeneity of sexual offenders (Knight & Prentky, 1990), that differences in perceptual abilities will characterize different offenders and that these differences will generate distinctive cognitive distortions. As we have noted, certain environmental contexts are also expected to be influential in shaping these distortions. For example, the problem of immediate gratification is again very likely to distort cognitive appraisals during the offense.

The *postoffense* stage is characterized by the types of cognitive distortions that Murphy (1990) describes as "self-statements made by offenders that allow them to deny, minimize, justify, and rationalize their behavior" (p. 332). As post hoc appraisals, these cognitive distortions serve to minimize the aversive emotional reactions and self-depreciation that the relapse engenders in the offender. Indeed, Ward, Hudson, and Siegert (1995) have suggested that for many sexual offenders, the AVE is actually more likely to occur at the point of relapse than at lapses earlier in the offense chain. Data reported by Ward et al. (1994) support this, and these researchers suggest that the AVE may actually facilitate an *intensification* of relapse behavior (i.e., frequency, severity). Denial, minimizations, and justifications result and serve to maintain the offending behavior. These postoffense cognitive distortions are evident in treatment (Barbaree, 1991; Winn, 1996). Denial of the act or some aspects of it represents an initial reaction in which the offender may seek to avoid a negative appraisal of his self-image. Denial of harm is an attempt to reduce feelings of guilt or shame (Bumby, Marshall, & Langton, 1999) by minimizing the perceived negative consequences for the victim. An offender's selective recall of elements of the offense, such as passivity or compliance on the part of the victim, serves to maintain his perception of the offense as an acceptable interaction. Justifications, drawn from the offender's schema, often use moral or psychological excuses to avoid responsibility and project blame (Murphy, 1990).

As a last thought, it is worth noting here that although cognitive distortions presented in treatment clearly serve as rationalizations and justifications for deviant sexual behavior, research has yet to determine whether such self-statements represent only post hoc formulations or actually constitute etiological factors in the sexually assaultive behavior (Bumby, 1996).

Before we consider intervention strategies to counter these various types of cognitive distortions, we review some of the recent attempts to assess them.

The Assessment of Cognitive Distortions

Much of the initial research on the cognitions of sexual offenders focused on their deviant attitudes and beliefs (e.g., Abel et al., 1984). Accordingly, efforts were made to devise paper-and-pencil measures that would assess the nature and degree of these distorted thoughts. Early measures include the Abel and Becker Cognition Scale (Abel et al., 1989) for use with child molesters; the Burt Rape Myth Scale (Burt, 1980), which is a measure of aggressive attitudes toward women and rape-supportive beliefs; and the Multiphasic Sex Inventory (Nichols & Molinder, 1984), consisting of a number of scales, the most relevant of which concern justifications and attributions. Although the psychometric properties of these measures appear adequate, they suffer from a number of limitations (Murphy, 1990). In particular, researchers have found that the items on these tests are subject to a social desirability response bias (Langevin, 1991). In addition, certain items lack face validity, and others are not limited to cognitive distortions related to sexual assault (Bumby, 1996). In general, the transparency and lack of discriminative utility of these measures limit their value both as assessment tools and as indicators of treatment progress.

Recent efforts have produced measures that attempt to address these limitations and to more directly investigate the cognitions of specific sexually assaultive populations. The Hanson Sex Attitude Questionnaire (Hanson et al., 1994) was developed to assess the deviant attitudes of incest offenders across a number of domains. Of the six scales in this measure, three demonstrated satisfactory psychometric properties and effectively distinguished incest offenders from comparison males: sexual entitlement, children as sexual agents, and appreciation of sexual harm. Although the sexual harm scale was significantly correlated with an index of social desirability, the two other scales appeared free of this response bias. However, the scales were validated with subjects who were promised anonymity, and their utility with offenders motivated to respond defensively remains to be determined.

Bumby (1996) developed a similar questionnaire. He generated a set of items thought to represent the cognitive distortions specific to child molesters (the MOLEST Scale) and rapists (the RAPE Scale). These scales included items from earlier measures that were modified in an attempt to reduce transparency. Bumby's data demonstrated strong internal consistency and reliability for both scales, with responses being unaffected by social desirability. Although the convergent and divergent validity of the MOLEST Scale was high, scores on the RAPE Scale did not correlate significantly with scores on Burt's (1980) Rape Myth Scale. The latter observation may not, however, constitute a threat to the RAPE Scale because Burt's measure includes items not directly concerned with sexually assaultive behavior. Most important, scores on the scales significantly differentiated sexual offenders from nonsexual offenders. However, our clinical experience with Bumby's measures suggests that they remain limited by the fact that the prosocial answers are obvious. Consequently, we have not found them to pick up the distortions offenders subsequently display in treatment.

McGrath and her colleagues also have attempted to develop tools that assess the distorted cognitions of sexual offenders. In a recent study, McGrath, Cann, and Konopasky (1998) reported on the use of tests addressing cognitive distortions, empathy, and defensiveness. The Child Molester Scale attempted to remove the transparency of other measures of cognitive distortions by incorporating justification in the items. The Empathy Test measures the respondent's capacity for general empathy and for empathy toward victims of sexual abuse. The Sexual Social Desirability Scale assesses acquiescence and denial, specifically in relation to sexuality, rather than more the general issues presented in most measures of social desirability. The psychometric properties of these measures appear satisfactory, and McGrath et al.'s research suggests that these tests reliably discriminate child molesters from comparison groups. However, the data on the cognitive distortions measure revealed a significant difference between the responses of child molesters promised anonymity and those facing parole assessments, suggesting that the scale is not entirely immune to a response bias.

A promising alternative approach involves the use of vignettes. In an early study, Stermac and Segal (1989) constructed 12 vignettes of sexual contact between adults and children. They found that child molesters' evaluations of the benefits to the child, as well as their view of the child's complicity and responsibility, were less affected than were the evaluations of a nonoffender group by the amount of sexual contact described. The child molesters' evaluations were only modified when the child's response was clearly negative and unambiguous. Hanson and Scott (1995) also used vignettes. Their written descriptions depicted interactions between a male and a female (Empathy for Women Test) for rapists and between an adult and a child for child molesters (Child Empathy Test). These interactions ranged from clearly sexually abusive to clearly nonsexual, nonabusive actions. Although the discriminative validity of the Child Empathy Test was poor, incest offenders made significantly more errors on the incest items than did other groups. The Empathy for Women Test afforded somewhat greater discriminative power, with rapists making significantly more errors across all items than nonoffender groups but not more than nonsexual offenders or child molesters. It is perhaps somewhat inaccurate to call these two tests measures of empathy when they might more reasonably be seen as examining perceptual accuracy. As we noted earlier, misperceptions about the lack of harm to victims might be better construed as a cognitive distortion rather than as a failure of empathy.

In general, the results of the measures discussed so far are somewhat disappointing, and it remains to be seen if any self-report measure can overcome the problem of response bias and accurately identify the cognitive distortions of sexual offenders.

A contrasting approach is provided by studies that address the perceptual accuracy of sexual offenders (see McDoncl, 1995). Although this work has not been generally recognized as investigating cognitive distortions, the failure to accurately perceive and interpret verbal and nonverbal cues, as we have already argued, can be usefully examined within the concept of cognitive distortions. Abbey and her colleagues (e.g., Harnish, Abbey, & DeBono, 1990) have repeatedly demonstrated that nonoffending males perceive interactions with females in predominantly sexual terms and impute sexual interest to females regardless of whether it is intended. The videotapes used in the Lipton et al. (1987) study with convicted rapists and Malamuth and Brown's (1994) research on self-reported sexual aggression in community males have been shown to demonstrate good discriminative validity. One advantage afforded by these procedures is that by requiring "best guesses" across a range of interactions, rather than self-disclosure of beliefs, these measures diminish the influence of a socially desirable response set. However, these measures are not currently used in assessments, and the processing aspects of cognition identified by these measures receive little or no attention in treatment. Nevertheless, the approach represents a promising source of new measures and warrants further research, particularly considering the absence of any similar assessment tools for use with child molesters.

Despite the limitations that characterize our presently available measures of cognitive distortions, Bumby (1996) notes that "it remains common practice to view these beliefs as genuine indicators of treatment motivation and progress,

degree of empathy and remorse, level of accountability, rehabilitation potential, and likelihood of recidivism" (p. 40). Clearly, there remains a need to
develop more powerful tools to assess cognitive distortions while controlling
for social desirability.

Notwithstanding this appropriate emphasis on reliable assessment tools, it is
worth noting that during interviews and particularly during treatment, offenders typically reveal many types of distortion, ranging from deviant core beliefs
to biased perceptions and attributions relating to the index offense. It is evident
that sexual offenders are capable of responding to tests in socially normative
ways that are often contradicted by what they say during interviews or treatment. Many offenders draw a distinction between what is generally unacceptable and what occurred in their own offense. To the extent that distortions are
specific to the offenders' own sexual assaults, general measures will be insensi-
tive and therefore of limited value. Specific distortions displayed at interviews
or during the course of treatment provide clinicians with their primary source of
knowledge about the attitudes sexual offenders hold regarding their victims and
their own behavior.

Having reflected somewhat negatively on the value of these measures as
general assessment tools, can they be said to be of any value as measures of
treatment change? Bumby (1996) reported a significant reduction in cognitive
distortions measured by his scales over the first 6 months of treatment and
concluded that both scales have utility in assessing treatment progress. However, the reductions in total scores might have resulted from the offenders simply learning the appropriate responses rather than by any real change in their
beliefs.

The results reported by McGrath and her colleagues (McGrath et al., 1998;
McGrath & Konopasky, 1997) suggest that their measures were useful indicators of treatment-induced reductions in cognitive distortions. However, the limited number of subjects in these analyses, all of whom were child molesters,
warrants caution, and, again, it may be that their clients simply learned what to
say. However, the reported reduction in social desirability responding at
posttreatment somewhat allays this concern. Furthermore, the possibility that
treatment simply trains clients how to respond to questionnaires is perhaps not
as fatal a flaw as might be thought. Certainly, a first step in attitude changes is to
learn what is appropriate. It usually takes repeated feedback triggered by inappropriate remarks (as typically happens in treatment) and subsequent repeated
expressions of appropriate thoughts to entrench attitude change at a deeper
level than is suggested by the previous criticism. In any event, there is no obvious way to discern the depth of cognitive change other than by what clients say
or report on questionnaires.

An alternative method has been used to assess treatment impact on denial.
Marshall (1994) reported significant therapy-induced reductions in denial and
minimization, as estimated by clinicians' ratings based on observing clients

throughout treatment. These ratings were demonstrated to be reliable by an independent judge who similarly observed the clients in treatment. The advantage of this procedure for estimating change is that it reduces the problem of offenders attempting to present in a socially desirable way because the evaluations are based on an extended period of observation. Unfortunately, ratings can readily be influenced by the therapist's natural desire to see his or her efforts as valuable. However, to the extent that existing empirical measures are limited, the inclusion of clinical ratings may be helpful.

Modifying Cognitive Distortions

A prefatory remark here seems necessary. Do cognitive distortions, whatever their form, reflect processes beyond the offender's awareness (as might be the case with deeply held attitudes or beliefs), or are they initiated voluntarily to justify past and future offending? Presumably, categorical denial of an actual assault is simply a lie, but is that true of misperceptions, minimizations, and justifications? Most therapists appear to believe that offenders are at some level aware of their distorting processes, but this might not always be true. It would seem to be a straightforward task to modify cognitions that the person realizes are false, but it may be a good deal harder to change firmly entrenched beliefs, and they may require an entirely different approach.

The application of relapse prevention (RP) approaches to treating sexual offenders has been quite varied. In some cases, RP has been considered the complete treatment package (Marques, Day, Nelson, & Miner, 1989), whereas in other instances of its application, RP serves a final integrating function aimed at maintaining, postdischarge, the benefits derived from a cognitive-behavioral program. In the former case, cognitive distortions are addressed throughout treatment as they arise or as they are prompted by the therapists. This approach lends itself to the process-oriented, open-ended group format (or "rolling" program) that we have adopted and that we advocate as the preferred treatment style (see Fernandez & Marshall, 2000 [this volume]). When RP serves as the final integrating feature of a cognitive-behavioral program, cognitive distortions are typically dealt with in a specific and distinct component of treatment. In either case, cognitive distortions are viewed as insidious threats to the future maintenance of the behavior changes induced by treatment. Not only must they be reduced, but cognitive distortions are also seen as one of the major risk factors whose early signs offenders must learn to identify and thereby abort the sequence of thoughts that initiates and maintains their offense chain and that culminates in the justification of offending.

Whichever way RP is construed, it is clear that the modification of cognitive distortions is seen as a crucial feature of treatment. Although changing cognitive distortions has been an important aspect of the treatment of sexual offenders for many years, even predating RP approaches, limited research has been devoted to describing and evaluating ways in which the distortions characteristic of this population can be altered. What follows is an overview of this limited literature.

Cognitive restructuring essentially involves the identification of dysfunctional thoughts, which are then challenged and alternatives offered (Meichenbaum, 1977). Analysis of the offense chain serves as a particularly useful framework for identifying and evaluating cognitive distortions in a collaborative fashion with the client (Hudson & Ward, 1996). With clients whose belief systems appear to be replete with underlying distortions, however, a more in-depth examination is afforded by working on an autobiography with the client (Long, Wuesthoff, & Pithers, 1989). Once identified, these thoughts are analyzed, their accuracy and utility are questioned, and the underlying logic is examined before more functionally useful thoughts are substituted for the inappropriate ones (Jenkins-Hall, 1989). With sexual offenders, Murphy (1990) emphasizes a Socratic approach, which can be seen as positive and motivational (Marshall, 1996), rather than the more confrontational rational emotive therapy of Ellis and his colleagues (Ellis & Grieger, 1977). Modifying distorted cognitions, then, involves techniques of supportive disputing and challenging engaged in by both the therapists and other group members. Within this general approach, three distinct but complementary methods to address cognitive distortions can be identified. The first is a direct intervention that discredits existing beliefs and attempts a wholesale replacement of the individual's belief system. The second involves providing evidence that is disconfirmatory of the client's beliefs, attitudes, and perceptions. The third is concerned with monitoring and altering the ways information is processed.

Jenkins-Hall (1989) describes a strategy that encourages offenders to develop objective counters to their dysfunctional thoughts. Specifically, offenders are required to evaluate these thoughts in terms of their "truthfulness." For example, if an offender declares that a child's hug was sexually motivated, the offender is required to review, along with the rest of the group, the evidence in support of this claim. He would then be challenged about the accuracy of his evidence and required to generate a more realistic appraisal. However, there is little evidence that this technique alone is sufficient. For change to result, it would seem necessary for the offender to actually internalize his appropriate response and change his deviant core belief that children seek adults to engage in sexual behavior. Without this change, the sexual offender may reoffend in a high-risk situation despite the more appropriate appraisal learned in treatment.

The underlying concern here is the finding that evidence that disconfirms strongly held beliefs is likely to be reinterpreted. Research on stereotyping with "normal" populations has suggested that in the face of disconfirming information, a core belief, or schema, may be differentiated rather than revised to include new subtypes that accommodate the disconfirming information (Johnston, 1996; Winfrey & Goldfried, 1986).

This discrediting method is an attempt to induce the client to make post hoc reinterpretations. Hollon and Garber (1988) express some pessimism about the utility of focusing on clients' beliefs regarding past experiences. The client has already formed and entrenched these beliefs by collecting what he perceives as confirmational evidence. What may happen in treatment is that the offender will learn what is required of him in terms of identifying and disputing cognitive distortions, but permanent change may not occur because the deep structures associated with these beliefs do not change. The discrediting approach, then, must be complemented by additional methods, such as those suggested by Hollon and Garber (1988). They develop multiple, concrete tests that the client must experience to disconfirm distorted thoughts. This is referred to as evidential disconfirmation. The reliance is on disconfirming experiences rather than on rational discussion of abstracted perceptions and beliefs.

In the treatment of sexual offenders, however, this "collaborative empiricism" between the therapist and the client presents something of a problem. Depressed patients can be assisted in testing the negative beliefs that maintain low self-esteem by conducting daily experiments to disprove their expectations. Unfortunately, in contrast, sexual offenders have already offended and demonstrate distorted attitudes and perceptions that too often cannot be readily tested in expectation-disproving experiments. One solution is the presentation of disconfirming material in the form of victim impact statements, video documentaries, and empathy-enhancing components. These represent appropriate and worthwhile attempts to change the offender's perspective and may serve to reduce cognitive distortions (Pithers, 1994). However, they do not enable disconfirmation of the offender's expectancies, and expectancy disconfirmation is said to be the mechanism for change (Hollon & Garber, 1988). Treatment providers have yet to develop optimal forms of evidential disconfirmation for use with sexual offenders.

Psychoeducational interventions, involving discussion of the way information is processed and the different meanings that others may attach to situations and events, represent a third potential method of addressing cognitive distortions. Empirical investigations into the efficacy of this type of approach have been limited mainly to nonoffending populations and use general persuasion rather than a collaborative analysis of information-processing biases (Gilbert, Heesacker, & Gannon, 1991). However, it is a recognized clinical intervention, and some evidence suggests that educational approaches that engage participants in experience-enhancing exercises may be effective in reducing cognitive distortions while enhancing empathy (Schewe & O'Donohue, 1993).

Johnston and Ward (1996) suggest introducing strategies to prevent normative heuristics and processing errors from facilitating distorted thinking. The aim is to teach the client to engage in more conscious, controlled processing. Such thinking is not immune to processing errors or biases but, relative to impulsive, automatic processing, the client is better able to identify distortions and counter them. Clearly, it requires motivated effort on the part of the client to use these strategies effectively. The psychoeducational approach is represented by treatment programs that place an emphasis on the self-monitoring and prevention of deviant thoughts and behaviors in the form of relapse prevention strategies. As Nelson and Jackson (1989) observe, "The construction of cognitive-behavioral offense chains is designed to actively engage and teach the offender to become an increasingly astute and responsible observer of his own past and present behavior" (p. 176). These strategies are used to enhance self-awareness, induce critical thinking, and develop coping strategies for high-risk situations (Steenman, Nelson, & Viesti, 1989).

MacDonald and Pithers (1989) outline procedures for teaching clients how to monitor their negative affective states, the content of fantasies, and offense planning. Such self-monitoring is clearly important if a client is to recognize the cognitive distortions that underlie apparently irrelevant decisions, the problem of immediate gratification, and the abstinence violation effect (Ward, Hudson, & Keenan, 1998). Recent work has examined the potential utility of thought suppression techniques (Johnston, Ward, & Hudson, 1998). However, a preliminary investigation of these techniques suggests that, paradoxically, suppression of sexual thoughts (many of which are typically deviant) may result in their greater accessibility (Johnston, Hudson, & Ward, 1997). This seems particularly likely in the high-risk situations during which the thought suppression techniques would be most crucial. In the presence of certain cues and a desire for immediate gratification, the client's ability to monitor and critically evaluate his cognitions might be seriously undermined. Furthermore, the technique appears to be contraindicated for certain types of sexual offenders (e.g., preferential child molesters). Although promising, then, the development of thought suppression strategies that will generalize from treatment and work in vivo requires additional research.

More general approaches to cognitive distortions, particularly those self-statements presented during treatment, included metaconfrontation (i.e., challenging the offender to challenge himself, as opposed to simply providing direct external challenges) and gaining permission to confront (Winn, 1996). In addressing those cognitive distortions that include aspects of denial, Hoke, Sykes, and Winn (1989) advocate a systemic approach that uses paradoxical strategies.

Conclusion

Although the cognitive distortions of sexual offenders are clearly an important target for assessment and treatment, a theoretical framework, from which to derive assessment tools and specific treatment interventions and within which we could investigate cognitions in a systematic fashion, has been lacking (Langton & Marshall, in press). Given this state of affairs, it is perhaps not surprising that the literature on the identification and assessment of cognitive distortions in sexual offenders is both limited and has produced inconsistent results. Similarly, the approaches to treatment have been characterized by rather vague descriptions of procedures aimed at changing these dysfunctional cognitions. Not surprisingly, there is little in the way of empirical support for any particular technique. These serious deficits in the literature have prevented the development of understanding cognitive distortions as they are manifest by sexual offenders, and this has impeded the effectiveness of our attempts to modify these cognitions. No doubt, the lack of specificity that characterizes discussions of cognitive distortions in the literature has discouraged researchers from a more detailed analysis of the issue, but careful research is desperately needed if we are to progress beyond our present state of confusion.

References

Abel, G. G., Becker, J. V., & Cunningham-Rathner, J. C. (1984). Complications, consent, and cognitions in sex between children and adults. *International Journal of Law and Psychiatry, 7,* 89-103.

Abel, G. G., Gore, D. K., Holland, C. L., Camp, N., Becker, J. V., & Rathner, J. (1989). The measurement of the cognitive distortions of child molesters. *Annals of Sex Research, 2,* 135-152.

Abelson, R. P. (1981). Psychological status of the script concept. *American Psychologist, 36,* 715-729.

Araji, S., & Finkelhor, D. (1985). Explanations of pedophilia: A review of empirical research. *Bulletin of the American Academy of Psychiatry and the Law, 13,* 17-37.

Bandura, A. (1986). *Social foundations of thought and action: A social cognitive theory.* Englewood Cliffs, NJ: Prentice Hall.

Barbaree, H. E. (1991). Denial and minimization among sex offenders: Assessment and treatment outcomes. *Forum on Corrections Research, 3,* 30-33.

Bem, S. L. (1981). Gender schema theory: A cognitive account of sex typing. *Psychological Review, 88,* 354-364.

Bumby, K. M. (1996). Assessing the cognitive distortions of child molesters and rapists: Development and validation of the MOLEST and RAPE scales. *Sexual Abuse: A Journal of Research and Treatment, 8,* 37-54.

Bumby, K. M., Marshall, W. L. & Langton, C. M. (1999). A theoretical model of the influences of shame and guilt on sexual offending. In B. K. Schwartz (Ed.), *The sex offender: Theoretical advances, treating special populations and legal developments* (Vol. 3, pp. 5.1-5.12). Kingston, NJ: Civic Research Institute.

Burt, M. (1980). Cultural myths and supports for rape. *Journal of Personality and Social Psychology, 38,* 217-230.

Burt, M. R. (1983). Justifying personal violence: A comparison of rapists and the general public. *Victimology, 8,* 131-150.

Cantor, N., Mischel, W., & Schwartz, J. (1982). Social knowledge: Structure, content, use, and abuse. In A. H. Hastorf & A. M. Isen (Eds.), *Cognitive social psychology* (pp. 33-72). New York: Elsevier.

Check, J. V. P., & Malamuth, N. M. (1983). Sex role stereotyping and reactions to depictions of stranger versus acquaintance rape. *Journal of Personality and Social Psychology, 45,* 344-356.

Darke, J. L. (1990). Sexual aggression: Achieving power through humiliation. In W. L. Marshall, D. R. Laws, & H. E. Barbaree (Eds.), *Handbook of sexual assault: Issues, theories, and treatment of the offender* (pp. 55-72). New York: Plenum.

Ellis, A., & Grieger, R. (Eds.). (1977). *Handbook of rational emotive therapy.* New York: Springer.

Feild, H. (1978). Attitudes towards rape: A comparative analysis of police, rapists, crisis counselors, and citizens. *Journal of Personality and Social Psychology, 36,* 156-179.

Fernandez, Y. M., & Marshall, W. L. (2000). Contextual issues in relapse prevention treatment. In D. R. Laws, S. M. Hudson, & T. Ward (Eds.), *Remaking relapse prevention with sex offenders: A sourcebook* (pp. 225-235). Thousand Oaks, CA: Sage

Fernandez, Y. M., Marshall, W. L., Lightbody, S., & O'Sullivan, C. (1999). The Child Molester Empathy Measure. *Sexual Abuse: A Journal of Research and Treatment, 11,* 17-31.

Fiske, S. T., & Taylor, S. E. (1991). *Social cognition* (2nd ed.). New York: McGraw-Hill.

Gilbert, B. J., Heesacker, M., & Gannon, L. J. (1991). Changing the sexual aggression-supportive attitudes of men: A psychoeducational intervention. *Journal of Counseling Psychology, 38,* 197-203.

Hall, R. L. (1989). Relapse rehearsal. In D. R. Laws (Ed.), *Relapse prevention with sex offenders* (pp. 197-206). New York: Guilford.

Hanson, R. K., Gizzarelli, R., & Scott, H. (1994). The attitudes of incest offenders: Sexual entitlement and acceptance of sex with children. *Criminal Justice and Behavior, 21,* 187-202.

Hanson, R. K., & Scott, H. (1995). Assessing perspective-taking among sexual offenders, nonsexual criminals and nonoffenders. *Sexual Abuse: A Journal of Research and Treatment, 7,* 259-277.

Harnish, R. J., Abbey, A., & DeBono, K. G. (1990). Toward an understanding of "the sex game": The effects of gender and self-monitoring on perceptions of sexuality and likability in initial interactions. *Journal of Applied Social Psychology, 20,* 1333-1344.

Hastorf, A. H., & Isen, A. M. (Eds.). (1982). *Cognitive social psychology.* New York: Elsevier.

Hoke, S., Sykes, C., & Winn, M. (1989). Strategic/systemic interventions targeting denial in the incestuous family. *Journal of Strategic and Systemic Therapies, 8,* 44-51.

Hollon, S. D., & Garber, J. (1988). Cognitive therapy. In L. Y. Abramson (Ed.), *Social cognition and clinical psychology* (pp. 204-253). New York: Guilford.

Hollon, S. D., & Kriss, M. R. (1984). Cognitive factors in clinical research and practice. *Clinical Psychology Review, 4,* 35-76.

Howells, K. (1978). Some meanings of children for paedophiles. In M. Cook & G. Wilson (Eds.), *Love and attraction: An international conference* (pp. 519-526). Oxford, UK: Pergamon.

Hudson, S. M., Marshall, W. L., Wales, D., McDonald, E., Bakker, L., & McLean, A. (1993). Emotional recognition in sex offenders. *Annals of Sex Research, 6,* 199-211.

Hudson, S. M., & Ward, T. (1996). Relapse prevention: Future directions. *Sexual Abuse: A Journal of Research and Treatment, 8,* 249-256.

Ingram, R. E., & Kendall, P. C. (1986). Cognitive clinical psychology: Implications of an information processing perspective. In R. E. Ingram (Ed.), *Information processing approaches to clinical psychology* (pp. 3-21). New York: Academic Press.

Jenkins-Hall, K. D. (1989). Cognitive restructuring. In D. R. Laws (Ed.), *Relapse prevention with sex offenders* (pp. 207-215). New York: Guilford.

Jenkins-Hall, K. D., & Marlatt, G. A. (1989). Apparently irrelevant decisions in the relapse process. In D. R. Laws (Ed.), *Relapse prevention with sex offenders* (pp. 47-55). New York: Guilford.

Johnston, L. (1996). Resisting change: Information-seeking and stereotype change. *European Journal of Social Psychology, 26,* 799-826.

Johnston, L., Hudson, S. M., & Ward, T. (1997). The suppression of sexual thoughts by child molesters: A preliminary investigation. *Sexual Abuse: A Journal of Research and Treatment, 34,* 303-319.

Johnston, L., & Ward, T. (1996). Social cognition and sexual offending: A theoretical framework. *Sexual Abuse: A Journal of Research and Treatment, 8,* 55-80.

Johnston, L., Ward, T., & Hudson, S. M. (1998). Suppressing sex: Mental control and the treatment of sexual offenders. *Journal of Sex Research, 34,* 121-130.

Knight, R. A., & Prentky, R. A. (1990). Classifying sexual offenders: The development and corroboration of taxonomic models. In W. L. Marshall, D. R. Laws, & H. E. Barbaree (Eds.), *Handbook of sexual assault: Issues, theories, and treatment of the offender* (pp. 23-52). New York: Plenum.

Langevin, R. (1991). A note on the problem of response set in measuring cognitive distortions. *Annals of Sex Research, 4,* 287-292.

Langton, C. M., & Marshall, W. L. (in press). Cognition in rapists: Theoretical patterns by typological breakdown. *Aggression and Violent Behavior.*

Laws, D. R. (1995). Theory of relapse prevention. In W. O'Donohue & L. Krasner (Eds.), *Theories of behavior therapy: Exploring behavior change* (pp. 445-473). Washington, DC: American Psychological Association.

Lipton, D. N., McDonel, E. C., & McFall, R. M. (1987). Heterosocial perception in rapists. *Journal of Consulting and Clinical Psychology, 55,* 17-21.

Long, J. D., Wuesthoff, A., & Pithers, W. D. (1989). Use of autobiographies in the assessment and treatment of sex offenders. In D. R. Laws (Ed.), *Relapse prevention with sex offenders* (pp. 88-95). New York: Guilford.

MacDonald, R. K., & Pithers, W. D. (1989). Self-monitoring to identify high-risk situations. In D. R. Laws (Ed.), *Relapse prevention with sex offenders* (pp. 96-104). New York: Guilford.

Malamuth, N. M. (1981). Rape proclivity among males. *Journal of Social Issues, 37,* 138-157.

Malamuth, N. M. (1986). Predictors of naturalistic sexual aggression. *Journal of Personality and Social Psychology, 50,* 953-962.

Malamuth, N. M., & Brown, L. M. (1994). Sexually aggressive men's perceptions of women's communications: Testing three explanations. *Journal of Personality and Social Psychology, 67,* 699-712.

Malamuth, N. M., Sockloskie, R., Koss, M., & Tanaka, J. (1991). The characteristics of aggressors against women: Testing a model using a national sample of college students. *Journal of Consulting and Clinical Psychology, 59,* 670-681.

Marlatt, G. A. (1989). How to handle the PIG. In D. R. Laws (Ed.), *Relapse prevention with sex offenders* (pp. 227-235). New York: Guilford.

Marques, J. K., Day, D. M., Nelson, C., & Miner, M. H. (1989). The sex offender treatment and evaluation project: California's Relapse Prevention Program. In D. R. Laws (Ed.), *Relapse prevention with sex offenders* (pp. 247-267). New York: Guilford.

Marques, J. K., & Nelson, C. (1989). Elements of high-risk situations for sex offenders. In D. R. Laws (Ed.), *Relapse prevention with sex offenders* (pp. 35-46). New York: Guilford.

Marshall, W. L. (1994). Treatment effects on denial and minimization in incarcerated sex offenders. *Behaviour Research and Therapy, 32,* 559-564.

Marshall, W. L. (1996). The sexual offender: Monster, victim, or everyman? *Sexual Abuse: A Journal of Research and Treatment, 8,* 317-335.

McDonel, E. C. (1995). An information-processing theory of the measurement of social competence. In W. O'Donohue & L. Krasner (Eds.), *Theories of behavior therapy: Exploring behavior change* (pp. 415-443). Washington, DC: American Psychological Association.

McGrath, M., Cann, S., & Konopasky, R. (1998). New measures of defensiveness, empathy, and cognitive distortions for sexual offenders against children. *Sexual Abuse: A Journal of Research and Treatment, 10,* 25-36.

McGrath, M., & Konopasky, R. (1997, October). *Treatment to improve empathy, treatment to decrease cognitive distortions, and treatment to decrease response bias: It works, it works, it works.* Poster session presented at the annual conference of the Association for the Treatment of Sexual Abusers, Washington, DC.

McKibben, A., Proulx, J., & Lusignan, R. (1994). Relationship between conflict, affect and deviant sexual behaviors in rapists and pedophiles. *Behaviour Research and Therapy, 32,* 571-575.

Meichenbaum, D. M. (1977). *Cognitive-behavior modification: An integrative approach.* New York: Plenum.

Murphy, W. D. (1990). Assessment and modification of cognitive distortions in sex offenders. In W. L. Marshall, D. R. Laws, & H. E. Barbaree (Eds.), *Handbook of sexual assault: Issues, theories, and treatment of the offender* (pp. 331-342). New York: Plenum.

Murphy, W. D., Coleman, E. M., & Haynes, M. R. (1986). Factors related to coercive sexual behavior in a nonclinical sample of males. *Violence and Victims, 1,* 255-278.

Nasby, W., & Kihlstrom, J. F. (1986). Cognitive assessment of personality and psychopathology. In R. E. Ingram (Ed.), *Information processing approaches to clinical psychology* (pp. 217-239). New York: Academic Press.

Nelson, C., & Jackson, P. (1989). High-risk recognition: The cognitive-behavioral chain. In D. R. Laws (Ed.), *Relapse prevention with sex offenders* (pp. 167-177). New York: Guilford.

Nichols, H. R., & Molinder, I. (1984). *Multiphasic Sex Inventory manual: A test to assess psychosexual characteristics of the sexual offender.* Tacoma, WA: Nichols & Molinder.

Pithers, W. D. (1990). Relapse prevention with sexual aggressors: A method for maintaining therapeutic gain and enhancing external supervision. In W. L. Marshall, D. R. Laws, & H. E. Barbaree (Eds.), *Handbook of sexual assault: Issues, theories, and treatment of the offender* (pp. 343-361). New York: Plenum.

Pithers, W. D. (1994). Process evaluation of a group therapy component designed to enhance sex offenders' empathy for sexual abuse survivors. *Behaviour Research and Therapy, 32,* 565-570.

Proulx, J., McKibben, A., & Lusignan, R. (1996). Relationships between affective components and sexual behaviors in sexual aggressors. *Sexual Abuse: A Journal of Research and Treatment, 8,* 279-289.

Russell, K., Sturgeon, V. H., Miner, H., & Nelson, C. (1989). Determinants of the abstinence violation effect in sexual fantasies. In D. R. Laws (Ed.), *Relapse prevention with sex offenders* (pp. 63-72). New York: Guilford.

Schank, R. C., & Abelson, R. P. (1977). *Scripts, plans, goals and understanding.* Hillsdale, NJ: Lawrence Erlbaum.

Schewe, P. A., & O'Donohue, W. (1993). Sexual abuse prevention with high-risk males: The roles of victim empathy and rape myths. *Violence and Victims, 8,* 339-351.

Schewe, P. A., & O'Donohue, W. (1998). Psychometrics of the Rape Conformity Assessment and other measures: Implications for rape prevention. *Sexual Abuse: A Journal of Research and Treatment, 10,* 97-112.

Scully, D., & Marolla, J. (1984). Convicted rapists' vocabulary of motive: Excuses and justifications. *Social Problems, 31,* 530-544.

Segal, Z. V. (1988). Appraisal of the self-schema construct in cognitive models of depression. *Psychological Bulletin, 103,* 147-162.

Segal, Z. V., & Stermac, L. E. (1984). A measure of rapists' attitudes towards women. *International Journal of Law and Psychiatry, 7,* 437-440.

Segal, Z. V., & Stermac, L. E. (1990). The role of cognition in sexual assault. In W. L. Marshall, D. R. Laws, & H. E. Barbaree (Eds.), *Handbook of sexual assault: Issues, theories and treatment of the offender* (pp. 161-172). New York: Plenum.

Sherman, S. J., Judd, C. M., & Park, B. (1989). Social cognition. *Annual Review of Psychology, 40,* 281-326.

Steenman, H., Nelson, C., & Viesti, C. (1989). Developing coping strategies for high-risk situations. In D. R. Laws (Ed.), *Relapse prevention with sex offenders* (pp. 178-187). New York: Guilford.

Stermac, L. E., & Segal, Z. V. (1989). Adult sexual contact with children: An examination of cognitive factors. *Behavior Therapy, 20,* 573-584.

Stermac, L. E., Segal, Z., & Gillis, R. (1990). Social and cultural factors in sexual assault. In W. L. Marshall, D. R. Laws, & H. E. Barbaree (Eds.), *Handbook of sexual assault: Issues, theories and treatment of the offender* (pp. 143-159) New York: Plenum.

Thorndyke, P. W., & Hayes-Roth, B. (1979). The use of schemata in the acquisition and transfer of knowledge. *Cognitive Psychology, 11,* 82-106.

Turk, D. C., & Salovey, P. (1985). Cognitive structures, cognitive processes, and cognitive-behavior modification: I. Client issues. *Cognitive Therapy and Research, 9,* 1-17.

Tversky, A., & Kahneman, D. (1974). Causal schemata in judgements under uncertainty. In M. Fishbein (Ed.), *Progress in social psychology* (Vol. 1, pp. 49-72). Hillsdale, NJ: Lawrence Erlbaum.

Ward, T., Fon, C., Hudson, S. M., & McCormack, J. (1998). A descriptive model of dysfunctional cognitions in child molesters. *Journal of Interpersonal Violence, 13,* 129-155.

Ward, T., & Hudson, S. M. (1996). Relapse prevention: A critical analysis. *Sexual Abuse: A Journal of Research and Treatment, 8,* 177-200.

Ward, T., Hudson, S. M., Johnston, L., & Marshall, W. L. (1997). Cognitive distortions in sex offenders: An integrative review. *Clinical Psychology Review, 17,* 479-507.

Ward, T., Hudson, S. M., & Keenan, T. (1998). A self-regulation model of the sexual offense process. *Sexual Abuse: A Journal of Research and Treatment, 10,* 141-157.

Ward, T., Hudson, S. M., & Marshall, W. L. (1994). The abstinence violation effect in child molesters. *Behaviour Research and Therapy, 32,* 431-437.

Ward, T., Hudson, S. M., & Marshall, W. L. (1995). Cognitive distortions and affective deficits in sex offenders: A cognitive deconstructionist interpretation. *Sexual Abuse: A Journal of Research and Treatment, 7,* 67-83.

Ward, T., Hudson, S. M., & Siegert, R. J. (1995). A critical comment on Pithers' relapse prevention model. *Sexual Abuse: A Journal of Research and Treatment, 7,* 167-175.

Ward, T., Louden, K., Hudson, S. M., & Marshall, W. L. (1995). A descriptive model of the offense chain for child molesters. *Journal of Interpersonal Violence, 10,* 452-472.

Winfrey, L. P. L., & Goldfried, M. R. (1986). Information processing and the human change process. In R. E. Ingram (Ed.), *Information processing approaches to clinical psychology* (pp. 241-258). New York: Academic Press.

Winn, M. E. (1996). The strategic and systematic management of denial in the cognitive-behavioral treatment of sexual offenders. *Sexual Abuse: A Journal of Research and Treatment, 8,* 25-36.

CHAPTER 10

Managing Resistance and Rebellion in Relapse Prevention Intervention

RUTH E. MANN
H. M. Prison Service, London

Auniversal problem for sex offender treatment clinicians is that many sex offenders do not fully engage in the treatment process. For example, most sex offenders do not enter voluntarily into treatment but are required to do so by the courts. In these cases, it cannot be assumed that their goals match those of the treatment providers. Even sex offenders who do enter treatment voluntarily and who profess agreement with the goal of stopping offending may have hidden agendas that impair their full participation in treatment.

In this chapter, I am first concerned with the ways in which relapse prevention interventions can fail to engage sex offenders. Second, I aim to give clinicians strategies for overcoming client resistance to relapse prevention work. The underlying principle is that resistance to treatment is a product of the interaction between the client, the therapist, and the treatment goals. If treatment and its goals can be made appealing and the therapist can adopt a treatment style that facilitates change, then client resistance can be significantly minimized.

The first step in making better connections with treatment clients is to examine the aims and methods of relapse prevention from a client's point of view. What issues may block a client from full participation in relapse prevention work?

The Conditions of Relapse Prevention and Why They Are Resisted

Relapse prevention refers to a treatment intervention that aims to equip clients who have addictive behavior problems with the skills and knowledge they need to avoid relapsing (Marlatt, 1985). During relapse prevention intervention, the client learns about the process of relapse and plans for his own likely experiences of lapses, abstinence violation effect, problems of immediate gratification, and so on.

Relapse prevention is linked to the transtheoretical model of change (Prochaska & DiClemente, 1982). This model proposes that behavior change involves movement through different stages. Clients who have not begun to consider the need for change are at the stage of *precontemplation*. Once the problem is acknowledged, the client moves through a stage of *contemplation* to the point where he makes a decision to change. After that decision is acted on, the client must maintain his behavior change for the rest of his life in what is known as the *maintenance* stage. Relapse prevention intervention is intended to give a client the skills and knowledge he needs to manage the maintenance stage of change and is focused specifically on that stage. It is important to note that it is not intended to help clients acknowledge their problems or make decisions about changing.

Three conditions must therefore be in place for relapse prevention to be an effective intervention:

1. The client must have as his goal the wish to avoid relapsing. He must have moved properly through the previous stages of change; that is, he must have properly contemplated his problem behavior and must have made the decision that he wishes to stop the behavior.

2. The client must accept the model of relapse on which relapse prevention is based. He must therefore accept that lapses are inevitable. He must believe that he is likely to experience high-risk feelings and thoughts again and that he will continue to experience urges for gratification through sexual offending.

3. The client must accept relapse prevention methods. He must believe that the best way to manage high-risk thoughts and feelings is through self-monitoring, cognitive control, and enactment of preplanned behavioral strategies. He must be committed to avoiding high-risk situations for the rest of his life and to escaping from them or otherwise managing them if he cannot avoid them.

If any of the above conditions are not met, then relapse prevention is probably not going to be an effective intervention for that client to undertake at that time. Unfortunately, however, these conditions are strict. It is quite likely that many sex offenders will not meet all three conditions, as the following case examples show.

Clients Who Do Not Have a Goal of
Wishing to Avoid Relapse

George is a sex offender convicted for sexual attacks on adult female strangers. During his imprisonment, George spent time in a therapeutic community, a cognitive-behavioral treatment program, and a prerelease relapse prevention program. In all of these treatment environments, he was apparently cooperative and keen to overcome his urges to commit further sexual offenses. However, after release from prison, George reoffended with little delay. In a letter to one of his prison therapists, he explained that mostly he had participated genuinely in treatment, but throughout all his time in treatment, he had secretly continued to indulge in immensely gratifying sexual fantasies about attacking women. He had hidden this information from his therapists because he did not want to give up the fantasies. George's performance in treatment was not necessarily a sham. In fact, he may have had two conflicting goals: to avoid reoffending but also to act out a fantasy. When he was forced to choose between the goals, he chose to pursue the one that offered the strongest gratification. None of his therapists had been aware of this conflict, so they had failed to help him resolve it before it was put to the test.

Clients Who Do Not Accept the Model on Which
Relapse Prevention Is Based

Matthew was also incarcerated for a violent sexual attack on an adult female. He too had spent time in a therapeutic community before entering H. M. Prison Service's cognitive-behavioral Sex Offender Treatment Program (SOTP) (Mann & Thornton, 1998). In SOTP, Matthew worked hard to overcome excuses, denial, and minimization surrounding his offending, and he also made good progress in developing victim empathy. However, he forcefully resisted the relapse prevention model. He was sure that his time in a therapeutic community had "turned him into a different person." He could not imagine any circumstances under which he was likely to have similar thoughts and feelings to those that preceded his offense. He consequently did not believe that any situation would be high risk for him.

Clients Who Do Not Accept Relapse
Prevention Methods

Lenny was incarcerated for committing a rape during a burglary. He attended SOTP with some initial "hiccups" (e.g., threatening to leave the group when put under pressure by their questions) but eventually making good progress toward most treatment goals. He did not deny the likelihood that he would experience high-risk situations, thoughts, and feelings in the future; in fact, he generated a veritable directory of them. However, he was put off by the idea of constant self-vigilance and cognitive control. He preferred to "see what happens, and hope I do the right thing when the crunch comes." Although he completed a relapse prevention plan in the group, his heart was not in it, and the plan was vague, repetitive, and failed to take sufficient account of the problem of immediate gratification.

How Clients Resist

Clients such as George, Matthew, and Lenny are not unusual. Indeed, a survey of experienced treatment providers (Mann, 1997) showed that about 50% of sex offender clients demonstrate some form of resistance to the conditions of the relapse prevention model. The problem of resistance, therefore, is a significant clinical issue neglected at our peril and not contemplated in the typical relapse prevention program for sex offenders.

DiClemente (1991) suggested a typology of resistance that I have adapted for the sex offender client group (Mann, 1997). This typology, which he describes as the "Four Rs" system, contains four types and is described in Table 10.1.

Note that the category labels (e.g., rebellious) refer to the style with which the resistance is demonstrated rather than the reason for the resistance. The style with which resistance is demonstrated may be related to the client's personality rather than his underlying reasons for resisting relapse prevention.

Understanding Resistance to
Relapse Prevention: Summary

It has been asserted that the conditions of the traditional relapse prevention intervention are such that many sex offender clients might not meet them. They may not share the goal of wishing to avoid relapsing, or they may not buy the assumptions of the model that lapses are inevitable and that self-management is the only way to control them. Clients who do not meet the conditions of relapse prevention may show this through active resistance in treatment such as rebelliously refusing to complete treatment tasks. Alternatively, clients may passively resist relapse prevention by apparently completing work but doing so without energy or investment. It seems that such active or passive resistance may be present in up to half of sex offenders undergoing a relapse prevention intervention.

In the remainder of this chapter, I present strategies for reducing resistance and for making relapse prevention a more attractive treatment intervention to sex offenders without compromising on its essential message. Two types of

TABLE 10.1   Typology of Resistance: The Four Rs

Type of Resistance	Reason for the Resistance	How the Resistance Is Shown
1. Reluctant	Client is at the precontemplation stage of change. He is not fully committed to change.	May fail to complete treatment tasks or only do so after persuasion. Tasks may be sketchily completed. Lack of energy and investment in relapse prevention work.
2. Rebellious	Client has a heavy investment in the problem behavior and does not want to stop, or client hates being told what to do and is therefore resisting the process rather than the content of treatment.	Fails to complete relapse prevention tasks. Responds to attempts to persuade with argument and forceful resistance. Probably this client resists all treatment tasks, not just relapse prevention work.
3. Resigned	Client lacks confidence in his ability to change. He feels that it is too late for him to change.	Lack of energy and investment in completing relapse prevention work.
4. Rationalizing	May be any of the above reasons.	Provides reasons galore why a certain task is not relevant, necessary, or useful. Uses cognition rather than emotion to block therapeutic work.

treatment strategy are proposed. The first is for treatment providers to redesign their relapse prevention goals and methods so that relapse prevention becomes a more attractive and flexible intervention. The second is for treatment providers to recognize resistance in individual clients and adapt their treatment style accordingly.

Redesigning Relapse Prevention to Reduce Client Resistance

It was hypothesized earlier that the aims and methods of relapse prevention produce resistance rather than resistance being part of the client's pathology. It is not my intention to argue that the aims of relapse prevention are incorrect. Clearly, sex offender treatment should aim to reduce the incidence of sexual offending. However, to minimize client resistance, it is important to present treatment aims and treatment tasks in a way that appears attractive to the client.

To do this, an understanding of the ways people set and define their goals is necessary. Ward and Hudson (2000 [this volume]) have drawn our attention to the importance of understanding our clients' offense-related goals. Understanding our clients' change-related goals, as well as ensuring that treatment offers them the opportunity to set the kinds of goals that will be most helpful to them, is equally important.

There is a well-established literature on the psychology of goal setting. In the next section, I briefly review that literature before discussing ways in which the psychology of goal setting should inform relapse prevention.

Understanding Goals and Goal Setting

Emmons (1996) defines *goals* as "desired states that people seek to obtain, maintain or avoid" (p. 314). He adds that people's lives are structured around the pursuit of goals and that this is affected by the type or orientation of goals they pursue. *Approach* goals are positive appetitive goals that people strive toward, and *avoidance* goals are negative aversive goals that people strive to avoid. The difference between approach and avoidance goals can sometimes sound merely semantic, but that difference reflects a psychological reality. For instance, "keep calm always" is an approach goal, whereas "try not to let anything upset me" is an avoidance goal. Although the desired psychological state may sound the same, the way in which the goal is stated affects the methods adopted and the likely success of those methods. According to Emmons, a person trying to keep calm always has one route to achieving that goal, and he knows that in any situation he is trying to do the same thing. A person who is trying not to get upset faces a whole range of possible ways in which his goal could be disrupted, and thus he must constantly scan his environment for threats against goal achievement. It is hypothesized that this difference accounts for the finding that "individuals concerned with avoiding negative outcomes have higher levels of distress compared to persons with primarily approach orientations" (Emmons, 1996, p. 322; Emmons & Kaiser, 1994).

People who expect that they can achieve their goals keep trying even when they meet adversity (Carver & Scheier, 1990). Expectations of success seem to be self-fulfilling and are therefore an important aspect of goal setting.

Disengagement from a goal after failure can be prevented if the goal holder has a learning orientation rather than an achievement orientation (Dweck & Leggatt, 1988). In other words, people keep trying if they see the learning process as part of the goal. People give up more easily if their goals are static in definition, so that in their minds the goal is not achieved at all until the final state is reached. The former (learning orientation) experience success as they learn; the latter (achievement orientation) experience success only when they have learned. Therefore, achievement-oriented people see themselves as losers when they hit setbacks, whereas learning-oriented people directly confront setbacks through effort and problem solving (Dweck, 1996).

"Ideal" goals, those to which a person intrinsically aspires, produce greater effort toward achievement than do "ought" goals, those to which one agrees just to avoid criticism or disapproval (Higgins, 1996). According to Higgins, this is

because people with predominately ideal-goal systems focus on positive outcomes and therefore persist longer on goal-related tasks than do people with
predominately ought-goal systems.

Applying Goal-Setting Theory to
Relapse Prevention With Sex Offenders

Relapse prevention could be made a more attractive and successful intervention if the importance of goal type is properly considered. This has previously
been proposed in relation to relapse prevention with alcohol abusers (Cox,
Klinger, & Blount, 1991). Cox et al. (1991) cite studies indicating that an
enhanced satisfaction with life and with goal-directed activities is linked to
greater resistance to relapse (e.g., Sanchez-Craig, Wilkinson, & Walker, 1987;
Tucker, Vuchinich, & Harris, 1985). Although similar lines of enquiry have yet
to be followed in studies of sex offenders, there seem to be good grounds for
expecting these sorts of findings to be applicable.

Theoretical and empirical observations about goals can be translated into
practice. Below are some suggestions for influencing relapse prevention practice with an understanding of the psychology of goal setting.

Change the Goal of Relapse Prevention to an Approach Goal. Traditional
relapse prevention has, by definition, an avoidance goal. The goal is the avoidance of a relapse, that is, the avoidance of further sex offending. Bearing in
mind the differences between goal orientations described earlier, this suggests
that sex offenders who have an avoidance-goal orientation to change will find
success harder to achieve than those with an approach-goal orientation. Traditional avoidance-oriented relapse prevention work requires clients to monitor
their environment constantly for any signs of threat in the form of impending
lapses. Assuming Higgins (1996) is correct, we are setting clients up for
greater levels of distress and lower likelihood of success by encouraging such
a strategy.

There are ethical and moral implications to changing the goal of relapse prevention. How content would sex offender treatment providers be (not to mention the public) with an intervention that did not have the avoidance of further
sex offending as its goal? Laws, Hudson, and Ward (2000 [this volume]) discuss some of these issues. They argue, persuasively, that it is more important to
conduct treatment that works than it is to conduct treatment that sounds politi-
cally acceptable. Furthermore, it is not suggested here that the purpose of sex
offender treatment should be anything other than to reduce the incidence of
sexual crime in society. That must never be compromised. However, as the
example cited earlier shows ("keeping calm always"), goal orientation refers to
the way in which the goal is defined, not to the actual desired state. The same
desired states can be defined in an avoidance or an approach manner. The

challenge facing sex offender treatment providers is to restate the avoidance goal—to "avoid reoffending" as an approach goal.

A rephrased approach version of the goal of sex offender treatment might be for the client "to become someone who lives a satisfying life that is always respectful of others." Such a goal is appropriate because it is defined in approach terms, and, if achieved, it is incompatible with sexual offending. Approach goals sound more appealing than avoidance goals, and this may be particularly important for sex offenders whose offending has followed an approach path because they are likely to require a considerable incentive to give up offending.

Interestingly, in Marlatt's (1985) original description of relapse prevention, he defines three aims to the intervention: "acquiring adaptive coping skills . . . fostering new cognitions . . . and developing a daily lifestyle that includes positive self-care activities and nondestructive ways of achieving personal care and satisfaction" (Marlatt & Gordon, 1985, p. xiii). All of these aims are approach goals. Perhaps it is not the original conceptualization of relapse prevention intervention that needs attention but the way in which it has come to be delivered.

Once the overall goal of relapse prevention has been reoriented, then clients should be encouraged to frame their subgoals as approach goals. The importance of shifting from an aversive to an appetitive lifestyle has been stressed for problem drinkers (Cox et al., 1991). Cox et al. (1991) cite Klinger (1977), who demonstrated that people absorbed in avoiding negative goals are more likely to attempt using alcohol than those working toward positive, attractive goals. Sex offenders, then, once they have established an overall goal that is incongruent with offending, should be encouraged to break this down into a number of attractive, appetitive subgoals. For instance, a client may decide that his goals are to become more confident and competent in socializing with adult women, to turn a creative hobby into a skill that can pay a wage, and to become more generous and caring toward adult family members. These goals are all positive and appetitive, and as soon as they begin to be achieved, they will allow the client to experience benefits in return, both financial and social.

Offer Treatment in a Way That Ensures Clients Choose Personally Meaningful and Valuable Goals. This refers to the necessity that clients' goals are intrinsically important to them and not imposed on them. Like all human beings, sex offenders are likely to resist being told that they should change in certain ways. However, in our experience, asking clients to define their own life goals is often fruitful. Rarely do they select goals that are compatible with offending.

A good example of a forum for encouraging sex offenders to set themselves personally meaningful approach goals is the treatment strategy "New Me," developed by Jim Haaven (Haaven, Little, & Petre-Miller, 1990). In this strategy, the client is first asked to describe or draw himself as he was when offending and to label this "Old Me." In our experience, the best Old Me descriptions are created in the form of a drawing or collage. Next, the client is asked to describe or draw himself as he would like to be in the future. Note that this "New Me" description must relate *to the future* to avoid complications of clients believing they are cured. Clients are told that New Me must be realistic, but otherwise they are given no constraints to this task. In our experience, if the client is allowed free choice in the construction of New Me, he is likely to describe personally valuable and meaningful goals. In defining New Me, it is possible to teach clients the difference between approach and avoidance goals and to encourage them to describe New Me with a predominately approach orientation.

Encourage a Learning Orientation Rather Than an Achievement Orientation. This is important to ensure that clients persist toward their goals and do not give up easily. Encouraging a learning orientation should result in clients gaining satisfaction from the change process in itself because they experience feelings of success regularly, and these feelings boost energy and motivation. This is particularly important for sex offenders, who can be habitually all-or-nothing thinkers, unused to recognizing and appreciating small prosocial successes.

One way in which a learning orientation can be encouraged is through the setting of subgoals, also known as "goal laddering" (Cox et al., 1991). In this procedure, clients are encouraged to break their long-term goals down into hierarchical steps. This process should continue until the very first steps can be specified (the term *baby steps* is often useful to demonstrate to clients how they should expect themselves to progress). Such first steps can be set as between-session treatment goals, and the client can then receive positive feedback from the group as he achieves each step. This is particularly important in the early days of the relapse prevention intervention because it allows the client to experience success early in treatment, which will motivate him to continue.

With the New Me methodology described earlier, clients can be asked to envisage subgoals as stages or steps along their journey toward New Me. This reinforces the notion that New Me is not yet achieved but sets the client in a context of progression that can be very motivating. For example, one client described New Me as someone who cared for and appreciated others. He specified as his first step toward this ultimate goal that he would remember to thank the fellow prisoner who every morning passed on a newspaper to him. Every time he achieved this goal, he shared his success with the treatment group, who reinforced his behavior with positive feedback.

Help Clients Develop Positive Expectancies for Their Potential to Achieve New Goals. Often, sex offenders experience relapse prevention as a negative message. One group of treatment "graduates" memorably described the re-lapse prevention part of their treatment program as "that bit where they told us all the things we couldn't do anymore"; another group complained that "we spent all that time learning about the damage we had done to people and how we had to change, and then we were told that we were probably going to offend again." Often, treatment providers are unwilling to foster too much confidence about coping in their clients because of the dangers of overconfidence. These dangers are very real. Hanson and Harris (1998), for example, found that pro-testations of being at no further risk were significant immediate precursors of recidivism. There is a thin therapeutic line to tread between helping clients believe they have the power to change and having them believe they are cured.

How to Manage Overconfidence. The psychology of goal setting tells us that clients need to believe they can achieve their goals even when they meet adver-sity. This may mean that we should encourage more optimism about change in our clients, rather than warning them repeatedly that they will inevitably fail to control risk factors.

Again, we have found metaphor to be a useful way of communicating an optimistic but realistic expectation to clients. In one treatment exercise, clients can be asked to prepare for a bicycle journey up a very high mountain. They can be asked to brainstorm all the different things that might go wrong on such a journey. Lists should include external things that might go wrong (punctures, bad weather) and internal things (lose motivation, get lonely). Their second task is then to plan for the journey, listing ways to prepare for each possible trib-ulation. There are two messages to be learned from this exercise. First, "if you really want to get up the mountain, you can." Second, "you're more likely to be successful and achieve your goals if you plan ahead."

Strategies for Working With Resistant Individuals

In addition to redefining the aims and methods of relapse prevention, it is also important for sex offender treatment providers to be equipped with an understanding of individual resistance and strategies for responding to it. This section refers particularly to the principles and strategies of motivational inter-viewing, a treatment approach that is specifically designed for overcoming resistance to change in clients with addictive behavior problems. Motivational interviewing is now well recognized as applicable to the sex offender client group (Garland & Dougher, 1991; Mann, 1995, 1997).

Motivational interviewing (MI) was developed around the same time as relapse prevention. It first appeared in the literature in 1983 when Miller (1983) advocated a move away from traditional approaches to understanding denial in alcohol abusers. In 1991, when a comprehensive theoretical and practical guide to MI was published (Miller & Rollnick, 1991), MI was explicitly linked to Prochaska and DiClemente's transtheoretical model of change (DiClemente, 1991). Although MI is often thought to be most applicable to clients at the pre-contemplation stage of behavior change, motivational strategies are also used for responding to client resistance during treatment (Miller & Rollick, 1991). Some of these are the following:

1. Understand Resistance as Ambivalence. Motivational interviewing reframes resistance as ambivalence. This encourages the therapist to approach resistance in a positive way. Understanding a client's ambivalence is a central tenet of motivational interviewing. A client can be helped to articulate his ambivalence by simple counseling techniques such as open questions followed by reflective listening:

> You've talked in the past about your commitment to not reoffending. I can see you're not happy with working out your risk factors. Can you tell me some more about why you're not happy with this work?

Reflective listening, an essential skill in motivational interviewing, develops empathic understanding of the client by the therapist and trust of the therapist by the client. It is the best way for the therapist to see the factors in the client's ambivalence. Through this procedure, the therapist can decide what aspect of relapse prevention the client is resisting (i.e., the goal, the model, or the methods).

2. Do Not Attempt to Persuade the Client. This is important with all resistant clients but particularly so with rebellious clients, whose resistance springs directly from attempts to get him to do something, and with rationalizing clients who love a good debate. Instead, the therapist needs to facilitate the client to present arguments for change, rather than the therapist presenting the reasons to the client:

> I can see that you're not happy with the idea of planning for your high-risk situations. What sort of planning does make sense to you, if you're going to have a better life without offending?

In this example, the therapist has decided to start where the client is and find out his priorities. A skillful therapist can then work with the client's priorities so that treatment becomes meaningful for the client rather than imposed on him.

3. Revisit Motivational Statements. Clients whose motivation is shaky (reluctant resistors) or who lack confidence in their ability to change (resigned resistors) can find it helpful to revisit motivational statements they made earlier in treatment. These statements might include statements about reasons to change or statements of optimism about change. Note that it is important that such statements are revisited by the client himself. A common error is for the therapist to take the responsibility for reminding the client or group about the need for relapse prevention work, rather than questioning clients so that they develop their own motivational statements. Useful questions for helping clients revisit their motivation include the following:

- What are my goals, and why are they important?
- How hard am I prepared to work to achieve my goals?
- Is there anything I would not want to do even if it helped achieve my goals?
- When I find myself resisting something in therapy, what might be going on?
- When I feel myself losing confidence in myself or my goals, what could I do?

4. Provide Opportunities for Discovery Rather Than Teaching. A common misconception about relapse prevention, or indeed any cognitive-behavioral intervention, is that it is a psychoeducational rather than a psychotherapeutic intervention. This means that in many programs, relapse prevention concepts are taught by the therapists rather than discovered by the client. Motivational interviewing, in contrast to the psychoeducational approach, emphasizes the Socratic method (Overholser, 1993). The basic tenet of this approach is that a person understands, internalizes, and remembers best ideas discovered by his or her own reasoning process. The bicycle-up-the-mountain exercise described earlier is an example of a Socratic exercise. During this exercise, sex offenders in treatment discover the value of preparation for themselves.

The difference between the psychoeducational approach and the Socratic approach can also be illustrated by using as an example the task of teaching sex offenders about urge management. A traditional method of teaching clients about urges is to use the "wave" metaphor. Marlatt (1985) suggests that

> the therapist can describe the urge as a response that grows in intensity, peaks and then subsides. . . . The client is instructed to imagine that an urge is like a wave and that he or she is learning to be a surfer. (p. 241)

This is clearly a didactic teaching method—the therapist describes and instructs. The same metaphor could be taught Socratically. In this alternative approach, the therapist would ask the client to describe the way in which an urge grows. The client should first be asked what he feels is going to happen if he does not give in to his urge. As the client describes the experience of an urge, the therapist can draw a line of increasing intensity on a chart to illustrate what the client is saying (even better if the client can draw the urge himself). Then the client should be asked to describe circumstances when he has not given in to an urge, perhaps when he had an urge to smoke but had no cigarettes, or when he had an urge to offend but no opportunity. The client should describe the experience of the urge gradually subsiding. Again, the therapist or the client himself can draw a graph to represent this experience. Finally, the therapist finishes the exercise with the Socratic question, designed to help the client make the link between the exercise and his life. For example, "So if this is what an urge feels like when it's happening, and if this is what happens if you don't give in to an urge, what could you do or say to yourself during an urge to help you get through it without offending?"

The result is the same: The client realizes that urges will diminish if not indulged and that he can talk himself through an urge by remembering this. However, the psychoeducational approach has told the client what to do, whereas through the Socratic approach, he has worked out what to do for himself. The Socratic method not only diffuses rebellious or rationalizing resistance (because clients are not being told what to do), but all clients also learn the message more thoroughly, whether or not they are resistant.

Conclusions

The conditions of traditional relapse prevention can be hard for sex offenders to accept. First, the relapse prevention model takes an avoidance orientation, which may not be the most therapeutically successful approach to take. Second, offenders' goals are assumed to be the same as the therapist's when in fact there is often little reason to suppose this to be the case. To reduce the incidence of resistance and rebellion in a relapse prevention program, I have suggested transforming the goals of relapse prevention and encouraging clients to take an approach orientation to personal change. Furthermore, therapists who understand the principles of motivational interviewing, particularly the nature of ambivalence and the importance of self-discovery, are more likely to deliver relapse prevention interventions in more effective ways.

References

Carver, C. S., & Scheier, M. F. (1990). Principles of self regulation: Action and emotion. In R. Sorrentino & E. T. Higgins (Eds.), *Handbook of motivation and cognition: Foundations of social behaviour* (Vol. 2, pp. 3-52). New York: Guilford.

Cox, M., Klinger, E., & Blount, J. P. (1991). Alcohol use and goal hierarchies: Systematic motivational counselling for alcoholics. In W. R. Miller & S. Rollnick (Eds.), *Motivational interviewing: Preparing people to change addictive behavior* (pp. 260-271). New York: Guilford.

DiClemente, C. C. (1991). Motivational interviewing and the stages of change. In W. R. Miller & S. Rollnick (Eds.), *Motivational interviewing: Preparing people to change addictive behavior* (pp. 191-202). New York: Guilford.

Dweck, C. S. (1996). Implicit theories as organizers of goals and behavior. In P. M. Gollwitzer & J. A. Bargh (Eds.), *The psychology of action: Linking cognition and motivation to behavior* (pp. 69-90). New York: Guilford.

Dweck, C. S., & Leggatt, E. L. (1988). A social cognitive approach to motivation and personality. *Psychological Review, 95,* 256-273.

Emmons, R. A. (1996). Striving and feeling: Personal goals and subjective well-being. In P. M. Gollwitzer & J. A. Bargh (Eds.), *The psychology of action: Linking cognition and motivation to behavior* (pp. 313-337). New York: Guilford.

Emmons, R. A., & Kaiser, H. (1994, August). *Approach and avoidance strivings and subjective well being.* Poster presented at the 102nd Annual Convention of the American Psychological Association, Los Angeles.

Garland, R. J., & Dougher, M. J. (1991). Motivational intervention in the treatment of sex offenders. In W. R. Miller & S. Rollnick (Eds.), *Motivational interviewing: Preparing people to change addictive behavior* (pp. 303-313). New York: Guilford.

Haaven, J., Little, R., & Petre-Miller, D. (1990). *Treating intellectually disabled sex offenders: A model residential program.* Orwell, VT: Safer Society.

Hanson, R. K., & Harris, A. (1998). *Dynamic predictors of sexual recidivism* [Online]. Available: http://www.sgc.gc.ca/epub/corr/e199801b/e199801b.htm (downloaded from the Web site of the Solicitor General of Canada).

Higgins, E. T. (1996). Ideals, oughts and regulatory focus: Affect and motivation from distinct pains and pleasures. In P. M. Gollwitzer & J. A. Bargh (Eds.), *The psychology of action: Linking cognition and motivation to behavior.* New York: Guilford.

Klinger, E. (1977). *Meaning and void: Inner experience and the incentives in people's lives.* Minneapolis: University of Minnesota Press.

Laws, D. R., Hudson, S. M., & Ward, T. (2000). The original model of relapse prevention with sex offenders: Promises unfulfilled. In R. D. Laws, S. M. Hudson, & T. Ward (Eds.), *Remaking relapse prevention with sex offenders: A sourcebook* (pp. 3-24). Thousand Oaks, CA: Sage.

Mann, R. E. (1995). *Motivational interviewing with sex offenders: A practice manual.* Hull, UK: NOTA.

Mann, R. E. (1997, October). *When they don't want to change: Techniques for relapse prevention intervention with reluctant or rebellious clients.* Paper presented at the 16th annual conference of the Association for the Treatment of Sexual Abusers, Arlington, VA.

Mann, R. E., & Thornton, D. (1998). *The evolution of a multisite sexual offender treatment program.* In W. L. Marshall, Y. M. Fernandez, S. M. Hudson, & T. Ward (Eds.), *Sourcebook of treatment programs for sexual offenders* (pp. 47-58). New York: Plenum.

Marlatt, G. A. (1985). Relapse prevention: Theoretical rationale and overview of the model. In G. A. Marlatt & J. R. Gordon (Eds.), *Relapse prevention* (pp. 3-70). New York: Guilford.

Marlatt, G. A., & Gordon, J. R. (1985). Preface. In G. A. Marlatt & J. R. Gordon (Eds.), *Relapse prevention* (pp. xii-xiv). New York: Guilford.

Miller, W. R. (1983). Motivational interviewing with problem drinkers. *Behavioural Psychotherapy, 1,* 147-172.

Miller, W. R., & Rollnick, S. (Eds.). (1991). *Motivational interviewing: Preparing people to change addictive behavior.* New York: Guilford.

Overholser, J. (1993). Elements of the Socratic method 1: Systematic questioning. *Psychotherapy, 30*(1), 67-74.

Prochaska, J. O., & DiClemente, C. C. (1986). Transtheoretical theory: Toward a more integrative model of change. In J. C. Norcross (Ed.), *Psychotherapy: Theory, Research, and Practice, 19,* 276-288. New York: Brunner/Mazel.

Sanchez-Craig, M., Wilkinson, D. A., & Walker, K. (1987). Theory and methods for secondary prevention of alcohol problems: A cognitive approach. In W. M. Cox (Ed.), *Treatment and prevention of alcohol problems: A resource manual* (pp. 287-331). Orlando, FL: Academic Press.

Tucker, J. A., Vuchinich, R. E., & Harris, E. V. (1985). Determinants of substance abuse relapse. In M. Galizio & S. A. Maisto (Eds.), *Determinants of substance abuse: Biological, psychological and environmental factors* (pp. 383-421). New York: Plenum.

Ward, T., & Hudson, S. M. (2000). A self-regulation model of relapse prevention. In D. R. Laws, S. M. Hudson, & T. Ward (Eds.), *Remaking relapse prevention with sex offenders: A sourcebook* (pp. 79-101). Thousand Oaks, CA: Sage.

CHAPTER 11

Complementing Relapse Prevention With Medical Intervention

DON GRUBIN
University of Newcastle

Before the introduction of classical relapse prevention principles to the treatment of sex offenders, the psychiatric treatment of sex offenders
generally followed one of two mutually exclusive models. The first was
psychodynamic psychotherapy, in which the roots of offending behavior were
sought deep in the individual's developmental history in the belief that with
insight came cure, or at least change. The second model was a more typically
medical one, whereby the cause of offending was believed to lie in organic
pathology, and treatment was based on physical interventions, either in the
form of medication or in more extreme measures such as castration. Neither
approach was subjected to well-designed outcome studies, and both tended to
rely on their face validity for their continued support. Unfortunately, face validity did not translate into a reduction in recidivism (Furby, Weinrott, &
Blackshaw, 1989), and medical models of sex offender treatment lost much of
their credibility.

The application of relapse prevention and associated cognitive behavioral
techniques to sex offender treatment shifted the focus of work with sex offenders onto behavior. It emphasized that offenders are responsible for and capable
of controlling their actions. This model not only had the advantage of defining

clear treatment targets that could be measured, but it was also demonstrably effective (Nagayama Hall, 1995).

Although there are individual exceptions, psychiatrists as a group have tended not to be providers of relapse prevention types of treatment, even when they acknowledge its success and accept its rationale. There are a number of reasons for this, but two are probably most important: First, the training and work of psychiatrists are concerned with the treatment of mental illness rather than the modification of offending behavior. Second, psychiatric skills themselves have been seen as largely unnecessary for the delivery of successful relapse prevention programs. The original relapse prevention models as applied to sex offenders, targeting self-control and personal responsibility, had little room for medical intervention and its suggestion that individuals are the passive victims of their histories and their hormones.

In general, there are few psychiatrists who only or even primarily assess and treat sex offenders. Instead, they become involved in sex offender management as part of their general, psychotherapeutic, or forensic practice. As such, their approach to treatment tends to reflect the way in which they work generally, and psychodynamic and medical interventions are thus still common in the psychiatric world, albeit less dominant than they once were. Some psychiatrists, of course, have played a role in the delivery of relapse prevention programs, but in this capacity, they usually function on the psychological rather than the medical end of the spectrum. Others have hovered on the margins, providing input when specific psychiatric problems develop in individual participants, using their knowledge of the relapse prevention model primarily to ensure that their intervention does not undermine the goals of treatment.

As relapse prevention has evolved, it has become clear that the model does not provide an all-encompassing explanation of sex offending, nor does it address all aspects of treatment (Ward, Hudson, & Keenan, 1998). In particular, the complexity underlying the etiology of sex offending has meant that focusing on a small number of high-profile variables, such as cognitive distortions or negative mood states, has proven inadequate in meeting the treatment needs of many offenders. The cloth of a single paradigm does not readily fit all offenders without alteration, and the need for tailoring has become increasingly apparent. Programs often take up the slack by bolting on additional modules, such as those that address self-esteem, intimacy deficits, or assertiveness.

Perhaps the main difficulty with relapse prevention is its tendency to ignore factors that may contribute only indirectly to offending, whereas those that appear to have no relationship with offending behavior are not addressed at all. This might make sense if one could be confident that the assessment process was sufficiently detailed to ensure that the relapse pathway for a particular individual was well understood, but this is usually not the case. Medical approaches to assessment and treatment, which are in general more broadly based and encompass a wider context, can enhance this understanding, but they are not easily accommodated by the traditional model. Those that are more organically based do not fit well with the psychological orientation of relapse pathways, and those that are psychodynamic in nature seem too vague to be made part of a relapse prevention strategy.

Some of the gaps that have become evident in the treatment fabric, however, are well suited for plugging with psychiatric or medical intervention. This does not mean that medical and cognitive-behavioral models need to compete for supremacy. The model remains cognitive-behavioral, but it gains an additional set of medical tools. When this is recognized and acted on, psychiatrists can make a constructive contribution to modern relapse prevention. In our program, for example, we believe that psychiatrists can do more than simply ensure that they do no harm.

The Psychiatric Context

In North America and Great Britain, perhaps the greatest impact on psychiatric practice in recent years has been the shift of emphasis from institutional to community care and the corresponding unease that has been engendered in the public by the perception that dangerous, mentally disordered individuals are being allowed to wander uncontrolled in the streets. For example, in response to a small number of high-profile cases in England and Wales where psychiatric patients have killed while living in the community, it has been government policy since 1994 to hold an independent inquiry, chaired by a judge or lawyer, into the circumstances of cases in which such a homicide has occurred—by the end of 1998, more than 50 inquiry reports had been published, and another 30 inquiries were in progress (*zt monitor,* 1999). The belief of many is that the purpose of such inquires is to ensure that responsibility can be attributed to named individuals when things go wrong, resulting in a subtle shift of blame from the perpetrator to those who have been involved in his or her care.

It is perhaps not surprising, therefore, that psychiatrists in Britain have started to take a keen interest in risk assessment and risk management. There are now numerous clinical protocols for dealing with potentially dangerous patients, designed to ensure that risk factors for individual patients are understood and responded to when they become apparent. These are strongly influenced by a careful consideration of phenomenology, that is, the description of the nature of psychiatric symptoms and mental states. Critically, however, it is no longer the case that symptoms alone are the benchmark of treatment—behavior and the prediction of future behavior are of equal priority with symptom control in the psychiatric management of dangerous individuals.

Although many of the concepts associated with relapse prevention, particularly those relating to the description of offending cycles or chains, and the identification of high-risk situations can be readily applied to the management of potentially dangerous patients, pure relapse prevention models present a fundamental problem in psychiatry—the assumption that "relapse prevention" means total "abstinence" is simply not feasible, whether this is in terms of symptom recurrence or reengaging in dangerous behaviors. Psychiatrists talk of reducing and managing risk, not eliminating it, in a manner similar to the "harm reduction" model well outlined by Laws (1996). With the shadow of an inquiry always in the background, it is a brave and probably foolhardy practitioner who implies a guarantee of the safety of his or her patients.

Sex offenders are potentially dangerous individuals. Although the majority are not mentally ill, an understanding of how they perceive the world (both symbolically and practically), a knowledge of the mental phenomenology that underlies their offending and their response or resistance to treatment, and the possibility of using medication as an adjunct to psychological treatment can all contribute to their long-term management, taking it beyond the relatively narrow confines of relapse prevention. Used appropriately, psychiatry can broaden the scope of relapse prevention significantly.

Psychiatry and Relapse Prevention

The core of any sex offender relapse prevention program is its concentration on factors such as cognitive distortions and on high-risk thoughts, emotional states, and situations, with the aim of developing coping strategies. It is about self-management. This is not terribly psychiatric, and it will never become so. Once an established relapse prevention plan is in place, psychiatric input will often be irrelevant unless mental illness complicates the relapse prevention plan. But relapse prevention does not exist in isolation, and for any individual its components only become clear after a good deal of preceding work has been carried out. If the possibility of psychiatric input is ignored at this stage, it is unlikely that any potential benefits will be recognized later.

Assessment

There are two components to assessment: the assessment of treatment needs and the more basic assessment of whether an offender has the potential to benefit from the treatment offered. Neither is typically seen as a psychiatric task. As Marshall, Laws, and Barbaree (1990) point out, however, the recognition that some men will not respond effectively to a specific program should not result in their exclusion from treatment but in the provision of alternative programs more appropriate for them. In some cases, this might mean preparatory work to enable them to engage in relapse prevention treatment, but in other cases an entirely different strategy may be necessary. Traditional relapse prevention models tend to lack the flexibility needed to accommodate such individuals.

Mentally Ill Sex Offenders

One reason why offenders are typically excluded from treatment is because they are believed to suffer from some form of mental illness, and there is concern that either they will disrupt the treatment program, or they will decompensate under it (Grubin & Thornton, 1994). But although "mental illness" is an exclusionary criterion in many sex offender programs, the question of psychiatric symptomatology is invariably dealt with only superficially. Although in some cases psychotic symptoms may be the direct cause of offending (e.g., when delusional ideas lead to an attack on a victim) (Smith & Taylor, 1999), psychiatric illness can also be contributory or even coincidental rather than causal to the offending behavior. There is no reason to believe that the underlying distortions and pathways to offending are any different in mentally ill sex offenders than in those who are not; indeed, when looked for, few differences are found (Sahota & Chesterman, 1998). Simply treating acute symptoms is unlikely to be sufficient in reducing sexual risk. Why, then, automatically exclude the mentally ill from sex offender treatment programs?

Of course, not all mentally ill offenders are appropriately managed within a relapse prevention-type program, but in our experience, the proportion who are not is much lower than many would predict. Blanket exclusion is unnecessary if informed psychiatric assessment and proper mental state examination take place to elucidate the relationship between psychiatric symptoms and offending. Provided that offenders are not acutely ill, most are able to deal with the concepts of relapse prevention; visions of massive decompensation or bizarre behavior within the group are more often part of the fantasy of psychiatrically inexperienced therapists than reality.

The role of mental illness is further complicated by some offenders who use psychiatric symptoms as an excuse for their offending. Clearly, an accurate assessment of mental state is essential, both in terms of determining whether there is a fundamental mental illness that requires treatment in its own right and dismissing definitively at an early stage recourse to illness as a means of avoiding responsibility. Indeed, in refusing to accept disease explanations for offending when opportunistically presented by an offender, the medical model of sexual offending is flipped onto its head. This is almost certainly best achieved by a psychiatrist, who can definitively address the issue of mental illness.

Understanding the Past

Sex offenders are more than bundles of cognitions and behaviors. An important aspect of assessment is gaining an understanding of what makes an individual vulnerable to carrying out a sexual offence. As Ward et al. (1998) point out, a multitude of branch points and pathways leads to offending behavior in general, as well as within a single offender. Deciphering these requires an appreciation of the schema with which the individual interprets the world, his immediate aims, and his more abstract, higher-level goals (Ward & Hudson, 1998). Although Ward and his colleagues would probably not go so far, this may require interpretation of the sort that psychiatrists—and, more particularly, psychotherapists—are comfortable with. For some individuals, the symbolism of some aspects of their environment may be more important than the reality—an offending pattern may be a recapitulation of early experience.

Relapse prevention typically focuses on the present and the future. The origins of dysfunctional behavior are of little relevance, and much energy often needs to be expended in distracting offenders from the question of "why." Although we agree that there is little to be gained in offenders focusing on the speculative early roots of their offending, the same is not truc in the case of those carrying out the assessment. Apart from assisting in the identification of factors that may trigger the ignition of a chain of events leading to offending, such an analysis may also reveal symptoms that need treatment in their own right. A good example of this relates to offenders' own histories of victimization.

It is now well established that childhood sexual abuse, particularly if protracted or frequent and when carried out by a family member or someone else in a position of trust, can be associated with significant psychiatric symptomatology, both at the time of the abuse and later in the life of the victim (Watkins & Bentovim, 1992). Adult psychiatric problems have been best studied in women (Romans, Martin, & Mullen, 1997) but are also often described in men. These symptoms range from self-destructive behavior, aggression, and inappropriate sexual behavior to the development of specific mental illnesses (although it can be difficult to disentangle the effects of childhood sexual abuse from other adverse childhood experiences such as physical abuse and poor parenting).

Childhood sexual abuse could contribute to adult sexual offending against children in a number of ways. Most straightforward are "cycle of abuse" theories that suggest that children learn behaviors that are modeled for them. Alternatively, it may be that men with a history of sexual abuse discharge the confusion engendered in them by victimizing others, either negatively through the expression of anger or, in a sense, positively, by rationalizing that their experiences were beneficial and hence should be repeated with others. Another possibility, of course, is that premature sexual experience interferes with the future development of intimate sexual and emotional relationships, perhaps by interfering with childhood attachment processes. Each of these alternatives is equally possible, and none can be proved or disproved. In specific cases, however, in the context of an offender's history, one or the other may make more sense for that particular individual and provide a route to uncovering the cognitive distortions and emotional states that fuel his offending. None of this needs to be shared with the offender, but this type of psychiatric perspective is a valuable component to a multidisciplinary case conference.

Even when an individual may appear to have overcome issues associated with a history of victimization, at times of stress he may decompensate in a wide variety of ways, ranging from self-destructive behavior to feelings of intense depression or anger, any of which may manifest themselves in offending. Relapse prevention strategies may recognize particular stresses as risk factors, but the individual's vulnerability to a range of stresses associated with his abuse history will be missed if his own victimization is not dealt with properly. If childhood abuse has been severe enough to affect adult behavior, then it clearly is likely to have an important influence on the way in which that individual views the world. An awareness by the offender of this can be a useful ingredient in a relapse prevention strategy if it helps him make sense of the emotions he experiences, especially when these increase his risk of engaging in deviant behavior.

Offenders may also use a history of abuse to excuse their behavior. If associated with genuine psychiatric symptoms, the balance between acknowledging the effects of the abuse, on one hand, and not allowing it to hinder the acceptance of responsibility, on the other hand, can be problematic. To manage this, there must be a realistic appraisal of the symptoms and a clear distinction in the therapist's own mind between treating symptoms and understanding the cause. This can be difficult, if not impossible, if the psychiatrist sits outside the treatment team.

Thus, in addition to providing input in relation to the nature of any real or claimed psychiatric symptomatology, assessing an individual from a psychiatric perspective can provide insight into what an individual is trying to "achieve" by his offending. Such insight needs then to be fed into the relapse prevention process, rather than being viewed as an end in itself.

Treatment

Medication

Perhaps the most obvious contribution psychiatrists can make to a relapse prevention program is through their ability to prescribe medication. This, however, is something that is sometimes frowned on by strict adherents to the model. Because the use of medication suggests short-term improvement in the absence of long-term psychological change, extreme cognitive-behaviorists perceive it as cheating, even if effective. The use of medication also carries the risk of suggesting to the offender that his drives are not wholly under his power, and he has only a limited ability to control his offending.

Provided that medication is prescribed in a manner that complements rather than distracts from the main body of treatment work, however, we have found that it can usefully facilitate relapse prevention work. Indeed, in some cases in which sexual thoughts are intrusive or sexual arousal is excessive, it can make cognitive-behavioral treatment possible where otherwise an offender is inaccessible to psychological intervention.

Medication can be used in three ways: to help regulate mood, to reduce sexual drive, and to lessen sexual preoccupation when it is associated with obsessive thinking processes and compulsive behavior. Antiandrogens such as cyproterone acetate and Depo-Provera® (medroxyprogesterone acetate) are most frequently associated with sex offender treatment, but selective serotonin reuptake inhibitors (SSRIs) such as fluoxetine (Prozac®) and major tranquilizers such as haloperidol or trifluoperazine, if used appropriately, can also be of benefit. Even more traditional antidepressants may have a role. The problem tends to be that those who are unable to prescribe medication often do not consider it as part of a treatment package.

The antiandrogens reduce sexual drive as well as the ability to respond physically with an erection to sexual stimuli. In addition, they are reported to reduce sexual fantasies and to lower sexual "tension" generally (Bradford, 1988). In motivated offenders with high sexual drive, their use allows them to focus on the concepts of relapse prevention without these concepts themselves causing sexual arousal. They are not a long-term solution because invariably men at some stage want a trial without medication, either as a "test" or because of frustration with their asexuality; in the absence of a relapse prevention strategy, the return of sexual feelings makes reoffending more likely.

Thus, antiandrogens may be an effective adjunct to the initiation of cognitive-behavioral treatment and allow a relapse prevention strategy to be put in place. Ideally, if for no other reason than the long-term risk of physical side effects, their use should be relatively brief—about a year—and cessation carried out in a controlled manner. For some men, it may be appropriate for them to decide when to stop and start medication as part of their relapse prevention strategy itself, for although the effects on sexual response are not immediate, this gives them a sense of being able to control a drive that, rightly or wrongly, they believe is otherwise uncontrollable. In this way, one of the putative disadvantages of using medication, the abrogation of responsibility by the offender, is in fact turned into an advantage.

The SSRIs are used in a variety of psychiatric disorders, primarily those involving either mood or impulse control, including depression, anxiety, panic, bulimia, and obsessive-compulsive disorder. Serotonin itself is known to have a role in appetitive behaviors such as appetite and sex. In a number of open studies, SSRIs have been used to treat exhibitionists, fetishists, voyeurs, and child molesters with favorable results, reporting a reduction in fantasies, sexual urges, masturbation, and paraphilic behavior (reviewed in Greenberg & Bradford, 1997). It has also been suggested that the SSRIs have a specific effect on sexual deviancy, with paraphilic fantasies, urges, and arousal reduced but not those associated with conventional sexuality (Kafka & Prentky, 1992), although these findings need to be replicated in larger numbers of patients.

The mode of action of the SSRIs in the treatment of paraphilia is unclear. Despite the reports referred to earlier that they may have a primary effect on the deviant sexual behavior itself, our experience is that they are most beneficial in those whose sexual offending has an obsessive-compulsive quality to it, characterized by brooding, preoccupation, and repetitive ritual: These men offend over many years but without marked escalation in their behavior. Certainly, doses used are those typical of treating conventional obsessive-compulsive disorder.

Like the antiandrogens, the SSRIs can instill in an offender a sense of control, and they can interrupt the abnormal thinking processes that block other types of intervention. Provided that they are viewed by the offender as a component of relapse prevention rather than as a cure for sexual offending, there is little risk of their use undermining a psychologically based program. The offender's perception of this, of course, reflects the views of the prescriber and the message given by him or her.

One final class of drugs of which we make use is the major tranquilizers. These agents tended to be popular in the 1960s, when the intention was to lower sexual drive, one of their common side effects (Tennent, Bancroft, & Cass, 1974). Overall, however, the reduction in sexual drive is unpredictable and often minor, and other side effects such as tremor, rigidity, and restlessness make these drugs uncomfortable to take in the doses required. In our clinic, however, we use the major tranquilizers not for their effects on sexual drive but for their sedative action—in low doses (e.g., trifluoperazine 2 mg twice a day), they reduce arousal generally and anger more specifically.

One of the components of relapse prevention treatment is to help the offender recognize a link between mood and reoffending. Risk factors, behavioral and coping strategies, and resilience vary with different emotional states. The problem for many is that having identified the link, they may be unable to do anything about it. Anger control work, for example, tends to be effective in respect to specific triggers but not for the chronic anger many of them experience. Reducing this allows them to address other aspects of relapse prevention.

Whereas a general reduction in anger and arousal provides a backdrop on which relapse prevention can take place, major tranquilizers and antidepressive medication can also have a more direct role in relapse prevention strategies.

Hanson and Harris (1998), for example, demonstrated that although the presence of psychiatric symptoms as a whole were not predictive of sexual reoffending, a "change for the worse" in psychiatric symptomatology was particularly "negative mood" and "anger." It is of course possible to address these factors cognitively; this is a long-term task that often requires abilities that many of these men simply do not possess. Medication, therefore, by lifting mood or damping anger, can contribute to behavioral regulation. As with medication generally when used in sex offenders, the crucial step is incorporating it into a relapse plan that places the onus on the offender to recognize a change in mood.

Long-Term Management

Treatment gains, in relapse prevention as with anything else, diminish over time. Maintenance requires either further treatment or some form of ongoing external supervision and monitoring to identify the emergence of offense precursors (Pithers, 1990). Those working within criminal justice agencies can find both difficult to provide, particularly when an offender's obligation to remain in contact with them lapses. Close contacts of the offender are often recruited to assist in external supervision, and although they are in a good position to do this, like the offender the abilities and motivation of these contacts also decrease over time.

Psychiatrists and mental health services are used to providing long-term care for individuals with chronic disorders, with community follow-up lasting for many years in some cases. Although sex offenders may not present with symptoms, they remain a long-term risk for relapse and, at least in our clinic, justify continued appointments on that basis. Little in the way of "therapy" takes places during these sessions, but we use them both to monitor an offender's situation generally and to provide a reminder to him of his continued risk. Although psychiatric intervention is not the only way to achieve this, it is hard to see how else this function can be readily carried out. In addition, those who are on medication or who stop and start medication as necessary require some form of medical oversight, and although in the United Kingdom this can be provided by the man's general practitioner (GP), the GP would generally lack an understanding of how the mediation was being used.

It is also worth remembering that a number of these men are isolated, with little in the way of social interactions. When necessary, we can increase the amount of contact through the input of a community psychiatric nurse. Psychiatric outpatient appointments may be the only time when these men have an opportunity to talk about themselves or to seek help when things are beginning to go wrong. They can provide a human face to what can become a mechanical relapse prevention process.

Expectations of Others

Although not part of treatment per se, the expectations of others have a bearing on how and whether treatment can be delivered at all. Courts, parole boards, and tribunals, among others, look to experts to help them reach decisions about disposal or release. In the United Kingdom, at least, this often takes the form of a request for a psychiatric report. Having psychiatry as an integral part of a sex offender treatment program means that one can effectively counter those who advocate unproven medical approaches to sexual offenders, which may be either overoptimistic or overpessimistic, on their own terms.

Conclusion

Relapse prevention, of course, usually comes at the end of a treatment program in which a variety of factors that contribute to sexual offending have been addressed; as described by Pithers (1990), it is a method for maintaining earlier therapeutic gains. It relies on the motivation of offenders to avoid further offending, but it is not simply about suppressing behavior. Instead, it seeks to identify goals, of which an avoidance of offending may be just one and perhaps subsidiary to other higher-level aims (Ward & Hudson, 1998; Ward et al., 1998). Self-regulation lies at its core. Psychiatric input can assist in identifying the thoughts and emotions that can disrupt self-regulation, as well as provide a means to facilitate it.

Someday there may be a pill that will cure sexual offending, but one would be ill advised to hold one's breath waiting for it. Medication, however, can affect sexual function, often as a side effect of other intended treatment. As we become more aware of the possibilities offered by drugs, it may be possible to use medication in increasingly subtle and effective ways as part of larger treatment programs. This will require cooperation between psychiatrists and probably other medical specialists with other disciplines working with sex offenders.

To contribute effectively to sex offender treatment programs, psychiatrists have to be prepared to work within multidisciplinary and often multiagency teams and to resist dominating the clinical process. Psychiatry will never occupy center stage in programs that are essentially cognitive-behavioral in nature. Given the current tendency to attribute blame when things go wrong, however, psychiatrists should have little difficulty in signing up to this approach. In an area where risk can be reduced but not eliminated, one wants as many hands as possible on the tiller if the ship does hit the rocks. The alternative is to withdraw altogether, which in the long run helps neither the offender nor the society in which he lives.

References

Bradford, J. M. W. (1988). Organic treatment for the male sexual offender. In R. A. Prentky & V. L. Quinsey (Eds.), *Human sexual aggression: Current perspectives* (Vol. 258, pp. 193-202). New York: New York Academy of Sciences.

Furby, L., Weinrott, M. R., & Blackshaw, L. (1989). Sex offender recidivism: A review. *Psychological Bulletin, 105,* 3-30.

Greenberg, D. M., & Bradford, J. M. W. (1997). Treatment of the paraphilic disorders: A review of the role of the selective serotonin reuptake inhibitors. *Sexual Abuse: A Journal of Research and Treatment, 9,* 349-360.

Grubin, D., & Thornton, D. (1994). A national program for the assessment and treatment of sex offenders in the English prison system. *Criminal Justice & Behavior, 21,* 45-61.

Hanson, R. K., & Harris, A. (1998). *Dynamic predictors of sexual recidivism* (Cat No. JS42-82/1998-01E). Ottawa: Department of the Solicitor General of Canada, Corrections Research.

Kafka, M. P., & Prentky, R. A. (1992). Fluoxetine treatment of non paraphilic sexual addictions and paraphilias in men. *Journal of Clinical Psychiatry, 53,* 351-358.

Laws, D. R. (1996). Relapse prevention or harm reduction? *Sexual Abuse: A Journal of Research and Treatment, 8,* 243-247.

Marshall, W. L., Laws, D. R., & Barbaree, H. E. (1990). Present status and future directions. In W. L. Marshall, D. R. Laws, & H. E. Barbaree (Eds.), *Handbook of sexual assault: Issues, theories, and treatment of the offender* (pp. 389-395). New York: Plenum.

Nagayama Hall, G. C. (1995). Sex offender recidivism revisited: A meta-analysis of recent treatment studies. *Journal of Consulting and Clinical Psychology, 63,* 802-809.

Pithers, W. D. (1990). Relapse prevention with sexual aggressors: A method for maintaining therapeutic gain and enhancing external supervision. In W. L. Marshall, D. R. Laws, & H. E. Barbaree (Eds.), *Handbook of sexual assault: Issues, theories, and treatment of the offender* (pp. 343-361). New York: Plenum.

Romans, S., Martin, J., & Mullen, P. (1997). Childhood sexual abuse and later psychological problems: Neither necessary, sufficient nor acting alone. *Criminal Behaviour and Mental Health, 7,* 327-338.

Sahota, K., & Chesterman, P. (1998). Mentally ill sex offenders in a regional secure unit: Cognitions, perceptions and fantasies. *Journal of Forensic Psychiatry, 9,* 161-172.

Smith, A. D., & Taylor, P. J. (1999). Serious sex offending against women by men with schizophrenia: Relationship of illness and psychotic symptoms to offending. *British Journal of Psychiatry, 174,* 233-237.

Tennent, T. G., Bancroft, J., & Cass, J. (1974). The control of deviant sexual behaviour by drugs: A double-blind controlled study of benperidol, chlorpromazine and placebo. *Archives of Sexual Behavior, 3,* 261-271.

Ward, T., & Hudson, S. M. (1998). The construction and development of theory in the sexual offending area: A meta-theoretical framework. *Sexual Abuse: A Journal of Research and Treatment, 10,* 47-63.

Ward, T., Hudson, S., & Keenan, T. (1998). A self-regulation model of the sexual offense process. *Sexual Abuse: A Journal of Research and Treatment, 10,* 141-157.

Watkins, B., & Bentovim, A. (1992). The sexual abuse of male children and adolescents: A review of current research. *Journal of Child Psychology and Psychiatry, 33,* 197-248.

zt monitor: The Monthly Digest From the Zito Trust. (1999, January-February). London: The Zito Trust.

CHAPTER 12

Competency-Based Assessment

MICHAEL H. MINER
University of Minnesota

In 1989, David Day, Mary Nafpaktitis, and myself reported on the development of the Sex Offender Situational Competency Test (SOSCT) (Miner, Day, & Nafpaktitis, 1989). The SOSCT was developed using the behavioral-analytic method described by Goldfried and D'Zurilla (1969). This method involved four steps: (a) situational sampling, (b) selection of situational attributes, (c) development of a pool of test items, and (d) construction of the assessment instrument itself. In our 1989 chapter, we described each of these steps and how they lead to the development of a test for measuring competency in sex-offending risk situations (see Miner et al., 1989, for details).

Clearly, the domain assessed by the SOSCT is dependent on the domain of situations sampled during the first phase of test development. In our initial work, we used a structured interview to identify a wide range of high-risk situations for sex offending. Thus, the SOSCT is a measure of the competency of an individual to cope with situations that could lead directly to sexual offending. The reformulation of relapse prevention leads to a broadening of the scope of competencies needing to be assessed as part of a complete evaluation. In this chapter, I intend to explore the use of competency-based assessment within the context of planning sex offender treatment. In developing the SOSCT, competency was operationally defined in terms of an individual's interactions with his or her environment, that is, by the occurrence of adaptive behaviors in a specific situation or class of situations (Hops, 1983; Scheidt & Schaie, 1978). Thus, the

SOSCT assessed the effectiveness in terms of behaviors within a specified class of situations directly related to the commission of a sex crime. In this chapter, I draw on a broader definition of competency. That is, competence can be seen as an asset or characteristic of a person—an ability or capacity that exists in the person. A competency, therefore, can consist of a motive, trait, skill, aspect of self-image, social role, or body of knowledge that leads to effective performance (Wexley & Klimoski, 1984). Although competency can be measured within the context of specific situations, this is often difficult within a clinical context. In addition, the behavioral analogue procedures used in such assessments often have limited generalizability and unproven predictive validity. Necessary competencies can also be described in terms of the tasks and characteristics required of an individual within a specified context but can be measured in a less situation-specific manner. Thus, assessment within a competency-based model can involve the selection of instruments that reflect the behavior repertoire of an examinee, measuring the kind of things an examinee can do, rather than his or her relative standing in a defined group of other examinees (Nitko, 1980). For example, the fact that a particular individual's score on a measure of emotional empathy is lower than 50% of a norming population is less important than knowing that this particular individual is generally unable to understand other people's emotional reactions.

Criterion-Referenced Tests

Before beginning a discussion of competency assessment, we must explore the issue of criterion-referenced tests and criterion-based validity. Because our interest in competency assessment is the measurement of behavior repertoire and attributes that lead to effective performance within selected contexts, our tests must measure these factors. Test norming generally involves providing a *derived score* that allows testers to interpret the meaning of the *raw score,* that is, the actual score obtained when summing across items on a test. These derived scores (e.g., percentile rank, linear standard scores, normalized standard scores, grade equivalents, IQs) define an individual's relative standing in a defined group (Nitko, 1980). For example, an individual who obtains a full-scale IQ of 70 is defined as mentally retarded. We do this because his or her intelligence quotient is two standard deviations below the mean (IQ on Wechsler tests have a mean of 100 and a standard deviation of 15) of the general population. That is, this person is less smart than more than 95% of us. However, this score tells us nothing about what this particular individual can or cannot do.

It may be possible to develop derived scores that reflect the behavior repertoire of an individual—that is, the kinds of things he or she can do, rather than his or her relative standing in a particular group (Glaser & Klaus, 1962). Specifically, criterion-referenced measures provide information on where an individual lies on a continuum of skill attainment or the degree of competence that has been obtained by a particular individual, independent of references to the performance of others (Glaser, 1963). An example of this, with which many of us are familiar, is the Examination for the Professional Practice of Psychology (EPPP) administered in the United States as part of state licensure procedures for psychologists. Other examples include college entrance examinations, such as the American College Test (ACT) and the Scholastic Aptitude Test (SAT), which can be part of college admission criteria in the United States. These tests predict performance in a given context, professional psychology for the EPPP, and college grade point averages for the ACT and the SAT. This is what we are interested in when we perform competency-based assessment.

Criterion-referenced tests measure performance within a particular domain of behaviors. To develop a test and provide meaning to the score obtained, it is necessary to be able to articulate and define the behaviors within the domain to be measured. Without well-defined domains, it is impossible to develop a criterion-referenced assessment strategy (Nitko, 1980). In addition, because our goal with criterion-referenced assessment is to measure a behavior repertoire or the competence with which an individual performs within a given environmental context, not only must the behavior, cognitive, or attitudinal domains be defined, but they also must be ordered in some meaningful way such that higher test scores correspond with increased ability to reach a specific behavioral end point.

Measurement domains can be ordered in a number of ways, depending on the goals of the assessment. Behavior domains can be ordered in terms of the social or aesthetic quality of one's performance (e.g., the techniques necessary to produce a virtuoso violin performance), the difficulty or complexity of the subject matter (e.g., assessment of mathematics attainment by beginning with addition, then moving to subtraction, multiplication, and division), the degree of proficiency with which complex tasks are performed (e.g., the judges' scoring at a figure skating or gymnastics meet), the prerequisite learning or developmental sequences necessary to attain competent performance (e.g., ability to float, then to swim), or along some dimension or hypothetical factor, a latent trait (see Nitko, 1980, for an explanation of these).

Although a complete explanation of the process of developing and standardizing a criterion-referenced test or assessment process is beyond the scope of this chapter, it is my goal to explain the process and to provide strategies for conducting competency-based assessment of sex offenders. Of particular interest is the ordering of a competency domain with respect to latent traits. That is important for sex offender assessment because of the paucity of available criterion-referenced tests and the complexity of the behavioral domains in which assessment is necessary. Nitko (1980) explains this process as linking latent trait levels to well-defined subdomains of behaviors or skills. This can be very difficult when one conceptualizes the assessment process as relying on a single scale. However, as will be explained later in this chapter, this task is less diffi-cult when one looks at the behavioral domain as being reliant on multiple latent traits. Thus, the level of each trait, as well as the number of necessary traits pres-ent in the individual, may indicate competence within the defined domain.

In summary, competency-based assessment relies on the concept of crite-rion-referenced testing. Our goal, when assessing the level of competence of offenders, is to determine whether they can perform a certain set of tasks effec-tively; we are not interested in their standing relative to other individuals on such performance, except to the extent that their relative standing indicates an inability to do what is required within the context being measured.

Competency-Based Sex Offender Assessment

Miner et al. (1989) described the development of a situational competency test for assessing the coping skills of sex offenders. This behavioral-analogue assessment measured the ability of individuals to identify situations that could lead to sexual offending and to develop and articulate appropriate coping strate-gies. The situations included in this test were obtained by careful evaluation of the types of situations that preceded the commission of sex offenses by a sample of incarcerated offenders (see Day, Miner, Nafpaktitis, & Murphy, 1987; Miner et al., 1989). As described in Miner et al. (1989), the SOSCT is administered via audiotape, and the responses of the offenders can be recorded on either audio- or videotape. Trained raters, who provide scores on a variety of scales, then observe the tapes.

The easiest and most reliable measures are latency (or time from the end of the prompt to the beginning of the offender's response) and duration (the elapsed time of the response). Recent preliminary data analysis indicates that the cumulative latency measure is associated with success after release from treatment (Marques & Day, 1998). Although these are the easiest scores to obtain and show positive psychometric properties, they are of little value to the clinician. Even if the preliminary predictive validity holds up with later analy-ses, the latency and duration measures will still be of limited utility in clinical settings because they provide no information on the quality of a response or of response topography.

Early investigation of the psychometric properties of the SOSCT indicated a wide variability in the reliability coefficients for effectiveness ratings across test items, with many items showing poor interrater agreement (Day & Miner, 1989). In general, the level of reliability was related to the location of a risk situ-ation on a conceptual behavior chain. The more proximal risk situations (e.g., you are helping a neighbor with a kid's birthday party and you run out of ice cream) showed higher interrater reliability than more distal risk factors (e.g., you have just had an argument with your partner). The further development of the SOSCT, including better anchoring of the effectiveness ratings and more explicit scoring criteria, has awaited other priorities of the staff conducting California's Sex Offender Treatment and Evaluation Project. Thus, the problems that existed in the scoring protocol in 1989 have yet to be addressed.

The test presented in our 1989 chapter (Miner et al., 1989) assesses the coping skills of sex offenders within a domain of situations generated by sampling sex offenders' offending patterns. The sampling frame for developing the SOSCT was appropriate to the conceptualization of relapse prevention described in Laws (1989). That is, the intervention focused and was guided by the behavior chain (see Nelson & Jackson, 1989) constructed by an offender to describe the events leading up to his offenses. In our reconceptualization of the process of relapse, we have broadened our focus beyond a singular path, hypothesizing multiple domains and different types of risks, depending on the goals of an individual (Ward & Hudson, 1998). Certainly, as we look at relapse prevention from a more broad perspective, we see that coping is required in a range of situations and not simply limited to those proximal to offending. The clinician interested in a competency-based assessment would look to other situations in which coping is necessary and the skills and other characteristics necessary for successfully negotiating such situations. In our development of the SOSCT, we attempted to include items that would reflect situations that were not just immediately proximal to an offending opportunity but also reflect more distal situations, such as a conflict with an intimate partner (Miner et al., 1989). It was our thought that such a strategy would make the SOSCT more reflective of the range of skills that offenders would require to avoid high-risk situations and to avoid reoffending. Research, to date, on the SOSCT does provide some data on our success in reaching this goal (Marques & Day, 1998).

The behavioral-analytic model used to develop the SOSCT would appear to be an important and useful strategy for developing assessment tools. However, its weakness, as reflected in the experience with the SOSCT, is that it provides no mechanism for explicitly ordering the skills necessary for a competent response; it simply provides a method for identifying appropriate situational contexts.

Competency-based assessment typically involves the measurement of skills expressed in terms of behavioral objectives (Kennedy, 1976). Competency can also be more broadly defined such that it consists of motives, traits, skills, aspects of self-image, social role, and bodies of knowledge that lead to effective performance within a specified domain (Wexley & Klimoski, 1984). In the remainder of this chapter, I build on the knowledge gained from the SOSCT and describe a process by which one might develop a competency-based assessment of sex offenders.

Identifying Relevant Domains and Component Skills

Relapse prevention is and always has been a social-cognitive framework (Nelson, Miner, Marques, Russell, & Achterkirchen, 1989; Ward & Hudson, 1998). Thus, the assessment of competency is, by definition, an assessment of behaviors within a social domain. However, the clinician will wish to investigate a range of social competencies when evaluating any type of sex offender.

Social competence has been described in a recent study of risk factors for child molesters in terms of the quality of peer relationships, the level of heterosexual attachments, and the number of marriages (Prentky, Knight, & Lee, 1997). One often includes under this domain the ability to acquire and maintain employment. The domain of social competency, therefore, involves a range of skills, knowledge, and attitudes that would lead to effectively developing peer relationships, being able to develop and maintain involvement with members of the opposite gender, and having an ability to maintain intimate relationships. In addition, the socially competent individual would need the skills and knowledge necessary to acquire and maintain gainful employment as well as the motivation to do so.

Viewing social competence within the seven-phase relapse framework proposed by Ward and Hudson (1998), one can see that the ability of the offender to function in socially proscribed roles will readily affect his reaction to life events and whether these events lead to desires for offending. In addition, the ability of an offender to function on a day-to-day basis further influences the type of goals he might adopt with respect to reoffending. That is, the less socially competent the offender, the less he has to lose by engaging in sexually abusive behavior.

As defined here, social competence reflects the ability of the individual to engage in behaviors that will allow him to develop meaningful interpersonal relationships, maintain intimate relationships with others, and maintain gainful employment. That is, how does the offender function in society in areas other than sex offending?

The goal of assessment within this domain is to determine the weaknesses and strengths of the individual in fulfilling his various social roles. For example, does the offender have the level of social skills necessary to make a reasonable impression on perspective friends, partners, or employers? Are his assertiveness skills such that he can effectively function with adults? Does he have marketable job skills? Table 12.1 presents an example of the skills that one might want to assess to determine the competence of an individual for developing and maintaining interpersonal relationships.

Empathy

Within the overall domains described earlier, subareas reflect constellations of skills. One example of this is empathy. Empathy has been described as

TABLE 12.1   Specific Skills for Assessment of Peer and Intimate Relationships

Conversation skills

Assertiveness skills

Ability to negotiate

Ability to express feelings

Ability to identify others' feelings and nonverbal cues

involving four types of skills: the ability to recognize another person's distress, the ability to take the other's perspective and see events from his or her point of view, the ability to generate the same or similar emotions as those observed in the other, and the ability to take action to alleviate the observed person's distress (Davis, 1983; Marshall, Hudson, Jones, & Fernandez, 1995). It is not clear whether sex offenders have an overall deficit in empathy or whether their lack of ability to empathize is limited to victims of sexual abuse or, even more specifically, to their victims (see Marshall et al., 1995, for a review of this literature). It may also be that empathic deficits are temporally specific and influenced by other variables such as sexual arousal. Although empathy deficits may not be a common element to sex offenders, some evidence shows that those who lack the capacity for empathy (e.g., those defined as psychopaths or having antisocial personality disorder) are more likely to reoffend (Gretton, McBride, & Hare, 1995; Rice & Harris, 1997). In addition, empathy training is a common element in sex offender treatment (Freeman-Longo, Bird, Stevenson, & Fiske, 1995) and may be especially important to the development of approach goals in the reformulated model presented in this book.

Although a number of measures exist to assess empathy, their relevance to sex offenders is questionable. As indicated earlier, there is accumulating evidence that sex offenders do not have general empathy deficits, but their issues of empathy are related directly to their offenses and to the victims of those offenses. Therefore, constructing an assessment strategy for measuring empathy deficits in a sex offender population presents some unique problems.

Basing our strategy for ordering skill measurement on Marshall et al. (1995) and Davis (1983), we can construct a sequence of skills for assessing an individual's empathic competency. A precursor to being competent in empathy is the ability to identify one's own emotional reactions (Ward, Keenan, & Hudson, in press). The individual who is capable of this may then be able to identify the emotional reactions of others. Those unable to identify their own emotions would not be likely to be aware of others' emotional reactions. Thus, measuring one's awareness of his or her own emotional reactions is an important first step in a competency-based assessment of empathy. The next level of competence would be the ability of an individual to identify the emotional reactions of others. Although Marshall and Maric (1996) did find deficits in child molesters using the Hogan (1969) Empathy Scale, it may be that measuring this ability to identify the emotional reactions of others in some general way may not be effective in identifying empathy deficits in sex offenders. Research does indicate that offenders may be able to identify emotional reactions in most circumstances, but they are deficient in such assessment when confronted by potential victims or in offending situations. Lipton, McDonel, and McFall (1987) found that rapists have problems identifying indicators of negative mood states in first-date situations, and Malamuth and Brown (1994) suggest that sexually aggressive men are relatively incompetent in decoding women's emotions, specifically seeing fear as surprise and friendly behavior as seductive. Hudson et al. (1993) found a more general inability for sex offenders to identify emotions, most likely confusing surprise and anger with disgust.

The individual who is able to identify emotions in others must then be able to take another's perspective to be competent in expressing empathy. This perspective taking forms a third level of competency. Again, as with identification of emotions, it is possible that the deficits of sex offenders are not in their ability to take another's perspective in most situations but may be related specifically to sexual offending situations. Thus, assessment may need to consider the characteristics of an offending situation, not just the ability to take another's perspective in any emotional situation.

The competency-based assessment of empathy then involves the measurement of an individual's ability to generate the emotions that another is feeling—that is, to feel their pain. This may again need to be measured within the context of the offending situation. Finally, the competent individual would do something to alleviate the hurt felt by the other person.

Fernandez, Marshall, Lightbody, and O'Sullivan (1999) report on the development of an empathy measure for child molesters. Using three vignettes—one describing a child-accident victim, one describing a child-molest victim, and one specific to the offender's offense—the measure assesses the ability of an individual to identify a child's feelings and how the individual feels about the child. This measure, which assesses two of the five tasks described earlier in this section, has shown good reliability and the ability to show treatment changes and differences between child molesters and controls. This instrument is a good example of a competency-based assessment tool, which can be used in assessing empathy.

Decision Making

An important concept in relapse prevention is the idea of the problem of immediate gratification (PIG). The PIG implies a decision-making process that focuses on the immediate positive outcome of a set of alternatives while ignoring the long-term aspects of the decision. Assessment of the decision-making domain can be used as another example of how to develop a competency-based assessment. The first step in being able to make a decision is assessing the ability to see alternatives. That is, can the individual identify a number of possible behaviors available in a particular situation? Then, the next task in decision making is to identify the consequences of each alternative. The next level of competence would be an ability to determine the positive and negative aspects of each consequence and to see both long-term and short-term consequences. The next step in an assessment would be to measure the ability of an individual to value the various types of consequences. That is, what are the relative weights given to short-term positive, short-term negative, long-term positive, and long-term negative consequences? Finally, the last step would be the ability to choose behaviors that balance all four types of consequences and advance a long-term agenda. This process is taught and can be assessed using the decision matrix (Jenkins-Hall, 1989). Certainly, effective decisions about offending behaviors, avoiding risky situations, or keeping a balanced budget depend on the degree of cognitive distortions (see Langton & Marshall, 2000 [this volume]), issues of denial (see Mann, 2000 [this volume]), and skills such as reality testing and objectivity. Certain personality traits, such as low self-esteem, narcissism, impulsivity, and psychopathy, would interfere with the therapeutic process and interfere with decision-making competency.

Implications for Assessment Strategies

In the preceding section, I outlined the process of identifying the elements to be assessed using a competency-based assessment strategy and the ordering of these elements so that one can arrive at a meaningful measure of competence. The above areas are meant as examples, and many experts and clinicians can likely come up with other domains to be assessed. The key element in a competency-based assessment is the focus on outcome, not characteristics. In the general psychological assessment process, one looks to describe individuals in terms of their characteristics, then to categorize them in some meaningful way. In a competency-based assessment, the task is to describe the skills possessed by individuals, their motivations to use those skills, and any intra- or interpersonal characteristics that might interfere with their using these skills within a specified set of life situations. Although one generally looks to criterion-referenced tests in such an assessment, one does not have to exclusively rely on such procedures. Because criterion-referenced tests within the domains described in this chapter are often rather cumbersome, relying on behavioral-analogue procedures, the outpatient clinician may choose to use more standard paper-and-pencil measures of the domains of interest, as well as the results of clinical interviews and record reviews. Those working in settings that allow for direct observation may find themselves able to use observational sampling procedures to assess offenders in their daily routines on many of the important skills, knowledge, and characteristics.

A competency-based assessment strategy is an integral part of a relapse prevention orientation toward intervention. Relapse prevention is a competency-based intervention, focusing on self-regulation (Ward & Hudson, 1998). That is, the interventions to be applied must be guided by assessing the skills that an offender brings to treatment and the motivations that the offender has to use those skills in multiple contexts.

Conclusions

In this chapter, I have outlined the major concepts of a competency-based strategy toward assessment. Competency-based assessment has its foundation in two areas: the recent move in education toward accountability and the movement within professional training toward competency-based training programs. Within forensic psychology and psychiatry, we have a long history of competency-based assessment, that is, assessments of competency to stand trial. Such assessments have, by statute and legal precedent, needed to focus on the abilities of the defendants, not just their personality or psychiatric characteristics. It has never been sufficient to determine that an individual suffered from schizophrenia; it is necessary for the assessor to show that the characteristics of this disorder within this individual interfere with his or her ability to perform the tasks necessary to contribute to his or her defense. That is, the competency assessor must show that the individual is unable to understand the proceedings, is unable to perform specified tasks, and lacks the abilities necessary to cooperate with an attorney and mount an effective, not necessarily a successful, defense.

Relapse prevention, as described initially (Laws, 1989; Nelson et al., 1989; Pithers, Marques, Gibat, & Marlatt, 1983) and in its reformulation (Hudson & Ward, 1996; Ward & Hudson, 1996, 1998; Ward, Hudson, & Marshall, 1994, 1995; Ward, Louden, Hudson, & Marshall, 1995), can be viewed as a competency-based intervention strategy. That is, the focus is on helping individuals develop specific skills and knowledge that will allow them to perform effectively within a range of domains that have been identified as leading to reoffending. The clinician working within such a framework emphasizes performance goals—that is, does the client "walk the walk," rather than just "talk the talk"? Assessment within such a framework, therefore, must be performance based as well. By this, I do not mean that we must directly assess the performance of an individual within real-life situations, although that certainly would be optimal. However, when developing our assessment strategies, we can take a competency-based approach. Such an approach requires that we, as clinicians, be cognizant of the skills, knowledge, cognitive styles, and personality traits necessary for an individual to effectively function within the multiple domains that comprise their everyday existence and will allow them to avoid future criminal behavior.

Clearly, there is a need for much more research in the area of assessment. We have identified a number of variables that are important to evaluate when assessing sex offenders. However, our instrumentation for such assessments is either lacking or has poor or as yet untested psychometric properties. Assessments based on the factors leading to successful performance within identified social domains will lead directly to appropriate intervention strategies and provide feedback to both the client and the clinician on progress toward completion of treatment. These benefits, however, are only possible with well-designed, reliable, and valid assessment tools.

References

Davis, M. H. (1983). Measuring individual differences in empathy: Evidence for a multidimensional approach. *Journal of Personality and Social Psychology, 44,* 113-126.

Day, D. M., & Miner, M. H. (1989). [Kappa statistics for SOSCT item effectiveness ratings]. Unpublished raw data.

Day, D. M., Miner, M. H., Nafpaktitis, M. K., & Murphy, J. F. (1987). *Final report: Development of a situational competency test for sex offenders.* (Available from David M. Day, California Department of Mental Health, 1600 Ninth Street, Sacramento, CA 95814)

Fernandez, Y. M., Marshall, W. L., Lightbody, S., & O'Sullivan, C. (1999). The child molester empathy measure: Description and examination of its reliability and validity. *Sexual Abuse: A Journal of Research and Treatment, 11,* 17-31.

Freeman-Longo, R. W., Bird, S. L., Stevenson, W. R., & Fiske, J. (1995). *1994 nationwide survey of treatment programs and models.* Brandon, VT: Safer Society.

Glaser, R. (1963). Instructional technology and the measurement of learning outcomes. *American Psychologist, 18,* 519-521.

Glaser, R., & Klaus, D. J. (1962). Proficiency measurement: Assessing human performance. In R. Gagné (Ed.), *Psychological principles in systems development* (pp. 419-474). New York: Holt, Rinehart & Winston.

Goldfried, M. R., & D'Zurilla, T. J. (1969). A behavior-analytic model for assessing competence. In C. D. Spielberger (Ed.), *Current topics in clinical and community psychology* (Vol. 1, pp. 151-196). New York: Academic Press.

Gretton, H., McBride, M., & Hare, R. D. (1995, October). *Psychopathy in adolescent sex offenders: A follow-up study.* Paper presented at the annual conference of the Association for the Treatment of Sexual Abusers, New Orleans, LA.

Hogan, R. (1969). Development of an empathy scale. *Journal of Consulting and Clinical Psychology, 33,* 307-316.

Hops, H. (1983). Children's social competence and skills: Current research practices and future directions. *Behavior Therapy, 14,* 3-18.

Hudson, S. M., Marshall, W. L., Wales, D., McDonald, E., Bakker, L. W., & McLean, A. (1993). Emotional recognition skills of sex offenders. *Annals of Sex Research, 6,* 199-211.

Hudson, S. M., & Ward, T. (1996). Relapse prevention: Future directions. *Sexual Abuse: A Journal of Research and Treatment, 8,* 249-256.

Jenkins-Hall, K. D. (1989). The decision matrix. In D. R. Laws (Ed.), *Relapse prevention with sex offenders* (pp. 159-166). New York: Guilford.

Kennedy, D. A. (1976). Some impressions of competency-based training programs. *Counselor Education and Supervision, 5,* 245-250.

Langton, C. M., & Marshall, W. L. (2000). The role of cognitive distortions in relapse prevention programs. In D. R. Laws, S. M. Hudson, & T. Ward (Eds.), *Remaking relapse prevention with sex offenders: A sourcebook* (pp. 167-186). Thousand Oaks, CA: Sage.

Laws, D. R. (1989). *Relapse prevention with sex offenders.* New York: Guilford.

Lipton, D. N., McDonel, E. C., & McFall, R. M. (1987). Heterosocial perception in rapists. *Journal of Consulting and Clinical Psychology, 55,* 17-21.

Malamuth, N. M., & Brown, L. M. (1994). Sexually aggressive men's perceptions of women's communications: Testing three explanations. *Journal of Personality and Social Psychology, 67,* 491-503.

Mann, R. E. (2000). Managing resistance and rebellion in relapse prevention intervention. In D. R. Laws, S. M. Hudson, & T. Ward (Eds.), *Remaking relapse prevention with sex offenders: A sourcebook* (pp. 182-200). Thousand Oaks, CA: Sage.

Marques, J. K., & Day, D. M. (1998). *Sex offender treatment and evaluation project. Progress report.* (Available from Program Development and Evaluation Branch, California Department of Mental Health, 1600 Ninth Street, Room 350, Sacramento, CA 95814)

Marshall, W. L., Hudson, S. M., Jones, R., & Fernandez, Y. M. (1995). Empathy in sex offenders. *Clinical Psychology Review, 15,* 99-113.

Marshall, W. L., & Maric, A. (1996). Cognitive and emotional components of generalized empathy deficits in child molesters. *Journal of Child Sexual Abuse, 5,* 101-110.

Miner, M. H., Day, D. M., & Nafpaktitis, M. K. (1989). Assessment of coping skills: Development of a situational competency test. In D. R. Laws (Ed.), *Relapse prevention with sex offenders* (pp. 127-136). New York: Guilford.

Nelson, C., & Jackson, P. (1989). High-risk recognition: the cognitive-behavioral chain. In D. R. Laws (Ed.), *Relapse prevention with sex offenders* (pp. 167-177). New York: Guilford.

Nelson, C., Miner, M., Marques, J., Russell, K., & Achterkirchen, J. (1989). Relapse prevention: A cognitive-behavioral model for treatment of the rapist and child molester. *Journal of Social Work and Human Sexuality, 7,* 125-143.

Nitko, A. J. (1980). Distinguishing the many varieties of criterion-referenced tests. *Review of Educational Research, 50,* 461-485.

Pithers, W. D., Marques, J. K., Gibat, C. C., & Marlatt, G. A. (1983). Relapse prevention with sexual aggressives: A self-control model of treatment and maintenance of change. In J. G. Greer & I. R. Stuart (Eds.), *The sexual aggressor: Current perspectives on treatment* (pp. 214-234). New York: Van Nostrand Reinhold.

Prentky, R. A., Knight, R. A., & Lee, A. F. S. (1997). Risk factors associated with recidivism among extra familial child molesters. *Journal of Consulting and Clinical Psychology, 65,* 141-149.

Rice, M. E., & Harris, G. T. (1997). Cross-validation and extension of the Violence Risk Appraisal Guide for child molesters and rapists. *Law and Human Behavior, 21,* 231-241.

Scheidt, R. J., & Schaie, K. W. (1978). A taxonomy of situations for an elderly population: Generating situational criteria. *Journal of Gerontology, 33,* 848-857.

Ward, T., & Hudson, S. M. (1996). Relapse prevention: A critical analysis. *Sexual Abuse: A Journal of Research and Treatment, 8,* 177-200.

Ward, T., & Hudson, S. M. (1998). A model of the relapse process in sexual offenders. *Journal of Interpersonal Violence, 13,* 700-725.

Ward, T., Hudson, S. M., & Marshall, W. L. (1994). The abstinence violation effect in child molesters. *Behaviour Research and Therapy, 32,* 431-437.

Ward, T., Hudson, S. M., & Marshall, W. L. (1995). Cognitive and affective deficits in sexual aggression: A cognitive deconstructionist analysis. *Sexual Abuse: A Journal of Research and Treatment, 7,* 67-83.

Ward, T., Keenan, T., & Hudson, S. M. (in press). Understanding cognitive, affective, and intimacy deficits in sex offenders: A developmental perspective. *Aggression and Violent Behavior.*

Ward, T., Louden, K., Hudson, S. M., & Marshall, W. L. (1995). A descriptive model of the offense chain for child molesters. *Journal of Interpersonal Violence, 10,* 452-472.

Wexley, K. N., & Klimoski, R. (1984). Performance appraisal: An update. In A. P. Brief (Ed.), *Managing human resources in retail organizations* (pp. 75-93). Toronto: Lexington Books.

CHAPTER 13

Contextual Issues in Relapse Prevention Treatment

YOLANDA M. FERNANDEZ
W. L. MARSHALL
Queen's University, Ontario

We believe that the context within which treatment is provided, whether for sexual offenders or for any other group of clients, can have a significant influence on the degree to which the clients change. Contextual issues influence the enthusiasm with which therapists deliver treatment and the ease with which therapeutic interventions can be implemented. These same issues affect the participation of our clients in treatment and the extent to which they can comfortably carry out homework assignments.

A number of yet unexamined contextual features might influence the overall effectiveness of treatment. The structural aspects of treatment (i.e., the manner in which clients are allocated to treatment and the support of other staff in institutions or other agencies in the community) are quite important, and yet have received very little attention in the literature.

In addition to the structural aspects of the context of treatment, there are the features of the actual delivery of treatment. The questions here are the following: Is it best to adopt an individual one-on-one approach or do all or most of treatment in groups? Should we employ open- (sometimes called "rolling") or closed-group formats? Or should treatment be seen as a set of psychoeducational components or as a therapeutic process having as a guide a set of treatment targets? Whichever option is chosen, the questions become, "How can we create the most facilitative therapeutic environment?" and "What characteristics should the therapist display to be most effective?" Finally, there is the postrelease context to be considered. Are any postrelease (or postdischarge from a community clinic) conditions necessary, such as restrictions on the client's behavior, supervision by a parole officer or a client-identified support group, and additional community treatment or booster courses?

In the course of this chapter, we hope to raise the relevant issues for each of these topics in a way that will allow the reader to come to his or her own conclusions. We will, however, quite clearly state our position on these matters.

The Structural Aspects of Treatment Provision

The first aspect of these structural issues within an institutional setting concerns the advantages or disadvantages of creating a sexual offender-specific institution. One of us (Marshall) has had the opportunity of working within two such institutions: Kia Marama, New Zealand's institution, where imprisoned child molesters receive treatment (Hudson, Marshall, Johnston, Ward, & Jones, 1995), and Scotland's Peterhead Prison (Spencer, 1998). In Kia Marama, security and other nontherapy staff were selected because they were willing to work supportively with these offenders and with therapy staff, and at Peterhead, staff were persuaded by the excellent governor (Alec Spencer) to be supportive. A separate sexual offender-specific institution is, we believe, the ideal setting in which to run treatment programs for sexual offenders. However, it does bring some problems, not the least of which is that many offenders are removed from ready access by their families. As an alternative mixed-offender program, Bath Institution, in which we operate our treatment programs, is a programs-devoted prison where security staff wear street clothes, address inmates by their first names, and are supportive of treatment. Harassment of sexual offenders by other prisoners is kept to a minimum by the threat of transfer of the harasser to a less hospitable institution. Within Bath Institution, all offenders (who also wear street clothes) have the opportunity to have frequent face-to-face visits with their families and reasonably frequent conjugal visits. These opportunities encourage our clients to implement many of the skills they are acquiring in treatment, particularly those having to do with the enhancement of intimacy and social skills. In any event, having a treatment-supportive environment, where the administrative and security staff attempt to facilitate effective treatment, provides an environment where treatment participation and effectiveness are maximized, whether it be within a sexual offender-specific institution or one where there are other prisoners.

Earlier, we (Marshall, Eccles, & Barbaree, 1993) outlined what we called a "three-tiered" approach that had been implemented within the Ontario Regional Penitentiaries. Although that structure is still in place, there have been some modifications and expansions of treatment opportunities. The aim of the structure is to direct sexual offenders to the treatment program most suited to their needs in an institution that meets their security requirements. When sexual offenders enter the Ontario region, they participate in the Millhaven Institution's Assessment Unit, where they are interviewed and phallometrically assessed, and they complete a battery of paper-and-pencil tests. On completion of this assessment, sexual offenders are placed in one of several maximum-, medium-, or minimum-security institutions according to estimates of their treatment and security needs, as well as according to their potential to create management problems. High-needs sexual offenders are sent to an institution (high medium security) that has an extensive program adapted to their needs. Moderate-needs offenders go to an institution (low medium security) that has a somewhat less extensive program, and low-needs offenders are placed where their limited problems can be effectively addressed (minimum-security institution).

As to the extent of treatment, a high-needs sexual offender can be expected to spend 6 months in sexual offender-specific treatment and an additional 12 months in other relevant programs (e.g., anger management, substance abuse, cognitive skills) before being transferred to a lower-security institution, where he will complete another 3 to 4 months of what is essentially a prerelease program. Moderate-needs offenders will spend 4 months in sexual offender-specific treatment, plus another 8 to 10 months of ancillary treatment, and the low-needs offenders will spend a total of 6 months in programs. As the readers of the chapter by Marshall and Anderson (2000 [this volume]) will see, we believe that any more extensive involvement in treatment (including limited community treatment) may be counterproductive.

If a client adamantly refuses to participate in treatment, he will likely be sent to a medium- or maximum-security institution that has no sexual offender program. If he changes his mind at any time, he will be transferred to a treatment institution. Refusal to enter treatment is not always matched by denial, nor is denial always matched by a refusal to enter treatment. Because there is evidence that denial does not predict recidivism (Hanson & Bussière, 1998), we have essentially abandoned our attempts to get deniers to admit their guilt while allowing them to participate in a program that addresses their criminogenic needs.

This overall approach not only maximizes the effective use of limited resources, but it also addresses the obvious heterogeneity of sexual offenders, at least in terms of their varied treatment needs. Correctional Services of Canada, it should be understood, provides a remarkable range of treatment opportunities for all offenders, including sexual offenders, so we are not suggesting that they provide insufficient resources; it is just that resources will always be limited in some way because society must spend its funds sensibly on many things. When a sexual offender who has been determined to have extensive treatment needs has completed the high-needs program, he will be transferred to one of the lower-level programs as a preparation for subsequent release into the community. When released into the community, he will be carefully supervised for the first 6 months and involved in treatment, with both treatment and supervision being gradually reduced according to the progress displayed. When moderate-needs offenders complete their somewhat less-extensive program, they may be transferred to minimum-security institution for a prerelease program or released directly to the community, depending on how well they did in treatment. Some of these moderate-needs offenders may be required to enter a community program, and all will receive less-intensive supervision on release. Low-needs offenders receive minimal institutional treatment, no postrelease treatment, and minimal supervision. Again, these strategies are meant to put our resources where they are most needed.

We have had the fortunate opportunity to see Correctional Services of Canada move from offering a single institutional program for sexual offenders in the Ontario region, with no collateral programs and no community programs, to a full array of programs in seven prisons and community programs in numerous cities throughout the province. This expansion of programs has also occurred in all other provinces of Canada. Most of this considerable expansion began in 1989 under the wise direction of the then-Commissioner Olè Ingstrup, who fortunately has now returned as commissioner. The framework for treatment that we have described has had a positive effect on the way offenders view the system, making them more cooperative with treatment. In general, it has fostered in the inmates a view of the system (and, by corollary, society in general) as more just and reasonable than were the procedures in the past. The percentage of sexual offenders receiving appropriate treatment has increased remarkably from the start of limited treatment in 1973 to the extensive treatment opportunities offered today. Furthermore, as noted by Marshall and Anderson (2000), Correctional Services of Canada's programs for sexual offenders are very effective.

The Delivery of Treatment

Timing of Treatment

In prison settings, a problem arises concerning when treatment should be implemented. This is most problematic with those offenders who have received long sentences. For instance, if a sexual offender is given a 10-year sentence and he is determined to have extensive treatment needs, he will enter an extensive sexual offender program at the appropriate institution. In addition, he will be directed to enter one or more other programs. In all our institutions, numerous collateral programs also meet some aspects of the needs of sexual offenders (e.g., substance abuse, conflict resolution, cognitive skills, and living without violence). These programs are 6 weeks long and psychoeducational in format, typically involving five full-day sessions per week. Even when our hypothetical high-needs sexual offender is required to complete several of these collateral programs and the extensive sexual offender-specific program, the completion of all programs will take no more than 18 months. The question we are faced with concerns whether it is better to do any or all of these programs early in a long sentence or shortly before release. If we have the offender commence treatment early in his 10-year sentence, this will reduce the likely apathy and resentment that may onset with a long delay in entry to treatment. Because treatment is reasonably close in time to the offense, it should be relatively easy for the client to recall details of the offense and concurrent problems in his life at the time of the offense. However, the processes of institutionalization may erode some of the benefits gained from treatment by the long delay from treatment termination to release. If we delay the onset of treatment until near-imminent release, we may have to overcome an entrenched, resentful attitude and a loss of memory for relevant details. This is a dilemma for which there is no ready solution.

What the high-needs institution does in the Ontario regional penitentiaries is have a long-termer's pretreatment program facilitated by one of the exemplary graduates of their extensive program. This is intended to encourage optimism, instill and maintain a positive approach to treatment, and accustom the new-comers to group processes. In our institutions, we also provide maintenance programs for successful graduates of the sexual offender programs. The aim of these programs is, of course, to ensure that treatment benefits are not eroded before release. These maintenance programs meet once every 2 weeks, so they are not taxing on our resources.

Open Versus Closed Groups

In our programs at Bath Institution, we have elected to follow an open (or "rolling") format of treatment. We will begin by briefly describing an open for-mat, and then we will discuss some of the reasons why this approach may have advantages over the closed-group format.

Typically in closed groups, all clients begin the treatment program together and progress simultaneously through various treatment components (i.e., dis-closure, cognitive distortions, victim empathy, social and relationship skills, offense cycle, relapse prevention), eventually completing treatment within a predetermined period. The hallmark of an open group is that offenders do not begin treatment at the same time. Instead, as group members complete the treatment program and space becomes available, new members are added to the group. Similar to the closed group, each subject completes the same treatment components. In contrast, however, at any one time, different group members may be providing disclosures, addressing distortions, working on victim empathy and intimacy issues, creating an offense cycle, or discussing relapse prevention strategies. The feature targeted for a particular offender during a session depends on how far along he is in the treatment program.

There are several advantages to open-format groups. To begin with, in closed groups, an offender is usually in treatment for a predetermined period (e.g., 6 months), whereas in open-ended groups, the amount of time spent in treatment can be adjusted according to the needs of the individual. As mentioned previously, in the Ontario region of the Correctional Services of Canada, all incoming sexual offenders are thoroughly assessed and allocated to the appropriate institution based on a variety of criteria. Although the most salient feature for placement should be and typically is the extent of the offender's treatment needs, other important factors (i.e., institutional adjustment, escape risk) may have a strong influence on the placement of an individual. Consequently, a treatment group in any particular institution may have greater differences between group members in terms of risk and treatment needs than might be preferred. In an open group, because offenders do not progress through treatment components simultaneously, individual components may be expanded to accommodate offenders with higher needs without slowing the progress of other lower-needs members. Also, an open-ended format allows brighter offenders to progress more rapidly, whereas lower-functioning clients can take their time without feeling singled out. In addition, as offenders move through the system (i.e., cascade from higher- to lower-security institutions), most will have participated in several treatment programs at the various stages in this movement. At each of the lower stages, then, these offenders may not need another full program but could benefit from specific aspects of treatment in which they did not do well in the earlier program.

Sexual offenders are also quite heterogeneous. As Marshall, Anderson, and Fernandez (1999) noted, the responses of sexual offenders to almost all measures demonstrate a greater degree of variability than conformity. Open groups lend themselves to working with such heterogeneous populations because the therapist has much greater flexibility in adapting the program to the particular needs of each client. Consequently, the therapist is able to avoid a "cookbook" approach in which all subjects are treated with exactly the same techniques at exactly the same time regardless of their problems, personal style, attitude, or readiness for change. That is, open groups have the flexibility to customize the treatment program to the clients' needs.

An important aspect of group therapy is to encourage mutual support and assistance among clients, both within and between therapy sessions. In open groups, some offenders are nearing the end of their treatment program, and others are just beginning. This structure offers the more "senior" members of the group an opportunity to encourage and support the newer group participants. The senior members have the opportunity to demonstrate their newly acquired knowledge and to behave in a nurturing fashion toward another member. The ability to be nurturant is related to effective social and intimacy skills and to the capacity for empathy, all of which are goals of therapy (Marshall, Anderson, & Fernandez, 1999). Such "success" experiences, with which these men are not usually familiar, contribute to improved self-esteem. As newer members progress through treatment and become senior members, they too have the opportunity to take on the role of "mentor" to new group members. An additional benefit for the therapist is that, in our experience, senior group members provide poignant and constructive challenges to new group members. Senior members are typically able to empathize with the new offenders' reasons for engaging in denial or cognitive distortions and provide appropriate challenges based on their own similar experiences. Such challenges are generally considered more credible by the offenders than the challenges offered by therapists. These challenges also assist both the person being questioned and the questioner because the latter relies on his own experience to provide his challenge. Moreover, this process provides vicarious learning for all group members.

Active participation is considered essential to most treatment programs. Participation facilitates the acquisition of new skills and attitudes (Bandura, 1986) and appears to promote self-awareness and self-confidence (Marshall, Anderson, & Fernandez, 1999). It also provides the therapist with an opportunity to judge how deeply the offender has internalized prosocial treatment-oriented attitudes. In open groups, the senior members, who may have been in treatment for several weeks to months, are typically comfortable enough with the treatment process to actively engage in discussions. Consequently, they are able to model active participation for newer group members. In addition, the therapeutic rapport already established with senior members provides the therapist with an opportunity to show the newer group members that active participation will be rewarded and encouraged.

So far, we have outlined many of the benefits open groups offer the offenders. However, open groups also provide benefits for the therapists. As mentioned earlier, we have noticed that open groups appear to encourage more active participation and effective challenges from the senior group members. Consequently, the therapist does not have to break down denial and challenge cognitive distortions alone. This collaborative approach can accelerate some offenders' progress through the denial, minimization, and cognitive distortion aspects of treatment. Therapists who use open groups have reported that treatment sessions seem more interesting because they deal with a variety of issues within one session rather than focusing on a single topic for a significant length of time. Finally, therapists indicate that the open format provides ample opportunity to deal with important issues as they arise, facilitating a better therapeutic relationship. For example, if a client comes to the group and discloses that his wife has suddenly left him, the therapist can immediately address the problem and simply allow extra time for the distressed client to progress to the next stage of treatment. The other group members may benefit from a discussion dealing with relationship difficulties without affecting the timeline of the group as a whole.

When discussing open groups, the concern voiced most often by therapists is that they will not remember which aspect of the program each group member is to be working on during a session. For a variety of reasons, this happens far less often than this concern might suggest. However, when the therapist does forget, the best way to deal with it is to simply ask the offender. This strategy allows the therapist to show that he or she is human and makes mistakes, just like the offender, and it provides an appropriate model for dealing with mistakes, that is, to ask for clarification and admit when help is needed.

Process of Treatment

Most sexual offender treatment programs are cognitive-behavioral in design (Marshall & Fernandez, 1998) and emphasize the use of specific procedures. As a result, interest in therapeutic processes appears to have been neglected in recent years (Marshall, Anderson, & Fernandez, 1999). However, it has been shown that therapist style and client-therapist relationship characteristics contribute to the variance in outcome displayed by behavioral interventions (Schaap, Bennum, Schindler, & Hoogduin, 1993), and sexual offender therapists are beginning to recognize the importance of therapist features for changing the behavior and cognitions of their clients (Marshall, Mulloy, & Serran, 1999).

Although confrontational approaches to therapy remain popular, emerging research suggests that such a style will elicit limited, if not negative, effects on sexual offenders. Beech and Fordham (1997) found that a confrontational approach to treating sexual offenders failed to produce the hoped-for improvements on various measures of treatment change. Kear-Colwell and Pollack (1997) point out that a therapist using a confrontational style approaches therapy with negative assumptions about the client that, they suggest, hinders treatment progress. Such therapists behave in authoritarian and aggressive ways to "break through" the client's denial. Kear-Colwell and Pollack claim that this unempathic style leads self-confident or assertive offenders to become resistant and argumentative. As a result, the client is then considered to be uncooperative and is removed from treatment. Those confident clients who remain in treatment, Kear-Colwell and Pollack suggest, adopt a manipulative strategy of pacifying the therapist by simply agreeing on all issues. In contrast, clients who lack self-confidence simply yield to the therapist's demands, thereby further eroding their self-esteem. Either way, it is unlikely clients will benefit from a confrontational style.

Marshall (1996) has proposed that sexual offender therapists discard the confrontational approach and instead rely on therapeutic styles that have been shown to maximize treatment benefits. Marshall, Anderson, and Fernandez (1999) provide a list of therapist behaviors that lead to the creation of a positive therapeutic climate. Most of the identified features have long been held as necessary characteristics of an effective therapist (Butler & Strupp, 1986; Frank, 1973). For example, warmth, empathy, and acceptance of the client by the therapist have been considered critical by most earlier schools of psychotherapy, and recent research suggests the same is true for cognitive-behavioral therapy (Safran & Segal, 1990; Schaap et al., 1993).

When challenging sexual offenders regarding issues to do with denial, minimization, or other examples of cognitive distortions, we suggest that it is best to do so in a supportive and nonthreatening way. The same is true for other embarrassing or distressing issues. In sexual offender treatment, the therapist may begin this process by clearly distinguishing the offender from his or her offensive behavior. In our treatment program, this is achieved in part by enforcing a rule that participants do not describe themselves in derogatory terms. That is, we do not allow clients to describe themselves as sexual offenders, child molesters, or rapists; in particular, we do not permit them to use colloquial descriptors, such as "diddlers" or "rape hounds." The therapist instructs the client to think of himself as someone who has engaged in unacceptable behavior but is not an unacceptable person. In fact, these clients have characteristically engaged in far more prosocial than antisocial activities, and their strengths are all too frequently overlooked by sexual offender therapists. Bumby (1994) has suggested that perceiving oneself as an offender may be expected to engender shame, which implies that he is unchangeable. In contrast, if the client perceives that his behavior is problematic, he will likely feel guilt, which facilitates a belief in the potential for change. In addition, the enforcement of the above rule indicates to the client that the therapist is both understanding and sympathetic to his problem while nonjudgmental of him as a person.

Throughout treatment, we attempt to promote an appropriate therapeutic climate by enhancing clients' self-confidence. We specifically adopt those therapist characteristics that have been demonstrated to facilitate behavior change. In particular, we emphasize a respectful, empathic, and rewarding approach to clients and encourage clients to model our style of interaction with each other. We also encourage all other institutional staff to behave respectfully toward the group participants. Men who have been incarcerated for a sexual offense often expect to be condemned by others. In an effort to reduce the likelihood of rejection and negative feedback, the offender may adopt problematic strategies. For example, an offender who is worried about being condemned for molesting his daughter might describe the victim in negative terms and portray himself in a positive light, thereby avoiding discussion of important issues. We suggest that providing feedback in a manner that enhances rather than degrades clients' self-esteem is crucial to allowing them to face the reality of their offenses. In an effort to further enhance self-esteem, clients are encouraged to attend to personal appearance and self-presentation, as well as upgrading educational and vocational skills. We also require our clients to rehearse throughout each day a list of positive features about themselves. This combination of strategies has been shown to effectively enhance the self-esteem of our clients (Marshall, Champagne, Sturgeon, & Bryce, 1997), and these changes in self-esteem are related to improvements in other treatment targets (Marshall, Champagne, Brown, & Miller, 1997), including reductions in deviant arousal (Marshall, 1997).

Finally, as part of a more positive approach to therapy, our treatment program now focuses on approach goals rather than avoidance goals. Mann (1998) noted that current relapse prevention models focus on negative issues by requiring offenders to identify obstacles to remaining offense free. Although this is obviously quite sensible, Mann pointed out that the evidence from other bodies of literature indicates that approach goals are more readily attained than avoidance goals. Consequently, she suggested that treatment should focus on identifying and building on clients' strengths rather than focusing only on problems. Marshall, Anderson, and Fernandez (1999) suggest that concentrating on clients' deficits may inadvertently imply that we do not believe our clients have the ability to meet their needs in prosocial ways. This is obviously not a message we wish to convey. As part of our effort to emphasize strengths, for example, we explore situations with our clients in which they had the opportunity to offend but did not. Such situations aid in identifying future strategies for remaining offense free.

Conclusions

In this chapter, we have discussed the structural and delivery aspects of treatment. We believe that, in conjunction with the type of relapse prevention model we have noted in another chapter of this book (Marshall & Anderson, 2000), the allocation to different levels of intensity of treatment outlined earlier and the approach to treatment we have described provide an optimal therapeutic environment for treating sexual offenders. Presently, however, much of what we have had to say in this chapter reflects what we think makes good sense. What is now essential is that these ideas be put to empirical test. We have begun the arduous task of ascertaining the effects of various therapeutic processes, but no single group of researchers could possibly address more than limited features of the possible factors that influence outcome. Therefore, we encourage others to take up the investigation of these important issues.

References

Bandura, A. (1986). *Social foundations of thought and action: A social cognitive theory.* Englewood Cliffs, NJ: Prentice Hall.

Beech, A., & Fordham, A. S. (1997). Therapeutic climate of sexual offender treatment programs. *Sexual Abuse: A Journal of Research and Treatment, 9,* 219-237.

Bumby, K. M. (1994, November). *Cognitive distortions of child molesters and rapists.* Paper presented at the 13th Annual Research and Treatment Conference of the Association for the Treatment of Sexual Abusers, San Francisco.

Butler, S. F., & Strupp, H. H. (1986). Specific and nonspecific factors in psychotherapy: A problematic paradigm for psychotherapy research. *Psychotherapy, 23,* 30-40.

Frank, J. D. (1973). *Persuasion and healing.* Baltimore, MD: Johns Hopkins University Press.

Hanson, R. K., & Bussière, M. T. (1998). Predicting relapse: A meta-analysis of sexual offender recidivism studies. *Journal of Consulting and Clinical Psychology, 66,* 348-362.

Hudson, S. M., Marshall, W. L., Johnston, P., Ward, T., & Jones, R. (1995). Kia Marama: New Zealand Justice Department's programme for incarcerated child molesters. *Behaviour Change, 12,* 69-80.

Kear-Colwell, J., & Pollack, P. (1997). Motivation and confrontation: Which approach to the child sex offender? *Criminal Justice and Behavior, 24,* 20-33.

Mann, R. E. (1998, October). *Relapse prevention? Is that the bit where they told me all the things I couldn't do anymore?* Paper presented at the 17th Annual Research and Treatment Conference of the Association for the Treatment of Sexual Abusers, Vancouver, British Columbia.

Marshall, W. L. (1996). The sexual offender: Monster, victim, or everyman? *Sexual Abuse: A Journal of Research and Treatment, 8,* 317-335.

Marshall, W. L. (1997). The relationship between self-esteem and deviant sexual arousal in nonfamilial child molesters. *Behavior Modification, 21,* 86-96.

Marshall, W. L., & Anderson, D. (2000). Do relapse components enhance treatment effectiveness? In R. D. Laws, S. M. Hudson, & T. Ward (Eds.), *Remaking relapse prevention with sex offenders: A sourcebook* (pp. 39-56). Thousand Oaks, CA: Sage.

Marshall, W. L., Anderson, D., & Fernandez, Y. (1999). *Cognitive behavioural treatment of sexual offenders.* London: Wiley.

Marshall, W. L., Champagne, F., Brown, C., & Miller, S. (1997). Empathy, intimacy, loneliness, and self-esteem in nonfamilial child molesters. *Journal of Child Sexual Abuse, 6,* 87-97.

Marshall, W. L., Champagne, F., Sturgeon, C., & Bryce, P. (1997). Increasing the self-esteem of child molesters. *Sexual Abuse: A Journal of Research and Treatment, 9,* 321-333.

Marshall, W. L., Eccles, A., & Barbaree, H. E. (1993). A three-tiered approach to the rehabilitation of incarcerated offenders. *Behavioral Sciences and the Law, 11,* 441-445.

Marshall, W. L., & Fernandez, Y. M. (1998). Cognitive-behavioural approaches to the treatment of the paraphiliacs: Sexual offenders. In V. Caballo (Ed.), *International handbook of cognitive and behavioural treatments for psychological disorders* (pp. 281-312). Oxford, UK: Elsevier Science.

Marshall, W. L., Mulloy, R., & Serran, G. (1999). *The identification of treatment-facilitative behaviors enacted by sexual offender therapists.* Unpublished manuscript, Queen's University, Kingston, Ontario, Canada.

Safran, J. D., & Segal, Z. V. (1990). *Interpersonal process in cognitive therapy.* New York: Basic Books.

Schaap, C., Bennum, I., Schindler, L., & Hoogduin, K. (1993). *The therapeutic relationship in behavioural psychotherapy.* New York: John Wiley.

Spencer, A. (1998). Peterhead Prison Program. In W. L. Marshall, Y. M. Fernandez, S. M. Hudson, & T. Ward (Eds.), *Sourcebook of treatment programs with sexual offenders* (pp. 29-46). New York: Plenum.

CHAPTER 14

External Supervision

How Can It Increase the Effectiveness of Relapse Prevention?

GEORGIA F. CUMMING
Vermont Center for the Prevention and Treatment of Sexual Abuse

ROBERT J. McGRATH
Vermont Treatment Program for Sexual Aggressors

Convicted sex offenders typically undergo a period of correctional supervision in the community. Some are sentenced directly to community supervision, but others are returned to the community on supervision following a period of incarceration. Even in the United States, where incarceration rates are among the highest in the world, recent estimates indicate that more than one half of sex offenders are serving their sentences in the community under probation, parole, or some other community release status (Greenfeld, 1997). Of those sex offenders who are incarcerated in the United States, sentencing practices allow almost every one of them to eventually return to the community, typically after serving only a portion of his or her original sentence (Maguire & Pastore, 1995). Given these practices and numbers, society has a vested interest in ensuring that effective strategies are used to manage sex offenders while they are being supervised in the community.

This chapter details supervision practices that may be used to effectively manage sex offenders in the community to enhance public safety. The supervision practices described have evolved from the initial application of the relapse prevention model to supervising sex offenders pioneered in Vermont in the early 1980s (Pithers, Cumming, & Martin, 1989; Pithers, Marques, Gibat, & Marlatt, 1983). We will discuss how this model has evolved over the past several years and how it is now applied on a day-to-day basis to manage sex offenders. Our description of the practical application of this model includes how offenders are prepared to transition from prison to the community and how offenders are supervised in the community. In addition, data on the effectiveness of various supervision models are reviewed. Because most identified sex offenders are male, male pronouns will be used. The term *supervising officer* is used to identify community correctional officers, whether they are probation, parole, furlough, or some other type of community supervision officer or agent.

Evolution of the External Supervision Dimension

In 1982, the Vermont legislature appropriated funds to create the Vermont Treatment Program for Sexual Aggressors (VTPSA). The VTPSA began as a 16-bed prison-based treatment program and soon evolved into the first integrated statewide system of inpatient and outpatient sex offender treatment programs. Currently, Vermont's continuum of care for sex offenders comprises a 36-bed intensive prison program for higher-risk offenders, a 32-bed short-term prison program for moderate-risk offenders, and 11 geographically dispersed outpatient programs. During a typical year, approximately 90 sex offenders receive treatment in prison programs and 325 in outpatient treatment programs. The outpatient programs offer varying levels of service intensities for offenders who are released to the community from prison and for lower-risk offenders who are given probationary sentences. Treatment in each of these programs is typically delivered in a group format and is informed by treatment guidelines developed by Vermont's network of treatment providers (McGrath, 1995).

The original application of relapse prevention with sex offenders in the prison-based VTPSA emphasized teaching offenders self-control strategies (Pithers et al., 1983). This aspect of the model, now known as the internal self-management dimension (Pithers, Cumming, Beal, Young, & Turner, 1988), relied solely on the offender and therapist to identify problematic behaviors and apply appropriate coping strategies. Unfortunately, when offenders were released to the community, they often did not fully discuss lapses with their outpatient therapist and supervising officer. Their reticence to discuss such problem behavior and thinking patterns was often related to the fear that reporting lapses might result in their return to prison. Although understandable, this type of secrecy probably increased their risk of returning to prison. Concerns with how to more effectively identify lapses by the offender, enhance community safety, led to the development of the external supervisory dimension of the relapse prevention model (Pithers et al., 1988).

The external supervisory dimension originally comprised three elements, and a fourth element has been added recently. In the first of these four elements, officers are taught the principles of relapse prevention and learn to use these to supervise each sex offender on their caseload. Second, officers assist each offender in creating an informed network of individuals to assist in supporting him and monitoring his behavior in the community. Third, officers refer each offender to a specialized sex offender treatment program and develop a collaborative relationship with the mental health professionals conducting the therapy. Fourth, officers refer offenders for polygraph examinations to monitor their compliance with supervision conditions. These four elements comprise the "supervision diamond" detailed in Figure 14.1.

To implement the external supervisory dimension, it was necessary to develop a training program that would provide supervising officers with the skills to use the principles of relapse prevention. The training program is divided into a three-part series. The first part, titled "Sex Offender Profiles," introduces officers to the typologies and characteristics of sex offenders and compares their similarities and differences. The trainers give an overview of the Vermont Department of Corrections' (DOC) treatment programs and policies on risk reduction and risk control. The second part is titled "Assessment of Sex Offenders" and details how to complete a specialized presentence report. This report will determine amenability to treatment, type of risk the offender poses to the community, and specialized conditions of probation needed to manage risk if a probationary sentence is ordered. The third part is titled "Supervision of the Sex Offender" and covers relapse prevention principles, identification of risk factors, and implementation of supervision strategies to monitor those risk factors as described by Cumming and Buell (1997).

Our experience in training supervising officers has been that they are not particularly interested in recent theoretical debates about the sequencing and subtleties of the relapse prevention model. We continue to keep the application of relapse prevention principles as concrete and practical as possible. We begin with the premise that a sex offender's deviant sexual behavior is typically preceded by an identifiable and predictable chain of behaviors, emotions, and cognitions. Although initial formulations of the relapse prevention model theorized a relapse pathway common to all sex offenders (e.g., Pithers et al., 1988), not surprisingly, recent research suggests that there are multiple pathways to relapse among sex offenders (e.g., Ward, Louden, Hudson, & Marshall, 1995). Hence, our training emphasis with supervising officers is on learning to examine the particular offense patterns of each of their supervisees and developing supervision plans accordingly.

Another shift in our training of supervising officers is to encourage them to help offenders develop healthy lifestyles and positive coping strategies. These

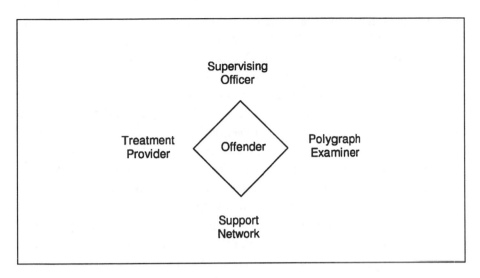

Figure 14.1. Supervision Diamond

types of interventions were highlighted in the development of the relapse prevention model with sex offenders (Pithers et al., 1983). However, our experiences in supervising staff in Vermont and conducting training throughout the
United States and Canada suggest that such approach goal-oriented interventions take a backseat to an emphasis on avoidance strategies. Understandably,
supervising officers do not want their supervisees to reoffend, and considerable
supervision efforts are focused on ensuring that offenders do not engage in certain types of risk behaviors. Thus, sex offenders typically have conditions that
begin with phrases such as "You shall not . . ." and "You may not . . . ." Pro-
hibiting sex offenders from engaging in high-risk behaviors such as having
contact with victims, loitering around potential victims, and abusing alcohol
are reasonable and appropriate types of community supervision conditions.
And monitoring and enforcing such conditions is an appropriate part of a supervising officer's responsibilities. However, these types of avoidance strategies,
by themselves, probably have limited value in helping sex offenders develop
long-term changes.

In addition to saying "no" to offenders, supervising officers should help
offenders develop a positive and balanced lifestyle. These approach interventions include traditional supervision activities such as brokering education, job
training, employment, and mental health services. In addition, they should
include the development of leisure time activities, healthy friendships, and
appropriate civic involvement.

The second element of the external dimension, the development of a community-based collateral network, also emphasizes the development of positive
approach strategies in addition to including a monitoring function. The steps to
develop a community-based collateral network are included in the portion of

the training dealing with supervision strategies. The collateral network is made up of the important people in the offender's life who interact with him on a regular basis. These individuals could include a spouse, family members, friends, employer, Alcoholics Anonymous sponsor, and church members. As will be discussed later, one purpose of the network is to assist the offender in making and supporting positive lifestyle changes. Another purpose of the network is to assist the officer in gaining information regarding the offender's adjustment in the community. Lapses can be more easily identified and effectively dealt with early in the relapse process so that the offender does not relapse. Network members are educated about the relapse prevention model, with a particular focus on the offender's individual risk factors. In addition, they are taught how to look for warning signs of possible relapse. Members of the network become involved because they care about the offender and want to assist him in this process. Thus, it is important for the officer to explain how collaboration can help the offender be successful in the community without relapsing.

The third element of the external dimension is specialized sex offender treatment and the officer's liaison with the treatment providers. Officers refer sex offenders to mental health clinicians that provide specialized sex offender treatment under contract with the DOC. The DOC provides a minimum payment for each treatment group. Thus, although each offender is expected to pay at least a portion of his treatment fees according to sliding fee scales, if these fees do not add up to the agreed-on contract amount, the DOC will make up the difference to the provider. Contract providers are located in both the private and public sectors.

The contracted providers agree to follow treatment guidelines that use a cognitive-behavioral relapse prevention treatment model. The development of these guidelines was a collaborative effort among Vermont's prison- and community-based treatment network (McGrath, 1995). As recommended in these guidelines, treatment is conducted primarily in a group format, and offenders sign authorizations of disclosure that enable open and frequent communication between the treatment provider and supervising officers. Such communication is deemed essential and focuses on the offender's application of skills learned in treatment. Equally important is communication about the offender's ongoing risk factors so that treatment and supervision interventions can be adjusted as needed for community protection.

To support consistency and quality among treatment programs, contract providers attend monthly supervision meetings facilitated by the VTPSA clinical director. These supervision meetings occur in three different locations around the state so that travel time is not a significant impediment to the provider. The focus of these meetings is on treatment planning, reviewing recent research findings, and addressing any current systems concerns, such as problematic prosecution or sentencing practices. In addition, these meetings serve as an opportunity for providers to receive emotional support from other professionals who are also working with this difficult population.

Once a year, treatment providers and supervision officers are invited to VTPSA-sponsored statewide 2-day training events. The first day of these joint training sessions usually involves workshops by local professionals on assessment, supervision, treatment, or program development topics. The second day typically involves a presentation by a nationally or internationally known clinician or researcher in the sex offender or criminology field. Our most valuable resources in managing sex offenders are our staff. Our modest investment in training our teams of clinicians and supervision officers offers an improved quality of services. Such training also enhances an esprit de corps among staff that can positively influence staff commitment to providing quality services.

The fourth element of the external supervisory dimension is the use of polygraphy. Although polygraphy has been used in a variety of ways with sex offenders (Blasingame, 1998), the Vermont programs have limited use of this tool to what has been termed *monitoring examinations*. These exams are typically administered to higher-risk sex offenders released from prison, on furlough, or on parole. During a monitoring examination, a sex offender on community supervision is asked questions concerning whether he has followed his supervision and treatment conditions since being placed in the community or since his last polygraph exam. Typical exam questions target issues such as unauthorized contact with potential victims, criminal behavior, pornography use, and substance abuse. Supervision and treatment staff use test results to modify treatment and supervision plans to better manage the risk factors of each offender. It is important to note that we do not use polygraph test results in any legal proceeding and do not consider polygraph results to be sufficient evidence to determine facts or to serve as the basis for terminating an offender from treatment. Polygraphy is only one of several tools used in the supervision of sex offenders and does not replace the field supervision provided by officers.

The application of the four supervision elements has evolved considerably over the years. When the Vermont treatment programs were developed, we were influenced by the prevailing belief that most sex offenders posed a very high risk for reoffense. We accordingly tended to supervise all sex offenders at a high level of supervision. As research more clearly identified sex offender risk factors, we began to match the intensity of supervision services to the risk level of the offender. Applying this principle (Andrews, Bonta, & Hoge, 1990), the VTPSA now uses assessment tools such as the Vermont Assessment of Sex Offender Risk (McGrath & Hoke, 1997), the Rapid Risk Assessment for Sex Offense Recidivism (Hanson, 1997), and the Violence Risk Appraisal Guide (Quinsey, Harris, Rice, & Cormier, 1998).

Because the predictive validity of each of these risk tools is far from perfect and because we would initially rather err on the side of providing too much supervision than too little, all sex offenders initially start out under a high level of supervision. If a sex offender scores low risk on these instruments, his level of supervision is reduced when he has entered treatment, established an appropriate residence, obtained employment, and is compliant with supervision. Sex offenders who score in the high range on these instruments are maintained under a high level of supervision for 12 months before a reduction in supervision level is considered. Any offender, regardless of his initial risk assessment, who begins to evidence an increase in his risk is returned to a higher level of supervision. Indications of an offender's increased risk focus on an analysis of his dynamic risk factors. Hanson and Harris (1998) have identified the dynamic factors that appear to be most related to sexual reoffense risk.

In addition, we now emphasize and attend to the learning style of each offender and strive to improve officers' skills in the interactional elements of the supervision process. Andrews et al. (1990) have argued that correctional programs that attend to these responsivity factors have more positive outcomes than those that do not. All supervising officers are trained in motivational interviewing (McGrath, 1990; Miller & Rollnick, 1991), and supervising officers are encouraged to strive to develop a collaborative working relationship with their supervisees rather than one that is based purely on authority. Positive reinforcers are valued over punishers, and supervising officers are encouraged to interact with offenders in a direct, open, respectful, and nonpunitive manner. When limits need to be set, however, supervising officers are asked to deliver them in as firm, fair, and swift manner as possible. Similar to many other jurisdictions, graduated sanctions have taken a prominent role in our overall supervision strategy by matching the sanction to the severity of the infraction and risk of the offender.

Transition From Prison to Community

For an offender who has been incarcerated for an extended period, the first several months in the community are a critical transition period. Early in the development of our program, it was not uncommon for a sex offender transitioning from our prison-based program to the community to experience some backsliding. Out from under the constraints as well as the psychological safety and familiarity of the regimented prison lifestyle, some offenders would begin to act out. Some would become more argumentative and begin to break community supervision rules. We now anticipate and plan for this.

Six months prior to release, the focus in treatment begins to shift to planning more explicitly for the offender's transition to the community. The facility treatment team, composed of the program director, clinical director, assistant prison superintendent, treatment staff, and institutional caseworker, reevaluate the offender's treatment progress. Staff conduct an updated risk assessment that addresses both static and dynamic risk factors to assist in this planning process. The offender updates and presents his relapse prevention plan to his peers and treatment staff. Because we believe it is important for offenders to disclose their offenses and risk factors to employers and landlords, in preparation for release we ask them to role-play situations they are likely to encounter when applying for a job or looking for an apartment. Each offender is expected to participate actively in the selection and development of his support network. Often, sex offenders who have transitioned to the community from one of the prison programs come back to talk to program participants about their experiences of returning to society.

The offender's support network can include spouse, extended family member, friends, Alcoholics Anonymous sponsor, and pastor. Members of the support network are introduced to one another and work together as a team to help the offender transition safely back into the community. We have more recently added correctional volunteers to some of our support teams as we find many of our multiconvicted and higher-risk offenders no longer have family and friends who maintain contact. For these men, we have developed support teams composed almost entirely of correctional volunteers.

Volunteers have had an important role in Vermont corrections since the early 1970s. Using volunteers as part of a sex offender's support team was a natural extension of the DOC's philosophy of involving the community in rehabilitation efforts. Criteria for being accepted as a DOC volunteer include undergoing an NCIC record check and submitting a minimum of three references. Volunteers who are accepted by the DOC through this process and express an interest in working with sex offenders receive additional training. This training parallels the training that officers receive on sex offender typologies, characteristics, and the relapse prevention model, except that it is presented at a more basic level. Emphasis is placed on the role of the volunteer as a member of the offender's support network. The training highlights differences in working with the general correctional offender versus a sex offender involved in a treatment program. The collaborative relationship the volunteer will have with the supervising officer and other support network members is also highlighted. In earlier years, the focus for the network members was to identify lapse behavior and have them disclose this information to the supervising officer. Although this continues to be important, it is equally important for the network to help the offender reintegrate safely back into the community and provide opportunities for safe social interaction and friendship. Volunteers provide a significant social link to a "regular life." For this reason, the "collateral" network referred to in earlier relapse prevention literature (Pithers et al., 1988) is now referred to as the "support" network.

Three months prior to release, each offender is assigned to a parole officer. The prison caseworker sends the offender's treatment summary to the parole officer. This treatment summary details the offender's offense history, progress in treatment, identified risk factors, and relapse prevention plan. The supervising community officer has responsibility for verifying and giving final approval to the offender's residence and employment plan. Within that 3-month period, the supervising officer will meet with the facility treatment team and the offender. The purpose of the meeting with the offender, which the offender's primary therapist facilitates, is for the offender to outline his offense history, his risk factors, and his coping strategies. A similar meeting also takes place with the support network.

We have found that this combination of meetings reduces splitting by the offender after his release and is often the first opportunity for the support network to develop the sense of being part of a team. The relationship between the officer and the support network is critical in the success of this approach. The network must feel valued and respected by the officer. For higher-risk offenders, the support network will continue to meet as a team with both the offender and the supervising officer after the offender's transition into the community. The frequency of meetings is determined by the risk and needs of each offender. For example, sex offenders who have no family support and have served many years in prison will need more assistance. They may need help learning bus routes, shopping for food, cooking, and going for job interviews. They may also need help in dealing with predictable failures, such as being turned down for employment. The support network for this type of offender may meet together with the offender once a week to plan for the upcoming week and review the previous week.

We suggest that in areas that are more geographically disperse than Vermont, an alternative to face-to-face planning meetings with treatment staff, supervising officers, and the support network could be either videoconferences or phone conferences. We view such personal contacts as very important because written reports often do not adequately convey all of the information that is helpful to those who will be charged with supervising the offender in the community.

As part of the release plan, the supervising officer contacts an approved treatment provider to arrange treatment in the community. The supervising officer becomes the primary link between the prison program and the community-based treatment provider. In Vermont's more urban areas, offenders will attend up to three treatment groups per week for 6 to 9 months before transferring to a weekly group that then includes offenders on probation. In addition, offenders undergo a maintenance polygraph every 6 months and receive random home and employment checks from his officer.

As previously discussed, our supervision model requires monitoring according to the risk the offender presents. Supervision consists of supporting the offender in the change process, holding the offender accountable for even small infractions, and verifying compliance or noncompliance through direct observation, third-party communication, and the polygraph examination. A lapse is not necessarily viewed as a program failure or a personal failure on the part of the offender. We view lapses as an opportunity for offenders to learn and incorporate more readily the skills they have acquired in treatment. The supervision approach is one of support combined with high accountability for even minor transgressions.

Infractions are evaluated according to risk and needs. A graduated sanction approach is used if the lapse or parole infraction is assessed as allowing for a community-based response. Using a graduated sanction approach allows for a response that is geared to the seriousness of the lapse and the learning style of the offender. Typical graduated sanctions may result in a higher level of supervision, community service, restitution to the victim compensation fund, and increased attendance at Alcoholics Anonymous or other substance abuse-related treatment. In addition, the offender may be given assignments in the treatment group to address lapse behavior and develop new coping strategies for a particular risk factor.

Community Supervision

For the offender moving from prison to the community, the framework for supervision is established prior to the offender's release. While in prison, the offender reads and agrees to the conditions of furlough or parole supervision. Community-based treatment begins immediately on release. The support network has been selected and trained, and the supervising officer has been made aware of the potential pitfalls that the offender is likely to encounter.

Setting up the supervision framework with a probationer is another matter, especially under circumstances in which a presentence investigation has not been ordered by the court. Many sex offenders are able to present in a socially acceptable manner, and they frequently demonstrate low scores on general correctional risk assessment instruments. The risk they pose to the community may not be readily apparent. Consequently, we encourage judges and prosecutors to order a presentence investigation report on every sex offender. The presentence report enables the probation officer to begin to establish the framework for supervision. The suitability of the offender's current residence and employment is evaluated. Members of the offender's family and circle of friends are interviewed not only to verify the offender's self-report but also to assess their appropriateness and willingness to be part of the offender's support network. For a family member or friend to be part of the offender's support network, he or she must believe the offender committed the offense, be knowledgeable about the offender's offense dynamics, recognize risk factors, and be willing to speak with the supervising officer about the offender's activities. The offender is evaluated for special needs that he may have, such as substance abuse or mental health counseling, and whether volunteer services would be beneficial.

It is critical that the presentence report evaluates the offender's amenability to treatment. Three factors seem important in this determination (McGrath, 1991). The offender must acknowledge that he committed a sexual offense and accept responsibility for his behavior. The offender must consider his sexual offending behavior to be a problem that he wants to stop. And the offender must be willing to participate in treatment and abide by the special conditions of supervision.

Although recent research indicates that denial, in and of itself, may not be correlated with sexual offense recidivism (Hanson & Bussière, 1998), most sex offender treatment programs require sex offenders to acknowledge committing a sexual offense as part of the program admission criteria. This is notwithstanding the fact that deniers can be provided pretreatment intervention services that may assist them in overcoming denial. In Vermont, the DOC made a decision early in the development of treatment programs that an offender in denial will not be recommended for a community-based sentence. This decision is based on the belief that sex offenders who are placed in the community on probation should be actively participating in programs, including sex offender treatment, that are designed to reduce their risk. Consequently, the presentence report becomes another tool to break through a sex offender's denial with the possibility of incarceration becoming a motivation to disclose. This is particularly effective with sex offenders who take responsibility for their criminal behavior only when it is in their own best interests to do so. The presentence report also provides officers an opportunity to educate the legal system by explaining in lay language the rationale for their recommendation and the reasons for requesting the special conditions for community supervision. The report, as a result, can affect sentencing decisions and may motivate the sex offender to engage in treatment. Those few offenders who are placed on probation and are in denial typically receive a high level of supervision.

If probation is recommended, the supervising officer will include in the presentence report the special conditions of probation that will address the offender's precursors to deviant behavior. For example, a child molester may not be allowed to participate in friendships or relationships with women or men who have children, and a rapist may not be allowed to frequent bars, taverns, or businesses whose primary function is to serve alcoholic beverages. Just as the sex offender may fall through the cracks on standard corrections risk assessment instruments, standard probation conditions do not always provide the probation officer with the needed tool to intervene in the offender's relapse cycle. Thus, careful attention must be given to developing conditions that will be most effective in helping the offender not reoffend.

Although volunteers have become an essential part of the support network for many of the men in our prison-based programs, the majority of men on probation do not participate in our volunteer program. Understandably, sex offenders who receive probationary sentences commonly are first-time offenders with prosocial lifestyles and have an already existing and appropriate support network. Probationers who have developmental or psychiatric disabilities are the main recipients of our volunteer services. Typical services provided to these more needy offenders include assistance with treatment homework assignments and help with developing appropriate socialization activities. Both these activities provide ample opportunity for volunteers to encourage the offender in the treatment process and decrease the sense of isolation and rejection that many sex offenders feel as a result of their sexual offense conviction.

Because isolation and rejection are risk factors for some offenders, this is an important task not only for volunteers but also for the support network as a whole. The identified support network is educated about the relapse prevention model and receives information regarding the offender's offense and risk factors. Whenever possible, the sex offender makes the disclosure to individual members of his support network. The supervising officer verifies that the disclosure has been truthful and complete.

Ongoing Supervision

The case-planning process forms the basis for sex offender supervision and, as outlined in this chapter, is best developed in conjunction with the offender. This is not to say that offenders determine how they will be supervised. Rather, the most effective case plans are developed with the full awareness and understanding of the offender regarding his requirements and responsibilities during the duration of supervision. During the course of an offender's supervision, his case plan will reflect information that either supports the direction of the initial case plan or requires the use of a different approach. The case plan is not a fixed document. Changes occur in the case plan as new information is discovered, such as when the offender is making positive strides or when the offender is displaying high-risk behavior.

The success of the supervision network is dependent on the willingness and cooperation of the individuals involved to share information, as well as on the reliability of the information they provide. It is important for network members to know how the information they provide will be used and with whom it will be shared. Network members are encouraged to report any lapse behavior or other possibly important information to the supervising officer. They need to know that they may have only one piece of the puzzle, whereas the officer is the recipient of a wide range of information that is more telling of the offender's overall level of risk.

In evaluating problem behaviors, our officers are asked to consider the following:

(a) Is the offender self-reporting the lapse behavior?
(b) Is he keeping secrets that are being disclosed by third parties such as a network member or police officer?
(c) How serious is the lapse?
(d) To what extent does the lapse compromise community safety?
(e) What level of responsibility is the offender taking for the lapse behavior?
(f) Is the offender able to develop a plan to address the lapse behavior?
(g) Is the plan realistic?

Depending on the seriousness of the lapse, the supervising officer may need to take immediate action without consulting with the therapist or network members until after the fact. More frequently, because supervision is proactive rather than crisis driven, the officer is able to consult with the treatment provider and develop a coordinated response to the lapse behavior. Lapses provide the opportunity to reevaluate the offender's status and make changes in the case plan or treatment plan. Lapses become a reminder for the officer to confer with other network members as to the offender's overall behavior in the community.

Developing the case plan and the support network is initially time intensive. However, once the network is established and trained and the offender is in treatment, the officer's time involvement per month should decrease. It will always remain important for the officer to maintain regular contact with the offender, but it is equally important for the officer to have regular contact with the support network, law enforcement personnel, and the therapist. Supervision of sex offenders requires verifying what the offender says during office and field visits and focusing the discussion on the offender's sexually deviant behavior. Collectively, the network members will observe and interact with the offender for significant blocks of time during the week. This interaction is indicative of how well the offender is incorporating real change in his life.

Effectiveness of External Supervision

Having described and recommended a model of external supervision, a fair question is whether empirical support exists for the efficacy of this approach. First, we examine this issue by broadly reviewing what we know about the effectiveness of community supervision practices in general. We then narrow our focus to the effectiveness of community supervision strategies with sex offenders employing a relapse prevention model.

Several studies have evaluated the effectiveness of community supervision practices. Notably, in the largest randomized social science experiment ever conducted in the United States, RAND Corporation evaluated intensive supervision programs (ISPs) in 14 jurisdictions in nine states (Petersilia & Turner, 1993a, 1993b). Although this study's experimental design excluded sex offenders, given its size, quality, and scope, the results are instructive to those interested in ISPs with sex offenders as well. In brief, the study concluded that although ISPs were successful at holding offenders accountable for their offenses, they did not decrease recidivism rates. More encouraging, however, was the finding that ISP participants who were also involved in treatment recidivated at significantly lower rates than those who did not. Support for these findings is found in Gendreau's (1998) recent extensive meta-analytic review of the correctional outcome literature. His review also found that a combination of treatment and supervision was associated with reduced reoffense rates among the general criminal population, of which sex offenders were included, whereas supervision alone showed comparatively little or no benefit in reducing recidivism rates. Likewise, Cullen, Wright, and Applegate (1996) have reviewed this literature. One of their major recommendations for improving the effectiveness of community correctional practices is the coupling of treatment services and supervision.

Unfortunately, very few empirical studies have focused solely on the community supervision of sex offenders. Of these few, Romero and Williams (1983) conducted the earliest. They randomly assigned a group of 231 sex offenders to either probation with group psychotherapy or to probation only. At 10-year follow-up, they found no significant differences in the sexual recidivism rates between the two groups. Of course, sex offender treatment and supervision practices have evolved considerably from the ones that they described.

Compared to the practices described by Romero and Williams (1983), a treatment and supervision approach that is much more similar to the one we have outlined in this chapter was recently evaluated by Gordon and Packard (1998). They examined the recidivism rates of 306 men who completed an incarcerated sex offender treatment program. On release from prison, 209 of these offenders received up to 3 years of relapse prevention-based maintenance treatment and community supervision. The services provided to the other 97 offenders were typically limited to supervision by a community corrections officer. Although not randomly assigned, the two groups were similar on most variables measured. At a 5-year follow-up, statistically significant differences were found in the sexual recidivism rates between the two groups. The sexual recidivism rate of the treatment plus supervision group was 2% versus 8% for the supervision-only group.

Perhaps the most well-known relapse prevention-based sex offender treatment outcome study is California's Sex Offender Treatment and Evaluation

Project (e.g., Marques, 1984; Marques & Day, 1998). This rigorously designed study involved random assignment of sex offenders who volunteered to either treatment or no-treatment conditions. The treatment group participated in an intensive 2-year incarcerated program followed by 1 year of community-based relapse prevention treatment. While in the community, both the treatment and no-treatment groups received standard parole supervision. Although this longitudinal study is still in the follow-up phase of data collection, the lower rates of sexual reoffending among treated subjects is promising (Marques & Day, 1998). We can speculate that in addition to treatment, the collaborative effort of the treatment provider and supervision officer contributed to this lower recidivism rate. The community treatment provider's knowledge of each offender's relapse cycle helps to inform the parole officers how to more effectively supervise each parolee.

In Vermont, early evaluation of relapse prevention supervision and treatment programs was encouraging. Although one of these initial studies did not include a comparison group (Pithers & Cumming, 1989), it suggested that the sexual reoffense rate of the treatment sample was lower than the reoffense base rates of what would be expected among a comparable untreated sample. In the absence of a comparison sample, such an approach at estimating program effectiveness is justified, although certainly less than ideal. Another of these initial studies included a comparison group composed primarily of treatment dropouts (Hildebran & Pithers, 1992). Over an average follow-up period of 7 years, 6% of 60 treated offenders reoffended versus 33% of 40 untreated offenders. Of course, the treatment dropouts, by virtue of the fact that they had dropped out of treatment, were likely a higher risk group than the treatment group.

More recently, McGrath, Hoke, and Vojtisek (1998) evaluated an outpatient program in Vermont that was composed primarily of probationers. Of 122 sex offenders at risk in the community for an average of over 5 years, 71 participants enrolled in a comprehensive cognitive-behavioral and relapse prevention-based supervision and treatment program that employed the model described in this chapter. An additional 32 participants were referred to this program but were allowed to enter less specialized treatment services primarily due to geographic or scheduling reasons. The remaining 19 participants received only supervision services because they either denied their sexual offense or refused treatment. Except for the no-treatment group, whose members had more extensive nonsexual criminal histories, there were no other identified differences among factors related to reoffense risk found between the three groups. At follow-up, the group that received comprehensive cognitive-behavioral and relapse prevention-based treatment and supervision services demonstrated a statistically significant treatment benefit. In terms of sexual recidivism, 1.4% of the cognitive-behavioral treatment and supervision group subjects recidivated versus 15.6% of the nonspecialized group subjects and

10.5% of the no-treatment group subjects. The no-treatment group had the highest rate of nonsexual criminal convictions.

Unfortunately, the design of this recent Vermont study (McGrath et al., 1998) did not allow for the identification of the specific treatment or supervision variables that may have contributed to the differing recidivism rates among the three groups. However, for the purpose of this chapter, a few important hypotheses emerged in the study. Among the specialized treatment and supervision group, treatment and probation staff shared a common approach, a relapse prevention model, and conducted frequent case meetings. These elements were postulated as important contributing factors in the low sexual recidivism rates of the specialized treatment group. Conversely, poor and infrequent communication between treatment providers and probation officers in the less-comprehensive group resulted in delayed or no reporting of offender lapses to the probation officer. This may have contributed to the lower success of this group.

In the future, an important issue to examine will be how well sex offenders are able to maintain abstinence from sexual offending once off supervision. Of the sex offender outcome studies reviewed, only California's Sex Offender Treatment and Evaluation Project (Marques & Day, 1998) appears to have followed a large number of sex offenders after they have completed a period of community supervision. Their results suggest that recidivism rates rise considerably once supervision ends. That ongoing external supervision strategies may help sex offenders control their deviant sexual behavior is encouraging. That the effects of treatment may not be long lasting, without external supervision to enforce compliance, is obviously a concern. An emphasis on fostering continuing offender motivation and self-management skills is an important goal. However, if such interventions do not prove effective, extending periods of parole or probation supervision may be warranted.

Summary

There is currently strong evidence in the general criminology literature that a combination of community supervision and treatment is associated with reduced rates of recidivism. There is emerging evidence that this combination is also a productive approach with sex offenders. The promise of how community supervision of sex offenders using a relapse prevention model can be efficacious has been the topic of this chapter.

Currently, almost all outcome studies and meta-analyses on the effectiveness of community supervision in general and supervision of sex offenders in particular have limited their evaluations to broad classes of interventions. They do not focus attention on the specific components of these interventions. This is certainly the case with the elements of the external supervision dimension of relapse prevention that we have detailed in this chapter. However, although we await a more precise analysis of several specific external supervision components, practitioners on the front line must still supervise sex offenders, and they should use those approaches that appear to hold the most promise.

On the basis of results of current research findings and our belief in a set of commonsense supervision principles, it is our opinion that several broad practices that we have reviewed are warranted. Officer training should be a priority, and such training will result in better services to offenders. All sex offenders should be assessed using validated risk instruments, and the intensity of supervision services should be congruent with each offender's risk level. Supervising officers should target their supervision efforts to the needs of offenders that are believed to be most related to offending. Supervising officers should strive to develop prosocial collaborative relationships with offenders because this will enhance supervision outcomes. Sex offenders must inform family, friends, volunteers, and significant others about their relapse prevention plans, and these support persons should hold the offender accountable for leading a prosocial lifestyle. Supervision should not only be concerned with assisting offenders in avoiding high-risk scenarios but also emphasize helping offenders develop positive support systems and positive coping responses. Finally, frequent and close communication between the supervising officer, treatment provider, polygrapher, and support network can improve the ability of the offender to lead an abuse-free life.

References

Andrews, D. A., Bonta, J., & Hoge, R. D. (1990). Classification for effective rehabilitation: Rediscovering psychology. *Criminal Justice and Behavior, 17,* 19-52.

Blasingame, G. D. (1998). Suggested clinical uses of polygraphy in community-based sexual offender treatment programs. *Sexual Abuse: A Journal of Research and Treatment, 10,* 37-45.

Cullen, F. T., Wright, J. P., & Applegate, B. K. (1996). Control in the community: The limits of reform. In A. T. Hartland (Ed.), *Choosing correctional options that work: Defining the demand and evaluating the supply* (pp. 69-116). Thousand Oaks, CA: Sage.

Cumming, G. F., & Buell, M. M. (1997). *Supervision of the sex offender.* Brandon, VT: Safer Society.

Gendreau, P. (1998, October). *Making corrections work.* Paper presented at the 17th Annual Conference of the Association of the Treatment of Sexual Abusers, Vancouver, British Columbia.

Gordon, A., & Packard, R. (1998, October). *The impact of community maintenance treatment of sex offender recidivism.* Paper presented at the 17th Annual Conference of the Association for the Treatment of Sexual Abusers, Vancouver, British Columbia.

Greenfeld, L. A. (1997, February). *Sex offenses and offenders: An analysis of data on rape and sexual assault* (Report No. NCJ-163392). Washington, DC: U.S. Department of Justice.

Hanson, R. K. (1997). *The development of a brief screening scale for sexual offense recidivism.* Ottawa: Solicitor General of Canada.

Hanson, R. K., & Bussière, M. T. (1998). Predicting relapse: A meta-analysis of sexual offender recidivism studies. *Journal of Consulting and Clinical Psychology, 66,* 348-362.

Hanson, R. K., & Harris, A. (1998). *Dynamic predictors of sexual recidivism.* Ottawa: Solicitor General of Canada.

Hildebran, D. D., & Pithers, W. D. (1992). Relapse prevention: Application and outcome. In W. O'Donahue & J. G. Geer (Eds.), *The sexual abuse of children: Clinical issues* (Vol. 2, pp. 365-393). Hillsdale, NJ: Lawrence Erlbaum.

Maguire, K., & Pastore, A. L. (1995). *Sourcebook of criminal justice statistics—1994.* Washington, DC: Government Printing Office.

Marques, J. K. (1984). *An innovative treatment program for sexual offenders: Report to the legislature.* Sacramento: California Department of Public Health.

Marques, J. K., & Day, D. M. (1998). *Sex offender treatment and evaluation project: Progress report (May, 1998).* Unpublished report, California Department of Mental Health.

McGrath, R. J. (1990). Assessment of sexual aggressors: Practical clinical interviewing strategies. *Journal of Interpersonal Violence, 5,* 507-519.

McGrath, R. J. (1991). Sex offender risk assessment and disposition planning: A review of clinical and empirical findings. *International Journal of Offender Therapy and Comparative Criminology, 35,* 329-351.

McGrath, R. J. (Ed.). (1995). *Vermont clinical practices guide for the assessment and treatment of adult sex offenders.* Williston: Vermont Center for the Prevention and Treatment of Sexual Abuse.

McGrath, R. J., & Hoke, S. E. (1997). Vermont assessment of sex-offender risk. In G. F. Cumming & M. M. Buell (Eds.), *Supervision of the sex offender* (pp. 145-147). Brandon, VT: Safer Society.

McGrath, R. J., Hoke, S. E., & Vojtisek, J. E. (1998). Cognitive behavior treatment of sex offenders: A treatment comparison and long-term follow-up study. *Criminal Justice and Behavior, 25,* 203-225.

Miller, W. R., & Rollnick, S. (1991). *Motivational interviewing: Preparing people to change addictive behavior.* New York: Guilford.

Petersilia, J., & Turner, S. (1993a). Evaluating intensive supervision probation/parole: Results of a nationwide experiment. In *Research in brief.* Washington, DC: National Institute of Justice.

Petersilia, J., & Turner, S. (1993b). Intensive probation and parole. In M. Tonry (Ed.), *Crime and justice: A review of research* (Vol. 17, pp. 281-335). Chicago: University of Chicago Press.

Pithers, W. D., & Cumming, G. F. (1989). Outcome of the Vermont Treatment Program. In D. R. Laws (Ed.), *Relapse prevention with sex offenders* (pp. 313-325). New York: Guilford.

Pithers, W. D., Cumming, G. F., Beal, L., Young, W., & Turner, R. (1988). In B. K. Schwartz & H. R. Cellini (Eds.), *Relapse prevention* (pp. 123-140). Washington, DC: U.S. Department of Justice, National Institute of Corrections.

Pithers, W. D., Cumming, G. F., & Martin, G. R. (1989). Vermont treatment program for sexual aggressors. In D. R. Laws (Ed.), *Relapse prevention with sex offenders* (pp. 292-310). New York: Guilford.

Pithers, W. D., Marques, J. K., Gibat, C. C., & Marlatt, G. A. (1983). Relapse prevention with sexual aggressives: A self-control model of treatment and maintenance of change. In J. G. Greer & I. R. Stuart (Eds.), *The sexual aggressor: Current perspectives* (pp. 241-239). New York: Van Nostrand Reinhold.

Quinsey, V. L., Harris, G. T., Rice, M. E., & Cormier, C. A. (1998). *Violent offenders: Appraising and managing risk.* Washington, DC: American Psychological Association.

Romero, J. J., & Williams, L. M. (1983). Group psychotherapy and intensive supervision with sex offenders: A comparative study. *Federal Probation, 47,* 36-42.

Ward, T., Louden, K., Hudson, S. M., & Marshall, W. L. (1995). A descriptive model of the offense chain for child molesters. *Journal of Interpersonal Violence, 10,* 452-472.

PART V

SEXUAL PREFERENCE ASSESSMENT

CHAPTER 15

Remaking Penile Plethysmography

ROBERT J. KONOPASKY
Saint Mary's University, Nova Scotia

AARON W. B. KONOPASKY
Princeton University

Common Applications of Penile Plethysmography (PPG)

PPG Uses

Case 1: "Can PPG, a measure of penis size, identify sexual preference for men or women?"

Case 2: "Do PPG scores correlate with sexual paraphilias?"

Case 3: "Do PPG scores correlate with past criminal sexual behavior or future criminal sexual behavior?"

PPG Abuses

Case 4: "This man denies touching the boy. He says that he is not attracted to boys or men, just women. Does PPG contradict his report?"

Case 5: "This man denies molesting three female children. Does PPG indicate pedophilia?"

Case 6: "This sex offender denies raping her and says she consented. The parole board wants to know whether he will do it again. What does PPG say?"

AUTHORS' NOTE: Special thanks to Abby Wildman for her contributions to this research project.

Discussion of the Uses and Abuses of PPG

Because sexual offenses cause great and enduring harm, phallometrics, or penile plethysmography (PPG), has been used to provide information about these and even more kinds of cases. In this chapter, we argue that these three uses and these three abuses have shaped our understanding of PPG and led us to declare the test to be useful (Abel, Becker, Murphy, & Flanagan, 1981; Avery-Clark & Laws, 1984; Freund, 1965; Freund & Blanchard, 1989; Lalumière & Quinsey, 1994; Quinsey & Laws, 1990), and to conclude exactly the opposite, by issuing dire warnings about the lack of PPG reliability (Barbaree, Baxter, & Marshall, 1989), the lack of PPG validity (Hall, Proctor, & Nelson, 1988), and ethical problems related to PPG (Schouten & Simon, 1992).

Why are some applications, specifically—Cases 4 through 6—labeled as abuses? What would be wrong with using PPG in all the above kinds of cases? After all, we need information about sexual offenders, especially information that they cannot deny. Our need for such information does not mean, however, that PPG can provide it. At the same time, PPG may be useful even if it does not always identify pedophiles or rapists and even if it does not make very accurate predictions about who will rape. We suggest that there can be good clinical use of PPG if it is modified and if the sexual arousal scores are interpreted cautiously.

Organization of the Chapter

Hundreds of PPG studies have attempted to demonstrate the use of PPG in deciding about one or another of Cases 4 through 6. Some articles support the use of PPG in such cases (Abel, Barlow, Blanchard, & Guild, 1977; Harris, Rice, Quinsey, Earls, & Chaplin, 1992; Quinsey & Chaplin, 1984; Quinsey, Chaplin, & Upfold, 1984; Rice, Chaplin, Harris, & Coutts, 1994; Rice & Harris, 1997), but others do not (Blader & Marshall, 1989; Murphy, Krisak, Stalgaitis, & Anderson, 1984). The reviews, which summarize broader PPG issues (e.g., type of apparatus, PPG stimuli, scoring, and standardization) suggest that different methodologies produce different results (Murphy & Barbaree, 1994). Given the mixed messages in opposing studies and the many issues raised by reviews, the clinician is left unsure about what PPG can and cannot deliver.

A strategy had to be found to protect this chapter from being drawn into controversies—for example, whether PPG can discriminate between rapists and nonrapists—and/or reviewing the already good reviews of PPG. As an alternative, we concede that there are PPG controversies and that PPG has not delivered all of what we wanted, but we argue that research has supported PPG as a measure of sexual arousal and preference. The existence of some positive demonstrations of PPG validity makes it unreasonable to simply abandon this test (Quinsey & Laws, 1990). After the Wright brothers got their plane off the ground even a few times, no one could deny that it did fly. (Freund [1957] did demonstrate that PPG could measure sexual orientation.) And if the Wright brothers' plane had been tested as a boat and sank after it had flown, it would not have made sense to abandon the plane as a flying machine. (If PPG cannot discriminate between rapists and nonrapists, it might not make sense to abandon it as a measure of sexual arousal and sexual preference.) The strategy should instead be to uncover the tacit instructions in the negative studies, for making proper use of PPG. This chapter was written as a challenge: to rethink PPG, to retest it, and to revalue it.

Rethinking PPG

Before suggesting how to remake PPG, it is useful to discriminate among three hypothetical constructs (O'Donohue & Letourneau, 1992)—sexual arousal, sexual preference, and sexual paraphilia—and between those three constructs and sexual behavior. Afterwards, PPG uses are suggested.

Sexual Arousal

Sexual arousal is relatively straightforward and operationally defined as a substantial increase in penis size (see below).

Sexual Preference

Sexual preference means greater sexual arousal to a stimulus than others that are sexually arousing. A stimulus that is not preferred may still be highly arousing. Given that sexual preference could refer to anything from a preference for one gender over the other, a partner of one age over another, or even a partner with one hair color over another, the construct is so inclusive that it lacks value. In this chapter, we suggest that sexual preference be used only to refer to gender preference.

Sexual Paraphilia

A person might show a paraphilia even though the individual might not prefer that paraphilic sexual activity to other sexual activity. An important difference between these two constructs is the variables one must consider in identifying a

TABLE 15.1   PPG Accuracy as a Function of PPG Use and Subject Cooperation

	Subject Cooperation	
PPG Use	Subjects Select Stimuli[a]	Experimenter Selects Stimuli[b]
Sexual preference/orientation	High accuracy	Moderate accuracy
Sexual paraphilia	Moderate accuracy	Poor to moderate accuracy
Prediction of criminal behavior	Poor accuracy	Poor accuracy

a. Subjects attend to the PPG stimuli and do not fake.
b. Subjects might not attend to the PPG stimuli and might fake.

sexual paraphilia, in addition to sexual arousal: the distress caused the individual by such arousal and the duration of time that the individual has experienced such arousal (*DSM-IV*, American Psychiatric Association, 1994).

Criminal Sexual Behavior

Between the above three hypothetical constructs and behavior, there is no reason to assume that the relationships are simple. One might show sexual arousal in reaction to a stimulus, a sexual preference for that stimulus, or even a paraphilia in regard to that sexual object but not necessarily show criminal sexual behavior in reaction to that stimulus. For example, one could be sexually aroused by the next-door neighbor but not rape that neighbor. The opposite is also true. One might not show a paraphilia but act as if one did, at least for a time (Quinsey, Chaplin, & Carrigan, 1979). One might even engage in a criminal sexual activity with someone who is not of much sexual interest.

Why is there a loose fit between sexual preferences, sexual paraphilias, and criminal sexual behavior? The answer is that criminal sexual behavior is multidetermined: The reasons for the behavior have as much to do with opportunity, the threat of punishment, attitudes, values, morals, and so on, as with sexual arousal and preference (Quinsey, Rice, Harris, & Reid, 1993).

PPG Uses

PPG has been used to provide information about (a) sexual preference (Cases 1 and 4), (b) paraphilias (Cases 2 and 5), and (c) criminal sexual behavior (Cases 3 and 6) (see Table 15.1). Some sexual acts (e.g., child molesting) might be part of a paraphilia and unlawful. Others (e.g., rape) would be unlawful but not part of a paraphilia.

Clearly, Cases 4 through 6 suggest the use of PPG to collect information that might be used against the client—for example, identifying the sexual orientation of soldiers (Case 4), diagnosing a father who wants unsupervised access to his child as pedophilic (Case 5), or finding that an unrepentant sex offender shows high arousal to sadistic rape stories.

In contrast, Cases 1 through 3 seem to reflect only curiosity about whether PPG scores provide certain kinds of information. If subjects understand that the experimenter is interested in the relationships between sexual arousal in a laboratory and other behaviors (e.g., sexual orientation), not in gathering information to be used to make decisions about the subjects, then subjects might feel free to help the experimenter test PPG. If subjects cooperate, there can be a fair assessment of PPG's reliability and its validity as a measure of sexual arousal and sexual preference.

Retesting PPG

The strategy is to review PPG methodology and then to proceed from simpler and less demanding goals (Case 1) to the more difficult ones (Case 6). Table 15.1 organizes the six PPG cases according to two variables: what PPG is being used to determine and whether the client is being cooperative in certain ways. It is argued that there is a relationship between the types of PPG applications, certain kinds of subject cooperation, and PPG validity: Accuracy will fall as one moves from using PPG to identify sexual orientation to paraphilias, and accuracy will fall when the subjects do not cooperate (i.e., experimenter selects the stimuli and subjects fake).

PPG as a Measure of Penis Size

This section offers a brief history of PPG only to argue that PPG's apparatuses and methods offer prima facie evidence of high interscorer reliability. A first basic question is the following: Can PPG reliably measure changes in penis size? The reader is referred to Freund, Sedlacek, and Knob (1965) for a detailed description of an apparatus to measure changes in penis volume. To make PPG more convenient than the volumetric device developed by Freund, various strain gauges were constructed that measured only the change in circumference of the shaft of the penis (Murphy & Barbaree, 1994). It seems clear that either the volumetric or the strain gauge methods can reliably measure changes in whatever human appendage they surround, although exactly what is measured is different (Abel, Barlow, Blanchard, & Mavissakalian, 1975; Abel, Blanchard, Barlow, & Mavissakalian, 1975). O'Donohue and Letourneau (1992) suggested that the volumetric device was more subject to error, but these problems are reducible to the physical integrity of the equipment and can be avoided by proper maintenance and care attaching the apparatuses. Neither method seems to be subject to error as a result of the apparatus itself.

Naturally, the physical changes in the apparatus must be consistently scored if PPG is to be useful. To score a change in penis size, the physical apparatus is attached to a transducer, and the transducer is attached to an objective recording device, usually a computer, that records a measure (e.g., peak amplitude of the change in penis size). The methodology for changing analogue to digital data has been worked out, and there is no reason to expect a problem in computer scoring (Lalumière & Harris, 1998).

One problem that could threaten the consistency of scoring between researchers is that the apparatus might calculate scores based on different response data or use different statistics to calculate PPG scores (Murphy & Barbaree, 1994). A different issue is whether those scores are then compared within an individual or between individuals (Harris & Rice, 1996; Harris, Rice, Quinsey, & Chaplin, 1996). Still, all such problems can be easily avoided if we know the process by which a researcher calculates scores. Given the physical integrity of a PPG apparatus and the objectivity of the scoring, PPG should generate high interscorer reliability when penis size is measured.

The next basic question is the following: Can PPG reliably measure change in penis size as the subject reacts to a stimulus? This question about PPG reliability is peculiar because the question does not specify that the stimulus must have sexual content, the obvious content for PPG stimuli. (In this chapter, test-retest reliability is defined as a reliable relationship between a stimulus, sexual or not, and a PPG score.)

Various studies have required subjects to self-stimulate to measure the size of the penis at full erection (Abel et al., 1977; Barbaree, Marshall, & Lanthier, 1979). Other studies demonstrated that nonsexual stimuli (e.g., electric shocks or noxious odors) are reliably followed by detumescence (Barlow, Leitenberg, & Agras, 1969; McConaghy, 1969, 1970; McConaghy, Proctor, & Barr, 1972). Accepting those demonstrations, we conclude that PPG is test-retest reliable and that there is a stable relationship between changes in penis size and particular stimuli.

Some might complain that this is not an interesting sort of reliability for PPG to have. Indeed, all PPG studies, including reliability studies, typically identify the stimuli as having either sexual or neutral content and require that PPG scores properly line up with these types of stimuli before the test is declared test-retest reliable (Eccles, Marshall, & Barbaree, 1988; Farkas et al., 1979; Wormith, 1986). However, this requirement makes such studies more like validity than reliability studies: They actually test whether PPG measures what it purports to measure—the relationship between PPG scores, as measures of sexual arousal and sexual and neutral stimuli, not just a reliable change in PPG scores as the subject attends to one stimulus versus another.

Does PPG have this special sort of reliability? Marshall and Fernandez (in press) reported their surprise at studies finding few PPG reliability studies given the extensive period during which PPG has been used. But it seems that a demonstration of high test-retest reliability is predictable if one worked with male heterosexual subjects who selected 6 sexually arousing pictures of naked women out of a possible 100 pictures and 6 neutral pictures (Abel, Blanchard, et al., 1975). These stimuli would not have to be the same for all subjects. As a second part of cooperation, the subjects would agree to focus on the pictures and not fake. It is expected that the correlation of PPG scores between a first and second testing of the sexual stimuli would be highly significant; consistency in response to the neutral stimuli is also expected. Finally, given that the subjects selected the pictures because they were arousing, the difference between PPG scores in reaction to sexually arousing stimuli and neutral stimuli should be significantly different, which is evidence of validity.

Plenty of evidence supports this prediction. First, studies show PPG to be reasonably reliable, even though the stimuli in those studies were selected by the experimenter, and at least some subjects had a vested interest in deception (Barbaree et al., 1989). A very different line of reasoning also supports this prediction. When Freund (1963) reported that 85 subjects reacted differently to pictures of younger children and older adults and reported in a second study that PPG scores could be used to correctly classify all 31 heterosexual and 39 homosexual subjects who were shown paired pictures of males and females, it was understood that PPG made valid discriminations. Could PPG have been valid but unreliable in the Freund studies? The answer is no; if Freund's PPG lacked reliability, it is extremely unlikely that it would have made those near-perfect classifications (Anastasi, 1997). Subsequent demonstrations (Freund, Langevin, Cibiri, & Zajac, 1973; McConaghy, 1967, 1989) also argue against explanation by chance.

Oddly, the instructional faking studies do not provide evidence against this conclusion. Those studies asked subjects to control themselves, to be sexually aroused by the "right" stimulus and not sexually aroused by the "wrong" stimulus. That subjects could voluntarily control or fake their sexual responses (Henson & Rubin, 1971; Laws & Holmen, 1978; Laws & Rubin, 1969; Wydra, Marshall, Earls, & Barbaree, 1983) was understood to cast doubt on the validity of PPG (Alford, Wedding, & Jones, 1983). In this chapter, we take the opposite position. As those subjects achieved control by focusing on erotic fantasies when they wanted to show sexual arousal response and focusing on asexual ones when they wanted to show no sexual arousal (Laws & Rubin, 1969; Rubin & Henson, 1975), then certain fantasies were reliably followed by similar PPG scores. Along these lines, the antifaking studies also offer support for PPG reliability. Those studies demonstrated that voluntary control of sexual arousal is weakened when the subject is asked to engage in a task that interferes with a subject creating internal images—for example, having the client describe the picture in front of him (Henson & Rubin, 1971; Wormith, 1986) or pressing one or another button, depending on the content of the audiotape (Proulx, Cote, & Achille, 1993; Quinsey & Chaplin, 1988b). Because those tracking tasks did weaken voluntary control, it is likely that subjects were controlling changes in penis size by making use of erotic and asexual fantasies, which were reliably followed by a change in penis size. Together, the faking and antifaking studies also suggest that habituation is not a problem if the stimuli are very arousing.

These studies also demonstrate an additional quality of PPG: Subjects respond to what they think about the stimulus (i.e., there is cognitive mediation between the stimulus and arousal); sexual arousal is not simply elicited by the sexual stimulus. Establishing this cognitive link is important. Even though we may have hoped that paraphilic stimuli would elicit arousal in someone with a paraphilia, the faking and antifaking studies demonstrate that we cannot easily know why someone shows arousal to a stimulus.

The next question is the following: Does PPG have internal consistency and alternate-form reliability? This question can be answered quickly. If we accept that subjects can be aroused by more than one picture of a naked female and cooperative subjects select enough pictures to form two sets, then PPG scores for the two different sexually arousing stimulus sets should be highly correlated over time. PPG scores for the neutral sets should also be highly correlated over time. There would be high internal consistency for pictures within each set and even consistent responses to pictures in each set with the overall score for the two sets combined. As a psychometric device, it seems reasonable to conclude that PPG shows high internal consistency, high test-retest reliability, and high alternate-form reliability in subjects who select the stimuli and do not fake.

PPG as a Measure of Sexual Preference

PPG as a measure of sexual arousal is straightforward: Subjects should react to stimuli they find sexually interesting and not react to neutral stimuli. PPG as a measure of sexual preference is not so straightforward. So far, we have not described how PPG could discriminate between two classes of stimuli, both of which are sexually arousing. There was a notion of comparison, of course, in assessing PPG as a reliable and valid measure of arousal—a comparison between sexual arousal response to sexual stimuli) and sexual arousal response to neutral stimuli. Still, that comparison involves only the ability to test whether someone is aroused by a stimulus, not whether someone is aroused more by one stimulus than another. Given that our assumption so far is that subjects will select their own stimuli, it is reasonable to expect than any one of the many methods used to score responses would show significant differences.

For PPG to test sexual preference, sexual arousal to different sexual stimuli must be reliably and validly measured, and a reliable method must be found to discriminate among the PPG scores. Because a sexual arousal difference score for two sexually arousing stimuli is likely to be smaller than the difference score between a sexual and a neutral stimulus, the different sets of sexual stimuli should not be overly similar (Fuller, Barnard, Robbins, & Spears, 1988). If PPG is tested with classes of stimuli that are close to each other and PPG cannot make those discriminations (O'Donohue & Letourneau, 1992), one should avoid the wrong conclusion that PPG cannot validly discriminate between any sexually arousing and very sexually arousing stimuli.

The potential problem of habituation was dismissed earlier in regard to PPG testing of sexual arousal. Habituation may pose a bigger problem for sexual preference testing. Let us assume that a man has sexual interests in two women, Ms. X. and Ms. Y., and that his sexual interests in these women vary in strength: He prefers Ms. X. Notwithstanding his clear preference for Ms. X, he might date Ms. Y once in a while, just because he habituates to Ms. X. It gets worse: He may cancel a date with Ms. X to spend time with Ms. Y., even though he has not yet grown weary of Ms. X., if he knows that Ms. Y will soon leave the country. Like sexual arousal, sexual preference seems to be subject to habituation and, worse, subject even to the anticipation of habituation.

There are studies that report PPG's ability to identify sexual preferences (Quinsey et al., 1979; Quinsey, Steinman, Bergersen, & Holmes, 1975). Even so, because it is true that a measure of sexual preference (see Case 1) is much more complicated than a measure of sexual arousal, the following study is proposed.

Proposed Study to Demonstrate the Use of PPG as an Indicator of a Sexual Preference in Cooperative Subjects (Case 1)

A researcher would recruit cooperative male subjects who prefer adult females (HEAF) and male subjects who prefer adult males (HOAM). All subjects would select 12 out of 100 pictures of attractive naked adult females, 12 out of 100 pictures of attractive adult males, and 12 out of 100 neutral pictures. The stimuli would not have to be the same for each subject. These sets could be divided to make two alternate sets, and these two sets could be administered a month apart to the subjects who would agree to attend to the stimuli and not fake. The measure taken would be penis volume.

It is expected that a wide variety of PPG scores (e.g., average peak amplitude, average area under the curve, average z-score, etc.), in response to these stimulus sets, would have high internal consistency within sets, high alternate-form reliability across sets, and high test-retest reliability across time. It is expected that HEAF subjects would show significantly greater sexual arousal to the adult females than the adult males. It is expected that the HOAM would show a different pattern (i.e., greater arousal to the adult males) than the adult females (Freund et al., 1973). The slopes of the two curves might be also be different for the two groups (e.g., the HEAF showing a bigger difference in arousal to the sexual stimulus sets and the neutral set than the HOAM).

PPG as a Measure of a Paraphilia

Even if the results were as predicted—that PPG could identify sexual orientation—we want more from PPG: We want PPG to identify sexual paraphilias (see Case 2).

It seems worthwhile to consider how a test of sexual preference could possibly identify a paraphilia. The reasoning might be that paraphilic sexual behaviors are a subset of preferred sexual behaviors, themselves subsets of sexually arousing behaviors. The picture is an inverted triangle, with sexually arousing stimuli being at the top and paraphilic behavior—preferred sexual behaviors that happen to have paraphilic content—at the bottom (Freund, 1981). With this model, the notion is that if we presented clients with paraphilic stimuli (e.g., pictures of naked children), and the individual showed a sexual preference for those stimuli (Quinsey & Lalumière, 1996), then we could identify the person as paraphilic.

This reasoning does not stand up to scrutiny. It is not true that paraphilic behaviors are a subset of sexually preferred behaviors. A client can prefer sexual activity different from his paraphilic activity. A client might prefer sex with a young woman but molest a young female (Freund, McKnight, Langevin, & Cibiri, 1972; Quinsey et al., 1993).

As an alternative, one could argue that showing any substantial sexual arousal to a paraphilic stimulus reveals the person to be paraphilic. But there is a flaw in this reasoning too: Some clients might find children somewhat sexually interesting or arousing but not act on their feelings; they would not be diagnosed as showing pedophilia. Instead, they would show arousal to adults and engage in sex with adults. How could one tell the difference between the client who does show a paraphilia, but paraphilic activity is not preferred, and the client who does not show a paraphilia but feels some arousal to the paraphilic stimuli (O'Donohue & Letourneau, 1992)?

The real story may be that PPG can identify some clients who show paraphilias, some who do not, and others for whom the data are ambiguous. After all, it might be that for many men who show a paraphilia, though not all, the paraphilic stimuli are also preferred stimuli. Perhaps for those men who show a paraphilia but for whom the paraphilic stimuli are not preferred, some might show greater arousal to such paraphilic stimuli than nonparaphilic men, but men who find the paraphilic stimuli sexually interesting. In short, PPG may be accurate, but not very accurate in classifying people as paraphilics (Murphy & Barbaree, 1994); this accuracy will likely be less than PPG classifications of sexual orientation.

There is another problem. To be diagnosed as showing a paraphilia, one has to have shown the relevant behavior for at least 6 months, and those behaviors must have caused problems, such as distress or impairment of the individual's functioning. But even if all paraphilias were subsets of preferred sexual activities (e.g., sexual preference for children), how could PPG, a measure of arousal, determine how long a client has shown this preference for children? Similarly, how could PPG show that one's pattern of sexual arousal causes distress or functional impairment?

In light of this reasoning, PPG cannot claim to identify paraphilias in simple ways. Notwithstanding this, it is easy to understand why clinicians hope for PPG to be able to identify paraphilias directly and simply. The hope should be tested again.

Proposed Study to Demonstrate the Use of PPG as an Indicator of a Sexual Paraphilia in Cooperative Subjects (Case 2)

The proposed study, which focuses on the identification of men with a paraphilia, is different from other studies because it would employ cooperative subjects who would select the stimuli and would agree not to fake.

A researcher could ask for the aid of three groups: one whose members show homosexual pedophilia and who have little interest in sex with anyone else (HOMC), one whose members are homosexual (HOAM), and one whose members are heterosexual (HEAF). Subjects would be offered the assurance of confidentiality regarding any information gathered in the study, including disclosures of inappropriate activity. Subjects would be asked to honestly report their sexual histories and their feelings about various classes of people (e.g., male children, female children, male adults, and female adults).

Marshall and Fernandez (in press) reported the use of screening to eliminate from the control group subjects who have unidentified problems. We do not propose such strict controls. To make this study more representative of the field, some heterogeneity would be tolerated in the groups—for example, some subjects in the HOMC reporting arousal toward little girls, at least sometimes. For the HOAM and HEAF groups, what counts is that none would ever have been diagnosed as showing a paraphilia, been charged with molesting a child, or felt persistent, strong urges to touch a child after becoming an adult. There would be one kind of screening out: Consistent with McAnulty and Adams (1990), Quinsey and Laws (1990), and Seto and Kuban (1996) but inconsistent with Hall (1990) and Hall et al. (1988), subjects who did not show any arousal to any stimuli would be excluded from the analysis.

The subjects would be asked to select 12 of 100 pictures of attractive young boys, 12 of 100 pictures of attractive young girls, 12 of 100 pictures of attractive adult females, 12 of 100 pictures of attractive men, and 12 neutral pictures. Two sets of stimuli could be formed for each subject for each class of stimuli. Subjects could be tested twice using these alternate forms, a month passing between each test. Penis size would be measured when the stimuli were shown, and z-scores would be calculated and averaged for each class of stimuli.

It is expected that there would be high internal consistency in the stimulus sets, high alternate-form reliability across sets, and high test-retest reliability across time. It is also expected that the PPG scores could be used to correctly classify most of the members in the two groups because there would be a relationship between sexual arousal to the stimuli or sexual preference for some of the stimuli and the subject's prior report of homosexual paraphilia. As studies report PPG's accuracy at discriminating between normals and groups showing paraphilias, between subgroups of a paraphilia (Barsetti, Earls, & Lalumière, 1998), or even between groups that show paraphilias (e.g., pedophilia) and those that engage in criminal sexual behavior (e.g., rape) (Wormith, 1986), these expectations seem reasonable. Still, it is expected that the accuracy of these classifications might be less than the identification of sexual preferences.

PPG as a Measure of Criminal Sexual Behavior

We want PPG to do more than identify paraphilias: We also want PPG to indicate, for example, whether a client committed rape and whether he is likely to rape again. It is worthwhile considering how PPG, a measure of sexual arousal, a presumed very good indicator of sexual preference, and a presumed good indicator of paraphilia, could possibly provide information about criminal sexual behavior. Would this not be like using IQ to predict a particular grade on a particular test in a particular course?

The modest relationship between sexual arousal in reaction to a stimulus, on one hand, and sexual behavior in reaction to the same stimulus, on the other, is bound to be a problem in using PPG scores to predict criminal sexual behavior. For example, some men, who are strongly aroused by depictions of forced sex (Seto & Kuban, 1996), might inhibit themselves (Quinsey et al., 1984), whereas others, who have less sexual interest in forced sex, might commit an offense because they think they can get away with it. Still, we might hope to identify those who have raped by testing reaction to forced sex. We might hope for the same simple inverted-triangle model suggested for identifying paraphilias; specifically, sexually preferred stimuli are a subset of sexually arousing stimuli, and certain sexually preferred stimuli are associated with criminal activity. The idea is that the client who is more aroused when listening to a rape story will rape, and the one who is less aroused will not (Abel et al., 1977; Hall, Shondrick, & Hirschman, 1993; Lalumière & Quinsey, 1994; Quinsey & Chaplin, 1982; Quinsey et al., 1984). But Baxter, Barbaree, and Marshall (1986) report that this is not so; many rapists are more aroused to consenting than forced sex; apparently, criminal sexual activity is not always a subset of preferred sexual activity. The second possibility is that even if the rape is not preferred, those who rape will show significantly more arousal to rape than to neutral stimuli, whereas those who have not raped will show a smaller difference (Abel et al., 1977; Abel, Becker, Blanchard, & Djenderedjian, 1978; Lalumière & Quinsey, 1994). The problem is that many men are aroused by the fantasy of rape, although they respond to those fantasies less than consenting sex, but will not rape (Malamuth, Heim, & Feshbach, 1980). The last possibility is that any arousal shown when listening to rape stories indicates a rapist, a strategy that would surely label too many clients as rapists (Malamuth et al., 1980).

The problem is compounded when one tries to discriminate between one type of criminal sexual behavior and another. Baxter, Marshall, Barbaree, Davidson, and Malcolm (1984) reported that child molesters who only offended against postpubescent females displayed preferences similar to rapists and dissimilar to offenders who molested children younger than age 12. This is not difficult to understand. Many of the men who offended against post-pubescent females might have a preference for women but are unable or un-willing to attempt force with an adult who will fight back. In this case, PPG might identify the sexual arousal patterns of men who offended against post-pubescent females as rapists, even though the law groups these men differently (i.e., according to the age of their victims, not what they want to do to their victims, and not those they want to victimize). Notwithstanding these difficulties, the hope that PPG can predict criminal behavior should be tested.

Proposed Study to Demonstrate the Use of PPG as an Indicator of a Criminal Sexual Behavior in Cooperative Subjects (Case 3)

This study would be different from most in the literature because it would ask subjects to select the stimuli and not to fake. A researcher could ask for the aid of two groups, one whose members have truthfully admitted to rape and a nonrapist group. Subjects would be offered the assurance of confidentiality regarding any information gathered in the study, including disclosures of inappropriate activity. Subjects would be asked to honestly report their sexual histories and their sexual feelings about various kinds of sexual activity.

Sexual sadists would be screened out of the rapist group, even though PPG has a better record of success discriminating between sadistic rapists and nonrapists than discriminating between nonbrutal rapists and nonrapists (Marshall & Fernandez, in press). Sadistic rapists would properly fit into a study about PPG's capacity to identify paraphilias (i.e., sadism) (see Case 2). The remaining rapists might have a dominant preference for forced sex and show little or no interest in consenting sex. Some of these rapists might be strongly aroused by rape but also strongly aroused by consenting sex.

The nonrapist group would be screened by asking potential clients to remove themselves if they had engaged in forced sex, even if they had not been caught. Some of those who remain have fantasized about forced sex, but none would ever have raped a woman, whether charged or not. Consistent with the last proposal, there would be one additional kind of screening out: Subjects who did not show any arousal to any stimuli would be excluded from the analysis.

The subjects would be asked to select the 12 most appealing audiotaped stories of rape out of 25 stories and the 12 most appealing stories of consenting sex out of 25 stories. There would also be 12 neutral stories. (If subjects reported that all of the stories about rape were disgusting, they would be asked to select the 12 least offensive.) The audiotaped stories about rape would be recorded in the voice of the victim and include details of the force used; the stories would focus less on the pleasure of the rapist and more on the discomfort of the women. None of these rape stories would be extremely brutal or extremely violent. (We are not targeting sadistic rapists in this study [see above] but, rather, nonbrutal rapists.) None would imply that it was the victim's suffering that was sexually arousing (Quinsey & Chaplin, 1984; Rice et al., 1994).

The stimulus sets could be divided to form two sets of rape stories, consenting sex stories, and neutral stories. The two sets would be administered a month apart. PPG would measure changes in penis volume.

It is expected that the PPG scores would demonstrate high internal consistency within stimulus sets, high alternate-form reliability, and high test-retest reliability. It is also expected that the PPG scores could be used to correctly classify some but certainly not all members of the rapist and nonrapist groups (i.e., there would be a modest but significant relationship between sexual arousal to the stimuli, sexual preference for the stimuli, and the subjects' prior history of rape). Given those studies that report differences between rapists and nonrapists, even when the experimenter selected the stimuli (Abel et al., 1977; Harris et al., 1992; Lalumière & Quinsey, 1994; Quinsey & Chaplin, 1984; Quinsey et al., 1984) and the subjects had reason to fake, these predictions seem reasonable. It is expected that PPG's ability to distinguish between these two groups would be less accurate than its ability to distinguish those showing paraphilias and normals (Murphy & Barbaree, 1994), which was in turn poorer than its ability to distinguish homosexuals from heterosexuals.

In this study, past criminal behavior is identified, although one could also try to predict the future. Given those studies that report modest success when PPG scores are used to make such predictions, it is expected that there would be a significant difference between these two groups (Quinsey, Rice, & Harris, 1995; Rice, Harris, & Quinsey, 1990; Rice, Quinsey, & Harris, 1991). The rapist and nonrapist groups could be followed up for 5 years after the conclusion of the study. Differences in the number of sexual offenses in the two groups could be analyzed. Such follow-ups may require an even longer period to determine PPG's value as a predictor of sexual offenses.

PPG as a Measure of Sexual Preference and Paraphilias and as a Predictor of Sexual Behavior When Subjects Fake

The three proposed studies have the subjects selecting the stimuli and the subjects agreeing not to fake, these being ideal conditions for PPG. Given that in most applications the experimenter selects the stimuli and the subjects may fake, the impact of these differences should be considered.

Experimenter Selection of PPG Stimuli

What seems a perfectly reasonable demand—that the sexual stimuli be selected by the experimenter and grouped by the experimenter according to classes such as "pictures that are arousing for pedophiles who prefer little girls" or "stories about rape that are arousing for rapists"—is actually very problematic. One issue is the content validity of classes of sexual stimuli: We cannot identify all stimuli associated with sexual preferences, paraphilias, or criminal sexual behavior and know the proportions represented by any particular stimulus (O'Donohue & Letourneau, 1992). At best, a stimulus set will have face validity and a range of stimuli.

The problem of content validity in one class is compounded if we create multiple classes of sexual stimuli. Do the stimuli in one class sample as effectively as stimuli in another class? If not, differences in response to different classes may reflect differences in sampling.

There is another sampling problem. Are the stimuli in one class as provocative as the stimuli in another? For example, a child could be presented in ways that would elicit more or less sexual arousal, and such differences can be confounded across classes of people. For this reason, O'Donohue and Letourneau (1992) criticized Hall et al.'s (1988) presentation of child stimuli for 4 minutes and adult stimuli for 2 minutes. If the experimenter does not create the stimuli but depends on public sources (Laws & Osborn, 1983), this problem of uneven sampling is likely.

If the experimenter selects the stimuli, an even more serious problem is created when it comes to scoring the client's response: The clients may show a wide range of arousal in reaction to one class of stimuli. After all, if experimenters select and group stimuli, they might group stimuli together that actually represent different classes from the point of view of the client. When a client responds to only one stimulus in a class of five chosen by the experimenter, it might be true that he does not show much arousal to that class. But why might a client respond to the one stimulus? One explanation of the high level of arousal to the one stimulus in a set is error, implausible unless erections are random (Zuckerman, 1971). Naturally, if we imagine that the one high-arousal response is error, responses to the class of stimuli are best represented by a summary statistic.

The real answer might be that the one stimulus represents a different class to the client; the experimenter and the client might have different ways of classifying pictures in terms of their ability to arouse. For example, the client might show strong sexual arousal to a picture of a 6-year-old girl because that girl has certain physical features, has a certain facial expression, and is standing a certain way. When the client sees a girl who looks that way, he thinks about her in certain ways, and these thoughts are followed by sexual arousal. The client might not respond much at all to children who look similar except for very small and particular differences. (The argument is against a normal gradient of stimulus generalization: Small differences in stimulus might make for big differences in reaction.) Not knowing these fine discriminations, thoughts, and feelings on the part of the client, the experimenter might lump this class of 6-year-old children in with another class (e.g., the class of all 6-year-old girls), even those who do not provoke the client. As a result, when responses to the class of 6-year-olds constructed by the experimenter are averaged, evidence of deviant arousal by the relevant subclass of little girls is lost.

Faking

The second major problem in common PPG applications is client faking. Faking in this area may be so widespread that it has dulled our sensitivity to the difficulty of validly testing subjects who have a vested interest in faking (Lalumière & Quinsey, 1994). Like other tests, the PPG apparatus itself cannot identify responses that are fake as opposed to those that indicate arousal. As in the case of the MMPI-2 validity scales, there would have to be an additional measure to assess faking (e.g., an informed technician who identifies certain patterns of arousal as faking).

Taken together, the experimenter selecting the stimuli, the averaging of high- and low-arousal responses to members of the same class of stimuli, and faking pose a serious problem for PPG. A decline in PPG accuracy is suggested (see Table 15.1), from the identification of sexual orientation (from Case 1 to Case 3) to the prediction of criminal behavior (from Case 3 to Case 6). Table 15.1 also predicts that PPG will be less accurate when the experimenter selects the stimuli (Orne, Thackray, & Paskewitz, 1972) and the subject tries to fake (Cases 4-6) than when the client selects the stimuli and does not fake (Cases 1-3). Meta-analyses seem to confirm this prediction (Lalumière & Quinsey, 1994).

Improving PPG to Handle These Problems

Only so much can be done to improve the basic functioning of a PPG apparatus. These are the location and general qualities of the PPG laboratory, instructions to the client, the way in which change in penis size is measured, what stimuli are presented to the client, and how the response is scored.

The PPG Laboratory. Psychologists who want to provoke a sexual response on the part of the client have chosen circumstances that are likely to dampen the client's sexual response rather than enhance it. The client, who knows he is being tested and that the information may be unfavorable to his life circumstances, is asked to attend a laboratory, to attach an apparatus to his penis, and to allow himself to be observed while he is presented erotic stimuli (Laws & Osborn, 1983). Such environments should be made friendlier by changing furniture, lighting, decorations, and so on.

Instructions. The client should be required to engage in a task that interferes with faking (Geer & Fuhr, 1976; Proulx et al., 1993; Quinsey & Chaplin, 1988a, 1988b). If faking is detected, it should be strongly discouraged. If the client will not stop faking, the test results should not be interpreted.

What Is Measured. Is there a measure of change in penis size other than by the volume or strain gauge method that would minimize the impact of the experimenter selecting the stimuli and faking? It seems that standard PPG apparatuses will remain the choice for now, although some researchers argue that of these, measuring penis volume is better than measuring penis circumference (Clark, 1972; Freund, Langevin, & Barlow, 1974; McConaghy, 1974, 1989; Rosen & Keefe, 1978).

Quality of the Stimulus. Care must be taken to create credible, attractive, and realistic stimuli.

Number of Stimuli Presented. It was argued earlier that a client might react very differently to pictures of people who seem to represent the same class (e.g., 6-year-old children) because the client might think very differently about one child than another. In proposed Studies 1 through 3, this problem was avoided by having subjects select the stimuli from a variety of pictures.

There is a way for the experimenter to select the pictures that represent a class of stimuli and still create slides that are likely to elicit sexual arousal if the client is aroused by some in that class: The experimenter could show four pictures of 6-year-old male children on each of six slides, making a total of 24 pictures of different males of this age. This massing of pictures increases the chance that at least one picture in each slide will be arousing (Lalumière & Quinsey, 1994; Quinsey & Chaplin, 1984). It might also be more difficult for the client to use internally generated images as a distraction if he is faced with multiple pictures on one slide. It is acknowledged that one would have to use the same technique across all classes, making for a large number of computer-generated pictures. This has proved difficult in the past when experimenters presented clients with pictures of real people. Computer generation of pictures of people who really do not exist allows for this number of pictures.

If the stimuli are stories about sex, it might be impractical to present many stories. The alternative is to carefully develop the story, a suggestion taken up under the next subheading.

Content of the Stimulus. As stated earlier, the problem with the experimenter selecting the stimuli is the idiosyncrasy of sexual arousal. For example, a particular story about rape might not arouse a rapist because the details are not right, even though many other circumstances and stories about rape would arouse the rapist. How can the experimenter select the stimuli and avoid decreasing the power of PPG to validly discriminate? What materials are chosen and how they are organized are determined by one's theory of sexual behavior and sexual offending. Some notions of what is sexually arousing might seem so straightforward that we do not need to think of them as theories (e.g., that homosexual men find pictures of naked males arousing). Even here, there might be ways of presenting such pictures that make a difference in arousal even for those people who are aroused by the class of the person depicted. When it comes to other kinds of sexual stimuli (e.g., rape vs. consenting sex stories), good theory (e.g., theory about what kinds of rape stories will be arousing to what kinds of rapists) seems critical.

The writing of consenting sex and rape stories could be guided by new relapse prevention theory—for example, the path analysis of sexual offending by Hudson and Ward (1997). At the very least, it would be interesting to connect PPG assessment and relapse prevention theory in this way.

When a picture is shown to a client, it is likely that the client will think that it is a real person even if the picture is computer generated. When it comes to stories about rape, however, the client might be likely to imagine that the story is nothing more than fiction, a perception that makes it less arousing. Rape stories could be presented as true accounts of a rape read by the actual victim (Lalumière & Quinsey, 1994; Malamuth & Check, 1980a, 1980b, 1983; Quinsey & Chaplin, 1982). Although it might be true that some nonrapists respond to fictitious accounts of rape, perhaps fewer of these would respond to what is described as a true account by the victim.

Also, the stimuli could be more provocative. For ethical reasons, psychologists do not make use of the obvious stimuli (i.e., real people to provoke the client), even though these stimuli would elicit greater response. This format would harken back to the work of Masters and Johnson (1966), who actually observed real instances of sexual behavior between partners, between a client and a sexual surrogate. Although this format is not advocated, within 5 years computer technology might allow for effective virtual reality stimuli, which allow interaction between the subject and the "person."

Scoring. The problem of averaging scores issues directly from the experimenter selecting the stimuli and probably doing a poor job of it. An alternative to averaging scores is to treat any heightened arousal (e.g., 10% of full erection to a picture of a 6-year-old girl) as important. Exclusive of the neutral stimuli, all low scores for a class of stimuli would be dropped. For neutral stimuli, any significant arousal would result in the test results being declared useless.

Proposed Study to Demonstrate the Use of PPG as an Indicator of a Sexual Paraphilia in Noncooperative Subjects (Case 5)

Suppose we follow all the suggestions described earlier. Then might PPG be used to test for things such as paraphilias when the experimenter selects the stimuli and when clients are likely to fake? One last study is proposed. This study would be similar to Case 5 in that it would test whether PPG can discriminate between clients who show homosexual pedophilia and heterosexuals who are attracted to adults, even when the clients are asked to fake. This seems a lot to ask of any test, but it is what we want. Cases 4 and 6 are skipped, although it is assumed that the format of this study could be used in Cases 4 and 6.

This study is similar to standard faking studies but with one critical difference: In this study, the experimenter would try to identify and stop faking, a common practice in clinical settings. A researcher could enlist the aid of two groups: one that shows homosexual pedophilia (HOMC) and the other control (HEAF) whose members have a sexual preference for adult females. Screening of the HOMC group would not be stringent. The members would have a dominant preference for male children younger than age 11 and would be diagnosed as showing pedophilia. Screening of the control group would not be excessive; the critical issue is that none of the members of HEAF would have been diagnosed as showing homosexual pedophilia or been charged with molesting a child, of course, no members of the control group would report irresistible urges to touch any child.

By computer, the experimenter would construct six slides depicting 9-year-old boys, six depicting girls, and slides for male and female adults. Each slide would show four pictures (e.g., four pictures of a boy, four pictures of a girl, etc.). There would also be six neutral slides, each of which would show four pictures of landscapes.

The PPG laboratory would be made to look as pleasant as possible. Half of the HOMC subjects would be told to fake high arousal to stimuli depicting sexual activity with adult women and low arousal to all other stimuli. The other half of the HOMC group and all of the HEAF group would be told to attend to the stimuli and not to fake. All subjects would also be told that in standard PPG the technicians identify faking when it happens and discourage it verbally. Subjects would be told that their technician would do the same. Subjects would also be informed that they would be given only $20 for participating and not $100 if it was determined that they were faking. Specifically, subjects who were caught faking by the technician would be given one more chance, but if they continued to fake, they would be told, then the test would be discontinued and they would not be given the larger fee.

In fact, the technician would not be informed about the faking instructions to some subjects. The technician would be told to identify faking, to document it, and to discourage it verbally (Quinsey & Chaplin, 1988b). The technician would also be told that if faking was missed for a subject and the subject reported it later, then the technician would only be paid $20 for conducting that test rather than the normal fee of $100.

The subjects would be given a tracking task (Quinsey & Chaplin, 1988b). Subjects would also be told that if they did not complete the tracking task, then they would be paid only the $20 and not the $100 fee. As a matter of fact, all subjects would be paid the $100 fee at the conclusion of the study even if they were identified as fakers and the test was discontinued, on the condition that they report whether they faked and how they faked or not.

This format is not the standard faking study format because, on one hand, the subjects would be instructed to fake and, on the other hand, the experimenter would also try to identify faking and would strongly discourage it. This latter practice is consistent with what is done clinically and makes for better field validity.

What would happen when members of the HOMC are told to fake *and* to keep it hidden, as well as when they are told to stop faking when they are caught? It is expected that many would stop faking after their first warning, some would fake again and their participation would stop, and some would continue to fake but their faking would not be detected. The following subjects would be excluded from the analysis: (a) subjects who continued to fake and were ejected, (b) subjects who showed no arousal to any stimuli, and (c) subjects who showed arousal of more than 10% erection to any neutral picture.

It would be of interest to compare the number of subjects who did fake, whether or not they were told to fake, in the honest HOMC group, the faking HOMC group, and the honest HEAF group. It would also be of interest to find out if those who were told to fake, did fake, especially those who were not detected and those who seemed to heed the discouragement after one warning.

Studies have reported that PPG has discriminated between pedophiles and controls (Barbaree & Marshall, 1989; Quinsey et al., 1975). Given the design of the above proposed study, it seems reasonable to predict that PPG scores would discriminate between subjects who show homosexual pedophilia, those who are homosexuals, and those who are heterosexuals.

If this study works as predicted, then studies that parallel Case 4 (the identification of sexual preference) and Case 6 (the determination of past criminal sexual behavior) could be carried out. Of course, a study to assess PPG's ability to determine criminal sexual behavior would require writing stories about sex. It is acknowledged that producing a sufficient number of stories might be impractical and that fewer stories would lessen the likelihood of finding significant differences between rapists and nonrapists.

Even if the last proposed study, the one to test PPG's capacity to identify homosexual pedophiles, works reasonably well, this might not be sufficient to allow clinicians and others to use PPG to make decisions with legal implications. Indeed, the bottom line seems to be that PPG probably works best where we need it least (i.e., identifying sexual orientation with cooperative subjects) and that PPG's worst performance is where we want it most, in making predictions of criminal behavior about subjects who fake. Is there a way to make good use of PPG in a clinical setting?

Reconceptualizing PPG

Supposed problems with PPG validity probably issue from the claim that PPG can measure something more than sexual arousal—for example, paraphilias or criminal behavior. Of course, we could use PPG as *part* of a test to diagnose paraphilias or to distinguish rapists from nonrapists. In the same way, we might use an IQ test as part of a test to predict grades in school. Rather than complain about PPG not being a valid test of paraphilic behavior, a better strategy is to ask how PPG, a measure of sexual arousal, might contribute to clinical diagnoses and our legal system.

Paraphilia Test

Some researchers may have hoped that PPG could provide a shortcut to diagnosis of paraphilias—in other words, that PPG is a paraphilia test. We have seen that this is not so or at least that it is not a very accurate paraphilia test. Does this mean that PPG can make no contributions to the diagnostic process? No. Let us assume that paraphilias are defined by the criteria stated in the *DSM-IV* (American Psychiatric Association, 1994). In the case of pedophilia, one of the criteria is the existence of sexual urges toward children. PPG may contribute to the diagnostic process if it demonstrates at least one response of sexual arousal to a picture of a naked child (Marshall & Eccles, 1991). It must be clear that in finding one significant display of sexual arousal to one picture of a naked child, one cannot know that the individual is paraphilic. Still, it is something for which the clinician would look for an explanation. Instead of simply concluding that high-arousal responses to paraphilic stimuli are explained by the client having a paraphilia, the clinician would have to properly weight this response as a descriptor of the client.

Criminal Behavior Test

Clinicians and those who make legal decisions about offenders want a test that can predict sexual criminal behavior. It was hoped that PPG would be that test; it is not. This does not mean, however, that PPG cannot comprise a very limited part or component of a criminal behavior test.

Suppose that a man is accused of molesting a child, and suppose PPG reveals that he has sexual urges toward children (PPG is a very good test of arousal). This would not be, of course, proof that he is guilty. It might not even be good evidence that he is guilty; few people who show such urges molest children. Still, it seems that PPG has told us something very important about the accused: that he has at least a minimal reason to molest a child. In this way, PPG establishes that the client had a motive to commit the crime of which he is accused.

Of course, showing that those who had a motive to commit a crime does not show that that person did commit that crime. Not all people with motives to commit crimes do so. But just as in a murder case, establishing a motive is important; it makes the idea that the person committed the crime prima facie plausible. Once motive is established, prosecutors might add to their case by citing physical evidence, the defendant's criminal history, and so on.

Treatment

One could change the focus from PPG as a test to PPG as an aid to treatment. The following are several suggestions about how PPG might contribute directly to treatment.

Overconfidence

Laws (1999) stated that cessation treatment in itself is not enough; relapse prevention (RP) is necessary. PPG should convince a client that this is so. If a client shows arousal to deviant stimuli after treatment (e.g., to a child), then the client and the therapist should expect that the client will show some arousal in the future. After all, most clients will find themselves in risky situations at some time and will feel aroused, and this arousal may cause an abstinence violation effect (AVE).

Dealing With Lapses

Laws (1999) argues that the AVE may be an important precursor and cause of offending: A client might decide that he has broken a rule, that breaking the rule means that he is not cured of his problems, and that he is out of control. This leaves him with no sense that he can resist his urges.

Because a PPG test involves real sexual stimuli and real sexual behavior, PPG can be used to work with clients in regard to the AVE. Suppose that a client thinks that he must never show arousal to a young child and that if he does, he is powerless to resist his urges. PPG could be used to convince the client that this is not so. After all, showing arousal to a child in the PPG laboratory would be considered by him to be a lapse or a breaking of the no-arousal rule. With such a display of arousal, however, the therapist can talk about the nature of conditioning, the modest impact of the passage of time on such conditioning, the lack of value in the idea of willpower, and so on. As important, the offender should be able to see that arousal, an urge, a real one, is not necessarily followed by relapse. Finally, the offender and the therapist together can work out a way for the offender to cope with such lapses.

What if the client does not feel discomfort after showing arousal, suggesting that there will not be an AVE if the client is aroused by something outside of the laboratory? If the client does not feel concern as a result of the show of arousal to deviant stimuli, again the therapist has important information and must address this problem.

Identifying Critical Cues

A sexual offender might not know exactly what cues trigger sexual arousal that are followed by rape. If the client knew, he could then be taught to watch for those cues and avoid them.

First, there might be situational cues. To figure out which situational cues are powerful for a given client, one might use the theory of self-regulation described by Hudson and Ward (1997) as a guide to writing rape or child molesting stories. Without the client's help, it is unlikely that an experimenter could guess at or cover all the possibilities. Even if one assigns a minimal number of positions across the different choice points (e.g., the salient events that begin the process, the different plans the offender might strike to respond to those salient events, the approach and avoidance styles, the active and passive styles, etc.), the number of stories that could be generated would be in the thousands. In a similar way, one might determine whether there are additional cues, such as physical characteristics, apparent age, and so on. If PPG is used as a therapeutic aid, then a positive reaction to a rape story that is written by the offender offers important information.

Avoiding Self-Awareness

Baumeister (1991) suggested that a common method of avoiding the discomfort of what one's behavior means is to narrow one's focus to a more concrete level of interpretation. For example, one might think "This ice cream tastes so creamy" rather than "This ice cream is full of saturated fat and I know that for people with my cholesterol, more fat raises the risk of heart attack." Offenders may do similar things when offending, but the experience and results of PPG can reverse this tendency. The client is unlikely to be able to avoid the more abstract meaning of being aroused by a deviant stimulus in the PPG laboratory. If the client can somehow ignore the deviance of the stimulus, the therapist can easily review the implications of the client's arousal by saying things such as "This is a picture of a 5-year-old whom you do not know. Your arousal to the child cannot be love for the child."

Positive Emphasis

Thornton (1997) criticizes RP for putting too great an emphasis on risk. PPG can change this emphasis. If a client can demonstrate control over his arousal, something the faking studies suggest, then that demonstration should convince the client that what he thinks is a way to control himself.

Summary

Issues concerning the proper use of PPG were reviewed. Three hypothetical constructs—specifically, sexual arousal, sexual preference, and sexual paraphilia—and the relationship between these constructs and criminal sexual behavior were discussed. Six cases of PPG use, three of which appear to be abuses, were outlined. Studies were proposed that would shed light on PPG reliability—specifically, internal consistency, test-retest reliability, and alternate-form reliability. Problems in PPG validity were isolated: If the experimenter selects the stimuli and the subject fakes, PPG validity is diminished. Improvements (e.g., the use of multiple pictures, theory-guided rape stories, an absolute method of scoring, and the use of new technology) were outlined. Finally, the relationship between PPG and revised RP was considered.

References

Abel, G. G., Barlow, D. H., Blanchard, E. B., & Guild, D. (1977). The components of rapists' sexual arousal. *Archives of General Psychiatry, 34,* 895-903.

Abel, G. G., Barlow, D. H., Blanchard, E. B., & Mavissakalian, M. (1975). Measurement of sexual arousal in male homosexuals: Effects of instructions and stimulus modality. *Archives of Sexual Behavior, 4*(6), 623-629.

Abel, G. G., Becker, J. V., Blanchard, E. B., & Djenderedjian, A. (1978). Differentiating sexual aggressives with penile measures. *Criminal Justice and Behavior, 5*(4), 315-332.

Abel, G. G., Becker, J. V., Murphy, W. D., & Flanagan, B. (1981). Identifying dangerous child molesters. In J. R. Stuart (Ed.), *Violent behavior: Social learning approaches to prediction, management and treatment* (pp. 116-137). New York: Brunner/Mazel.

Abel, G. G., Blanchard, E. B., Barlow, D. H., & Mavissakalian, M. (1975). Identifying specific erotic cues in sexual deviation by audiotape descriptions. *Journal of Applied Behavior Analysis, 8,* 246-260.

Alford, G. S., Wedding, D., & Jones, S. (1983). Faking "turn-ons" and "turn-offs." *Behavior Modification, 7,* 112-125.

American Psychiatric Association (APA). (1994). *Diagnostic and statistical manual of mental disorders* (4th ed.). Washington, DC: Author.

Anastasi, A. (1997). *Psychological testing* (7th ed.). Upper Saddle River, NJ: Prentice Hall.

Avery-Clark, C. A., & Laws, D. R. (1984). Differential erection response patterns of sexual child abusers to stimuli describing activities with children. *Behavior Therapy, 15,* 71-83.

Barbaree, H. E., Baxter, D. J., & Marshall, W. L. (1989). The reliability of the rape index in a sample of rapists and nonrapists. *Violence and Victims, 4,* 299-306.

Barbaree, H. E., & Marshall, W. L. (1989). Erectile responses among heterosexual child molesters, father-daughter incest offenders, and matched non-offenders: Five distinct age preference profiles. *Canadian Journal of Behavioural Science, 21*(1), 70-82.

Barbaree, H. E., Marshall, W. L., & Lanthier, R. D. (1979). Deviant sexual arousal in rapists. *Behavior Research and Therapy, 17,* 215-222.

Barlow, D. H., Leitenberg, H. S., & Agras, W. S. (1969). Experimental control of sexual deviation through manipulation of the noxious scene in covert sensitization. *Journal of Abnormal Psychology, 74,* 596-601.

Barsetti, I., Earls, C. M., & Lalumière, M. L. (1998). The differentiation of intrafamilial and extrafamilial heterosexual child molesters. *Journal of Interpersonal Violence, 13,* 275-286.

Baumeister, R. F. (1991). *Escaping the self.* New York: Basic Books.

Baxter, D. J., Barbaree, H. E., & Marshall, W. L. (1986). Sexual responses to consenting and forced sex in a large sample of rapists and non-rapists. *Behavior Research and Therapy, 24,* 513-520.

Baxter, D. J., Marshall, W. L., Barbaree, H. E., Davidson, P. R., & Malcolm, P. B. (1984). Deviant sexual behavior: Differentiating sex offenders by criminal and personal history, psychometric measures, and sexual response. *Criminal Justice and Behavior, 11,* 477-501.

Blader, J. C., & Marshall, W. L. (1989). Is assessment of sexual arousal in rapists worthwhile? A critique of current methods and the development of a response compatibility approach. *Clinical Psychology Review, 9,* 569-587.

Clark, T. O. (1972). Penile volume response, sexual orientation, and conditioning performance. *British Journal of Psychiatry, 120,* 126.

Eccles, A., Marshall, W. L., & Barbaree, H. E. (1988). The vulnerability of erectile measures to repeated assessments. *Behavior Research and Therapy, 26*(2), 179-183.

Farkas, G. M., Evans, I. M., Sine, L. F., Eifert, G., Wittlieb, E., & Vogelmann-Sine, S. (1979). Reliability and validity of the mercury-in-rubber strain gauge measure of penile circumference. *Behavior Therapy, 10,* 555-561.

Freund, K. (1957). Diagnostika homosexuality u muszu. (Diagnostics of homosexuality in men.) *Ceskoslovak Medicine, 53,* 382-393.

Freund, K. (1963). A laboratory method of diagnosing predominance of homo- and heteroerotic interest in the male. *Behavior Research and Therapy, 1,* 85-93.

Freund, K. (1965). Diagnosing heterosexual pedophilia by means of a test for sexual interest. *Behavior Research and Therapy, 3,* 229-234.

Freund, K. (1981). Assessment of pedophilia. In M. Cook & K. Howells (Eds.), *Adult sexual interest in children* (pp. 139-179). London: Academic Press.

Freund, K., & Blanchard, R. (1989). Phallometric diagnosis of pedophilia. *Journal of Consulting and Clinical Psychology, 57*(1), 100-105.

Freund, K., Langevin, R., & Barlow, D. (1974). Comparison of two penile measures of erotic arousal. *Behavior Research and Therapy, 12,* 355-359.

Freund, K., Langevin, R., Cibiri, S., & Zajac, Y. (1973). Heterosexual aversion in homosexual males. *British Journal of Psychiatry, 122,* 163-169.

Freund, K., McKnight, C. K., Langevin, R., & Cibiri, S. (1972). The female child as a surrogate object. *Archives of Sexual Behavior, 2,* 119-133.

Freund, Sedlacek, and Knob. (1965). A simple transducer for mechanical plethysmography. *Journal of the Experimental Analysis of Behavior, 8, (3),* 167-170.

Fuller, A. K., Barnard, G., Robbins, L., & Spears, H. (1988). Sexual maturity as a criterion for classification of phallometric stimulus slides. *Archives of Sexual Behavior, 17*(3), 271-276.

Geer, J. H., & Fuhr, R. (1976). Cognitive factors in sexual arousal: The role of distraction. *Journal of Consulting and Clinical Psychology, 44,* 238-243.

Hall, G. C. N. (1990). Validity of physiological measures of pedophilic sexual arousal in a sexual offender population: A reply to Quinsey and Laws. *Journal of Consulting and Clinical Psychology, 58*(6), 889-891.

Hall, G. C. N., Proctor, W. C., & Nelson, G. M. (1988). Validity of physiological measures of pedophilic sexual arousal in a sexual offender population. *Journal of Consulting and Clinical Psychology, 56*(1), 118-122.

Hall, G. C. N., Shondrick, D. D., & Hirschman, R. (1993). The role of sexual arousal in sexually aggressive behavior: A meta-analysis. *Journal of Consulting and Clinical Psychology, 61,* 1091-1095.

Harris, G. T., & Rice, M. E. (1996). The science in phallometric measurement of male sexual interest. *Current Directions in Psychological Science, 5*(5), 156-160.

Harris, G. T., Rice, M. E., Quinsey, V. L., & Chaplin, T. C. (1996). Viewing time as a measure of sexual interest among child molesters and normal heterosexual men. *Behavior Research and Therapy, 34*(4), 389-394.

Harris, G. T., Rice, M. E., Quinsey, V. L., Earls, C., & Chaplin, T. C. (1992). Maximizing the discriminant validity of phallometric assessment data. *Psychological Assessment, 4*(4), 502-511.

Henson, D. E., & Rubin, H. B. (1971). Voluntary control of eroticism. *Journal of Applied Behavior Analysis, 4*(1), 37-44.

Hudson, S. M., & Ward, T. (1997, October). *Relapse prevention: Conceptual revisions.* Paper presented at the meeting of the Association for the Treatment of Sexual Abusers, Arlington, VA.

Lalumière, M. L., & Harris, G. T. (1998). Common questions regarding the use of phallometric testing with sexual offenders. *Sexual Abuse: Journal of Research and Treatment, 10*(3), 227-237.

Lalumière, M. L., & Quinsey, V. L. (1994). The discriminability of rapists from non-sex offenders using phallometric measures: A meta-analysis. *Criminal Justice and Behavior, 21,* 150-175.

Laws, D. R. (1999). Relapse prevention. *Journal of Interpersonal Violence, 14,* 285-302.

Laws, D. R., & Holmen, M. L. (1978). Sexual response faking by pedophiles. *Criminal Justice and Behavior, 5*(4), 343-356.

Laws, D. R., & Osborn, C. A. (1983). How to build and operate a behavioral laboratory to evaluate and treat sexual offenders. In J. G. Greer & I. R. Stuart (Eds.), *The sexual aggressor: Current perspectives on treatment* (pp. 293-335). New York: Van Nostrand Reinhold.

Laws, D. R., & Rubin, H. B. (1969). Instructional control of an autonomic sexual response. *Journal of Applied Behavior Analysis, 2*(2), 93-99.

Malamuth, N., & Check, J. (1980a). Penile tumescence and perceptual responses to rape as a function of victims' perceived reactions. *Journal of Applied Social Psychology, 10,* 528-547.

Malamuth, N., & Check, J. (1980b). Sexual arousal to rape and consenting depictions: The importance of the woman's arousal. *Journal of Abnormal Psychology, 89,* 763-766.

Malamuth, N., & Check, J. (1983). Sexual arousal to rape depictions: Individual differences. *Journal of Abnormal Psychology, 92,* 55-67.

Malamuth, N. M., Heim, M., & Feshbach, S. (1980). Sexual responsiveness of college students to rape depictions: Inhibitory and disinhibitory effects. *Journal of Personality and Social Psychology, 38,* 399-408.

Marshall, W. L., & Eccles, A. (1991). Issues in clinical practice with sex offenders. *Journal of Interpersonal Violence, 6*(1), 68-93.

Marshall, W. L., & Fernandez, Y. M. (in press). Phallometric testing with sexual offenders: Limits to its value. *Clinical Psychology Review.*

Masters, W., & Johnson, V. (1966). *Human sexual response.* Boston: Little, Brown.

McAnulty, R. D., & Adams, H. E. (1990). Patterns of sexual arousal of accused child molesters involved in custody disputes. *Archives of Sexual Behavior, 19,* 541-556.

McConaghy, N. (1967). Penile volume change to moving pictures of male and female nudes in heterosexual and homosexual males. *Behavior Research and Therapy, 5,* 43-48.

McConaghy, N. (1969). Subjective and penile plethysmographic responses following aversion-relief and apormorphine aversion therapy for homosexual impulses. *British Journal of Psychiatry, 115,* 723-730.

McConaghy, N. (1970). Penile response conditioning and its relationship to aversion therapy in homosexuals. *Behavior Therapy, 1,* 213-221.

McConaghy, N. (1974). Measurements of change in penile dimensions. *Archives of Sexual Behavior, 3*(4), 381-388.

McConaghy, N. (1989). Validity and ethics of penile circumference measures of sexual arousal: A critical review. *Archives of Sexual Behavior, 18*(4), 357-369.

McConaghy, N., Proctor, D., & Barr, P. (1972). Subjective and penile plethysmography responses to aversion therapy for homosexuality: A partial replication. *Archives of Sexual Behavior, 3,* 67-78.

Murphy, W. D., & Barbaree, H. E. (1994). *Assessments of sex offenders by measures of erectile response: Psychometric properties and decision making.* Brandon, VT: Safer Society.

Murphy, W. D., Krisak, J., Stalgaitis, S., & Anderson, K. (1984). The use of penile tumescence measures with incarcerated rapists: Further validity issues. *Archives of Sexual Behavior, 13*(6), 545-554.

O'Donohue, W., & Letourneau, E. (1992). The psychometric properties of the penile tumescence assessment of child molesters. *Journal of Psychopathology and Behavioral Assessment, 14*(2), 123-174.

Orne, M. T., Thackray, R. I., & Paskewitz, D. A. (1972). The detection of deception: A model for the study of the physiological effects of psychological stimuli. In N. S. Greenfield & R. S. Sternbach (Eds.), *Handbook of psychophysiology* (pp. 743-786). New York: Holt, Rinehart & Winston.

Proulx, J., Cote, G., & Achille, P. A. (1993). Prevention of voluntary control of penile response in homosexual pedophiles during phallometric testing. *Journal of Sex Research, 30,* 140-147.

Quinsey, V. L., & Chaplin, T. C. (1982). Penile responses to nonsexual violence among rapists. *Criminal Justice and Behavior, 9*(3), 372-381.

Quinsey, V. L., & Chaplin, T. C. (1984). Stimulus control of rapists' and non-sex-offenders' sexual arousal. *Behavioral Assessment, 9,* 169-176.

Quinsey, V. L., & Chaplin, T. C. (1988a). Penile responses of child molesters and normals to descriptions of encounters with children involving sex and violence. *Journal of Interpersonal Violence, 3*(3), 259-274.

Quinsey, V. L., & Chaplin, T. C. (1988b). Preventing faking in phallometric assessments of sexual preference. In R. A. Prentky & V. L. Quinsey (Eds.), *Human sexual aggression: Current perspectives* (pp. 49-58). New York: New York Academy of Sciences.

Quinsey, V. L., Chaplin, T. C., & Carrigan, W. F. (1979). Sexual preferences among incestuous and nonincestuous child molesters. *Behavior Therapy, 10,* 562-565.

Quinsey, V. L., Chaplin, T. C., & Upfold, D. (1984). Sexual arousal to nonsexual violence and sadomasochistic themes among rapists and non-sex-offenders. *Journal of Consulting and Clinical Psychology, 52*(4), 651-657.

Quinsey, V. L., & Lalumière, M. L. (1996). *Assessment of sexual offenders against children.* Thousand Oaks, CA: Sage.

Quinsey, V. L., & Laws, D. R. (1990). Validity of physiological measures of pedophilic sexual arousal in a sexual offender population: A critique of Hall, Proctor, and Nelson. *Journal of Consulting and Clinical Psychology, 58*(6), 886-888.

Quinsey, V. L., Rice, M. E., & Harris, G. T. (1995). Actuarial prediction of sexual recidivism. *Journal of Interpersonal Violence, 10*(1), 85-105.

Quinsey, V. L., Rice, M. E., Harris, G. T., & Reid, K. S. (1993). The phylogenetic and ontogenetic development of sexual age preferences in males: Conceptual and measurement issues. In H. E. Barbaree & W. L. Marshall (Eds.), *The juvenile sex offender* (pp. 143-163). New York: Guilford.

Quinsey, V. L., Steinman, C. M., Bergersen, S. G., & Holmes, T. F. (1975). Penile circumference, skin conductance, and ranking responses of child molesters and "normals" to sexual and nonsexual visual stimuli. *Behavior Therapy, 6,* 213-219.

Rice, M. E., Chaplin, T. C., Harris, G. T., & Coutts, J. (1994). Empathy for the victim and sexual arousal among rapists and nonrapists. *Journal of Interpersonal Violence, 9*(4), 435-449.

Rice, M. E., & Harris, G. T. (1997). Cross validation and extension of the Violence Risk Appraisal Guide for child molesters and rapists. *Law and Human Behavior, 21,* 321-241 .

Rice, M. E., Harris, G. T., & Quinsey, V. L. (1990). A follow-up of rapists assessed in a maximum security psychiatric facility. *Journal of Interpersonal Violence, 5,* 435-448.

Rice, M. E., Quinsey, V. L., & Harris, G. T. (1991). Sexual recidivism among child molesters released from a maximum security psychiatric institution. *Journal of Consulting and Clinical Psychology, 59*(3), 381-386.

Rosen, R. C., & Keefe, F. J. (1978). The measurement of human penile tumescence. *Psychophysiology, 15*(4), 366-376.

Rubin, H. B., & Henson, D. E. (1975). Voluntary enhancement of penile erection. *Bulletin of the Psychonomic Society, 6*(2), 158-160.

Schouten, P. G. W., & Simon, W. T. (1992). Validity of phallometric measures with sex offenders: Comments on the Quinsey, Laws, and Hall debate. *Journal of Consulting and Clinical Psychology, 60*(5), 812-814.

Seto, M. C., & Kuban, M. (1996). Criterion-related validity of a phallometric test for paraphilic rape and sadism. *Behavior Research and Therapy, 34*(2), 175-183.

Thornton, D. (1997, October). *Is relapse prevention really necessary?* Paper presented at the 16th Annual Meeting of the Association for the Treatment of Sexual Abusers, Arlington, VA.

Wormith, J. S. (1986). Assessing deviant sexual arousal: Physiological and cognitive aspects. *Advances in Behavior Research and Therapy, 8,* 101-137.

Wydra, A., Marshall, W. L., Earls, C. M., & Barbaree, H. E. (1983). Identification of cues and control of sexual arousal by rapists. *Behavior Research and Therapy, 21,* 469-476.

Zuckerman, M. (1971). Physiological measures of sexual arousal in the human. *Psychological Bulletin, 5,* 297-329.

CHAPTER 16

Polygraphy

Assessment and Community Monitoring

MICHAEL A. O'CONNELL
Mill Creek, Washington

In any endeavor, one should expect some tension between theory and practice. This is especially true in the case of the evaluation and treatment of sexual deviancy. Here, the negative consequences of incorrect or misapplied theory can have dramatic and devastating consequences. Historically, clinical approaches to working with sex offenders had been shaped by the theories that sought to make sense of what motivated sexual offending. For example, Groth's (1979) typology sought to differentiate among men who raped on the basis of their psychological motivation. Groth followed up with coauthors Hobson and Gary (Groth, Hobson, & Gary, 1982) to present a theory of child molester types.

The notion of distinct sex offender typologies fits an older tradition that expected a narrow range of sexually deviant outlets. Kinsey, Pomeroy, and Martin (1948) described child molesters as "sexually thwarted, incapable of winning attention from older females and reduced to vain attempts with children who are unable to defend themselves" (p. 238). Frisbic (1966) and Hammer and Glueck (1957) proposed that sex offenders have arrested psychological development. Supported by single case studies with discussions of the theoretical implications (Barnett, 1972; Salzman, 1972; Socarides, 1973; Zechnich, 1971), sexually deviant behavior and sex offending were typically seen as a symptom of an underlying emotional pathology. This meant that the motivation to commit sex offenses was narrow, unusual, and aberrant. Those who would molest only boys could be differentiated from those who would only molest girls. Child molesters who had offended against children outside the family would pose little risk to their own children. Men who exposed their genitals might be regarded as pursuing a particular psychological need that was satisfied by exhibitionism to adults and would present no risk to children.

Abel and his colleagues created a furor when they presented a paper at the World Congress of Behavioral Therapy (Abel, Mittleman, Becker, Cunningham-Rathner, & Lucas, 1983). This presentation and subsequent publications (Abel et al., 1987; Abel, Becker, Cunningham-Rathner, Mittleman, & Rouleau, 1988; Abel & Osborn, 1992; Abel & Rouleau, 1990) reported extensive histories of previously undetected and unreported sex offenses. Moreover, participants reported a wide range of deviant sexual behavior. Other investigators, using somewhat less complex and sophisticated procedures, found similar although much less dramatic results (Freund, 1990; Laws, 1994; Weinrott & Saylor, 1991). In a study, described below, I corroborate the more dramatic results of Abel and his colleagues regarding the range and extent of sexual deviancy among sex offenders. These more recent studies have supported models of sexual deviancy that suggest that repeated sex offending behavior is driven more by behavioral reinforcement rather than more complex psychological motivations.

Relapse prevention with sex offenders was adapted from use with substance and other addiction-like, behaviorally reinforced problem behaviors (George & Marlatt, 1989). This approach distinguished cessation of addictive behaviors from the maintenance of change (relapse prevention). Relapse prevention has been especially useful with its attention on precursors to relapse, such as emotional states and environments that present high-risk situations. In addition, relapse prevention has helped clarify some mechanisms that work to extend lapses into repeated relapses: short-term gratification and the abstinence violation effect.

However, relapse prevention has come under scrutiny and criticism in recent years. Maletsky (1998) comments on the limitations of thinking about cycles, which suggests the inevitability of repeated unpleasant outcomes. Ward and Hudson (1998a) note that the original relapse prevention model fails to cover all the possibilities involved in reoffending. These limitations, in practice, lead to some compelling problems. Many offenders, who having completed relapse prevention treatment, often in classroom settings, report confidence in their capacity to avoid reoffense "because I learned my relapse cycle." However, when asked to describe their cycle, they say, "But, I don't have it with me." These men can also place themselves in risky circumstances that may not have been identified as high-risk situations. In addition, probation officers often limit their assessment of treatment progress to what amounts to a vocabulary

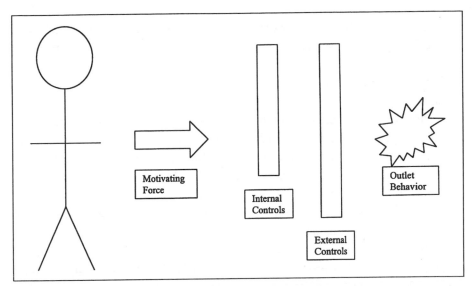

Figure 16.1.   Model of Child Molestation
SOURCE: Adapted from Finkelhor (1984).

test. For example, if an offender is familiar with relapse prevention terms, then all is well. However, if an offender is acting in accordance with relapse prevention principles but is not using the nomenclature of the model, then the probation officer can misunderstand the man to be "back in cycle."

As the above examples show, relapse prevention has been easy and tempting to oversimplify. Its attractive simplicity can lead to misuse. Much of relapse prevention subject matter lends itself to classroom presentation. This can lead to the mistaken assumption that preventing reoffenses can be accomplished by simply teaching relapse prevention.

Thus, relapse prevention has been a useful Level III microtheory (see Ward & Hudson, 1998b) insofar as it attempts to describe the offending process. It can help shape and implement protective maintenance strategies. An alternative model of the process that I have found useful, given its simplicity and ease with which clients understand it, is based on Finkelhor's (1984) model of child molestation. Figure 16.1 is a slightly modified version of the one Finkelhor presented. I use this model as a way of introducing treatment objectives to new clients as they are about to begin therapy. It is also helpful when meeting with a client's friends or family members, as they receive direction about how to monitor the offender in moderate-risk situations.

This model shows how the potential offender is affected by competing forces: First is the motivating force propelling him in the direction of committing the *outlet behavior.* This could be a sex offense or any attractive but irresponsible activity. This could include abusing alcohol or drugs, robbing a bank, or driving at high speed on the highway. The motivating force is whatever makes the outlet behavior attractive. In the case of robbing a bank, the attraction is the prospect of obtaining a lot of money. In the case of a sex offense, the motivating force could be sexual arousal and pleasure or meeting some emotional need.

For everyone, barriers stand in the way of their acting on these attractions. Most obvious are external controls. Although most people can appreciate the attraction of taking possession of the bank's money, they also realize the money is locked up. If you attempt to take it and get caught, you will get into a lot of trouble. The same is true with sex offenses. High on the list of the external controls is the realization that you could get into a lot of trouble if you try to have sex with a child. Besides, you would need to have an opportunity to be alone with potential child victims and be sure they will not tell anybody what happened before you could go ahead with the offending behavior.

In addition to external controls is the reality that most people believe sex offending and bank robbery are wrong and would never seriously consider engaging in that behavior. They have internal controls that kick in before they need the external controls to prevent them from molesting a child or robbing a bank. Nevertheless, most of us do check the speedometer when we see a police car on the highway. So, external controls do have an effect on our internal controls.

In fact, most internal controls are internalized external controls. For example, if you are like most people, somewhere around age 3 or 4, you learned to look both ways before you crossed the street. That lesson was probably learned under the supervision of a parent or other adult. You were not allowed to cross the street unless you looked both ways. These days, you probably look both ways before you cross the street without giving it much thought. You have thoroughly internalized this rule, and it probably serves you well.

Whenever a sex offense occurs or, for that matter, whenever anyone engages in any pleasurable but irresponsible behavior, the strength of the motivating force, whatever it is, is stronger than the combination of internal and external controls. Put another way, to prevent a sex offense, the controls must be strong and resilient enough to resist the force that propels a potential offender in the direction of the proscribed behavior.

Interventions to prevent reoffense must begin with the understanding that the offender had some combination of strong enough motivation and insufficient controls. Thus, interventions should be directed at strengthening controls and reducing attraction to the behavior. As a practical matter, the most obvious place to begin is with external controls. The main attraction of external controls is that they do not depend on the offender to implement them, and, compared to reduced motivation to offend or increased internal controls, it is easier to see when external controls are in place.

But how stringent must those external controls be? Certainly, confinement in prison substantially reduces the likelihood of reoffense. For some offenders, that degree of external control may be required over a lifetime. Others may need to be in a secure setting while they develop more reliable internal controls and reduce the attraction to the offending behavior. Others may be able to avoid reoffense with much less in the way of externally imposed constraints. But how do you know?

The Need for Accurate Assessment Information

Risk assessment and prediction of violent reoffense have received increasing attention. With the expansion of civil commitment statutes for sexually violent predators, actuarial methods to predict risk to the community have become valuable tools. Hanson and Bussière's (1998) meta-analysis of 61 follow-up studies found sexual recidivism was best predicted by deviant sexual preference and prior sexual offenses. Risk assessment instruments (e.g., Hanson, 1997; Quinsey, Harris, Rice, & Cormier, 1998) spotlight factors that address *deviant sexual arousal* or *relevant offending history*. In other words, the attractiveness of sex offending and the frequency of past offending are likely to be important in assessing risk.

Deviant Sexual Arousal

Several methods can be used to determine which deviant sexual stimuli appeal to a particular man. His self-report has the attraction of being direct and relatively simple. However, when it comes to deviant sexual arousal, self-report by sex offenders can significantly underestimate deviant arousal compared to physiological measurements (Laws, 1989; Murphy & Barbaree, 1988; Pithers & Laws, 1989). Penile plethysmograph, even with its limitations requiring the man's cooperation, provides an objective means to assess sexual interest. In recent years, the Abel Screen has shown some promise as a less intrusive alternative (Abel, Huffman, Warberg, & Holland, 1998; Abel, Lawry, Karlstrom, & Osborn, 1994). With either of these instruments, it can be instructive to compare the client's self-report of sexual interest to the physiological measurement. The comparison can shed light on two important questions: How realistic is the man about his own arousal? Can he be counted on to see a potential problem developing?

Relevant Offending History

Having a reliable and relevant behavioral history in this context means knowing how often a man has engaged in what kind of sex-offending behavior. This information serves two assessment purposes: (a) It offers another indication of attraction. When it comes to repeated incidents of sexually deviant behavior, people seldom return to behavior they found completely unappealing. (b) A complete and accurate sexual history provides a clear indication of gaps in the controls that were in operation at the time of the deviant activity.

Using Polygraph for Assessment

An archival study of 127 files of men referred for evaluation of amenability for community-based sex offender treatment (O'Connell, 1998) described what these men reported about their deviant sexual behavior at three different points in the evaluation process: (a) on referral, (b) after clinical interviews, and (c) after sexual history polygraph testing. The polygraph testing was conducted at the end of the evaluation process and after the participant had reviewed his sexual history in clinical interviews with the evaluator.

A comprehensive prepolygraph interview with the polygraph examiner essentially replicated the sexual history discussed in the earlier clinical interviews. The polygrapher reviewed and summarized sexual history with the client before the instrumentation began. During the polygraph instrumentation, the man is asked a number of questions, to which he is expected to answer no. The questions are crafted to corroborate his self-report of general sexual history, as well as those parts of the sexual history or referral problem that are of greatest concern.

This study suggested that polygraph testing elicited significantly more information regarding sexually deviant behavior and lifetime sexual offending. On average, more than three times the number of incidents of sexually deviant behavior had been reported after polygraph testing than were known before. In addition, polygraph testing led to disclosures of more different types of sexual deviancy: The average number of different paraphilias reported was doubled after polygraph testing. Nearly half of the men were found to be deceptive on the initial polygraph instrumentation, leading to additional testing. They required as many as four separate test administrations, admitting more information with each succeeding test, to pass. In addition to those whose initial testing resulted in a deceptive finding, many participants reported more deviant history when they realized withholding the information would result in polygraph charts indicating deception. These results suggest that sex offenders who are taking polygraph exams to corroborate their self-report of sexual history have a high base rate (46%) of attempting deception. This lowers the probability of false-positive results with this population.

Fourteen of the 127 participants in this outpatient sample ultimately ended up with polygraph charts indicating either deception or inconclusive results. Yet most of these ended up being accepted, by the treating agency and the referring criminal justice institution, for community-based treatment. Even in these cases, polygraph testing encouraged clients to disclose important new information, such as additional victims, more incidents of offending, and additional paraphilias. Thus, polygraph testing was not used as a means to make definitive judgments of the truth but rather was a means to encourage clinically important disclosures. Sex offenders probably have more extensive deviant histories than would be known without polygraph testing. A more complete report of deviant sexual history during pretreatment evaluation will help clinicians understand important issues related to treatment planning and risk assessment.

Risk Assessment and Treatment Planning

Polygraph testing to corroborate sexual history should be part of a comprehensive evaluation that should precede specialized treatment for sexual deviancy (see O'Connell, Leberg, & Donaldson, 1990, for a more thorough discussion of this point). Of course, during and throughout the course of treatment, the sex offender client will provide additional and more detailed information about himself and his offending. This will add new insights about his life, his offending patterns, and his risk factors. However, the "heavy lifting" of assessment should occur before therapy begins in earnest. There are several reasons for this.

First, actuarial risk prediction studies have indicated that static factors, such as pretreatment deviant sexual arousal and relevant offending history, are the most powerful predictors of recidivism. This information can usually be gathered before therapy. There are no clinical reasons not to accumulate as much of this important information as possible. Sexual history polygraph testing is an excellent vehicle for obtaining a rich data set of this important information. Failure to obtain this information could result in treatment that does not address important clinical and risk-related issues.

When treatment is conducted in an outpatient, community-based setting, this is all the more important. In this setting, unidentified risks can have immediate and potentially dangerous consequences. For the therapist treating sex offenders in the community, the first order of business is to ensure that the likelihood of reoffense is at a manageable and acceptable level.

The importance of pretreatment evaluation and risk assessment may be less critical in a secure, institutional setting in that the dangers of reoffense are likely to be substantially less in the short run. Perhaps with the luxury of a more leisurely assessment schedule, within a treatment setting, the therapist could obtain more complete data and information of a subtler dimension. Risk to the community and the likelihood of reoffense are not significant until after the offender is released from the institution. However, there are still problems potentially associated with failing to conduct a thorough evaluation prior to beginning treatment. Therapy involves establishing a relationship with the client to help the man understand himself better and to make some difficult changes in his life. Many if not most sex offenders are human beings with genuinely likeable qualities. They want and need to be liked for both healthy reasons and manipulative ones. Effective therapists come to know and care about their clients. If therapists are attempting to both establish a therapeutic relationship and assemble risk-related information, there is the danger that important assessment information could be contaminated or narrowed by interpersonal factors.

This may be one of the reasons why clinical judgment alone has been shown to be an unreliable means of assessing risk of violent and sexual reoffense (Monahan, 1981). Indeed, studies (e.g., Barbaree, 1999) indicate that the predictive power of purely actuarial risk assessment methods can be diluted or contaminated by "clinical judgment." Therefore, not only is it important to conduct thorough pretreatment evaluations and risk assessments, but clinicians should also be very cautious about assuming that treatment compliance or therapeutic progress should override pretreatment risk assessment when crafting long-term planning about community placement.

Using polygraph testing has another advantage in assessing deviant sexual history as part of a comprehensive evaluation. Contrary to what many would expect, it can be employed in a very noncoercive, "nothing personal" sort of way. There is less need and temptation for aggressive confrontation of denial and minimization in a way that can be wearing and demeaning. Clients can be told simply that they need to take a polygraph exam as part of the evaluation for community-based treatment. Consider the following, for example:

> I know this is very embarrassing stuff to talk about and admit to. Most people in your situation naturally want, if they can, to hold back some information. But I really need to know that what you tell me about your offending history is really all there is. If you take and "pass" a polygraph exam on this issue, I will have much greater confidence that you are, indeed, telling me the whole truth about this. On the other hand, if you show deception on the exam, I will know that you are likely withholding information that is important for us to be talking about in treatment. So, after we go over your sexual history, I will refer you to a polygraph examiner. If, for some reason, you withhold something from me, by all means be sure to tell the truth to the polygrapher. Because if you don't, the polygraph charts will indicate a problem. Then we'll just have to figure out what you didn't report. And then you'll have to take another polygraph exam to show me that information is the whole story. So, save yourself the trouble and the expense of taking follow-up tests by telling the whole truth about your sexual history the first time through.

Rather than suggesting that the therapist does not trust the client, this approach conveys an appreciation and understanding of the difficult situation he finds himself in. At the same time, this approach communicates that the therapist is uncompromising about the need to get important information out on the table to understand the level of risk and reduce the likelihood of reoffense.

As noted earlier, using polygraph testing to corroborate the client's self-report of deviant history substantially increases what is known about his attraction to deviant sexuality and the range and extent of his deviant history. What effect will this additional information have on risk assessment models? It is probable that risk prediction models, all of which were developed on the basis of official records and offender self-reports, will need to be recalibrated to accommodate the increased base rates of deviant behavior that will result from polygraph-assisted assessments. Furthermore, not only therapists treating sex offenders but also judges, prosecuting attorneys, and other community protection agents have an interest in these sexual histories. It is vital that they also expect to see increased disclosures with sexual history polygraph exams. It would be counterproductive if they imposed severe consequences and discouraged disclosures that are important for evaluation and treatment.

The resulting expanded report of deviant sexual history during a pretreatment assessment helps to shape our understanding of two important treatment issues: deviant sexual arousal and high-risk situations.

Deviant Sexual Arousal

Of course, sexual history should be compared to the results of the physiological assessment of sexual arousal. If, for example, plethysmograph testing shows highest arousal to prepubescent boys and he acknowledges acting on this many times, then treatment intervention can begin with a high degree of confidence that sexual attraction to boys is a major risk consideration. Whether or not a client says he is sexually attracted to boys and whether or not physiological testing shows attraction to that particular stimulus, if he fondled the penis of an 8-year-old boy once, the behavior was attractive enough for him to do it. If he did it twice, it was attractive enough to come back for more. Greater numbers of incidents suggest an even greater level of attraction. Therefore, frequency of offending is likely to be a meaningful indication of the level of deviant sexual arousal. Moreover, the higher the frequency, the stronger the association between the sexual attraction and deviant behavior.

Knowing about the client's deviant arousal logically leads to establishing some specific treatment conditions, which can then be monitored, as discussed below. These external controls should be designed to advance the treatment goal of reducing deviant arousal. For example, whether or not the client has the opportunity to offend (he may be well supervised), an offender with a strong attraction to prepubescent children should probably not attend family swim sessions at the community pool. Nor should he, even if he is in a secure, institutional setting, masturbate to images of a child in a swim suit that he sees in a magazine. Either case would likely reinforce and strengthen his attraction to offending stimuli.

High-Risk Situations

The expanded self-report of sexual history provides important insights about holes in the controls that govern a person's behavior. No matter how strong the attraction, every time an offender engaged in sexually deviant behavior, the combination of internal and external controls in place was insufficient to prevent that behavior from occurring. This is especially important information in assessing risk and amenability to treatment in less restrictive settings such as community-based programs.

For example, if we have a high degree of confidence an offender has molested only children he has known quite well and where he assumed a caregiving role, then additional external controls should focus particular attention on his avoiding those situations. It is relatively uncomplicated to develop and implement rules that proscribe being alone with children in private settings and acting as a caregiver. The risks would be quite different if the offender had befriended children playing videogames at a convenience store and groomed them for molestation. The additional external controls needed in this second example would cast a much wider net of prohibited activities.

Polygraph corroboration of deviant sexual history introduces more confidence and greater precision in crafting rules, whether they come from a court order, probation conditions, or a treatment contract. External controls should be crafted with an eye on both the offender's potential attraction to the offending behavior and how controls failed to deter past offending situations. Of course, the new rules should include a built-in margin for error. The costs for being wrong in this business are very great.

On the other hand, overuse of external controls can have the undesirable effect of lessening the likelihood they will be internalized. After all, most interventions involving sex offender treatment and supervision are time limited. At some point, most offenders will need to function successfully without official, external surveillance. We want offenders to assume more responsibility for implementing and managing their own internal controls. We create a problem if the external controls are too onerous and prohibit activities that are clearly unrelated to risk. Offenders are likely to stop following these kinds of rules as soon as they are able (e.g., at the end of mandated treatment or when completing court-ordered supervision). If so, they risk "throwing out the baby with the bath water" if they stop observing rules that are truly essential for them to avoid tempting, risky situations.

Treatment and supervision rules should help the offender practice a lifestyle that lessens the opportunities and temptations to offend. This is similar to recovering alcoholics who may want to develop a social circle and lifestyle that minimize the situations in which they may need to turn down offers of a drink. Likewise, child molesters may be well served to think about themselves as people who generally avoid situations with children. Consider the case of a man who has enjoyed officiating youth sports activities but sexually offended against his children. He may be well monitored on the playing field and may never find himself alone with children. The objective level of risk may be quite low. But what message is he sending himself and those who know him? It may be better to practice and internalize the notion, "I'm careful to limit my activities with children" rather than "I'm OK around kids."

Sexual history polygraph testing can help provide an additional measure of confidence in crafting external controls, especially when deciding *not* to include a prohibition. An exhibitionist or voyeur may not need extensive prohibitions to avoid children. If, for example, polygraph testing corroborates an exposer's self-report that deviant history did not include child victims, this information can provide therapists and community supervision agents (e.g., probation officers) with the confidence to avoid imposing rules that do not address likely areas of risk.

In conclusion, when treating an offender in the community, the first order of business is to ensure that he does not act in a way that increases the likelihood of reoffense. The rules or external controls that you hope he will practice and internalize should provide a barrier to placing himself in high-risk situations. If these rules are well crafted and are meaningful to the man himself, it is vitally important that they be followed. How do you know if they are?

Using Polygraph for Monitoring

Besides helping with assessment and treatment planning, polygraph is a useful tool for monitoring participation in treatment. Periodic, rule-compliance polygraph exams offer an additional measure of oversight and quality control for treatment and community placement rules. Although the literature is not extensive, one small published study (Abrams & Ogard, 1986) indicates that polygraph monitoring is associated with lower levels of reoffending. A number of articles (e.g., Blasingame, 1998; Hagler, 1995) have indicated polygraph can be a useful adjunct to community-based treatment and monitoring.

Rule-compliance polygraph testing focuses on the offender's adherence to the external controls. As discussed earlier, these controls are a way to help the client avoid high-risk situations and ensure he is appropriately managing his deviant sexual arousal (see O'Connell et al., 1990, for an outline of recommended conditions for community-based treatment). For example, child molesters would be prohibited from unsupervised contact with children. Exposers might be prohibited from having unstructured time driving around in their car, if that was part of their offending pattern. Most offenders in treatment would be prohibited from using disinhibiting drugs or alcohol. Rules for institutional treatment are likely to be less extensive because there are fewer opportunities for clients to place themselves in risky situations. All offenders, in whatever treatment setting, would be expected to refrain from masturbating to deviant fantasies and required to report deviant impulses.

Before the test instrumentation, the polygraph examiner should conduct a prepolygraph interview with the man to review all relevant rules: court orders, probation rules, and treatment directives. Some examiners and programs have him fill out a written questionnaire, listing all violations of the rules. If this tool is used, care must be taken that it does not undermine the effectiveness of the polygraph exam to detect deception.

Polygraph testing is a measure of emotional distress at the prospect of being caught in a lie. If the offender is withholding important information and has lied about that, it is important that he be worrying about getting caught in that lie at the time of testing. If he filled out a questionnaire a week earlier and the polygraph test is about whether he lied on that questionnaire, the emotional saliency of that lie could be less than if he had just looked the examiner in the eye and said something he knew was false. So, if a questionnaire is used to ensure completeness or for record-keeping purposes, it is important that the man's answers on that questionnaire be discussed in detail at the prepolygraph interview.

At the prepolygraph interview, the man will report any violations of the rules during some defined period of time, usually since the last polygraph exam. The polygraph examiner will craft relevant questions for the testing, based on (a) information from the therapist or community supervision agent (e.g., probation officer) about areas of greatest concern and (b) incorporating information from the prepolygraph interview. The examiner will review the questions with the client before the test instrumentation. This is done to ensure a shared understanding of the meaning of the questions and so the subject is not surprised by any of the questions. This ensures that any physiological responses are to fears of being caught in a lie, not due to surprise at the question.

Test validity is enhanced when the test questions are limited in scope. Therefore, the preferred method for question composition involves several different ways of asking him if he lied on the prepolygraph interview regarding rule compliance. Consider the following, for example:

1. Regarding this history, did you lie to me about not violating your rules of either probation or treatment?
2. Regarding this history, did you lie to me about your contact with minors?
3. Other than what you told me today, did you lie about your honesty with your therapist and group about your sexual activity?
4. Regarding this history, did you lie to me about your use of either alcohol or illegal drugs?

Purposes of Periodic Polygraph Exams

Monitoring polygraph exams serves several important but distinctly different purposes: uncovering problems, encouraging rule compliance, and increasing self-disclosure in therapy.

Discovering Problems

At the most basic level, deceptive polygraph findings can alert therapists and community supervision agents that something is amiss. Of greater value are admissions the client makes at the prepolygraph interview to "pass" the exam. These bring attention to problems in the client's approach to treatment or adherence to external controls. Acknowledging he has consumed alcohol or drugs, especially for someone who has a history of offending while intoxicated, can bring attention to this concern. A child molester acknowledging previously unreported, unsupervised contact with children can alert community supervision agents to potential high-risk situations. These rule violations indicate that an offender is failing to respect the boundaries that have been put into place to contain his placement in the community.

Encouraging Rule Compliance

Another value of periodic polygraph testing is the extra measure of motivation it provides sex offenders to adhere to the external controls (see Abrams & Ogard, 1986, for a modest study that provides some evidence of this). Knowing that he has to take a polygraph exam can give the offender an additional reason to think twice before crossing the line into prohibited activity. We want offenders in treatment and on community placement to follow the rules. We want them to practice operating within those constraints with the hope they will make them a habit. Just as most drivers will check their speedometer if they believe a trooper with speed-detecting radar may be around the bend in the highway, understanding that a polygraph exam is in the offing can help sex offenders check their behavior.

Increasing Self-Disclosure in Therapy

Periodic polygraph testing helps encourage the sex offender in treatment to report relevant information to his therapist. This includes not only information about rule compliance but also information about sexual activity and sexual fantasies. Mental rehearsal of deviant sexual behavior is believed to mediate and increase the probability of sexual aggression (Laws & Marshall, 1990). Sexual history polygraph testing (see O'Connell, 1998) demonstrated that a majority of subjects in a community-based sample of sex offenders came to acknowledge that sex offenses did not just happen but were accompanied by covert rehearsal and reinforcement of sexually deviant arousal. Treatment interventions should include prohibitions against reinforcing deviant sexual arousal. This includes rules about not masturbating to deviant fantasies.

If an offender is masturbating to appropriate fantasies but finds that deviant, offense-related fantasies intrude, this important information needs to be discussed in treatment. If an offender client finds he is getting sexually aroused when he drives past a school bus stop, this is information vitally important for reducing the impulse to offend. How is a therapist to know whether or when a client is experiencing these sexually arousing thoughts? Typically, therapists want their clients to report their sexual thoughts, feelings, and behaviors as a way of monitoring this important area and encouraging the client to begin self-monitoring his sexual interests. But this is asking a lot. Most people regard their sexual fantasies as their private affair, and few of us want to discuss the themes that are part of our sexual impulses. Sex offenders in treatment are typically reluctant to acknowledge that they are still experiencing deviant sexual arousal. At the very least, they arc embarrassed about this. They are also likely to fear that information of this sort could negatively affect their legal and treatment status.

Many therapists using periodic or rule-compliance polygraph testing address this problem by first having a treatment rule that sex offender clients report sexual activities, fantasies, and impulses by way of a daily journal or weekly check-in sheet. Self-report of all sexual activities provides the raw material for treatment intervention. The client must be talking with his therapist about what is arousing and what is not. Clients' self-report of deviant or gray-area sexual interests allows potential problems to be addressed before they are acted on or progress to even more serious problems.

Compliance with the rule requiring a full and complete report of sexual thoughts, feelings, and behaviors can then be corroborated on the periodic polygraph testing. As with other rule-compliance issues addressed this way, the preferred outcome is a no-deception result on the polygraph charts and no information reported at the prepolygraph interview that had not been thoroughly discussed in treatment. This result tells the therapist and the community supervision agent that all has been going as was previously thought.

Interventions: New Information and Deceptive Findings

If the client needed to report new information at the prepolygraph interview to "pass" the test, this information gets factored into what the therapist and community supervision agents know about the offender's treatment progress and rule compliance. If the polygraph charts show deception, then the interested parties only know that something is amiss. What the offender says to explain the deceptive results in the posttest interview and on subsequent occasions should be regarded with caution. This should begin a process leading to follow-up polygraph testing to corroborate the client's self-report.

The severity of the rule violation and the assessment of risk will be included in my decision of what to make of troubling polygraph results. It is rare for offenders to "pass" all of their periodic tests without reporting new information in treatment sessions just before the test or at the prepolygraph interview. For example, it is not uncommon for clients to report in the beginning stages of treatment that they have stopped having any sexual impulses, fantasies, or urges. The fear associated with the investigation of their offense, their arrest, and conviction occasionally causes offenders to lose interest in sexual matters. But this fear-induced aversion to all things sexual, especially sexually deviant arousal, tends to wear off over time.

Polygraph testing is often necessary to get these clients to admit that deviant sexual impulses have returned. It can be good news when a client *finally* reports occasional deviant impulses to "pass" a monitoring polygraph exam. This can be the beginning of meaningful and fruitful treatment interventions to better manage and reduce deviant sexual arousal.

On the other hand, there are times when I find myself with little room for error. I may have decided to work with an offender who is only marginally acceptable for community-based treatment. It is made clear to such a client that he has little room for mistakes. Community safety may require that he demonstrate the willingness and capacity to have no rule infractions. I may place this person on a period of probationary treatment while I see if he can operate within the confines of treatment rules (see O'Connell et al., 1990, for an outline of typical community-based treatment rules). Early, periodic polygraph testing may uncover rule-compliance problems and convince me that this is a person who is not suitable for outpatient treatment.

Sex offending is, among other things, the result of offenders doing what felt good rather than what was right. Treatment interventions and community supervision should, among other things, help offenders learn to do the right thing, even when that may not feel as good. Rule compliance or periodic polygraph testing helps reinforce this principle.

Testing Frequency

Although rule-compliance polygraph testing is a valuable tool, more is not necessarily better. Polygraph testing risks losing potency and validity when conducted too frequently. Six-month intervals are generally recommended. Some standards allow 3-month intervals between examinations. I recommend having the first administration of periodic rule-compliance testing no more than 6 months into treatment. If there are concerns about the client's willingness or ability to be honest about rule adherence, then a monitoring polygraph exam 3 months into treatment is required. It is best to avoid a sex offender beginning treatment, especially if he is living in a community setting, having a lot of early practice at breaking the rules, or failing to report important information. Having the client know a polygraph test is coming in the foreseeable future may lessen the temptation to get away with something. But if the client is trying to avoid reporting important information or operating outside the containment vessel of established safety rules, we need to know about that sooner rather than later.

Summary

Polygraph testing can help focus attention on critical aspects of relapse prevention with sex offenders. Assessment testing can help clarify an individual's attraction to sexual deviancy and particular high-risk situations. Polygraph monitoring can help ensure offenders refrain from reinforcing sexual deviancy and avoid risky situations.

Sexual history polygraph testing also helps therapists and other interested parties know more about the client's offending and deviant history. The more complete self-report of deviant history provides important information about the offender's attraction to offending behavior. This information also helps identify an individual's specific high-risk situations, those circumstances that are truly on the road to reoffense. This can help with the development of treatment interventions and strategies to contain the potential risk to the community.

Defining the truly risky circumstances an offender should avoid can help shape meaningful external controls. These include rules the offender should practice while in treatment and under supervision. Periodic rule-compliance polygraph testing increases the likelihood of offenders adhering to externally imposed controls. Polygraph monitoring can increase the probability that offenders will internalize the external controls through practice and habituation. This is especially important over the long haul, as the external structure recedes.

On the other hand, polygraph monitoring of rule compliance can bring attention to the fraying of external controls. If an offender is not willing or able to operate within the existing structure, then it may be necessary to impose additional external controls. Reducing the likelihood of reoffense to acceptable levels includes recognizing when an offender is at too high a risk of relapse. It may not feel like a therapeutic victory, but knowing that a sex offender needs to remain in a secure setting to avoid high-risk situations is still very important information. Polygraph monitoring is but one part of a web of intervention and containment strategies. Nevertheless, this tool can help elicit important information that is otherwise difficult to obtain.

References

Abel, G. G., Becker, J. V., Cunningham-Rathner, J., Mittelman, M. S., & Rouleau, J. L. (1988). Multiple paraphilic diagnoses among sex offenders. *Bulletin of the American Academy of Psychiatry and the Law, 16,* 153-168.

Abel, G. G., Becker, J. V., Mittelman, M., Cunningham-Rathner, J., Rouleau, J. L., & Murphy, W. D. (1987). Self-reported sex crimes of nonincarcerated paraphiliacs. *Journal of Interpersonal Violence, 2,* 3-25.

Abel, G. G., Huffman, J., Warberg, B., & Holland, C. L. (1998). Visual reaction time and plethysmography as measures of sexual interest in child molesters. *Sexual Abuse: A Journal of Treatment and Research, 10,* 81-95.

Abel, G. G., Lawry, S. S., Karlstrom, E., & Osborn, C. A. (1994). Screening tests for pedophilia. *Criminal Justice and Behavior, 21,* 115-131.

Abel, G. G., Mittelman, M., Becker, J. V., Cunningham-Rathner, J., & Lucas, L. (1983, December). *The characteristics of men who molest children.* Paper presented at the World Congress of Behavior Therapy, Washington, DC.

Abel, G. G., & Osborn, C. (1992). The paraphilias: The extent and nature of sexually deviant and criminal behavior. In J. Bradford (Ed.), *The psychiatric clinics of North America: Clinical forensic psychiatry* (pp. 675-687). Philadelphia, PA: W. B. Saunders.

Abel, G. G., & Rouleau, J. L. (1990). The nature and extent of sexual assault. In W. L. Marshall, D. R. Laws, & H. E. Barbaree (Eds.), *Handbook of sexual assault: Issues, theories and treatment of the offender* (pp. 9-21). New York: Plenum.

Abrams, S., & Ogard, E. (1986). Polygraph surveillance of probationers. *Polygraph, 15,* 174-182.

Barbaree, H. E. (1999, April). *Classifying and managing risk for reoffense amongst adult and adolescent sexual offenders: Combining actuarial methods and clinical realities.* Paper presented at the Children's Justice Conference, Bellevue, WA.

Barnett, I. (1972). The successful treatment of an exhibitionist: A case report. *International Journal of Offender Therapy and Comparative Criminology, 16,* 125-129.

Blasingame, G. D. (1998). Suggested clinical uses of polygraphy in community-based sexual offender treatment programs. *Sexual Abuse: A Journal of Research and Treatment, 10,* 37-45.

Finkelhor, D. (1984). *Child sexual abuse: New theory and research.* New York: Free Press.

Freund, K. (1990). Courtship disorder. In W. L. Marshall, D. R. Laws, & H. E. Barbaree (Eds.), *Handbook of sexual assault: Issues theories and treatment of the offender* (pp. 195-208). New York: Plenum.

Frisbie, L. V. (1966). Studies on sex offending in California: 1954-1966. *California Mental Health Research Digest, 4,* 135-141.

George, W. H., & Marlatt, G. A. (1989). Introduction. In D. R. Laws (Ed.), *Relapse prevention with sex offenders* (pp. 1-31). New York: Guilford.

Groth, A. N. (1979). *Men who rape.* New York: Plenum.

Groth, N. A., Hobson, W., & Gary, T. (1982). The child molester: Clinical observations. *Journal of Social Work and Human Sexuality, 1,* 129-144.

Hagler, H. H. (1995). Polygraph as a measure of progress in the assessment, treatment and surveillance of sex offenders. *Sexual Addiction and Compulsivity, 2,* 98-111.

Hammer, E. F., & Glueck, B. C., Jr. (1957). Psychodynamic patterns in sex offense. *Psychiatric Quarterly, 3,* 325-345.

Hanson, R. K. (1997). *The development of a brief actuarial risk scale for sexual offense recidivism* (Cat. No. JS4-1/1997-4E). Ottawa: Public Works and Government Services Canada.

Hanson, R. K., & Bussière, M. T. (1998). Predicting relapse: A meta-analysis of sexual offender recidivism studies. *Journal of Consulting and Clinical Psychology, 66,* 348-362.

Kinsey, A., Pomeroy, W., & Martin, C. (1948). *Sexual behavior in the human male.* Philadelphia, PA: W. B. Saunders.

Laws, D. R. (1989). Direct monitoring by penile plethysmography. In D. R. Laws (Ed.), *Relapse prevention with sex offenders* (pp. 105-114). New York: Guilford.

Laws, D. R. (1994). How dangerous are rapists to children? *Journal of Sexual Aggression, 1,* 1-14.

Laws, D. R., & Marshall, W. L. (1990). A conditioning theory of the etiology and maintenance of deviant sexual preference and behavior. In W. L. Marshall, D. R. Laws, & H. E. Barbaree (Eds.), *Handbook of sexual assault: Issues, theories, and treatment of the offender* (pp. 209-229). New York: Plenum.

Maletsky, B. M. (1998). Defining our field II: Cycles, chains and assorted misnomers. *Sexual Abuse: A Journal of Research and Treatment, 10,* 1-3.

Monahan, J. (1981). *Predicting violent behavior: An assessment of clinical techniques.* Beverly Hills, CA: Sage.

Murphy, W. D., & Barbaree, H. E. (1988). *Assessment of sexual offenders by means of erectile response: Psychometric properties and decision making* (Contract No. 86M0506500050lD). Washington, DC: National Institute of Mental Health.

O'Connell, M. A. (1998). Using polygraph testing to assess deviant sexual history of sex offenders (Doctoral dissertation, University of Washington, 1997). *Dissertation Abstracts International, 58,* A3023.

O'Connell, M. A., Leberg, E., & Donaldson, C. R. (1990). *Working with sex offenders: Guidelines for therapist selection.* Newbury Park, CA: Sage.

Pithers, W. D., & Laws, D. R. (1989). The penile plethysmograph: Uses and abuses in assessment and treatment of sexual aggressors. In B. Schwartz (Ed.), *A practitioner's guide to treatment of the incarcerated male sex offender* (pp. 83-91). Washington, DC: National Institute of Corrections.

Quinsey, V. L., Harris, G. T., Rice, M. E., & Cormier, C. A. (1998). *Violent offenders: Appraising and managing risk.* Washington, DC: American Psychological Association.

Salzman, L. (1972). Psychotherapy with patients with sexual disorders. In M. Hammer (Ed.), *The theory and practice of psychotherapy with specific disorders* (pp. 273-301). Springfield, IL: Charles C Thomas.

Socarides, C. W. (1973). Sexual perversion and the fear of engulfment. *International Journal of Psychoanalytic Psychotherapy, 2,* 432-448.

Ward, T., & Hudson, S. M. (1998a). A model of the relapse process in sexual offenders. *Journal of Interpersonal Violence, 13,* 700-725.

Ward, T., & Hudson, S. M. (1998b). The construction and development of theory in the sexual offending area: A metatheoretical framework. *Sexual Abuse: A Journal of Research and Treatment, 10,* 47-63.

Weinrott, M. R., & Saylor, M. (1991). Self-report of crimes committed by sex offenders. *Journal of Interpersonal Violence, 6,* 286-300.

Zechnich, R. (1971). Exhibitionism: Genesis, dynamics and treatment. *Psychiatric Quarterly, 45,* 70-75.

CHAPTER 17

The Abel Screen

A Nonintrusive Alternative?

LANE FISCHER
Brigham Young University

In this chapter, I consider the contribution of the recently developed Abel Screen to the remaking of relapse prevention. I briefly review the general function of sexual preference assessment in the context of relapse prevention and the use of penile plethysmography as an objective measure of sexual preference. The need for a less-intrusive procedure is highlighted with a review of the history of sustained visual attention as an alternative measure of sexual preference. Finally, I review the technical adequacy of the Abel Screen with conclusions as to how well it satisfies the demands of relapse prevention.

Relapse prevention assumes that deviant sexual behavior is similar to an addiction that persists across the life span and must be managed through adaptive coping behavior. Abstinence from deviant sexual behavior is the goal. Relapse prevention assumes that there is a predictable course to repeated offending with attendant affective, cognitive, social, and behavioral chains at each stage of the process. The predicted course toward relapse can be made explicit for each individual client, and he can be taught alternative cognitions and behaviors that will alter the predicted course and result in sustained abstinence. Relapse prevention does not assume that the personality or preferences of the perpetrator will be restructured but that sexual offending, like an addiction, will pose a perpetual risk that must be managed.

The assessment of sexual preference serves relapse prevention by identifying a sex offender's preferred sexual object or deviant sexual behavior. Once the preferred sexual object or behavior is identified, then the seemingly irrelevant decisions that lead sex offenders into high-risk situations can be illuminated. For example, if a sex offender's preferred sexual object is 2- to 4-year-old boys, then the seemingly irrelevant decision to walk home from work along a route that passes a neighborhood preschool takes on significance. Although familiarity with the schedule and location of the preschool is in itself harmless, such familiarity may become replete with potential harm when a sex offender is under stress. Deviant fantasies of 2- to 4-year-old boys in general or of particular boys who attend the preschool represent a lapse that may lead to relapse and a sexually aggressive act. Having knowledge of a sexual offender's preference for 2- to 4-year-old boys allows the client and clinician to identify the seemingly irrelevant decisions, high-risk situations, and lapses that involve such children.

Ward, Louden, Hudson, and Marshall (1995) posited an offense chain that sex offenders may follow. The chain includes several stages, including distal planning, contact with potential victims, proximal planning, offending, cognitive restructuring, and future resolution. An offender may follow several possible pathways through the various stages. A positive affect pathway includes entrenched preference for adult-child contact with attendant belief systems and explicit planfulness. A negative affect pathway includes more implicit planning, interpersonal neediness, and negative evaluation of self and offending. Laws (1999) associated those two pathways with two types of offenders. The positive affect pathway is the more likely course, followed by pedophiles who have a fixated preference for a particular sexual object. The negative affect pathway is the more probable course for incest offenders whose behavior is more likely regressed and situationally determined.

Assessment of sexual preference is more helpful when there is a true focal sexual preference. Assessment of sexual preference is analogous to identifying the "drug of choice" in chemical dependency treatment. It is probably more effective with offenders who have clearly defined preferences of sexual objects or deviant behaviors than with those who manifest more diffuse and situationally reactive behaviors. As Marshall (1996) opined, "If sex offenders typically are polymorphously perverse . . . then this would demand a rather different approach to assessment" (p. 176). Clinicians who work with sex offenders have typically relied on clinical interviews, analysis of records, self-report, and penile plethysmography (PPG) to assess sexual preference (Laws, 1989). Although clinical interviews and self-reports are somewhat subjective and may be compromised by dissimulation, PPG seems, on face value, to be more objective and resistant to distortion.

Penile Plethysmography

Singer (1984) hypothesized three stages of males' sexual behavior. Stage 1 involves sustained attention to possible sexual attractors. Stage 2 involves movement toward that attractor. Stage 3 involves resultant physiological response, sexual arousal, and penile engorgement. PPG measures male sexual behavior at Singer's Stage 3. Measures of penile tumescence are recorded in reaction to audio and/or video depictions of various sexual objects or behaviors.

Although PPG has the appeal of being an objective measure of sexual preference, concerns have been voiced about the use of PPG for both ethical and psychometric reasons. Primarily, PPG is extremely invasive, and it uses sexually explicit stimuli to elicit penile tumescence. Marshall (1996) was particularly concerned about the use of PPG with adolescents. Exposing adolescents to explicit images of deviant sexuality may inadvertently introduce, stimulate, or ratify such behavior. Marshall and Fernandez (in press) reviewed the extant evidence regarding the psychometric properties of PPG and identified problems with its standardization, data formats, internal consistency, temporal stability, and criterion validity.

Given the invasiveness of PPG, the limited empirical evidence of its actual reliability and validity, and the ethical concerns related to exposing adults and adolescents to such experiences, it seems reasonable to find other objective measures of sexual preference that might circumvent these problems. The Abel Screen is a device that purports to measure sustained visual attention as an indicator of sexual interest. If effective, the Abel Screen would be a less-intrusive alternative consonant with Singer's (1984) Stage 1. The Abel Screen would have particular application to the assessment and treatment of adolescents.

History

Before considering the nature of the Abel Screen, it is important to review the literature and highlight what we know about sustained visual attention as a predictor of sexual preference. Rosenzweig (1942) devised an instrument that he called the "photoscope" to test changes in sexual interest as a response to hormone therapy. His validation of the instrument is of interest. He used 20 inpatient males who had been diagnosed with schizophrenia from a pool of 58 on the ward. The 20 participants were divided into two groups: the 10 most and the 10 least interested in sexual behavior. Interest in sexual behavior was determined by the staff having observed patients' masturbation and heterosexual or homosexual overtures to staff members or other patients.

The instrument used essentially two types of stimuli: 10 nonsexual and 10 sexual photographs, including heterosexual and homosexual content. The photographs were mounted on cards set into a Rolodex-type device that were displayed one at a time in a box. Patients controlled the length of time any photograph was displayed and were allowed to view the slides up to three times in a single sitting. An observer watched through a one-way mirror and timed how long each photograph was displayed.

The author used various analytical methods to determine the reliability and validity of the instrument. The average reliability coefficient from four different approaches was 0.54, which was marginal at best. Rosenzweig (1942) demonstrated that the photoscope differentiated between the high sexual group and low sexual group by comparing the average time each spent on the sexual and nonsexual pictures. The high group observed the sexual pictures for an average of 40 seconds and observed the nonsexual photographs for only 19 seconds. The low group observed the sexual pictures for an average of 13 seconds and the nonsexual for 19 seconds. He concluded, importantly, that although the test could discriminate between the two groups, it could not really discriminate the underlying difference between them. The photoscope may have been actually measuring the inhibition of sexual interest rather than sexual interest itself. It was unclear whether the low group was as interested in sexual behavior as the high group but simply more inhibited in their expression thereof. That question is still relevant. Sustained visual attention scores may indicate disinhibition more than sexual preference per se. In the absence of a baseline, it may be impossible to tell the difference.

Zamansky (1956) developed a more sophisticated technique in which he observed the eye movements of participants while observing pairs of photographs that had either male, female, or neutral content. His objective was to eventually determine whether he could identify the covert homosexual interests of patients suffering from paranoid schizophrenia. The development of the instrument is of interest. He compared 20 homosexual males with 20 heterosexual males. No participants showed evidence of psychopathology. The author hypothesized that homosexual men would spend relatively more time than heterosexual men observing photographs of males versus females, males versus neutral stimuli, and neutral stimuli versus female photographs. It was assumed that preference for a neutral photograph over a female image would indicate resistance to attraction to women as sexual objects. The predominant psychoanalytic theory of the time hypothesized that male homosexuality was more related to feeling repulsed by women than feeling attracted to men.

Zamansky (1956) predicted correctly in every case. Discrepancies in visual attention time between types of slides significantly discriminated the homosexual group from the heterosexual group and showed apparent attraction toward the preferred sexual object and resistance to the nonpreferred object when compared to neutral stimuli. The author's paired item approach allowed him to address whether visual attention represents attraction toward or repulsion by a possible sexual object. That question is also still relevant. For a client that is generally repulsed by all objects, an increased visual attention score may simply represent relatively less repulsion (double negative) than actual positive sexual attraction.

Ware, Brown, Amoroso, Pilkey, and Pruesse (1972) and Brown, Amoroso, Ware, Pruesse, and Pilkey (1973) measured sustained visual attention and semantic meaning associated with sexually explicit photographs. Forty male college students individually controlled the slide projector, viewed 15 slides, and rated them along several dimensions. The slides varied in sexual explicitness and ranged from a heterosexual couple that was clothed and embracing to a nude female on a bed with her genitals exposed.

Ware et al. reported the results of the total group, and Brown et al. reported the results of the same group divided into two conditions: alone or in the presence of others. Visual attention was significantly correlated with the degree of sexual explicitness ($r = .66$). It was very strongly correlated ($r = .93$), with the semantic dimension labeled *activity*. Activity was measured by three differentials: stimulating versus nonstimulating, active versus passive, and hot versus cold. The results indicated that males extended their visual attention to slides that were more explicit and stimulating to them. The authors had hypothesized a curvilinear relationship between degree of explicitness and visual attending time. However, a direct linear correlation was observed. Brown et al. (1973) reported that viewing time was generally longer and more variable when participants were alone than in the presence of other people.

Love, Sloan, and Schmidt (1976) used subjects' degree of sex guilt as a covariate of viewing time and the degree of sexual explicitness of photographic slides. The content of the slides "varied from photographs of pretty girls in bikinis to graphic portrayals of heterosexual sexual activity" (p. 625). The authors sampled 35 undergraduate males and divided them into three groups (low, moderate, and high) according to their responses to the Sex Guilt Subscale of the Mosher Forced-Choice Guilt Inventory (Mosher, 1966). In general, the three groups did not differ in their average viewing time of the slides, yet when covarying the degree of explicitness of each slide, differences between groups emerged. Although the high-sex guilt group generally viewed the slides equally regardless of the degree of sexual explicitness, the low-sex guilt group generally viewed the slides longer as the degree of explicitness increased. The moderate-sex guilt group showed a curvilinear pattern of increasing viewing time that peaked at mid-range explicitness and decreased with the most sexually explicit slides. By considering subjects' degree of sex guilt, Love et al. (1976) were able to find the curvilinear relationship between visual attention and degree of sexual explicitness that Brown et al. (1973) had hypothesized.

Quinsey, Rice, Harris, and Reid (1993) measured viewing time of slides along with reports of physical and sexual attractiveness as dependent variables related to heterosexual males' and females' preferences of age and gender of sexual objects. They used slides of nude male and female children, adolescents, and adults. Because none of the models was photographed in flirtatious poses, they were not considered to be sexually explicit. Although visual attention was significantly correlated with the participants' ratings of sexual arousal, stimulation, and attractiveness, there was little variation in viewing time across the gender and age conditions. The exception was that slides of adults and pubescents of the preferred gender were observed longer than all categories of nonpreferred gender. In contrast to previous studies (Brown et al., 1973; Love et al., 1976), when sexual explicitness was controlled, visual attention decreased in variability and usefulness as a predictor. Visual attention to the nonexplicit material used in this study was not deemed by the authors to be a strong measure of sexual preference.

Wright and Adams (1994) used visual attention as one correlate of sexual attraction. They sampled 20 adults in each of four groups: male heterosexuals, male homosexuals, female heterosexuals, and female homosexuals. They used three types of slides: neutral and male and female nudes from *Playgirl* and *Playboy* magazines, respectively. They hypothesized that viewing time would be significantly increased to slides that represented the preferred sexual object versus those of the nonpreferred sexual object. In each of the four groups, there were clearly significant differences in mean attention times, with greater sustained attention occurring to slides of the preferred sexual object.

Harris, Rice, Quinsey, and Chaplin (1996) used viewing time as a factor to discriminate between child molesters and normal heterosexual men. The authors sampled 26 child molesters and 25 community volunteers who reported being heterosexual. They presented neutral slides and slides of nude male and female children, pubescents, and adults. They monitored penile tumescence, subjective ratings of sexual attractiveness, and visual attention to each slide.

The nonoffenders' penile tumescence, ratings, and visual attention were concordant across stimulus categories. Normal heterosexual males showed greatest arousal, attention, and report of sexual attractiveness to slides of nude adult females with decreasing arousal to pubescent and child females and least arousal, attention, and attractiveness ratings to males of any age. The molesters' profiles were discordant among the three variables across the stimulus categories. The measures of penile tumescence did not match the ratings of sexual attractiveness. The measures of visual attention showed very little variation, averaging only 1.87 seconds with a restricted range. The authors were able to significantly discriminate between the offenders' and nonoffenders' patterns of visual attention because although the nonoffenders showed variability with a decreasing curve across conditions, the offenders showed a very low baseline with extreme restriction of variability across stimulus conditions. In fact, if the authors had conducted a test of the differences between the two groups' sustained visual attention to pubescent or child females, they would have discovered that the nonoffenders actually paid more attention to such slides than did the child molesters. The molesters' average attention to the slides of adolescents and children was less than the nonoffenders' attention.

Quinsey, Ketsetzis, Earls, and Karamanoukian (1996) reported two elegant studies of viewing time, ratings of sexual attractiveness, and penile tumescence that tested hypotheses emerging from Symons's (1979) evolutionary theory. In Study 1, they used 24 normal heterosexual males and 24 normal heterosexual females to compare how they would rate and attend to slides of nude male and female adults, pubescents, and children. They discovered a general concordance between ratings and viewing time. When considering subjects' responses to slides of preferred objects, there was a consistent pattern of longer viewing time toward adult models with decreasing time across age of the object. When considering subjects' responses to slides of their nonpreferred objects, there was shorter time and a generally flat curve across all ages of objects.

In Study 2, the authors used 24 normal heterosexual males to assess how they responded to slides of nude male and female adults, pubescents, prepubescents, and children. The variables measured were subjective ratings of attractiveness, sustained visual attention, and penile tumescence. They demonstrated general concordance between ratings, viewing time, and penile tumescence as well as a consistent pattern of longer viewing time toward adult models that decreased with the age of model and flattened out across nonpreferred objects of all ages. Quinsey et al. (1996) produced perhaps the best studies of visual attention to date. The studies are grounded in a theory of normal sexual behavior, and they show replication of findings.

Summary of Visual Attention Research

What do we know about visual attention as a predictor of sexual preference, sexual attractiveness, or sexual arousal?

- Visual attention discriminated between high and low sexual interest or perhaps between low and high inhibition of sexual interest (Rosenzweig, 1942).
- Visual attention discriminated between heterosexual and homosexual males (Zamansky, 1956).
- Visual attention increased with degree of sexually explicit content and when people were alone rather than in the presence of others (Brown et al., 1973; Ware et al., 1972).

- People with different degrees of sex guilt showed different patterns of visual attention as sexual explicitness increased (Love et al., 1976).

- Sexually nonexplicit material was a less effective predictor of sexual preference because it elicited limited variability (Quinsey et al., 1993).

- Increased visual attention was associated with preferred versus nonpreferred sexual objects in normal heterosexual and homosexual adults (Wright & Adams, 1994).

- Normal heterosexual males and females showed a clear pattern of increased visual attention to adult sexual objects with decreasing attention across age and nonpreferred objects (Quinsey et al., 1996).

- Child molesters showed a restricted flat pattern of visual attention across age categories reminiscent of subjects with high sex guilt and of normals viewing their nonpreferred objects (Harris et al., 1996; Love et al., 1976; Quinsey et al., 1996).

Quinsey et al. (1996) summarized the state of the art well when they concluded that

the coherence of the measures of sexual interest and the differences between males and females observed in this study indicate that covertly measured viewing time can serve as a measure of males' sexual preferences. Although its sensitivity and specificity may not be good enough yet for clinical applications . . . they are good enough for group research and show promise for the study of sexual preferences among children and adolescents. (p. 352)

The Abel Screen

The Abel Screen has been labeled by several different names, including the Abel Screen (Abel, Lawry, Karlstrom, Osborn, & Gillespie, 1994), the Abel Assessment for Interest in Paraphilias (Abel, 1995), and the Abel Assessment for Sexual Interest (Abel, 1997a, 1997b, 1997c). For simplicity, I shall refer to it as the Abel Screen. The Abel Screen is a creative instrument that uses self-report of attraction to 22 categories of possible sexual stimuli, as well as a surreptitious measure of sustained attention to photographs of the stimuli. It also includes a questionnaire regarding sexual behavior. The test uses 160 slides in 22 categories of possible sexual attractors that include 2- to 4-year-old children, 8- to 10-year-old children, 14- to 17-year-old adolescents, and adults of both genders, both African American and Caucasian. All models are clothed and photographed in similar lighting, and none of the poses is sexually explicit. In addition, there are photographs of clothed models depicting images of six paraphilias, including frotteurism, sadomasochism against females, sadomasochism against males, exhibitionism, fetishism, and voyeurism against females.

Although the system does present a questionnaire, the heart of the instrument is its measure of sustained visual attention. To complete that portion of the test, clients sit alone at a screen that is attached to a carousel slide projector and laptop computer. Clients have unlimited time to view each slide, and they advance the carousel at their own pace by pressing the return key on the computer. Clients view a small set of practice slides and then view the 160 slides twice. On the second viewing, they also report how sexually arousing or disgusting each slide is to them on a 7-point Likert-type scale. They respond by pressing keys 1 to 7 on the keyboard. The computer measures in milliseconds how long each image is projected on the screen. When completed, the data are sent to Abel, Inc. via modem or disk, where they are tabulated, and a report is subsequently faxed to the clinician.

Psychometric Adequacy of the Abel Screen

Fischer and Smith (1999) reviewed the test publisher's data supporting the technical adequacy of the Abel Screen. The test had been marketed as serving screening functions, diagnostic functions, and prognostic functions. They enumerated concerns about the instrument's data format, reliability, validity, and normative base.

Regarding the Abel Screen's data format, it is important to note that the research regarding visual attention has analyzed between-group differences. For example, comparisons were made between high and low sexual interest groups, normal and pathological groups, or heterosexual and homosexual groups. The variation has always been between groups. The Abel Screen does not rely on between-group variation but creates scores that are ipsative (i.e., scores have reference to intraindividual variance only). Abel Screen z-scores are created by subtracting the grand mean of categories from the mean viewing time in each category and dividing that difference by the standard deviation of category means for each individual.

If one considers the conversion of raw scores to Abel Screen z-scores, then two major problems become apparent. For example, if Client A has a grand mean viewing time of 2 seconds with a standard deviation of 2 milliseconds, and Client A views a given category of slides for a mean of 2.008 seconds, then his Abel Screen z-score for that category would be 4 standard deviations above the mean and appear to be extremely deviant. If Client B has a grand mean viewing time of 20 seconds with a standard deviation of 20 seconds, and Client B observes the same category of slides for an average of 100 seconds, then his Abel Screen z-score would be 4 standard deviations above the mean. Clients A and B both receive Abel Screen z-scores of 4 for the same category of slides.

The first problem that emerges is that the apparent variance in Client A's scores is an artifact of the computational procedure. The procedure forces scores to appear variable when the underlying variation is minuscule. Because the Abel Screen does not report the underlying raw scores, means, or standard deviations for each subject, there is no raw score baseline or interval with which to ground the interpretation of the scores.

The second problem that becomes apparent is that Abel Screen z-scores are not commensurate across clients. Clients A and B have identical z-scores of 4, but Client A's real viewing behavior of 2.008 seconds is dramatically different than Client B's viewing time of 100 seconds. Although their ipsative profiles might be identical, the same score or profile represents different behavior for each client. Because clinicians are familiar with norm-referenced z-scores used by many psychological tests, it is tempting to interpret Abel Screen z-scores as though they were norm referenced when, in fact, they are not. Clinicians cannot compare any given client to another. There is no normative baseline or interval with which to ground the interpretation of the scores.

Clemans (1956) outlined the necessary procedures to create "ipsative-standard scores" that might compensate for both of the above problems. His technique allows patterns of ipsative scores to be compared to a standard pattern. As yet, Abel Screen z-scores have not been converted to ipsative-standard scores, and both problems persist.

Regarding the Abel Screen's reliability, it was noted that no internal consistency reliability coefficients were reported for the test as it was marketed. There were no estimates of temporal stability either. Test-retest reliability is crucial to the development of any instrument that serves to predict behavior across time and setting. If an attribute such as sexual preference is assumed to be relatively constant and perennial, as relapse prevention assumes, then an instrument that purports to measure that attribute must produce highly similar results time after time. It was unknown whether the instrument could produce a temporally stable estimate of sexual interest.

When considering the validity of the Abel Screen, Fischer and Smith (1999) noted that the same two studies were reported in each iteration of the technical manual to support the three functions of the instrument. Neither study used the test as it was marketed with 22 categories of slides. There was no evidence of validity of the current incarnation of the instrument to fulfill its purported screening, diagnostic, or prognostic functions.

Perhaps most alarming was the observation that although the test was actively marketed for use with adolescents there were no samples of adolescents in any study of the reliability or validity of the pilot slides. There was no evidence about how adolescents responded to the procedure.

Fischer and Smith (1999) made the following six recommendations to improve the empirical base of the instrument:

1. Research is necessary to establish a normative expectation that will make the data interpretable. Scores can be used as ipsatives if there is a normative expectation about what the ordinal patterns should look like regardless of means and standard deviations. With sufficient data, scores could be converted to true norm-referenced z-scores.

2. Internal consistency studies should be conducted on the full test as it is currently marketed.

3. Data should be gathered that justify the use of 22 categories as orthogonal constructs. If such data cannot be obtained, the test should be refined to match the true underlying structure of the categorical model.

4. Test-retest reliability studies should be conducted on the instrument as it is currently marketed.

5. Screening and diagnostic validity studies will also be necessary using the test as marketed.

6. All of the above analyses should be performed separately for populations of adults and adolescents.

Some progress has been made in response to some of these recommendations. Although the test publishers have not chosen to pursue Clemans's (1956) technique, they have proposed another strategy. Abel, Phipps, Hand, and Jordan (1999) presented a strategy that approximates a normative process. They created four prediction models using both questionnaire and visual attention data. The models predicted which subjects had molested girls younger than age 14, boys younger than age 14, adolescent girls, and adolescent boys. On the basis of the models, they proposed to create a probability estimate that any new client has "actually committed the child molestation behavior in the past." Whether the new strategy can be applied to relapse prevention remains to be seen. For example, in the model that predicted molesters of adolescent boys, the visual attention score that was predictive was sustained attention to young girls, not adolescent boys. The new strategy is an empirical norm-referenced approach that represents a theoretical shift away from an ipsative sexual interest approach. The publishers of the test have deferred questions about such artifacts until further study (G. G. Abel, personal communication, September 23, 1999).

Abel et al. (1999) presented internal consistency and test-retest reliability coefficients for a subset of 16 categories ignoring the 6 paraphilia categories. These data have yet to be scrutinized by peer review, and the publisher has deferred questions about the computation of the coefficients (G. G. Abel, personal communication, September 23, 1999). The use of a subset of categories continues to be problematic because the ipsative z-scores are dependent on responses to 22 categories. If the 6 paraphilia categories are not to be included in the test, then the variance associated with them should not be included in the ipsative scoring procedure. Relatedly, Abel et al. (1999) presented models to predict molesters of children younger than age 14 or older than age 14. It seems that the test may not be adequate to actually assess the putative categorical model that includes 22 categories of attractors.

Abel Screen Relapse Prediction Score

Abel (1997c) recently developed a relapse prediction score (RPS). The RPS is designed to assess the relapse risk of any subject who takes the test. The RPS is a composite score created from 20 items in the questionnaire or viewing time scores. The items are weighted by the correlation coefficients associated with factors found to be significant in Hanson and Bussière's (1998) meta-analysis of relapse predictors.

Only two components of the RPS originate from the viewing time results. These are sexual interest in children and sexual interest in boys as measured by Abel Screen ipsative scores. The remaining 18 variables arc static and emerge from the patient or therapist portion of the questionnaire. Abel (1997c) reported that the composite score was norm referenced to 1,454 cases. However, no validity data have been reported as to the efficacy of the RPS in actually predicting relapse. It is undetermined whether the composite score has any prognostic validity. The RPS is a creative idea that needs to be empirically validated before it is used clinically.

Independent Evaluation of the Abel Screen

Several authors have recently begun to evaluate the technical adequacy of the Abel Screen as it is currently configured. Smith and Fischer (1999) estimated the test-retest reliability, screening validity, and diagnostic validity of the Abel Screen as used with adolescents. They sampled 40 nonoffenders and 41 sexual offenders in day treatment facilities. They administered the test on two occasions with an average test-retest interval of 14 days. Because the scores reported to clinicians are ipsative, no norm-referenced reliability coefficient could be calculated. The authors created a distribution of ideographic correlation coefficients with an average coefficient to estimate the temporal stability of the test. The average test-retest reliability coefficient was +0.63 with a range from −0.09 to +0.96. The median correlation coefficient was +0.58. This means that some subjects' test-retest reliability was as low as −0.09, whereas others' were as high as +0.96. Anastasi (1988) sets the desirable range of test-retest reliability at +0.80 and above. The Smith and Fischer (1999) data indicate that, although some trends exist toward temporal stability, the average coefficient was below the standard, and there was a wide distribution around the average, with some scores even being in the negative range.

Smith and Fischer (1999) estimated the screening validity of the Abel Screen using two methods at test and retest to determine the deviant status of subjects. Of the four analyses, no significant prediction was obtained. The efficiency rates that estimate the ratios of error and true decisions ranged from 52% to 58% among the various methods. This indicates a 48% to 42% error rate in screening decisions. Smith and Fischer (1999) also tested the diagnostic validity of the test using two methods at test and retest. They found no significant correlations at any time between the actual reported victims and the type of victims predicted by the Abel Screen.

Kaufman, Rogers, and Daleiden (1998) assessed the test-retest reliability of the Abel Screen using raw scores and correlated categories rather than individual profiles. They sampled 119 incarcerated adolescents, 67 of whom were sexual offenders and 52 nonoffenders. The participants were tested twice with an average test-retest period of 2 weeks. The test-retest coefficients of the various categories ranged from +0.32 to +0.73 for the offender group and from +0.24 to +0.75 for the nonoffender group. They also aggregated the coefficients from deviant and nondeviant stimuli and obtained average correlation coefficients ranging from +0.55 to +0.67. Although the Kaufman et al. (1998) analytical approach was different from Smith and Fischer's (1999) approach, the estimates are very similar. They concluded that their results "did not reveal highly reliable two-week test-retest reliability findings with incarcerated sexual offender and non-offender samples. In fact, only 25% to 45% of the variance on retest was accounted for by initial viewing times" (p. 4).

Several independent studies of how the Abel Screen compares with PPG with adults have recently been reported. Smith and Annon (1998) compared the performance of penile plethysmography and the Abel Screen by sampling 96 males referred to the Forensic Behavioral Science Institute. All participants had admitted to inappropriate sexual behavior. The analysis resulted in a significant correlation between the PPG response to adolescent females ages 14 to 17 and the admission of sexual behavior with adolescent females. The Abel Screen showed no significant correlations between the admitted sexual behavior and sustained viewing time or self-reported interest in any Abel Screen category.

Johnson and Listiak (1999) conducted a pilot comparison of the Abel Screen and PPG using two sets of stimulus materials. They tested 63 incarcerated adults who were participating in a sex offender treatment program. The perpetrators had molested female children, male children, adolescent females, or adolescent males. They concluded that the results obtained by the Abel Screen were comparable to those obtained by phallometric assessment.

Gray (1999) conducted an exploratory study with 39 outpatient pedophiles and administered both the Abel Screen and a version of PPG. He concluded that both instruments were operating in similar fashion and identifying 65% to 79%

of the pedophiles by their response to any child category. A very helpful aspect of Gray's study is his analysis of dissimulation. Although Abel (1996) reported that clients were unable to alter their results on the Abel Screen, Gray demonstrated that there is a discernable pattern to dissimulation. By applying his formula to the Abel Screen data, the author removed 11 of the 39 subjects as dissimulators. Of the remaining 28 subjects, the Abel Screen identified 96% as pedophiles. Of the 11 dissimulators, the Abel Screen only identified 36% as pedophiles. The author recommended that users of the Abel Screen "reevaluate their Abel protocols in terms of the potential for dissimulation" (p. 12).

Seghorn and Weigel (1999) conducted four discriminant function analyses using Abel Screen and PPG data. They discriminated among five clinician-defined groups: pedophiles, offenders (molesters), accused, child pornography, and sexual compulsive disorders (e.g., exhibitionism). Using one subset of Abel Screen data from 183 participants, the authors had a 36% hit rate, but with another subset, they had a 62% hit rate. Using PPG data from 33 subjects, they achieved a 78% hit rate. Using both Abel and PPG data from 27 subjects in the discriminant analysis, they achieved a 96% hit rate. The authors' results depend on discriminant function analysis, which is not the data typically reported to clinicians, but the implication is that the best results will be obtained by using both instruments.

Letourneau (1999) conducted a study using 58 incarcerated adults who were administered both the Abel Screen and PPG. Molesters had victimized one of three groups: male children, female children, or female adolescents. Employing several analytical procedures, she found that the tests performed similarly and were better at identifying perpetrators who had molested male children than those who had offended against female children or adolescents. She concluded that "it will be important to demonstrate whether the [Abel Screen] and the PPG can categorize offenders with comparisons more finely tuned than these" (p. 39).

Conclusions

The Abel Screen presents two advantages over PPG. It is less invasive. It does not present sexually explicit material to clients. However, it has technical and practical limitations. It is not based in the group difference literature, and its computation of ipsative scores distorts the underlying variance that is never reported. The 22 categories of attractors probably represent an overly complex and inaccurate model. Its reliability is still in question. It can be dissimulated. The RPS has not been validated. There is no support for its use with adolescents.

Marshall and Fernandez (in press) criticized the use of PPG for similar technical and practical reasons. The extant evidence seems to indicate that the Abel Screen operates similarly to PPG. The remaking of relapse prevention seems to require better technical adequacy than either PPG or the Abel Screen can currently provide. Of course, dismissal of both instruments leaves the clinician with a void. Should we prefer an imperfect assessment to no assessment at all? Probably. The demand is for those who market and use such instruments to be very clear about their limitations. It is extremely dangerous to claim more psychometric adequacy for an instrument than is supported by the evidence or to make decisions ignorant of the limitations of the device. Clinicians should demand clarity and responsiveness from those who market psychometric instruments. Developers have an ethical demand to be open and accurate in their claims. The effort to remake relapse prevention is grounded in such an ethic. It is a response to the outcome data and an attempt to refine the model appropriately.

References

Abel, G. G. (1995). *New technology: The Abel Assessment for Interest in Paraphilias.* Atlanta, GA: Abel Screening, Inc.

Abel, G. G. (1996). *A new objective test for youthful offenders: The Abel Assessment for Interest in Paraphilias.* Atlanta, GA: Abel Screening, Inc.

Abel, G. G. (1997a). *Abel Assessment for Sexual Interest: Judges' product information.* Atlanta, GA: Abel Screening, Inc.

Abel, G. G. (1997b, July-August). *Abel screening news.* Atlanta, GA: Abel Screening, Inc.

Abel, G. G. (1997c, September-October). *Abel screening news.* Atlanta, GA: Abel Screening, Inc.

Abel, G. G., Lawry, S. S., Karlstrom, E., Osborn, C., & Gillespie, C. F. (1994). Screening tests for pedophilia. *Criminal Justice and Behavior, 21*(1), 115-131.

Abel, G. G., Phipps, A., Hand, C., & Jordan, A. (1999, September). *The reliability and validity of visual reaction time as a measure of sexual interest in children.* Paper presented at the annual meeting of the Association for the Treatment of Sexual Abusers, Orlando, FL.

Anastasi, A. (1988). *Psychology testing* (6th ed). New York: Macmillan.

Brown, M., Amoroso, D. M., Ware, E. E., Pruesse, M., & Pilkey, D. W. (1973). Factors affecting viewing time of pornography. *Journal of Social Psychology, 90,* 125-135.

Clemans, W. V. (1956). An analytical and empirical examination of some properties of ipsative measures. *Psychometric Monographs, 14.*

Fischer, L., & Smith, G. M. (1999). Statistical adequacy of the Abel Assessment for Interest in Paraphilias. *Sexual Abuse: A Journal of Research and Treatment, 11*(3), 195-206.

Gray, S. (1999, September). Outcomes of the Abel assessment and the penile plethysmograph in a sample of sex offenders in outpatient treatment. In S. Johnson (Chair), *Current research comparing plethysmography with the Abel Assessment for Sexual Interest.* Symposium conducted at the annual meeting of the Association for the Treatment of Sexual Abusers, Orlando, FL.

Hanson, R. K., & Bussière, M. T. (1998). Predicting relapse: A meta-analysis of sexual offender recidivism studies. *Journal of Consulting and Clinical Psychology, 66,* 348-362.

Harris, G. T., Rice, M. E., Quinsey, V. L., & Chaplin, T. C. (1996). Viewing time as a measure of sexual interest among child molesters and normal heterosexual men. *Behaviour Research and Therapy, 34,* 389-394.

Johnson, S. A., & Listiak, A. (1999, September). Comparing outcomes of plethysmographic assessment with the Abel assessment in a prison based sex offender sample. In S. Johnson (Chair), *Current research comparing plethysmography with the Abel Assessment for Sexual Interest.* Symposium conducted at the annual meeting of the Association for the Treatment of Sexual Abusers, Orlando, FL.

Kaufman, K. L., Rogers, D., & Daleiden, E. (1998, October). *Sexual interest in incarcerated adolescent offenders: A test-retest analysis.* Poster session presented at the annual meeting of the Association for the Treatment of Sexual Abusers, Vancouver, British Columbia.

Laws, D. R. (1989). *Relapse prevention with sex offenders.* New York: Guilford.

Laws, D. R. (1999). Relapse prevention: The state of the art. *Journal of Interpersonal Violence, 14,* 279-296.

Letourneau, E. J. (1999, September). A comparison of the penile plethysmograph with the Abel Assessment for Sexual Interest on incarcerated military sex offenders. In S. Johnson (Chair), *Current research comparing plethysmography with the Abel Assessment for Sexual Interest.* Symposium conducted at the annual meeting of the Association for the Treatment of Sexual Abusers, Orlando, FL.

Love, R. E., Sloan, L. R., & Schmidt, M. J. (1976). Viewing pornography and sex guilt: The priggish, the prudent, and the profligate. *Journal of Consulting and Clinical Psychology, 44,* 624-629.

Marshall, W. L. (1996). Assessment, treatment, and theorizing about sex offenders: Developments during the past twenty years and future directions. *Criminal Justice and Behavior, 23,* 162-199.

Marshall, W. L., & Fernandez, Y. M. (in press). Phallometric testing with sexual offenders: Limits to its value. *Clinical Psychology Review.*

Mosher, D. L. (1966). The development and multitrait-multimethod matrix analysis of three measures of three aspects of guilt. *Journal of Consulting Psychology, 30,* 25-29.

Quinsey, V. L., Ketsetzis, M., Earls, C., & Karamanoukian, A. (1996). Viewing time as a measure of sexual interest. *Ethology and Sociobiology, 17,* 341-354.

Quinsey, V. L., Rice, M. E., Harris, G. T., & Reid, K. S. (1993). Conceptual and measurement issues in the phylogenetic and ontogenetic development of sexual age preferences in males. In H. E. Barbaree, W. L. Marshall, & S. M. Hudson (Eds.), *The juvenile sex offender* (pp. 143-163). New York: Guilford.

Rosenzweig, S. (1942). The photoscope as an objective device for evaluating sexual interest. *Psychosomatic Medicine, 4,* 150-158.

Seghorn, T. K., & Weigel, M. (1999, September). Comparative use of Abel assessments and penile plethysmograph laboratory assessments in an outpatient forensic practice. In S. Johnson (Chair), *Current research comparing plethysmography with the Abel Assessment for Sexual Interest.* Symposium conducted at the annual meeting of the Association for the Treatment of Sexual Abusers, Orlando, FL.

Singer, B. (1984). Conceptualizing sexual arousal and attraction. *Journal of Sex Research, 20,* 230-240.

Smith, G., & Annon, J. (1998, October). *Abel assessment and penile plethysmography: A comparison of instrument sensitivity.* Poster session presented at the annual meeting of the Association for the Treatment of Sexual Abusers, Vancouver, British Columbia.

Smith, G. M., & Fischer, L. (1999). Assessment of juvenile sexual offenders: Reliability and validity of the Abel Assessment for Interest in Paraphilias. *Sexual Abuse: A Journal for Research and Treatment, 11*(3), 207-215.

Symons, D. (1979). *The evolution of human sexuality.* New York: Oxford University Press.

Ward, T., Louden, K., Hudson, S. M., & Marshall, W. L. (1995). A descriptive model of the offense chain for child molesters. *Journal of Interpersonal Violence, 10,* 342-372.

Ware, E. E., Brown, M., Amoroso, D. M., Pilkey, D. W., & Pruesse, M. (1972). The semantic meaning of pornographic stimuli for college males. *Canadian Journal of Behavioral Science, 4,* 204-209.

Wright, L. W., & Adams, H. E. (1994). Assessment and sexual preference using a choice reaction time task. *Journal of Psychopathology and Behavioral Assessment, 16,* 221-231.

Zamansky, H. S. (1956). A technique for measuring homosexual tendencies. *Journal of Personality, 24,* 436-438.

PART VI

PROGRAMS: MAJOR INTERVENTIONS USING RELAPSE PREVENTION

CHAPTER 18

Preventing Relapse in Sex Offenders

What We Learned From SOTEP's Experimental Treatment Program

JANICE K. MARQUES
California Department of Mental Health

CRAIG NELSON
JAN-MARIE ALARCON
Atascadero State Hospital

DAVID M. DAY
California Department of Mental Health

The Sex Offender Treatment and Evaluation Project (SOTEP) is a longitudinal research program that was designed to evaluate the effectiveness of an innovative relapse prevention (RP) program for sex offenders (see Marques, Day, Nelson, Miner, & West, 1991, for a detailed description of the project). The SOTEP treatment program, housed at Atascadero State Hospital in California, operated from 1985 until the treatment phase of the project ended in 1995. The project is now in the follow-up phase, in which recidivism data are being collected on both treated and untreated study participants.

AUTHORS' NOTE: The views expressed are those of the authors and do not necessarily reflect the policies of the California Department of Mental Health. We thank the SOTEP clinical staff for their efforts in providing the treatment program and in helping us evaluate it.

In this chapter, we describe some of the lessons we have learned from SOTEP, particularly those that highlight the strengths and weaknesses of the RP model as we applied it in our treatment program. Although some of this information is based on preliminary analyses of our recidivism data, much of it is from more informal and qualitative data sources, such as interviews with SOTEP clinicians at the end of the treatment program and with participants who reoffended after their release to the community. In addition to describing some of the problems we found in our RP program, we indicate some specific ways that we believe the model could be improved. Finally, we describe our newest application of RP in a program specifically designed for the treatment of sex offenders who are under civil commitment as sexually violent predators.

Overview of SOTEP

As both a treatment and research project, SOTEP has included the following key elements: (a) an experimental design that required random assignment of volunteers to either treatment or no-treatment conditions; (b) an intensive, cognitive-behavioral inpatient treatment program designed specifically to prevent relapse among sex offenders; (c) a 1-year aftercare program in the community; and (d) a comprehensive evaluation of both in-treatment changes and long-term treatment effects (including a follow-up period in which recidivism rates for treated and untreated subjects are measured for at least 5 years).

Sample. Participants for SOTEP were recruited from California prisons between 1985 and 1994. Qualified offenders were rapists and child molesters who were within 18 and 30 months of release and who met several other screening criteria (e.g., no more than three felony convictions, IQs 80 and above, no organic or major mental disorders, and no recent history of severe management problems in prison). Offenders who qualified and volunteered for the project were matched on the variables of age, criminal history, and type of offense. One member of each matched pair was assigned at random to our treatment group and the other to the untreated volunteer control group. In our outcome study, we have also followed a third group, the nonvolunteer control group, consisting of matched offenders who did not want treatment.

Treatment. Once selected, members of the treatment group participated in an intensive inpatient program at Atascadero State Hospital, a secure forensic treatment facility in central California. From the beginning (Marques, 1984), SOTEP was designed to provide a comprehensive treatment program that was based on our adaptation of Marlatt's RP model (Marlatt, 1980; Marlatt &

Gordon, 1985). The program embraced the basic theoretical concepts of RP, emphasized the long-term risk of reoffending, and explicitly targeted the problem of relapse. All of the program's components, which included a variety of cognitive, behavioral, and skill-training elements, were organized around the RP framework. Both assessment and treatment procedures focused on the individual's specific risk factors for reoffense, from broad lifestyle factors and cognitive distortions to deviant sexual arousal patterns and deficits in coping skills.

SOTEP's primary treatment structure was the core RP group, which met for three 90-minute sessions each week throughout the program. This highly structured group was the setting in which each participant's cognitive-behavioral offense chain was constructed and used to identify the risk factors and patterns that his RP program needed to address. It was also the setting in which we worked on the important elements of motivation and responsibility. The offender was encouraged to learn, in detail, how he set up his past crimes and what he needed to do differently to avoid reoffense.

In addition to this intensive RP training, treatment group subjects participated in other program components that addressed common determinants of sex offending. The project's specialty groups were designed to provide the specific knowledge, attitudes, and skills that the offender needed to identify and cope with potential high-risk situations. These included groups on sex education, human sexuality, relaxation training, stress and anger management, and social skills. A prerelease class designed to prepare the offender for "life on the streets" was also mandatory. Other specialty groups (e.g., substance abuse) and individualized treatment components (e.g., behavior therapy to alter deviant sexual arousal patterns) were offered on a prescriptive basis. To maintain consistency and fidelity in the program, all treatment services (with the exception of individual psychotherapy) were provided according to structured treatment manuals.

After completing the hospital program, treatment subjects participated in the Sex Offender Aftercare Program (SOAP) for 1 year. These services, which were provided in the offender's community by clinicians who were trained in the use of RP by SOTEP clinical staff, were a condition of the participants' parole. This meant that failure to attend SOAP could result in a parole revocation and return to prison.

The SOTEP treatment unit at Atascadero closed in June 1995, completing the 10-year treatment phase of the project. By March 1996, the subjects in all three experimental groups had been released from the hospital or prison to the community.

Evaluation. Our most important program evaluation effort is the ongoing measurement of long-term outcomes to determine whether (and for which types of offenders) our treatment has reduced recidivism. We also included measures of in-treatment changes in our design to learn more about which treatment components and goals are related to long-term outcomes. During the treatment phase, we used relevant pre-post measures for each of the program's groups and the behavior therapy component. We also used a number of measures to determine the extent to which treatment group members achieved the following overall goals of the program: (a) an increased sense of personal responsibility and decreased use of justifications for sexual deviance, (b) a decrease in deviant sexual interests, (c) an understanding of and ability to apply the basic concepts and techniques of RP, (d) an improved ability to identify high-risk situations, and (e) better skills in the areas of avoiding and coping with high-risk situations.

SOTEP Findings Regarding What Worked

Program Evaluation Findings

Recidivism Data

Our most recent recidivism data (Marques & Day, 1998) showed that after about 5 years at risk, the 167 subjects who completed treatment had a lower sex reoffense rate (10.8%) than did the 225 volunteer control subjects (13.8%) or the 220 nonvolunteer controls (13.2%). This trend has continued for several years (see Marques, Day, Nelson, & West, 1994) but has not reached statistical significance. Another consistent finding over our years of follow-up has been that the 37 treatment dropouts have demonstrated the poorest outcomes (18.9% sex reoffense).

Our data also suggest that our program was more successful with certain offender subgroups than with others. For example, one high-risk subgroup, molesters with male victims, appears to be more responsive to treatment than molesters with female victims (although this trend is also not statistically significant at this point). Offenders in the treatment group with substance abuse problems or prior treatment experience have done significantly better than their counterparts in the two control groups. On the other hand, the small subgroup of offenders with evidence of thought disorder has not responded well to the SOTEP program. Among these offenders, treatment subjects have a higher rate of reoffense than do the control subjects.

In-Treatment Changes

In general, our evaluation data have indicated that treatment subjects made significant progress toward the five goals listed earlier, including the understanding of RP concepts and the acquisition of some RP skills. Because we have previously reported our in-treatment change data in considerable detail (see Marques et al., 1991; Marques, Nelson, West, & Day, 1994), we focus here on findings that are directly relevant to the RP model. The most important measures of the extent to which participants learned RP concepts and skills were (a) two written assignments (the cognitive-behavioral chain and the decision matrix), in which subjects demonstrated their ability to apply RP to their own lives, and (b) the Sex Offender Situational Competency Test (SOSCT), in which subjects were asked to describe what they would do in a number of high-risk situations presented to them on audiotape.

The most pressing question about these measures concerns their relationship to reoffense: Are participants who are skilled in RP at a lower risk of reoffense? We have not completed the analyses that address this question using the SOSCT data, but we have examined the relationships between the two written RP assignments and reoffense. In our earlier analyses (Marques, Nelson, et al., 1994), we found that these ratings were related to reoffense: Subjects who had learned the program's RP model well were less likely to reoffend than those who had not. Although subsequent analyses have not found this effect for the whole treatment group, there is evidence that it applies to a very important subgroup. Among the more chronic offenders (e.g., individuals with a more extensive history of sex crimes), we have continued to find that those who mastered the RP model had a lower risk of reoffense. For the less chronic offenders, however, those who did well on the RP measures had about the same reoffense rate as those who did not do well.

Qualitative Analyses

Clinical Analyses of Treatment Failures

Just before the treatment program closed in 1995, we met with SOTEP's treatment staff and conducted psychological "postmortems" on our known treatment failures. We discussed the 21 individuals in the treatment group (including dropouts) who had been returned to custody for new sex offenses and another 4 who had engaged in "high-risk behaviors" (offense precursors such as cruising or annoying a child). The discussion included both the individual's performance in treatment as well as what was known about his situation after release. In each case, we tried to determine what we "missed" in the individual's relapse prevention program. Although the focus was on identifying what our program lacked, we also invited discussion of what our program had done well.

These clinical analyses yielded a number of common themes about how and why offenders failed and some conclusions about the strengths and weaknesses of our program. These conclusions are summarized next.

What We Did Well in the SOTEP Program. Our review of cases indicated that our program was strong in several ways and that we had successfully done the following:

1. Taught the relapse prevention model. Nearly all of the participants indicated that the RP model made sense to them and that the skills taught in the program could help them avoid reoffending. All of them passed our basic mastery test of RP and showed some ability to apply the model to their own and others' behavior. Some became experts in the RP model.

2. Taught offenders about their risk factors. Over their time in treatment, most improved significantly in their abilities to analyze the chain of events that led up to their offenses and to identify a variety of risk factors that could precipitate relapse.

3. Set a supportive tone. As the RP model prescribes, our core groups were generally problem-solving, collaborative efforts, with therapists and other members helping the offender construct his cognitive-behavioral offense chain and improve it over time.

4. Taught coping skills. Again, as RP suggests, our focus was on identifying specific coping skills that could be used to interrupt the chain of events leading to relapse. Offenders who completed treatment left with what appeared to be a toolbox full of cognitive and behavioral coping strategies.

5. Confronted criminal attitudes and distortions. Although our tone was supportive, much of the time in the core group was spent identifying and confronting denial, minimization, and offense-supportive attitudes. Participants showed improvements in their ability to identify cognitive distortions and to verbalize more accurate and appropriate views.

What We Could Have Done Better in the SOTEP Program. Our case reviews suggested several areas of weakness in our program. We concluded that treatment would have been more effective if we had done the following with our participants:

1. Strengthened their commitment to abstinence. Our participants were all highly motivated to avoid rearrest and imprisonment, but many showed little motivation that was not fear based. Among treatment failures, there was a notable lack of commitment to abstinence regarding high-risk behaviors. They did not appear motivated to avoid identified risk factors such as substance abuse, a criminal lifestyle, or access to potential victims. They may have left with tools for recognizing and coping with high-risk situations, but many did not use the tools. Even after considerable exposure to treatment, some offenders were still in the early stages of change (see Prochaska & DiClemente, 1982). We concluded that motivation and commitment to abstinence should remain primary targets of treatment throughout the program, including aftercare.

2. *Stressed and challenged participants more.* Some clinicians felt that SOTEP's highly structured program allowed participants to "succeed" in the program while avoiding difficult therapeutic work. Depending on the offender, this might have been work on their own victimization experiences, resolution of family problems, or development of a nondeviant lifestyle. An attitude of "I'll deal with that when I get out" (e.g., "I'll find a woman and have a great relationship") was common among the treatment failures. Our conclusion was that we should have challenged this avoidance more strongly and insisted that these individuals take on such important and difficult problems during their inpatient treatment.

3. *Focused more on affective factors.* This is another weakness related to the highly structured nature of the SOTEP program and to the fact that length of treatment was predetermined by the individual's release date. This program structure did not allow us to provide dosed levels of intervention (e.g., longer and more intensive treatment for those who needed it). Given the cognitive-behavioral focus of our RP program, it is not surprising that this need for more intensive work was clearest in the affective area. Many participants were not skilled at identifying and modifying emotional elements in their offense chains and decision matrices. Perhaps the most difficult task in this area was the development of empathy in offenders who maintained that their own victimization was positive. In some cases, these men understood that sexual abuse can have negative effects, but they did not see their own victims as harmed. This seemed to us to be a significant risk factor that we could have addressed more thoroughly.

4. *Emphasized practice of coping skills.* SOTEP's core group focused on recognizing and analyzing risk and on learning coping responses. We made sure that all cognitive-behavioral chains included coping responses for each step leading to the offense. What we did not ensure was that participants were prepared to use the coping skills they identified. It is easy to write down "I would recognize and defeat that cognitive distortion by telling myself it is wrong to think about a child that way." It does not follow, however, that the individual could do that quickly and effectively in a high-risk situation. There was a strong consensus among SOTEP clinicians that more actual practice of identified coping skills was needed.

5. *Provided a strong conditional release component.* SOTEP treatment subjects experienced an abrupt transition from the heavy structure of the hospital to minimal supervision and treatment in the community. Many offenders were released into the community without adequate housing, employment, and social support, and some rather quickly were facing high-risk situations on a regular basis. Our clinicians agreed that more transitional work needed to be

done, followed by a longer aftercare program that required return to a more restrictive treatment setting if a participant began to flounder in the community.

Interviews With Reoffenders

Also near the end of SOTEP's treatment phase, we undertook a small study of treatment group subjects who reoffended to learn more about the relapse process (Russell, Marques, Murphy, & Potash, 1994). Nine subjects (three rapists and six child molesters) who had returned to prison because of new sex crimes participated in structured interviews that consisted of (a) construction of the cognitive-behavioral chain that led up to their new crimes and (b) interview probes regarding motivation, commitment to abstinence, high-risk behaviors, lapses, and aspects of their reoffenses. It should be noted that these nine individuals were not representative of the SOTEP treatment group in several ways; most important, rapists, child molesters with male victims, and those with many prior sex offenses were overrepresented in the interview sample. This small group appeared to include a number of men who were continuing a long pattern of sex offending. It also included two men who had begun but failed to complete the hospital program.

The most striking finding from our interview data was that despite the fact that the average time to rearrest was 28 months, six of the nine subjects had returned to high-risk behaviors within 1 month of their return to the community. The most common of these behaviors was alcohol or drug use, followed by befriending adults with children, buying pornography, or having sex with prostitutes. When asked about their commitment to abstinence, only one subject indicated that he had made a commitment to avoid high-risk behaviors, despite our emphasis on this in the program. Only five reported having made a commitment to abstinence with respect to sex offending. When asked about their motivation, all of the interviewees described themselves as very motivated to change when they began treatment, but most were unable to sustain their motivation over time. Some offenders continued to experience deviant fantasies or urges during treatment, saw this as an indication that they were incapable of change, and believed that it was useless to struggle against their longstanding deviant interests. For these individuals, reoffense appeared to be just a matter of time.

When subjects were asked to describe the impact of their reoffenses, six reported that their victims had suffered no harm, and the other three reported only minimal impact. None described the impact of the reoffense on the victim as moderate to severe. Four perceived their victims as mutually consenting.

These SOTEP reoffenders, then, appeared to be men with long-standing patterns of sex offending who had volunteered for treatment but were unable to sustain their motivation to change. Despite a significant exposure to treatment, almost half of these subjects left the program without a strong commitment to abstinence, most of them failed to avoid obvious high-risk behaviors, and all of them showed a lack of victim empathy. These individuals clearly did not "get" the program that we provided.

Enhancing the RP Model

As the preceding section indicates, our experience with RP in SOTEP's experimental program revealed some weaknesses in the model as we applied it, as well as some ways in which our model could be enhanced. In this section, we describe a number of areas in which modifications, additions, and changes in emphasis may improve the effectiveness of RP with sex offenders.

Introducing Treatment

Because RP is a cognitive-behavioral treatment approach (Marlatt, 1985a; George & Marlatt, 1989), it is important to introduce offenders to this type of treatment and its basic precepts, such as the following: (a) beliefs organize thoughts, (b) thoughts determine feelings and behaviors, (c) beliefs and thoughts are under one's voluntary control, and (d) correcting irrational thoughts and modifying self-statements can change feelings and behaviors (Beck, 1976; Ellis, 1962; Meichenbaum, 1977). Presenting offenders with examples of everyday occurrences in which people reacted in different ways due to their unique beliefs and interpretations is one way of accomplishing this without engendering resistance. One example that can be used is of a man who was buying a muffin and told by the cashier that he should pick another one. The customer became angry, stating, "No one tells me what I should do." Offenders are asked to provide examples of these everyday situations and interpretations and to explore how a benign interpretation (e.g., "The muffin may not be fresh") will produce a very different reaction than a malignant one (e.g., "The cashier is saving this muffin for himself") will produce. Many examples of this type of non-sex-offending material can be given to offenders in a nonthreatening way until they have internalized the concept that beliefs and thoughts determine feelings and behaviors. Such examples also help them distinguish between events and their interpretations of those events, a distinction that is necessary if offenders are to learn how to control the high-risk thoughts that lead to offending.

Although external supervision and monitoring are essential parts of an adequate sex offender treatment regime, RP is predominantly a self-control treatment model. It aims to teach offenders how to manage their behaviors and urges by coping more effectively with high-risk situations. By accepting that thoughts determine feelings and behaviors and that thoughts are under the offender's voluntary control, a foundation for developing a sense of self-control is established.

Enhancing Motivation

As we described earlier, one of the most salient correlates of relapse among SOTEP participants was simply not being motivated to change their behavior. In some cases, motivation was hampered by a belief that treatment would not be efficacious in light of their own perceived inability to resist deviant impulses. An even more basic problem was that although they had learned ways to reduce temptation, some reoffenders did not believe that their behavior was really undesirable. Or, they simply did not want to stop. It cannot be assumed, even in voluntary programs, that offenders are intrinsically motivated to abandon what for many has been a lifelong pattern of sexual deviance. It is our view that RP needs to be enhanced by placing more emphasis on the beliefs that underlie these motivational deficits.

Of course, the problem of motivating clients is not unique to sex offender treatment, and we may well benefit from work that has been done in related fields. For example, health educators also face the challenges of enhancing motivation and changing ingrained, unhealthy beliefs and behaviors. One approach that has been developed is the Health Belief Model (Rosenstock, Strecher, & Becker, 1988), a theoretical framework that guides behavioral interventions in the field of public health. Essentially, the Health Belief Model holds that people are rational and will change their behavior when they perceive themselves as susceptible to a condition that poses a substantial threat—but only if they perceive the prescribed intervention as efficacious and themselves as capable of undertaking the recommended action. We expect that these conditions also hold for sex offenders and their application of RP interventions.

The problem of motivational deficits has also plagued those treating addictive behaviors for years and has provoked the development of an approach, motivational interviewing, that specifically targets the problem of developing and maintaining motivation to change (Miller & Rollnick, 1991). Motivational interviewing is a nonauthoritarian approach that helps clients identify their own concerns about their behavior, articulate their own reasons for change, and reach a decision to change. This approach, which is closely linked to Prochaska and DiClemente's (1982) transtheoretical stages of change (see also Prochaska, DiClemente, & Norcross, 1992), fits quite well with an overall RP approach in which the therapist encourages and guides clients but does not try to force-feed them. As we learned from our treatment failures, offenders who have not arrived at their own sources of motivation are at considerable risk when they leave the supervised treatment setting.

Many offenders initially express the desire to change to avoid future punishment (especially in an age of increasingly severe prison sentences for sex offenses) or to avoid social and family rejection. Such motivation must be considered suspect and highly variable. It is a well-known behavioral principle that the effects of punishment dissipate over time. Hence, it can be expected that the fear of future incarceration or social rejection will also eventually wear off. More intrinsic and internal rewards for success must be developed and encouraged if motivation is going to be sustained.

In developing motivation, it is important to emphasize the positive aspects of behavior change (see Marlatt, 1985a). The successful application of RP strategies does not just lead to a life of deprivation from the sexual behavior that offenders have found so satisfying in the past. It can also lead to improved social relationships, job performance, and overall life satisfaction. Instead of just taking away something that was enjoyable, successful treatment needs to focus on replacing the past deviant behavior with other positive and enjoyable behaviors. Although it can be difficult, we believe that this aspect of treatment deserves more attention if offenders are to remain motivated for change.

Defining Key RP Concepts

Abstinence. Our experience has identified a need to define carefully the concept of abstinence and spend more time on each of its components. Just as motivation to change cannot be assumed, neither can the commitment to abstinence. In many ways, commitment to abstinence goes hand in hand with motivation. As motivation waxes and wanes, so does the personal vow not to reoffend. One technique that is incorporated in many programs is a regular affirmation of the vow of abstinence. This may take the form of a restatement during each treatment session about why the offender has come to treatment, along with a personal reminder that managing deviant sexual impulses is a lifelong endeavor.

It may also be necessary to adopt a broader concept of abstinence. Instead of simply making a commitment not to reoffend or engage in deviant fantasies, offenders should also make a commitment not to intentionally engage in the high-risk behaviors that have preceded their offenses (spending time with children, alcohol or drug intoxication, etc.).

It is important to define abstinence not as depriving oneself of an act of pleasure but as gaining control of one's life and the increased self-esteem that accompanies achieving life's goals. Offenders must first establish some broader life goals and learn how sex offending is incompatible with these goals. Focus is then placed on increasing self-esteem by teaching offenders to keep promises to themselves.

Solidifying the commitment to abstinence is an important task that continues throughout treatment. Offenders are taught that a true commitment to abstinence means that one will maintain abstinence, whatever the cost.

Although this level of commitment may seem alarming at first, the therapist can demonstrate that there are already areas of their lives in which they have firmly and successfully made such commitments. A favorite example is coming to work with clothes on. Offenders readily agree that, no matter what happens, they are committed to wearing clothes to work and will find a way to do so. In a similar manner, offenders must be willing to take extreme steps to avoid children or other high-risk situations in their lives. They can also explore the tools they would use to maintain their self-promise to wear clothes and see that many of the same tools could be used to refrain from sex offending.

Lapse. The definition of *lapse* seems to have been a continuing source of confusion in RP programs, ours included. In the original (Marlatt, 1985b) model, a lapse was an obvious first break in the commitment to abstinence, such as the first drink after a period of sobriety. It was also an opportunity for growth and understanding of the relapse process and a time for interventions designed to avoid a full-blown relapse. When we started our program (Marques, 1984), we defined lapse as "the step (usually a cognitive event, such as a fantasy, thought or plan) which immediately precedes an offense." Over the years, however, the term came to be more broadly defined as our concept of commitment to abstinence also broadened. Many clinicians in our program began identifying the lapse as the intentional placing of oneself in a high-risk situation. By acting on a high-risk factor, such as entitlement thinking or putting oneself in the proximity of children, offenders are intentionally escalating their offending patterns. They have breached their commitment to abstinence.

We are aware that broadening the definition of a lapse to "intentionally acting on a high-risk factor" lacks precision and is theoretically awkward. It is also in conflict with the definition used in the most advanced RP models that have been developed recently by Ward, Hudson, and their colleagues (Ward & Hudson, 1998). Perhaps the best solution is to leave the *lapse* where it was (an immediate precursor to the offense) and find a better term for this earlier step in the cognitive-behavioral chain. Terminology aside, we feel strongly that this is a critical point in the chain and that work on such "early lapses" can help offenders learn how to intervene and seek outside help before they are close to relapse. Even this early in the offense chain, it can be appropriate for offenders to seek assistance from outside sources such as counselors, probation officers, and support groups. Not only will they have more time to get help, but they also may be more receptive to cognitive interventions as well.

Abstinence Violation Effect. As initially conceived, the abstinence violation effect (AVE) consisted of the thoughts and feelings an offender experienced after committing a lapse. These feelings were typically seen as negative self-esteem, expectations of failure, and an impaired sense of self-control (Marques, 1984; Marques & Nelson, 1989; Nelson, Miner, Marques, Russell,

& Achterkirchen, 1988). Offenders were taught to prepare for these negative feelings and to learn skills for avoiding the lapse propelling them onto a full-blown relapse. Since the initial theoretical descriptions of RP with this population, however, research has suggested that lapses may actually be associated with a state of excited anticipation. The cognitive dissonance and negative emotional consequences that characterize the AVE seem to be more likely to follow relapse than a lapse (Ward, Hudson, & Marshall, 1994). A lapse, such as a deviant fantasy, may not be accompanied by a negative affective state but may well be experienced quite positively as immediate gratification (Ward, Hudson, & Siegert, 1995). Obviously, this requires adjustments to the way programs prepare individuals to cope with lapses and the reactions that they experience.

Practicing and Internalizing RP Skills

Institutional programs in particular need to emphasize the importance of getting offenders to internalize RP tools by employing them in their everyday lives. Offenders are taught that most of the same high-risk factors and cognitive distortions that led to their sex offenses also affect how they manage all other aspects of their lives, including those within the institution. Offenders frequently see the techniques and strategies being provided as only applicable to their lives after their release to the community. As a result, they may delay and resist actual behavior changes in the present. To counter this, institutional treatment staff must be alert to each individual's most salient cognitive distortions and risk factors and must address them when they occur. Even though an offender may not have ready access to potential victims in the controlled treatment environment, he must practice employing corrective thinking and avoiding risky behaviors in everyday circumstances. For example, an offender who has a high-risk factor of feelings of entitlement may be observed to insist on being first in line to a meal or getting the newest hospital-issued uniforms. Another offender with a high-risk factor of seeking immediate gratification may be seen spending his monthly allowance the first day he receives it. A third offender with the distorted belief that rules are only for other people may be observed breaking a rule when he feels he can get away with it. In a comprehensive RP program, offenders must be taught to identify high-risk factors as they occur daily and apply appropriate corrective actions without prompting. Keeping daily journals and logs can help them identify the risk factors they encounter and the coping responses they used in response to them. They should also practice using RP tools, such as developing cognitive-behavioral chains or decision matrices, when problem behaviors occur.

If our experience is typical, it is seductive for clinicians to concentrate their RP work with sex offenders on identifying high-risk factors, often to the exclusion of practicing and overlearning coping responses to these factors. The process of identifying high-risk elements can be likened to many insight-oriented approaches that center on helping clients ascertain why they did what they did as opposed to concentrating on developing the skills needed to act differently in the future. Many clinicians find the work of practicing and developing coping skills tedious and time-consuming. Yet, the development of adequate coping skills to high-risk elements in the offending pattern is one of the most critical interventions.

Our experience suggests that RP programs should spend more time and energy on practicing and sharpening coping responses than on identifying high-risk elements and factors. Offenders must be able to *behave* differently, not just intellectually grasp how they can behave differently. It is essential that they practice the skills that are needed to maintain abstinence in the community while still in the institution. It is also important to anticipate and rehearse responses to many scenarios that could occur in the community. For example, those being discharged to urban areas with public transportation can be asked what they would do if they were on a bus going to work and it was filled with children on a field trip.

Community Transition

Institutional RP programs also need to build in the structures needed for offenders to make a smooth transition to outpatient treatment and supervision. Ideally, the community therapist and supervisors should become involved early in the treatment process. They must be aware of the offender's progress in identifying high-risk situations and the coping responses to minimize the chances that these will result in relapse. The model, vocabulary, and techniques used in treatment should be consistent across both the residential and outpatient settings. The outpatient clinician or supervisor should take an active role in identifying potential high-risk scenarios for the offender to practice before his community release. Adequate housing, occupational or vocational plans, and social support services must be arranged before an offender is released. If an offender begins to lapse, it is imperative that outpatient services have the option of returning the offender to a controlled environment.

A New RP Program

Since the end of the treatment phase of the SOTEP study, we have been involved in the development of a new treatment program at Atascadero State Hospital, the Sex Offender Commitment Program (SOCP). This program is designed to treat men who are being civilly committed as "sexually violent predators" under a 1995 law (codified in the California Welfare and Institutions Code,

1999) that is similar to those in other jurisdictions (Lieb, Quinsey, & Berliner, 1998). In this section, we describe this new program, with an emphasis on how we have adapted and extended our RP framework to accommodate this new commitment process and offender population.

Before describing the new program, we want to point out that the populations treated in SOTEP and SOCP are quite different. First, unlike SOTEP participants, the new SOCP participants have been involuntarily committed. Many believe they have been wrongfully detained past their prison terms and are openly hostile and resistant to any form of evaluation or therapy. It is not uncommon for SOCP participants to view the treatment program with distrust and skepticism. Second, the SOCP participants are a higher risk group than the SOTEP participants were. For example, although more than a third of the SOTEP participants had only one felony conviction, this new group averaged more than eight arrests and six convictions before their commitment. To be committed as a sexual predator, the offender must have had at least two victims who were either strangers or individuals with whom a relationship was established for the purpose of victimization. It must also be determined, based on two independent clinical evaluations, that the offender suffers from a mental disorder and is likely to commit new sex crimes in the future. The evidence must be sufficiently strong to be able to convince a judge or jury beyond a reasonable doubt that they meet these criteria.

There are also important structural differences between SOTEP and SOCP, such as the length of treatment, release criteria, and outpatient treatment requirements. SOTEP participants were in treatment only until their parole dates regardless of treatment progress. SOCP participants are committed for a 2-year period, but the commitment can be extended every 2 years until the court determines that the offender can be released. Even with its relatively stringent commitment criteria, the offenders entering SOCP are a diverse group, and there will be significant differences in the length of time that they require to complete the program. Finally, there is a much more highly structured and extensive aftercare structure in the new program. Unlike SOTEP participants, who were seen by private clinicians for 1 year after release, SOCP will have a comprehensive, state-provided community treatment program, and treatment will continue until the patient successfully completes the outpatient phase of the program.

Program Requirements

We have designed the new treatment program to meet both statutory requirements (see California Welfare and Institutions Code, 1999) and the recommendations for civil commitment that have been made by the Association for the Treatment of Sexual Abusers (ATSA, 1997). As required by statute, the program is based on a structured protocol that describes assessment procedures, treatment components, and measures of treatment progress. Consistent with ATSA recommendations, the program (a) is provided by qualified and licensed staff in a mental health treatment facility, (b) employs individualized treatment planning and systematic measurement of progress, (c) includes the components that are recognized for maximum treatment potential, and (d) has identifiable phases of treatment, including an aftercare program in the community.

The program includes the two approaches (cognitive-behavioral and hormonal) that Hall's (1995) meta-analysis identified as promising interventions with sex offenders. Like SOTEP, the cognitive-behavioral strategies are provided in group settings and are organized within an RP framework. Unlike SOTEP, the use of both antiandrogens (Fedoroff, Wisner-Carlson, Dean, & Berlin, 1996) and selective serotonin reuptake inhibitors (Greenberg & Bradford, 1997) is emphasized in the new program.

Program Structure

SOCP has adopted a five-phase treatment structure, with specific treatment tasks and goals set out for each phase. Recurring themes are also addressed in all phases, including cognitive restructuring, victim empathy, and relapse prevention. The first four phases occur in the institutional setting and are to be successfully completed before the individual moves to the final outpatient component. Again, although the program is highly structured, the course and pace of treatment will be guided by individualized treatment plans and assessments of progress. Because of the diversity of the offenders in the program, some offenders will require more time to complete each of the phases than will other offenders. The program's phases consist of the following:

1. Treatment Readiness. This is designed to facilitate the transition from the prison culture to a treatment environment. Due to the resistance of many SOCP participants, the primary group activity in this phase is largely didactic and educational in format. Information is presented on the commitment law, the most common mental disorders (paraphilias and personality disorders) that are the bases for commitment, and the typical cognitive distortions that are used by sex offenders. Foundations for enhancing victim empathy are laid through relatively matter-of-fact descriptions of the common repercussions of rape and molestation. Cognitive-behavioral treatment is introduced, as are RP assumptions and terms. The emphasis in this phase of treatment is on helping the offender gain an intellectual and cognitive understanding of the overall treatment process.

2. Skills Acquisition. This marks the transition to a more active phase of the treatment process. To advance to this second phase, the offender must (a) acknowledge committing past sex offenses and express a desire to reduce his risk of reoffending, (b) be willing to discuss his past offenses, (c) agree to participate in required sex offender-specific assessment procedures (including penile plethysmography), (d) pass a test on the basic tenets of RP and the Sexually Violent Predator law, and (e) conduct himself appropriately in a group setting. During this phase, offenders begin to apply RP techniques to their individual cases. They complete an autobiography (Long, Wuesthoff, & Pithers, 1989) that describes the development of their sexually deviant patterns, along with cognitive-behavioral offense chains (Nelson & Jackson, 1989) and decision matrices (Jenkins-Hall, 1989), to identify their personal high-risk factors and potential future coping strategies. Specific cognitive distortions and justifications the offender has used are identified and confronted, and information on sexual victimization is presented and processed in terms of its impact on each offender personally.

Treatment in this phase requires the offender to become more personally invested in the treatment process. He must accept and identify that he remains at risk for reoffending in the future and that there are steps he can take to reduce the likelihood that he will commit another sexually violent act. It is, however, still possible for those in this phase to maintain a fairly detached and intellectual stance (e.g., to verbally describe risks and coping strategies without intending or having the requisite skills to change their patterns of behavior).

3. Skills Application. In this phase, offenders integrate and apply the skills they have learned. To progress into this phase of treatment, the offender must (a) make a commitment not to reoffend, (b) understand that the goal of treatment is to manage and control his deviant sexual urges (as opposed to believing that he will be "cured"), (c) complete all prescribed assessment procedures, (d) successfully complete (as determined by an interdisciplinary treatment team) the cognitive-behavioral chain and decision matrix assignments, and (e) be able to recognize and correct the cognitive distortions that led him to sexual victimization.

Treatment in this phase focuses on practicing the coping responses identified in the previous phase of treatment. Structured exercises are used to help offenders overlearn these coping strategies so they become strong habits in high-risk situations (Hall, 1989; Steenman, Nelson, & Viesti, 1989). Offenders also begin a process of keeping logs and journals (Long, Wuesthoff, & Pithers, 1989) that are regularly reviewed in a group setting to identify potential high-risk thinking and behaviors. The offenders continue to develop victim empathy skills through exercises that help them personalize how they have harmed their specific victims. Victim empathy and clarification letters are used to facilitate this process.

This phase of treatment clearly differentiates RP as it is delivered in SOCP from SOTEP. Because SOTEP was time limited, there was often too little time to ensure that the participant had integrated the treatment interventions. In contrast, SOCP has the ability, through the constant observation that occurs in an institutional program, to determine that the offender is "walking the talk." That is, we can observe whether the coping responses he has articulated are actually being applied in his day-to-day life. Without this daily evidence of changed thinking and behavior, offenders are not able to progress to the next step in the treatment program.

4. Transition. Transition focuses on preparation for release to community treatment. Advancement to this phase requires a determination by the offender's treatment team that he has met all of the criteria for the inpatient phases of treatment. He must demonstrate that he is strongly committed to abstinence, able to identify all of his relevant high-risk factors, and consistently able to cope with risky situations and thinking in ways that reduce his likelihood of reoffending. Also, the local program must be willing to accept him for outpatient treatment, supervision, and monitoring.

During this phase, offenders complete a detailed maintenance manual that is used to solidify their treatment gains. In conjunction with the community program, an in-depth release plan is developed, which covers treatment and supervision, living situation, employment, and safe community activities. Community notification and registration laws are thoroughly reviewed so he is clear about his responsibilities as well as potential community reactions on his release. Members of the offender's social support network are made aware of his high-risk factors and offending patterns and are instructed in the mechanisms for intervening in the offense chain as needed.

5. Community Outpatient Treatment. This involves intensive monitoring and supervision as well as treatment in the community-based program. To progress to this less-restrictive setting, the offender's institutional treatment team and community provider must recommend it, and the court must approve. The major treatment task in this phase is to extend treatment gains made in the institution to the community setting. Having community treatment providers who are fully acquainted with the SOCP participants facilitates this task. Each offender has an outpatient provider who is identified at the beginning of treatment and who meets every 6 months with the offender and treatment team throughout the institutional program.

In addition to continuing RP and possibly pharmacological interventions, the community programs will provide ongoing supervision and monitoring. Devices such as electronic bracelets, around-the-clock supervision, and periodic polygraphs may be required. This level of supervision is gradually reduced as warranted by the offender's behavior and adjustment in the community. This phase of the program may continue indefinitely until it is terminated by the court. It may also result in the participant returning to earlier phases of treatment in the institution, should he show signs of engaging in risky behavior in the community.

Conclusions

In this chapter, we have provided what is definitely a "mixed review" of our application of the RP model with sex offenders. On the positive side, SOTEP participants found the model intuitively appealing and relevant, and most of them made significant progress in learning RP skills and achieving other program goals. Also, the treatment group is continuing to show somewhat lower (although not significantly so) reoffense rates than their control group counterparts. On the negative side, our clinical analyses of treatment failures have revealed that some offenders who completed the 2-year program did not use the RP skills they learned and began engaging in high-risk thoughts and behaviors soon after their release. Although obviously discouraging in some ways, this information has led to some positive developments in our research and clinical work. For example, we have begun to examine our treatment group more closely with respect to the extent to which participants actually "got treatment." To this end, we plan in our next recidivism analyses to compare the outcomes of SOTEP participants who achieved most program goals with the outcomes of participants who did not. On the clinical side, our treatment failures have led us to a number of ideas for enhancing RP that we have presented in this chapter. Finally, we have used our SOTEP data and experience to design a new multiphased and intensive RP program for high-risk offenders who are being civilly committed for treatment.

References

Association for the Treatment of Sexual Abusers (ATSA). (1997). *Civil commitment of sexually violent offenders.* Beaverton, OR: Author.

Beck, A. T. (1976). *Cognitive therapy and the emotional disorders.* New York: International Universities Press.

California Welfare and Institutions Code, chap. 2, article 4, sections 6600-6608 (1999).

Ellis, A. (1962). *Reason and emotion in psychotherapy.* New York: Lyle Stuart.

Fedoroff, J. P., Wisner-Carlson, R., Dean, S., & Berlin, F. S. (1996). Medroxy-progesterone acetate in the treatment of paraphilic sexual disorders: Rates of relapse in paraphilic men treated in long-term group psychotherapy with or without medroxy-progesterone acetate. In E. Coleman, S. M. Dwyer, & N. J. Pallone (Eds.), *Sex offender treatment: Psychological and medical approaches* (pp. 109-123). New York: Haworth.

George, W. H., & Marlatt, G. A. (1989). Introduction. In D. R. Laws (Ed.), *Relapse prevention with sex offenders* (pp. 1-31). New York: Guilford.

Greenberg, D. M., & Bradford, J. M. W. (1997). Treatment of the paraphilic disorders: A review of the role of the selective serotonin reuptake inhibitors. *Sexual Abuse: A Journal of Research and Treatment, 9*(4), 349-360.

Hall, G. C. N. (1995). Sexual offender recidivism revised: A meta-analysis of recent treatment studies. *Journal of Consulting and Clinical Psychology, 63,* 802-809.

Hall, R. L. (1989). Relapse rehearsal. In D. R. Laws (Ed.), *Relapse prevention with sex offenders* (pp. 197-206). New York: Guilford.

Jenkins-Hall, K. (1989). The decision matrix. In D. R. Laws (Ed.), *Relapse prevention with sex offenders* (pp. 159-166). New York: Guilford.

Lieb, R., Quinsey, V., & Berliner, L. (1998). Sexual predators and social policy. *Crime and Justice: A Review of Research, 23,* 43-113.

Long, J. D., Wuesthoff, A., & Pithers, W. D. (1989). Use of autobiographies in the assessment and treatment of sex offenders. In D. R. Laws (Ed.), *Relapse prevention with sex offenders* (pp. 88-95). New York: Guilford.

Marlatt, G. A. (1980). *Relapse prevention: A self-control program for the treatment of addictive behaviors.* Unpublished manuscript, Department of Psychology, University of Washington, Seattle.

Marlatt, G. A. (1985a). Lifestyle modification. In G. A. Marlatt & J. R. Gordon (Eds.), *Relapse prevention* (pp. 280-348). New York: Guilford.

Marlatt, G. A. (1985b). Relapse prevention: Theoretical rationale and overview of the model. In G. A. Marlatt & J. R. Gordon (Eds.), *Relapse prevention* (pp. 3-70). New York: Guilford.

Marlatt, G. A., & Gordon, J. R. (Eds.). (1985). *Relapse prevention: Maintenance strategies in the treatment of addictive behaviors.* New York: Guilford.

Marques, J. K. (1984). *An innovative treatment program for sex offenders: Report to the legislature.* Sacramento: California Department of Mental Health.

Marques, J. K., & Day, D. M. (1998). *Sex Offender Treatment and Evaluation Project: Progress report.* Unpublished manuscript, California Department of Mental Health.

Marques, J. K., Day, D. M., Nelson, C., Miner, M. H., & West, M. A. (1991). *The Sex Offender Treatment and Evaluation Project: Fourth report to the legislature in response to PC 1365.* Sacramento: California Department of Mental Health.

Marques, J. K., Day, D. M., Nelson, C., & West, M. A. (1994). Effects of cognitive-behavioral treatment on sex offender recidivism: Preliminary results of a longitudinal study. *Criminal Justice and Behavior, 21,* 28-54.

Marques, J. K., & Nelson, C. (1989). Understanding and preventing relapse in sex offenders. In M. Gossop (Ed.), *Relapse and addictive behaviour* (pp. 96-106). Beckenham, UK: Croom-Helm.

Marques, J. K., Nelson, C., West, M. A., & Day, D. M. (1994). The relationship between treatment goals and recidivism among child molesters. *Behavior Research and Therapy, 32*(5), 577-588.

Meichenbaum, D. (1977). *Cognitive-behavior modification.* New York: Plenum.

Miller, W. R., & Rollnick, S. (1991). *Motivational interviewing: Preparing people to change addictive behavior.* New York: Guilford.

Nelson, C., & Jackson, P. (1989). High-risk recognition: The cognitive-behavioral chain. In D. R. Laws (Ed.), *Relapse prevention with sex offenders* (pp. 167-177). New York: Guilford.

Nelson, C., Miner, M., Marques, J., Russell, K., & Achterkirchen, J. (1988). Relapse prevention: A cognitive-behavioral model for treatment of the rapist and child molester. *Journal of Social Work and Human Sexuality, 7,* 125-143.

Prochaska, J. O., & DiClemente, C. C. (1982). Transtheoretical therapy: Toward a more integrative model of change. *Psychotherapy: Theory, Research, and Practice, 19,* 276-288.

Prochaska, J. O., DiClemente, C. C., & Norcross, J. C. (1992). In search of how people change: Applications to addictive behavior. *American Psychologist, 47,* 1102-1114.

Rosenstock, I. M., Strecher, V. J., & Becker, M. H. (1988). Social learning theory and the health belief model. *Health Education Quarterly, 15,* 175-183.

Russell, K., Marques, J. K., Murphy, J., & Potash, L. (1994, November). *The road to relapse: Factors that erode commitment to abstinence.* Poster session presented at the annual meeting of the Association for the Treatment of Sexual Abusers, San Francisco.

Steenman, H., Nelson, C., & Viesti, C. (1989). Developing coping strategies for high-risk situations. In D. R. Laws (Ed.), *Relapse prevention with sex offenders* (pp. 178-187). New York: Guilford.

Ward, T., & Hudson, S. M. (1998). A model of the relapse process in sexual offenders. *Journal of Interpersonal Violence, 13,* 700-725.

Ward, T., Hudson, S. M., & Marshall, W. L. (1994). The abstinence violation effect in child molesters. *Behaviour Research and Therapy, 32,* 431-437.

Ward, T., Hudson, S. M., & Siegert, R. J. (1995). A critical comment on Pithers' relapse prevention model. *Sexual Abuse: A Journal of Research and Treatment, 7,* 167-175.

CHAPTER 19

An Evidence-Based Relapse Prevention Program

RUTH E. MANN
DAVID THORNTON
H. M. Prison Service, London

H. M. Prison Service (England and Wales) introduced a comprehensive sex offender treatment strategy in 1991. The aim of the strategy was to provide a multisite, consistently delivered, manual-based treatment program for sexual offenders. In particular, the strategy emphasized that the program would be committed to periodic revision, based on empirical evidence and other worldwide developments in treatment theory and practice.

Since 1991, there have been several significant developments to the Sex Offender Treatment Program (SOTP). The structure of the SOTP and some of the lessons learned from it are described in Mann and Thornton (1998). Basically, from an initial single-program provision, intended to meet the needs of all sex offenders, the SOTP has grown into a family of five interlinked treatment programs, which ensure that high-risk, high-need offenders receive a high-intensity program, and lower-risk, lower-need offenders receive shorter, more needs-focused programs.

The content of each individual treatment program is subject to constant monitoring against research findings and clinical developments elsewhere in the world. In this chapter, we describe the way in which our Core Program (the entry point into treatment for all sex offenders) has been revised to take account of such developments. In particular, we focus on the revisions to the relapse prevention component of the Core Program. The relapse prevention component is preceded by components addressing denial, minimization and rationalization, and victim empathy. The entire program was revised 3 years after its introduction and is currently undergoing a second revision.

These revisions have been based on two types of evidence. First, we have remained committed to reviewing our practice against published research findings or theoretical developments. Second, we have established within our program a practice of collating clinical experience across the 25 treatment sites. We call such information "replicated clinical experience." Replicated clinical experience is discovered through annual surveys of all program therapists, analysis of treatment reports, videomonitoring of all programs, and regular meetings of the treatment managers from each site.

Version 1 of the Core Program

In this program, written in 1991, the relapse prevention component was minimal. The content of the program mainly reflected then current habits of practice in the United Kingdom.

The relapse prevention component of the program was based on the notion of the offense cycle (Wolf, 1988). Group members were required to present their sexual offending in terms of 13 stages: motivation, fantasy, internal inhibitions, trigger, excuse to contemplate offending, fantasy rehearsal, targeting, grooming, offending, fantasy reinforced by immediate gratification, guilt, push guilt away, and return to preoffense phase. This cycle was assumed to be relevant to all types of offenders from child sexual molesters to rapists.

Following presentation of offense cycles, group members participated in a discussion about "cure versus control" and looked at a sample case of a child molester who reoffended after release from a treatment program. Group members discussed this case in terms of steps that the child molester should have taken to move away from risk. Finally, a group brainstorm was conducted on the topic "What I need to do to control my offending." An emphasis was placed on "things to avoid" and working with their probation officers.

The First Revision

This version of the Core Program ran for about 2 years until it became apparent from our reading of the literature that the relapse prevention component was inadequate. In particular, we were aware of evidence from two main sources: the SOTEP program in California and the British STEP Research Team evaluation of community sex offender treatment programs. The need for a revision was also supported by members of a recently appointed advisory panel, which was convened to bring the SOTP up to the best standards of practice worldwide. The panel was an international group of recognized experts in treatment provision or sex offender research who met twice yearly to examine quality of delivery and program design. The first revision of the Core Program took place in 1994.

Evidential Basis for the First Revision

The SOTEP program (see Marques, Nelson, Alarcon, & Day, 2000 [this volume]) reported in 1994 that the success with which two written assignments (the cognitive-behavioral chain and the decision matrix) were completed was related to recidivism (Marques, Nelson, West, & Day, 1994). These two assignments were seen as epitomizing the extent to which program participants understood the RP model. Although our first-version Core Program contained a simple decision matrix exercise, it used the concept of offense cycle rather than cognitive-behavioral chain as a basis for relapse prevention.

Also in 1994, the British-based STEP Research Team published its report on the effectiveness of community-based treatment for sex offenders (Beckett, Beech, Fisher, & Fordham, 1994). One of the key findings of this report was that insufficient time was devoted in therapy to helping offenders "acknowledge the possibility of future risk, recognize potential risk situations and acquire the behavioural skills to avoid, escape or cope with risky situations" (p. 81). The report recommended that treatment programs should extend their duration to devote more time to relapse prevention training, and if this was not possible, treatment goals should be reprioritized so that a greater proportion of treatment time was devoted to relapse prevention.

Clinical Basis for the First Revision

The most often reported clinical problem with the first version of the Core Program related to the offense cycle methodology. Clinicians reported that offenses did not commonly follow the 13 steps outlined. If they did, the steps often happened in a different order, which resulted in therapists having to amend their presentation of the model. Furthermore, the offense cycle did not seem to make sense of more impulsive offenses in which conscious targeting and grooming had not occurred or in which the offense had not been rehearsed in fantasy.

Clinicians also reported dissatisfaction with the shortness of the relapse prevention sessions and felt that work achieved in these sessions was too general and did not allow for sufficiently individualized application.

Second Version of the Core Program

This version of the Core Program was introduced in late 1994 and accompanied by a program of training for all therapists to ensure that they fully understood the changes to the program and the evidential and clinical bases for the changes. This version of the program also incorporated significantly more intensive work focusing on the development of victim empathy.

The relapse prevention component of the program increased in length from a handful of sessions to about 40 two-hour sessions. The offense cycle method was removed from the program. The program was then expanded to include the construction of cognitive-behavioral chains (Nelson & Jackson, 1989). In our program, we referred to this exercise as "the decision chain" to highlight the extent of personal choice involved in offending and in avoiding reoffending. Group members were taught the concept of the cognitive-behavioral chain, learning to understand the link between situations, interpretations, feelings, and behaviors. Each group member produced a first draft of his chain, which was then worked on in the group. Once all chains had been enhanced to a reasonable standard, taking into account the recommendations of Nelson and Jackson (1989), each group member then identified, for each step in the chain, alternative thoughts and behaviors that he could have used to reverse rather than increase the momentum toward offending. This exercise is therefore a retrospective "what I could have done differently" type of analysis.

Following the construction of the chains, the group was introduced to the concept of risk factors, and each group member examined his chain to identify risk factors both early and late in the pathway toward offending. Risk factors were grouped under four headings: situations, thoughts, behaviors, and feelings. Group members were encouraged to identify at least 4 risk factors in each group, leading to a total list of about 16 risk factors. Each group member also described the recognition cues for each risk factor in terms of how he would feel, look, think, and behave when the risk factor was present.

Third, group members worked on developing coping strategies for each risk factor. This was done as a theoretical exercise and completed on paper. Group members were asked to think of ways to avoid, ways to control, and ways to escape from each risk factor. After a piloting of this procedure, one group came up with the acronym ACE to refer to this system of identifying coping strategies.

Fourth, following the ACE sessions, group members participated in a discussion about the abstinence violation effect (AVE) (Russell, Sturgeon, Miner, & Nelson, 1989) and some mini-role-plays intended to help them practice talking themselves out of the AVE as a preparation for any eventual occurrence. Group members also kept a risk diary for 2 or 3 weeks, in which they were asked to record any times when they experienced risk factors, the coping strategies that they tried to use, and how well their strategies worked.

The Second Revision

The second revision of the Core Program is currently under way. In this revision, the relapse prevention component of the program is receiving special attention. Although the program is not being lengthened, the content of the relapse prevention component is significantly different in many ways from its predecessor.

Evidential Basis for the Second Revision

The evidential basis for revision can be subdivided into four areas: (a) theoretical challenges to the relapse prevention model, (b) internal clinical impact research, (c) recent SOTEP findings, and (d) uncertainty regarding the necessity of traditional relapse prevention as a treatment component for sex offenders.

Theoretical Challenges to the Relapse Prevention Model. These are described in detail elsewhere in this volume. In essence, theoretical challenges to the model have undermined the traditional relapse prevention (RP) assumption that all offenders attempt to avoid reoffending. Instead, there is now a recognition that many offenders are still motivated to offend and actively make decisions that take them nearer offending, rather than relapse being the result of a series of weak, unconscious, or poorly planned decisions. The nature of the abstinence violation effect has also been challenged, and it is now thought that lapses toward offending are associated with positive appetitive urges rather than negative experiences of guilt and failure (Ward, Hudson, & Marshall, 1994).

Internal Clinical Impact Research. Three internal studies in particular indicated that certain aspects of our relapse prevention component were flawed. First, we found that approximately one in five program participants still believed themselves to be at absolutely no risk of reoffending on completion of treatment (Mann, 1996). It is assumed that such clients are therefore unlikely to engage in self-monitoring because they would see no reason to do so. Second, we found that the types of (supposedly individualized) risk factors identified by program participants were actually related more to the prison in which they received treatment than to their own offending pattern (Thornton, 1998). In other words, some different treatment sites seemed to have developed their own theories about risk factors for sexual offending, which were then expressed through their clients' RP plans. A third relevant internal project identified that about 50% of SOTP clients demonstrated some kind of resistance to relapse prevention (Mann, 2000 [this volume]).

Recent SOTEP Findings. Marques et al. (2000) report the latest wave of findings from the SOTEP project. They highlight the importance of strengthening commitment to abstinence, focusing more on affective factors, emphasizing the practice of coping skills, and conducting treatment in a motivational manner. The last of their findings is supported by social psychological principles about motivation and goal setting (Mann, 2000).

Uncertain Necessity of Relapse Prevention as a Treatment Component for Sex Offenders. For instance, Marshall and Anderson (1996) suggested that there was no compelling evidence for the benefits of detailed internal management training, nor was there a remarkable treatment effect in those programs with elaborate external supervisory relapse prevention components. They concluded that "the present review indicates that the costs of engaging in detailed training in RP concepts and providing extensive aftercare for all sexual offenders are not presently justified" (p. 219).

Clinical Basis for the Second Revision

Information from a number of sources has indicated strongly to us that there are several clinical problems with the delivery of the current RP component of our program.

Survey Information. A survey of all SOTP therapists (Mann, 1995) indicated that the relapse prevention sessions were repetitive and tedious for both group members and therapists. The same survey also indicated that therapists had a poor understanding of the concept of the abstinence violation effect.

Analysis of Program "Products" (the Work Produced by Program Participants). In particular, it was apparent that decision chains were poorly completed and comprised mainly planning thoughts rather than clearly revealing, more complicated cognitive patterns preceding sexual offenses. This problem was highlighted further by one particular treatment site producing quite exceptional decision chains, thereby showing up the very limited usefulness of the rest (see Table 19.1 for a comparison of good and bad examples of decision chains).

Analysis of treatment products also indicated that risk factor lists were too long for their content to be retained by the offenders and were usually poorly differentiated from one another. For instance, an offender would include anger as a high-risk feeling and, in describing that risk factor, would write down the thoughts associated with his feeling angry. These same thoughts would also be recorded in their own right as high-risk thoughts. As a result, risk factor lists were repetitive and unnecessarily complicated.

TABLE 19.1   Examples of Decision Chain Links

Comprehensive Chain	Poor Chain
Situation: Staying with John and his wife, Anne. John has asked me to find somewhere else to live.	*Situation*: Jane brings me a cup of tea.
Thoughts: I don't want to leave. I'd love to have sex with Anne. F***ing hell, why does he keep on to me about leaving? I've done him favors before. I wish I was in his place. It's not fair. I'm not doing any harm. I don't really want to work because I like being near Anne. I'll have to get by on my welfare. Sometimes I think she fancies me. I've done some things for her; I should get something back in return. I feel worthless, inadequate. Why the f*** can't I do these things (car, house, job, etc.)? It's not my fault, I need a good f***. I'd like to do it to Anne but she would say no and probably tell John.	*Thoughts*: I like her; she likes me.
Behavior: Fantasize about raping Anne. Pretend to look for work, apartment. Stay around house to be near Anne. Watch her intently.	*Behavior*: Continue to dig garden. Get an erection.

Finally, analysis of treatment products revealed universally poorly kept risk diaries. The purpose of this exercise had not been adhered to. Program participants were using the exercise to attempt to demonstrate to their therapists that they had benefited from treatment. They therefore only contained entries relating to events that had been successfully coped with. Furthermore, nearly all diary entries referred to supposed risk factors that actually were not the kinds of events that increase the risk of sexual offending (see Table 19.2 for an example of this type of entry). In this case, the risk factor described in the diary was not even one of the 16 risk factors identified in the program.

Videomonitoring Evidence. This provided further examples of the difficulties therapists were having with the relapse prevention component of the Core Program. Therapists who usually adopted a Socratic approach to treatment were observed suggesting strategies to their group members for coping with risk and, in particular, trying to persuade group members to give up certain activities (e.g., coaching football) or avoid certain places (e.g., candy shops, swimming pools). Decision chains, first drafted as a homework exercise, were observed being redrafted almost entirely in group sessions, so that program clients appeared deskilled and self-conscious about their work.

TABLE 19.2   Example of Poor Risk Diary Entry

Day	Risk Factor You Experienced	How It Came About	How You Tried to Cope	How Well Your Strategy Worked
Monday	Frustration	Given a vegetarian meal when I am a vegan	Listened to classical music and did breathing exercises. Self-talk: Some things aren't worth rocking the boat for.	Effective in the short term

Third Version of the Core Program

In the third version of the Core Program, decision chains have been moved to an earlier stage in the program and are no longer first drafted as a homework exercise. Instead, group members either talk through or walk through their offense disclosure, and therapists translate the information into a decision chain format at the same time. This allows for greater probing of thought processes underlying each interpretation, as shown in the good example in Table 19.1.

Sessions identifying risk factors, recognition cues, and coping strategies all as theoretical exercises have all been dropped. Instead, we have adopted the "Old Me, New Me" methodology first developed for learning disabled clients (Haaven, Little, & Petre-Miller, 1990). As described in another chapter (Mann, 2000), clients identify important attributes of their offending selves and set approach goals for nonoffending futures. A racecourse analogy is used to represent the idea of clearing hurdles (achieving subgoals) and managing setbacks. A significant proportion of sessions is devoted to practicing New Me skills through role-play. During role-plays, another group member is assigned to play the voice of Old Me and encourages the offender to return to old ways by stating his positive appetitive feelings about offending. Offenders therefore have to practice engaging cognitive and behavioral strategies at the same time. The risk diary is replaced by a New Me diary, in which group members record their achievement of subgoals set in group sessions. An example of a typical New Me diary entry is shown in Table 19.3. This diary format not only promotes positive behaviors and achievements of goals, but it also encourages articulation of positive emotional consequences of achieving subgoals.

Finally, a relapse prevention board game, "The Lifestyle Challenge" (Mann, Wheatley, & Hirons, 1999), is played. In this game, participants have to progress around a Monopoly-style board, encountering various high-risk situations, thoughts, and feelings as they go. Their strategies are examined by the group, and self-praise cards are awarded for the enactment of positive, realistic, workable strategies.

TABLE 19.3   New Me Diary Entry

Day	New Me Goal	Subgoal	What I Did Today	How I Felt
Monday	Good adult relationships	Saying thank-you	1. Wrote to my visitors thanking them for visiting me. 2. Thanked another group member for keeping me a seat in the TV room.	1. Satisfied 2. Appreciated, bonded, appreciative
		Giving support	1. Saw that the man in the next cell looked miserable. Said to him that I was happy to listen if he wanted to talk about anything.	1. Nervous but pleased when I did it and he thanked me.

Although the full revised program has not yet been implemented, several sites have piloted the new relapse prevention component with apparent success. Although the impact of the new sessions has yet to be formally evaluated, both therapists and clients report a greater sense of engagement in the new treatment sessions, and this is supported by videomonitoring observations.

Conclusion

In this chapter, we have attempted to outline the way in which a large multisite treatment program can adapt to changes in theoretical understanding, new empirical studies, and new treatment methodologies. A commitment to evidence-based treatment is, in our minds, a duty of all sex offender treatment providers. As much as we would like to treat sex offenders according to our whims, our preferences, or our personal theories, we do not serve society responsibly in so doing. As behavioral scientists, our treatment programs must advance on the basis of evidence.

References

Beckett, R., Beech, A., Fisher, D., & Fordham, A. S. (1994). *Community-based treatment for sex offenders: An evaluation of seven treatment programmes.* London: Home Office. (Available from the Home Office Publications Unit, 50 Queen Anne's Gate, London, England, SW1H 9AT)

Haaven, J., Little, R., & Petre-Miller, D. (1990). *Treating intellectually disabled sex offenders: A model residential program.* Orwell, VT: Safer Society.

Mann, R. E. (1995). *What's difficult about working with sex offenders?* Paper presented to the annual conference of the British Society for Criminology, Loughborough, England.

Mann, R. E. (1996, November). *Measuring the effectiveness of relapse prevention intervention with sex offenders.* Paper presented at the Association for the Treatment of Sexual Abusers' 15th Annual Research & Treatment Conference, Chicago.

Mann, R. E. (2000). Managing resistance and rebellion in relapse prevention intervention. In R. D. Laws, S. M. Hudson, & T. Ward (Eds.), *Remaking relapse prevention with sex offenders: A sourcebook* (pp. 187-200). Thousand Oaks, CA: Sage.

Mann, R. E., & Thornton, D. (1998). *The evolution of a multisite sexual offender treatment program.* In W. L. Marshall, Y. M. Fernandez, S. M. Hudson, & T. Ward (Eds.), *Sourcebook of treatment programs for sexual offenders* (pp. 47-58). New York: Plenum.

Mann, R. E., Wheatley, M. P., & Hirons, D. (1999). *The lifestyle challenge: A relapse prevention boardgame for sexual offenders.* London: H. M. Prison Service.

Marques, J. K., Nelson, C., Alarcon, J. -M., & Day, D. M. (2000). Preventing relapse in sex offenders: What we learned from SOTEP's experimental treatment program. In R. D. Laws, S. M. Hudson, & T. Ward (Eds.), *Remaking relapse prevention with sex offenders: A sourcebook* (pp. 321-340). Thousand Oaks, CA: Sage.

Marques, J. K., Nelson, C., West, M. A., & Day, D. M. (1994). The relationship between treatment goals and recidivism among child molesters. *Behaviour Research & Therapy, 32*(5), 577-588.

Marshall, W. L., & Anderson, D. (1996). An evaluation of the benefits of relapse prevention programs with sexual offenders. *Sexual Abuse, 8*(3), 209-221.

Nelson, C., & Jackson, P. (1989). High-risk recognition: The cognitive-behavioral chain. In D. R. Laws (Ed.), *Relapse prevention with sex offenders* (pp. 167-177). New York: Guilford.

Russell, K., Sturgeon, V. H., Miner, M. H., & Nelson, C. (1989). Determinants of the abstinence violation effect in sexual fantasies. In D. R. Laws (Ed.), *Relapse prevention with sex offenders* (pp. 63-72). New York: Guilford.

Thornton, D. (1998, October). *Relapse prevention as an assessment technique.* Paper presented at the Association for the Treatment of Sexual Abusers' 17th Annual Research & Treatment Conference, Vancouver, British Columbia.

Ward, T., Hudson, S. M., & Marshall, W. L. (1994). The abstinence violation effect in child molesters. *Behaviour Research and Therapy, 32,* 431-437.

Wolf, S. (1988). A model of sexual aggression/addiction. *Journal of Social Work and Human Sexuality, 7,* 1.

PART VII

RELAPSE PREVENTION APPLIED TO SPECIAL POPULATIONS

CHAPTER 20

Relapse Prevention With Adolescent Sex Offenders

WILLIAM D. MURPHY
I. JACQUELINE PAGE
University of Tennessee, Memphis

Current data would suggest that 30% to 50% of child molestations and up to 20% of rapes are committed by adolescents (Barbaree, Hudson, & Seto, 1993; Vizard, Monck, & Misch, 1995; Weinrott, 1996). Abel, Osborn, and Twigg (1993) report that more than 40% of their sample of adult offenders report the onset of paraphilias before age 18. The recognition of the seriousness of the problem of adolescent offenders led from a situation in which the legal system and the mental health system tended to minimize the problem (Atcheson & Williams, 1954) to an explosion of treatment programs (Freeman-Longo, Bird, Stevenson, & Fiske, 1995) and an explosion of assumptions regarding this population (National Council on Juvenile and Family Court Judges, 1993). Weinrott (1996), in a somewhat critical comment, noted that the National Task Force on Juvenile Sex Offending (National Council on Juvenile and Family Court Judges, 1993) had more assumptions (387) than studies in the literature.

Regardless of data and empirical support, groups such as the National Task Force on Juvenile Sex Offending did raise the awareness of the problem of juvenile sex offending and the need to address the problem. The awareness of the problem, as noted, also led to an explosion of "offender-specific" treatment programs. Because little data guide the development of truly "adolescent sex offender-specific" programs, there was a tendency to apply those theories and techniques developed by adult offenders to the juvenile population. This included using behavioral approaches to reduce deviant arousal (Hunter & Goodwin, 1992; Weinrott, Riggan, & Frothingham, 1997), modifying cognitive distortions (Becker & Kaplan, 1993), and using the relapse prevention (RP) model (Gray & Pithers, 1993) as an overriding guide to treatment.

The purpose of this chapter is twofold but is primarily to present clinical approaches to adapting the RP concepts to adolescents. However, in a manner that may seem contradictory, we will first review some characteristics of the RP model and of adolescent offenders. This review should serve to temper the view of the RP model as the "truth" of the offense process. Rather, it is the current pragmatic guide to the recognition of the precursors to offending behavior.

Relapse Prevention and the Offending Process With Adolescent Offenders

Within the adolescent sex offender field, two models are used to identify patterns and precursors to sexual offenses. Although these models are different, they are typically discussed as part of relapse prevention treatment in the adolescent offender area, and therefore both are described. The two models are the relapse prevention model (Gray & Pithers, 1993) and the concept of the sexual abuse cycle (Ryan, Lane, Davis, & Isaac, 1987), more recently updated by Lane (1997). The sexual abuse cycle in its latest presentation (Lane, 1997) basically describes three phases. Initially, there is a precipitating phase in which the offense cycle is triggered by an event that leads to feelings of powerlessness and low self-esteem, which in turn leads the offender to take a "poor me" stance, assuming or expecting the worse, feeling helplessness, and beginning to withdraw and isolate. This is followed by a compensatory phase in which the offender begins blaming others for his problems and engages in behaviors in an attempt to gain power and control. He then begins having retaliation fantasies that are sexual in nature and starts mentally rehearsing sexual offenses that in turn lead to setting up the offense, which leads to the sexual abuse. Finally, there is an integration phase in which the offender first affirms his adequacy but then begins to develop fears of being caught and other negative consequences. These fears are then dealt with by cognitive distortions about not getting caught, followed by ambivalent feelings of increased self-doubt and self-criticism. These are dealt with by what is termed *suppression distortions* ("I don't have a problem" or "I'll never do it again").

The major presentation of the application of relapse prevention to adolescents is by Gray and Pithers (1993). In this presentation, there is a mixture of the original RP model and the cycle model. For example, the original description of the relapse prevention model (Pithers, Marques, Gibat, & Marlatt, 1983) suggested that relapse follows from seemingly unimportant decisions through high-risk situations (which are primarily negative emotional states or interpersonal conflict) to a lapse, which is followed by the abstinence violation effect together with the problem of immediate gratification, leading to relapse. Gray and Pithers (1993) expand the overall concept of risk factors in the RP model by describing three classes of risk factors. These include predisposing risk factors (e.g., sexual or physical abuse, family chaos, absence of empathy skills and social skills, low self-esteem), precipitating risk factors (emotional misman-agement, thinking errors, opportunity, low control of impulse and urges, absence of conflict resolution skills, fantasies about sexual abuse), and perpetu-ating risk factors (lack of supervision, gratification from emotional and sexual release, lack of information about positive sexuality, displacement of responsi-bility, gender shame).

Although different in many ways, both models share certain characteristics. First, they both suggest that negative affect primarily triggers sex offending, that there is a single pattern of relapse, that skills deficits are extremely impor-tant, and that cognitive distortions play a major role in the offense process.

These models have had a very significant impact on the field. Ryan et al. (1987) were one of the first to attempt to organize clinical observations of the adolescent offender population and to provide a treatment framework. Simi-larly, Gray and Pithers's (1993) work not only has provided a model of relapse but also has expanded this to provide an integrated approach to treatment. Both had significant heuristic value in helping to guide treatment programs. How-ever, at this time, some adjustment to these models may be necessary, and fur-ther research is needed to support them.

Critique

One of the first problems with both models is the lack of empirical support for some of the proposed variables. In both the description of the sexual abuse cycle and Gray and Pithers's (1993) description of precipitating risk factors, there is a blending of etiology with the relapse process. Specifically, the sexual abuse cycle model focuses on issues such as self-esteem and feelings of power-lessness, whereas the relapse prevention model, as presented by Gray and Pithers, focuses on a number of predisposing and perpetuating risk factors that have no clear support in the literature. There is very mixed evidence (Murphy, Haynes, & Page, 1992; Weinrott, 1996) as to whether adolescent offenders dif-fer on a number of these variables from other types of offenders. In addition, both models posit the importance of cognitive distortions, although there is lit-tle to no evidence regarding cognitive factors in juvenile offenders (Hunter, Becker, Kaplan, & Goodwin, 1991; Weinrott, 1996).

Ward, Hudson, and associates (Ward & Hudson, 1996; Ward & Hudson, 1998; Ward, Hudson, & Siegert, 1995; Ward, Louden, Hudson, & Marshall, 1995) have extensively critiqued the relapse prevention model, and much of this critique is already reviewed in this volume. However, some specific issues seem relevant to adolescent offenders. These include the following: (a) There is a single model or process of relapse, (b) relapse is always triggered by negative events or affect, (c) all offenders are attempting to avoid offending, and (d) the original relapse model is based largely on skills deficits.

Our current knowledge of adolescent offenders makes it clear that they are a very heterogeneous group. Both clinical descriptions (O'Brien & Bera, 1986) and empirical evidence (Knight & Prentky, 1993) suggest a variety of types of juvenile sex offenders. Also, a variety of reviews (Murphy et al., 1992; Vizard et al., 1995; Weinrott, 1996) suggests a great deal of heterogeneity in this population. Given this heterogeneity, it is highly unlikely that there is one relapse process. As Weinrott (1996) has pointed out, the notion of the sexual abuse cycle would only fit a few of the typologies described by O'Brien and Bera (1986) and similarly does not fit many of the typologies described by Knight and Prentky (1993). In addition, this literature makes it clear that not all adolescent offenders suffer from coping skills deficits; Knight and Prentky's typology suggests that some offenders are quite competent socially, which is consistent with clinical observation.

In addition to the heterogeneity issues, there are also questions as to whether adolescent sex offenders are a specialized group or part of a larger group of conduct-disordered youths (Milloy, 1998; Ryan, 1998). The rates of recidivism for general delinquency is much higher than rates for sex offending (Lieb, 1997; Weinrott, 1996), and many adolescent offenders have previous arrests for nonsexual behavior (Weinrott, 1996). Although probably true for adults also, the issue of lifestyle impulsivity and generalized delinquency is extremely important to adolescents and is not clearly addressed in either the relapse prevention model or the sexual abuse cycle model. Although there is no clear answer, it is likely that data will show that there is a subgroup of adolescents identified for sex-offending behavior that is primarily paraphilic, a group that is primarily conduct disordered, and a group that is mixed. The model of relapse proposed by Ward and Hudson (1998) more clearly describes an impulsive path that seems clinically consistent with some subset of adolescent offenders. Neither the abuse cycle nor the relapse prevention model clearly addresses these issues.

It is also not clear that adolescent offenders' behavior is always triggered by some negative emotional state, such as loss of self-esteem or interpersonal rejection. As Ward and Hudson (1998) have suggested, some offenders are guided by approach goals; that is, they want to offend and are not attempting to avoid. Although similar data are not available at this time for adolescents, clinical experience would suggest that some adolescents have set attraction patterns to children; their sexual offending behavior is not based on negative emotional states but primarily on their sexual attraction.

Another issue, related less to the relapse prevention model or sexual abuse cycle model but more to their application, is the rate of learning or high base rate of scholastic problems in this population. Although there are no clear data, Weinrott (1996), in reviewing Graves's (1993) meta-analysis, suggested that among undifferentiated adolescent sex offenders, 59% had been retained in a grade, 41% were diagnosed as learning disabled, and 53% qualified for special education or other forms of remediation. In programming or addressing relapse prevention with adolescents, it is very important to recognize the fact that a number of the offenders will have significant learning problems.

There are therefore a number of concerns regarding relapse prevention in adolescent offenders. The major issue we feel that has not been addressed is the heterogeneity of this population and the consequent assumption of a single pathway to offending or relapsing. The next section of this chapter presents clinical approaches to teach relapse prevention to adolescent sex offenders. The clinical exercises described are geared to presenting material in a way that is both understandable to adolescents and that will help engage the adolescents in the treatment process. In addition, we attempt not to make assumptions about the relapse process. It has been our clinical experience that if adolescents are exposed to standard sexual abuse cycles or standard relapse prevention chains, they tend to produce patterns that are not very individualized. Finally, in doing relapse prevention with adolescents, we feel it is important not only to focus on risk to sexually reoffend but also on broader delinquent behavior and lifestyle impulsivity as risk factors in and of themselves.

Clinical Approaches

Teaching the Language

To develop relapse prevention plans, adolescents need a foundation, and a cornerstone of the foundation is the language used in sex offender-specific treatment. Therefore, we begin treatment by identifying basic terms and concepts that will be used throughout the treatment program. Although many terms and concepts are used in sex offender-specific treatment, choosing a few basic words provides a basic foundation, keeps the adolescent from being overwhelmed by a long list, and provides an opportunity for early success.

Five basic terms—*risk factor, minimization, cognitive distortion, relapse prevention plan,* and *seemingly unimportant decision*—are generally sufficient to get the adolescent started. To assist the adolescent in learning these terms, we have found that the development of flashcards with the word on one side and the definition on the reverse can be very helpful. In general, we use a flashcard that is half the size of a regular sheet of paper, that is on different-colored paper for visual appeal, and that is laminated. The definition used can be adjusted based on the cognitive level of the adolescents in the program. For example, the definition of a risk factor might be "any person, place, situation, thought, feeling, or thing that increases your risk to reoffend." However, a simpler definition might be "things that increase your risk to reoffend." We have also found it very helpful for those offenders with possible intellectual or learning difficulties to use substitute language that is nontechnical. For example, distortions and minimizations may be replaced by the term *SOB* (sex offender bull), or relapse prevention plan can be replaced by *plan of action,* which has a more natural meaning to the adolescent.

The use of flashcards by the adolescent, with his parents or with other group members, allows sharing of the learning experience. They also serve as a good tool for encouraging the parents to be involved and to understand the way the words apply in sex-offender-specific treatment. After the adolescents have learned the basic definitions, Step 2 is for them, in at least a very basic fashion, to give an example of how each of the words applies to them. At this point, the adolescent may identify a risk factor, such as being around small children, or some distortions that he may have used.

Other educational approaches also can be usefully employed. Such things as crossword puzzles, word searches, and matching games can be developed using the language from sex offender treatment. Again, these methods introduce the adolescents to the concepts of relapse prevention and provide them with some early successful learning experiences. These approaches are quite adaptable depending on learning styles, intellectual levels, or learning disabilities of the adolescents in a program. The therapist can adjust the complexity of the definition and use substitute terminology to engage the adolescent in these activities.

Maps

Relapse prevention primarily involves recognizing the precursors to offending, but it also involves the concept of choice. Once the adolescent has some basic understanding of terminology, we move to the idea that offending involves choices—more specifically, that certain risk factors and choices increase the chance of relapsing.

To introduce this concept, the idea of two roads in life is introduced along with the concept that the adolescent has a choice in which road he takes. Maps involve examining the offending and nonoffending road. The active component of this project easily engages the adolescents and allows for them to learn while they are working on the project. Adolescents often believe that on the nonoffending road, they simply do not encounter any risk rather than recognize that risk does exist, and their decision of how to handle it determines which road they are on. During this project, clients actually draw out maps for the offending and nonoffending roads. In general, these are drawn starting with a road that branches into two roads, the offending road and the nonoffending road. Risk situations and factors need to be included on both roads, with the client providing healthy ways to deal with these on the nonoffending road. This forces the clients to begin thinking of choices and recognize that they are responsible for the choice they make as well as beginning to look at how to handle different risky situations.

Oversight of the project is provided by the therapist; however, the client needs to be challenged to be creative. For example, drawing "poor me potholes," "distortion ditches," "pornography ponds," and playgrounds all help to visually recognize the concepts of risk factors. The adolescent is also encouraged to represent coping strategies on the nonoffending road. Initially, these may be simple strategies such as avoidance or escape, which may be represented by detours around or tunnels under risk factors. We also encourage the adolescent to draw roads connecting the offending and nonoffending roads. This represents how one can return to the nonoffending road even if he has made unhealthy decisions on the offending road. As treatment progresses and the adolescent learns other coping strategies, the maps can be reviewed and added to. Similarly, they can be used to add more individualized risk factors as treatment progresses. The ends of the roads are represented by consequences, jail, victim impact, family pain, or the positives associated with an abuse-free lifestyle.

The therapist may need to prompt the adolescent to include situations and other risk factors that are more linked to lifestyle choices than to specific sex offender issues. Examples may include gang affiliation, poor school attendance, and so on. This helps reinforce the notion that he makes choices in all aspects of his life, not just in regard to sex offending. Including lifestyle and life stressors also serves as a building block to recognizing that a decision in one aspect of our lives affects other aspects. It also raises the issue that the goal of treatment is not just reduction of sex offending but reduction in all forms of abusive behavior.

Basic Relapse Prevention Plan

After the adolescent has developed some skills in basic terminology, such as risk factors and relapse prevention plan, we then move to what we call our basic relapse prevention plan. We have found that in working with adolescents, it is important not to become overly complicated and that, in general, certain types of high-risk situations and fantasies or thoughts are commonly associated with offending. Situations such as being alone with children, being in places that attract children, and sexual fantasies of children are generally seen as risk factors or high-risk situations for most offenders against children. At this basic level, the adolescent can begin to accept that being alone with a child does increase his risk, as does thinking about offending. Also consistent with the notion that not all offenses are related to negative emotional states, we try not to tie the presence of deviant sexual fantasies or the placement of oneself in high-

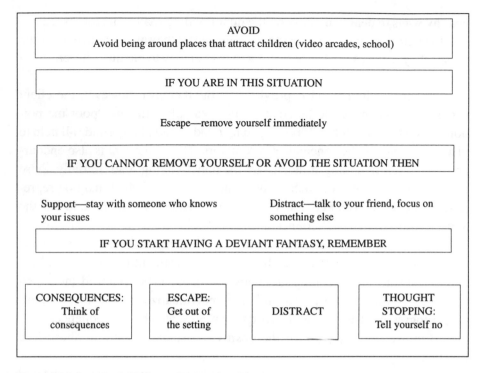

Figure 20.1.   Basic Relapse Prevention Plan

risk situation to any specific emotional state. We, at this point, focus on rule-bound learning and, at least for child molesters, define being with younger children and engaging in deviant sexual fantasies as risk factors that must be coped with.

To present this concept, what we term our *basic relapse prevention plan,* along with simple coping strategies, is included in Figure 20.1. The figure focuses primarily on those individuals who sexually molest children, but it can be adapted for other types of victims. We also, out of our experience, combine high-risk situations with children and deviant fantasies because many of these coping strategies are similar for these two types of risk factors.

As can be seen in Figure 20.1, a flowchart is presented, beginning with attempting to avoid high-risk situations with children, followed by escape if he finds himself in such a situation and the use of specific strategies if he cannot remove or avoid these. The two basic strategies we teach are external support and the use of distraction. Also in the flowchart, specific strategies are outlined for dealing with deviant sexual fantasies. These include thinking of consequences, escaping if he is having a fantasy in a situation with children, using distraction techniques, and using thought stopping.

Once the basic flowchart is presented, the adolescent individualizes this chart for himself. For example, under the "Avoid" box, he would specifically situations in his neighborhood, community, or family situations that he would need to avoid. Under the "Support" section, he would list his specific support people and could also list individuals that he felt need to be informed and educated about his offending issues. Also under "Distract," he would specifically list activities that would help distract him from focusing on small children. Similarly, under the deviant fantasy section of thinking of consequences, he would outline some specific consequences that he would imagine and would write these out in detail and rehearse them similar to covert sensitization. He is asked to create a visual image that would have an emotional impact. Similarly, he would list specific activities that could be used to distract him from deviant sexual fantasies.

A significant therapeutic aspect of this flowchart involves the processing of those situations that are to be avoided versus those situations the adolescent cannot avoid. In general, when they start, most adolescent offenders against children, at least on the surface, will accept that they cannot be alone with children. However, when he starts looking at specific situations that he may have to avoid, he can become more resistant. Although he may accept that he cannot be alone with his specific victim, he can become much more resistant when the group starts identifying the need to avoid places such as video arcades and skating rinks that tend to attract much younger children. At this point, the adolescent offender has to begin to accept that living a nonoffending lifestyle will require sacrifices on his part and a change in his lifestyle. This issue is not one that will necessarily be resolved easily and will continue throughout treatment. An important aspect of addressing this issue, however, is to maintain some hope in the adolescent and not allowing him to focus only on what he has to "give up" but also the many things that are still available to him in his life. It is very easy for the adolescent and sometimes his family to only focus on the negative (i.e., things he cannot do or should not do), losing sight that many of these things only represent a small part of his life.

Introduction to Immediate Precursors

Our next step in dealing with adolescent offenders is to introduce the notion of immediate precursors to offending. To do this, we have adopted as a model the four preconditions of sexual abuse as outlined by Finkelhor (1984). These involve four factors: motivation to sexually abuse, overcoming internal inhibitions, overcoming external inhibitions, and overcoming the victim's resistance.

A similar model is being used by the British prison system. We have adopted certain terminology used by them, in which (a) motivation becomes "what makes you want to do it," (b) internal inhibitions become "giving yourself permission," (c) overcoming external inhibitions is "getting access to the victim," and (d) overcoming resistance is "making the victim go along." This can be presented either on a worksheet or visually with walls drawn that the offender has to overcome to offend.

The purpose of this assignment, within the overall prevention framework, is to identify that abuse does not "just occur," but a sequence requires some planning, even though at times the sequence may occur quite rapidly and impulsively. In general, under motivation, we tend to get the offender to focus on sexual motivation rather than other potential motivators that are important for offending, such as power and control issues or low self-esteem. We believe that at this early point in treatment, some of these factors can quickly be used as excuses. Under giving yourself permission, we tend to focus on distortions and minimizations, and under getting access, the focus is on the overall grooming process such as the general way the offender sets up the situation, gets access to the victim, and manipulates the family. Finally, in overcoming the child's resistance, we continue the focus on the grooming process, but at this point we introduce the concept of force being more than the use of physical force (i.e., the use of such things as bribery) and the power inherent in age differences.

Again, at this point in treatment, our focus is on getting the offender and the family to recognize that the abuse may not have been as impulsive as it seemed and that there had to be at least some planning. It is our belief that this model sets up the next stage of treatment, which looks at more individualized risk factors and more detailed patterns leading up to the offense.

Individualized Risk Factors and Individualized Relapse Prevention Plans

The final step with the adolescent offender is identifying what we term *individualized risk factors*, both in terms of sex offending and general lifestyle (e.g., gang involvement). We find this aspect of treatment the most complicated and the most time-consuming. It is also at times problematic because many times the therapist's model of how sex offenses occur can very much influence what gets identified as risk factors or behavioral chains. It is also at times very difficult for some of the lower-functioning offenders to see the connection between certain life events (e.g., thought patterns or emotional states) and the final act of offending. Finally, when we are doing such activities in the group, we need to guard against offenders patterning their offense chains or individualized risk factors after other group members, that is, not copying. Given the heterogeneity in the offender population, we have not found any one approach that will work with all offenders. We have also learned to accept that some offenders may not have complicated, negatively emotional driven chains and, as Ward and Hudson (1998) pointed out, may be more driven by approach motivation than any type of desire to avoid. In such cases, we tend to focus on having very strong basic relapse plans and for the offender and the offender's support system to clearly understand the immediate precursors to the offending so that these can be closely monitored.

TABLE 20.1   Psychosexual Homework Sheet (completed daily)

Areas of content

- Things I liked

- Things I didn't like

- Sexual thoughts/fantasies that I had

- Did you masturbate to the thought/fantasy?

- How did you deal with the thought/fantasy?

- Risk factors that I had today

- How I dealt with the risk factors

- Other healthy ways I could have dealt with the risk factor

One of the first steps we take to identifying individualized risk factors is the use of a daily homework sheet that the adolescent begins when entering our program. Table 20.1 is an example of the type of homework sheet with the areas of content. Within each of these areas, space is provided for him to write in answers to each of the questions. Initially in treatment, the focus is on examining whether there is any connection between things the offender liked or did not like and types of sexual thoughts and fantasies he may have had. In a number of instances, the offender describes daily events during his day-to-day life, which have been associated with some type of deviant sexual fantasy. When the offender is being honest about his sexual thoughts and fantasies, such recordings can help guide both the adolescent and the therapist toward possible links between life events and potential precursors to the sexual offending. The other areas on the homework sheet become more relevant as the offender begins to identify specific risk factors that he can then monitor.

Another early step in developing individualized plans is helping the adolescent recognize the connection between certain situations, thoughts, feelings, and behaviors. Many times, we begin this process by analyzing nonoffending situations using a situation, thought, feeling, behavior worksheet. This worksheet has categories listed where the offender fills in specific situations and thoughts, feelings, and behaviors associated with the situations. Within a residential treatment program, there are ample opportunities to analyze the emotional reactions the adolescent has to daily events. For example, if there is an anger outburst or some aggressive behavior, he can be asked to look at what occurred prior to the behavior, what thoughts he had about the situation, and what feelings were elicited. Similarly, if he self-reports a deviant sexual fantasy, we can look at situations that proceeded that and thoughts and feelings about the situation. Using the situation, thought, feeling, behavior chain is a simplified way of beginning to build potential longer chains of behavior.

To begin to look at more extensive chains of behavior, we have adopted two basic approaches. One is a fairly simple technique used by many programs that has the offender verbally walk through his offense. We will ask him to begin the day of the offense and begin describing all the events he can remember occurring and the thoughts and feelings associated with the events. While this is happening, one member in the group is asked to write down the significant events the offender describes. This can then be expanded by getting him to describe what was happening a week or a month prior to the offense, depending on the therapist's perceptions of what type of time frame needs to be used. An offender with multiple offenses can be asked to do this for a number of the offenses, and the other group members and the therapist can begin to look for potential patterns. It is very important, in doing this assignment or any assignment for that matter, not to be judgmental and to encourage the offender to focus on things they perceive as negative, as well as all events that occurred. This helps avoid the therapist projecting his or her belief or implicit model of the offense chain onto the adolescent.

A second method that we have found quite helpful is what we call the cycle sequence strip. This basically requires the offender, rather than verbally walking through the offense, to draw out all the events that occurred in a set time period prior to the offense. We find it helpful to have the offenders do this in panels, almost like a comic strip, with each panel representing an event and at the top of the panel having him list the thoughts, feelings, and behaviors that are going on in the picture that he drew. It is stressed that drawing skills are not important, and those adolescents who may not have artistic skills are encouraged to simply draw stick figures. For some of our clients, this type of assignment is quite engaging, and they can be quite creative in drawing out events of their day. Again, this is repeated for different offenses, and again these are presented in the group with an attempt to analyze potential patterns.

Once some specific patterns emerge, some offenders will be asked to complete a typical behavioral chain. However, rather than using what we consider more complex chains, we tend to simplify this by using a series of stop signs (see Figure 20.2) that on the left-hand side are events, thoughts, and feelings, whereas the right-hand side includes coping strategies. Although the example shows a chain of three stop signs, additional pages can be added. It should be noted that for some of the lower-functioning clients or those with severe learning disabilities, these chains need simplification.

The final step is the development of a specific relapse prevention plan for the risk factors that have been identified up to this point. It is our strong feeling that most adolescent offenders (and probably adult offenders) are not going to remember complex chains, nor are they going to remember multiple risk factors, particularly when under stress. Therefore, we attempt to integrate all the previous work or simplify the number of risk factors for each client. We term

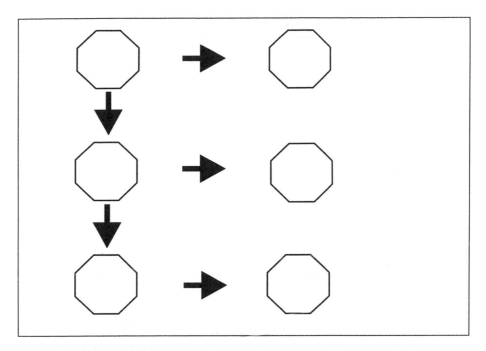

Figure 20.2.   Behavior Chains

factors, particularly when under stress. Therefore, we attempt to integrate all
the previous work or simplify the number of risk factors for each client. We term
this the *working relapse prevention plan.* We use this term to communicate our
philosophy that relapse prevention plans need to be adjusted throughout one's
life as situations change. Table 20.2 is a copy of the categories we use in the
working relapse prevention plan. First is the identification of the risk factor,
which is the name applied to it. We attempt to apply names that have meaning to
the offenders and to reflect their own personal experience. For example, for a
certain offender, we may need a term such as *the not good enough syndrome*
rather than low self-esteem. For another offender who identified a pattern that
involved his offending being preceded by a number of poor decisions in various
aspects of his life, we termed his risk factor as the *slipping and sliding pattern.*
For this offender, the notion of slipping and sliding down a hill was a strong
visual image of his pattern. Second, the offender is asked to identify, when this
is appropriate, events that trigger the risk factor. In the next section of the
worksheet, he is asked to identify how he will recognize the risk factor, which is
usually broken down into thoughts, feelings, and behaviors that are associated
with it. We require all our clients to specify the behaviors that would be observable to others as part of the monitoring system. The last three sections of this
plan are specific coping strategies. We ask each offender to develop a minimum
of three coping strategies for each offense. At this point, it is very important to

TABLE 20.2   Working Relapse Prevention Plan

Areas of Content
Identification of risk factor
Triggers
How to recognize
Thoughts
Feelings
Behaviors
How to Deal With It 1
How to Deal With It 2
How to Deal With It 3

stress the importance of developing competing behaviors. At times, this can be the most difficult part of the process because there is a tendency for both adolescents and adult offenders to use overly simplified coping strategies.

What we attempt to accomplish by our final relapse prevention plan is to summarize the work the offender has done into a product that can be used. We use the signs, or "how to recognize," as a means of not ending up with too many risk factors. For example, we have seen adolescent programs that have lengthy lists of what are identified as risk factors. These may include things such as anger, "poor me" feelings, engaging in negative self-talk, and so on. These are really reactions and signs of a specific risk factor, which is triggered by specific situations. We find that it is much easier to approach this by minimizing the number of risk factors the offender has to remember. In general, if the therapist can help the offender identify the more general risk factor, this can trigger remembering the thoughts, feelings, and behaviors that are associated with the risk factor.

Summary

We have outlined in this chapter the very limited literature on relapse prevention with adolescent sex offenders. We have noted some of the limitations of this model but also recognize that at this time it has significant heuristic value within the adolescent field, and, until other models are available or further data are available, it is the most empirical guide we have for treatment. We have described our approach to implementing the notion of relapse prevention with adolescent offenders, taking into account their heterogeneity and some of the other concerns that have been raised about relapse prevention as a model with the adult offender. Our methods are designed to provide approaches that will engage the adolescent, provide successful experiences, and attempt to avoid assuming there is only one relapse process.

References

Abel, G. G., Osborn, C. A., & Twigg, D. A. (1993). Sexual assault through the life span: Adult offenders with juvenile histories. In H. E. Barbaree, W. L. Marshall, & S. M. Hudson (Eds.), *The juvenile sex offender* (pp. 104-117). New York: Guilford.

Atcheson, J. D., & Williams, D. C. (1954). A study of juvenile sex offenders. *American Journal of Psychiatry, 111,* 366-370.

Barbaree, H. E., Hudson, S. M., & Seto, M. C. (1993). Sexual assault in society: The role of the juvenile sex offender. In H. E. Barbaree, W. L. Marshall, & S. M. Hudson (Eds.), *The juvenile sex offender* (pp. 1-24). New York: Guilford.

Becker, J. V., & Kaplan, M. S. (1993). Cognitive behavioral treatment of the juvenile sex offender. In H. E. Barbaree, W. L. Marshall, & S. M. Hudson (Eds.), *The juvenile sex offender* (pp. 264-277). New York: Guilford.

Finkelhor, D. (1984). Sexual abuse as a moral problem. In D. Finkelhor (Ed.), *Child sexual abuse: New theory and research* (pp. 14-22). New York: Free Press.

Freeman-Longo, R. E., Bird, S., Stevenson, W. F., & Fiske, J. A. (1995). *1994 nationwide survey of treatment programs and models.* Brandon, VT: Safer Society.

Graves, R. E. (1993). *Conceptualizing the youthful male sex offenders: A meta-analytic examination of offender characteristics by offense type.* Unpublished doctoral dissertation, Utah State University.

Gray, A. S., & Pithers, W. D. (1993). Relapse prevention with sexually aggressive adolescents and children: Expanding treatment and supervision. In H. E. Barbaree, W. L. Marshall, & S. M. Hudson (Eds.), *The juvenile sex offender* (pp. 289-319). New York: Guilford.

Hunter, J. A., Becker, J. V., Kaplan, M., & Goodwin, D. W. (1991). Reliability and discriminative utility of the Adolescent Cognitions Scale for juvenile sexual offenders. *Annals of Sex Research, 4,* 281-286.

Hunter, J. A., & Goodwin, D. W. (1992). The clinical utility of satiation therapy with juvenile sexual offenders: Variations and efficacy. *Annals of Sex Research, 5,* 71-80.

Knight, R. A., & Prentky, R. A. (1993). Exploring characteristics for classifying juvenile sex offenders. In H. E. Barbaree, W. L. Marshall, & S. M. Hudson (Eds.), *The juvenile sex offender* (pp. 45-83). New York: Guilford.

Lane, S. (1997). The sexual abuse cycle. In G. Ryan & S. Lane (Eds.), *Juvenile sexual offending: Causes, consequences, and correction* (pp. 77-121). San Francisco: Jossey-Bass.

Lieb, R. (1997). *Findings from the community protection research project: A chartbook.* Olympia: Washington State Institute for Public Policy.

Milloy, C. D. (1998). Specialized treatment for juvenile sex offenders. *Journal of Interpersonal Violence, 13,* 653-656.

Murphy, W. D., Haynes, M. R., & Page, I. J. (1992). Adolescent sex offenders. In W. O'Donohue & J. H. Geer (Eds.), *The sexual abuse of children: Clinical issues* (Vol. 2, pp. 394-429). Hillsdale, NJ: Lawrence Erlbaum.

National Council on Juvenile and Family Court Judges. (1993). The revised report from the National Task Force on Juvenile Sexual Offending, 1993, of the National Adolescent Perpetrator Network. *Juvenile and Family Court Journal, 44,* 1-120.

O'Brien, M., & Bera, W. H. (1986). Adolescent sexual offenders: A descriptive typology. *Preventing Sexual Abuse: A Newsletter of the National Family Life Education Network, 1,* 2-4.

Pithers, W. D., Marques, J. K., Gibat, C. C., & Marlatt, G. A. (1983). Relapse prevention with sexual aggressives: A self-control model of treatment and the maintenance of change. In J. G. Greer & I. R. Stuart (Eds.), *The sexual aggressor: Current perspectives on treatment* (pp. 214-234). New York: Van Nostrand Reinhold.

Ryan, G. (1998). What is so special about specialized treatment? *Journal of Interpersonal Violence, 13,* 647-652.

Ryan, G., Lane, S., Davis, J., & Isaac, C. (1987). Juvenile sex offenders: Development and correlation. *Child Abuse and Neglect, 11,* 385-395.

Vizard, E., Monck, E., & Misch, P. (1995). Child and adolescent sex abuse perpetrators: A review of the research literature. *Journal of Child Psychology and Psychiatry, 36,* 731-756.

Ward, T., & Hudson, S. M. (1996). Relapse prevention: A critical analysis. *Sexual Abuse: A Journal of Research and Treatment, 8,* 177-200.

Ward, T., & Hudson, S. M. (1998). A model of the relapse process in sexual offenders. *Journal of Interpersonal Violence, 13,* 700-725.

Ward, T., Hudson, S. M., & Siegert, R. J. (1995). A critical comment on Pithers' relapse prevention model. *Sexual Abuse: A Journal of Research and Treatment, 7,* 700-725.

Ward, T., Louden, K., Hudson, S. M., & Marshall, W. L. (1995). A descriptive model of the offense chain for child molesters. *Journal of Interpersonal Violence, 10,* 452-472.

Weinrott, M. R. (1996). *Juvenile sexual aggression: A critical review.* Boulder, CO: Center for the Study and Prevention of Violence.

Weinrott, M. R., Riggan, M., & Frothingham, S. (1997). Reducing deviant arousal in juvenile sex offenders using vicarious sensitization. *Journal of Interpersonal Violence, 12,* 704-728.

CHAPTER 21

Treatment of the Developmentally Disabled Sex Offender

JAMES L. HAAVEN
Oregon State Hospital

EMILY M. COLEMAN
Clinical & Support Options, Inc.

The developmentally disabled sex offender (DDSO) has received increasing attention over the past 10 to 15 years primarily due to the deinstitutionalization movement. There has been a significant move to close large developmentally disabled (DD) institutions and to provide support systems for DD persons to live in the community in small group homes, foster care, or independent-supported living. With this welcome transition also comes the problem of providing adequate community safety through supervision of DDSOs who have been in institutions for years without receiving any sex-offender-specific treatment. Historically, DD persons have been at the greatest risk from caregivers and other DD persons who were sexually offending (Furey, 1994). The denying and minimizing of this "in-house" problem has finally taken a turn, and DD professionals and advocates are now addressing this issue. However, a negative consequence created by this deinstitutionalization is that more DD sex offenders are being redirected to correctional and psychiatric settings that are not designed to meet their needs. Therapists and educators in treatment programs integrate DD persons with the nondisabled in these facilities and then attempt to "dummy down" the information. This rarely will constitute adequate treatment for DDSOs.

Throughout this chapter, persons who have demonstrated sexual offending behaviors and who diagnostically fall within the mild to borderline level of mental retardation are referred to as DDSOs. Use of the term DDSO is not intended to imply that the person is defined solely by these aspects; the therapeutic approach inherent in the described programming requires seeing the person in a respectful and holistic manner. The focus in this chapter is on adult male DDSOs. Although the material is applicable to adolescent and female developmentally disabled offenders, it is beyond the scope of this chapter to address the significant differences that exist among these populations. It is important to note that we are addressing sexual offending behavior that is motivated by sexually deviant impulses. This is differentiated from those sexually inappropriate behaviors that violate standard social norms without intent to harm but reflect deficits in social skills, lack of limit setting, environmental restriction, and institutionalization. Treatment strategies for sexually inappropriate behavior typically involve social skills training and sex education. More information and treatment approaches are available for sexually inappropriate behavior than sexually offending behavior in DD populations.

Barriers to Treatment

Professionals and advocates in the DD field have been slow to address this serious problem due in part to concern about creating a new category of sex offenders within the DD population. It is believed that the public views developmentally delayed persons as sexually out of control and that labeling them also as sex offenders would only serve to increase this perception. Presently, there are little data from which to draw a conclusion concerning the prevalence of sexual offending behavior of DDSOs compared to non-DDSOs. Some studies have indicated a higher prevalence of sexual offending by this population (Day, 1993; Koller, Richardson, Katz, & Haynes, 1982). Overall, there is little clear evidence of overrepresentation of developmentally disabled persons within the sex offender population (Griffiths, Hingsburger, & Christian, 1985; Murphy, Coleman, & Abel, 1983).

Advocates for the DD population are concerned that any differences of sexual offending prevalence might be attributed to the disability itself, without taking into account other critical factors: lack of opportunities for social or sexual development, past victimization, and destructive public attitudes toward disabled persons. Knowing and understanding these concerns should not divert efforts to address this problem of sexual offending behavior of DD persons.

Other attitudes in the developmental disability field have also inhibited attention to the problem of sexual abuse. These include denying and minimizing the impact of individuals' offensive behavior and assuming DDSOs are not responsible for their actions. These attitudinal barriers are diminishing, and treatment for DDSOs has started to be given the attention it demands.

Unfortunately, little information concerning the appropriate theoretical models, treatment strategies, monitoring tools, or research in any of these areas exists. The focus in this chapter is on certain theoretical constructs and treatment interventions that have been used and show promise with DDSOs. Due to the limited information in this field, it is necessary to draw on the readings and research in the nondisabled field. It is important for professionals in the DD field to not only learn about nondisabled sexual offender treatment and juvenile sexual offender treatment but also to reevaluate traditional DD paradigms. For example, most Departments of Mental Retardation and DD agencies have policies that promote individual freedom. Therefore, it can be difficult for the professional immersed in the DD field to see the value of restricting DD pedophiles from child-oriented activities.

Utility of the Relapse Prevention Model for DDSOs

To acquaint the experienced DD and inexperienced sexual offender professional with the field, we briefly review the most influential model currently available, relapse prevention (Pithers, Marques, Gibat, & Marlatt, 1983).

Relapse prevention (RP) is an approach to the conceptualization and treatment of compulsive disorders and was originally developed for individuals with substance abuse (Marlatt & Gordon, 1985). It was subsequently modified for application with sex offenders as a self-management model (Pithers et al., 1983).

A number of tenets are central to the RP model: It is a self-management approach, and the approach is individually prescriptive. In addition, it is based on the concept that abuse is not committed on impulse but that offense precursors (small steps) can be identified and addressed. There is a psychoeducational thrust that combines behavioral skill training with cognitive intervention techniques. To be effective, clients must be self-disclosing and motivated to change (Marlatt & Gordon, 1985).

Simply put, RP is a self-control approach for sex offenders designed to prevent high-risk behavior from escalating to a sexual offense. This is accomplished by helping the offender to understand the factors leading to relapse and learning to intercede early in the cycle. The RP model has been further defined as a single-relapse pathway, emphasizing an implicit and covert route to offending (Pithers, 1990). Attention was given to the importance of apparently irrelevant decisions in setting up high-risk situations (HRS) leading to relapse. Identified as the major HRS has been negative emotional states, interpersonal conflict, and environmental situations (Pithers, 1990). In this RP model (Pithers et al., 1983), there is a sequence of critical events in the reoffense cycle: abstinence, seemingly unimportant decisions (harmless looking but risky), high-risk situations, lapse (deviant fantasy or behavior very close to reoffending), abstinence violation effect (giving up), and reoffense. This process is facilitated by the client's initial tendency to focus on the prospect of immediate gratification (PIG) and to ignore the later, negative consequences of sexually offending (Pithers, 1990). Our intent is not to delve into the intricacies of the RP model as it has evolved but instead to provide some ideas concerning how the RP model could be adapted for DDSOs.

Many aspects of the RP model are compatible with the philosophy and past practice of treatment providers in the DD field. For example, traditionally in this area, great attention has been paid to the use of self-management techniques with DD persons. The emphasis on individual versus generic treatment planning because of the special needs and complexity of DD persons has always been a central issue and concern. Similarly, the use of behavioral antecedents in the design of intervention strategies has been an important aspect of treatment within the DD field. Traditionally, the first step in assessing aberrant behavior of DD persons is to complete a functional analysis of the target behaviors. A model commonly used to guide this process is the multicomponent model (Gardner & Moffatt, 1990). This model is based on a biopsychosocial perspective using biological and psychosocial constructs. It guides assessment and treatment by analyzing the events that instigate, strengthen, and decrease aberrant behavior. Treatment involves changing the person's reaction to external and internal conditions that instigate aberrant behavior and teaching new skills to replace dysfunctional behavior. This model, unlike the RP model, does not attempt to explain behavior in a sequential offense chain. However, like the RP model, it does focus on behavioral and cognitive skills training.

The RP model has been adopted in many new DDSO programs for sexual offending behavior due to its compatibility with the learning models typically used in the DD field. However, providers have quickly learned that the application of the traditional RP model to this population was not without its problems. This has been especially true with those providers who were less knowledgeable about the special needs of DD persons and were trying to simply "write down" nondisabled program formats.

Adapting the Relapse Prevention Model

Several critical areas of differences between DDSOs and nondisabled offenders need to be considered when adopting the RP model (Haaven, Little, & Petre-

Miller, 1990). These include learning capacity, self-esteem, and coping skills. The learning capacity and the speed by which new information is learned by DD persons are more limited than nondisabled persons, and they need to learn more slowly and use different strategies. Their ability to identify and understand chains of causal relationships is severely compromised. In addition, their ability to identify subtleties of behavior and its consequences is generally poor and affects their decision-making abilities. Also, most DDSOs have very low global self-esteem. They feel inadequate and fear that they will fail when required to learn new behaviors and perform. They react to this fear of being labeled "dumb" by exaggerating their accomplishments and being overly sensitive to criticism and resistant to change. DD persons also have greater social living skills deficits than nondisabled individuals. They have more difficulty meeting their needs through appropriate means, need to act out their frustrations, and have difficulty controlling negative affective states. This, in turn, affects their ability to retrieve and implement appropriate cognitive and behavioral coping skills. These factors combine to reduce the chances of such individuals coping effectively with high-risk situations and may lead to relapse. Because of these limitations, DD persons need support systems built around them such as case management, financial assistance, housing, leisure and social activities, and so on. It also becomes clear why DDSOs have difficulty adjusting to the traditional RP treatment format for nondisabled sex offenders. It is a self-management model that requires the ability to understand the sequence of events (reoffense chain)—the subtle behaviors, thoughts, and feelings leading to an offense—and then learning to intervene appropriately.

In the RP model (Pithers, 1990), an important precondition for applying RP interventions is that offenders are motivated to stop offending and to change sexual and nonsexual response patterns related to their offense pattern. We suggest that DDSOs have even greater resistance issues than nondisabled sex offenders due to their low self-esteem. They have learned that they frequently fail when attempting to change their behavior. One method commonly suggested in RP programs is to introduce empathy training early in the treatment process (Pithers & Gray, 1996). This is based on the rationale that offenders who are aware of the impact of sexual abuse on victims will be more motivated to change behavior. This may be more problematic with DDSOs because their capability to empathize is limited by an inability to view things from their victim's viewpoint and to experience the appropriate emotional responses. Although they are able to describe the effects of sexual offending on a victim, they are generally incapable of developing a truly empathetic response.

Certainly the efficacy of the RP model for sex offenders has its critics regarding the simplicity of a single-component model, inherent motivational problems, and propensity for plans to become unrealistic or simplistic. However, it provides a useful framework when working with DDSOs. Two elements of RP that are especially helpful are the self-management focus and the linking of offense precursors with corresponding interventions. Therefore, RP generally is used to teach DDSOs to identify and address high-risk situations and to arrange external support systems of monitoring and assistance around those high-risk situations.

A central element of adapting the RP model for DDSO persons is the acquisition of "success" identity. This approach was popularized by William Glasser's (1965) reality therapy and focuses on one's identity as a major contributor to all behaviors and emotions. Glasser hypothesized that everyone has an intrinsic drive toward achieving a distinct and unique identity. These success identities fulfill individuals' basic needs for love, power, fun, and freedom. Therefore, a failure identity can lead to psychological problems and maladjustment.

In addition to seeking success identities, DDSOs must also develop expectations that they are capable of reaching these goals. High levels of self-efficacy will increase individuals' efforts to adjust their actual behavior so that it more closely approximates their intended behavior (Carver & Scheier, 1990)—their success identity. Critical in this process is that DD persons set goals for their ideal self to which they aspire. Also, their goals must be realistic, and they must feel capable of actually achieving them.

Developmentally Disabled Sex Offender RP Model

To successfully adapt the RP sex offender model to this population, it must be presented in a way that can be understood and incorporated into daily use by DDSOs. The DDSO RP model outlined in Figure 21.1 identifies the critical treatment component areas.

This diagram does not imply a single pathway or necessarily a sequential offense cycle. The following are the components of the DDSO RP model:

1. New Me—Outline characteristics and prioritize New Me goals.
2. Setups—Understand both setups to (a) not attaining New Me goals (good life) and (b) high-risk/reoffending behavior (give up).
3. What-to-dos—Learn how to (a) reach New Me goals and maintain healthy life balance and (b) take action when there is danger.

Initially, DDSOs identify goals defined in terms and characteristics of the ideal New Me, the principles of this New Me, and the corresponding behaviors (Carver & Scheier, 1990). This ideal self is a desired self of the client that is expressed in abstract terms (e.g., powerful, wise, strong person). The corresponding principles are statements such as "I stand up for what's right" and "I can wait." Easier to understand for DDSOs are the behaviors that would reflect this New Me (personal grooming skills, communication skills, etc.) and provide them the life balance (good life) that they desire. They must develop goals

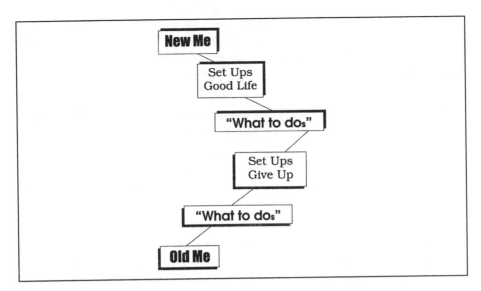

Figure 21.1.   Developmentally Disabled Relapse Prevention Model

and corresponding skills to achieve and maintain the "good life" but also must give attention to understanding the critical precursors (setups) that inhibit them from being the person they strive to be. The action or treatment strategies that they believe to constitute the desired person are identified as "what-to-dos." The treatment focus is on setting acquisitional goals involving approach behavior to meet needs and attain lifestyle balance as a New Me.

The next step in the process is to avoid "give-up" by giving attention to the setups or precursors (alcohol, deviant fantasies, access to victims, etc.) that the client needs to identify as serious danger signs. The interventions involve self-control and high-risk intervention skills. A distinction is made between setups that limit the client achieving New Me goals and the good life and setups indicating high-risk offending situations leading to give-up. Give-up is similar to the abstinence violation affect (Marlatt & Gordon, 1985) in which the DDSOs are at a stage in the offending chain where their self-esteem is lowered or they no longer view themselves as abstainers. The give-up what-to-dos are avoidance strategies such as escaping from high-risk situations, cognitive restructuring, sexual arousal control techniques, and so on.

The concept of the PIG is used to explain the urges that can take place at any time to fuel an offending pattern. The easy visualization and symbolism of a PIG can help explain to DDSOs how urges can happen and disrupt the New Me person. Therefore, the treatment dynamic is one of empowerment—to learn to be the person you want to be without letting the Old Me PIG control you. Old Me in the DDSO RP model indicates relapse—reoffending behavior.

Finally, several additional points need to be made about the DDSO RP model. There is no attempt to teach a specific chain of events (cycle) to reoffense because DDSOs find it difficult to learn and interpret such a sequence. Although they may be able to learn to recite the elements of a cycle in a classroom setting, they are unlikely to use this understanding in real-life situations. The clinician can identify a specific chain of events for the purpose of treatment planning, but one must keep in mind that sexually deviant behavior of DDSOs is a complex and covert process that does not lend itself easily to behavioral functional analysis. The wording in the DDSO RP model projects an empowering approach in which the person is actively defining what he wants to be in life and how to attain it. Again, this model focuses on a success-expectancy paradigm—the capability of living a responsible, meaningful life without hurting others.

A central theme of this model is personal responsibility and accountability. The approach to changing long-standing dysfunctional behavior requires more than just skill building and "feel-good" therapy. It demands accountability. New Me persons stand up for what is right and learn from their own mistakes. The idea of explaining treatment in terms of becoming a New Me can be a powerful and effective tool for change with DDSOs. This addresses one of the most difficult problems with the RP model. Without motivation, without reduction of resistance to change, especially in redefining dysfunctional goals, treatment with DDSOs will not be effective. The reason this Old/New Me approach is motivating is that it is understandable and empowering. It defines treatment in a less threatening way, and it allows an active partnership between DDSOs and therapists. Most important, it gives DD persons an opportunity to mold and embrace new identities—new labels that are success oriented and not restricting or embarrassing. In addition, it provides a common language to use throughout treatment to label behaviors, thoughts, and so on (Old Me thinking, New Me behavior, etc.).

The program components and strategies using the DDSO RP model will be summarized in the three stages of treatment: assessment, treatment, and transition/aftercare.

Assessment

Completing a sex-offender-specific evaluation is the first step in an effective intervention. The purpose of assessment is to determine the scope of sexual problems, risk levels, ability to benefit from treatment, and the appropriate treatment interventions. In reviewing and collecting information on the nature of the sexual problems, risk factors or precursors to the offending behavior are identified. The multicomponent (MC) model (Gardner & Moffatt, 1990) outlined earlier in the chapter provides a framework for identifying these factors and precursors. The MC model identifies (a) events that instigate or increase the probability of occurrence, (b) events that strengthen and maintain behavior, and (c) events that decrease behavior. To further structure the assessment and treatment process, the four preconditions model (Finkelhor, 1984) can be helpful. This model outlines the occurrence of sexual abuse by recognizing four conditions that need to be met prior to the offense. The four conditions provide a framework for organizing the collection of risk factor information for assessment. This visual representation of the model can also be helpful in explaining to caretakers, parents, and other support systems, as well as DDSOs, how this sexual behavior occurs.

Using the models outlined, assessment starts with analysis of clinical and criminal records that permit preliminary assessment of the client's high-risk factors. Records can also contain indications of deficits that have a significant effect on the client's sense of identity (self-esteem) in various domains (sexual, social, etc.) and self-efficacy. During the assessment process, the therapist can introduce the concept and language of Old Me and New Me and explain treatment within the context of the DDSO RP model.

The following is an outline of suggested evaluation practices (Coleman & Haaven, in press). After thoroughly reviewing third-party information, the clinician explains the evaluation purpose and process, its risks and benefits, and the confidentiality limits to the DDSO. The ability of the DDSO to give informed consent is evaluated. If he or she cannot give informed consent, a guardian ad litem needs to be appointed before proceeding with the evaluation.

Through a combination of the DDSO's self-report and third-party information, the evaluator then obtains a general history, information regarding current daily functioning, mental status examination, and sexual history. The evaluation may also include psychometric testing, the polygraph, and measurement of sexual arousal via the plethysmograph. General history information includes the family genogram, history of mental illness, substance abuse and other addictions, education, employment, criminal history, previous treatment interventions, medical history, and history of victimization, including physical, emotional, sexual trauma, or neglect. The sexual history is an opportunity for the DDSO to begin to take responsibility for his or her problem. However, in addition to the usual difficulty sex offenders initially have in being forthcoming about their problems, there are unique obstacles to gathering this information with the DDSO. Idiosyncratic language, increased anxiety in an unfamiliar situation, response to a situation's demand characteristics, more global denial, memory deficits, communication deficits, and attention deficits can interfere with the process of gathering accurate information. With knowledge, training, and practice, the evaluator can learn to anticipate, identify, and cope with these difficulties.

Most often, psychometric questionnaires used with DDSOs have been adapted from those employed with nondisabled offenders and the language or response mode simplified. There are a few tests designed for the developmentally disabled, including the Socio-Sexual Knowledge and Attitude Test (SSKAT) (Edmonson & Wish, 1975) and the Modified Cognition Scale for the Developmentally Disabled (Haaven, 1995). Developed for persons who are nonverbal, the SSKAT obtains information on knowledge and attitudes in 14 different areas, including dating and intimacy. On the SSKAT, the client responds to questions by pointing to one of four pictures presented by the clinician. The Modified Cognition Scale for the Developmentally Disabled provides information on attitudes toward pedophilia and rape of adult women.

A valuable tool with the nondisabled sexual offender, the plethysmograph can also be an important evaluation component for DDSOs. However, it is important to note the lack of norms for the developmentally disabled population. Therefore, the plethysmograph results must be interpreted much more conservatively. Also, certain adjustments are necessary in the use of the plethysmograph with DDSOs. They may need increased time to become comfortable in the laboratory. Other necessary factors to consider are accounting for medication effects, difficulty sitting still and focusing on the stimuli presentations, and difficulty accurately perceiving the stimulus and understanding the self-report process.

It is not uncommon for certain diagnoses to be missed during the assessment process, and therefore crucial offending precursors may remain undetected. Character disorders, substance abuse, depression, organicity, depression, and posttraumatic stress disorder are frequently underdiagnosed (Coleman & Haaven, in press). In contrast, schizophrenia appears to often be overdiagnosed in this population. The clinician needs to be mindful of these common errors.

In the final evaluation step, a feedback session during which the DDSOs are given the evaluation results and treatment recommendations is scheduled. Typically, DDSOs have worked hard throughout the evaluation process and have taken responsibility for their sexual problems. This should be recognized and their continuing efforts to deal with these sexual problems encouraged in the feedback sessions.

Treatment Phase

When designing a treatment program, the physical environment in which treatment takes place should not be overlooked. It is important to have a milieu that reinforces information being learned as well as providing motivation for change; DD persons are very sensitive to their surroundings. Whether treatment takes place in a therapist's office or in an institutional setting, the environment must first be perceived by the offender as a "safe" place: warm, respectful, and humane. The environment should be thematic, where visual representations of change and New Me identity (collages, pictures, awards, etc.) are celebrated (Haaven et al., 1990).

It is important to foster an environment in which self-management is reinforced, and staff should not do anything for clients that they can do for themselves. However, it may be helpful to use a peer buddy system. The treatment environment should be seen as a learning lab, a place where internal controls, peer group problem solving, and life balance are fostered. Values and themes (e.g., "Stand up for what's right") should be associated with the DDSOs' behaviors as part of their New Me. In this environment, people need to feel safe to make changes and to learn from mistakes—to learn for a living.

For most treatment activities, a group format is most effective with DDSOs. Group treatment provides a more powerful experience when addressing issues such as denial and deviant impulses, as well as fostering prosocial identities (New Me's). Group treatment allows for fostering and developing greater peer influence that can be used throughout treatment and in the community. Unlike nondisabled and especially adolescent offenders who are very susceptible to peer group influence, this has to be developed with DDSOs. DD persons historically have learned to respect authority figures (caregivers) and discount their own peers.

Groups should be relatively small, no more than eight clients, and generally brief and frequent sessions are preferable to longer and less frequent sessions. Four groups a week for 30 minutes are more effective than two groups a week for 1 hour (Brown, 1994), although this may be prohibitive in many outpatient settings. Group time can increase as members become more focused and motivated. In addition, use of creative and action-oriented methods such as drama therapy, mindfulness techniques, and refreshment breaks can also prolong group length without losing group members' attention. Common verbal statements represented by visuals (symbols) can be helpful in facilitating verbal expression. In general, the therapist must take a more active and directive role to facilitate redirection and pull out themes. However, initially not all DDSOs may be ready for group therapy, and individual counseling and peer support sometimes may be necessary before a client assumes group membership.

The different treatment components of the DDSO RP model should be introduced to DDSOs so that the mastery of information and skills build on each other. Certainly, the degree of risk and opportunity to offend also dictates how the components are sequenced. If clients are at greater risk or have opportunities to relapse, they will need to learn self-control and high-risk techniques as quickly as possible. As treatment progresses, components are reintroduced and integrated into the next component introduced. Therefore, opportunities to confront denial and cognitive distortions, as well as reinforcement of interpersonal relationship skills and other New Me skills, should be integrated in all of the components.

Development of a New Me

The treatment process is introduced to DDSOs with the construct of Old Me and New Me. The concept is explained as the way they do not want to be (Old Me) and the way they want to be (New Me). DDSOs begin by identifying the goals of their New Me. As mentioned earlier in this chapter, these goals include the ideal self and corresponding principles and behaviors of the New Me. It is not necessary to have the clients fully understand the abstract quality of the ideal self or principles but instead embrace the new labels they have chosen. Although DD persons will need assistance in identifying such labels or statements, it is important that such choices reflect their desires. The goals of the behaviors to achieve the New Me and the good life must be realistic so that they can continue to make progress toward them and recognize this progress. Some of the clients' New Me characteristics may be ones they already possess as well as new skills to be learned to compensate for existing Old Me characteristics. The new skills should be presented within the context of developing goals to approach this new identity. This activity can be part of homework, and a guardian or caretaker can assist the client if he or she is in an outpatient setting. Numerous activities can be used to complete an Old Me/New Me project: a collage depicting Old Me/New Me with a show-and-tell presentation, a hanging mobile in which Old Me characteristics balance New Me characteristics, and a tracing of a facial profile created with a projected light, with each side facing the other and writing or placing pictures on each side (Old and New Me). Activities such as fashion shows or role-plays that depict Old Me/New Me characteristics are just a few of the many ways this concept can be learned. These activities are most effectively accompanied by open discussions and explanations by the clients. Staff should resist attempting to overcontrol the process by demanding that certain characteristics be identified. This project is ideally an ongoing process continually modified by the clients. Clients should be provided with adequate assistance to complete such projects and should feel a sense of pride and ownership over their results. The initial perception of success by the clients is very important in providing motivation for the treatment process, and clients need to feel that treatment is an engaging, empowering journey. The public display of completed projects in the group or individual's home or facility can provide a degree of achievement and pride.

Identifying a specific coping skill for DDSOs gives increased emphasis to the new identity concept. Coping skills are defined in terms of specific goals, behaviors, and cognitions. Four examples of New Me coping skills are Cool Head (walk away), People First (help others), Do Right (stand up for what is right), and Can Wait (slow down). Figure 21.2 outlines the Old Me (Now) and New Me (Can Wait) thinking and behavior that correspond with a high-risk situation of "not getting own way."

OLD ME	NEW ME
Now . . . when not getting own way	**Can wait . . . when not getting own way**
<u>Thinking</u>: "I want what I want when I want it, and I want it right now."	<u>Thinking</u>: "I can wait. I don't need it now. I don't have to have my way."
<u>Behavior</u>: Demands, blows up, calls names, makes threats, takes from others	<u>Behavior</u>: Slows down, talks nicely, is willing to wait for things

Figure 21.2. Example of Generic Coping Skill

One coping skill is chosen as a primary New Me focus throughout treatment and community follow-up. A coping skill is chosen that is central to the DDSOs' pattern of behavior and fosters self-efficacy, especially in potential high-risk situations that test the client's self-control. In other words, this coping skill best describes the client's critical action that moves him closer to his New Me identity. Using this treatment tool, clients can be evaluated in terms of how often and effectively they use their New Me coping skills in various settings and activities. All caregivers and treaters are encouraged to focus on the same skill area, further reinforcing clients' new identities; this facilitates generalization of skills. A common evaluation system can be instituted to measure clients' success. To increase the sense of personal ownership by clients, they can make small laminated cards the size of a credit card. On one side, the card is personalized with artwork or pictures representing their New Me coping skills (e.g., "Cool Head") and, on the other side, their New Me behaviors and thoughts. DDSOs are now "card-carrying" New Me persons.

After completing the Old Me/New Me component, which includes defining the good life, DDSOs are introduced to the terms and meanings of the DDSO RP model. There are discussions on how life imbalance can lead to offending behavior. When explaining this model to DDSOs, we ask them to imagine themselves beginning as a New Me and living the good life without hurting others. They then discuss how life imbalance can develop and affect their good life. In this process, they are introduced to the term *setups,* which are risky situations (poor communication, "wrong" crowd, etc.) that may bring about a state of instability. *What-to-dos* are defined as their New Me skills that allow them to take action to maintain the good life. The next component of the DDRP model discussed is *give-up.* This is presented as those situations that spell danger and mean the DDSO is doing or thinking something deviant, which can lead to hurting another person. At this point, it is explained that the DDSO must take action by using his new avoidance skills and seeking help (give-up what-to-dos).

If action is not taken and immediate gratification urges are not controlled, relapse will occur. Two central themes are emphasized in explaining the process: making "smart choices" and "hanging in" during adversity.

Setups

In this treatment component, DDSOs identify setups (risky situations) in two areas: setups that keep them from having a good life (responsible, respected, and successful) and setups that put them in serious danger of reoffending. The most effective way to collect this information is by immersing DDSOs in projects and providing them with a sense of control over the process. To collect information about setups, it is necessary to address the issue of denial. First, DDSOs need to demonstrate that they assume responsibility and accountability for their actions. This is a "rite of passage" process establishing the idea that they are responsible to behave in a nonhurtful manner and to accept consequences for their own actions—a New Me. Second, addressing the issue of denial provides an opportunity to reinforce the values of openness, honesty, and trust that will be recurring themes throughout the treatment. Finally, confronting the denial of DDSOs provides an opportunity to collect information concerning the offense precursors, patterns of lifestyle imbalance, and desired personal characteristics. Therefore, confronting denial can be a process of exploring DDSOs in a comprehensive way.

We suggest that there are more similarities than differences in the dynamics of denial between DDSOs and nondisabled sex offenders. The different types of denial (fact, awareness, affect, etc.) exhibited are similar for both groups. However, what is different for DDSOs is that they may cling to their denial more rigidly in an attempt to defend themselves against anything that may seem threatening. Therefore, DDSOs may take longer to risk self-disclosure and totally share openly about their offenses. However, once self-disclosure occurs, there may be less minimizing than with nondisabled sex offenders.

We recommend that DDSOs should not be excluded initially from treatment simply because they strongly deny having committed an offense. DDSOs may just take longer to overcome their own fears of "looking bad." In most cases, they should be allowed to continue the treatment process even though they are still not fully open as to their offender activity. Ultimately, they are still expected to be open and take responsibility for their actions. It should be noted, however, that the likelihood of such individuals taking responsibility is much greater if they are receiving consistent messages to take responsibility from their environment.

The approach of the therapist in addressing denial should be firm without being condemning. The therapist should facilitate a discussion in which all interactions are respectful and at a pace that DD persons can cognitively manage. It is effective to have DDSOs assume a role (New Me) of challenging themselves (Old Me).

The format often used to address denial with nondisabled sex offenders is a group process in which the therapist facilitates group members to question, probe, and confront an individual. This confrontation approach has major limitations with DDSOs due to their limited verbal skills, low self-esteem, and performance anxiety. However, the process can be adapted and become effective with increased group structure, empowerment of the person disclosing, and an environment of understanding and support.

Group structure can be provided by identifying and subsequently focusing on categories of self-disclosure. These can include autobiography, setup (high-risk) thoughts/feelings/behaviors, identification of all victims, crime details, and masturbatory/fantasy practices. In each of these areas, DDSOs can make collages and, using a show-and-tell format, present their information. The autobiography can be a book that pictorially represents relevant stages and events of their lives. This includes what they see in the future for themselves as a New Me. Another way to structure this task can be to identify these same categories but group them into events prior, during, and after the crime. In either group structure, it is important to provide categories that can be understood by the clients. It is also essential to empower clients to persevere with difficult tasks until they have completed all of them. Ideally, the therapist encourages clients to go at their own pace with the encouragement and support of the group, but they are also required to address all of the areas adequately. Videotaping the disclosures and allowing clients to observe the tape and critique themselves can reduce denial throughout the self-disclosure process. The concept of New Me and self-efficacy is continually reinforced.

What-to-Dos

The next step in the treatment process is to identify those strategies (what-to-dos) that lead to their goals of being a New Me (good life) and to controlling deviant impulses. Teaching effective self-management skills to DDSOs is a critical element of the RP model. Although the learning capacity of DDSOs is less than nondisabled persons, they are more often hampered by inadequate methods of teaching than by their disability. Teaching DDSOs skills requires more than breaking down these skills into small steps and rewards; it requires engagement (Ferguson & Haaven, 1990). Linking emotion with the learning process provides this engagement. Without skills that can be effectively used by DDSOs in high-risk situations, RP is of limited value. The use of therapy animals (Coleman, 1997) can also be an effective method.

For DDSOs to meet their goals of being New Me persons, a critical area that must be considered is interpersonal skills. Interpersonal skills provide DDSOs with the ability to develop and maintain extensive support systems. Communication, anger/frustration management, and relationships are all addressed within interpersonal skills training. Within the context of relationships, sex education and sex therapy are introduced. DDSOs not only have serious deficits in sexual information but also often have developed sexually dysfunctional practices due to past institutionalization. In addition, studies of nondisabled sex offenders have indicated a link between attachment, intimacy, and sex offending (Ward, Hudson, & Marshall, 1996). DDSOs are especially at risk in this regard due to poor early infant and childhood attachments.

Also deserving attention are the skill areas of problem solving, seeking help, and any other area that is critical to the person's self-esteem and self-efficacy. Some research indicates that teaching nondisabled offenders to think before they act can decrease offending behavior (Ross & Fabiano, 1985). Because DDSOs are capable of learning problem-solving skills, it seems reasonable to assume that they can also benefit from them. Learning the specific skill of how to seek help is important for DDSOs as well as overcoming fears preventing them from using this skill. An area that should not be overlooked is addressing those skill areas or characteristics that have a significant effect on a DDSO's sense of New Me identity. These skills or habits, like changing one's appearance, may seem insignificant in addressing offending issues but are critical for positive identity development.

The next area of treatment focuses on developing skills to control deviant impulses. These give-up "what-to-dos" are avoidance strategies such as escaping from high-risk situations, cognitive restructuring, and sexual arousal control techniques. DDSOs are capable of learning to identify concrete, behavioral high-risk situations (i.e., staring at children) but are limited in identifying subtle precursors in their offending cycle. The literature with the nondisabled sex offenders indicates that the inability to effectively manage negative emotional states is a high-risk factor (Pithers et al., 1983). Unfortunately, DDSOs are especially handicapped in identifying emotional risk situations, the first step in managing them. Teaching clients to associate their particular physical manifestations of emotions with their emotional state (e.g., hand tremors with anxiety, blushing with sexual arousal) can be helpful in this process. However, it may be more productive to focus on identifying more concrete risk situations (such as being in the presence of a child, alcohol, or pornography) than attempting to teach DDSOs emotional recognition and regulation. This is not to say that an anxiety management technique such as relaxation training is not beneficial.

Didactic discussion is of limited value in teaching skills to DDSOs. Role-playing various avoidance and escape interventions is most effective when increasing the "drama" or exaggerating the activity. Board games can be developed in which clients draw game cards calling for relevant role-playing, problem solving, and answering yes/no questions. One of the most effective teaching tools is the use of a camcorder to videotape clients practicing escape behavior. Clients then review these tapes as homework. In addition, DDSOs can view television or videos and identify escape behaviors and their consequences. In another effective video approach, "feed forward" (Dowrick & Associates, 1991), new behavior is enacted on tape by combining individual existing component skills and editing them into a new sequence for review. Also, imagery facilitated by collages or tape recorders can be used by clients to practice escape and avoidance tactics. It is important to teach these skills within the context of the New Me identity. The practice behavior should end with scripts and scenes that are rewarding and foster self-efficacy.

Cognitive restructuring involves teaching the client to recognize cognitive distortions or thinking errors justifying sexual abuse and to develop more rational statements as replacements. DDSOs often err in interpreting sociosexual behavior, for example, thinking that a woman who smiles at him wants to have sex with him. The following differences with DDSOs should be noted. First, the understanding of the emotion-cognition link is not essential for therapeutic progress (Prout & Cale, 1994). DDSOs often times will confuse thoughts and feelings but can still benefit from cognitive restructuring. New statements should be taught to specific rather than global situations. Cognitive restructuring should be less intellectual and more concrete and behavioral, directly teaching alternative cognitions or language. This may require providing them with specific words or lists to choose from. Focusing on one or two critical distortions in the offense cycle may be most effective. Having clients dispute in a role-play using their New Me statements against the therapist using clients' Old Me cognitions can be very effective.

All sexual arousal control techniques used with nondisabled sex offenders should be considered for use with DDSOs. DDSOs should not be denied opportunities due to their disabilities. Rather, the various arousal control techniques available should be adapted to the specialized needs of DDSOs. Therefore, covert sensitization, minimal arousal conditioning, satiation techniques, odor aversion, hormonal drug therapy, and use of selective serotonin reuptake inhibitors should be given consideration.

Transition/Aftercare

Transition and ongoing care is absolutely critical with DDSOs. DDSOs have difficulty with change and do not generalize skills to new situations easily. Generalization training is necessary to transfer newly learned skills in simulated situations to a wide array of real-life situations. This training should be carefully controlled and monitored as the clients are exposed to high-risk situations. Clients should not be put into or put themselves (alone) into high-risk situations as a way of testing themselves (Griffiths et al., 1989). To facilitate this generalization process, therapists can introduce DDSOs to a variety of real-life situations. Clients may play an active role in planning community trips, but they must be closely supervised by the therapist. Once skill competency is demonstrated by the DDSO, the therapist can transfer supervision to the client's caregivers in the community. This gradual process of generalization training can then progress to a client going on a planned outing alone while a staff person, with the client's consent, covertly makes behavioral observations from a distance. This has been labeled the Harvey phenomena (Ward et al., 1992). Should any inappropriate behavior occur, further training is required before reintroducing another activity. The risk-to-benefit ratio must always be carefully evaluated in deciding the steps and level of supervision needed throughout the generalization process.

Group therapy is recommended during the transition phase and for an extended period of time while living in the community. Outpatient transition groups can focus on potential high-risk situations and provide opportunities to practice (role-play) situations. Clients report and discuss activities that support a balanced lifestyle. Attention is paid to maintaining a healthy sense of identity (New Me).

It is critical in the transition phase to provide support systems that meet the needs of the clients. Adequate external monitoring, controls, and continuity of treatment are also crucial. A sophisticated relapse prevention plan with detailed precursors to offending will facilitate the monitoring process. This is valuable even though a client may not understand his specific offense cycle at that depth. In addition, it is helpful to consider the entire community as potential members of a support system (Coleman & Haaven, 1998).

Some common system errors seriously compromise effective treatment and supervision in the community of DDSOs (Ward & McElwee, 1995). One such error is complacency within the support system, when staff "drop their guard" to indicators of relapse such as clients not using elementary controls. Other errors include breakdown of communication or support among caregivers and underestimating the effects of changes in the lives of clients. The most common error in the DDSO RP model we have outlined is the lack of attention given to clients maintaining a positive sense of self (New Me) and encouraging self-efficacy.

Conclusion

Clinical observation and experience indicate that RP is a clinically useful model for DDSOs, although research is sorely needed to explore this. We must keep in mind that RP is a self-management model requiring an external support system to be effective with DDSOs. We have proposed that the RP model be modified to focus on the development of a positive self-identity with DDSOs. We have also suggested that DDSOs do not necessarily need to understand a specific cycle of offense to effectively use this self-management model. Finally, there should be caution against identifying DD persons as having deviant patterns without closely assessing the impact and effect of their disabilities and experiences (Hingsburger & Tough, 1998).

It is important to note that assumptions about the DDSO have been based on studies and research on a population of people who have, for the most part, been raised in institutions. With deinstitutionalization, following generations of people with developmental disabilities will have significantly different "roots" and therefore characteristics.

RP has continued to evolve. A multiple-pathway self-regulation model (Ward, Hudson, & Keenan, 1998) has been introduced with new assumptions that may help explain the varied offense patterns of DDSOs. For the present, we must continue to attempt to adapt existing models to the unique needs and makeup of DDSOs.

References

Brown, T. B. (1994). Group counseling and psychotherapy. In D. C. Strohmer & H. T. Prout (Eds.), *Counseling & psychotherapy with persons with mental retardation and borderline intelligence* (pp. 195-233). Brandon, VT: Clinical Psychology Publishing.

Carver, S. C., & Scheier, M. F. (1990). Origins and functions of positive and negative affect: A control-process view. *Psychological Review, 97,* 19-35.

Coleman, E. M. (1997). Animal-facilitated sex offender treatment. In B. K. Schwartz & H. R. Cellini (Eds.), *The sex offenders: New insights, treatment innovations and legal developments* (pp. 21.1-21.11). Kingston, NJ: Civic Research Institute.

Coleman, E. M., & Haaven, J. (1998). Adult intellectually disabled sexual offenders. In W. Marshall (Ed.), *Sourcebook of treatment programs for sexual offenders* (pp. 273-285). New York: Plenum.

Coleman, E. M., & Haaven, J. (in press). Assessment and treatment of the intellectually disabled sex offender. In M. S. Carich & S. Mussack (Eds.), *Handbook on sex offender treatment.* Brandon, VT: Safer Society.

Day, K. (1993). Crime and mental retardation: A review. In K. Howells & C. R. Holland (Eds.), *Clinical approaches to the mental disorder offender* (pp. 111-144). Chichester, UK: Wiley.

Dowrick, P. W., & Associates. (1991). *Practical guide to using video in the behavioral sciences.* New York: John Wiley.

Edmonson, B., & Wish, J. (1975). Sex knowledge and attitudes of moderately retarded males. *American Journal of Mental Deficiency, 80,* 172-179.

Ferguson, E. W., & Haaven, J. (1990). On the design of motivating learning environments for intellectually disabled offenders. *Journal of Correctional Education, 41,* 32-34.

Finkelhor, D. (1984). *Child sexual abuse: New theory and research.* New York: Free Press.

Furey, E. M. (1994). Sexual abuse of adults with mental retardation: Who and where. *Mental Retardation, 8,* 173-180.

Gardner, W., & Moffatt, C. (1990). Aggressive behavior: Definition, assessment, treatment. *International Review of Psychiatry, 2,* 91-100.

Glasser, W. (1965). *Reality therapy.* New York: Harper & Row.

Griffiths, D., Hingsburger, D., & Christian, R. (1985). Treating developmentally handicapped sexual offenders: The York behavior management services treatment program. *Psychiatric Aspects of Mental Retardation Reviews, 4,* 49-54.

Griffiths, D., Quinsey, V., Hingsburger, D., & Christian, R. (1989). *Changing inappropriate sexual behavior: A community-based approach for persons with developmental disabilities.* Baltimore, MD: Brookes.

Haaven, J. (1995, October). *Treatment of intellectually disabled sex offenders.* Paper presented at the training workshop at the 14th Annual Conference of the Association for the Treatment of Sexual Abusers, New Orleans, LA.

Haaven, J., Little, R., & Petre-Miller, D. (1990). *Treating intellectually disabled sex offenders: Model residential program.* Orwell, VT: Safer Society.

Hingsburger, D., & Tough, S. (1998). Hey! Watch your mouth! *NADD Bulletin, 1,* 95-97.

Koller, H., Richardson, S. A., Katz, M., & Haynes, M. R. (1982). Behavioral disturbance in childhood and early learning adult years in populations who were and were not mentally handicapped. *Journal of Preventative Psychiatry, 1,* 453-468.

Marlatt, G. A., & Gordon, J. R. (Eds.). (1985). *Relapse prevention: Maintenance strategies in the treatment of addictive behaviors.* New York: Guilford.

Murphy, W. D., Coleman, E. M., & Abel, G. G. (1983). Human sexuality in the mentally retarded. In J. L. Matson & F. Andrasik (Eds.), *Treatment issues and innovations in mental retardation* (pp. 581-643). New York: Plenum.

Pithers, W. D. (1990). Relapse prevention with sexual aggressors: A method for maintaining therapeutic gain and enhancing external supervision. In W. L. Marshall, D. R. Laws, & N. E. Barbaree (Eds.), *The handbook of sexual assault: Issues, theories, and treatment of the offender* (pp. 343-361). New York: Plenum.

Pithers, W. D., & Gray, A. S. (1996). Utility of relapse prevention in the treatment of sexual abusers. *Sexual Abuse: A Journal of Research and Treatment, 8,* 223-230.

Pithers, W. D., Marques, J. K., Gibat, C. C., & Marlatt, G. A. (1983). Relapse prevention with sexual aggressives. In J. G. Greer & I. R. Stuart (Eds.), *The sexual aggressor* (pp. 214-239). New York: Van Nostrand Reinhold.

Prout, H. T., & Cale, R. L. (1994). Individual counseling approaches. In D. C. Strohmer & H. T. Prout (Eds.), *Counseling and psychotherapy with persons with mental retardation and borderline intelligence* (pp. 109-140). Brandon, VT: Clinical Psychology Publishing.

Ross, R. R., & Fabiano, E. A. (1985). *Time to think: A cognitive model of delinquency prevention and offender rehabilitation.* Johnson City, TN: Institute of Social Sciences and Arts.

Ward, K., Heffern, S. J., Wilcox, D. A., McElwee, D., Dowrick, P., Brown, T. D., Jones, M. J., & Johnson, C. L. (1992). *Managing inappropriate sexual behavior: Supporting individuals with developmental disabilities in the community.* Anchorage, AK: ASETS.

Ward, K., & McElwee, D. (1995, May). *Supporting individuals with inappropriate sexual behaviors in community based settings.* Paper presented at the training workshop at the ANCOR Conference on Intellectually Disabled Sex Offenders, New York.

Ward, T., Hudson, S. M., & Keenan, T. (1998). A self-regulation model of the sexual offense process. *Sexual Abuse: A Journal of Research and Treatment, 10,* 141-157.

Ward, T., Hudson, S. M., & Marshall, W. L. (1996). Attachment style in sex offenders: A preliminary study. *Journal of Sex Research, 33,* 17-26.

CHAPTER 22

Relapse Prevention With Sexual Murderers

JOANNA CLARKE
H. M. Prison Service, London

ADAM J. CARTER
H. M. Prison Brixton, London

In 1997, more than 3,500 life sentence prisoners were incarcerated in England and Wales, constituting approximately 6% of the total prison population. Of these, more than three quarters had been convicted of murder. The procedure is such in England that a vast majority of these life sentence prisoners (lifers) will be released under what is known as the "tariff" system. This is the process whereby the trial judge, when passing a mandatory life sentence for murder (or discretionary life sentence for a grave offence, e.g., arson, rape), will make a recommendation about the length of time that should be served in prison for retribution to be served. This will be based on the facts of the case, such as intent, extent of injury, culpability, and so on. Once this recommendation is endorsed by the home secretary, it becomes what is known as the tariff—that is, the length of time the prisoner must serve before release into the community under life license is considered. The tariff may be very short (e.g., 4 years). In a handful of cases, it will be for the prisoner's natural life, but for most it will fall somewhere between 10 and 20 years. Whether or not a man is released at his tariff will depend on a number of factors, not least of which is how successfully he has worked to reduce his risk. Even when a lifer is released, this will be on life license, and there will be conditions attached to which he must adhere if he is to avoid being recalled to prison. These conditions will be specific to the offender and his circumstances and should incorporate features aimed at preventing

reoffending. Until the introduction of the Sex Offender Treatment Program
(SOTP) (Mann & Thornton, 1998) to the English prison system in 1990, the
treatment technology through which risk was identified was vague and unsophisticated. It is not surprising, then, that up to 50% of life sentence prisoners
released between 1972 and 1991 who had a previous or current conviction for a
sexual or arson offense were eventually recalled or reconvicted in the long term
(Thornton, 1997). It is noteworthy that virtually no sexual reconvictions were
recorded in the first 4 years, the period for which supervision in the community
is at its most stringent. This contrasts considerably with determinate sentence
sexual offenders, in which reoffending is most likely within the first 2 years of
release from prison.

Despite what is known about the reconviction of lifers, there has been little
work undertaken in the United Kingdom to systematically investigate their
offending in a way that reliably identifies risk and comprehensively addresses
the issue of relapse prevention. This, in turn, has left us bereft of information
regarding motivation to offend. It is in fact difficult to assess the number of mur-
ders that occurs in any given year that may be classified as sexual. This is due in
part because when a sexual offense is committed in the context of a murder, it is
the murder charge that is pursued (Brownmiller, 1975; MacDonald, 1971). In
other cases, conclusive evidence of a sexual offense may be lacking (Groth &
Burgess, 1977). Even when sexual murderers have been identified, ways of categorizing them according to their motivation to offend and their distinct treatment needs had not been considered.

Most studies of sexual and serial murderers have focused on describing the
crime and demographic characteristics of the offender. For example, Ressler,
Burgess, and Douglas (1988) conducted a large-scale study of sexual homicide
over a 4-year period, which reviewed 36 sexual murderers and concentrated
primarily on the personal histories of the offender, profiling, and crime scene
analysis. They concluded from their work that a typology of sexual murder is
essential to provide "a focus for the intervention efforts that address the need to
monitor, evaluate, and change salient personality characteristics," arguing that
"measurements of these characteristics and methods of evaluating positive
change are essential to prevent the tragic reality of released violent criminals
repeating their crime." Grubin (1994) conducted another comprehensive study
of sexual murderers. He compared 21 sexual murderers with 121 offenders who
had raped but not killed and identified social and emotional isolation as the key
characteristics that distinguished the two groups. Grubin argues that this finding provides important insights into why some offenders go on to kill, and this
clearly has implications for interventions aimed at preventing relapse. However, a dearth of research focuses on the treatment needs of this distinct group
of offenders. That which does is generally based on single-case studies
and rarely reports on method (see, e.g., Schlesinger & Revitch, 1990). To
the authors' knowledge, there has not yet been any large-scale investigation

into treatment need or outcome. This may in part be due to strong arguments that sexual murderers are not treatable, based on assertions about the high incidence of psychopathy among sex killers. Also, it may be argued that in terms of numbers they constitute such a small group that resources would be better directed elsewhere. However, if we are ever to sensibly address the issue of relapse prevention for such a high-risk group whose reoffending can cause untold damage, we have a professional obligation to apply the most up-to-date treatment technology, comprehensively address treatment outcome, and adapt our treatment approaches as necessary.

In July 1996, a specialist unit was opened at Her Majesty's Prison Brixton, dedicated to the assessment and treatment of men who had killed in a sexual context. In this chapter, we review how the application of relapse prevention principles has affected sexual murderers, and we consider alternative approaches based on a developing understanding of this client group.

The Past

The treatment of sexual murderers as a distinct client group is a recent innovation in the English prison system, and as far as we are aware, the unit at Brixton (D Wing) is the only one of its type in the world.

The need for such a unit was precipitated by the identification of a number of life-sentence prisoners whose motivation for offending was unclear but in which some sexual element was indicated—for example, a victim found with clothing removed, exposing sexual parts of the body; bite marks to the breasts; bruising to the genital area; insertion of foreign objects into body cavities; evidence of oral, anal, and/or vaginal intercourse; and evidence of sadistic interest, such as the victim being bound and/or gagged.

With more and more staff from all disciplines being trained in the provision of the SOTP throughout the Prison Service (approximately 500 to date), the likelihood that the motivation for a murder would be questioned increased. Whereas in the past a defense such as "She insulted me during sex and I lost it" or "We were playing a (consenting) sex game and she died by accident" had been accepted, alarm bells would start to ring for trained staff on the receiving end of such a vague protestation. Examination of files might or might not indicate that sexual activity had taken place, but the fact that the murder had occurred in a sexual context was enough for an assessment to be deemed necessary. It is not difficult to imagine the resistance put up by a man to be assessed as a sex offender when no charge for a sexual offense was made at his conviction, and this, combined with the complexity of the offense, necessitated the creation of a specialized treatment facility.

D Wing houses 27 men at any one time and is staffed by a multidisciplinary team of 26 full-time staff and approximately 10 part-time staff, all of whom have been specially trained. This team comprises prison officers, psychologists, probation staff, education staff, and chaplains, all of whom are involved in the delivery of treatment to varying degrees.

There are four main categories of referral to the unit:

1. Lifers, for whom forensic evidence suggests a sex offense took place (they may or may not accept this) and/or about whom there is disagreement that sex offending is an area of concern

2. Lifers who have failed SOTP elsewhere and need to retake the program; they may or may not accept this to be necessary

3. Lifers for whom assessment and/or treatment is urgently needed

4. A small number of straightforward cases of lifers who accept the need for SOTP

Since D Wing's inception, 32 sexual murderers have undergone treatment at Brixton, consisting of the standard SOTP as applied to nonmurdering sex offenders, together with a 40-hour cognitive skills program. Of these men, 1 had murdered a child, and 2 had murdered men. The remaining 29 had murdered adult women (> age 14). What has become increasingly apparent is that the effectiveness of these programs in comprehensively addressing all the treatment needs of this complex and challenging client group is limited, and none more so than in the area of relapse prevention (RP). This concern has been raised as the heterogeneity of the group has become more obvious. Although we first considered the needs of those lifers referred to be the same, it is becoming increasingly clear that they have different and very distinct treatment needs. The application of traditional RP principles to these men presents a number of difficulties. Later in this chapter, using a number of cases, we illustrate our concerns and suggest alternative approaches to preventing relapse.

Relapse Prevention in the Core
Sex Offender Treatment Program

Relapse prevention is a major component of the core SOTP, currently being run by Her Majesty's Prison Service. It accounts for almost half of the 86 group work sessions that offenders undertake to complete the course. The emphasis of the RP intervention is on "control, not cure" (Mann, 1994). The first part of the RP process is the construction by the offender of a cognitive-behavioral offense chain (Nelson & Jackson, 1989). The chain consists of between 8 and 12 links, representing a sequence of decisions that resulted in the client offending. The chain will show a list of situations, each one with an accompanying set of thoughts and interpretations, the behavior that followed, and the resulting feelings or moods. The exercise aims to highlight the precipitants that place the offender at risk and thus enhance his feelings of control over his offending. This is achieved in two ways. First, the offender identifies specific factors within four categories that place him at risk, both early and late in his behavior chain. The categories are high-risk situations, thoughts, behaviors, and feelings. Once identified, the offender then generates a number of different strategies for managing these risk factors, if and when he encounters them in the future. The management strategies are divided into three. Primarily, the offender develops strategies to *avoid* risk factors. The strategies are largely behavioral, such as undertaking mood management courses or declining invitations that may lead to further risk, such as baby-sitting. It is understood that some risk factors may be unavoidable, or an offender may not manage to avoid them. In such circumstances, he will need to have developed a number of *control* strategies. These are largely cognitive and rely heavily on self-talk, visual imagery, urge management, and other similar strategies. In the event that the offender does not control a risk factor, he will also have developed a number of *escape* strategies, which are entirely behavioral and usually drastic (e.g., shouting loudly to draw attention to oneself).

Clinical data from the SOTP have indicated some success for nonmurdering sex offenders in developing an understanding of RP principles. They show significant posttreatment improvements in the recognition of risk situations ($p < .0001$), generation of coping strategies ($p < .0001$), and recognition of future risk ($p < .01$). Data concerning sexual murderers are less robust, and although they indicate change in a positive direction, they suggest that RP has not been as effective in improving offenders' relapse prevention knowledge.

It is our view that for many sexual murderers the current relapse prevention model, as described, is less effective for a number of main reasons that can be broadly divided into two key areas. The first relates to the barriers that exist for lifers to effectively address their offending, and the second relates specifically to the heterogeneity of the group.

Barriers to Relapse Prevention

The RP Process

The relapse prevention element of the core SOTP comes toward the end of the course, when it is assumed the offender has taken responsibility for the offense. For this to be achieved, patterns of thinking related to sexual offending must be recognized, and specific cognitive distortions comprising minimizations, excuses, and justifications (Murphy, 1990) used by the offender need to have been identified. This process will enable the client to identify risk factors that can be incorporated within the relapse prevention plan.

It is also assumed that victim empathy has been developed or heightened and that preventing the creation of more victims is integral to the RP plan, providing an incentive for its implementation. For effective RP plans to be developed within the current model, the offender must have engaged with the therapeutic process and have been open about his offending and the thinking and behavior that lay behind it. As George and Marlatt (1989) state, "An important precondition for applying RP interventions is that the offender be motivated to stop offending." He must be deemed to have developed a realistic attitude toward the risk of reoffending. This is necessary for the continued self-monitoring of his behavior, the sharing of his RP plan with significant others (e.g., supervisory officers), and assessment of risk and further treatment needs. It is also important that the offender does not become overconfident, considering himself no longer at risk or intentionally putting himself in testing situations in an attempt to prove he no longer poses a risk. Even following successful engagement with the therapeutic process, there are a number of barriers to successful RP for the offender from both internal and external sources. Some of these barriers are hard to overcome, regardless of the motivation of the individual. Others pose difficulties because of their consequences to the offender's life in prison and relationships with family and friends.

The Prison Environment

Incarceration itself presents barriers for RP. Prison life demands that those who commit sexual homicide live in a way that not only prevents RP being embarked on but also hinders its effective maintenance. Within the allocated prison, for the offender to stay within the general population with nonsexual offenders (where there is often an easy regime and no stigma), there will be pressure on him to deceive and become secretive about his offense. Given that the charge is often for murder, without any mention of the sexual element of the crime, this is not difficult. Furthermore, the offender is often provided with a very plausible account of his offending by his defending barrister, which he can then reiterate to any interested party (including, of course, his therapists). It is not surprising that, over time, after repeating a defensive version of his offense to survive in prison, the offender comes to believe it.

For those lifers known as sex offenders, there is an option to be located in units for vulnerable prisoners. They may have to move to these units in any case to complete treatment, and the likelihood is that the sex offender label will stay with them should they return to an ordinary location. To survive, the offender again has to become closed about his offending, which can have a considerably negative impact on maintaining progress made. In addition, any written work completed during treatment will usually be stored away from the prisoner's cell to reduce the risk of identification as a sex offender. This can hinder the practice and implementation of relapse prevention skills.

Family

The continued support of close family in the face of overwhelming evidence of their loved one's guilt can be instrumental in preventing the offender from being open about his crime. Family members can appear only too willing to accept the offender's version of the offense because accepting the reality is too much to bear. It is understandable that the mother of a son who has killed a child or mutilated a woman will seek an explanation where blame can be apportioned elsewhere and the offender is in some way exonerated, and it is equally understandable that the offender will allow that to happen. In such circumstances, easing an offender out of denial so that he can plan an offending-free future is a complex task.

For others, when family and friends are supportive of the treatment process, the offender's location in a prison a long distance away from such support can be demoralizing, thus affecting his motivation to make the best of the treatment process. It is recognized that undertaking treatment can be a difficult and painful process, which family support can act to ameliorate through being actively involved in relapse prevention plans and encouraging the offender toward an offending-free future.

Time Into Sentence

The identification of a sexual element to an offense, or the need to explore a case further when an individual is well into his sentence and previous explanations have not been contested, has led to considerable dispute between the offender and the professionals concerned with his treatment.

For the vast majority of lifers on D Wing, the SOTP and the concept of relapse prevention within it have not been an option for much of their sentence. For many, they have "progressed" through the lifer system, being transferred to lower-security prisons in response to favorable reports that they do not present a control problem and have engaged in some form of purposeful activity (e.g., full-time education). Myers, Reccoppa, Burton, and McElroy (1993) comment that after apprehension, these men are often perceived as model prisoners by staff. Evidence of a sexual element to his offense or inconsistencies in his account may have escaped any close scrutiny, leading him to believe that he is on target to be released at his tariff date. Against the background of denial described earlier, it is understandable then that the identification of a need for treatment late in the sentence can set up an adversarial relationship between the offender and prison service representatives. The offender and his supporters may spend considerable time and effort disputing the need for treatment and, once all avenues have been exhausted, enter treatment complaining of coercion and Home Office conspiracy. In these circumstances, he is quite likely to enter a program suspicious and resentful, protesting that he has only agreed to treat-ment to effect his release. Clearly, this is not conducive to effective treatment.

Acceptance of Risk

Offenders who accept responsibility for their offending but fail to recognize any risk of offending again may do well in the course up until relapse preven-tion. Here, their lack of acceptance of future risk can prevent them from ade-quately planning for relapse. Other offenders may be reluctant to describe devi-ant sexual fantasy for fear that they may be deemed more at risk by those responsible for making decisions about release.

Another way that failure to accept risk can manifest itself is in the lifer ques-tioning the efficacy of sex offender treatment and its relevance to him. Some lifers go to considerable lengths to research treatment programs and use any negative findings, regardless of their source, not to do all or part of the program. The uncooperative offender may continue to make complaints through his legal representative, questioning aspects of treatment and the competency of those involved. Behavior such as this is clearly a barrier to the development of a com-mitment to relapse prevention. In circumstances such as these, the offender often sees completion of the program, merely by his attendance, as adequate to fulfill the requirements of the professionals involved in his treatment and fails to recognize the need for continued self-monitoring of his behavior.

Heterogeneity of the Group

Since treatment began on D Wing, it has become increasingly apparent that treating the offenders as a homogeneous group is unhelpful and inadequate, both in terms of understanding their behavior and attempting to prevent its recurrence. Ressler et al. (1988) comment on the many different bases on which murderers have been typed by motive (Revitch, 1965), intent (Kahn, 1971), number of victims (Frazier, 1974), and type of victim (Cormier & Simons, 1969). However, not only do most studies fail to make a distinction between sexual and nonsexual murder (Perdue & Lester, 1974), but they also do not type cases in a way that informs treatment.

Based on experience to date, we have been working on such a typology, the validation of which is in progress. This typology is based on features that are likely to affect the way treatment interventions are applied and combines fea-tures of previous typologies (e.g., motivation, fantasy, and relationship with the victim). From the 32 cases so far treated at Brixton, four main categories have been identified.

Type 1: Sexually Motivated Murder

Characterized by the following:

- The primary sexual motivation is to kill.
- Sophisticated and detailed masturbatory fantasies are involved in the killing.
- Sexual offending is secondary. The victim may or may not be sexually assaulted, and this may occur before or after death.
- The victim is usually unknown and specifically targeted.
- The *method* of killing is sexually stimulating.

Type 2: Sexually Triggered—Aggressive Control

Characterized by the following:

- Primary motivation is to sexually offend.
- Sexual offending includes sadistic features.
- The offender is only briefly acquainted with victim, or the victim is unknown.
- Killing may be instrumental (e.g., to prevent detection, to shut victim up during the offense).
- Killing is intentional.

Type 3: Sexually Triggered—Aggressive Discontrol

Characterized by the following:

- There was no prior intention to kill or sexually offend.
- Killing is explained by the offender as having resulted from something the victim said or did in a sexual context, triggering a substantial sense of grievance held for some time against an intimate party.
- There is extreme violence/humiliation against the victim, suggesting loss of control and perspective.
- Offender is unlikely to exhibit a similar level of violence in a nonsexual context but is known to be aggressive.
- Sexual intercourse may or may not take place, but violence against the victim has sexual characteristics (e.g., mutilation to the genital area).

Type 4: Sexually Triggered—Neuropsychological Dysfunction

Characterized by the following:

- There is unclear motivation to kill or sexually offend.
- Offender either behaved sexually in an aggressive context or aggressively in a sexual context.
- Offender's life is characterized by a series of events in which sexual encounters led to feelings of aggression or aggressive encounters led to sexual arousal.
- Penile plethysmography (PPG) profile is likely to indicate highest arousal to aggression only.

Clearly, if sexual murderers do fall into the categories described, then their needs in terms of preventing relapse are substantially different. But what are the alternatives, and how are they most effectively applied?

Future Directions

To consider the application of alternative approaches to RP in the context of the typology described, a case example is helpful. We recognize that only the briefest descriptions are possible here, but we believe they adequately illustrate the points being made.

Case A

A was convicted of the murder of a 69-year-old female who was known to him as a consequence of his delivery work for a local butcher. There was no evidence of sexual assault, although the victim's underwear had been cut off, and she had one stab wound to the groin and another to the chest.

For 16 years, A denied any sexual motivation for his offending but once in treatment admitted that the sight and feel of blood always gave him an erection. He described explicit fantasies about offending both before this offense and once incarcerated, and the only thing that stopped him was lack of access to a weapon. The features of A's offending classify him as a Type 1 sexual murderer, whose primary motivation was to kill and for whom the method of killing was stimulating.

When considering the application of traditional RP methods to this case, we suggest that A's risk factors are too deep-rooted, general, and prevalent to be identified as specific precursors to offending. In addition, we would argue that for A to rehearse risk factors and coping strategies, as is required by the current RP model, would in fact facilitate the rehearsal of his fantasies and thus increase the possibility of offending (Thornton, 1997). We would advocate the targeting of criminogenic need, as described by Thornton (1997), as a more appropriate response to reducing the risk of A reoffending. Although some traditional RP principles are subsumed in this approach, it also incorporates more general self-management skills, together with issues of interpersonal conflict and emotional intimacy, which are intrinsic to A's functioning.

Case B

B was convicted of the murder of a woman in her 30s. She was found bound and gagged in the burnt remains of her bedroom. Forensic examination showed clear evidence of forced vaginal and anal penetration. B had previously refused treatment, saying the victim's death was an accident.

Once on the program, B acknowledged that his intention was to vaginally and anally rape his victim. He said he hit her when she would not do as he told her, made her sit naked with her legs wide apart, and left her tied up overnight. He strangled her to death the next morning when she started to scream.

B would be classified as a Type 2 sexual murderer. His primary motivation was to sexually offend; the murder was intentional and instrumental, and it included sadistic features. We would suggest that the RP model as it exists in the core SOTP would provide the necessary skills for B to use to prevent relapse. This is based on the premise that B is essentially a sex offender who has killed, and thus his motivation is similar to other nonmurdering sex offenders.

Case C

At the age of 19, C was convicted of the murder of a 17-year-old woman. He strangled her to death, forced a branch into her vagina, and pushed grass into her mouth. There was no evidence that sexual intercourse had occurred. C had spent some time in a therapeutic community but had not systematically addressed his offending.

During treatment, C described his murder of the victim as resulting from her trying to leave him when he had not wanted her to. He reported feelings of intense anger and rejection, stemming from his resentment of his wife and her perceived ill treatment of him. He explained killing his victim as "payback for all the times I've been scorned and rejected" and mutilating her body as "standing up" for himself.

C's overriding sense of grievance, mutilation of the victim, and extreme levels of violence would classify him as a Type 3 sexual murderer. His therapists accepted his claim that he had not intended to kill or sexually offend.

For C we would argue that the issue of emotional regulation is the most salient feature to be addressed if relapse is to be prevented. His offending stems from the development of a substantial sense of grievance, rather than specific risk factors, which was triggered by a set of circumstances that could not necessarily have been anticipated. Although it may be appropriate for him to apply RP principles to those factors relating to mood management early in his offense chain, we would argue that more comprehensive emotional regulation is required. Such intervention would involve a better understanding of general thinking patterns than is currently demanded in the RP section of the core program.

▚ Case D

D murdered a woman some 15 years his senior by throwing a concrete block at her head several times. There was evidence that sexual intercourse had occurred before death but no evidence that it was forced. At the time of the offense, D had been glue sniffing and drinking alcohol with his victim for most of the day. After the murder, D visited the body several times over the course of several months, removing parts of her skull, he says, to avoid detection.

D said in treatment that he killed his victim because she had not commented on the sex they had had. However, his account of his offense changed several times during treatment, and even when it became more consistent toward the end of the program, he was unable to make connections between his behavior early in his offense chain and later.

D has a history of violent and sexual behavior, and neuropsychological screening indicated that further assessment should be undertaken. These features clearly classify him as a Type 4 sexual murderer.

It is arguable that offenders such as D are able to successfully engage in cognitive-behavioral treatment, and thus the relevance of RP is disputed. Consideration could be given to pharmacological intervention in such cases.

Conclusions

We have argued that the application of RP principles to men who have killed in a sexual context presents a number of difficulties, and we have questioned the relevance of this approach to a proportion of this client group. Some of the difficulties relate to the context in which the work is undertaken; others relate to the complexity of these men and our limited understanding of their psychological functioning.

We recognize that prison is a far from ideal environment in which to undertake therapeutic interventions. However, for sexual murderers, little alternative exists, and much can be done to improve the treatment context. Structuring treatment expectations at the start of the sentence will go some way to reduce the denial, collusion, and resistance, which may be experienced by treatment providers, and will help all involved with the progression of the sexual murderer through the lifer system.

There are also advantages to locating sexual murderers together for treatment. First, it facilitates a more open therapeutic approach, allowing the offenders to be considerably more honest about their offending than has previously been the case. This overcomes some of the barriers previously outlined. Second, it focuses attention on the complexity of sexual murderers, providing a unique opportunity to increase our understanding.

However, developing an understanding of such needs is at the very earliest stages. Thornton's (1997) research indicates that the risk of relapse increases over time, suggesting that whatever work is undertaken needs to be in the long term, with a relapse prevention component at its core.

The fact that a majority of lifers will be released means we have an obligation to develop and provide the most sophisticated treatment technology possible. In the process of doing this, decisions need to be made about what constitutes successful relapse prevention for a man who has previously killed. We suggest that validation of the typology is required if alternative treatment approaches are to be explored. We would envisage that as a result of this continued research, a program tailored to the needs of this client group will develop that will incorporate a variety of relapse prevention approaches specific to the needs of each individual.

References

Brownmiller, S. (1975). *Against our will: Men, women and rape.* New York: Simon & Schuster.

Cormier, B. S., & Simons, S. P. (1969). The problem of the dangerous sexual offender. *Canadian Psychiatric Association, 14,* 329-334.

Frazier, S. H. (1974). Murder: Single and multiple aggression. *Aggression, 52,* 304-312.

George, W. H., & Marlatt, G. A. (1989). Introduction. In D. R. Laws (Ed.), *Relapse prevention with sex offenders* (pp. 1-31). New York: Guilford.

Groth, A. N., & Burgess, A. W. (1977). Sexual dysfunction during rape. *New England Journal of Medicine, 297,* 764-766.

Grubin, D. (1994). Sexual murder. *British Journal of Psychiatry, 165*(5), 624-629.

Grubin, D., & Thornton, D. (1994). A programme for the assessment and treatment of sex offenders in the English prison system. *Criminal Justice and Behaviour, 21*(1), 55-71.

Kahn, M. W. (1971). Murderers who plead insanity: A descriptive factor-analytic study of personality, social and history variables. *Genetic Psychology Monographs, 84.*

MacDonald, J. M. (1971). *Rape offenders and their victims.* Springfield, IL: Charles C Thomas.

Mann, R. E. (1994). *Sex Offender Treatment Programme training manual.* London: Internal Home Office.

Mann, R. E., & Thornton, D. (1998). *The evolution of a multi-site sex offender treatment programme.* (Available from Offending Behaviour Programmes Unit, H. M. Prison Service, 7th Floor, Abell House, John Islip Street, London SW1P 4LN, United Kingdom)

Murphy, W. D. (1990). Assessment and modification of cognitive distortions in sex offenders. In W. L. Marshall, R. D. Laws, & H. E. Barbaree (Eds.), *The handbook of sexual assault: Issues, theories, and treatment of the offender* (pp. 331-342). New York: Plenum.

Myers, W. C., Reccoppa, L., Burton, K., & McElroy, R. (1993). Malignant sex and aggression: An overview of serial sexual homicide. *Bulletin of the American Academy of Psychiatry Law, 21*(4), 435-451.

Nelson, C., & Jackson, P. (1989). High risk recognition: The cognitive behavioral chain. In D. R. Laws (Ed.), *Relapse prevention with sex offenders* (pp. 167-177). New York: Guilford.

Perdue, W. C., & Lester, D. (1974). Temperamentally suited to kill: The personality of murderers. *Corrective and Social Psychiatry, 1,* 13-15.

Ressler, R. K., Burgess, A. W., & Douglas, J. E. (1988). *Sexual homicide: Patterns and motives.* New York: Lexington.

Revitch, E. (1965). Sex murder and the potential sex murderer. *Diseases of the Nervous System, 26,* 640-648.

Schlesinger, L. B., and Revitch, E. (1990). Outpatient treatment of the sexually motivated murderer and potential murderer. In S. Chanales (Ed.), *Clinical treatment of the criminal offenders in outpatient mental health settings* (pp. 163-178). New York: Haworth.

Thornton, D. (1997, September). *Is relapse prevention really necessary?* Paper presented at 16th Annual Conference of the Association for Treatment of Sexual Abusers, Washington, D.C.

CHAPTER 23

Replacing the Function of Abusive Behaviors for the Offender

Remaking Relapse Prevention in Working With Women Who Sexually Abuse Children

HILARY ELDRIDGE
JACQUI SARADJIAN
The Lucy Faithfull Foundation

In remaking relapse prevention for women offenders, we have developed positive approach strategies tailored to intervene in the abusive patterns identified by the women themselves and to help them meet their needs in nonabusive ways. Most of the women we have worked with have experienced extensive abuse as children and as adults. Poor attachments and a history of meeting needs in destructive ways are integral to their offending patterns and are addressed as part of relapse prevention-focused intervention. They are invited to explore the possibility of an abuse-free "New Life" in the sense of freedom from being abused as well as from abusing others. Use of the term *abuse* in addition to *offense* is helpful in that many women who abuse their own small children sexualize all their behaviors. These behaviors are not necessarily criminal offenses, but they may be equally damaging. The "New Life Plan" is developed as an integral part of the intervention program with all new learning being related to it. A "New Life Collection" of what works for the woman is built up throughout the program. Emotional and physical risk factors are worked with as they are identified and matching management mechanisms are devised. Many women have more than one pattern of offending and have many subsets of emotions, moods, thoughts, and behaviors within each pattern. These become clear throughout intervention, and the New Life Plan is developed accordingly. The women have a *New Life Manual* (Eldridge & Saradjian, in press-b), which provides examples of other women's abusive patterns and self-management plans and encourages them to work out their own. Women in treatment for sex offending are in a minority and are often worked with individually rather than in groups. As a consequence, they describe feeling isolated and bizarre. The manual offers them hope by helping them see that they are not alone and that other female abusers have succeeded in achieving abuse-free lives. Much of the inaccessible jargon of traditional relapse prevention is replaced with more user-friendly language, often devised by the women themselves.

The "New Life," in its most positive sense, is about the woman learning how to lead a life in which sexually abusing a child is not a desirable option. To achieve this, she has to relinquish all distorted beliefs about the behavior itself. Crucially, she also needs to know the process by which she gets from the thought to the offense. For this to be more than an intellectual exercise, she has to recognize the needs she has met by offending. These are fundamental needs—for example, the giving and receiving of human care and cooperation and a need for a degree of power and control in the world, needs notably unmet in the lives of most of the women (Saradjian, 1996). Unmet needs are associated with aversive emotional states to which the woman may have responded by sexually abusing.

Sexual abuse therefore becomes a coping mechanism used to avoid feelings, such as fear, anger, and loneliness. Avoiding such feelings may have been functional as a means of past survival but in the present is dysfunctional and offense related. Sexual offending can become a perceived need that masks underlying needs. Insight does not of itself create change. The change process requires finding new practical ways toward nonabusive adult relationships, responsibility, and fulfillment. In this chapter, we describe how we have worked with women offenders to these ends.

Illustrative case examples from our work have been given throughout the text. These are drawn from women who gave permission for their stories to be told, provided their identities were protected. Thus, names have been changed and cases disguised. In some instances, composite cases based on actual cases are described to further protect the confidentiality of the women and their families.

Abusive Solutions to Unmet Needs

Established sexual offending is a very difficult behavior to eradicate. Haley (1990) proposes that any symptom, such as sexual offending, originates as an effective "personal solution" to a problem or problems within the life of the perpetrator. In the past, relapse prevention has focused mainly on stopping the use of the behavior to solve the offending problem without sufficient consideration of what problems the offender is trying to "solve" by sexually offending. When faced with painful situations, most human beings will revert to habitual methods of making themselves feel better, and in the case of sexual offenders, this often leads to reoffending.

Women who sexually abuse children behave in a way that is the antithesis of the stereotype and consequent expectation of the behavior of women toward children. Therefore, in working with such women, professionals have struggled to understand why they have transgressed those norms. It is perhaps because of this that research has addressed the women's life histories, relationships, beliefs, and motivations in much greater depth than most of the research carried out with male sexual offenders (e.g., Saradjian, 1996; Spletz, Matthews, & Mathews, 1989).

For both men and women, there are strong links between childhood experiences of pain, trauma, and distorted and disturbed attachments and the expression of such violent acts in the sexual assault of a child (de Zulueta, 1993). Research carried out with 52 women who have sexually abused children (Saradjian, 1996) and our long-term clinical work with such women have led to the conclusion that many do so because, through their life experiences, they have learned that they can meet their needs this way. This is undoubtedly also true of male sexual offenders. Relapse prevention will be vulnerable to failure unless the offender, whether male or female, can learn which personal needs are met by offending and how those needs can be met through nonabusive sources.

Theoretical Basis

Gilbert (1989) takes an ethnological approach to human motivation, stating that all living creatures, including human beings, have two ultimate goals: to survive as an individual and to survive as a species through reproduction. Research and clinical evidence support the notion that to meet these needs, humans have had to develop strong social networks. Consequently, four biosocial goals have evolved related to social interaction. These are (a) caregiving; (b) care receiving; (c) power over others, leading to a sense of status, and over the environment, leading to a sense of competence; and (d) cooperation. All behaviors, when thoroughly analyzed, can be traced to fulfilling one of the biosocial or primary goals. Behaviors that lead to meeting those biosocial goals lead to positive emotions and a feeling of well-being (reward) and thus tend to be repeated. Behaviors that go against fulfillment of those biosocial goals lead to negative or aversive emotional states and thus tend to be avoided or resisted. If there is conflict in the achievement of different biosocial goals, cognition, whether consciously processed or not, and emotion will affect the choice of behavior. The choice can be highly complex and will eventually be determined by the need which at that time is most important for survival. For example, a child may suffer humiliating sexually abusive experiences and thus forgo power and control over a situation in order not to alienate the abuser who may be meeting the child's affiliation needs. In some cases, when the abuser is a parent, he or she is perceived by the child as necessary for basic survival.

Julie felt isolated and alone. Her mother was "always out." She had no real friends. When she was 12 she "met a man of 43" who she said "fell in love with her." She said he made her feel "better than she ever had" in her life. When he wanted to have sex with her she agreed. She said, "I hated his smell and his taste and the feeling of his body on mine." He forced her to engage in more and more humiliating sadistic sex. Nevertheless, she said she wanted to be with him because "he loved me and took care of me and I'd have put up with anything for that."

Research shows that much social learning is achieved by direct experience, vicarious experience, and instruction (Akers, 1977; Bandura, 1969). From birth, a person is constantly learning through interactions with caregivers, other people, and the environment. This leads to the buildup of a body of knowledge: the person's models of the world, beliefs, knowledge, and attitudes, all of which are stored at various levels of consciousness. This knowledge develops and changes over time as new experiences are assimilated. However, models formed in early life are particularly resistant to change unless challenged by a powerful alternative source.

An individual's beliefs, attitudes, and consequent behaviors will develop due to experiences within his or her environment, mediated by rewarding or aversive emotions. However, there is now evidence to indicate that there are innate, individual differences in temperament, that is, in a person's emotional sensitivity and responsiveness (Goldsmith & Campos, 1982). Consequently, there will also be individual differences in people's emotional reactions to similar environmental experiences. Nevertheless, it has been shown that the most powerful continuing influence on behavior is environmental (Emde, 1989).

This model of human functioning stresses the interactions between a person's environment, both physical and social; the person's behavior, including beliefs, attitudes, thoughts, and actions; and the person's biological and physiological systems, each of which is equally reactive to and influential on the other (Sameroff, 1989).

Aspects of the Women's Lives That Contribute to the Development of Sexually Abusive Behavior

Saradjian's (1996) study showed that most of the women in the sample felt powerless, unloved, and isolated. They experienced childhood relationships in which their emotional needs were not appropriately met, although many of them idealized their relationships with at least one of their primary caregivers, despite being abused by them. The women had all experienced some form of childhood abuse, primarily emotional abuse, but most had also experienced physical and sexual abuse. These experiences left the women with intense feelings of rage, self-hate, and vulnerability that had to be repressed (Kohut, 1985). This rage may be repressed but lead to an intensely held need for reprisal to redress the injury (Miller, 1990). During their abusive experiences, the victims internalized both sides of the relationship and thus learned vicariously that dominance over a child can be rewarding and reduce intense emotional arousal.

The closest attachment figure in many of the women's lives was someone who had sexually abused them. In such situations, the victim may readily assimilate the identity projected onto her by the abuser (Salter, 1995). The women later projected similar thinking errors onto their victims, evidenced in their perceptions of their target children. In addition, during childhood, the women were expected to carry out tasks inappropriate for their age and developmental stage. It is likely that this was the origin of the women's own distorted expectations of and beliefs about children.

Due to the lack of emotional responsiveness of their caregivers, the women offenders had a limited sense of their own emotional needs. Consequently, they had difficulty in identifying and dealing with emotional arousal and lacked empathy with both themselves as victims of abuse and with their own victims (Block & Block, 1979). The women had poor relationships with siblings and peers and very few emotionally intimate relationships. Their adult relationships seemed to reinforce rather than challenge the distorted models of the world developed during childhood. They felt a lack of self-worth and formed sexual relationships with partners who were either directly abusive or by whom they felt neglected or rejected. They had few alternative emotionally rewarding relationships and learned that relationships with others usually brought pain. They had no model of their needs being met within relationships with peers. Regardless of how powerful and manipulative they may have appeared to others, they generally felt powerless. This feeling of powerlessness was exacerbated by the stereotypical role of women in society.

An analysis of the women's lives led to the conclusion that they could not meet their biosocial needs though normal sources. This resulted in the experience of negative emotional states, which they tried to reduce in some way to avoid emotional disorders such as anxiety or depression (Gilbert, 1989). Research and clinical work with these women indicated that they had learned to meet their needs for power, control, and affiliation through the sexual abuse of children (Saradjian, 1996).

Tina had been initially coerced into sexually abusing children by her husband, who was very controlling and abusive toward her. She felt a "deep intense anger and hatred," yet she was too afraid to direct those feelings at him. However, she said that during the sex with children, "to my shame, I felt highly sexually aroused." Tina said that she began to sexually abuse children when her partner was not there. She said, "It felt so good to be able to do something sexually I actually chose to do, to have my sexual needs met as I wanted them to be." She said she felt "amazing, I was in control."

Tina recounted a particularly sadistic feeling when sexually abusing one teenage girl whom she perceived as being all the things that she was no longer: "attractive, free, happy, independent." She said she "desperately wanted to hurt her."

Kay described only feeling "loved and cared for" when she was being sexual with the adolescent girl, a resident in the home in which Kay worked. She said she felt it was only through sex that "you could feel close to someone" and show "how much you love and care."

Some women who were initially coerced into sexually abusing did so to fulfill their affiliation needs by maintaining their relationships with their partners. They felt they would not cope alone and would do anything, no matter how initially aversive, to keep their partners.

Lionel coerced Joan into using her daughter in pornography. If she disobeyed him, he manipulated her by withdrawing attention and affection from her and talking about other women. She said she was terrified to refuse him because she felt she could not cope alone and could not bear to lose him.

Women involved in multiperpetrator, multivictim groups described very positive feelings not only from the abuse but also from being part of the group itself.

Moira was enticed into an organized abuse group when she was a young teenager. She had always been very isolated as a child and had felt rejected within her own family. She said that she was very socially anxious and suffered from panic attacks. She said that when she was first recruited to the group, she was made to feel important by the other group members. She said that she "did not really enjoy all the sex that much" but what she really enjoyed was being part of the group, feeling that she was "a member" and that she had "a role" within that group. She said that her confidence increased dramatically and that all her anxieties "seemed to disappear."

Some women who targeted adolescents met similar needs in these relationships as nonabusing women met with adult partners. The difference for the women offenders was that they felt they had the power within the relationships.

■■ Rhona, age 38, described being "in a relationship with" a 13-year-old boy in the
■■ class she taught. She described this boy as the person she felt "closest to in all the world." She said that it was in him that she could "confide" and share her "innermost thoughts, hopes, and fears." She described him as the person she would rely on for help if she was in any difficulties and him as the person who made her feel "loved, important, and special" and with whom she said she wanted to "share her body." She described an active sexual relationship between them within which she felt she could "have my sexual needs met in the way that I want them to be."

Some women said that the only form of closeness they ever felt was as a child within a sexually abusive relationship. These women described a need to re-create such a relationship to reestablish that sense of closeness.

■■ Karen described being sexually abused by her mother from infancy until 5 years
■■ of age. She described that as the only time in her life when she felt close to anyone. She said when her mother stopped abusing her, she felt abandoned and longed for a daughter of her own so that she could be sexual with her and gain that feeling of closeness again.

Some women experienced intrusive negative thoughts and associated feelings related to unresolved past abuse. Some said these thoughts and feelings initiated their first sexually abusive acts. They repeated the acts in an attempt to make sense of unresolved traumatic experiences of their own. These acts then became rewarding in themselves, and different triggers could lead to offending.

■■ Doreen frequently had images of being sexually abused by her father and foster
■■ father, which left her feeling the physical and emotional hurt that she felt during the actual experiences. Sometimes she would "dwell" on why they did it and would imagine herself doing the same things to a child. She did not masturbate to the thoughts, but she did have "good feelings." When she had her own child, she "found herself" touching him sexually and said how those acts released "feelings of tension" in her. She said she then "found herself" sexually abusing her son whenever she felt emotionally stressed and tense in any way.

Like Doreen, some women learned to regulate all forms of emotional arousal by sexually abusing or thinking about sexually abusing a child: They tended to be highly active sexual offenders. Other female offenders sexually abused in response to more specific emotional feelings. Some described meeting different needs by abusing the same child in different ways at different times or meeting different needs by abusing different children.

■■ Amanda sexually abused two of her sons. She sexually abused her older son when she felt angry. During those sexual acts, she fantasized about inflicting damage to the genitals of men who had abused her during her childhood. She described quite different motivations leading her to sexually abuse her younger son: feelings of loneliness, of wanting closeness with someone. While masturbating this child, she created graphic "romantic" fantasies. With both children, however, she described "feeling good" because she was the one in control. She described feeling a great sense of power that she could meet her needs and yet not risk being hurt and humiliated.

Some women described how their offending no longer met their needs as it had done previously, and they then adapted their behaviors to bring about the same feeling: They did this by targeting another child or by changing their behavior with the same child.

■■ Janine talked of how the older and more independent her son became, the more frequently she felt she needed to abuse him and the more intrusive the acts she "had to" engage in to feel as if she was "connected" to him still and could maintain control over him.

In summary, then, the women's offending was meeting a combination of unmet needs, both fundamental and perceived, which they had no mechanisms for meeting or dealing with in other ways. Figure 23.1 illustrates this.

A Needs-Based Model: Relapse Prevention Reframed

For an abuse-free life to be sustainable, it must be attractive and meet or replace the needs met by offending. Traditional relapse prevention has not focused on the function the abusive behavior serves for the offender. Without this consideration, it may fail. Traditional relapse prevention has also emphasized avoidance goals, which are less likely to be effective than approach goals (Mann, 1998). The prevention of reoffending can only be attractive if it offers the offender a new life that is both satisfying and attainable.

Remade relapse prevention is based on individual assessment of needs met by the offending behavior. Awareness of personal risk factors therefore

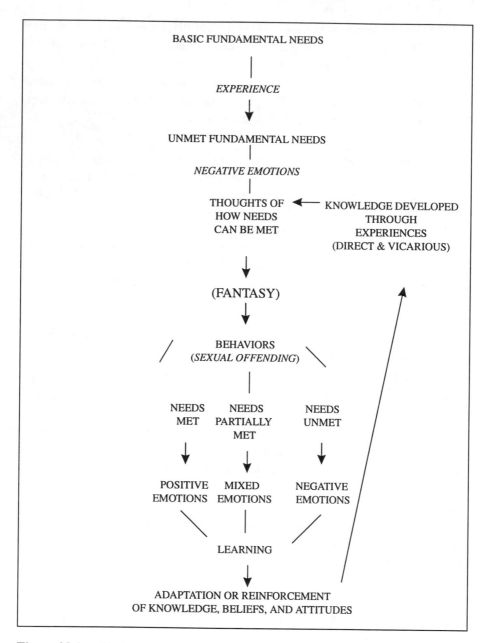

Figure 23.1. Diagram

includes recognition of the importance of either challenging perceived needs or
meeting them in other ways. The New Life Plan then concentrates on finding
positive ways of meeting fundamental needs. Harnessing positive qualities and
a sense of self-worth helps develop a self-image that fits with and enables the
woman to achieve an abuse-free lifestyle. The more traditional components of
relapse prevention are also essential because sometimes needs will not be met,
and the woman is tempted to resort to well-learned and seemingly successful

methods of meeting those needs. The habit may be well established, and an awareness of physical as well as emotional risk factors and accompanying practical coping strategies is required.

Integrating Relapse Prevention Into an Effective Treatment Program

We view relapse prevention as integral to treatment programs for female offenders. Throughout their work, the women are asked, "What have you learned from this? How does it relate to your abusive pattern and your plans for your New Life?" New knowledge and insights are applied continuously to practical everyday life changes. Research into the lives of the women and their behavior suggests that effective programs should focus on the following:

- Identifying abusive patterns, including thoughts, feelings, moods, and senses as well as behaviors
- Identifying the needs met by abusing children and dealing with what generated those needs:
  — factors related to present lifestyle—particularly current relationships
  — factors related to past abuse history
- Finding nonabusive ways of meeting needs
- Managing negative emotional states
- Challenging distorted abuse-related cognitions and beliefs
- Managing fantasy
- Identifying emotional and physical risk factors and matching coping mechanisms that work fast and effectively
- Developing a positive abuse-free new life
- Use of external monitors
- Testing relapse prevention plans in practice

Setting the Scene for Intervention

Effective work requires not only feeling and thinking change but also practical changes within the woman's life.

Protecting Children. The protection of children with whom she has contact must be given priority. Many women offenders are single parents, and the seriousness of their behavior is denied by people who, if the offender was male, would take clear action to protect the children. Thus, the therapist often has a teaching role in increasing the awareness of impact issues for children in all relevant parties, including colleagues.

Clear Ground Rules. The operating principles for work with male sex offenders described by Eldridge (1998, p. 7) also apply to work with women. Suitably adapted, these include the following:

- Professionals working with the woman take the view that they are first and foremost agents of child protection.
- In line with the above, professionals adopt a policy of responsible information sharing with appropriate child protection agencies.
- Intervention takes place within a therapeutic environment.
- The woman is encouraged to take a positive and active approach to herself and her treatment regardless of whether positive or aversive techniques are used.
- Remade relapse prevention is an integral part of the intervention program.
- Remade relapse prevention thinking is encouraged, and strategies are woven into the program from its beginning.
- From the midpoint of intervention (i.e., the point where the woman has developed a heightened awareness of the need to lead an abuse-free life), she should focus increasingly on developing New Life self-management strategies, and the emphasis on this should become increasingly greater as she progresses toward discharge.
- The woman develops a clear understanding of her offending pattern(s).
- The woman develops a clear understanding of her abusive process, her most likely routes to reabuse, and other possible main routes to reabuse.
- The woman recognizes and values reasons for leading an abuse-free new life.
- The woman has an active role in developing the New Life Plan.
- The woman learns to distinguish between emotional slides and physical steps toward abuse and abuse itself.
- The woman learns effective coping mechanisms to deal with emotional slides and physical steps.
- The woman learns effective coping mechanisms to deal with high-risk scenarios, both expected and unexpected.
- The woman recognizes the importance of and plans for a realistic and positive abuse-free lifestyle.
- The woman makes contingency plans to deal with setbacks and disappointments.
- The woman's New Life Plan is shared with a network of appropriate people who may act as external monitors.
- The woman attends formal "booster" sessions with those responsible for her treatment, at regular intervals thereafter.
- The woman has access to professional help after leaving her program.
- Professionals working with the woman operate an antidiscriminatory approach, taking account of specific issues for women, the woman's culture, relationships, and individual considerations such as age, learning abilities, and physical abilities.

- Professionals working with the woman challenge discriminatory attitudes, particularly those associated with sexuality and those which link to sexual abuse.

- Those involved in the woman's support and monitoring network liaise closely and share information about her with each other as appropriate.

The adoption of responsible information sharing with appropriate child protection agencies is vital. Women offenders in treatment can provide information about the scale and content of their abuse, hitherto undisclosed, which can be used to enhance the child victim's therapy and inform child protection decision making. For example, a woman who was initially thought to have begun abusing her child when he was age 4 later revealed in treatment that she had abused him since birth. This had major implications for his therapeutic needs and decisions relating to contact with his mother.

Ensuring the Woman Is Safe. To work effectively, the woman needs to feel psychologically and physically safe. For example, she may still be living with or dependent on someone who has sexually abused her as a child or may be in an abusive relationship. It is extremely difficult to work toward change if continuing messages in her life conflict with those being developed within the program.

Providing an Empathic, Noncolluding Therapeutic Environment. Women who sexually abuse children are aware that female offending is rarely discussed. When they label their own behavior as sexual abuse, they may view themselves as too abnormal to change. While maintaining a child protection perspective, the therapist needs to value and harness the woman's positive qualities and help her recognize that although she has done harm, she is nevertheless a worthwhile human being capable of change. While openly displaying a nontrusting approach—because it would be foolish to trust someone who cannot trust herself—it is essential to empathize with and have positive regard for the woman.

Using Accessible Language. In our experience, women work best when they can relate what they do in ordinary language. Thus, jargon such as *grooming* is replaced with *manipulation.* Traditional relapse prevention jargon such as *lapse* is replaced with *emotional slides and physical steps to abuse,* and *relapse* is replaced with *reabuse.*

Planning for Managing Feelings. Setting the scene for work includes an introduction to *managing feelings:* a crucial component of remade relapse prevention. Recognition that aspects of the program will be distressing is followed by a plan for how to deal with negative emotions while continuing the process of self-challenge.

Identifying Abusive Patterns

Effective plans for an abuse-free lifestyle are directly related to the woman's abusive pattern or patterns and to the kind of lifestyle that is practical and attractive to her. It is rare for any abuser to immediately disclose, to either her therapist or herself, all aspects of her pattern. Thus, assessment should be ongoing throughout the work, and the developing New Life Plan will change in line with the changing mutual understanding of the abusive pattern(s). Based on our clinical practice, we hypothesize that the following patterns are common and should be the subject of future research with women.

Approach Patterns (i.e., Continuous, Uninhibited by Attempts to Stop)

Historically, relapse prevention has emphasized avoidant goals in which negative mood states act as precursors to offending. However, the concept of approach goals is described in Eldridge (1992; Eldridge & Still, 1995, pp. 137-141) as "continuous or uninhibited cycles" and by Ward and Hudson (1998) as "approach pathways." Essentially, such offenders either plan their offending or have no interest in avoidance. Some of the planners may have an "umbrella" strategy. This means they engage in explicit planning related to getting access to children generally and can focus their planning around a child to whom they are particularly attracted. They have the added bonus of being approached by or having the opportunity to be alone with a child who they had not specifically targeted. The kind of thinking such women engage in can include "I want to do it, there's nothing wrong with it—must make sure I don't get caught because people won't understand."

> Kay, who was a residential worker in a children's home for children who had suffered sexual/emotional abuse and were seeking substitute mothers, did not need to engage in detailed planning because vulnerable children came to her. She was able to use the child's actions both to trap the child and keep her quiet and to justify the behavior to herself on the grounds that the child wanted it. However, she used clearly identifiable conscious "grooming" tactics to gain compliance and prevent disclosure.

Many women who target adolescent boys are in this category, and the denial of society that they are harming the boys supports their core beliefs.

Remade relapse prevention recognizes that although some women plan their offending in terms of an umbrella strategy or a clear plan in relation to one particular child, others do not. Some women who have approach goals do not really think too much about it—they just do it whenever they can. They tend to believe it does no harm, or they have a right to it anyway. Work with women who have approach goals to offending must concentrate on changing core beliefs before any attempt at prevention of reoffending can be effective.

Avoidant Patterns (i.e., Inhibited by Beliefs That the Behavior Should Stop)

This type of pattern is identified by Wolf (1984) and by Eldridge (1992, 1998; Eldridge & Still, 1995) and is further developed by Ward and Hudson (1998) as "avoidant passive" and "avoidant active." Some women know what they are doing is wrong and tell themselves they should not do it again. Some have active strategies for avoidance but often fail when they feel they have an excuse to offend, such as overwhelming emotions. For other women within this group, prevention is closer to wishful thinking. They delude themselves about how they get from the thought to the offense. They deny responsibility for the abuse they perpetrate and project it onto others: "I don't want to do it but I feel that a stronger force, real or imaginary, is making me do it." Some women set up situations so that a child behaves in a particular way, which means they can then project their own distorted beliefs onto the child. Thus, the power that *forces* them into abusing is the child. For example, "She came to me." Women who are initially coerced into offending by men often have a variant of this pattern. Some would not abuse except when subject to severe coercion, but others begin to abuse independently, nevertheless still insisting that it was because they were made to do it.

Offenders often have more than one pattern of offending in relation to different children, different circumstances, and mood states. In addition, there may be variants on the primary patterns. We have observed the following variants in women offenders.

"Zig-Zag" Patterns

Remade relapse prevention recognizes that some women seem torn between approach and avoidant goals. They offend without inhibition until an event occurs that challenges their core beliefs. For example, the child pulls away during the abuse. There are then attempts at avoidance until the desire to alleviate negative emotions becomes strong and inhibitors are overcome. The woman may then abuse continuously for a period until such a challenging event recurs. Her own desire to offend and the child's attempts to survive by, for example, pleasing mother or teacher combine to reinforce her pro-offending beliefs and approach goals.

Denial Patterns

This pattern occurs when a woman sexually abuses a child and then denies it to herself. She has no conscious intention of sexually abusing a child again and thus neither specifically approaches nor avoids situations that lead to offending. In fact, she puts it out of her mind and does not think about it. Women who have this pattern describe mood states leading to offense-linked daydreaming that occurs almost simultaneously with the offending behaviors. There is very little cognitive processing or conscious planning.

Identifying the Needs Met by Abusing Children: The Core of the New Life Plan

Whatever pattern(s) the women have, failure to recognize needs met by offending is likely to result in ineffective New Life Plans. Offenders with approach goals will have no inclination to change their core beliefs about abusive behavior if they believe that consequently their lives will be diminished by giving up something valued and perceived as necessary. The fear of a vacuum of unfulfilled need cannot be overestimated. Those women who already try to avoid the behavior will be likely to fail despite good intentions if unmet needs surface and have no alternative means of being met.

Thorough assessment involves detailed analysis of each individual woman's life and pattern of offending. It involves checking the precursors to her offending to assess which individual or combination of needs is met by it. Some women are very clear about their motivations to offend. Consider the following example:

> Sylvia said it was always when she felt isolated, alone, and lonely and wanted to feel close to another human being without the risk of being rejected that she sexually abused her son. She says that the only person she had ever felt really emotionally close to was her father and that was only during the times when he was sexually abusing her. She said that being sexual with her son was the only "real human connection" she had felt in her adult life.

Most women, however, need more help in understanding their own motivation. When they detail all the precursors, they often describe particular associated mood states. The focus then turns to finding out what triggers these mood states. A trigger can be an internal or external event. Internal events are those associated with a thought about previous experiences that has been a source of stress and distress. Intrusive thoughts associated with past unprocessed trauma from either the distant or more recent past are internal events that the women tell us are often associated with sexual offending. External events are current or recent events that lead the woman to perceive that her needs are unmet, and they are associated with negative emotions that she does not know how to manage.

In considering the needs met by offending, it is important to focus on current needs, with a focus on the past only when it intrudes on the present. For example, in examining the thoughts and feelings present within the mood states and sexual fantasies leading up to offending, it was apparent that the survival mechanisms Marion had used as a child to deal with her own abuse had become dysfunctional and offense related in her adult life. It became clear that Marion was experiencing triggers in her adult life leading to "emotional flashbacks" and the desire to act out sexually.

Marion talked about a low mood state in which she felt "isolated, in a bubble, and wanting contact, warmth, security and sex." Next, experiencing "a good feeling of getting sexually aroused, warming, not in the bubble, not watching" because she was "feeling the feelings." These feelings drew her back into "being real," keeping in contact with herself. She said, "Sexual feelings feel nicer, more comfortable. Sexual feelings are safer than angry ones." The thoughts associated with these feelings were her own childhood abuse. She said she would begin to imagine her own childhood abuse but would then switch instantly to thoughts of her son with herself in the role of abuser. During the sexual acts that were imposed on her as a child, she coped by suppressing her angry feelings in order not to alienate her abusers. She managed to do this by concentrating on the sexual feelings. Sex had become her coping mechanism for dealing with pain. By sexually abusing her son, she was able to meet her perceived needs but maintain power and control over the situation.

Some women are so cut off from their own emotions that they appear to behave as automatons with no understanding at all of any of the precursors to their behaviors. It is necessary to work in some depth on their own history, including sexual abuse history, before they are able to begin to identify the emotional states, thoughts, and beliefs that led to their abusive behavior. It is only subsequently that they can examine the needs met by their offending. The therapists' empathy with the women's abusive experiences plays a vital role in helping the women empathize with themselves as victims and thereby with their own victims.

Finding Nonabusive Ways of Meeting Needs

Work concentrates on helping the women to identify needs met by abuse and how to change their lives so that (a) their basic human needs can be met in other ways, and (b) some of the perceived needs that developed as a result of unresolved trauma can be changed by working through that trauma and learning positively from the past.

For many of the women, there is nothing in their lives, currently, through which they feel they can meet the needs met by offending. Many have had very aversive experiences within most relationships. This has to be addressed by examining their experience and beliefs about relationships. For example, some have become acclimatized to accepting high levels of abuse within relationships while clinging to unreal, romanticized daydreams of possible relationships that doom them to disappointment and failure. Those women who offend primarily or solely with adult partners are sometimes subject to the "Love's Illusion Route to Reabuse." This is described in the *New Life Manual* (Eldridge & Saradjian, in press-b) and matching *Therapist Guide* (Eldridge & Saradjian, in press-a). The women are given exercises to work out how they got into the situation, what made it difficult to escape, and what self-talk and what fears and feelings trapped them further. Was it fear of being alone, fear of losing that person, fear of being caught, or fear of being hurt or even killed? They are asked "How logical was the fear? What ways of escape did you have? What prevented you using them? What could you change about the way you think and the way you act to prevent yourself ever being in a situation like that again?"

In treatment, the women are encouraged to develop greater self-esteem and more realistic expectations of both sexual and nonsexual friendships. In addition, many of the women need practical help to experiment with more positive social interactions and to develop supportive networks. People become part of the "New Life Collection." At first, reliance may be placed on monitoring networks run by professionals such as social workers and parole officers, the support function of which can be replaced by developing social networks, which may include friends and neighbors.

For all the women in Saradjian's (1996) study who had themselves been sexually abused as children, there were unresolved needs related to those experiences and met through the sexual abuse they perpetrated. Almost all of the women who had been sexually abused in childhood reenacted some aspect of that abuse in the sexual acts that they perpetrated. For some, this was a near-exact replication of their own experience but with themselves in the role of abuser. For others, it was a less clear reenactment, such as initially targeting children who were the age they were when their own abuse first occurred—targeting a specific gender of child or repeatedly carrying out specific acts that they had experienced. Children use play to help them make sense of and integrate various aspects of their experience, and at times adults do the same. Their play, however, uses people rather than toys and relationships in which they have adult power. In a similar manner to children's play, the female offenders both created fantasies and reenacted their traumas (Saradjian, 1996).

■■ As a child Stephanie had told her mother that she was being sexually abused by her father. Her mother had told her that she must obey her father. As an adult she became preoccupied with the thought of what her mother must have felt knowing that her husband was having sex with her daughter. She said she went "over and over it" in her mind and fantasized the situation with her own husband in the role of abuser. Stephanie said that she eventually persuaded her husband to have sex with a teenage girl so that she could watch and see what her mother had felt like.

Almost all the women described feelings involving power and control as being related to their sexual abuse of children. Thus, it is important that the women are able to find alternative sources for such feelings. Stopping offending and finding other, more appropriate, and ultimately more effective ways of dealing with their emotions are likely to make them feel more in control. Working on their own issues of victimization enables them to become less troubled by uncontrollable intrusive thoughts and feelings. Learning to be assertive in relationships and solving problems effectively are also ways of improving a sense of competence and self-efficacy. Work on problem-solving strategies provides necessary skills and increases feelings of competence in and control over their world. The strategies and the exercises they have found effective become part of the "New Life Collection."

Managing Negative Emotional States

Negative emotions are functional in that they indicate when needs are not being met. They motivate people to find some way of addressing unmet need and thus reduce negative emotional arousal. However, realistically no one can ever meet all their needs all the time, and thus everyone experiences negative emotions sometimes and has their own ways of dealing with these emotions, some more effective than others. Female sexual offenders have rarely learned to deal with their emotions effectively. When they were not sexually abusing children, either they became very depressed or they were likely to employ other coping mechanisms known to reduce negative emotional arousal, such as self-mutilation, suicide attempts, substance abuse, chaotic sexual behavior with adult partners, aggressive behaviors, and so on. It is now known that all these behaviors release endogenous opioids, which bring about a sense of well-being and calm within a person (e.g., Rodgers & Cooper, 1988). Thus, in effective relapse prevention, it is necessary to help each woman recognize her emotions and deal positively with negative emotional states to prevent her from resorting to such behaviors.

Many of the women offenders react in extreme ways to their negative emotional states because they fear being overwhelmed. Hence, in remaking relapse prevention, we recognized that when this problem is part of a woman's pattern, she needs help in learning how to tolerate such feelings. In treatment, women can reduce fear of emotions by repeatedly practicing identifying those feelings, experiencing them, and letting them go. Some women find it easier to do this if they also work out for themselves the proximal source of that particular emotion. Each time a woman allows herself to have the feeling and let it go, she becomes less afraid of it and more able to recognize that she need not be overwhelmed by it. Through this technique, she begins to feel she can tolerate and express her feelings. Eventually some women are able to apply this technique of feeling it, letting it go, feeling it, and letting it go to manage intrusive thoughts related to the desire to sexually abuse children. Hanson (1998) describes using this approach with certain male sex offenders.

Many other coping strategies have been used to help with emotional regulation (e.g., Linehan, 1993), such as developing a vocabulary to enable the woman to talk about her emotions to others and to gain comfort from this. Linehan (1993) also describes techniques that can be used in crisis situations to try and change the emotion if it is becoming too aversive to let go. She describes using distress tolerance skills such as distracting or self-soothing behaviors—for example, looking at a beautiful flower, picture, or going to a positive place; listening to soothing music or focusing on sounds that are around; using favorite perfumes or having some very relaxing oils such as lavender to smell; eating or drinking something that is special and feels like it is a treat; or having a bubble bath or rubbing lotion onto the body. Linehan (1993) also encourages the use of imagery to mentally create a relaxing scene or safe place or, if possible, to "have a brief vacation" by getting into bed or going out for a period of time to a positive place. If the impulse to act becomes very pressuring, she suggests techniques such as "taking opposite action"—that is, behaving in a way that is inconsistent with the emotion, such as "doing something nice for someone she is angry at, [or] approaching what she is afraid of" (p. 151).

■■
■■ Sandra described how she now deals with her emotions. "I deal with my moods, I
        don't let myself get depressed or angry. I'm calmer, feel different. I don't let
        things wind me up. I work out what it is: sit down and write down what it is, or if I
        can't do that I'll do it in my head. I'm truthful with myself. If it's a big problem—
        I'll clean, paint the house, do anything to change my mood, run round the block,
        go to the park. I find when I'm calmed down enough to work it out I find it's only a
        little thing anyway. I think, why did I get all wound up over it? For example, if one
        of the neighbors is annoying me, I write down what has she done, what have I
        done, what was my reaction to her, how did I treat her? Is it my fault or hers?
        Maybe I need to apologize! If it's not my fault, that's when I have to be assertive
        and confront whoever has offended me in a polite but straightforward manner. I
        used to land myself in trouble all the time because I didn't think. Now I take my
        time to think things through. I'm more relaxed now! I've got some music I really

like. I sit with my headphones on. If I feel low I try to find someone to talk to. My feelings are like going to the center of a ball of wool. I used to back away because I hadn't gone all the way through it. I was afraid of the feelings. Now I've actually gone into that center part, it's easier for me to deal with them."

Challenging Distorted Abuse-Related Cognitions and Beliefs

As with male offenders, targeting abuse-related cognitive distortions is central to creating change. All the women in the study (Saradjian, 1996) had distorted cognitions and beliefs about children and about themselves. Analysis of their life histories clearly shows how these developed. Thinking errors implanted by their childhood abusers and distorted beliefs developed to cope with abuse can be particularly resistant to change. Knowledge gained in analyzing their development can be used to help the women challenge the validity of their current pro-offending beliefs.

Diane was coerced into sexually abusing her children by her husband. Diane believed the following:

1. She could not cope without a man in her life.
2. If only she was good enough and pleased the man enough, he would not beat her or emotionally torture and humiliate her.
3. He (and other men) could not control his sexual impulses.
4. If she was to be a good wife, she should help him meet these needs.
5. Children felt closer to parents with whom they had a sexual relationship.

Diane had been sexually abused by her own father but did not perceive it as sexual abuse. He was the only person with whom she had a close relationship as a child, and it was within her relationship with him that she developed the beliefs that facilitated the abuse she perpetrated, albeit initially coerced into doing so by her husband. Until Diane recognized that her father had sexually abused her and that what he had told her was to facilitate him doing so, it was impossible to challenge her beliefs.

Effective self-generated challenges to her most common abuse-related thinking errors form an invaluable part of the woman's "New Life Collection" and can be developed throughout the intervention program.

Managing Fantasy

Initial research led us to conclude that some female offenders masturbated to sexual fantasy about abusing children, but others did not. However, it became clear that although some may not have masturbated to such sexual thoughts, their fantasies formed part of their thinking and supported their offending. For many women, fantasy seems to be a stage between negative emotion and offending behavior. They describe their sexual fantasies as thoughts that become associated with feelings that make them feel as if they want or need to be sexual with a child. They describe thoughts of their own abusive experiences and coping with the negative feelings associated with those thoughts by imagining similar scenarios with themselves as the perpetrator. They describe thinking of abuse they have or would like to perpetrate and deriving positive feelings from these thoughts. Some imagine graphic sexual or sadistic acts they would like to perpetrate on an adult while they are sexually abusing a child. Fantasy is often an attempt to make sense of experience, daydreaming, wish fulfillment, and mental rehearsal. Covert sensitization is indicated in some cases to break the link between abusive fantasies and positive emotional and physical feelings. When an effective combination of aversive sequences and escape scenes has been identified, these become part of the woman's "New Life Collection" for use as required.

Identifying Emotional and Physical Risk Factors and Matching Coping Mechanisms

Women offenders have identified and related to the concept of emotional and physical risk factors. Physical risk factors are behavioral steps, and emotional risk factors are feelings that are associated with sexual offending. Some women recognize how emotional factors operate faster than physical steps toward offending, almost as an emotional slide.

Susanna saw the emotional slide as a "fast track," the consequence of which she described as "her body beginning to react to her thoughts." She recognized behaviors that reinforced low feelings, like not bothering to get up or to wash. This, in turn, reinforced a sense of being out of control and irresponsible, leading into a sense of feeling like an isolate: a direct precursor to her offending. She likened this to a "snakes-and-ladders" board. When a life event occurred, realistic self-talk took her up the rungs of the ladder to a positive place. Negative self-talk took her not only down the rungs but sometimes onto a snake, which propelled her beyond the bottom of the ladder.

It may be that so many of these women experience emotional slides because events trigger emotions that in turn trigger unresolved feelings related to earlier trauma.

■■ Hannah recognized that one of her emotional risk factors to offending was when
she felt in any way "abandoned" by her daughter whom she had sexually abused.
She described any incident such as the child turning away rather than toward her
when she walked into the room as evidence that the child did not want her. This
distorted thinking triggered feelings related to her perceived "abandonment" by
her mother who had sexually abused her and who she perceived as leaving her
because she, Hannah, had stopped wanting her. Hannah says that when she felt
"abandoned" by her daughter, she "needed" to be sexual with her to feel "one
with her again" and take away her "terrible loneliness and fear."

Remade relapse prevention recognizes that the emotion experienced does
not have to be negative. For example, Brenda, who had approach rather than
avoidant goals relating to offending, talked of risky emotions, including feeling
happy, warm, and sexual. Her only known way of sharing these feelings was to
be sexual with a child. The *New Life Manual* (Eldridge & Saradjian, in press-b)
lists common emotional patterns women have identified:

Misery me: This is a mixture of negative feelings and negative self-talk, including
   self-pity, fear, loneliness, and hopelessness.
I need, I want—you're there! This is a desire for comfort, warmth, security, and
   sex, rather than a desire for a particular person.
Seething cauldron: This is an angry route, often about a desire for revenge on
   someone who the woman believes has hurt her or on the child for having a
   childhood.
The treadmill: This appears to be about boredom, life is a drag, monotonous, no
   fun, nothing worth doing, and no thrills. Offending leads to an increase in emotional arousal. This seems common among women who target adolescents and
   see the relationship as a love affair.
Hypo: This is a "hyped" state in which the woman feels out of control and inclined
   to emotional extremes. She has a desire to indulge in abuse and believes this
   will "bring her down." Thus, she uses offending to calm her emotional arousal.

Emotional and physical risk factors combine to produce offending. Physical
risk factors may be in place but not be acted on until emotional factors are also
present. Even if emotional factors are present, they may not be acted on because
physical factors are not present.

■■ Maria said that for her, emotional risk times were when she felt unloved, not valued, frustrated with her personal life, in need of comfort, not coping with problems, or needing to feel power or to have some sort of control. She said that
physical risk times were when her child was undressed, being put to bed, during
bath times, and changing clothes after school, when no other adult was around
and she had scope to be more dominating.

The women need to recognize both types of risk factors. In the intervention program, they need to develop and practice a range of matching coping mechanisms for each risk factor that work fast and effectively. This includes changing their self-talk to alter their emotional reactions to thoughts and events as well as changing their lifestyles to reduce the number of opportunities for abusive behaviors.

Developing a Positive Abuse-Free "New Life"

Effective relapse prevention is greatly facilitated if the women develop a life in which their sense of "New Me" (Mann, 1998) is inconsistent with sexual abuse. To develop a positive abuse-free life, the women need to improve their self-esteem and confidence. The therapeutic process in which the women experience nonabusive, empathic relationships raises self-esteem. Making sense of life history, including victimization as well as offending, can raise self-esteem. Finding a sense of self other than as a victim or a perpetrator can provide a foundation to develop other aspects of self. This can be done by learning new skills and finding arenas in which these can be developed.

Sally said of her "New Life": "I've had the confidence to go to college, get a part-time job, mix easier with people, I'm not so frightened of my actions, feel more in control, won't make a fool of myself. I can handle myself." She saw sexually abusing her son as a habit and says, "A habit: You gave it the power, you can take the power away. It's something you do for yourself, and if you don't like that you can always stop it. Even though it's hard to stop, you've got to want to stop doing it yourself. I've broken a lot of habits. Habits like lounging around the house not getting dressed until late afternoon. I don't do things like that any more. I've got more self-dignity now. I get myself dressed. I won't sit around the house feeling sorry for myself."

Use of External Monitors

Despite a good "New Life Plan," stresses can become too great to deal with, and steps and slides may be taken down the path to reoffending. The support of others who also know the risk factors specific to that woman and the signs that she is not coping can be vital at this time. Knowledge and shared awareness of these factors can be built up throughout intervention programs that include the "New Life Plan" development as an integral component.

Sandra had the help and support of her social worker, support workers, and a neighbor. These people knew about Sandra's pattern, and she was able to tell them what signs they needed to look out for, which would indicate that she was not coping. She said, "If I let myself go, if I start drinking really heavy, if I let the house go, if I get irritable and ratty, if I can't be bothered, if I don't turn up for appointments on time (I'm usually very punctual), if I can't be bothered, it's about being down and depressed. If I got myself into a state like that, I'd be going back on all the work that I've done in the last 2 years."

As therapists we want to believe in change. We feel good when our clients say the *right* things, seem empathic, and complete the psychological treatment outcome tests showing a positive treatment effect. All of this is fakeable. Ultimately, monitoring behavior is the only real test of change.

Conclusion

Perhaps because there are fewer women offenders coming to professional attention, more individual in-depth work focusing on needs met by offending is carried out with them. Knowledge of these needs can be applied to help the women find more effective ways of changing their current thinking and their current situation—namely, developing a satisfying abuse-free new life. If this work is vital to remade relapse prevention with women, then the same must be true of men.

In our experience, it is easier to put together a support and monitoring group for a woman than it is for her male equivalent. It is easier to engage neighbors and friends, provided she has a social network. This may be because women generally find it easier to develop social networks than men. Alternatively, it may be that people find it harder to recognize and accept that women have sexually abused children and believe that women are more likely than men to be able to change and control their behavior. These may be distortions due to society's view of male and female sexual behavior, and so care must be taken to ensure that the support does not become collusive.

Media stereotypes associated with sex offending foster beliefs in monstrous individuals who are barely human. Public health education programs (Laws, 1998) can be developed to help people recognize and challenge behaviors in those close to them. If we are serious about the importance of positive abuse-free lives, then we have to deal with the way offenders are perceived. It is no good doing great treatment and putting together a superb "New Life Plan" if no one lets the perpetrator live it. Being allowed to live it does not mean putting children at risk: It simply means meeting human needs through relationships and activities that are satisfying and can be accomplished without causing harm.

References

Akers, R. L. (1977). *Deviant behavior: A social learning approach* (2nd ed.). Belmont, CA: Wadsworth.

Bandura, A. (1969). *Social learning theory.* Englewood Cliffs, NJ: Prentice Hall.

Block, J. H., & Block, J. (1979). The role of ego control and ego resiliency in the organization of behavior. In W. A. Collins (Ed.), *Minnesota symposium on child psychology* (Vol. 13, pp. 39-101). Hillsdale, NJ: Lawrence Erlbaum.

de Zulueta, F. (1993). *From pain to violence: The traumatic roots of destructiveness.* London: Whurr.

Eldridge, H. J. (1992, September). *Identifying and breaking patterns of adult male sex offending: Implications for assessment intervention and maintenance.* Paper presented at the annual conference of the National Association for the Development of Work with Sex Offenders, Dundee, UK.

Eldridge, H. J. (1998). *Therapist guide for maintaining change: Relapse prevention for adult male perpetrators of child sexual abuse.* Thousand Oaks, CA: Sage.

Eldridge, H. J., & Saradjian, J. (in press-a). *Assessment, treatment and relapse prevention with women who sexually abuse children: A therapist guide.* Thousand Oaks, CA: Sage.

Eldridge, H. J., & Saradjian, J. (in press-b). *New life manual.* Thousand Oaks, CA: Sage.

Eldridge, H. J., & Still, J. (1995). Apology and forgiveness in the context of the cycles of adult male sex offenders who abuse children. In A. C. Salter (Ed.), *Transforming trauma: A guide to understanding and treating adult survivors of child sexual abuse* (pp. 131-158). Thousand Oaks, CA: Sage.

Emde, R. N. (1989). The infant's relationship experience. In A. J. Sameroff & R. N. Emde (Eds.), *Relationship disturbances in early childhood* (pp. 33-51). New York: Basic Books.

Gilbert, P. (1989). *Human nature and suffering.* London: Lawrence Erlbaum.

Goldsmith, H., & Campos, J. (1982). Toward a theory of infant temperament. In R. N. Emde & R. J. Harmon (Eds.), *The development of attachment and affiliative systems* (pp. 161-193). New York: Plenum.

Haley, J. (1990). *Strategies of psychotherapy* (2nd ed.). Rockville, MD: Triangle Press.

Hanson, R. K. (1998, September). *Working with sex offenders.* Paper presented at the annual conference of the National Offender Treatment Association, Glasgow, UK.

Kohut, H. (1985). *Self psychology and the humanities: Reflections on a new psychoanalytic approach.* New York: Norton.

Laws, D. R. (1998, September). *Sexual offending as a public health problem.* Paper presented at the annual conference of the National Offender Treatment Association, Glasgow, UK.

Linehan, M. (1993). *Cognitive behavioral treatment of borderline personality disorder.* New York: Guilford.

Mann, R. (1998, October). *Relapse prevention? Is that the bit where they told me all the things I couldn't do any more?* Paper presented at the annual conference of the Association for the Treatment of Sexual Abusers, Vancouver, Canada.

Miller, A. (1990). *Banished knowledge, facing childhood injuries.* London: Virago.

Rodgers, R. J., & Cooper, S. J. (Eds.). (1988). *Endorphins, opiates and behavioral processes.* Chichester, UK: Wiley.

Salter, A. (1995). *Transforming trauma: A guide to understanding and treating adult survivors of child sexual abuse.* Thousand Oaks, CA: Sage.

Sameroff, A. J. (1989). Principles of development and psychopathology. In A. J. Sameroff & R. N. Emde (Eds.), *Relationship disturbances in early childhood* (pp. 17-32). New York: Basic Books.

Saradjian, J. (1996). *Women who sexually abuse children: From research to clinical practice.* London: Wiley.

Speltz, K., Matthews, J. K., & Mathews, R. (1989). *Female sexual offenders: An exploratory study.* Orwell, VT: Safer Society.

Ward, T., & Hudson, S. M. (1998). A model of the relapse process in sexual offenders. *Journal of Interpersonal Violence, 13,* 700-725.

Wolf, S. C. (1984). *A multifactor model of deviant sexuality.* Paper presented at the Third International Conference on Victimology, Lisbon, Portugal.

CHAPTER 24

Holism, Wellness, and Spirituality

Moving From Relapse Prevention to Healing

LAWRENCE ELLERBY
JACQUELINE BEDARD
Forensic Behavioral Management Clinic
Native Clan Organization, Winnipeg, Manitoba

SHIRL CHARTRAND
Correctional Service Canada, Saskatchewan

When the Native Clan Organization's Forensic Behavioral Management Clinic began providing programming for aboriginal and non-aboriginal men who had committed sexual offenses in 1987, the primary model of treatment was a cognitive-behavioral approach with a strong emphasis on relapse prevention (RP). The application of RP had much appeal and was heralded as *the* treatment modality for sexual offenders. RP had a credible lineage originating from the addictions field (Marlatt, 1982; Marlatt & Gordon, 1985), and the applicability to sexual offenders was presented in a thoughtful manner by Pithers, Marques, Gibat, and Marlatt (1983) and later in a comprehensive compilation focusing on RP with sexual offenders (Laws, 1989). The model offered what many treatment programs desired: a theory, a language, and a methodology for the provision of sexual offender treatment.

As a treatment program in Manitoba, a province in the Canadian prairies, a large number of the men in our sexual offender program are aboriginal (status and nonstatus Indians, Metis, and some Inuit). This is a reflection of the fact that aboriginal people have the highest arrest, incarceration, and crime rates of any group in Canada and that one in four aboriginal offenders have been identified as sexual offenders (LaPrairie, 1996; LeClair, 1996; Motiuk & Belcourt, 1996). As a result, it has been important for us to recognize the characteristics and needs of this particular client group and in turn consider how to offer treatment in a way that is meaningful, both in terms of facilitating change and in terms of risk management.

In our program's infancy, we were aware that the treatment needs and the intervention process for some of the aboriginal men in our program would differ from what was considered to be state-of-the-art sexual offender treatment, but we had little understanding or appreciation of how or what this would look like. As a result, we relied on the framework provided by the RP model as a basis while we learned and developed our skills and program structure. In this chapter, we discuss the ways our use of the RP model has evolved to be more useful and applicable for our program needs and discuss how the development of our treatment program has been influenced by our exposure to and involvement with Native Canadian teachings and healing approaches.

Beyond a Cognitive-Behavioral Relapse Prevention Approach: A Blending of the Contemporary and the Traditional

To expand beyond the dominant treatment model has been an evolutionary process. In the early stages of development, it was important for our program and for our clinicians to adhere to the recommended and recognized model for the treatment of sexual offenders. As our program matured, the increased level of experience, skill, and confidence among the members of the clinical team allowed us to become more secure, open, and willing to explore alternative forms of interventions and to move beyond a cognitive-behavioral RP approach to sexual offender treatment.

Intuitively, we felt strongly that we needed to be more responsive to the needs of the aboriginal men in our program and that we had to better understand how to design the treatment experience to fit the men we were working with rather than try to fit them into our preconceived notion of a treatment program. To determine if there was support for this position, we examined outcome data from our program between 1987 and 1994. Initially, our hypothesis did not appear to hold up because we found no significant difference in recidivism rates between aboriginal and nonaboriginal men who had completed the sexual offender treatment program. Both groups demonstrated similar low reoffense rates (Ellerby, 1994). However, on closer review, we found a striking difference in treatment completion rates. Although 84% of the nonaboriginal men completed the program, only 42% of the aboriginal offenders remained in treatment until completion. Aboriginal men were significantly more likely to be suspended for breaching conditions of parole, to drop out of treatment, and to commit a sexual offense while in the midst of the program (Ellerby, 1994). This suggested to us that, although the interventions appeared equally effective for those who completed the program, the therapeutic approach was not engaging as many of the aboriginal men.

In response to this and in an effort to determine what type of treatment experience would be more relevant and meaningful for this client group, we set out to explore the role of traditional healing among aboriginal peoples. We looked to native elders and healers for guidance and direction and invited them to become part of our treatment team. As we learned about aboriginal culture, spirituality, ceremonies, and teachings, we found a great deal of compatibility in our philosophy of treatment and in the beliefs that form the foundation of traditional healing among aboriginal people. Our affinity with traditional healing further encouraged us to consider ways of integrating what both contemporary sexual offender treatment and traditional healing offer.

We refer to this integrated approach within our program as a blended treatment and healing approach. We have used the term *blended* because it was important to us that the cultural aspect was not adjunctive to treatment but, rather, an integral part of the program. Although at times it has been difficult, we continue to strive to synthesize the Western treatment and traditional healing models.

By moving toward a blended treatment and healing approach, we hoped to engage aboriginal men into the treatment and healing process and to provide a more effective way of addressing their sexual offending behavior and their risk. Since adapting our program, the difference in completion rates between aboriginal and nonaboriginal offenders has been eliminated. This has meant a significant reduction in the number of aboriginal men who drop out of treatment, who are suspended while in treatment, and who are charged with a new offense during the course of treatment.

We have also found that by learning about traditional healing, we have pushed ourselves to continue to grow as professionals and have become more well rounded as a treatment program. We believe that this evolution has enabled us to provide a higher quality of treatment not only for aboriginal offenders who wish to participate in traditional healing within their treatment experience but also for the aboriginal and nonaboriginal offenders attending our program who are not directly involved in the blended contemporary-traditional component of the program. The lessons learned from the traditional healing perspective—advising of the need to assume a holistic approach to treatment and healing, to base treatment on a wellness model, and to appreciate the necessity of addressing spirituality as an integral aspect of treatment—have permeated and inspired all of our programming.

A Holistic Approach to Healing

In blending contemporary sexual offender treatment with aboriginal healing, we have evolved in the way in which we conceptualize our treatment program and approach. The vast majority of sexual offender treatment programs identify themselves as cognitive-behavioral/RP in their program orientation and interventions. In fact, this has become the expected theoretical and clinical orientation for sexual offender treatment. Programs describing themselves in any other terms risk being met with a quizzical eye and being questioned about the appropriateness and the efficacy of their programming. Although for years we too would proudly, and with a sense of authority, describe our program as cognitive-behavioral/RP, today we do not view our program as being limited to this approach but, rather, describe our theoretical and clinical orientation as *holistic*.

The concept of holism comes from the aboriginal perspective that all things in life are connected and make up the whole of our existence. In a holistic framework, to understand and address various life issues one must always consider the interconnectedness of all things and not maintain a perspective that isolates or compartmentalizes.

This teaching comes from what is called the medicine wheel (see Figure 24.1). The medicine wheel is an ancient symbol in the form of a circle divided into four equal quadrants. The four cardinal points or directions of the circle represent a range of life dimensions and have corresponding teachings. The medicine wheel is a tool for learning about and understanding creation, and it assists this learning process by providing a means of illustrating abstract life concepts. The medicine wheel teaches that, although you can identify separate areas and phases within life, all things lie on the circle and, as a result, are interconnected and part of the whole.

A number of examples of medicine wheel teachings demonstrate the connectedness and integration of life using the four directions along the circle. Some of these teachings include how the four different peoples of creation (mineral people, plant people, animal people, human people) all live together on Mother Earth and depend on each other, how the four distinct and powerful elements (earth, air, fire, water) make up the physical world and must be respected equally, how the plants and animals (these vary depending on the nation of aboriginal people) represented on the four directions symbolize life teachings, how the four symbolic races of people (black, white, yellow, red) are all part of the same human family, and how the four stages of life (childhood, youth, adulthood, eldership) are all connected and evolve (Bopp & Bopp, 1997; Bopp, Bopp, Brown, & Lane, 1984; Ellerby & Stonechild, 1998).

The medicine wheel is used by many aboriginal people and communities to address healing. The circle teaches that in treating dysfunction, healing must also occur in a holistic fashion. In this regard, human beings are described along

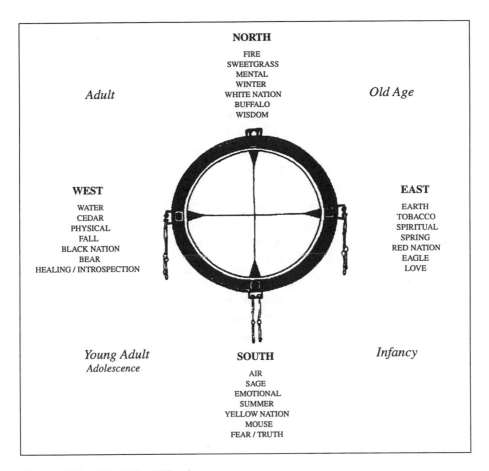

NORTH
FIRE
SWEETGRASS
MENTAL
WINTER
WHITE NATION
BUFFALO
WISDOM

Adult

Old Age

WEST
WATER
CEDAR
PHYSICAL
FALL
BLACK NATION
BEAR
HEALING / INTROSPECTION

EAST
EARTH
TOBACCO
SPIRITUAL
SPRING
RED NATION
EAGLE
LOVE

Young Adult
Adolescence

SOUTH
AIR
SAGE
EMOTIONAL
SUMMER
YELLOW NATION
MOUSE
FEAR / TRUTH

Infancy

Figure 24.1. Medicine Wheel

four dimensions of human nature: the mental, the spiritual, the emotional, and the physical. In a holistic approach to healing, each of these dimensions must be recognized and attended to for a person to develop into a healthy, well-balanced individual. It is the pursuit of balance or harmony among these qualities that results in awareness and recovery (Bopp & Bopp, 1997; McGaa, 1990; Ross, 1996; Warry, 1998; Wyse & Thomasson, 1999).

In addition to viewing the individual as a whole, a holistic model views the person as existing in the larger context of his or her family, community, and Mother Earth. If meaningful healing is to occur, each of these relationships must also be acknowledged and integrated into the treatment and healing process to move toward balance and harmony.

The adoption of a holistic approach to the treatment of sexual offending has contributed to how we view the men we work with, the process of treatment and healing, and the target areas for therapeutic intervention. Applying a holistic perspective requires moving beyond seeing clients as "sexual offenders." Rather, the men in treatment must be recognized as individuals who are more than the sum of their offending behavior. They must be seen as people who are unique (e.g., different strengths, weaknesses, different levels of risk and need) and as individuals who have relationships and connections with others and the world around them that go beyond their identity as that of an offender. In moving beyond viewing and labeling clients as primarily or exclusively sexual offenders to accepting them as human beings whose identities are diverse in their makeup, we are compelled to adopt a humanistic approach to treatment. In this regard, the process of treatment becomes one that is nonjudgmental, nonpunitive, respectful, and empathic while holding the individual fully accountable for his choices and behavior. This approach is the essence of traditional and holistic healing and is the basis of practice for native elders and healers (Ellerby & Ellerby, 1998). It is also a style of practice that we have found advantageous and an important means of engaging men in the therapeutic process (Ellerby, Gutkin, & Foss, 1994).

A holistic approach also suggests the need to address a broad range of life issues to restore balance and, in our context, to manage risk. Although treatment targets offense-specific factors, this is done within the larger context of considering the individual's overall functioning and personal history. In addition, a framework for approaching treatment and healing is provided that extends beyond a cognitive-behavioral approach to also highlight the need to attend to the emotional and spiritual dimensions of the individual within a healing process. In a holistic approach, the objective is to work toward addressing and bringing balance to the four human domains: mental, spiritual, emotional, and physical.

Given the significance of interconnectedness in a larger sense within the holistic model, it also became apparent that it was not ideal to treat the offender in isolation. The program needed to develop so those members of the individual's family of origin, his partner or wife, and his support people and community members could be involved in the treatment and healing process. Also, it was important to extend the supports beyond the confines of the treatment facility and to provide community outreach to assist the men to reintegrate with their community. It is our contention that a holistic approach facilitates client engagement in the treatment and healing process, enhances change, and strengthens the maintenance of change over time and across situations.

A Wellness Approach to Healing

Within aboriginal healing, the process of treatment is shifted from a "sickness" approach, in which treatment is very problem focused, to a "wellness" approach, in which treatment focuses on restoring health and balance. Bopp and Bopp (1997) note that "a sickness approach tends to focus on what is wrong, whereas a wellness approach focuses on building what is needed in order for things to be right" (p. 69). In adapting a wellness approach to sexual offender treatment, a major focus of the intervention becomes attending to an individual's potential and their ability to strive toward growth, stability, health, and long-term risk management.

To some extent, this is consistent with the RP model, which has been described as moving away from a medical-disease model (George & Marlatt, 1989). However, a wellness model is somewhat broader and brings with it a language that challenges some of the terminology associated with RP. Although the concepts are not that different, the connotations associated with the differing language is profound. Wellness provides a positive context for the process of change and risk management. A good example is the axiom "There is no cure for sexual offending behavior." Although this statement is commonly pronounced both in the treatment of offenders and in the education of the public to explain offending behavior and the need for long-term maintenance, such a phrase would not be judged a helpful way of explaining this concept in a wellness model. The connotations for the individual in treatment would be seen to be counterproductive to facilitating growth beyond their identity or label of that as an offender and thus counterproductive to long-term wellness and risk management. The implication of this language for the general public is the potential to incite fear and to create a lack of confidence in and support for the treatment of sexual offenders.

In contrast, a wellness model would communicate this by indicating to both men in treatment and the general public that to manage risk over time, individuals must live a healthy and balanced lifestyle. This means being aware of, monitoring, and managing the factors in their lives that have the potential to contribute to unhealthy coping, a disruption in personal balance, and an increase in risk. Although the concept of the need for ongoing maintenance is the same, the means and context of describing it are quite different. The shift is one from a pessimistic position of "no cure" to a motivating and hopeful stance asserting the "importance of and need to maintain wellness." The shift is one from focusing primarily on the prevention of a relapse to the overall healing of the individual. This perspective is also consistent with the notion that approach goals, being "well" in this case, are easier to achieve and are associated with more positive affective states than is the case with avoidance goals (Ward & Hudson, 1998b).

It has been our experience that the majority of men in our program have responded very well to a wellness orientation. For many, attending to what is needed to be well is a new perspective because historically they have encountered negative and punitive attitudes from others and been told what is wrong and what not to do. We have found this positive approach beneficial in engaging and motivating men in therapy, thus significantly reducing resistance and control issues.

Adopting a wellness approach does not mean "getting soft" with men who have offended. They are held accountable for their behavior and their choices, must identify and address offense precursors and risk factors, and have limits set to support the management of high-risk situations (e.g., not being alone with children, not picking up hitchhikers). All of this, however, is done within a larger context of working toward overall wellness. In addition, this approach is not naive and certainly acknowledges that some individuals are so damaged and defended that they are unwilling or unable to move toward wellness. These individuals are considered to be at high risk and must be responded to accordingly. In addition, some individuals do not respond to this orientation and its associated language. In these cases, we more closely follow aspects of the RP framework. Overall, however, a wellness approach supports offenders to address their deficit areas and risk factors and to move toward living a more balanced life without labeling them as perpetually sick or dangerous.

One of the challenges in working within a wellness perspective with elders and healers has been communication related to high-risk and high-need individuals. In a traditional model of healing, there is a reluctance to speak about an individual's weaknesses and problem areas or to raise concerns one may have about the individual (Ellerby & Stonechild, 1998). This is sometimes viewed as a breach of confidence, as potentially interfering with the healing relationship, as focusing on negative issues, and as being judgmental. Ross (1996) notes that aboriginal people seldom make judgmental comments and suggests that traditional people would tend to view a reliance on judgmental words as limiting the way in which we understand and deal with the people and world around us. He also notes that there is a greater focus on discussing the relationships of things versus the characteristics. Consistent with this, it is not uncommon for an elder to give feedback such as "He is on the path," "He has fallen off the path," and "He is getting back on the path."

Given the importance placed on the identification of risk factors in treatment and the evaluation of treatment progress to assist in decision making within the criminal justice system (e.g., for sentencing and parole), we have had much discussion about this topic. This issue has accented the importance of blending both traditional and contemporary approaches to treatment and healing and the need to have the elders working collaboratively with therapists. This cooperative and coordinated approach ensures that risk factors and treatment gains are being thoroughly addressed and evaluated in the best way possible while allowing for elders/healers and treatment providers to stay true to their treatment and healing orientation.

Although there are some challenges to a wellness approach, we believe that focusing on wellness is profoundly powerful to the individual. The message men in treatment receive is that if they work toward balance in their lives, healing and wellness are both possible and probable. By virtue of following a path toward balance, individuals become more aware and healthy—attributes that place them in a better position to both manage their risk and live a more prosocial, healthy, and satisfying quality of life.

The Role of Spirituality in Healing

Typically, the process of therapy and spirituality are viewed as separate enti-
ties having distinct roles. The separation of treatment and spiritual care is
particularly evident with forensic clients, including sexual offenders. Often,
offender treatment is seen to be provided by clinicians who focus on addressing
criminogenic risk factors. Spiritual care, on the other hand, tends to be viewed
as a "soft" form of support, unrelated to risk management, provided by well-
meaning but often ill-informed and naive spiritual leaders.

Early in the development of our treatment program, we too argued that, although spiritual care might be an important adjunct support for offenders, spirituality did not have a place within sexual offender treatment. As a result of
our involvement with aboriginal culture, traditional healing, and contact with
elders and healers, we learned to distinguish between religiosity and spirituality. Thus, we came to appreciate that attending to spirituality was not only a
legitimate element of treatment, but it was also a necessary component if treatment and healing were to occur in a profound and integrated manner.

In following a holistic approach, equal attention must be given to the mind,
body, emotion, and spirit. In an aboriginal approach, spirituality provides the
foundation of all healing. Renault and Freke (1996) nicely capture the essence of why this is so: "We are not human beings on a spiritual journey.
We are spiritual beings on a human journey" (p. 28). The exploration of self
and the process of personal growth are intrinsically linked to the spiritual
domain.

When discussing the importance of spirituality as part of the treatment and
healing process, we are not talking about religious affiliation or preaching
about faith. We simply see a need to acknowledge one's spiritual dimension, to
recognize the need for spiritual nurturing, and to be open to supporting individuals to nourish their spirit using the rituals, symbols, teachings, and ceremonies
that are meaningful to them. Consideration of the spiritual domain facilitates
moving beyond the intellectual and superficial to exploring deep-rooted emotional issues and core beliefs.

Although spirituality and spiritual care have not typically been identified as
a serious component of sexual offender treatment, there is growing interest in
the role and significance of spiritual care in general psychotherapy (Cornett,
1998; Pargament, 1997). The importance and relevance of addressing spirituality in sexual offender treatment, through the involvement of elders, traditional teachings, and ceremony for aboriginal men, have been previously noted
(Ellerby, 1994; Ellerby & Ellerby, 1998; Ellerby & Stonechild, 1998; Fournier
& Crey, 1997; Wyse & Thomasson, 1999).

Attending to the spiritual dimension of individuals in sexual offender treatment is viewed as particularly relevant in considering the evolution of RP
because, in our opinion, the spiritual component of healing is most strongly

associated with long-term maintenance of lowered risk as this healing goes beyond targeting high-risk factors and situations to addressing the underlying trauma from which these contributing and risk factors have their origins.

The Process of Healing

All too often, the focus of treatment programs is on program content, but much less attention is given to the process of delivering the programming. This is likely the case because it is much easier to describe, implement, and measure the content of a program than its process. In addition, when faced with the need to respond to a social problem by developing programs to intervene, many funders, organizations, administrators, program directors, and treatment providers want to find the "treatment recipe" that provides them with direction on what to do and what content to include. As described earlier, RP provides a theory, language, and methodology for sexual offender treatment. This is both a strength and a challenge for the model. The advantage is that RP has provided a guide and direction for clinicians to work with. The potential difficulty is in how treatment providers may choose to implement the model. Given the framework provided, there may be and has been a tendency to adopt and deliver a highly structured psychoeducational RP approach to treatment.

In providing treatment to aboriginal men who have committed sexual offenses, we have learned that this style of intervention is less useful and that attending to the process of the intervention is crucial to deliver effective programming. In this regard, we have found that the means of addressing a particular topic area (e.g., self-disclosure and accountability, identifying offense precursors and risk factors, developing risk management strategies) is every bit as important as the topic itself. As a result, to further our ability to engage men into treatment, we have moved more and more to an interactive style of therapy that is more process oriented and dynamic, allowing for the inclusion of elements of aboriginal tradition, ritual, and ceremony as part of the process.

Although a process-driven approach is by no means unique to traditional healing, within sexual offender treatment programs providing services to aboriginal offenders, aboriginal healing programs appeared far more process oriented than their contemporary sexual offender treatment program counterparts (Ellerby & Ellerby, 1998). In reviewing these programs and therapeutic styles, sex offender treatment providers tended to approach treatment in a goal-oriented and structured manner and conceptualized achieving the treatment targets as the means of facilitating change. In contrast, elders practicing in traditional programs tended to approach healing in an unstructured and process-oriented manner and viewed the process and means of addressing the treatment targets in healing as facilitating change (Ellerby & Ellerby, 1998).

Interestingly, Ross (1996) also described noting a more process-oriented style among aboriginal people and in a traditional healing process.

In developing our sexual offender treatment program, we have attempted to balance these two positions. We recognize the importance, with all of the offenders in our programs (traditional aboriginal, nontraditional aboriginal, nonaboriginal) to be attentive to both the goals of treatment and the process involved in working toward and achieving them. Although addressing the process of treatment and healing for sexual offenders is beyond the scope of this chapter, some key process issues are a fundamental part of the blended treatment and healing model. These include the composition of the clinical treatment team, the role of a therapeutic alliance in treatment and healing, and the inclusion of traditional healing rituals and ceremonies to facilitate learning and change.

Expanding the Treatment Team

Typically, when we consider the compilation of a sexual offender program treatment team, we think about mental health professionals (e.g., therapists, social workers, psychiatric nurses, psychologists, and psychiatrists). As an extension of the treatment team, Pithers and Cummings (1995) identify the importance of developing collaborative relationships between mental health professionals and probation and parole officers, as well as having other collateral contacts. These types of collaborative working relationships have been noted as important for clinical efficiency and improved risk management to implement the internal, self-management and external, and supervisory dimensions of RP, as well as for therapist self-care, providing a support network to assist in managing job-related fatigue and burnout (Ellerby, 1998; Pithers & Cummings, 1995).

In providing blended treatment and healing, we found other requirements useful to consider in compiling a treatment team. Most important has been the inclusion of native elders. Healthy elders bring with them the wisdom of traditional healing and spiritual leadership. They are able to provide advice and guidance on a range of issues from program development to approaches to treatment and healing to methods of evaluation. Elders have also provided clinical delivery in a variety of forms, among them offering individual counseling (at times as the primary therapist and at other times along with a sexual offender treatment provider), cofacilitating groups (with a contemporary-oriented sexual offender treatment provider), and organizing and performing the various ceremonies that are part of the healing process within the aboriginal culture.

Although one may not typically think of having a spiritual leader as part of the treatment team, elders bring invaluable experience, insights, and approaches to the treatment and healing process. However, there are some fundamental differences in how clinicians and elders work toward the process of change (Ellerby & Ellerby, 1998; Ellerby & Stonechild, 1998; Ross, 1992). Some of these differences are of tremendous value to the treatment process, but others present certain challenges. For example, sexual offender treatment providers tend to be cognitive-behavioral in their theoretical orientation, whereas elders tend to be spiritual-emotional. Sexual offender treatment providers tend to be clinical in their therapeutic relationships with offenders, but elders tend to be more personal and nurturing in their healing relationships. Consistent with this, it was interesting to note that sexual offender therapists often viewed offenders in a guarded and suspicious manner, whereas elders tended to perceive offenders with much more trust and compassion. In describing effective treatment approaches, therapists often described the use of challenging and cognitive-behavioral interventions as important treatment techniques, whereas elders often identified using warmth, humor, storytelling, self-disclosure, and ceremony as important healing techniques.

These comparisons are not to suggest that one style is superior to the other but to simply illustrate the possible differences in practice. When adding new members to a clinical team, there needs to be recognition of the potential differences in practice and clear understandings developed with respect to roles. These understandings are needed both to take advantage of the different skills available and to avoid any problems that result from differences in philosophy that may be incompatible with the needs of the program.

In addition to elders, we sought to include aboriginal clinicians as part of our treatment team. These individuals bring an awareness of cultural issues to treatment and enable some opportunity to provide ethnically similar therapists to clients, a match that may potentially be beneficial for clients (Atkinson & Lowe, 1995).

In adopting a holistic approach, we recognized the importance of attending not only to the offender as an individual but also to his connection to others and to the larger community. It became apparent that we needed to expand the support system into the community. As a result, we have encouraged men in treatment to include people they are connected to in their treatment healing. This could include partners, children, members of their family of origin, extended family members, friends, or other community support people. One member of our treatment teams runs a partner support group so that women involved in serious relationships with the men can be part of their treatment and healing experience. This group aims to provide support to these women and to help them become informed support people by teaching them about sexual offending, risk factors, and risk management strategies. They also have the opportunity to discuss a range of other issues, including their feelings about their partner's offending, coping with a partner's incarceration and subsequent release, discussing their own abuse histories, and addressing a host of relationship skills (e.g., communication and conflict resolution).

The holistic perspective has also meant that we consider practical stressors the men will face, in addition to treatment needs—for example, anxiety associated with release to the community after a lengthy period of incarceration, finding appropriate accommodations, navigating social service systems, budgeting and money management, personal hygiene, developing healthy prosocial recreational activities, and a host of general life skills. To assist this, we employed a community outreach support worker who provides clients with support and skill-building opportunities as part of their overall treatment and healing experience. This additional support system has been particularly relevant for men from rural areas who have been relocated to the city on parole, for those individuals with some degree of institutionalization, and for men with limited social skills.

Cultivating the Healing Relationship

The development of a strong therapeutic or healing relationship is fundamental to the blended treatment and healing model and is an area we have advocated as requiring further attention and recognition within the sexual offender treatment field (Ellerby et al., 1994). Although the significance of the therapeutic relationship has been emphasized in the general psychotherapy literature (e.g., Aponte & Winter, 1987; Kottler, 1993; Pearlman, 1979; Yalom, 1980), this is rarely discussed in relation to sexual offender clients. Blanchard (1995) provides the most thorough account of this.

The traditional approach to healing places great importance on the relationship between the healer and the person he or she is assisting. A relationship based on mutual respect is seen as a prerequisite to the healing process (Ellerby & Stonechild, 1998; Thin Elk, 1995). Within a blended treatment and healing model, a significant amount of care, consideration, time, and emotional energy is expended on implementing strategies to facilitate the development of a therapeutic alliance both on an individual therapist-client basis and in terms of our overall program culture. This investment sets the stage to facilitate the range of treatment strategies (contemporary treatment, including RP and modified RP strategies, and traditional healing) used in our program. It is our contention that establishing therapeutic relationships helps men in treatment feel a sense of acceptance for them as a person, not as an offender. It also creates an environment supportive of taking the emotional risks required to genuinely engage in the treatment and healing process.

Ceremony and Teachings as Part of the Healing Process

Within contemporary sexual offender programming, the primary modalities for treatment include group, individual counseling, and, at times, depending on the program and the need of the client, arousal modification sessions. In a blended approach to treatment and healing, there is a need to expand the interventions of treatment, to provide culturally appropriate programs, and to include ways of healing that are best suited to addressing some of the treatment and healing goals of a holistic approach. In this regard, we have incorporated aboriginal ceremonies and teachings as additional components of our program.

Within aboriginal healing, elders view any opportunity for learning, growth, and healing as a form of ceremony (Ellerby & Ellerby, 1998). As a result, even informal meetings, individual sessions, and groups are seen to have a ceremonial component. Within the blended group program and in individual sessions for some men, more formal elements of ceremony (e.g., smudging, prayer, use of an eagle feather) are incorporated to engage clients in the healing process, to foster a sense of cultural identity, and to create the opportunity for healing through the restoration of balance. In addition to the ceremonial component that occurs within individual and group sessions, additional ceremonies are conducted as part of the healing process. These include pipe ceremonies, sacred circle ceremonies, sweat lodge ceremonies, and fasts.

Although participation in ceremonies is part of an overall healing process and movement toward balance and wellness, the inclusion of ceremonies in our program has had a direct and significant connection to addressing issues relevant to sexual offending behavior and risk management. For example, one of the ceremonies often performed at the beginning of a meeting, gathering, or healing session is smudging. This involves the burning of the four sacred plants (tobacco, cedar, sweet grass, and sage) and using the smoke to smudge as a form of purification. This ceremony is in part directed at opening the individual so that he can participate in the healing process in an open, positive, focused, and genuine manner. As a result, this sets a high expectation in terms of the individual's level and quality of participation as they commence an individual or a group session.

In a similar vein, symbols such as an eagle feather or talking stone may be held during a healing process to bring strength and to facilitate openness and honesty. This is a powerful ritual in facilitating self-disclosure and accountability, both in supporting and directing people to be open and honest when discussing their personal and offending histories. One of the most important and sacred ceremonies is the sweat lodge (for a description, see Ellerby & Stonechild, 1998; Ross, 1992). Within the lodge, individuals are expected to be open and honest and to speak to the Creator about why they have come to the ceremony and to ask for help in healing. The men in treatment typically respond very well to this. The level of openness and sharing that occurs within this ceremony is often quite striking. In addition, the type of discussion and disclosure, both in content and in form, is typically very emotional.

Within the lodge, many different teachings may be given, and the elders will ask the participants to talk and pray about different issues in their lives. Elders in the blended program focus not only on general issues but also on issues specific to inappropriate sexual behavior. In this regard, men are asked to talk about the impact of their offending on their victims, on their families, and on their communities. During this process, they receive teachings; learn about the hurt they have caused and the need to be empathic, the importance of caring and respect, the significance of striving toward wellness and not reoffending; and pray for the recovery of those they have affected.

During the sweat lodge ceremony, issues related to identifying and addressing offense precursors and risk factors are also attended to. For example, sharing has included issues such as anger, self-centeredness, deviant sexual fantasies, and distorted thoughts about women and children. The elders provide teachings and prayers within the lodge that address ways of coping with these feelings and methods for challenging and correcting unhealthy thoughts and behaviors.

In addition, involvement in ceremony facilitates the men's level of participation in other components of his treatment and healing experience. For example, it is not uncommon for men in our institutional programs to be quite guarded and invested in denial and minimization during the beginning stages of treatment. We have seen that those individuals who participate in the sweat lodge ceremonies and who are working with the elder are often able to fairly quickly enhance their level of self-disclosure and accountability within the group process. Thus, involvement in traditional ceremonies facilitates men's participation in more contemporary aspects of the program.

It is also noteworthy that, on occasion, the sexual offender therapists also attend the sweat lodge ceremonies. During these times they have dual roles, both as a participant and as a guide who can also speak to the issues being addressed. The participation of therapists in ceremonies allows for greater blending of interventions and strengthening of therapeutic relationships.

A variety of sources describe the way in which ceremonies are used as an integral part of healing (e.g., Black Elk & Lyon, 1990; Hammerschlag, 1988; Kalweit, 1992; McGaa, 1990; Renault & Freke, 1996; Ross, 1992) and specifically in sexual offender treatment (Ellerby & Ellerby, 1998; Ellerby & Stonechild, 1998; Williams, Vallee, & Staubi, 1997).

Many teachings within the aboriginal culture are relevant to general personal growth and particularly applicable to sexual offender treatment. Some examples of the teachings elders have incorporated into the blended treatment and healing approach include focusing on history (e.g., the impact of colonialism and of the residential school system), culture (e.g., medicine wheel, spirituality, the importance of Mother Earth), and personal identity (who am I and what is my place in the world)—issues that are seen as providing the fundamental foundation on which to build toward wellness. Other important teachings are about honesty and truth, responsibility, respect (particularly for women and children), humility, trust, and kindness.

We have asked men participating in healing programs what teachings they have received and what issues they have worked on in their involvement with elders and through traditional ceremonies and teachings. A range of important issues was identified:

> becoming more willing to learn and to heal,
>
> becoming connected to their feelings,
>
> developing their spirituality,
>
> talking about their problems,
>
> having a better understanding of themselves and their behavior,
>
> reducing their experience of anger,
>
> addressing their victimization,
>
> learning self-control,
>
> learning to "think clearer,"
>
> becoming more positive,
>
> becoming more responsible,
>
> having a greater level of respect in their lives and a greater respect for women,
>
> learning about how to care (about themselves and others),
>
> learning to become more trusting,
>
> developing closer relationships with family,
>
> having a greater sense of hope,
>
> developing a sense of pride,
>
> feeling more at peace with themselves and their lives. (Ellerby & Ellerby, 1998)

Although the teachings and issues identified by elders and the men in traditional healing are certainly important general concepts in living a healthy and balanced lifestyle, the applicability for men who have engaged in inappropriate sexual behavior is evident. All of these teachings are seen to have relevance in addressing the treatment and healing needs of sexual offenders, and the majority of these are clearly related to moving toward wellness and long-term risk management.

The inclusion of ceremonies and teachings as part of the sexual offender treatment program accomplishes a number of goals. First, treatment and healing are framed in a meaningful context that engages men into the process. Second, it demonstrates a recognition of and respect for aboriginal culture and healing. This modeling of respect, openness, support, flexibility, and a willingness to accommodate the needs of the men in the program is seen to have been a powerful motivator, as further facilitating engagement, and as demonstrating the healthy styles of interpersonal interactions that we are trying to promote. Also, by blending the contemporary and traditional, the men in treatment gain the best of both worlds. They are challenged to understand their personal histories, the factors contributing to their offending, and future risk factors, and they strive toward wellness from a positive-oriented, cognitive-behavioral, and emotional-spiritual framework.

Reconceptualizing RP Concepts

The Language of Treatment

In the development of the blended treatment and healing program, we found a need to move away from the language and terminology of the RP model. Although the language of RP has been described as professionally neutral and as facilitating communication among treatment providers and between clinicians and corrections professionals about issues surrounding sexual offender treatment, case management, and supervision (Pithers & Cummings, 1995), we have found it to be an obstacle for many of the men in our program.

The language of RP has been problematic for a few reasons. For many of the aboriginal men, English is their second language, and for some of the men in treatment, literacy is an issue. For these individuals, terms such as *seemingly unimportant decision, problems with immediate gratification, abstinence violation effect, lapse,* and *relapse* are befuddling. The terminology, rather than the concepts, does not hold much meaning in their everyday lives and seems to do little to help them understand their offending behavior.

For those who are able to comprehend the RP terminology and provide eloquent descriptions of these concepts and how they are related to themselves and their offending, we have often been left feeling cautious about their degree of understanding rather than confident that they had mastered the RP model. In our experience, it has not been unusual for men to provide what appeared to be well-practiced definitions and descriptions that were more a reflection of memory and superficial insights rather than a thorough understanding of their relapse process.

We felt that by avoiding the jargon associated with the RP model while maintaining some of the concepts, our clients would not be in the position of having difficulty with the language, and we would reduce the likelihood of them memorizing terminology to satisfy the therapist. Moving away from this language also placed more of an emphasis on understanding, integrating, and internalizing the information and concepts that are the focus of treatment. Finally, much of the terminology and the connotations associated with the language of RP are negative. In contrast, reframing the concepts with language associated or consistent with a holistic and wellness approach provides for a more positive and motivating framework for treatment and healing.

Expanding the Offense Cycle

Identifying a sequence of offense precursors in an effort to enhance the ability to monitor, manage, and intervene has been a hallmark of the RP model. Over the years, there have been different conceptualizations about how to think about and illustrate pathways to offending (Bays & Freeman-Longo, 1989; Nelson & Jackson, 1989; Pithers, Cummings, Beal, Young, & Turner, 1989; Ward & Hudson, 1998a, 1998b; Ward, Hudson, & Keenan, 1998; Ward, Louden, Hudson, & Marshall, 1995).

In considering how best to provide a framework for understanding the precursors to sexual offending so that they can be monitored, identified, and managed, we felt it was necessary to illustrate the pathways to offending in a simple, easy-to-understand format that would be meaningful to the men in treatment. To this end, we developed an offense cycle that consisted of two connected cycles: an unhealthy life cycle and a crime cycle (see Figure 24.2) (Ellerby, 1993, 1996). This cycle is relatively straightforward and fits our work with aboriginal offenders. It is depicted in the form of a circle, an important concept in traditional healing, and is consistent with a holistic approach in that it illustrates the connectedness of an individual's overall functioning and coping (unhealthy life cycle) and the more immediate offense precursors (crime cycle).

In reviewing this offense cycle, the outer unhealthy life cycle consists of emotions, negative styles of thinking, and destructive behaviors or coping strategies. The emotions identified within this cycle are those feelings (both negative and positive) that contribute to unhealthy coping if not managed appropriately (e.g., worthlessness, loneliness, rejection, anger, resentment, shame, overconfidence, feelings of being superior or untouchable). Negative thinking within the unhealthy life cycle refers to negative self-statements and self-talk that typically involve the individual maintaining negative thoughts about themselves (e.g., "I am no good," "I am stupid," "I'm ugly"), about others (e.g., "Nobody likes me," "People don't understand me," "You can't trust people," "I'll show them"), or about the world around them (e.g., "Life's not fair"). It may also includes negative and distorted attitudes and beliefs (e.g., "My way or the highway," "Women are there to be used," "Why should I care about others?"). At times, there is some overlap between the negative thinking in the unhealthy life cycle and cognitive distortions in the crime cycle, but for the most part, negative thoughts are not as offense specific as cognitive distortions.

Destructive coping within the unhealthy life cycle identifies the range of ways in which an individual attempts to cope with his or her feelings and thoughts in unproductive and counterproductive ways. Rather than only focusing on the behaviors immediately connected to the sexual offending, we have found it beneficial to detail the range of a client's destructive behavior and coping styles

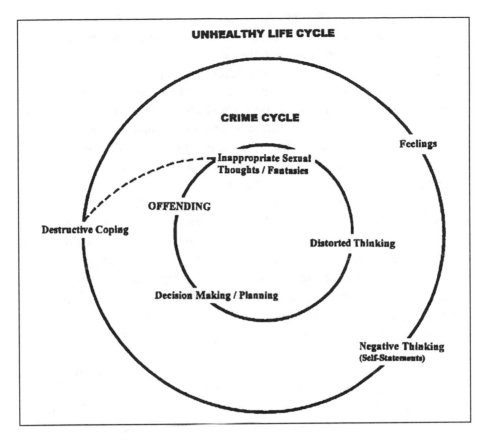

Figure 24.2.   Offense Cycle

(e.g., withdraw/isolate, suppress feelings, playing a role, substance abuse, controlling behaviors, aggressive behaviors, maintaining unhealthy relationships). This is important because the feelings and negative thinking that are offense precursors are also typically precursors to a variety of other forms of unhealthy behaviors. By identifying these destructive forms of coping, we highlight cycles within the cycle for sexual offending. Within a holistic approach to treatment and healing, these other deficit areas, which may or may not be directly connected with inappropriate sexual behavior, are identified as relevant areas for intervention.

In leading up to an offense, a transition is made from the unhealthy life cycle to the crime cycle. It is not necessary that an individual immediately proceed from one cycle into the next. When this transition occurs is determined by a variety of factors, but in our experience, the integral linking point into the inner crime cycle is the experience of inappropriate sexual thoughts or fantasies. This type of imagery is seen to represent a form of coping that moves from a general style of unhealthy behavior to a destructive coping strategy specifically associated with sexual offending. At this point, we loosely follow the sequence of precursors identified by Pithers et al. (1989), with fantasy being followed by cognitive distortions, planning, and then acting out.

There are some important theoretical and clinical points to be aware of and consider associated with how this cycle is conceptualized and used in our program. First, this cycle is designed to provide a framework for identifying factors that, when out of balance, can lead to unhealthy coping and increase the risk for reoffending. The cycle, as we use it, is not fixed or rigid. Although feelings, thoughts, behaviors, fantasies, distortions, planning, and acting out are ordered around the circle, there is no predetermined order to the process. An individual's experience of how he moves through the cycle or where he is in the cycle may vary. Also, this framework does not assume to describe the decision-making process or the pathways associated with the cycle that facilitates the avoidance of an offense versus relapse. Although a holistic approach would assert the need to consider multiple pathways to offending, consistent with the self-regulatory perspective (Ward & Hudson, 1998b; Ward et al., 1998), a traditional perspective would not define concrete pathways because of the complex, ever-changing interdependencies involved and the dynamic nature of the process (Ross, 1996).

Because this cycle illustrates a framework and is flexible in considering diversity within individuals and within various processes of offending, it is important clinically to be used in a very process-oriented manner. This allows for exploration of the factors pertinent to the individual and encourages a more in-depth and integrated understanding of the process.

Over the years of using this cycle, we have found it to be a helpful tool in a number of ways. Men in treatment have been able to quickly understand and identify with the process as it is illustrated. Also, they are able to see that there are a number of points, both along the unhealthy life cycle and crime cycle, at which they can intervene and break out of the cycle. Finally, this conceptualization helps men to appreciate the importance of managing their lives in a healthy manner and to clearly see how not coping with emotions, not challenging negative thinking, and engaging in destructive coping can easily lead them back into the inner crime cycle. This accents the need for the long-term maintenance of healthy coping strategies and the importance of wellness.

The Wellness Plan

A central feature of RP in sexual offender programs has been the development of the plan that outlines the coping strategies that have been identified and developed in treatment to assist the offender to avoid or manage their risk factors. This blueprint for risk management is referred to by various names such as a maintenance manual, control plan, and relapse prevention plan. Although the layout and format of these plans may vary, the objective is the same.

Although the development of RP plans has always been a component of our treatment program, we have experimented with different ways of constructing them so they would be clear and formatted in a manner that would enhance their practical utility, both for the client and for external supports such as probation or parole officers and community support people. For example, we wanted RP plans to highlight the most significant areas of risk and primary coping responses, rather than being overly inclusive, unwieldy, and so lengthy or complex in design that the men in treatment or their supports did not actually use them. Another concern in contemplating how best to develop a maintenance plan was to balance situationally specific coping strategies with more global and generalized coping responses. Although it is important to identify some very specific coping strategies, we wanted to ensure that men were learning how coping responses can be generalized across a range of situations. In very situationally specific RP plans, we have seen men become overly reliant on matching their coping response to the circumstances identified in their maintenance plan. If they do not learn to generalize the coping skills, they struggle, both in how to respond and in their level of confidence to respond appropriately when situations arise that they have not anticipated. For example, in developing coping strategies for anger and aggression, it is important to not only focus on a specific trigger (e.g., how to manage angry feelings toward your boss) but also to address the management of anger and aggression in a more global sense. This ensures that skills are developed to manage anger and aggression across situations, regardless of who the target is or what the anger was a result of.

Recently, we again turned to the teachings associated with aboriginal healing in an attempt to find ideas for reconceptualizing maintenance planning. We found that the concepts discussed earlier of holism, balance, and wellness were applicable for this purpose and have shifted from developing RP plans to wellness plans (see Figure 24.3). Wellness plans organize the recording of coping skills along the four aspects of an individual identified in traditional teachings (mental, spiritual, emotional, and physical).

In developing a wellness plan with a client, we examine what the individual must do within each personal domain to manage both his risk and his life in a healthy, balanced way. For example, in considering wellness in the physical domain, coping strategies can include behaviors that avoid and manage risk, as well as caring for and respecting one's body. These coping strategies include both offense-specific strategies (e.g., not being alone with children, not frequenting places where children are likely to congregate) and more general but relevant coping strategies (e.g., abstaining from consuming alcohol or drugs, attending to personal hygiene, and having proper sleep, exercise, and diet). In the mental domain, coping skills might include the use of thought-stopping and self-talk strategies. For example, this could include challenging and replacing negative self-talk and the use of positive self-talk, challenging and replacing distorted thoughts, and stopping or changing inappropriate thoughts and

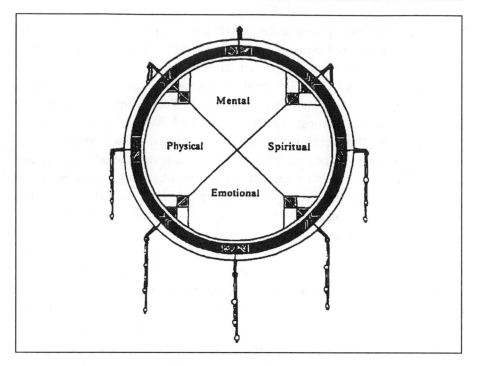

Figure 24.3.   Wellness Plan

fantasies (e.g., thoughts and fantasies with inappropriate sexual, aggressive, or revenge content). The emotional domain of wellness focuses on coping skills related to being aware of, recognizing, monitoring, understanding, and managing various emotions as they arise within a range of life situations and experiences.

Developing coping responses related to the spiritual domain has been the newest component of maintenance planning for us. The responses have been profound and are clearly related to working at an in-depth level in treatment and healing. Within the spiritual domain, coping responses have included introspection, developing a strong understanding of self, being honest and true to self, working toward a sense of peace and acceptance through resolving emotional pain and forgiveness, embracing the concepts of hope and faith, and having a positive attitude. For some individuals, coping strategies identified in this domain have consisted of prayer, commitment to faith through involvement in religion, and including spiritual leaders as part of their support team. For others, monitoring and avoiding tendencies to distort religious tenets are important components of healthy coping in this domain.

Attending to spiritual needs has been particularly critical for a number of the aboriginal men in treatment because this has offered a means for them to cope with and heal from the diverse life traumas that many of them have endured. These have included a range of traumas, including the ongoing effects of colonialism, the detrimental effects of the abuses perpetrated against them by individuals representing church and state through residential school experiences, and contact with missionaries, dislocation, loss of identity, racism and inordinate rates of addictions, and suicide. For aboriginal men participating in the blended treatment and healing program, coping strategies in the spiritual domain typically include involvement in traditional ceremonies and following teachings.

Within a traditional approach, the spiritual domain is the foundation for healing and change, and because it is connected to each of the other domains, it is viewed as the driving force of wellness. This is significant because elders and healers, although not advocating a cure, impart that the ability to strive toward wellness and to implement a wellness plan is always present as the Creator offers a constant source of motivation and strength to draw from (Ellerby & Stonechild, 1998).

As with the offense cycle, the development of a wellness plan is very process oriented. Men in treatment examine the ways they have coped successfully in the past and how the teachings and skills they have learned can help them to strive toward balance in the present and future. How healthy coping in each domain is connected to each other, to risk management, and to balance and wellness within one's self, one's family, and one's community is discussed and explored. Wellness plans are developed over time and are refined to include only those strategies that fit for the particular individual (vs. including group-generated ideas) and that are viewed as being realistic in terms of implementation (good ideas that are not likely to ever be applied are excluded). Wellness plans are developed within individual and group sessions and with the assistance of fellow group members, therapists, and elders. Typically, these plans include a range of both contemporary treatment and traditional healing strategies. Wellness plans are shared with other support people in the person's life. This could include correctional institution staff, a probation or parole officer, family members, and community members.

Men in treatment have responded well to the use of wellness plans. Although the concepts of an RP plan and a wellness plan are quite similar, the connotations for the men in treatment have been different. Wellness plans have been viewed as positive, proactive plans that highlight how various coping skills (offense specific and general) are interconnected. They illustrate the importance of attending to the different domains of balance in one's life and seek to have the individual focus on overall health and wellness in addition to risk management.

Conclusion

As with many other sexual offender programs, the RP model for treatment and the maintenance of change played a major role in our approach to treatment. As our program evolved, we realized the need to move beyond the cognitive-behavioral/RP model. Learning about and attending to the principles of holism, wellness, and spirituality has been an incredible learning experience and an asset, both to us as treatment professionals as well as to the men whose care we are charged with. It is our strong belief that programs orienting themselves around these principles and adopting a humanistic approach focusing not only on the level of risk of men in treatment but also on their needs will find considerable benefits. Although the development of our blended model has been influenced by our contact and relationships with aboriginal offenders and native elders, many of the lessons we have learned and the ways in which we have directed our programming have applicability to the treatment and healing of individuals from all backgrounds.

We have found that this treatment and healing approach has facilitated engagement in the treatment process, resulted in less resistance and fewer control issues, and supported men in treatment to take greater risks in striving toward personal growth. For us, this is what treatment and healing are about. In recognizing the identities and potential of the men we work with, we assist and support them to do the same, a process that is ultimately the foundation of both risk management and wellness.

References

Aponte, H., & Winter, J. (1987). The person and practice of the therapist: Treatment and training. In M. Baldwin & V. Satir (Eds.), *The use of self in therapy* (pp. 85-111). New York: Haworth.

Atkinson, D. R., & Lowe, S. M. (1995). The role of ethnicity, cultural knowledge and conventional techniques in counseling and psychotherapy. In J. G. Ponterotto, J. M. Cases, L. A. Suzuki, & C. M. Alexander (Eds.), *Handbook of multicultural counseling* (pp. 387-414). Thousand Oaks, CA: Sage.

Bays, L., & Freeman-Longo, R. (1989). *Why did I do it again? Understanding my cycle of problem behaviors: A guided workbook for clients in treatment.* Orwell, VT: Safer Society.

Black Elk, W., & Lyon, W. S. (1990). *Black Elk: The sacred ways of a Lakota.* San Francisco: HarperCollins.

Bopp, J., & Bopp, M. (1997). *Responding to sexual abuse: Developing a community based response team in aboriginal communities* (Aboriginal Peoples Collections Technical Series No. 1). Ottawa: Solicitor General of Canada.

Bopp, J., Bopp, M., Brown, L., & Lane, P. (1984). *The sacred tree.* Lethbridge, Alberta: Four Worlds Development.

Blanchard, G. T. (1995). *The difficult connection: The therapeutic relationship in sexual offender treatment.* Brandon, VT: Safer Society.

Cornett, C. (1998). *The soul of psychotherapy: Recapturing the spiritual dimension in the therapeutic encounter.* New York: Free Press.

Ellerby, L. (1993). *A revised offence cycle: Better understanding the relapse process.* Unpublished paper, University of Manitoba.

Ellerby, L. (1994). Community based treatment of aboriginal sexual offenders: Facing realities and exploring possibilities. *Forum on Corrections Research, 6*(3), 23-25.

Ellerby, L. (1996, October). *Extending the relapse prevention crime cycle: Model and application.* Paper presented at the 15th Annual Research and Treatment Conference of the Association for the Treatment of Sexual Abusers, Chicago.

Ellerby, L. (1998). *Providing clinical services to sexual offenders: Burnout, fatigue and moderating variables.* Unpublished doctoral dissertation, University of Manitoba.

Ellerby, L., & Ellerby, J. (1998). *Understanding and evaluating the role of elders and traditional healing in sexual offender treatment for aboriginal offenders* (Aboriginal Peoples Collections Technical Series No. 18). Ottawa: Solicitor General of Canada.

Ellerby, L., Gutkin, B., & Foss, H. (1994, November). *The role of therapeutic alliance in the treatment of sexual offenders.* Paper presented at the 13th Annual Research and Treatment Conference of the Association for the Treatment of Sexual Abusers, San Francisco.

Ellerby, L., & Stonechild, J. (1998). Blending the traditional with the contemporary in the treatment of aboriginal sexual offenders: A Canadian experience. In W. L. Marshall, Y. M. Fernandez, S. M. Hudson, & T. Ward (Eds.), *Sourcebook of treatment programs for sexual offenders* (pp. 399-415). New York: Plenum.

Fournier, S., & Crey, E. (1997). *Stolen from our embrace: The abduction of first nations children and the restoration of aboriginal communities.* Toronto: Douglas & McIntyre.

George, H., & Marlatt, G. A. (1989). Introduction. In D. R. Laws (Ed.), *Relapse prevention with sex offenders* (pp. 1-31). New York: Guilford.

Hammerschlag, C. A. (1988). *The dancing healers: A doctor's journey of healing with Native Americans.* San Francisco: HarperCollins.

Kalweit, H. (1992). *Shamans, healers, and medicine men.* Boston: Shambhala.

Kottler, J. A. (1993). *On being a therapist.* San Francisco: Jossey-Bass.

LaPrairie, C. (1996). *A state of aboriginal corrections.* Ottawa: Ministry of the Solicitor General of Canada.

Laws, D. R. (Ed.). (1989). *Relapse prevention with sexual offenders.* New York: Guilford.

LeClair, M. (1996). *Profile of aboriginal sexual offenders.* Ottawa: Correctional Service of Canada.

Marlatt, G. A. (1982). Relapse prevention: A self-control program for the treatment of addictive behaviors. In R. B. Stuart (Ed.), *Adherence, compliance and generalization in behavioral medicine* (pp. 329-378). New York: Brunner/Mazel.

Marlatt, G. A., & Gordon, J. R. (1985). *Relapse prevention.* New York: Guilford.

McGaa, E. (1990). *Mother Earth spirituality: Native American paths to healing ourselves and our world.* San Francisco: HarperCollins.

Motiuk, L., & Belcourt, R. (1996). *Homicide, sexual, robbery and drug offenders in federal corrections: End of 1995 review* (Research Brief B-13). Ottawa: Correctional Service Canada.

Nelson, C., & Jackson, P. (1989). High risk recognition: The cognitive-behavioral chain. In D. R. Laws (Ed.), *Relapse prevention with sexual offenders* (pp. 167-177). New York: Guilford.

Pargament, K. I. (1997). *The psychology of religion and coping: Theory, research and practice.* New York: Guilford.

Pearlman, H. H. (1979). *Relationship.* Chicago: University of Chicago Press.

Pithers, W. D., & Cummings, G. F. (1995). Relapse prevention: A method for enhancing behavioral self-management and external supervision of the sexual aggressor. In B. K. Schwartz and H. R. Cellini (Eds.), *The sexual offender: Corrections, treatment and legal practice* (pp. 20.1-20.32). Kingston, NJ: Civic Research Institute.

Pithers, W. D., Cummings, G. F., Beal, L. S., Young, W., & Turner, R. (1989). Relapse prevention: A method for enhancing behavioral self-management and external supervision of the sexual aggressor. In B. Schwartz (Ed.), *Sexual offenders: Issues in treatment* (pp. 292-310). Washington, DC: National Institute of Corrections.

Pithers, W. D., Marques, J. K., Gibat, C. C., & Marlatt, G. A. (1983). Relapse prevention with sexual aggressives: A self-control model of treatment and maintenance of change. In J. G. Greer & I. R. Stuart (Eds.), *The sexual aggressor: Current perspectives* (pp. 214-239). New York: Van Nostrand Reinhold.

Renault, D., & Freke, T. (1996). *Thorsons' principles of Native American spirituality.* San Francisco: Thorsons/HarperCollins.

Ross, R. (1992). *Dancing with a ghost: Exploring Indian reality.* Markham, Ontario: Octopus Publishing.

Ross, R. (1996). *Returning to the teachings: Exploring aboriginal justice.* Toronto: Penguin.

Thin Elk, G. (1995). Red Road approach. In D. Arbogast (Ed.), *Wounded warrior: A time for healing.* Omaha, NE: Little Turtle.

Ward, T., & Hudson, S. M. (1998a). The construction and development of theory in the sexual offending area: A meta-theoretical framework. *Sexual Abuse: A Journal of Research and Treatment, 10,* 47-63.

Ward, T., & Hudson, S. M. (1998b). A model of the relapse process in sexual offenders. *Journal of Interpersonal Violence, 13,* 700-725.

Ward, T., Hudson, S. M., & Keenan, T. (1998). A self-regulation model of the sexual offense process. *Sexual Abuse: A Journal of Research and Treatment, 10,* 141-157.

Ward, T., Louden, K., Hudson, S. M., & Marshall, W. L. (1995). A descriptive model of the offense chain for child molesters. *Journal of Interpersonal Violence, 10,* 452-472.

Warry, W. (1998). *Unfinished dreams: Community healing and the reality of aboriginal self-government.* Toronto: University of Toronto Press.

Williams, S., Vallee, S., & Staubi, B. (1997). *Aboriginal sexual offenders: Melding spiritual healing with cognitive-behavioural treatment.* Ottawa: Correctional Service Canada.

Wyse, M., & Thomasson, K. (1999). A perspective on sexual offender treatment for Native Americans. In A. D. Lewis (Ed.), *Cultural diversity in sexual abuser treatment: Issues and approaches.* Brandon, VT: Safer Society.

Yalom, I. (1980). *Existential psychotherapy.* New York: Basic Books.

PART VIII

THE BOTTOM LINE

CHAPTER 25

Maintaining Relapse Prevention Skills and Strategies in Treated Child Abusers

ANTHONY BEECH
University of Birmingham, England

DAWN FISHER
Llanarth Court Hospital, Wales

An issue for any form of therapy is the maintenance of treatment effects after therapy itself has ended. With sex offenders, this is obviously of paramount importance given the high cost of the commission of further offences to any future victims and also to the offenders. In the cognitive-behavioral approach to therapy, treatment for sex offenders is not a "cure" but, rather, a method of learning self-control (Pithers, Kashima, Cumming, & Beal, 1988). As such, urges to commit sexual assaults are not eliminated, and relapse will only be avoided if the offender continues to exercise the controls learned during treatment and is prepared for the fact that there is a likelihood of lapses (i.e., a return to the moods, fantasies, and thoughts associated with the relapse process). Known as relapse prevention (RP), this has become an integral component of cognitive-behavioral treatment programs for sex offenders in recent years.

The purpose of any RP training is to "enhance the maintenance of change of compulsive behaviors" (Marlatt, 1982). The first stage involves a detailed analysis of the precipitating situations, thoughts, and moods that occurred prior to previous offending. Thus, the offender learns to be aware of the "high-risk situations" that have led to his offending. Emphasis is then placed on teaching the offender the skills to prevent further offending. An additional component in RP with sex offenders is the involvement of significant others in any RP plan. Having identified the high-risk situations and any other identifiable precursors to offending, these are then communicated to those in supervisory roles and also to family and friends, as appropriate, who are instructed to report the presence of any of these factors when appropriate.

An ability to describe strategies to prevent future relapse, along with an awareness of risk situations and warning signs, has been shown to be correlated with future success in terms of preventing further offending (Marques, Nelson, West, & Day, 1994; Ryan & Myoshi, 1990). It would seem, therefore, that RP is an essential component of treatment, and it is important to have some mechanism whereby progress in this area can be assessed in a meaningful way. Pithers (1990) has described a comprehensive assessment procedure that involves a range of techniques, including self-report measures, self-efficacy ratings, relapse fantasies, a situational competency test, and an assessment of the determinants of sexual aggression. Although such methods are thorough, they are also extremely time-consuming and are often not practicable given the time constraints faced by those engaged in this kind of work.

Development of the RP Measure

With RP being such an integral part of cognitive-behavioral sex offender treatment programs, the development of a relatively brief but meaningful self-report assessment of RP knowledge from an offender would therefore be a valuable assessment tool. The second author has been extensively involved in devising such an instrument for use in both research and clinical settings. It was originally devised by Beckett and Fisher (1994) to examine the extent to which individuals participating in treatment programs were aware of their own high-risk situations and to what extent they had developed strategies to prevent reoffending. The instrument has recently been extensively revised and now includes a relatively easy scoring system. This version (Beckett, Fisher, Mann, & Thornton, 1998) comprises a number of questions and is divided into two main sections, which examine through a number of questions:

1. The offenders' awareness of the thoughts and feelings that lead to their offending, their willingness to admit to planning, recognition of where an offense is most likely to occur, and the characteristics of the victims they are most likely to offend against. They are also asked about how other people might know that they are at risk of reoffending and their motivation for offending.

2. The strategies the offender would use to cope with risk situations, deviant thoughts and feelings, and potential victims.

The offender is asked to generate at least two answers for each of the questions. The quality of the answers for each question (awareness or strategies) is rated on a 3-point scale as follows:

0—The offender refuses to recognize risk or the need to develop coping strategies (i.e., the offender shows no understanding of any relapse concepts).

1—The offender acknowledges some risk or has some understanding of what constitutes workable coping strategies. But, overall, the quality of the answer is general and unsophisticated and could do with further development.

2—The offender has a clear and appropriate understanding of his offending behavior, risk factors, and relapse prevention concepts or has well-thought-out realistic and workable coping strategies.

Answers are combined to give an overall score for awareness (of risk situations) and strategies (to get out of risk situations). There are nine questions about awareness, giving a maximum possible score of 18 on this subscale, and eight questions about strategies, giving a maximum possible score of 16 on this scale. As an adjunct to these main sections, the offender is also asked about his own perception of level of risk (in terms of the likelihood of reoffending) on a scale from 0 to 10, where 0 is *no risk* and 10 is *high risk*.[1]

As a note of caution about the scoring system as a whole, as Eldridge (1998) points out, "scorers should be trained in the use of the scoring and where possible inter-rater reliability should be carried out" (p. 137).

Measuring Treatment Effectiveness

In a study using the earlier version of this measure, it was found that in a sample of child molesters in community-run treatment programs, such programs appeared to have little impact in the area of RP (Beckett, Beech, Fisher, & Fordham, 1994). Only 18% of offenders improved by at least 1 standard deviation in terms of their pre- to posttest scores. However, it should be noted that data for this study were gathered when RP was only just starting to become incorporated into sex offender treatment programs in the United Kingdom. Plus, those programs that knew of the concept of RP tended to only include it as a brief section at the end of treatment.

More recently, we have been involved in long-term evaluation of treatment for sex offenders in English and Welsh prisons (Beech, Fisher, & Beckett, 1999) and have again used the RP questionnaire. This research was conducted in six prisons, and men were seen prior to entering and after they had completed the program.

The prison program in English and Welsh prisons, known as the Sex Offender Treatment Program (SOTP), was established in 1991 as part of a strategy for the integrated assessment and treatment of sex offenders in the United Kingdom (Grubin & Thornton, 1994; Mann & Thornton, 1998; Thornton &

Hogue, 1993). Currently, around 700 men receive therapy per year on the core component of the SOTP (Offending Behaviour Programmes Unit, H. M. Prison Service, personal communication, 1998), and it is probably the biggest multi-site treatment program for sexual offenders in the world at the present time, running in 26 prison establishments. The program is delivered to groups of usually about eight men, the majority of whom are child abusers. Treatment is delivered by trained staff (psychologists, probation officers, uniformed staff) working within the prison, supervised by a Treatment Manager, usually a psychologist.

The SOTP consists of a number of group work modules designed in line with current knowledge about criminogenic factors relevant to sexual offending (Mann & Thornton, 1998). The central part of the SOTP is the Core Program, whose primary purpose is to increase sexual offenders' motivation to avoid reoffending and to develop the self-management skills necessary to achieve this. The Core Program is divided into 20 blocks, half of which have some focus on RP. The areas covered in these blocks include the consequences of offending, decision chains, the development of alternatives at each of the decision stages, recognition of risk factors and development of effective strategies to deal with these, coping with the abstinence violation effect, and development of an individual's RP plan.

Motivation is developed by undermining the excuses and rationalizations (cognitive distortions) that offenders use to justify their offending, increasing empathy with their victims by creating an emotional awareness of the victim's experience of the offense and by examining the consequences of offending on their own lives to realize the negative effect offending has had. Self-management skills are inculcated by developing the offender's awareness of the behaviors, thoughts, feelings, and situations that increase the likelihood of offending and by teaching effective and realistic RP strategies to avoid, control, or escape from these risk factors.

One of the findings from our research was that in the sample of 77 child abusers seen as part of the project, there was significant improvement in nearly all of the men in awareness and strategies pre- to posttreatment. As a group, these men also evidenced having a truer insight into their problems by seeing themselves at a significantly higher level of risk (of reoffending) after treatment than they originally saw themselves prior to treatment. Although it may seem odd that offenders are rating themselves as being at greater risk of reoffending following treatment than prior to treatment, this observation is actually positive. Prior to treatment, offenders are typically defensive and denying, and many refuse to consider that they could pose a risk in the future. Therefore, a primary target of treatment is to enable offenders to acknowledge that they could reoffend. This awareness would then appear to motivate them to learn sensible strategies and to be willing to put them into practice.

Treatment effectiveness was also assessed by looking at change in a number of other areas, including denial, pro-offending attitudes, and social competence (see Beech et al., 1999, for these). Change was measured in terms of pre-post comparisons using statistical techniques as well as on an individual basis, which will be reported here. This is because not all offenders necessarily improve through treatment. Some offenders may stay the same, and some may actually get worse; so just looking at pre-post comparisons using statistical tests obscures this effect.

There has been a lot of work on the development of assessing individual change in psychotherapy outcome research using "clinically significant change" (see Hansen & Lambert, 1996, for review). This approach was used here to examine whether each offender had shifted significantly in his attitudes following treatment (i.e., whether his responses had moved from a range of scores more likely to be found among child abusers to a range of scores more likely to be found in nonoffenders) and whether any measured change was statistically reliable. The actual methodology is somewhat involved, but the full analysis can be found in Beech et al. (1999).[2]

Comparisons reported below are in terms of men who changed in terms of pro-offending attitudes from "offender responses" to "nonoffender responses" following treatment compared to those who had not changed. The scales that were used to measure change in pro-offending attitudes were as follows.

Cognitive Distortions Scale (from the Children and Sex Questionnaire; Beckett, 1987)

This scale is designed to measure the extent to which abusers portray their victims as in some way responsible for encouraging or initiating sexual contact and able to give consent. This scale, as have the other two scales reported below, has been extensively validated in offender and nonoffender populations.[3]

Victim Empathy Distortions Scale (Beckett & Fisher, 1994). This scale measures an offender's understanding of the effect that his abuses have had on his own victim(s) and how the victim(s) felt about such sexual contact.

Emotional Identification With Children Scale (from the Children and Sex Questionnaire; Beckett, 1987). This scale determines the emotional significance of children to the offender.

Therapeutic improvement was taken to have occurred when there was a decrease in these measures such that scores for an individual offender fell within a nonoffender range of responding after treatment. Using this procedure, a "treated sample" was identified. This treated sample consisted of 69% of the sample (53 out of 77 men). These were men who had improved in terms of the distorted thinking they used to justify their offending (decreased cognitive distortions), had increased insight into the effect their offending had had on their own victims (increased victim empathy), and, in pedophiles, had a decreased

TABLE 25.1 Comparison of RP Scores for the Treated and the Untreated Groups
Pre- to Posttreatment

	Pretreatment	*Posttreatment*	*Significant*
Treated group			
Awareness	4.53 (5.14)	11.32 (5.04)	Yes
Strategies	4.26 (4.46)	10.63 (4.43)	Yes
Risk	0.42 (0.84)	0.63 (0.83)	Yes
Untreated group			
Awareness	5.50 (5.09)	11.18 (4.47)	Yes
Strategies	5.14 (3.99)	9.59 (4.09)	Yes
Risk	0.62 (0.92)	0.62 (0.91)	No

NOTE: Standard deviation shown in parentheses.

level of identification with children (decreased emotional congruence). In comparison, the other 24 men showed no change on these measures. These men were termed the *untreated sample.*

In terms of change on the RP measure, both treated and untreated groups showed significant change on both awareness and strategies, suggesting that both groups had worked hard on identifying high-risk situations and the genera- tion of (sensible) strategies to deal with such high-risk situations. The mean scores for these two groups are shown in Table 25.1 together with an indication of whether the change was statistically significant. The figures in parentheses are standard deviations and basically reflect the spread of scores on the measures.

Interestingly, it can be seen from Table 25.1 that it was only in the treated sample that there was a statistically significant increase in level of risk (of reoffending) pre- to posttreatment. Level of risk in the untreated sample re- mained at the same level, showing no change at all. This latter result suggested that the untreated sample had not taken on board the messages of treatment (i.e., that they will always be at risk).

Long-Term Follow-Up Using the RP Measure

A further objective of the research was to retest offenders some time after treat- ment had ended to measure whether the treatment effects were maintained. This was considered an important part of the study because testing immediately following treatment obviously partly reflects the motivation and enthusiasm that, it is hoped, have been engendered during the treatment program. Also, by retesting a considerable period after treatment had finished, we thought it would be possible to see how much of the posttreatment gains had been retained. Here it was felt that these gains would be a truer reflection of how an individual would cope in the future. Plus, it was also possible to compare the attitudes of those who were still in prison compared to those who had been released. The thinking here was that perhaps those who were still in prison when retested were perhaps more able to idealize how they would cope,

TABLE 25.2   Comparison of RP Scores for Treated Versus Untreated Groups at
                 Posttreatment and Follow-Up

	Posttreatment	Follow-Up	Significantly Worse
Treated group			
Awareness	12.71 (4.38)	12.83 (4.35)	No
Strategies	11.44 (4.10)	11.73 (3.66)	No
Risk	0.60 (0.78)	0.60 (0.85)	No
Untreated group			
Awareness	12.19 (4.73)	10.31 (4.79)	Yes
Strategies	11.44 (3.66)	7.80 (4.34)	Yes
Risk	1.10 (1.00)	1.10 (1.00)	No

NOTE: Standard deviation shown in parentheses.

whereas those in the community were being faced with the reality of their situations and were having to put what they had gained from the treatment program
into practice.

Slightly less than two thirds (49) of the men who completed pre- and
posttesting on the questionnaires agreed to be retested 9 months after completing their treatment program. Of these, 36 were in the original treated group, and
13 were in the untreated group. Overall, no significant deterioration had taken
place in the total sample, suggesting that the overall gains in awareness, strategies, and level of risk had been maintained over time.

However, when the group was split into treated men and untreated men, a different pattern emerged. Table 25.2 shows the comparison of these two groups
from posttreatment to 9-month follow-up.

It can be clearly seen from Table 25.2 that the untreated group had significantly deteriorated in terms of both awareness and strategies, although their
own perceived level of risk remained the same. In comparison, the treated group
did not show any change on its scores from the end of treatment to the 9-month
follow-up period. This set of results clearly indicates that RP skills had only
stuck with the men who had shown changes in terms of pro-offending attitudes.
Thorton (November 1999, personal communication) adds further weight to
these findings where he analyzed in detail the RP plans of a sample of me who
had been through the SOTP and had not changed through treatment. Again he
found that this sample had reasonable RP plans at face value, but tended to be
superficial. On close questioning with their men's therapists he found that often
these men had not come up with RP plans themselves, but these tended to be
generated in conjunction with other group members and/or therapists. Thorton
argues from this that as these men did not necessarily own their RP plans these
are less likely to stick with them after the end of their treatment.

Thornton (November 1999, personal communication) adds further weight
to these findings where he analyzes in detail the RP plans of a sample of men
who had been through the SOTP and had not changed through treatment. Again
he found that this sample had reasonable RP plans at face value, but tended to be
superficial. On close questioning with their men's therapists he found that often

TABLE 25.3 Comparison of RP Scores in the Treated Sample
on Long and Short Programs at Posttreatment and Follow-Up

	Posttreatment	*Follow-Up*	*Significantly Worse*
Long treatment			
Awareness	13.20 (3.22)	13.21 (3.22)	No
Strategies	11.42 (4.19)	12.30 (3.18)	No
Risk	0.63 (0.84)	0.67 (0.77)	No
Short treatment			
Awareness	12.13 (5.30)	12.20 (4.50)	No
Strategies	12.43 (2.77)	9.93 (4.10)	Yes
Risk	0.60 (0.96)	0.73 (0.96)	No

NOTE: Standard deviation shown in parentheses.

these men had not come up with these RP plans themselves, but these tended to be generated in conjunction with other groups members and/or therapists. Thornton argues from this that as these men did not necessarily own their RP plans these are less likely to stick with them after the end of treatment.

Comparing Longer and Shorter Therapy in Terms of Producing Effective RP Skills

Other comparisons were looked at in terms of whether men had had a comparatively short amount of treatment (approximately 80 hours) or longer treatment (160 hours). Comparing the treatment effect between the longer and the shorter groups found that both groups were able to engender a significant improvement on awareness and strategies. From this result, it may seem that running the much longer program, which focused heavily on RP, was unnecessary. However, a closer examination of the results revealed that the picture was more complicated. When the shorter and longer groups were compared at the 9-month follow-up, the results showed that, although there was no significant deterioration in the scores, the men in the shorter program had lower scores than those in the longer program on awareness, and their scores on strategies had also deteriorated slightly when compared to their scores at posttreatment.

However, more interestingly, when treated men who had either undergone shorter or longer therapy were compared, it was found that awareness and strategies held up far better in the longer groups than in the shorter groups. These results are shown in Table 25.3.

It can be seen from Table 25.3 that treated men in the shorter groups actually got significantly worse in terms of being able to generate sensible strategies 9 months after the end of treatment. This result suggests that the longer treatment regime is more successful in making the RP side of training stick.

TABLE 25.4   Comparison of Community/Prison Sample
at Follow-Up

	Posttreatment	Follow-Up	Significantly Worse
Community sample			
Awareness	12.81 (4.46)	10.71 (5.04)	Yes
Strategies	11.38 (4.26)	9.29 (4.57)	Yes
Risk	0.76 (0.94)	0.71 (0.96)	No
Prison sample			
Awareness	12.43 (4.43)	13.19 (3.85)	No
Strategies	11.43 (3.85)	11.71 (3.51)	No
Risk	0.68 (0.86)	0.64 (0.78)	No

NOTE: Standard deviation shown in parentheses.

Comparing RP Skills in Men Still in the Community or in Prison

When the men were split into those who were still in prison at follow-up and those who had returned to the community, a much clearer picture emerged. These results are shown in Table 25.4.

It can clearly be seen from Table 25.4 that those who remained in prison showed no deterioration in their RP scores, but those who had returned to the community had significantly deteriorated on both awareness and strategies. This result indicates how the stresses and strains of the real world clearly had an impact on what they had learned.

When the community sample were split into those who had been on the longer versus the shorter program, it emerged that those men who had attended the longer program showed no deterioration in their scores. Those men who had attended the shorter program, however, did show significant deterioration on their scores on both awareness and strategies. This strongly suggests that the longer program is superior in maintaining treatment effects once men are returned to the community and subject to the stresses and pressures that this brings.

When looking at treated men who had been released into the community in terms of whether they had undergone longer or shorter therapy, even though this was a very small sample of men (eight had undergone shorter treatment and nine had undergone longer treatment), RP skills stuck with men who had undergone longer therapy. In comparison, in treated men who were back in the community, their RP skills had deteriorated. These results suggest that to inculcate reasonable RP skills that will hold up in the community, quite a long dose of therapy is needed.

Summary

In this chapter, we described a relatively quick and easy way of evaluating the extent to which offenders have successfully engaged in the RP part of treatment by using a newly developed questionnaire that assesses offenders' awareness of their own risk situations and use of appropriate coping strategies to deal with such risky situations.

An evaluation of a treatment program for sex offenders in U.K. prisons found that this instrument was effective in measuring changes in RP skills from the beginning to the end of treatment. More interestingly when completed again some months after the end of treatment, results from the measure indicated that only men who had also shown significant changes in other areas typically targeted in cognitive-behavioral therapy (i.e., reductions in pro-offending attitudes) maintained their RP skills. Men whose pro-offending attitudes had not changed, although evidencing good RP skills at the end of treatment, were found to have lost these some way down the line. This was most noticeable among men who were no longer in prison and who had gone through a fairly brief treatment regime.

These would seem to be important findings in that they demonstrate how the impact of therapy is maintained after the end of treatment. Thus, fairly long treatment is needed to make RP skills stick, and reentry into the community has a detrimental effect on the maintenance of these skills. The findings also indicate that men who have genuinely changed in their attitudes during treatment are more likely to maintain their RP skills. Therefore, these men may be in a better position to avoid reoffending than the men who had not changed during treatment and who had subsequently "lost" their RP skills.

These findings also have resource implications, in that they indicate that there is little point in undertaking RP training in short treatment programs or with men who have not demonstrated any change in other areas targeted in treatment. The results also support the need for both maintenance programs to prevent deterioration in the community and follow-up testing to assess current level of RP skills.

Notes

1. The scoring system here is 0 points for no risk; 1 is given if an offender rates himself as 1; 2 is given if he rates himself 2 or above.

2. To assess this clinically significant change, two things need to be assessed for each variable of interest: (a) determining a cutoff point between normal and dysfunctional responding on the particular measure of interest and (b) assessing, if an individual crossed the cutoff point, whether that change was reliable.

The cutoff points were determined in the following way:

$$Cutoff = \frac{(SD^1)(Mean^2) + (SD^2)(Mean^1)}{SD^1 + SD^2},$$

where SD^1 and $Mean^1$ are from data gathered from 81 U.K. nonoffenders (Fisher, Beech, & Browne, in press) and $Mean^2$ and SD^2 from 106 untreated child abusers (Beech et al., 1999).

The reliability of any change (Reliability Change Index [RC]) was determined in the following way:

$$RC = \frac{(posttreatment) - (pretreatment)}{S_E}.$$

Here, any pre-post change is significant if RC is greater than 1.64 for a one-tailed test.
The method of calculating S_E was as follows:

$$S_E = SD\sqrt{(1 - r_{xx})},$$

where r_{xx} is the test-retest reliability of the measure, and SD is the pretreatment standard deviation for the measure in the offender sample.

3. See Beech (1998).

References

Beech, A. R. (1998). A psychometric typology of child abusers. *International Journal of Offender Therapy & Comparative Criminology, 42,* 319-339.

Beech, A. R., Fisher, D., & Beckett, R. C. (1999). *An evaluation of the Prison Sex Offender Treatment Programme* (U.K. Home Office Occasional Report). (Available from Home Office Publications Unit, 50, Queen Anne's Gate, London, SW1 9AT, England, and from www.homeoffice.gov.uk/rds/publf.htm)

Beckett, R. C. (1987). *The Children and Sex Questionnaire.* (Available from R. C. Beckett, Oxford Regional Forensic Psychology Service, Oxford Clinic Room FS39, Littlemore Mental Health Centre, Sandford Road, Littlemore, Oxford, OX4 4XN, England, and from www. homeoffice.gov.uk.rds/publf.htm)

Beckett, R. C., Beech, A. R., Fisher, D., & Fordham, A. S. (1994). *Community-based treatment for sex offenders: An evaluation of seven treatment programmes* (Available from Home Office Publications Unit, 50 Queen Anne's Gate, London, W1H 9AT, England)

Beckett, R. C., & Fisher, D. (1994, November). *Assessing victim empathy: A new measure.* Paper presented at the 13th Annual Conference of the Association for the Treatment of Sexual Abusers, San Francisco.

Beckett, R. C., Fisher, D., Mann, R., & Thornton, D. (1998). The relapse prevention questionnaire and interview. In H. Eldridge (Ed.), *Therapist guide for maintaining change* (pp. 138-150). London: Sage.

Eldridge, H. (1998). *Therapist guide for maintaining change.* Thousand Oaks, CA: Sage.

Fisher, D., Beech, A. R., & Browne, K. D. (in press). The effectiveness of relapse prevention training in a group of incarcerated child molesters. *Crime, Psychology and Law.*

Grubin, D., & Thornton, D. (1994). A national program for the assessment and treatment of sex offenders in the English prison system. *Criminal Justice and Behavior, 21,* 55-71.

Hansen, N., & Lambert, M. (1996). Clinical significance: An overview of methods. *Journal of Mental Health, 5,* 17-24.

Mann, R., & Thornton, D. (1998). The evolution of a multi-site offender treatment program. In W. L. Marshall, S. M. Hudson, T. Ward, & Y. M. Fernandez (Eds.), *Sourcebook of treatment programs for sexual offenders* (pp. 47-58). New York: Plenum.

Marlatt, G. A. (1982). Relapse prevention: A self-control program for the treatment of addictive behaviors. In R. B. Stuart (Ed.), *Adherence, compliance and generalization in behavioral medicine* (pp. 329-378). New York: Brunner/Mazel.

Marques, J. K., Nelson, C., West, M. A., & Day, D. M. (1994). The relationship between treatment goals and recidivism among child molesters. *Behavior Research and Therapy, 32,* 577-588.

Pithers, W. (1990). Relapse prevention with sexual aggressors: A method for maintaining therapeutic gain and enhancing external supervision. In W. L. Marshall, D. R. Laws, & H. E. Barbaree (Eds.), *Handbook of sexual assault: Issues, theories and treatment of the offender* (pp. 343-362). New York: Plenum.

Pithers, W., Kashima, K. M., Cumming, G. F., & Beal, L. S. (1988). Relapse prevention: A method of enhancing maintenance of change in sex offenders. In A. C. Salter (Ed.), *Treating child sex offenders and victims: A practical guide* (pp. 131-170). London: Sage.

Ryan, G., & Myoshi, T. (1990, January). Summary of a follow-up study of adolescent sexual perpetrators after treatment. *Interchange,* pp. 6-8.

Thornton, D., & Hogue, T. (1993). The large scale provision of programmes for imprisoned sex offenders: Issues, dilemmas and progress. *Criminal Behaviour and Mental Health, 3,* 371-380.

CHAPTER 26

How Does Recidivism Risk Assessment Predict Survival?

JEAN PROULX
Université de Montréal and Institut Philippe-Pinel-de-Montréal, Canada

MONIQUE TARDIF
BERNADETTE LAMOUREUX
Institut Philippe-Pinel-de-Montréal, Canada

PATRICK LUSSIER
Université de Montréal, Canada

Last night a 22-year-old woman was brutally raped in Eastmount Park. The young woman, a nurse, was walking home after work when a man, armed with a knife, forced her to get into his car. He then handcuffed her, put a blanket over her and drove to Eastmount Park where he physically aggressed and raped her. Afterwards, the victim pretending to be dead, the aggressor hid her body behind a rock and left. The victim limped with difficulty to a gas station nearby from where she was transported to a hospital. Because the victim had noted the aggressor's car licence number, the police arrested him the following morning. The aggressor, John Doe, was on conditional release in the course of a four-year sentence for a sexual assault against a woman. Furthermore, he had been previously sentenced for another sexual assault. This man was a dangerous offender and it was obvious that he would reoffend! Why was he free? Who must be blamed for this inadmissible mistake? The members of the Conditional Release Commission who had decided to release him, the probation officer in charge of this criminal, or both? An inquiry should be carried out to find out who made the mistake.

—*Local newspaper report, October 1998*

According to this journalist, the prediction of recidivism is an exact science. Consequently, it must be possible to identify which sexual aggressor will recidivate and which one will not. Therefore, if a sexual aggressor reoffends after his release from jail, it is because somebody had committed a professional mistake. If the journalist's premise is correct, sexual recidivism may even be prevented. Unfortunately, the exact prediction of recidivism is an expression of wishful thinking rather than an empirical reality. The scientific studies as to the prediction of recidivism, however, provide information that may be used to improve the accuracy of the decisions of the practitioners who have to manage sexual aggressors.

The aim of this chapter is to review the results of recidivism studies and provide guidelines for practitioners to assess and manage the recidivism risk presented by the sexual aggressors on their caseload. This chapter includes the following sections: (a) methodological issues, (b) recidivism rates and survival curves, (c) static and dynamic (stable) predictors of sexual recidivism, (d) actuarial prediction of sexual recidivism, (e) dynamic (acute) predictors of sexual recidivism, (f) recidivism risk predictors and the relapse prevention model, (g) recidivism risk assessment and management in the community, and (h) future research areas in the assessment of recidivism risk in sexual aggressors.

Methodological Issues

Definition of Recidivism

First, we must define which type of behavior is considered a reoffense. Among the possibilities are the following: (a) a reconviction for the same type of sexual aggression (against a child or a woman), (b) a reconviction for any type of sexual aggression, (c) a reconviction for any sexual offense (a sexually aggressive act or a sexual nuisance crime such as exhibitionism or voyeurism), (d) a reconviction for any violent offenses (e.g., assault, murder), and (e) a reconviction for any criminal offense. According to Furby, Weinrott, and Blackshaw (1989), it is "advisable to define recidivism as the recommission of any sex offense" (p. 8). Although this suggestion seems appropriate, Rice and Harris (1997) noted "that because of plea bargaining and difficulties in determining motivation, the categorization of offenses as sexual or not, is more methodologically difficult than is categorizing them as violent" (p. 239). Furthermore, according to Quinsey, Harris, Rice, and Cormier (1998), "Although overinclusive, violent recidivism is likely to capture significantly more sexual reoffenses than the more commonly used sexual recidivism definition" (p. 129). On the other hand, because the predictors correlated with sexual recidivism and those correlated with nonsexual violent recidivism are only partially the same (Hanson & Bussière, 1998), an undifferentiated analysis of these two types of recidivism is questionable. These two most frequently used definitions of recidivism in sexual aggressors have both strengths and weaknesses, and further studies are therefore necessary to clarify this controversy.

Measurement of Recidivism

The most conservative operational measurement of recidivism is a reconviction listed in police records. Besides these official sources of information, there are also nonofficial sources (e.g., self-report by the aggressor, a report from a social or a mental health professional familiar with the aggressor, and information from a relative, a coworker, or a friend of the aggressor). Police records are the most frequently used measurement of recidivism because they are convenient. Unfortunately, official recidivism rates are "inherently noisy as they reflect police efficiency, the offender's luck and a variety of other uncontrolled factors" (Quinsey, 1983, p. 30). In fact, approximately 10% of sexual assaults are reported to the police, and only approximately half of these result in a conviction (Ouimet, 1998). Consequently, Marshall and Barbaree (1988) have suggested the use of nonofficial records instead of official ones. This suggestion may be relevant for some specific contexts (e.g., the follow-up of sexual aggressors voluntarily involved in an outpatient treatment program) but may not constitute a standard rule for the measurement of recidivism because nonofficial records may not always be available and contain bias as well. Despite their weaknesses, official records are, in our opinion, the most practical, reliable, and valid measures of recidivism in sexual aggressors.

Follow-Up Period and Time at Risk

The follow-up period for an aggressor starts after his release from institutional confinement (e.g., jail, psychiatric hospital) and ends at the time the follow-up data are gathered (Rice, Harris, & Quinsey, 1990). The follow-up period may include a treatment period in the community and a mandatory supervision period (Furby et al., 1989). Because the follow-up period may also include periods when an aggressor had no opportunity to reoffend (e.g., time spent in jail for a nonsexual offense, hospitalization), to obtain a precise "time at risk," we should subtract these periods from the follow-up period (Marshall & Barbaree, 1988).

Predictors of Recidivism

Two types of variables can be used to predict sexual recidivism: static predictors and dynamic predictors. *Static predictors* are unchangeable variables such as criminal history (sexual and nonsexual offenses), age, and demographic characteristics. *Dynamic predictors,* however, are changeable variables; they may be relatively stable, such as sexual preferences, personality disorders, and cognitive distortions (stable dynamic predictors), or they may be rapidly changing, such as emotional states, victim access, and sexual preoccupations (acute dynamic predictors). Static predictors permit assessment of risk status only, whereas dynamic predictors permit assessment of both risk status and changes in risk status (Hanson & Harris, in press; Quinsey, Rice, & Harris, 1995; Zamble & Quinsey, 1997).

Base Rate Problem

The base rate is the percentage of aggressors who recidivate during a specific mean follow-up period. If the base rate is too low, it is difficult to find any statistically significant relationship between the predictors and the outcome (recidivist vs. nonrecidivist) (Quinsey, Harris, et al., 1998). Therefore, in a recidivism study, a follow-up period of at least 5 years is recommended to obtain a higher enough base rate (Quinsey, Lalumière, Rice, & Harris, 1995).

Recidivism Rates and Survival Curves

Answering any questions regarding recidivism rates is meaningless if we do not refer to a specific follow-up period. In a mixed group of sexual offenders ($N = 28,972$), Hanson and Bussière (1998) found a sexual recidivism rate of 13.4% for a mean follow-up period between 4 and 5 years. In sexual aggressors against children (17 studies, $N = 4,483$), the weighted average sexual reconviction rate was 20.4% (range of 4% to 38%) (Quinsey, Lalumière, et al., 1995). Furthermore, the results of a study carried out by Hanson, Steffy, and Gauthier (1993) showed that in child molesters "the rate of reconviction was 5.2% per year for the first six years, and then dropped to about 1.8% per year for the next 20 years" (p. 648). Therefore, although child molesters had higher annual rates of recidivism during the 6 years following their release from prison, they remained for a long time at risk to reoffend.

In sexual aggressors against women (seven studies, $N = 458$), the weighted average sexual reconviction rate was 22.8% (range of 10% to 36%) (Quinsey, Lalumière, et al., 1995). According to Prentky, Knight, Lee, and Cerce (1995), "The high impulsivity offenders were almost three times (35%) (for a follow-up period of five years) more likely to commit a new sexual offense than the low impulsivity offenders (13%)" (p. 117). Furthermore, "group differences in survival rates reached an asymptote at five years for all victim-involved crimes and these differences, and the overall survival rates, remained relatively constant for these offenses over the next 15 years" (p. 122).

Sexual aggressors against children have a lower recidivism rate than sexual aggressors against women (Quinsey, Rice, & Harris, 1995). For example, in a study carried out by Proulx et al. (1997), for a mean follow-up period of 5.3 years (range: 1-155 months), the sexual recidivism rate was 13.0% for child molesters and 21.2% for sexual aggressors against women. Furthermore, the survival curve dropped faster in rapists than in child molesters (Proulx et al., 1999; Rice & Harris, 1997; Sturgeon & Taylor, 1980), but child molesters continued to recidivate far longer than the rapists (Rice & Harris, 1997).

Static and Dynamic (Stable) Predictors of Sexual Recidivism

We have limited the scope of this chapter to the prediction of sexual recidivism because of some evidence that the predictors of sexual and violent recidivism do differ (Hanson & Bussière, 1998; Quinsey, Khanna, & Malcolm, 1998). First, we present two recent studies (Hanson & Bussière, 1998; Quinsey, Khanna, & Malcolm, 1998) that examined recidivism in samples undifferentiated by age of victim. Second, we present the results obtained separately with samples of sexual aggressors of children and with samples of sexual aggressors of women, thus highlighting the predictors that are specific to each type of aggressor.

Mixed Samples of Sexual Offenders

Hanson and Bussière (1998) carried out a meta-analysis of sexual recidivism studies. This meta-analysis included 61 studies carried out between 1943 and 1995 (median = 1989), mainly in North America ($N = 46$) and in the United Kingdom ($N = 10$). These studies provided data on 28,972 sexual offenders (child molesters, rapists, exhibitionists, and voyeurs). Most of these studies did not present separate data for each type of sexual offender, precluding separate analyses. Weighted averaged r was used to aggregate findings of the 61 studies. This method permitted the assessment of the strength of the correlation between a predictor and the recidivism status. For example, a correlation of .30 means a difference of 30% in the recidivism rate between the offenders with a characteristic and those without. Furthermore, weighted averaged r permits taking into account factors that may influence a correlation such as recidivism base rate and sample size. Correlations of less than .1 were considered trivial.

Table 26.1 summarizes the nontrivial results obtained in the Hanson and Bussière (1998) meta-analysis. The best predictors of sexual recidivism are sexual deviancy assessed by phallometric assessment, history of sexual crimes (prior sexual offenses, stranger victim, male victim), psychological characteristics (any personality disorders, MMPI-4 and MMPI-5 scales), negative relationship with mother, and a failure to complete treatment. Among the psychological characteristics trivially related to recidivism are anxiety and depression. These results are astonishing because according to the relapse prevention

TABLE 26.1   Predictors of Sexual Recidivism

Predictors	Weighted Averaged r
Demographic factors	
Age	−.13
Marital status (single)	.11
General criminality (nonsexual)	
Number of prior offenses	.13
Sexual history crime	
Prior sexual offenses	.19
Stranger victim	.15
Female child victim	−.14
Early onset of sex offending	.12
Related child victim	−.11
Male child victim	.11
Diverse sex crimes	.10
Sexual deviancy	
Phallometric assessment—children	.32
Any deviant sexual preference	.22
Phallometric assessment—boys	.14
Treatment history	
Failure to complete treatment	.17
Developmental history	
Negative relationship with mother	.16
Psychological characteristics	
Any personality disorders	.16
Antisocial personality disorder	.14
MMPI-4—psychopathic deviate	.10
MMPI-5—masculinity/femininity	.27
Anger problem	.13

SOURCE: Hanson and Bussière (1998).

model, these emotions are precursors of deviant sexual fantasies (McKibben, Proulx, & Lusignan, 1994; Proulx, McKibben, & Lusignan, 1996) and of sexual assaults (Pithers, Kashima, Cumming, Beal, & Buell, 1988). A possible explanation for these results is that the assessment devices, used in the studies included in the meta-analysis, only assessed relatively stable emotional states such as depression rather than the transitory emotional states (acute dynamic predictor) that are posited by the relapse prevention model. For additional information as to static and stable dynamic predictors trivially related to recidivism in this meta-analysis, see Hanson and Bussière (1998).

Since the data collection of this meta-analysis, Quinsey, Khanna, and Malcolm (1998) have carried out a recidivism study based on a sample of 483 sexual aggressors from the Regional Treatment Center (RTC), a maximum-security correctional institution in Ontario, Canada. Several of the results obtained in this study are in agreement with those of the above-mentioned meta-analysis. Consequently, only the results that are different or those that concern variables not included in the above-mentioned meta-analysis are discussed.

Regarding their criminal history, the sexual recidivists had more juvenile incarcerations and were younger both at first arrest and incarceration than the nonrecidivists. Furthermore, the recidivists had inflicted more injuries to their victims than had the nonrecidivists. In the meta-analysis, however, the level of victim injury did not correlate with the recidivism rate. A possible explanation for this discrepancy may be sample selection. In fact, the Quinsey, Khanna, and Malcolm (1998) study included sexual aggressors but not sexual nuisance offenders. As to the developmental history, the recidivists had suffered a higher frequency of parental physical abuse and of parental emotional abuse and neglect. As to the psychological characteristics, the recidivists also had a higher score than the nonrecidivists for the Loss of Sex Control Scale of the Thorne Sex Inventory. These results "seem to indicate that sex offenders who state that they need to be supervised to not reoffend should be believed" (Quinsey, Khanna, & Malcolm, 1998, p. 639).

In both the Hanson and Bussière (1998) meta-analysis and the Quinsey, Khanna, and Malcolm (1998) study, predictors of sexual recidivism were identified in mixed groups of sexual offenders but not in specific types of sexual offender. This situation results from factors out of the researchers' control, such as the content of institutional files collected retrospectively and the sampling procedure in the original paper published. There may well be different factors associated with recidivism depending on the age of victim. Consequently, we will continue presenting the results of studies carried out with distinct samples of sexual aggressors against women and of sexual aggressors against children. We again present only the results that are different from those obtained with mixed groups of sexual offenders or that concern variables not included in the above studies.

Sexual Aggressors Against Children

Concerning general criminality, the recidivists have more previous property convictions than the nonrecidivists (Proulx et al., 1997; Rice, Quinsey, & Harris, 1991). These results differ from those obtained in the Hanson and Bussière (1998) meta-analysis. These discrepancies may be due to sample bias because the participants in these two studies were in maximum-security psychiatric institutions (Institut Philippe Pinel de Montréal, Mental Health Center in Penetanguishene). Furthermore, a large proportion of them were multirecidivist offenders convicted for both property and violent crimes.

Concerning the sexual history crimes, Hall and Proctor (1987) reported that sexual aggressors against children have a proclivity to reoffend sexually against children rather than against both child and adult victims. The number of victims and the magnitude of force used during the offense are positively correlated with the rate of recidivism (Barbaree & Marshall, 1988). Moreover, the sexual recidivism rate was higher in those who had genital-to-genital contacts with their victims (Gibbens, Soothill, & Way, 1981; Marshall & Barbaree, 1988). Finally, incest offenders have a lower rate of sexual recidivism than extrafamilial sexual child molesters (Fitch, 1962; Frisbie & Dondis, 1965; Hanson, Steffy, & Gauthier, 1993; Marshall & Barbaree, 1988; Rice et al., 1991; Sturgeon & Taylor, 1980).

Regarding sexual deviancy, Prentky, Knight, and Lee (1997) reported that the recidivists had a higher level of fixation to children than did the nonrecidivists. They defined the level of fixation to children as "the extent to which children are a major focus of the offender's thoughts and attention" (sexual and interpersonal) (p. 142).

Sexual Aggressors Against Women

As to their criminality, the recidivists had more previous sexual offenses, violent offenses, and nonsexual nonviolent offenses (Rice et al., 1990). Furthermore, the sexual aggressors against women had a proclivity to reoffend sexually against women (Hall & Proctor, 1987). Regarding sexual deviancy, Rice et al. (1990) found that recidivists had a higher nonsexual violence toward women index (assessed phallometrically) than nonrecidivists. However, contrary to what was expected, the rape index did not permit discrimination between recidivists and nonrecidivists (see also Proulx et al., 1997).

As to psychological characteristics, Rice et al. (1990) reported that the recidivists had a higher Psychopathy Checklist mean score than the nonrecidivists. Furthermore, high-impulsivity aggressors had a higher rate of recidivism than the low-impulsivity aggressors (Prentky et al., 1995). Impulsivity had two components: impulsive unplanned offense style and pervasively impulsive lifestyle. Consequently,

> it would appear from the results of the present study, as well as those of Rice et al. (1990), that psychopathy in general, and lifestyle impulsivity (factor 1 of the Psychopathy Checklist) in particular may be critically important risk markers for sexual recidivism. (Prentky et al., 1995, p. 124)

More precisely, "sexual deviance may be a more important factor for child molesters than for rapists; whereas general criminal deviance, lack of self-control and psychopathy may be more important for rapists" (Rice & Harris, 1997, p. 239). Based on the static and dynamic (stable) predictors of recidivism presented above, actuarial instruments have been developed (Hanson, 1997; Quinsey, Harris, et al., 1998).

Actuarial Prediction of Sexual Recidivism

Actuarial prediction is an objective, valid, and reliable procedure to predict recidivism. Such a procedure is based on rules for combining variables already demonstrated to predict recidivism. Actuarial instruments designed for general offenders, such as the Statistical Information on Recidivism (SIR) Scale (Nuffield, 1982), are not effective in predicting sexual recidivism (Bonta, Harman, Hann, & Cormier, 1996). The SIR Scale correlated .41 with general recidivism, .34 with nonsexual violent recidivism, and .09 with sexual recidivism (Bonta & Hanson, 1995). Furthermore, actuarial instruments designed for violent offenders such as the Violent Risk Appraisal Guide (VRAG) (Quinsey, Harris, et al., 1998) are not effective in predicting sexual recidivism (Rice & Harris, 1997). The VRAG Scale correlated .44 with violent recidivism (sexual and nonsexual) and only .17 with sexual recidivism (Rice & Harris, 1997). Such results are not surprising because the VRAG was developed with a sample of mentally disordered offenders ($N = 625$) admitted to a maximum-security psychiatric institution (Penetanguishene) and was designed to assess violent recidivism risk status in these men. Consequently, actuarial instruments specifically designed to assess sexual recidivism risk status in more general populations must be favored in the assessment of sexual aggressors.

Hanson (1997) has developed the Rapid Risk Assessment for Sexual Offense Recidivism (RRASOR), an actuarial instrument specifically designed for sexual offenders. The RRASOR has four items: (a) prior sex offenses, (b) age at release (younger than 25 years), (c) victim's gender, and (d) relationship to victim. The scores range from 0 to 5. With a 10-year follow-up period, those with a score of 0 have a 6.5% probability to recidivate, whereas those with a score of 5 have a 73.4% probability to recidivate sexually. The main limitation of this instrument is its reliance on static predictors only, which means that the deviance index derived from phallometric assessment, the best predictor of recidivism in the Hanson and Bussière (1998) meta-analysis, is not among the items included in the scale. Furthermore, it also means that the RRASOR is not useful to assess posttreatment changes in risk status because treatments address dynamic factors but not static predictors. Nevertheless, this instrument, developed with seven different samples from two countries (Canada and United Kingdom) ($N = 2,919$), may be useful in various settings.

Quinsey, Harris, et al. (1998) developed the Sex Offender Risk Appraisal Guide (SORAG), another actuarial instrument specifically designed for sexual aggressors. The SORAG has 14 items (see Table 26.2). The scores range from 1 to 9. With a 10-year follow-up period, those with a score of 1 have a 9.0% probability to recidivate, whereas all those with a score of 9 recidivate. The major strength of the SORAG is its reliance on both static and dynamic (stable) predictors. Unfortunately, this instrument had been developed with only one

TABLE 26.2   Items of the SORAG

Item
1. Lived with both biological parents to age 16
2. Elementary school maladjustment
3. History of alcohol problems
4. Marital status
5. Criminal history score for nonviolent offenses
6. Criminal history score for violent offenses
7. Number of previous convictions for sexual offenses
8. History of sex offenses only against girls younger than age 14
9. Failure on prior conditional release
10. Age index offense (negatively scored)
11. Meets *DSM-III* criteria for any personality disorder
12. Meets *DSM-III* criteria for schizophrenia (negatively scored)
13. Phallometric test results
14. Psychopathy Checklist score

Source: Quinsey, Harris, et. al., (1998).

sample of sexual aggressors admitted to a maximum-security psychiatric institution.

These actuarial instruments are landmarks in the development of assessment methods to predict sexual recidivism. They are particularly useful in determining the long-tem risk of sexual recidivism (Quinsey, Harris, et al., 1998). These instruments may be used by parole board officers who have to make decisions regarding releasing incarcerated sexual aggressors into the community. Unfortunately, actuarial instruments relying on static and dynamic (stable) predictors are not sensitive to change in the risk status of sexual aggressors (Boer, Hart, Kropp, & Webster, 1997; Zamble & Quinsey, 1997). Consequently, to assess risk status in sexual aggressors we must also consider acute dynamic predictors of recidivism such as emotional states and treatment compliance.

Acute Dynamic Predictors of Sexual Recidivism

Acute dynamic predictors are defined as proximate causes of recidivism. They are changes in the conditions of the aggressor (e.g., negative emotional state, alcohol intoxication) or changes in his environment (e.g., victim access, employment problem). These acute factors have to be the main focus during a treatment program, which means that an offender has to learn to identify his specific acute predictors of recidivism, and he also has to learn the skills necessary to cope appropriately with these risk factors (e.g., social skills, anger management). Furthermore, these acute predictors provide "targets for supervision and cues as to when supervision may be relaxed or needs to be intensified" (Quinsey, Harris, et al., 1998, p. 37). Consequently, therapists and

TABLE 26.3   Statistically Significant Point-Biserial Correlations Between Stable Dynamic Predictors and Sexual Recidivism

Predictor	Rapists	Homosexual Child Molesters	Heterosexual Child Molesters
Frequency unemployed	.31	—	—
Substance abuse	.22	.26	—
Ever used antiandrogens	.19	—	.19
Intimacy problem	.18	—	—
Number of positive influences	−.45	−.32	—
Number of negative influences	.23	.29	.18
Low remorse/victim blaming	.37	.37	—
Rape attitudes	.32	.22	—
Child molester attitudes	—	.36	.18
Sexual entitlement	.33	.32	.23
See self as no risk	.43	.52	.22
Victim access	.28	.37	.17
Sexual preoccupations	.28	.22	—
Dirty, smelly	.24	—	—
Improvement in appearance	−.21	−.25	—
Antisocial lifestyle	.38	.34	—
Uncontrolled release environment	—	.31	—
Cooperation with supervision			
Disengaged	.40	.39	—
Manipulative	.27	.47	.16
No show/late	.18	.36	—
Total noncooperation	.36	.50	.24

SOURCE: Hanson and Harris (2000).

practitioners, who supervise sexual aggressors in the community, definitely need information about the acute dynamic predictors of sexual recidivism.

Hanson and Harris (2000) carried out an important study about the dynamic (stable and acute) predictors of sexual recidivism. A total of 409 sexual aggressors (208 recidivists and 201 nonrecidivists) from different types of settings participated in this study. Their sample did not include incest offenders. For the recidivists, information was collected for two time periods—6 months and 1 month—before their reoffenses. For the nonrecidivist, it was collected at two time periods—6 months and 1 month—to the end of community supervision. The sources of information were interviews with the supervising officers and their supervision notes. Recidivism was defined as any charges or convictions for a sexual offense, as well as self-reports. Separate data were presented for rapists, homosexual child molesters, and heterosexual child molesters, including both stable and acute dynamic predictors of sexual recidivism.

Although this part of this chapter is about acute dynamic predictors of recidivism, we also present the results of Hanson and Harris (in press) as to the stable dynamic predictors to present the complete study and to highlight links between stable and acute risk factors. Table 26.3 summarizes the statistically significant point-biserial correlations between stable dynamic predictors and sexual recidivism in three groups of sexual aggressors. In rapists, the best stable dynamic predictors of sexual recidivism were the following: antisocial

TABLE 26.4 Statistically Significant Point-Biserial Correlations Between Acute Dynamic Predictors and Sexual Recidivism

Predictors	Rapists	Homosexual Child Molesters	Heterosexual Child Molesters
Employment problems	.23	—	—
Substance abuse	—	.32	—
Negative mood	—	.32	—
Anger	.25	.30	—
Social problem (isolation, conflict)	—	.27	—
Low remorse/victim blaming	—	.24	.18
See self as no risk	—	.27	—
Victim access	.18	.36	—
Sexual preoccupations	—	.29	—
Dirty, smelly	—	.25	—
Cooperation with supervision			
Disengaged	.28	.17	.20
Total noncooperation	.32	.19	.18

SOURCE: Hanson and Harris (2000).

lifestyle, low remorse/victim blaming, number of significant positive influences (negatively correlated), seeing self as no risk, and noncooperation with supervision (disengaged). In homosexual child molesters, the best predictors were low remorse/victim blaming, child molester attitudes, victim access, seeing self as no risk, and noncooperation with supervision (disengaged, manipulative, total noncooperation). Finally, with heterosexual child molesters, the best predictors were a sense of sexual entitlement, seeing self as no risk, and noncooperation with supervision (total noncooperation). These results strongly suggest that for these three types of sexual aggressors, the different forms of noncooperation with supervision are particularly accurate predictors of sexual recidivism. In addition, the practitioners have to pay attention when the sexual aggressors they supervise claim that they are not at risk to reoffend.

Table 26.4 summarizes the statistically significant point-biserial correlations between acute dynamic predictors and sexual recidivism in three groups of sexual aggressors. In rapists, the best acute dynamic predictors of sexual recidivism are anger, employment problems, and poor cooperation with supervision (disengaged, total noncooperation). In homosexual child molesters, the best predictors are negative mood (e.g., depression, hopelessness, anxiety, loneliness), anger, substance abuse, sexual preoccupations, and victim access. In heterosexual child molesters, the stronger predictors are low remorse and poor cooperation with supervision (disengaged, total noncooperation). These results indicate that "most of the factors that were stable (dynamic) risk factors were also acute (dynamic) risk predictors. In other words, the ongoing (stable) problems that differentiate the recidivists and nonrecidivists tended to get worse just prior to the recidivism event" (Hanson & Harris, 2000, p. 24).

Because acute dynamic predictors are labile and transitory, they have to be assessed frequently. Unfortunately, "risk prediction instruments have generally neglected the dynamic nature of recidivism processes, and this limits their ability to predict correctly in some cases" (Zamble & Quinsey, 1997, p. 137). In fact, no actuarial instrument includes acute dynamic predictors permitting the assessment of changes in recidivism risk status.

Recently, however, an assessment procedure has been developed to monitor acute dynamic risk factors in sexual aggressors—the Fantasy Report (McKibben et al., 1994; Proulx et al., 1996). This instrument permits assessing risk factors daily if necessary; however, it does not indicate the level of recidivism risk. The Fantasy Report is a self-report, consisting of questions listed on a computer screen, to be answered by the aggressor directly into the computer. First, the aggressor has to evaluate the frequency of his deviant and nondeviant sexual fantasies during the past day using a scale made up of five categories for both types (nondeviant and deviant) of fantasies: (a) much more than usual, (b) more than usual, (c) same as usual, (d) less than usual, and (e) much less than usual. Next, the aggressor has to indicate whether he masturbated (simply recorded as did or did not) while having these deviant or nondeviant fantasies. The aggressor then has to evaluate his mood during the past day, using another scale made up of five categories: (a) much worse than usual, (b) worse than usual, (c) same as usual, (d) better than usual, and (e) much better than usual. Finally, the aggressor has to indicate whether he has interpersonal conflicts (simply recorded as present or absent) during the past day and, if so, which of the following emotions they aroused: humiliation, oppression, rejection, anger, feelings of inadequacy, and loneliness. Using the Fantasy Report, Proulx et al. (1996) demonstrated that in rapists and heterosexual pedophiles, negative moods and conflicts coincided with overwhelming deviant sexual fantasies, whereas in homosexual pedophiles, negative mood but not conflicts coincided with such fantasies. Although this assessment procedure permits assessing acute dynamic risk factors, it may be falsified by an aggressor motivated to hide his genuine emotional and cognitive states.

Recidivism Risk Predictors and the Relapse Prevention Model

Acute dynamic predictors link studies of the prediction of recidivism with the relapse prevention model (RPM), which is a microtheory of the sequence of behaviors ending in a sexual assault (Laws, 1989; Pithers, 1990; Pithers et al., 1988). In the original model, the first component of that sequence is a high-risk situation (HRS), defined as a situation that threatens the aggressor's expectation of self-control over his deviant sexual behaviors. HRSs most frequently observed are negative emotional states and interpersonal conflicts. External situations difficult to avoid or to anticipate (e.g., a single mother with three children moves next door to the aggressor's apartment) may also be considered as an HRS. If the sexual aggressor fails to cope appropriately with an HRS, a lapse follows. A lapse, the second component of the relapse sequence, usually consists of deviant sexual fantasizing. Following a lapse, an abstinence violation effect (AVE) is thought to occur. This effect consists of two reactions to a lapse: (a) the cognitive dissonance between the offender's self-perception of being cured and his awareness of the lapse and (b) his attribution to the cause of the lapse. The problem of immediate gratification (PIG) is also involved—that is, selective attention by the aggressor to the immediate positive consequences of the sexual aggression as opposed to the delayed negative ones. The fourth component of the relapse sequence concerns cognitive distortions, justifying his sexual aggression. The fifth component, conscious planning of the future offense, is often associated with masturbatory activities. Finally, a relapse occurs—a reoffending, the last component of the relapse prevention model.

Several acute dynamic predictors, identified by Hanson and Harris (in press), fit with some of the components of the RPM. In fact, negative moods, anger, social problems, and victim access are HRSs; sexual preoccupation is a lapse; and victim blaming is a cognitive distortion.

Although the RPM is useful in understanding the offending process in sexual aggressors, it is a general model and does not include specific pathways (Ward & Hudson, 1996). As an example, Ward, Louden, Hudson, and Marshall (1995) found two pathways in the offending process of child molesters: (a) the positive affect pathway, characterized by positive affective states, explicit planning, the presence of cognitive distortions (e.g., the victim is a willing lover), a high level of sexual arousal, the use of deviant fantasies related to the victim, and an offense of long duration involving a low level of coercion and (b) the negative affect pathway, characterized by a diversity of negative affective states (i.e., depression, anxiety, guilt), implicit planning, alcohol intoxication, and an offense of short duration involving a high level of intrusiveness and the perception of the victim as an object. Consequently, different pathways in the offending process may exist (see also Hudson, Ward, & McCormack, 1999; Proulx, Perreault, & Ouimet, 1999; Ward & Hudson, 1998), and each probably has its own specific recidivism risk factors. In the pathways presented above, negative mood is probably a risk factor for the child molester using a negative affect pathway, whereas deviant sexual fantasies and cognitive distortions are probably risk factors for those using the positive affect pathway.

The RPM is also a framework for the treatment of sexual aggressors, which has two dimensions. First, an offender has to understand the recidivism risk factors in his offending process. Second, he has to learn the skills to cope appropriately with these risk factors. These two dimensions are necessary to reduce the risk of recidivism in sexual aggressors. In fact, if an offender claims that he is not at risk, he will not identify his own risk factors, and he will not use appropriate coping strategies to deal with them. Furthermore, if he is aware of his risk factors but he had never learned the skills to cope appropriately with them because he did not cooperate with supervision or any other reasons, he will continue to be at a high risk to recidivate. Finally, because there are several pathways in the offending process of sexual aggressors, treatment targets must be determined as a function of the specific recidivism risk factors in each of these pathways.

Recidivism Risk Assessment and Management in the Community

Beyond the validity of recidivism risk factor assessment procedures, recidivism risk management strategies are based on an interactive process involving clinical and legal issues. When a sexual aggressor returns to the community, he may be worried for some time about a possible future incarceration; thus, deviant sexual fantasies may be temporarily inhibited. Consequently, the aggressor may erroneously think that he is definitely cured. The practitioner in charge of this aggressor must inform him that his deviant sexual fantasies may come back. In that event, he has to consider them as an alarm signal rather than as a treatment failure. Furthermore, the practitioner has to encourage the aggressor to discuss openly the recurrence of his deviant sexual fantasies to get support to cope appropriately with this crucial risk factor.

Under the best conditions, the aggressor will give genuine information as to his deviant sexual fantasies to the practitioner in charge of his social reintegration. When deviant sexual fantasies recur, their contents as well as the events, cognitions, and emotions preceding them have to be investigated. Moreover, these risk factors have to be compared with those that occurred during the initial phases of past offending processes. The aim of this analysis is to clarify the nature of the recidivism risk factors (e.g., an interpersonal conflict, an occupational failure) currently present in this aggressor's life. The practitioner's next step is to evaluate whether the aggressor has the coping skills necessary to manage appropriately the recidivism risk factors (e.g., social skills to solve an interpersonal conflict). Finally, the practitioner has to judge whether the aggressor is willing to use these coping strategies. If the aggressor understands his offending process, has the coping skills necessary to manage the risk factors, and is willing to use them, the practitioner's tasks are limited to social reinforcements of the aggressor's prosocial actions. Unfortunately, it is rarely that easy.

When an aggressor identifies his risk factors but does not possess the coping skills to manage them or the motivation to use these skills, practitioners should take immediate actions to prevent recidivism. These actions may be the following: (a) If the aggressor lives with a potential victim, he should never be with her except when a responsible adult is present; (b) when such a condition is not possible, the aggressor has to move to another place; (c) an aggressor may have to move to another town to avoid a risk environment (e.g., relatives, friends) that favors drug and alcohol abuse and violence as problem-solving strategies for emotional and interpersonal problems; (d) some aggressors may have to take antiandrogen medication if deviant sexual fantasies are overwhelming; and (e) if none of these actions is effective, which means that the aggressor is still at risk to recidivate, he has to be incarcerated temporarily. If an aggressor recognizes his risk factors but is unable to cope with them, the reasons for the actions chosen by the practitioner must be discussed with him to ensure his voluntary commitment to comply with them. This means explaining to him the necessity of these actions to prevent recidivism and to take time to develop skills to cope with the risk factors adequately. Furthermore, it is important to listen to the aggressor's distress related to his risk factors and also to the consequences of his inability to cope with them. If practitioners do not follow these strategies, the aggressor may be reluctant to cooperate in the future with a practitioner who had previously decided to return him to jail or had taken him away from his home. Because lack of cooperation is a strong predictor of recidivism (Hanson & Harris, in press), cooperation must be achieved.

Another situation practitioners frequently face is an aggressor in the community who states that there are no more risk factors in his life. Such a statement may be truthful, a lie, or a genuine unawareness of the presence of risk factors. In such an event, practitioners must have other sources of information such as the aggressor's relatives, friends, and wife to assess recidivism risk factors. These persons have the possibility to observe indirect cues of the recurrence of deviant sexual fantasies such as time spent listening to programs involving children, frequent use of pornography, or the introduction of sadomasochistic practices with a consenting partner. Furthermore, these information sources may note the presence of other risk factors such as victim access and alcohol abuse. An aggressor may perceive the role of these information sources as a betrayal and become manipulative or coercive with them to stop their cooperating with the practitioner. Consequently, the practitioner must have a strong link to his sources of information. He should share with them his knowledge about the aggressor's risk factors and be involved and supportive when actions are taken to cope with these risk factors.

Other dimensions must be considered in managing recidivism risk factors of an aggressor in the community—the capabilities of the aggressor and the quality of his environment. In particular, the aggressor's intellectual capacities, level of sexual deviance, and social support from his relatives and friends must be considered. The aggressor and the practitioner therefore must have realistic expectations and never consider that there is no longer a risk for recidivism. An aggressor with a high score on an actuarial scale, however, may not recidivate if he has learned coping skills, has social support, and has cooperated honestly with a practitioner. Consequently, in sexual aggressors, recidivism is a function of stable risk factors and of changes in acute dynamic predictors. Furthermore, the aggressor's awareness of the recidivism process in daily life is of great importance in managing recidivism risk skills, as well as social support and cooperation with his practitioner.

Future Research Areas in the Assessment of Recidivism Risk in Sexual Aggressors

During the past 10 years, the field of recidivism risk assessment has grown rapidly. More research studies, however, are necessary to improve sensitivity (proportion of recidivists correctly classified: the true positive) and specificity (the percentage of false negative subtracted from one) of instruments designed to assess sexual recidivism risk. First, recidivism studies should be carried out with different types of sexual aggressors (Hudson et al., 1999; Knight & Prentky, 1990; Ward & Hudson, 1998) to identify predictors specific to each type. Second, because survival analysis has shown that recidivism rates vary as a function of time, we must verify whether recidivism predictors also vary as a function of time. Finally, new instruments to predict recidivism rates must include acute dynamic predictors (Zamble & Quinsey, 1997).

Coming back to the journalist's questions—"Why was he free?" and "Who must be blamed for this inadmissible mistake?"—the only answer is the limitations of our actual knowledge in the field of recidivism risk prediction. In fact, we will probably never achieve perfect risk predictions with any sexual aggressors. As practitioners, however, our responsibility is to base our risk assessment decisions on the results reported in the scientific literature.

References

Barbaree, H. E., & Marshall, W. L. (1988). Deviant sexual arousal, offense history, and demographic variables as predictors of reoffense among child molesters. *Behavioral Sciences & the Law, 6,* 267-280.

Boer, D. P., Hart, S. D., Kropp, P. R., & Webster, C. D. (1997). *Manual for the Sexual Violence Risk-20: Professional guidelines for assessing risk of sexual violence.* Vancouver, BC: Mental Health, Law, and Policy Institute, Simon Fraser University.

Bonta, J., & Hanson, R. K. (1995, August). *Violent recidivism of men released from prison.* Paper presented at the 103rd Annual Convention of the American Psychological Association, New York.

Bonta, J., Harman, W. G., Hann, R. G., & Cormier, R. B. (1996). The prediction of recidivism among federally sentenced offenders: A re-validation of the SIR scale. *Canadian Journal of Criminology, 38,* 61-79.

Fitch, J. H. (1962). Men convicted of sexual offenses against children: A descriptive follow-up study. *British Journal of Criminology, 3,* 18-37.

Frisbie, L. V., & Dondis, E. H. (1965). *Recidivism among treated sex offenders* (California Mental Health Research Monograph No. 5). Sacramento, CA: Department of Mental Hygiene.

Furby, L., Weinrott, M. R., & Blackshaw, L. (1989). Sex offender recidivism: A review. *Psychological Bulletin, 105,* 3-30.

Gibbens, T. C. N., Soothill, K. L., & Way, C. K. (1981). Sex offenses against young girls: A long-term record study. *Psychological Medicine, 11,* 351-357.

Hall, G. C. N., & Proctor, W. C. (1987). Criminological predictors of recidivism in a sexual offender population. *Journal of Consulting and Clinical Psychology, 55,* 111-112.

Hanson, R. K. (1997). *The development of a brief actuarial risk scale for sexual offense recidivism* (User Report No. 97-04). Ottawa: Department of the Solicitor General of Canada.

Hanson, R. K., & Bussière, M. T. (1998). Predicting relapse: A meta-analysis of sexual offender recidivism studies. *Journal of Consulting and Clinical Psychology, 66,* 348-362.

Hanson, R. K., & Harris, A. J. R. (2000). Where should we intervene? Dynamic predictors of sex offense recidivism. *Criminal Justice and Behavior, 27,* 6-35.

Hanson, R. K., Steffy, R. A., & Gauthier, R. (1993). Long-term recidivism of child molesters. *Journal of Consulting and Clinical Psychology, 61,* 646-652.

Hudson, S. M., Ward, T., & McCormack, J. (1999). Offense pathways in sexual offenders. *Journal of Interpersonal Violence, 14,* 779-798.

Knight, R. A., & Prentky, R. A. (1990). Classifying sexual offenders: The development and corroboration of taxinomic models. In W. L. Marshall, D. R. Laws, & H. E. Barbaree (Eds.), *Handbook of sexual assault: Issues, theories and treatment of the offenders* (pp. 23-52). New York: Plenum.

Laws, D. R. (Ed.). (1989). *Relapse prevention with sex offenders.* New York: Guilford.

Marshall, W. L., & Barbaree, H. E. (1988). The long-term evaluation of a behavioral treatment program for child molesters. *Behaviour Research and Therapy, 26,* 499-511.

McKibben, A., Proulx, J., & Lusignan, R. (1994). Relationships between conflict, affect and deviant sexual behaviors in rapists and pedophiles. *Behaviour Research and Therapy, 32,* 571-575.

Nuffield, J. (1982). *Parole decision-making in Canada: Research towards decision guidelines.* Ottawa: Supply and Services Canada.

Ouimet, M. (1998). *L'agression sexuelle, la violence conjugale et la toxicomanie: portrait statistique* (Sexual aggression, spouse abuse, and drug abuse: A statistical portrayal). Unpublished manuscript.

Pithers, W. D. (1990). Relapse prevention with sexual aggressors: A method for maintaining therapeutic gain and enhancing external supervision. In W. L. Marshall, D. R. Laws, & H. E. Barbaree (Eds.), *Handbook of sexual assault: Issues, theories, and treatment of the offender* (pp. 343-361). New York: Plenum.

Pithers, W. D., Kashima, K., Cumming, G. F., Beal, L. S., & Buell, M. (1988). Relapse prevention of sexual aggression. In R. A. Prentky & V. L. Quinsey (Eds.), *Human sexual aggression: Current perspectives* (pp. 244-260). New York: New York Academy of Sciences.

Prentky, R. A., Knight, R. A., & Lee, A. F. S. (1997). Risk factors associated with recidivism among extrafamilial child molesters. *Journal of Consulting and Clinical Psychology, 65,* 141-149.

Prentky, R. A., Knight, R. A., Lee, A. F. S., & Cerce, D. D. (1995). Predictive validity of lifestyle impulsivity for rapists. *Criminal Justice and Behavior, 22,* 106-128.

Proulx, J., McKibben, A., & Lusignan, R. (1996). Relationships between affective components and sexual behaviors in sexual aggressors. *Sexual Abuse: A Journal of Research and Treatment, 8,* 279-289.

Proulx, J., Ouimet, M., Pellerin, B., Paradis, Y., McKibben, A., & Aubut, J. (1999). Posttreatment recidivism rates in sexual aggressors: A comparison between dropout subjects and nondropout subjects. In B. K. Schwartz (Ed.), *The sexual offender: Theoretical advances, treating special populations and legal developments* (pp. 15.1-15.13). Kingston, NJ: Civic Research Institute.

Proulx, J., Pellerin, B., Paradis, Y., McKibben, A., Aubut, J., & Ouimet, M. (1997). Static and dynamic predictors of recidivism in sexual aggressors. *Sexual Abuse: A Journal of Research and Treatment, 9,* 7-27.

Proulx, J., Perreault, C., & Ouimet, M. (1999). Pathways in the offending process of extrafamilial sexual child molesters. *Sexual Abuse: A Journal of Research and Treatment, 11,* 117-129.

Quinsey, V. L. (1983). Prediction of recidivism and the evaluation of treatment programs for sex offenders. In S. Verdun-Jones & A. A. Keltner (Eds.), *Sexual aggression and the law* (pp. 27-40). Burnaby, BC: Simon Fraser University Criminology Research Center.

Quinsey, V. L., Harris, G. T., Rice, M. E., & Cormier, C. A. (1998). *Violent offenders: Appraising and managing risk.* Washington, DC: American Psychological Association.

Quinsey, V. L., Khanna, A., & Malcolm, B. (1998). A retrospective evaluation of the Regional Treatment Centre Sex Offender Treatment Program. *Journal of Interpersonal Violence, 13,* 621-644.

Quinsey, V. L., Lalumière, M. L., Rice, M. E., & Harris, G. T. (1995). Predicting sexual offenses. In J. C. Campbell (Ed.), *Assessing dangerousness: Violence by sexual offenders, batterers, and child abusers* (pp. 114-137). Thousand Oaks, CA: Sage.

Quinsey, V. L., Rice, M. E., & Harris, G. T. (1995). Actuarial prediction of sexual recidivism. *Journal of Interpersonal Violence, 10,* 85-105.

Rice, M. E., & Harris, G. T. (1997). Cross validation and extension of the Violence Risk Appraisal Guide for child molesters and rapists. *Law and Human Behavior, 21,* 231-241.

Rice, M. E., Harris, G. T., & Quinsey, V. L. (1990). A follow-up of rapists assessed in a maximum security psychiatric facility. *Journal of Interpersonal Violence, 5,* 435-448.

Rice, M. E., Quinsey, V. L., & Harris, G. T. (1991). Sexual recidivism among child molesters released from a maximum security psychiatric institution. *Journal of Consulting and Clinical Psychology, 59,* 381-386.

Sturgeon, V. H., & Taylor, J. (1980). Report of a five-year follow-up study of mentally disordered sex offenders released from Atascadero State Hospital. *Criminal Justice Journal, 4,* 31-63.

Ward, T., & Hudson, S. M. (1996). Relapse prevention: A critical analysis. *Sexual Abuse: A Journal of Research and Treatment, 8,* 177-200.

Ward, T., & Hudson, S. M. (1998). A model of relapse process in sexual offenders. *Journal of Interpersonal Violence, 13,* 700-725.

Ward, T., Louden, K., Hudson, S. M., & Marshall, W. L. (1995). A descriptive model of the offense chain for child molesters. *Journal of Interpersonal Violence, 10,* 452-472.

Zamble, E., & Quinsey, V. L. (1997). *The process of recidivism.* Cambridge, UK: Cambridge University Press.

CHAPTER 27

Treatment Outcome and Evaluation Problems (and Solutions)

R. KARL HANSON
Department of the Solicitor General of Canada

In the conclusion of the 1989 edition of *Relapse Prevention With Sex Offenders,* Laws notes that the enthusiasm for relapse prevention does not rest on a solid research base. He sagely cautions readers that it would "be wise to consider this book not as set of statements about treatment efficacy but rather as a set of marching orders" (Laws, 1989, p. 327). He further exhorts clinicians to test and revise as necessary the original relapse prevention (RP) formulations.

The work described in this volume is evidence that many heeded his call. Elements of the original RP theory have been questioned, and new features have been proposed. The new work appears to be a significant step forward. It is not clear, however, that the research base for the revisions is much firmer than it was 10 years ago for the original version. Central elements of RP theory have never been tested. There have been so few high-quality outcome studies that it is easy for skeptics to question whether RP treatment is effective at all (Harris, Rice, & Quinsey, 1998). It seems that some of us have been marching without looking where we are going.

Combining service delivery and research is never easy, but it is important. Given that treatment efficacy has yet to be firmly established, I believe that sex offender treatment providers have an ethical responsibility to contribute to new knowledge. Within the cognitive-behavioral tradition, there is no inherent conflict between treatment and research. Many of the tasks required by the research enterprise (e.g., clear record keeping, pre-post assessments) reinforce good service delivery. The purpose of this chapter is to outline a research strategy to be followed so that readers of the 2009 edition (*Re-Remaking Relapse Prevention?*) will find not only marching orders but also statements concerning empirically validated treatment procedures.

Testing Basic Assumptions

Before considering whether RP treatment is effective, it is first worth considering whether its basic assumptions are sound. The available research has provided some support for the usefulness of the RP model with sex offenders. McKibben, Proulx, and Lusignan (1994; Proulx, McKibben, & Lusignan, 1996) found that sex offenders increased their deviant sexual fantasies following interpersonal problems experienced on an inpatient treatment unit. Hanson and Harris (2000) found that recidivism on community supervision was associated with poor self-management skills, exposure to high-risk situations, and an acute worsening of mood—all factors consistent with the RP model.

Other parts of RP theory have not held up well to empirical scrutiny. RP describes a gradual, covert process through which the offender's motivation to prevent offending is gradually eroded by passive planning, seemingly irrelevant decisions, and poor coping skills (George & Marlatt, 1989; Laws, 1995). Interviews with offenders often suggest a more direct route. It is not uncommon for child molesters to describe feeling good before, during, and after a carefully planned offense (Ward, Louden, Hudson, & Marshall, 1995).

Some of the most basic assumptions of RP have received surprisingly little research attention. Although motivation to prevent recidivism is a precondition of the RP model, little is known about how often this requirement is met. Less is known about how motivation changes through the course of RP treatment or how it could interact with coping skills deficits. There have been few attempts to systematically measure motivation, apart from some structured clinical ratings used by particular treatment settings (e.g., Anderson, Gibeau, & D'Amora, 1995).

The theoretical foundations of a treatment approach should be plausible before it is subjected to clinical trials. As I have argued elsewhere (Hanson, 1996), RP is firmly rooted in the (highly plausible) social learning tradition. Some of RP's most distinctive features, however, may have limited applicability to sex offenders (such as the abstinence violation effect). RP is certainly plausible enough to be implemented, and in some jurisdictions, it is considered the standard practice. However, it is not a standard above serious scrutiny.

Confidence in the RP approach is influenced by the plausibility of its assumptions as much as by the results of outcome studies.

More and Better Outcome Studies

The primary goal of sex offender treatment is to reduce sex offense recidivism. Consequently, the evaluation of treatment programs appears rather straightforward: Compare the recidivism rates of treated and untreated offenders. Given such an obvious research design, it is tempting to attribute the lack of good outcome studies to ignorance, apathy, or arrogance. Such judgments, however, would be premature. Low-recidivism base rate means that exceptional efforts are required before treatment effects are likely to be found.

Contrary to what is commonly believed, approximately 15% of sex offenders are detected committing a new sex offense after 4 to 5 years at risk (Hanson, 1997a; Hanson & Bussière, 1998). The observed rates are underestimates because many offenses are never reported (Bonta & Hanson, 1994). The observed rates, however, are the only rates available. Even the routine use of polygraph examinations does not substantially increase the observed sex offense recidivism rate (K. English, personal communication, December 15, 1998). Consequently, evaluators wishing to demonstrate treatment effects need large sample sizes, long follow-up periods, high-risk offenders, or exceptionally effective treatments. Under normal circumstances, statistically significant treatment effects are not to be expected. For example, a treatment program that reduced recidivism by 40% (15% to 9%) over a 5-year follow-up period would require sample sizes of 200 per group (400 total) to have even a 50% chance of finding a treatment effect (two-tailed alpha of .05; Cohen, 1988). Most studies include substantially smaller samples.

Even though small studies may not find significant results, such studies can nevertheless make an important contribution when pooled with other research results. An evaluator who compares 30 treated sex offenders to 30 untreated offenders will most likely find nothing at all. Three offenders may recidivate in the treatment group compared to four in the comparison group. Although the study demonstrated a 25% reduction in recidivism, funding agencies and journal editors will be unimpressed. I believe, however, that it is crucial that such small studies be conducted and reported.

Types of Research Designs

Completers Versus Dropouts

The easiest form of outcome study compares treatment completers to dropouts and/or refusers. The main advantage of this approach is that the comparison group can be formed from existing records; recidivism data are the only new information required. Comparisons between dropouts and completers have consistently found lower recidivism rates among those who complete treatment (average $r = .17$; six studies, $p < .001$; Hanson & Bussière, 1998). Such results are difficult to interpret, however, due to the likelihood of preexisting group differences. The offenders who fail to complete treatment may be comparatively high risk due to lack of motivation, impulsiveness, or general belligerence. Alternately, some low-risk men could fail to attend treatment when they accurately perceive that they do not have the problems being targeted in that particular program.

Successful Versus Unsuccessful Completers

An alternate treatment design compares offenders who have been successfully treated with those who have not made adequate progress. Like the completer/dropout design, the results of such studies can also be attributed to preexisting offender characteristics (e.g., general compliance, IQ). Furthermore, if treatment is effective, comparisons between successful and unsuccessful completers would be expected to show relatively weak effects because both groups received the same type and amount of treatment.

Studies that compare successful and unsuccessful treatment candidates have typically found similar recidivism rates for both groups (Quinsey, Khanna, & Malcolm, 1998; Rice, Quinsey, & Harris, 1989; Seto, 1998). Ryan and Miyoshi (1990), in a pilot study of 69 treated adolescent sex offenders, found the lowest recidivism rates among those judged able to "identify the triggers of their offending behavior" and "interrupt their offense cycles." Nevertheless, they found that other similar ratings were unrelated to recidivism, including "ability to monitor self," "accepts responsibility for the assault," and the overall rating of success in treatment. In initial analyses of the Sex Offender Treatment and Evaluation Project (SOTEP) treatment outcome study, those offenders who mastered certain RP skills recidivated less often than others (Marques, Nelson, West, & Day, 1994). These encouraging effects, however, disappeared in subsequent analyses of the same study using additional subjects and an extended follow-up (Marques, 1999).

At the very least, it appears difficult to evaluate whether sexual offenders have benefited from RP treatment (see also the review by Hanson, 1998). The high failure rates among "successfully" treated candidates may also indicate a significant problem with the RP approach. Even if the treatment works, it is not for the reasons RP considers important.

Incidental Comparison Groups

To determine whether RP treatment reduces recidivism rates, however, studies require a comparison group that has not been exposed to RP treatment.

Researchers can deliberately assign offenders to treatment or no-treatment conditions, but it is also possible to construct comparison groups by capitalizing on natural experiments. These "incidental" comparison groups are formed when neither the offender, the therapist, nor the experimenter determine who receives treatment. Examples of such incidental groups include (a) offenders from the same jurisdiction before and after the implementation (or change) of a treatment program, (b) offenders from parallel jurisdictions who receive different (or no) services, and (c) offenders who receive better or worse versions of the same treatment due to variable treatment integrity, staff shortages, or facilities problems. One advantage of the incidental groups design is that the comparison groups can often be created after a program has been in operation for a number of years.

A promising example of the incidental groups design is the recent study by McGrath, Hoke, and Vojtisek (1998). Rural Vermont may seem a difficult setting to conduct treatment outcome research because Vermont's correctional policy directs all sex offenders to receive treatment. Not everyone, however, receives the same treatment. McGrath et al. (1998) were resourceful enough to take advantage of this natural experiment. Retrospective record reviews found that offenders participating in the specialized cognitive-behavioral treatment had a significantly lower sex offense recidivism rate (1.4%) than those receiving generic counseling (15.6%). These results were particularly encouraging, considering that there were no significant group differences on the preexisting risk factors examined in this study.

Statistically controlling for preexisting risk factors, however, is no guarantee that the groups are really equivalent. There could always be some unmeasured factor that contributes to group differences. As our knowledge of risk assessment improves, however, we can be increasingly confident that major risk factors have not been overlooked.

Random Assignment

The most direct method of generating similar groups is through random assignment. Random assignment is never popular; some even argue that it is unethical. I disagree. The moral requirement to provide empirically supported treatment justifies serious efforts to determine whether treatment works. We cannot assume that what *should* work *does* work. Also, there are obvious examples in which random assignment would not even result in a reduction in service delivery (e.g., insufficient space in program, alternate treatments available). Nevertheless, it is often difficult to sustain enthusiasm for random assignment because the results of any single study are likely to be inconclusive. After years of struggle to maintain the support of case managers, curb innovation among treatment providers, appease funding agencies, and retain disorderly clients, researchers can expect to be rewarded by a nonsignificant trend.

The most impressive random assignment study is California's SOTEP (see Marques, Nelson, Alarcon, & Day, 2000 [this volume]). SOTEP is a big project. Initial planning for the project began in the early 1980s, treatment was provided between 1985 and 1995, and the final results are expected sometime after the millennium. When the program was in full operation, the annual costs were slightly more than $2,000,000 for the research, inpatient treatment, and after-care services (J. Marques, personal communication, September 23, 1996). This excellent study will be highly influential, but it will not silence the debate on treatment effectiveness. If treatment effects are found, skeptics will point to special features of the program that limit its generalizability (e.g., type of follow-up supervision). If no treatment effects are found, treatment advocates will similarly suggest that the setting was artificial, clients were difficult, or the treatment was based on the 1989, not 1999, edition of *Relapse Prevention*.

Research Synthesis

Knowledge proceeds by orderly replication (Lakatos, 1970). Skeptics can dismiss any single study, but accumulated evidence from diverse studies can be persuasive. Traditionally, the integration of research results has been addressed through narrative reviews (e.g., Marshall, Jones, Ward, Johnston, & Barbaree, 1991; Quinsey, Harris, Rice, & Lalumière, 1993), and some even conduct narrative reviews of narrative reviews (U.S. General Accounting Office, 1996). More recently, researchers have turned to quantitative analyses (meta-analyses) as a method of systematically summarizing the results of previous research (Cooper & Hedges, 1994). Although meta-analysis can be more objective than narrative reviews, meta-analyses still require numerous coding decisions, decisions that may or may not be accepted by colleagues. Secondary analysis of data is a powerful research strategy, but the results of such analyses need to be scrutinized with the same care accorded primary research studies.

At least three meta-analyses of sex offender treatment outcome have been performed (Alexander, 1995; see summary by McGrath, 1995; Hall, 1995; Thornton, 1994), although Hall's (1995) is the only completed, published study. Hall analyzed 12 studies that appeared after Furby, Weinrott, and Blackshaw's discouraging 1989 review. Hall reported a small but significant treatment effect ($r = .12$). Furthermore, he concluded that cognitive-behavioral treatments and hormone-based treatments were more effective than strictly behavioral treatments.

Hall's (1995) meta-analysis has been welcomed by treatment advocates, but skeptics remain, well, skeptical. Reanalyses of Hall's 12 studies by Harris et al. (1998) found that the treatment effect could be wholly accounted for by studies that used dropouts/refusers as the comparison group. Also, Hall's classification of treatments into "behavioral" or "cognitive-behavioral" has been questioned (Becker & Murphy, 1998; Hanson, 1997b; Harris et al., 1998), shedding doubts over Hall's conclusions regarding the relative inferiority of behavioral treatment.

Hall's (1995) study, nevertheless, makes an important contribution by demonstrating how meta-analysis can help organize the sex offender treatment outcome literature. Unfortunately, his review also demonstrates one of the weaknesses of meta-analysis: The information presented in the original studies can be poorly matched to the meta-analyst's goals. Considerable inference is often required to extract the information desired for the secondary analysis from the concise descriptions in the original published reports.

ATSA Collaborative Outcome Research Project

Questions concerning the effectiveness of treatment for sexual offenders are unlikely to be resolved in the near future. Despite disagreements on many points, all reviewers agree that there have been insufficient studies to justify clear conclusions (Marshall et al., 1991; Quinsey et al., 1993). Consequently, the Association for the Treatment of Sexual Abusers (ATSA) has initiated a long-term project aimed at promoting quality outcome studies and synthesizing the results of all relevant outcome research.[1]

The minimum requirement for inclusion in this project is a comparison of the recidivism rates of sexual offenders who received some form of treatment with a group who did not receive that treatment. Studies are categorized into those that used (a) random assignment, (b) incidental assignment/matching, and (c) dropouts/refusers. A coding manual has been developed to guide the development of new studies and summarize existing studies. The coding manual uses standard categories to describe the intensity and nature of treatment and identifies a number of factors that can be used evaluate the equivalence of the treatment and comparison conditions. To avoid misrepresenting studies, the original researchers are being asked (whenever possible) to complete or verify the coding for their studies. Only grouped data are collected from local research sites to minimize problems of confidentiality and security of personal information.

The ATSA project is just beginning. The overall design of the project has been carefully reviewed, and the coding and analytic procedures appear feasible (Hanson et al., 1998). Too few studies have been processed, however, to justify even preliminary conclusions. It is hoped, however, that in the years to come, researchers, clinicians, and policymakers will increasingly turn to the ATSA collaborative project for the best-available evidence on the effectiveness of treatment for sex offenders.

Within-Treatment Change

Long-term outcome studies are important for determining whether treatment reduces recidivism. They are silent, however, on the effectiveness of current interventions. Unlike many forms of psychological treatment, the "problem" is not directly observable. Therapists who treat depression, for example, may see symptom improvement in a single session. In contrast, therapists who treat sex offenders may never see a sex offense. All sex offender treatment is, in this sense, relapse prevention. Instead of directly monitoring the problem behavior, therapists can only address factors that are presumed to be related to offending. Such factors have been called criminogenic needs (Andrews & Bonta, 1998) or stable dynamic risk factors (Hanson & Harris, 2000). Therapy is only as good as the criminogenic needs that it targets. Sex offenders have a variety of personal and life problems, but not all their problems are related to sexual offense recidivism. Treatments that target noncriminogenic needs cannot be expected to reduce recidivism.

Figure 27.1 presents a research strategy designed to determine whether particular factors are criminogenic. Although some of the activities would require separate research resources, many of the activities are an integral part of good clinical practice. Therapists who maintain records consistent with this model could not only improve service delivery but also make important contributions to new knowledge.

The first stage of this research strategy involves specifying the criminogenic needs targeted in treatment: What changes do we hope to see? These criminogenic needs can be further divided into factors that initiate the behavior (e.g., deviant sexual interests) and those that prevent relapse (e.g., self-management strategies). If a factor is associated with the initiation of sex offending, then it should be found more frequently among sex offenders than other groups, and it should predict recidivism. Relapse prevention factors need only predict recidivism; comparisons with nonoffenders are meaningless on factors such as victim blaming, knowledge of offense cycle, and cooperation with supervision. It is important that both initiation and relapse factors be considered current characteristics, not simply historical factors. Historical factors may signal the presence of current problems, but only current characteristics can change.

Once treatment targets have been defined, they need to be reliably measured. Constructing reliable measures is time-consuming and requires some specialized training. Consequently, programs often use existing measures even when the constructs assessed by these measures are poorly matched to the goals of treatment. Rather than tolerating measures of questionable utility, the field would benefit from sustained efforts to develop good measures of the constructs that sex offender therapists are really interested in.

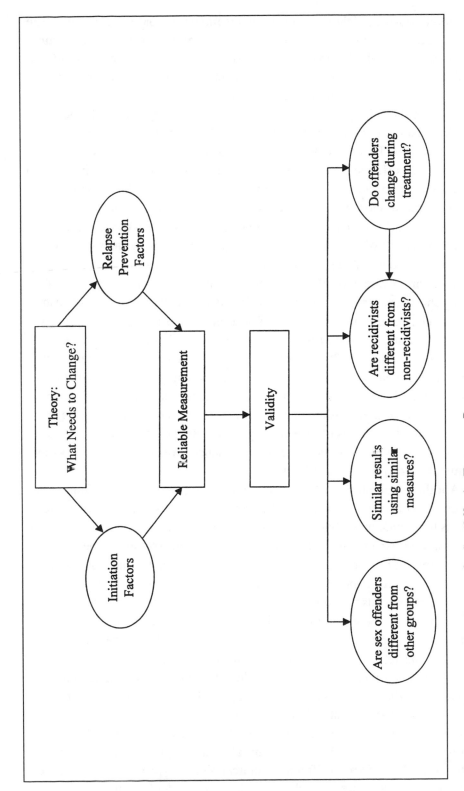

Figure 27.1. An Evaluation Strategy for Sex Offender Treatment Programs

Good measures of the right constructs are important for several reasons. The struggle to select or develop sound measures forces therapists to clearly articulate treatment goals. Sound measures are obviously necessary to assess offenders' progress in treatment. Furthermore, sound measures provide the opportunity to test theories and learn from mistakes.

As Meehl (1978) pointed out, progress in psychology is often hindered by weak measurement. Imagine that Dr. Smart believes that victim empathy inhibits recidivism. To test this hypothesis, he assesses victim empathy in a large group of sex offenders and then collects recidivism information. If he finds an association between low victim empathy and recidivism, his hypothesis receives some support. But what if no relationship is found? Should he abandon victim empathy training, or should he question his measures of victim empathy and recidivism? We would want to know about the reliability and validity of his measures before making such a decision.

There are several procedures for determining whether a measure is credible. In psychometric language, reliability refers to the extent to which the same individual receives the same scores each time he or she is assessed; validity refers to the extent that a measure assesses the construct it claims to assess (Ghiselli, Campbell, & Zedeck, 1981). The simplest approach to validity is face validity: Are knowledgeable judges able to guess what the scale is intended to measure? Face validity is important when deciding whether a measure meets the needs of a treatment program. Although clinicians should feel confident that the items are relevant, high levels of face validity are not necessarily desirable. If clinicians can guess what a scale is measuring, chances are offenders can too—and adjust their responses accordingly.

Another straightforward approach to assessing validity is to compare one measure to other similar measures. Consequently, it is useful for routine assessments to include more than one measure of important constructs. Considering the results of two measures not only improves clinical assessments but also provides important research information. Similarly, pretest and posttest evaluations bracketing individual treatment modules are not only good clinical practice but can also shed light on the validity of the measures used.

Comparisons between sex offenders and other men are another approach to estimating validity. The comparison groups could include other problematic populations (e.g., alcoholics, nonsexual criminals), socioeconomic status (SES)-matched nonoffenders, or samples of "normal" community men. No ideal comparison group is possible. Groups will always differ on a number of factors, and efforts to match the offenders on one characteristic will necessarily result in a systematic mismatch on other characteristics (Meehl, 1970). When group differences are observed, many alternate explanations are available. However, a lack of group differences indicates serious problems with the measure. How can sex offenders change if they already look normal?

The crucial test of sex offender measures is predictive validity. Sex offenders with the most criminogenic needs should recidivate most rapidly. If treatment changes risk factors, then posttreatment assessments should predict recidivism better than pretreatment measures. Recidivism information is not a routine item in clinical records, but it would be good practice if it were. We need feedback to keep our intuition from drifting into irrelevance.

The evaluation strategy outlined in Figure 27.1 includes a number of ways to test the merits of a particular measure. The more tests passed, the greater the confidence in the measure. Solid measures provide information not only about whether a particular treatment program is effective but also about whether particular offenders have benefited from treatment. Consequently, clinicians should ask themselves the following questions when conducting evaluations of treatment outcome:

1. What changes are needed to reduce the offenders' recidivism risk?

2. How well do the assessment procedures target the important factors?

3. Are the evaluation procedures reliable (same results each time)?

4. Do different measures yield similar results?

5. Do sex offenders differ from other groups?

6. Do sex offenders change during treatment?

7. Do pretreatment evaluations predict recidivism?

8. Do posttreatment evaluations predict recidivism better than the pretreatment evaluations?

Unfortunately, I do not know of a single measure that meets all these criteria (Hanson, 1998; Hanson, Cox, & Woszczyna, 1991). Reliable measures are relatively easy to find, as are those that correlate with similar measures. Also, a number of measures differentiate sex offenders from other groups (e.g., Bumby, 1996; Hanson, Gizzarelli, & Scott, 1994). Many measures change during the course of treatment (Hanson, Steffy, & Gauthier, 1993; Quinsey et al., 1998). Very few potentially dynamic measures, however, have been shown to predict sex offense recidivism (Hanson & Bussière, 1998). Phallometric assessments of sexual interest in children are one of the most well-established measures, but recidivism is best predicted by pretreatment rather than posttreatment evaluations (Rice et al., 1991). Some of the variables most commonly cited in risk evaluations, such as denial or victim empathy, have never been shown to predict sex offense recidivism (Hanson & Bussière, 1998).

So what needs to be done? As tempting as it is to question the research findings, it is also possible that there are serious flaws with the measures, the treatment, or both. Minimally, clinicians need to be exceedingly cautious when making judgments about whether sex offenders have changed (for better or worse). Better research is clearly needed.

There has been surprisingly little research designed to assess dynamic risk factors with sex offenders. The typical long-term follow-up study is unable to detect the rapidly changing risk factors observed using other types of research designs (Hanson & Harris, 2000; Quinsey, Coleman, Jones, & Altrows, 1997). Also, the measures considered in previous research have often been poorly matched to treatment goals. Most of the discouraging results have examined measures of general psychological distress or interpersonal functioning. Furthermore, the few attempts to create measures specifically tailored to sex offenders often produce measures with unknown reliability and validity. It is my contention that commitment to the research strategy outlined in Figure 27.1 will, in the long term, provide the feedback needed to lead clinicians and researchers in the right direction.

Although research support remains tentative, I believe that five factors could plausibly be considered dynamic risk factors for sexual offenders (Hanson, 2000):

1. Intimacy deficits (Seidman, Marshall, Hudson, & Robertson, 1994)
2. Negative social environment (Hanson & Harris, in press)
3. Attitudes tolerant of sex offending (e.g., Bumby, 1996)
4. Emotional/sexual self-regulation (Cortoni, 1998; McKibben et al., 1994)
5. General self-regulation deficits (Hanson & Harris, 2000)

Relapse prevention treatment tends to concentrate on self-regulation deficits, although broader cognitive-behavioral approaches can easily address all five factors.

Conclusions

Low recidivism rates present special challenges for the evaluation of sex offender treatment programs. Researchers have the option of either conducting new studies or using existing data. Each of these approaches presents its own limitations. New studies take many years; existing records may be inadequate. Nevertheless, progress is possible through the collective efforts of clinicians and researchers. Programs that maintain reliable records of client change provide a solid foundation for future evaluation efforts.

Almost all the information required for productive research can be drawn from well-documented clinical records. The only additional research costs are for comparison groups and recidivism data. It is relatively easy to find comparison groups for validity studies (e.g., SES-matched controls, nonsexual criminals). Comparisons between sex offenders and others can quickly reveal whether the proposed measures of criminogenic needs have promise. On the other hand, some ingenuity may be required to find comparison groups of untreated sex offenders for treatment outcome studies. Furthermore, comparisons between treated and untreated offenders will likely be inconclusive for most programs due to low statistical power (Barbaree, 1997). The accumulated evidence from these small outcome studies can, nevertheless, make an important contribution to knowledge. Recidivism data are not readily available in all jurisdictions, but it is good practice for those working with sex offenders to know who recidivates or not. Learning requires feedback.

This whole chapter can be read as a plea for clinicians to participate in research. Sometimes, research is perceived as a luxury, an interesting side activity that takes resources away from the pressing demands of service delivery. Often, the only perceived benefit of research is a few conference invitations and possibly the respect (or resentment) of colleagues. I hold a different view. More than 1,500 treatment programs for sex offenders are currently operating in the United States (Freeman-Longo, Bird, Stevenson, & Fiske, 1995). Daily, hundreds of therapists are writing treatment outcome reports for hundreds of judges, child welfare workers, and community supervision officers. Information about the offenders' amenability to treatment is routinely incorporated into decisions concerning sentencing, parole, family reunification, and community supervision. Until we are able to demonstrate that our reports are worth reading, the need for better research information is not a luxury but an emergency.

Note

1. For more information about the Collaborative Outcome Research Project, contact ATSA, 10700 S. W. Beaverton-Hillsdale Highway, Suite 26, Beaverton, OR 97005-3035, or the project manager, Andrew Harris, Corrections Policy, Department of the Solicitor General of Canada, 340 Laurier Avenue West, Ottawa, Ontario, Canada, K1A 0P8. Currently, the steering committee consists of Arthur Gordon, Karl Hanson, Andrew Harris, Janice Marques, William Murphie, Vernon Quinsey, and Micheal Seto.

References

Alexander, M. (1995, September). *Sex offender treatment: Does it work?* Paper presented at the NOTA/ATSA 1st Joint International Conference, Cambridge, UK.

Anderson, R. D., Gibeau, D., & D'Amora, D. A. (1995). The Sex Offender Treatment Rating Scale: Initial reliability data. *Sexual Abuse: A Journal of Research and Treatment, 7,* 221-227.

Andrews, D. A., & Bonta, J. (1998). *The psychology of criminal conduct* (2nd ed.). Cincinnati, OH: Anderson.

Barbaree, H. E. (1997). Evaluating treatment efficacy with sex offenders: The insensitivity of recidivism studies to treatment effects. *Sexual Abuse: A Journal of Research and Treatment, 9,* 111-128.

Becker, J. V., & Murphy, W. D. (1998). What we know and do not know about assessing and treating sex offenders. *Psychology, Public Policy, and Law, 4,* 116-137.

Bonta, J., & Hanson, R. K. (1994). *Gauging the risk for violence: Measurement, impact and strategies for change* (Corrections Branch User Report 1994-09). Ottawa: Department of the Solicitor General of Canada.

Bumby, K. M. (1996). Assessing the cognitive distortions of child molesters and rapists: Development and validation of the MOLEST and RAPE scales. *Sexual Abuse: A Journal of Research and Treatment, 8,* 37-54.

Cohen, J. (1988). *Statistical power analysis for the behavioral sciences* (2nd ed.). Hillsdale, NJ: Lawrence Erlbaum.

Cooper, H., & Hedges, L. V. (Eds.). (1994). *The handbook of research synthesis.* New York: Russell Sage.

Cortoni, F. A. (1998). *The relationship between attachment styles, coping, the use of sex as a coping strategy, and juvenile sexual history in sexual offenders.* Unpublished doctoral dissertation, Queen's University, Kingston, Ontario, Canada.

Freeman-Longo, R. E., Bird, S., Stevenson, W. F., & Fiske, J. A. (1995). *1994 nationwide survey of treatment programs & models.* Brandon, VT: Safer Society.

Furby, L., Weinrott, M. R., & Blackshaw, L. (1989). Sex offender recidivism: A review. *Psychological Bulletin, 105,* 3-30.

George, W. H., & Marlatt, G. A. (1989). Introduction. In D. R. Laws (Ed.), *Relapse prevention with sex offenders* (pp. 1-31). New York: Guilford.

Ghiselli, E. E., Campbell, J. P., & Zedeck, S. (1981). *Measurement theory for the behavioral sciences.* San Francisco: Freeman.

Hall, G. C. N. (1995). Sexual offender recidivism revisited: A meta-analysis of recent treatment studies. *Journal of Consulting and Clinical Psychology, 63,* 802-809.

Hanson, R. K. (1996). Evaluating the contribution of relapse prevention theory to the treatment of sexual offenders. *Sexual Abuse: A Journal of Research and Treatment, 8*(3), 201-208.

Hanson, R. K. (1997a). *The development of a brief actuarial risk scale for sexual offense recidivism* (User Report 97-04). Ottawa: Department of the Solicitor General of Canada.

Hanson, R. K. (1997b). How to know what works with sex offenders. *Sexual Abuse: A Journal of Research and Treatment, 9*(2), 129-145.

Hanson, R. K. (1998). What do we know about sexual offender risk assessment? *Psychology, Public Policy and Law, 4,* 50-72.

Hanson, R. K. (2000). *The Sex Offender Need Assessment Rating (SONAR): A method for measuring change in risk levels.* (User Report 2000-01). Ottawa: Department of the Solicitor General of Canada.

Hanson, R. K., & Bussière, M. T. (1998). Predicting relapse: A meta-analysis of sexual offender recidivism studies. *Journal of Consulting and Clinical Psychology, 66*(2), 348-362.

Hanson, R. K., Cox, B., & Woszczyna, C. (1991). Assessing treatment outcome for sexual offenders. *Annals of Sex Research, 4,* 177-208.

Hanson, R. K., Gizzarelli, R., & Scott, H. (1994). The attitudes of incest offenders: Sexual entitlement and acceptance of sex with children. *Criminal Justice and Behavior, 21,* 187-202.

Hanson, R. K., & Harris, A. J. R. (2000). Where should we intervene? Dynamic predictors of sex offense recidivism. *Criminal Justice and Behavior, 27,* 6-35.

Hanson, R. K., Harris, A., Marques, J., Murphie, W., Gordon, A., Quinsey, V., & Seto, M. (1998, October). *Collaborative data base of sex offender treatment outcome.* Paper presented at the 17th Annual Research and Treatment Conference of the Association for the Treatment of Sexual Abusers, Vancouver, British Columbia, Canada.

Hanson, R. K., Steffy, R. A., & Gauthier, R. (1993). Long-term recidivism of child molesters. *Journal of Consulting and Clinical Psychology, 61,* 646-652.

Harris, G. T., Rice, M. E., & Quinsey, V. L. (1998). Appraisal and management of risk in sexual aggressors: Implications for criminal justice policy. *Psychology, Public Policy, and Law, 4,* 73-115.

Lakatos, I. (1970). Falsification and the methodology of scientific research programs. In A. Musgrave & I. Lakatos (Eds.), *Criticism and the growth of knowledge* (pp. 91-195). New York: Cambridge University Press.

Laws, D. R. (Ed.). (1989). *Relapse prevention with sex offenders.* New York: Guilford.

Laws, D. R. (1995). Central elements in relapse prevention procedures with sex offenders. *Psychology, Crime & Law, 2,* 41-53.

Marques, J. K. (1999). How to answer the question, "Does sex offender treatment work?" *Journal of Interpersonal Violence, 14,* 437-451.

Marques, J. K., Nelson, C., Alarcon, J. -M., & Day, D. M. (2000). Preventing relapse in sex offenders: What we learned from SOTEP's experimental treatment program. In D. R. Laws, S. M. Hudson, & T. Ward (Eds.), *Remaking relapse prevention with sex offenders: A sourcebook* (pp. 321-340). Thousand Oaks, CA: Sage.

Marques, J. K., Nelson, C., West, M. A., & Day, D. M. (1994). The relationship between treatment goals and recidivism among child molesters. *Behaviour Research and Therapy, 32,* 577-588.

Marshall, W. L., Jones, R., Ward, T., Johnston, P., & Barbaree, H. E. (1991). Treatment outcome with sex offenders. *Clinical Psychology Review, 11,* 465-485.

McGrath, R. J. (1995, Winter). Sex offender treatment: Does it work? *Perspectives,* pp. 24-26.

McGrath, R. J., Hoke, S. E., & Vojtisek, J. E. (1998). Cognitive-behavioral treatment of sex offenders: A treatment comparison and long-term follow-up study. *Criminal Justice and Behavior, 25,* 203-225.

McKibben, A., Proulx, J., & Lusignan, R. (1994). Relationships between conflict, affect and deviant sexual behaviors in rapists and child molesters. *Behaviour Research and Therapy, 32,* 571-575.

Meehl, P. (1970). Nuisance variables and the ex post facto design. In M. Radner & S. Winokur (Eds.), *Minnesota studies in the philosophy of science* (Vol. 4, pp. 373-402). Minneapolis: University of Minnesota Press.

Meehl, P. (1978). Theoretical risks and tabular asterisks: Sir Karl, Sir Ronald and the slow progress of soft psychology. *Journal of Consulting and Clinical Psychology, 46,* 806-834.

Proulx, J., McKibben, A., & Lusignan, R. (1996). Relationships between affective components and sexual behaviors in sexual aggressors. *Sexual Abuse: A Journal of Research and Treatment, 8,* 279-289.

Quinsey, V. L., Coleman, G., Jones, B., & Altrows, I. (1997). Proximal antecedents of eloping and reoffending among supervised mentally disordered offenders. *Journal of Interpersonal Violence, 12,* 794-813.

Quinsey, V. L., Harris, G. T., Rice, M. E., & Lalumière, M. L. (1993). Assessing treatment efficacy in outcome studies of sex offenders. *Journal of Interpersonal Violence, 8,* 512-523.

Quinsey, V. L., Khanna, A., & Malcolm, P. B. (1998). A retrospective evaluation of the Regional Treatment Centre Sex Offender Treatment Program. *Journal of Interpersonal Violence, 13,* 621-644.

Rice, M. E., Quinsey, V. L., & Harris, G. T. (1989). *Predicting sexual recidivism among treated and untreated extrafamilial child molesters released from a maximum security psychiatric institution* (Research Report No. VI-III). Ontario, Canada: Mental Health Centre.

Rice, M. E., Quinsey, V. L., & Harris, G. T. (1991). Sexual recidivism among child molesters released from a maximum security institution. *Journal of Consulting and Clinical Psychology, 59,* 381-386.

Ryan, G., & Miyoshi, T. (1990). Summary of a pilot follow-up study of adolescent sexual perpetrators after treatment. *Interchange, 1,* 6-8.

Seidman, B. T., Marshall, W. L., Hudson, S. M., & Robertson, P. J. (1994). An examination of intimacy and loneliness in sex offenders. *Journal of Interpersonal Violence, 9,* 518-534.

Seto, M. (1998, February). *The Multifactorial Assessment of Sex Offender Risk for Reoffense (MASORR): A retrospective study.* Paper presented at the 51st Annual Convention of the Ontario Psychological Association, Toronto, Canada.

Thornton, D. (1994, September). *A review of treatment outcome with sexual offenders.* Paper presented at the Home Office Sex Offender Treatment Conference, Coventry, UK.

U.S. General Accounting Office. (1996). *Sex offender treatment: Research results inconclusive about what works to reduce recidivism.* Washington, DC: Author.

Ward, T., Louden, K., Hudson, S. M., & Marshall, W. L. (1995). A descriptive model of the offense chain for child molesters. *Journal of Interpersonal Violence, 10,* 452-472.

PART IX

THE WAY FORWARD

CHAPTER 28

Whither Relapse Prevention?

STEPHEN M. HUDSON
University of Canterbury, New Zealand

TONY WARD
University of Melbourne, Australia

D. RICHARD LAWS
Forensic Psychiatric Services Commission, British Columbia

Unfulfilled Promises

We begin this final chapter by posing the question "Are the promises made by relapse prevention (see Laws, Hudson, & Ward, 2000 [this volume]) at risk of being kept in the near future?" The companion query or even better question perhaps is, "What do we have to do to keep the faith with the optimism, as well as resources, that has been the result of adopting relapse prevention as the primary model?" The unfulfilled promises we have identified in Chapter 1 center on three major themes: Has relapse prevention reduced the reoffense rate, has it provided an adequate guide to structuring treatment, and is it adequate as a theory? We deal with each of these themes in turn, although they are clearly interrelated.

Reducing Reoffending

The first and arguably the most central promise relapse prevention made was to help our clients maintain the typically hard-won change generated by the

AUTHORS' NOTE: Portions of this manuscript were abstracted from D. R. Laws (1998a, 1998b).

intervention—in a nutshell, to reduce recidivism. The most recent answer to this has been provided by Marshall and Anderson (2000 [this volume]), who suggest that provided we do not take an excessively purist methodological view, the evidence supports the notion that programs with an internal self-management component of relapse prevention do reduce recidivism over the medium term. They also suggest that the available evidence for the requirement of significant follow-up postrelease (external supervision dimension) may be having paradoxical effects on reoffense rates. They provide an intriguing logical argument in support of this interpretation of these data as well. It probably pays us to be cautious in the face of just one study, but if this is indeed the case, then managing the transition from prison to community, at the very least, needs to be restructured in a manner that encourages and enhances self-regulation rather than diminishing it. They conclude by recommending that what remains is a need to evaluate the effects of the presence and absence of various relapse prevention components on long-term reoffending rates.

These points are well taken. Moreover, we believe this to be a fair evaluation of the current situation. However, there are additional issues to consider. For example, there is a need to link the amount of progress made by a man undergoing treatment and his subsequent behavior with respect to offending; in other words, we need to carry out our evaluations in a manner that is sensitive to dose relationships. Evidence collected in this manner might also provide some support for the model in the face of the trenchant criticisms that exist with respect to efficacy and the need for methodological rigor (see, e.g., Marshall & Anderson, 2000; Quinsey, 1998; Quinsey, Harris, Rice, & Lalumière, 1993). Indeed, this is implicit in some of the critical comments in Marshall and Anderson (2000).

The need for this type of evaluation is also supported by recent data collected within the British prison-based sexual offender program (Beech, Fisher, & Beckett, 1999). Although most of the participants were able to articulate adequate relapse prevention plans at the end of treatment (a within-treatment change), only those who also showed significant collateral positive changes in attitudes toward offending retained these skills at 9 months postrelease. This is also consistent with the motivational perspective implicit in the self-regulatory model (Ward & Hudson, 1998b) with its primary emphasis on goals.

The additional issue that this raises is how these changes in attitudes come about. Pithers (1990) has recommended that interventions relevant to victim harm issues need to occur prior to the central relapse prevention components, for motivational purposes. We have found an association between cognitive distortions (pro-offending attitudes at least in part), a measure of the amount of offending (number of victims), and some aspects of generalized empathy in men whom we would classify as approach explicit in their offending process (Hudson, Jones, & Ward, 1997). These observations are suggestive of goals (approach and avoidance in our model terms) and the mechanisms that "correct" these goals being the really core issue in treatment. Moreover, we have recently suggested that the central process that may well link empathy deficits (victim specific or more generalized to classes of potential victims) and intimacy deficits may be a function of a lack of awareness of other people's beliefs, desires, perspectives, and needs. That is, sexual offenders' problems in these domains can be viewed as partially arising from deficits in one central mechanism, the ability to infer mental states in others. Thus, the central component to treatment, especially for men with approach goals, and entrenched implicit theories that are offense supportive (Ward, in press) is likely to assist in convincing them of the harm they do.

In addition to suggestions for fine-tuning our focus in treatment and evaluation, what all of these issues raise is the need for "psychological autopsies" in the face of our inevitable failures. We are likely to learn more from a detailed analysis of one of our clients who has failed to use or access the needed skills than we will ever learn from meeting up with one of them who has remained offense free. Which is not to say that asking a successful client how he has managed to restrain or avoid behaving in an abusive manner is not of value. Clearly, it is. With a client who has reoffended, we simply have more opportunities to examine the adequacy of our interventions. We may find, for example, that a significant proportion of the failures reported an approach-explicit pathway in treatment. This has implications for how we structure the intervention (see Hudson & Ward, 2000 [this volume]).

More generally, improvements in intervention are likely to be an issue of which components are needed for which type of offender. As we have noted before, grapeshot approaches are not really enough. There are numerous references to the heterogeneity exhibited by offenders, as well as some work with respect to taxonomies (e.g., Knight & Prentky, 1990). However, there seems little impact of this type of work on interventions. We ought to be getting our taxonomic act together and using it to inform the adequate targeting of treatment. We (Ward, Nathan, Drake, Lee, & Pathé, 1999) have suggested that manual-based interventions are preferable, outside of some very specific circumstances, to the detailed, time-consuming, and frequently inadequate formulation-based approaches. However, we need to do better than to pretend that sexual offenders are all the same. Indeed, our major criticism of Pithers's (1990) model is that it only really allows for one offense process, and we know that is not the case. We know that sexual offenders are a diverse population, yet there is little published indication that we have any rational and explicit criteria for how to partial this variance meaningfully, what to do to these groups or get them to do, how much to do, and to what standard to reduce risk. It is high time we did.

Structuring Treatment

A second promise, albeit more implicit than the reduction of reoffending concerns, was to structure treatment in a manner that was particularly

compatible with thorough care. To achieve this promise, treatment providers
needed to also accept that the core issue was adequate modeling of the offense
process. Acceptance of this has been variable to say the least. If this issue had
been taken seriously, then considerably more work would have probably been
done in describing the processes involved. As it stands, we need to do a lot more
work refining Level 3 offense process models (Ward & Hudson, 1998a). As we
have argued on several occasions, the adequate modeling of the actual processes involved is the central underpinning to relapse prevention as a model of
treatment (Hudson & Ward, 1996; Ward & Hudson, 1996). We (Hudson &
Ward, 1998; Hudson, Ward, & McCormack, 1999; Ward, Louden, Hudson, &
Marshall, 1995; Ward & Hudson 1998b) and others (Proulx, Perreault, &
Ouimet, 1999) have gone some way along this path, but this work predominantly has focused on child molesters. However, much work needs still to be
done. Polaschek (1999) has recently completed a study modeling offense processes in incarcerated New Zealand Pakeha (white) males who have raped adult
women. This study identified 21 discriminable steps in the offending processes
described by these men. These steps could be summarized into six phases:
background, goal formation, approach, preparation, offense, and postoffense.
In addition, and most relevant to the argument being presented here, is that she
found three pathways: seeking sexual gratification to enhance positive mood,
escaping negative mood through sexual gratification, and redressing harm to
self by harming others (Polaschek, 1999).

Our own work has spanned developing a model, using the qualitative technique grounded theory, of offending processes in a group of incarcerated child
molesters (Ward, Louden, et al., 1995). We have used that model to explore
offense pathways in a group of child molesters and rapists (Hudson et al., 1999)
and found evidence of three major pathways. Approximately one third
reflected an appetitive, positive affect pathway, which was associated with a
resolution to continue offending. As we keep noting, this pathway is outside the
current scope of the relapse prevention model. Only a quarter of the sample
reflected the traditional covert-planning, negative-affect, restraint pathway.
The third major pathway reflected negative restraining processes but with
explicit planning. The remaining minor pathways reflected either a positive to
negative shift about the offense or were essentially positive pathways with negative beginnings. Most recently (see Chapters 2 and 3), we have been exploring
a self-regulatory based model of offending processes. Again, the preliminary
evidence we have collected (Hudson & Ward, 1998) suggests that of 44 men
who had offended sexually (30 child molesters and 14 rapists), more than three
quarters (76%) evidenced one of the two approach pathways. Proulx et al.
(1999) used cluster analysis offense details of 44 extrafamiliar child molesters
and detected two pathways, essentially with or without planning. In this case,
the proportions were reversed with 30 of the men reporting minimal planning.

That these proportions are unstable and probably sample dependent, as well as reflecting the difficulties in getting good-quality information of what are subtle aspects of offending, should not worry us very much. We do not know enough about these processes, most particularly how to classify them, and until we do, this is to be expected. Moreover, all of these attempts to chart the territory have identified *some* offending processes *not* currently covered by the relapse prevention model.

Marshall and Anderson (2000) very rightly suggest that if treatment providers do not use relapse prevention or offending process to ground their provision of interventions, then they need to use something else (e.g., a generic social learning model). An adequate model of the offense process is likely to be best practice. Group facilitators (therapists) need to have some framework to guide their facilitation of the disclosure. If the model is too detailed, then the result of the process has little portability. It needs to be portable if it is going to guide the man's behavior for any significant length of time (see Marshall & Anderson, 2000, for an excellent discussion of this point). Similarly, if the template carried by the facilitator is unduly narrow, regardless in which direction, then there is a risk that men will be encouraged to "fit the mold." Thus, we argue that facilitators' theory of offending process needs to be adequate. How else are they going to be able to recognize that a man has "jumped" a piece of time in his description and needs to be gently brought back to enrich the picture in meaningful ways? Moreover, we would argue that the facilitator has some theory, even if it is implicit (see Ward, in press). Finally, we would argue that no provider should be delivering treatment-labeled relapse prevention without an explicit model of the process. This would go some way toward the overuse (misuse) of the term in areas in which it is difficult to see the likely relevance.

Theoretical Adequacy

The final theme we suggested as being in need of review was that of theoretical adequacy. That is, is the theory of relapse prevention coherent and comprehensive? Sometimes, there is a negative reaction to the issue of theory, but it is our view (see Ward & Hudson, 1998a) that without a coherent model of what underlies the phenomenon we have been given the professional responsibility to deal with, we are unlikely to be successful. Moreover, we will not be in a good position to profit from our client's failures, inevitable that they are (see above). As we noted earlier, all therapists are likely to have a set of beliefs about what causes sexual offending, the processes involved as well as what are the appropriate things to be doing about them. It should be the case that the dominant model encapsulates those beliefs and does so in a manner that genuinely describes the territory, organizes relevant knowledge, and tells us what to do.

As Marshall and Anderson (2000) observe, the limited numbers of criticisms published of relapse prevention have been in terms of these issues (Hudson & Ward, 1996; Hudson, Ward, & Marshall, 1992; Mann, 1998; Ward & Hudson, 1996; Ward, Hudson, & Siegert, 1995). We have dealt with these issues in considerable detail in Chapter 1 and presented some of our suggestions for ways to overcome the problems that have been identified. Some progress has been made, but much remains to be done.

Sexual Offending as a Public Health Problem

A Different Emphasis

Laws (1998a, 1998b) recently argued that treating sexual deviation solely as a legal, medical, or psychological problem keeps it isolated from public consideration. Sexual deviation, like alcoholism and drug addiction, is (or should be) everybody's concern and everybody's problem. If sexual deviation cannot be seen, then no one has to deal with it. It is something that is happening to someone else, in another town, certainly not on their street, at their workplace, or in their children's school. Viewed in this way, it is a problem best left to those who are capable and willing to deal with it. Laws (1998a, 1998b) argued that sexual deviation should be brought into the open and dealt with as a public health problem.

Public health is usually defined as what a society does to ensure that its citizens are healthy. Applied to interpersonal violence, the focus is primarily on prevention. The public health model has three levels of prevention: primary, secondary, and tertiary.

At the *primary* level, the goal is to stop deviant behavior before it gets started. This requires early identification of the problem, usually in childhood, and prompt intervention. The *secondary* level of prevention overlaps the first to some extent. Here the concern is with persons who have engaged in deviant sexual behavior. They may be children, adolescents, or young adults. The assumption is that deviant behavior is not entrenched, that nondeviant alternatives are available, and that the individual may be amenable to treatment, possibly relapse prevention. At the *tertiary* level of prevention, we find the chronic, preferential sex offenders whose inclination toward deviant behavior is deeply entrenched. These are the persons most often seen in confinement or in the community after release from prisons or hospitals. Persons at this level have been major candidates for relapse prevention treatment. Unfortunately, most of our treatment efforts have been applied at the secondary and tertiary levels—a large proportion toward the tertiary, where they are least likely to succeed.

Public Health Violence Prevention Goals

It is necessary to make people aware of the magnitude and characteristics of sexual offending. As mentioned earlier, many people believe that sex offenders are somewhere that they are not. In fact, sex offenders are everywhere. Sexual deviation cuts across all social class lines, across all demographic variables. The public must learn what the characteristics of sex offending are. They must learn the strategies that offenders use to gain access to victims and carry out offenses. When they see these strategies at work, they must report them.

It is necessary to inform communities that there are interventions that work with sex offenders. Many people believe that these offenders are mentally ill and cannot profit from treatment. They get much of their information from biased reports in the print and television media, which focus on highly sensational cases that represent about one half of 1% of all sex crimes. Everyday sexual abuse does not sell newspapers. The message that needs to be communicated is that the resources are there (see, e.g., Freeman-Longo, Bird, Stevenson, & Fiske, 1994, on the availability of programs).

It is necessary to provide information on what works to prevent or deter sexual deviation. Although the resources are there (Freeman-Longo et al., 1994), they are not of equal value. Basically, for the treatment of sex offenders to be effective, it should be matched with offender risk level, be behavioral in nature and target criminogenic need, and be delivered in a manner that promotes prosocial skills (Andrews & Bonta, 1994; Gendreau, 1994). Regrettably, high-risk, high-need offenders who need the treatment most are often the ones least likely to get it.

Primary intervention efforts to prevent sexual abuse refer to public education and sex education in the schools. Included in such a curriculum would be misconceptions about rape and child abuse; the elements of consent, forced sex, and sexual harassment; the distinction between healthy and unhealthy sexual behavior; and the impact and consequences to victims of sexual abuse and sexual harassment.

Providing the public with information on the effectiveness of intervention programs is not easy. Fortunately, the use of meta-analysis permits the evaluation of large bodies of data to assess treatment outcome (e.g., Hanson & Bussière, 1996). On the other hand, simpler descriptive accounts of how various treatment interventions work with specific clientele are also useful (e.g., Grossman, Martis, & Fichtner, 1999). The information from such studies is commonly summarized in newspaper and magazine feature articles and so reaches a wider public. This, however, does not absolve professionals of the responsibility to provide information on treatment effectiveness at every opportunity.

Minimizing Harm Through Public Health Approaches

By using a public health perspective, it is possible to contain the number of new sex offenders entering the system. The point here is to interfere with a potential abuser to prevent him or her from crossing over from contemplation to actual offending (e.g., an option in low-level policing might be referring a potential offender to a treatment resource rather than making an arrest). The issue is to avoid a rush to judgment. If the problem can be dealt with short of introducing one more individual to the criminal justice system, that is probably an option that should be exercised.

Sex offenders can be encouraged to take early retirement. It is no wonder that sex offenders do not come forward and identify themselves. They are often unaware of treatment resources. Their image of what happens to apprehended sex offenders is shaped by what they see and read in the media. They fear being identified in their home communities, losing their jobs, losing their families, and being mistreated in custody.

A public health approach would prominently display information on the availability of treatment resources. This could be done on billboards or radio and television spot announcements. The public health approach to using seat belts, engaging in safe sex, and quitting smoking have all had an impact. What sponsors of such an effort are likely to forget, however, is that those earlier approaches only worked when the messages were hammered home day after day and night after night. The messages on treatment for sexual deviation must be incessant, and they must be brief and unambiguous. For example, when cigarette package notices read "The Surgeon General has determined that there is a link between smoking and lung cancer," many people focused on the word *link* and determined that the message did not apply to them. When the message eventually became "Smoking can kill you" or "Smoking can hurt your baby," it hit closer to home. Similarly, a public health message about sex offending would have to read "If you're molesting children and feeling bad about it, help is available. Call this number" or "Do you ever get the urge to have sex with children? We can help. Call this number."

The counterproductive effects of law enforcement can also be minimized. We mentioned earlier that police or social service agencies can directly refer individuals to a treatment resource rather than make a complaint that will result in arrest. Often, police officers will be aware that a given individual is highly likely to be engaging in deviant sexual behavior. However, he or she is never directly caught in the act, and no one has complained. The individual cannot be charged with a criminal offense. Some countries have a provision in their criminal codes that allow concerned professionals (police, forensic services, and family and children's services) to present evidence to a court that a given individual is likely to commit an offense or cause injury to another person. The court may then place the individual under a recognizance with elaborate conditions. Should the individual fail to observe the conditions of the order, criminal charges may then be laid.

All of the preceding suggestions are public-health-related approaches to the management of sexual deviation. All have a dual emphasis: preventing relapse and minimizing harm. A public health approach is, simply stated, a healthier way of dealing with our faulted and troublesome fellow humans. We do not deny the need to make society safer. We deny the necessity of using punishment to do it.

Does Relapse Prevention Prevent Relapse or Reduce Harm?

The notion of harm reduction (Marlatt, 1998), particularly when applied to sexual offending (Laws, 1996, 1999), is often seen as threatening by therapists who endorse relapse prevention. However, as presently conceived (see, e.g., George & Marlatt, 1989), therapists routinely fail to acknowledge that relapse prevention is stated as a zero-tolerance position: No sexually deviant behavior of *any* sort can be tolerated. This is a distortion of what actually happens in sex offender treatment. The notion of harm reduction would state that sexual offending occurs on a continuum ranging from total indulgence through abstinence. The more the client can be moved away from excess to moderation, the greater the amount of harm reduced. This is a public health perspective that recognizes human frailty but encourages people to moderate their behavior to do less harm to themselves and others.

Laws (1996) suggested that we abandon the term *treatment* and substitute *management* in its place. This would mean that our therapeutic efforts would be directed toward *reducing harm* rather than *eliminating harm.* This is, in fact, what we do in treating sex offenders. It is a bit of a paradigm shift to reframe what we do as relapse management or minimization rather than relapse prevention. It does not mean giving up on relapse prevention or attempting to prevent lapses and relapses. It simply acknowledges that we are not always going to be successful. That is hardly a radical position. However, numerous misconceptions surround the application of harm reduction to sexual offending. A consideration of a few of these misconceptions follows.

It is said that harm reduction *normalizes* deviant behavior, and this is unacceptable. Much of what was once considered deviant behavior (e.g., homosexuality, recreational drug use) is now ignored, tolerated, or simply accepted. It is easy to speak of harm reduction when one is talking about alcoholism, gambling, or shoplifting; it is much less easy to speak of sexual deviation in the same way. However, it may eventually prove necessary to normalize or decriminalize some aspects of sexual deviance, where the impact on others is limited. We will probably have to adopt a more European perspective that acknowledges that it is not necessary to medicalize and label sexual deviance to treat it or legalize and criminalize it to control it. We may simply have to accept that some deviant sexual behavior is part of the social landscape.

It is said that relapse is treatment failure. It is as easily argued that a person who gains some degree of control over a troublesome behavior, then loses it, is not the same person who entered treatment. The so-called "relapse" may be viewed as providing additional information on self-control and therefore has therapeutic value. Marlatt (1985) has referred to this process as a *prolapse*. It is also related to Prochaska and DiClemente's (1986) statement that it may take many attempts to finally achieve abstinence. From this perspective, relapse is an expected and manageable part of treatment (Marlatt, 1985).

It is said that there is a big difference between annoying and offensive behavior and devastating behavior. This is obviously true. The fear is that harm reduction will be accepting of devastating behavior. This is not true. We should continue to attempt to eliminate deviant thinking and deviant behavior, but we are not always going to be successful. We prevent some relapse, and we reduce a great deal of harm. But zero tolerance is an impossible goal, and pretending we can achieve this risks alienating rather than assisting.

It is said that harm reduction does more harm than good because it says that deviant behavior is okay. People become very upset if one says that harm reduction is a more sensible way of looking at the effects of treatment. The fear is that this really means that some sex offending is okay. Harm reduction openly recognizes that no matter what we do, no matter how good we are, a little bit of sex offending is going to occur. The notion of harm reduction came from the alcohol and drug treatment movement. If we apply those original principles to sexual deviation, it looks like the following (Des Jarlais, 1995, pp. 10-12):

1. Harm reduction is a public health alternative to the moral/criminal/political/ disease models of sexual deviation.

2. Harm reduction recognizes abstinence as an ideal outcome but accepts harm-reducing alternatives.

3. Harm reduction is a bottom-up approach, based on a realistic view of client behavior.

4. Harm reduction promotes low-threshold access to services as an alternative to high-threshold approaches.

5. Harm reduction is based on the principles of compassionate pragmatism rather than moralistic idealism.

When we reduce harm, we do not ignore harm. Nothing in the harm reduction approach says that harming other people is acceptable. What it does say is that we should continue to use the revised model of relapse prevention as our strategy and reduce as much harm as we possibly can.

Future Promises

We have already traversed some of the unfulfilled promises we believe were made and noted at that time what needs to be achieved if relapse prevention is to live up to expectations that accompanied the model's adoption by treatment providers in the sexual aggression area. In this final section, we note some additional things that we believe can reasonably be expected from relapse prevention in the next few years if we are to continue to strive to reduce harm.

Treatment Evaluation

The first item on the agenda must be the need for continued work on treatment evaluation. We have dealt with a number of issues related to this need at the beginning of this chapter, but there are some outstanding issues. The statistical problems that accrue from low base rates and the moral problems associated with the use of traditional random allocation to group types of experimental design remain with us. We agree with Marshall and Anderson (2000) that if the methodological requirements are too zealously applied, the net result will be a lack of effective progress in solving this substantial social problem. Although single-case designs (the usual solution to this dilemma that faces clinicians all too often) do offer some alternatives, the inherent problems in generalization, particularly in face of the taxonomic problems we face, limit their utility.

We have made some suggestions earlier with respect to some directions that could be taken in this regard. In addition, we need to learn more from our "mistakes," although it is a significant misnomer to call them such. We are in a more difficult position than most intervention areas insofar as the consequences of treatment failure are typically horrendous. The public outcry over our inability to predict well (see Proulx, Tardif, Lamoureux, & Lussier, 2000 [this volume]) and the fact that we have "failed to treat adequately" are both understandable reactions to the distress we all feel when someone innocent is abused. This should not mean that we avoid what we are professionally obligated to do. The analysis of "failures" needs to be in terms of any of the following processes: loss of skills acquired during intervention, a failure to generalize acquired skills, a motivationally driven failure to use existing skills, or, as raised earlier, the possibility of a new offense process exposing skills deficits.

Treatment Provision

The provision of treatment should be grounded on an adequate understanding of the offense process exhibited by the man undergoing treatment. This again raises the issue of treatment-related changes in offense processes. There is as yet no evidence for this, but given the typical singularity with which treatment providers appear to have been comfortable construing the offending process, this is probably not surprising. Both our descriptive model (Ward, Louden, et al., 1995) and the more recent self-regulatory model (Ward & Hudson, 1998b, 2000 [this volume]) describe multiple pathways. We have argued earlier for the possibility that the positive-emotion, approach-goal, explicit-planning pathway is likely to be disrupted in the face of good information concerning victim harm. It is frequently difficult for these men to change these deeply entrenched beliefs, often involving notions that their own abuser was the only one who really loved them and they were not harmed themselves. However, doing so is probably essential to reduce the risk they pose in the future. This change from an approach goal to one of avoidance is fundamental. Investigation of these two possible pathways for men classified as approach explicit in treatment—that is, still approach explicit or one of the two avoidant pathways—has considerable significance for how we structure treatment. Although this possibility is being argued for theoretically, it seems not unreasonable to think that a man who has derived most of his social and emotional contact from being in, for example, mentoring roles with children may well feel lonely and isolated in his new offense-free lifestyle. The risks this poses are substantially different from what existed previously.

A related issue concerns Marshall and colleagues' notion of tiered treatment (Marshall, Eccles, & Barbaree, 1993). This very useful suggestion for allocating resources that are almost inevitably restricted may well not be as straightforward as first thought. The notion that men can be assigned a level of need, according to the severity of their offense-related as opposed to offense-specific needs, is potentially problematic. That is, those men who have offended sexually and show evidence of only offense-specific deficits are thought to be relatively deficit free with respect to offense-related problems, such as problem solving and communication skills. What we are suggesting is that treatment-induced changes in the offending process makes this a more open question (see above). Again, "psychological autopsies" will assist us in making these issues clearer and will enable us to structure treatment in a more rational, empirically based manner.

A more peripheral issue but still related in the sense of modeling the processes involved, a central theme for relapse prevention, has been the criticism that these models do not provide enough detail with respect to vulnerability factors (Eccles, in press). This really refers to the distal versus proximal distinction we have drawn with respect to theory (Ward & Hudson, 1998a). Distal factors attempt to answer "why" questions and address vulnerability factors such as hostile attitudes toward women or intimacy deficits, whereas proximal factors address "how" questions (Alessi, 1992)—for example, how negative affect, perhaps arising from attachment difficulties (a vulnerability factor), functions to trigger disinhibition. The criticism that Level 3 or microtheory (see Ward &

Hudson, 1998a, for details of this nomenclature) models of the offending process lack detail with respect to vulnerability factors misunderstands what theories at this level are intending to achieve. What they are responsible for is the articulation of proximal factors involved and how they are temporally linked into a coherent process. We have been critical regarding how successful relapse prevention has been in this regard, but that is another issue. What it does raise is the more general point that our understanding of the initiating causes of sexual aggression, as opposed to maintaining factors, is still very primitive. It is unfair to hold relapse prevention responsible for these deficits in our broad etiological frameworks (Level 1) or single-factor theories (Level 2), but we would be remiss if we did not note the central puzzles that remain. We have suggested that we do not know enough about how vulnerability to offending develops (Hudson & Ward, 1997a) or indeed the converse—that is, how resilience develops in the face of those factors such as being sexually abused (see Lambie, 1998). Nor do we know much about the offender-specific processes that turn this vulnerability into an initial offense. We also do not know much about that initial offense—specifically, the offense process or pathway typically involved and its relationship to latter offense processes—although initial data suggest that there may well be little relationship (Hudson & Ward, 1999). This refers to the issue of escalation but in a broader and more grounded sense.

Finally, we know far too little about the temporally unstable and situationally specific factors that function as triggers to the initial experience of deviant desire. In contrast to some of the points made earlier, this is an important issue for relapse prevention. The divergence of the literature with respect to the prediction of future offending (e.g., Hanson & Bussière, 1996) and that of modeling the offending process (e.g., Pithers, 1990; Ward & Hudson, 1998b; Ward, Louden, et al., 1995) is salutary. For example, the absence of any predictive relationship between single-occasion measures of mood state administered early in the treatment process (e.g., Beck Depression Inventory) and reoffending has been taken as evidence against the need to address the issue of mood in treatment. We believe that transient and quite possibly situationally specific, strong affective states (positive or negative) are likely to be the proximal initiating cause or trigger of an offense process. The absence of a relationship between a one-off state mood measure during assessment for treatment and reoffending is quite predictable, given the nature of the tasks involved. It is not evidence about initiating causes of any offending process. It is equally premature and potentially dangerous to conclude that interventions aimed at affect and mood regulatory skills are unwarranted. The more general issue, deserving of substantial research effort, is that we are sadly lacking in assessment tools that do other than rely on self-report and are sensitive to both states and the meta-issue of state regulation (see Hudson & Ward, 1997a, for more details).

On a similar theme, although we have made progress with respect to modeling the process involved, at least at the broad level, there is much detail yet to be unpacked. Group facilitators need a relatively generic map of the territory to know when to ask probing questions and when they can safely move on. Marshall and Anderson's (2000) point is well taken—that every detail of an offending process does not need to be known. Indeed, a too fine-grained approach risks being counterproductive by virtue of the nonportability of the resulting map. However, research needs to unpack the issues of what events trigger or provide the excuse for a man to begin contemplating offensive acts. Similarly, we need to know a lot more about what processes actually go on in setting up high-risk situations—in other words, getting access to potential victims—and we lack any models of coercive processes involved in gaining victim compliance both during and after offending. The deepening of our understanding of these processes does not need to translate into an over-obsessional approach to the man concerned, but it would help us in asking the right questions to develop an appropriate understanding of what he actually did. This remains a central challenge for relapse prevention and for those who provide training to treatment providers.

Taxonomy and Assessment

All of these issues inform the broader concern about taxonomy. Ward et al. (1999) have argued persuasively that comprehensive case formulation is both difficult to do well and, moreover, time-consuming. Therefore, they suggest that the most rational strategy may well be to base treatment on diagnosis. This approach to treatment, called in this case a manual-based intervention, is preferred to treatment being based on formulation, unless exceptional circumstances exist. This is essential prescriptive treatment predicated on the determination of class membership. However, very few men who have offended sexually reach criteria for a *DSM-IV* diagnosis of paraphilia (American Psychiatric Association, 1994). Although there are existing attempts at classification (e.g., the work of Knight & Prentky, 1990, and their colleagues), the relapse prevention approach has the capacity to offer the offense process as a potential taxon. We have argued (Hudson & Ward, 2000 [this volume]) that the four proposed pathways, based on a self-regulatory model, have the capacity to articulate both offense-specific and offense-related treatment needs. This classificatory approach has the potential to be used in a manual-based fashion, but the caveats mentioned earlier need to be considered with respect to the possible instability of the offense process.

The other assessment issues involve most centrally deviant sexual arousal (see Konopasky & Konopasky, 2000 [this volume]) and risk assessment (see Proulx et al., 2000 [this volume]). Again, the relationship between the various offense processes that map the territory may be able to be usefully related to both of these issues. Phallometric assessment may help in deciding who should be assessed in this fashion and targeted for arousal reduction interventions. In addition, phallometric assessment has the potential to assist treatment indirectly. For example, the experience of sexual arousal in the laboratory can be used as an illustration of a lapse. This lapse may also have the potential to illustrate the other collateral effects of lapsing, such as the abstinence violation effect and cognitive deconstruction (Ward, Hudson, & Marshall, 1995), which are more likely in the real world (Konopasky & Konopasky, 2000). Moreover, these authors sensibly suggest that attending to the probable offense process in generating the stimuli used in the assessment of sexual arousal is likely to be helpful in comparison to the use of a standardized set that may or may not have any significance to the man undergoing the assessment. Both of these procedures (assessment and intervention) for deviant sexual arousal are contentious and expensive; hence, any means of rationally deciding the smallest number of men to expose to them is likely to be helpful.

Similarly, we have argued that there are good logical grounds for expecting dissimilar rates of reoffending across the differing offense processes. To use that information, as well as to differentially weight treatment responses in light of our concerns about treatment-induced change for some pathways, would be useful to investigate. The interface between relapse prevention and these issues is therefore particularly with respect to the future research agenda.

Implicit in these suggestions is the "what works for whom" question. This is the fundamental question we need to continue to strive toward answering if we are to retain any credibility. We have argued for this in the context of differing offense processes (see Chapter 3) but will not repeat those points here. Outside of those concerns, culture issues are especially important in this regard (see Ellerby, Bedard, & Chartrand, 2000 [this volume]). A major growth point for service delivery in the area of sexual aggression has involved special groups (see Marshall, Fernandez, Hudson, & Ward, 1998). Men from nondominant cultural backgrounds have been of particular interest. As we have argued before, modifications to the basic relapse prevention framework may be needed at three differing levels. Contextual features such as community consultation and involvement, location of treatment facilities, and entry and farewell rituals are all likely to be very important in recruiting the men to the program. This has been described as an issue of cultural safety and attends to the issue of access to services. Second, the style of our intervention may be inappropriate across cultures. For example, although the treatment process we strive to achieve is respectful of the man's dignity and reflects the belief that self-confidence precedes behavior change (Hudson, Marshall, Ward, Johnston, & Jones, 1995), it is still direct and facilitatively confrontational. These characteristics are not appropriate in some cultures and therefore may have a negative effect on treatment processes. Finally, our etiological and offense process models may simply be wrong and culturally inappropriate, and therefore the derived intervention may be in error even if the goals remain acceptable (i.e., reduced reoffending rates). However, each of these levels of potential program and theory modification needs to be driven by evidence, not sentiment. Indigenous cultures have frequently been badly treated by the dominant culture, but this is not a reason for abandoning good clinical evidence-based practice in favor of positive emotional gestures, no matter how well meant.

Finally, with respect to issues specific to relapse prevention is the concerns that various authors have raised recently about the inherent negativity (Mann, 1998) and almost solitary focus on risk (Thornton, 1997). Avoidance goals are associated more often with negative affect and failure. Therefore, a significant challenge for relapse prevention is to relanguage and refocus the model in a positive fashion; an offense-free lifestyle ought to become the slogan rather than a list of things "I am not allowed to do."

A New Model of Delivery

More generally, and very much for the future, is the possibility of an integrated intervention applicable to a number of the related problems for which relapse prevention is ideally suited. Our work on broad aspects of social competency (Hudson & Ward, 1997b, in press; Ward, Hudson, & Marshall, 1996; Ward, McCormack, & Hudson, 1997), particularly on the theoretical work in attachment and intimacy deficits in sexual offenders (Ward, Hudson, Marshall, & Siegert, 1995), has suggested that there may be fewer differences in psychologically oriented treatment needs across offender categories determined by current or predominant offense type. We have typically allocated men to an offense category on the basis of a hierarchical system that fully weights any sexual offense in the man's history. Provided he has no sexual offenses, then any nonsexual violent offending is identified and used to categorize. Those who remain after these two processes have been carried out are labeled nonviolent and nonsexual. This group typically includes men incarcerated for burglary or thefts and drug-related offending. Having allocated men to an offense category in this fashion, we have found few significant differences in the variables we examined (Hudson & Ward, 1997b). For example, out of level and style of dealing with anger, attitudes toward women and sexual assault, loneliness, and fear of intimacy, only anger related both to the predominant type of criminal activity they had committed and to their attachment style. Moreover, we found attachment style had considerably more clinical utility than offense type insofar as it was a better predictor of the individual's experience of interpersonal relationships and general interpersonal style. This clearly reflects the heterogeneity problem that has been referred to many times in the literature. The interesting question is what to do about it.

One possibility is an integrated core program. The essence of what we are suggesting derives quite directly from the underlying central principle of relapse prevention mentioned earlier. If one accepts that a rational strategy on which to base any intervention is a thorough understanding of the offense process, then to categorize according to models of these processes is likely to be a good way to proceed. The obvious limitation to this argument is that we have, as yet, few models of the offense process that have been developed in an adequate fashion. The work that we have done, using grounded theory analyses and offense descriptions or transcripts, is a beginning in this regard. Moreover, our recent theoretically driven model of the offending processes involved in sexual offending extends this using self-regulation as a central construct. This model may indeed have some applicability to the offense process, outside of the sexual area. Similarly, work recently completed by Polaschek (1999) has enriched our understanding of the processes involved in the sexual assault of adult women by white male offenders, at least within the New Zealand context. We have also begun the process of building descriptive models of followed offending both domestically and more generally (Hudson, Dolieslager, & Ward, 1999; Hudson, Drummond, & Ward, 1999).

The rational application of the central principles embodied in the relapse prevention model, at least as it informs treatment, should await the significant work that is required to articulate the offense processes in a broad range of areas. However, there is the intriguing possibility that were we to work with a range of men who had committed various offenses, we may find some strong commonalities both within the processes exhibited by them during their offending and, more critically, the treatment needs they exhibit. For example, it may well be the case that in terms of the self-regulatory model, men who show intact self-regulatory skills while being incarcerated for violent, drug-related, driving-related offending and sexual offending also show very similar treatment needs. The implications of this may mean that for all of these men, the primary focus of the intervention needs to be with respect to goal selection rather than intensive skill acquisition. Conversely, it may be the case that within this range of offender types, there are men who have committed these crimes in a way that reflects considerable skill deficits and relative absence of self-regulatory control—in other words, underregulation. These men likely need to be exposed to different types of intervention when compared with men with intact self-regulation—that which emphasizes the needed skills rather than problems with goals.

An integrated core program, for example, within a correctional system, may well involve motivationally oriented pretreatment work, followed by any intervention that is designed to explicate each man's offense process and the related treatment needs. Subsequent work has the capacity to be highly modularized, and most probably should be psychoeducationally oriented. The exception may be those offenders whose primary problem revolves around the goals they choose to pursue and the related needs. It may be a waste of therapeutic resources, which are never likely to be abundant, to put these men through intensive skill training experiences, given that it is at least possible that such work is irrelevant for them. Of course, this does not negate the point we made earlier that changing these men's goals may expose skill deficits previously hidden by the distorted lifestyles that they have typically created. This remains a fundamental empirical question.

Conclusion

It is appropriate to suggest that there is no such thing as a dumb question. The pioneers in this critical social business of ours did not break through the beliefs that sex offenders could not be treated by simply accepting these beliefs as accepted wisdom. We do not honor the responsibility we have to the women and children who will be abused if we behave as if we have all the answers to the complex set of puzzles sex offending poses for us. Relapse prevention has assisted us in developing what understanding we have managed to achieve so far, and we believe it has the potential to assist us further. The public health perspective, together with the fine-grained attention to detail about what the men we chose to work with actually do, will help us manage better in the future and so continue to justify the resources entrusted to us.

References

Alessi, G. (1992). Models of proximate and ultimate causation in psychology. *American Psychologist, 47,* 1359-1370.

American Psychiatric Association. (1994). *Diagnostic and statistical manual of mental disorders* (4th ed.). Washington, DC: Author.

Andrews, D. A., & Bonta, J. (1994). *The psychology of criminal conduct.* Cincinnati, OH: Anderson.

Beech, A., Fisher, D., & Beckett, R. (1999, September). *Putting back relapse prevention back where it belongs: As a necessary adjunct to successful treatment.* Paper presented at the 18th Annual Research and Treatment conference of the Association for the Treatment of Sexual Abusers, Orlando, FL.

Des Jarlais, D. C. (1995). Editorial: Harm reduction: A framework for incorporating science into drug policy. *American Journal of Public Health, 85,* 10-12.

Eccles, A. (in press). Relapse prevention. In W. L. Marshall, D. Anderson, & Y. M. Fernandez (Eds.), *Cognitive behavioural treatment of sexual offenders.* London: Wiley.

Ellerby, L., Bedard, J., & Chartrand, S. (2000). Holism, wellness, and spirituality: Moving from relapse prevention to healing. In D. R. Laws, S. M. Hudson, & T. Ward (Eds.), *Remaking relapse prevention with sex offenders: A sourcebook* (pp. 427-452). Thousand Oaks, CA: Sage.

Freeman-Longo, R., Bird, S. L., Stevenson, W. F., & Fiske, J. A. (1994). *Nationwide survey of treatment programs and models serving abuse-reactive children and adolescent and adult offenders.* Brandon, VT: Safer Society.

Gendreau, P. (1994, November). *The principles of effective intervention with offenders.* Paper presented at the International Association of Residential and Community Alternatives, Philadelphia, PA.

George, W. H., & Marlatt, G. A. (1989). Introduction. In D. R. Laws (Ed.), *Relapse prevention with sex offenders* (pp. 1-31). New York: Guilford.

Grossman, L. S., Martis, B., & Fichtner, C. G. (1999). Are sex offenders treatable? A research review. *Psychiatric Services, 50,* 349-361.

Hanson, R. K., & Bussière, M. T. (1996). *Predictors of sexual recidivism: A meta-analysis.* Ottawa: Solicitor General of Canada.

Hudson, S. M., Dolieslager, B., & Ward, T. (1999). *A model of offending process in non-domestically violent men.* Unpublished data.

Hudson, S. M., Drummond, S., & Ward, T. (1999). *A model of offending process in domestically violent men.* Unpublished data.

Hudson, S. M., Jones, R., & Ward, T. (1997, October). *Cognitive distortions and generalized empathy deficits in child molesters.* Paper presented at the 16th Annual Research and Treatment Conference, Arlington, VA.

Hudson, S. M., Marshall, W. L., Ward, T., Johnston, P. W., & Jones, R. (1995). Kia Marama: A cognitive behavioural program for incarcerated child molesters. *Behaviour Change, 12,* 69-80.

Hudson, S. M., & Ward, T. (1996). Relapse prevention: Future directions. *Sexual Abuse: A Journal of Research and Treatment, 8,* 249-256.

Hudson, S. M., & Ward, T. (1997a). Future directions. In D. R. Laws & W. T. O'Donohue (Eds.), *Handbook of sexual deviance: Theory and application* (pp. 481-500). New York: Guilford.

Hudson, S. M., & Ward, T. (1997b). Intimacy, loneliness, and attachment style in sex offenders. *Journal of Interpersonal Violence, 12,* 323-339.

Hudson, S. M., & Ward, T. (1998, October). *The self-regulatory model of the relapse process: Empirical evidence.* Paper presented at the 17th Annual Conference of the Association for the Treatment of Sexual Abusers, Vancouver, British Columbia.

Hudson, S. M., & Ward, T. (1999). *Offense process and the self-regulatory model.* Unpublished data.

Hudson, S. M., & Ward, T. (2000). Relapse prevention: Assessment and treatment implications. In D. R. Laws, S. M. Hudson, & T. Ward (Eds.), *Remaking relapse prevention with sex offenders: A sourcebook* (pp. 102-122). Thousand Oaks, CA: Sage.

Hudson, S. M., & Ward, T. (in press). Interpersonal competency in sex offenders. *Behavior Modification.*

Hudson, S. M., Ward, T., & Marshall, W. L. (1992). The abstinence violation effect in sex offenders: A reformulation. *Behaviour Research and Therapy, 30,* 435-441.

Hudson, S. M., Ward, T., & McCormack, J. (1999). Offense pathways in sexual offenders. *Journal of Interpersonal Violence, 8,* 779-798.

Knight, R. A., & Prentky, R. A. (1990). Classifying sexual offenders: The development and corroboration of taxonomic models. In W. L. Marshall, D. R. Laws, & H. E. Barbaree (Eds.), *Handbook of sexual assault: Issues, theories, and treatment of the offender* (pp. 25-32). New York: Plenum.

Konopasky, R. J., & Konopasky, A. W. B. (2000). Remaking penile plethysmography. In D. R. Laws, S. M. Hudson, & T. Ward (Eds.), *Remaking relapse prevention with sex offenders: A sourcebook* (pp. 257-284). Thousand Oaks, CA: Sage.

Lambie, I. (1998). *Resilience and sexual offending.* Ph.D. thesis, University of Auckland, Auckland, New Zealand.

Laws, D. R. (1996). Relapse prevention or harm reduction? *Sexual Abuse: A Journal of Research and Treatment, 8,* 243-247.

Laws, D. R. (1998a, February). *Going for the silver: Harm reduction and sex offender management at the millennium.* Keynote address to the 2000 Beyond Conference, Department of Clinical Psychology, University of Liverpool, and Stockton Hall Hospital, Liverpool, UK.

Laws, D. R. (1998b, September). *Sexual offending as a public health problem.* Keynote address to the meeting of the National Organization for the Treatment of Abusers, University of Glasgow, Glasgow, Scotland.

Laws, D. R. (1999). Harm reduction or harm facilitation? A reply to Maletzky. *Sexual Abuse: A Journal of Research and Treatment, 11,* 233-241.

Laws, D. R., Hudson, S. M., & Ward, T. (2000). The original model of relapse prevention with sex offenders: Promises unfulfilled. In D. R. Laws, S. M. Hudson, & T. Ward (Eds.), *Remaking relapse prevention with sex offenders: A sourcebook* (pp. 3-24). Thousand Oaks, CA: Sage.

Mann, R. (1998, October). *Relapse prevention: Is that the bit where they told me all the things I couldn't do anymore?* Paper presented at the 17th Annual Research and Treatment Conference of the Association for the Treatment of Sexual Abusers, Vancouver, British Columbia.

Marlatt, G. A. (1985). Relapse prevention: Theoretical rationale and overview of the model. In G. A. Marlatt & J. R. Gordon (Eds.), *Relapse prevention* (pp. 3-70). New York: Guilford.

Marlatt, G. A. (1998). *Harm reduction: Pragmatic strategies for managing high-risk behaviors.* New York: Guilford.

Marshall, W. L., & Anderson, D. (2000). Do relapse prevention components enhance treatment effectiveness? In D. R. Laws, S. M. Hudson, & T. Ward (Eds.), *Remaking relapse prevention with sex offenders: A sourcebook* (pp. 39-55). Thousand Oaks, CA: Sage.

Marshall, W. L., Eccles, A., & Barbaree, H. E. (1993). A three-tiered approach to the rehabilitation of incarcerated offenders. *Behavioral Sciences and the Law, 11,* 441-445.

Marshall, W. L., Fernandez, Y. M., Hudson, S. M., & Ward, T. (Eds.). (1998). *Sourcebook of treatment programs for sexual offenders.* New York: Plenum.

Pithers, W. D. (1990). Relapse prevention with sexual aggressors: A method for maintaining therapeutic gain and enhancing external supervision. In W. L. Marshall, D. R. Laws, & H. E. Barbaree (Eds.), *Handbook of sexual assault: Issues, theories, and treatment of the offender* (pp. 343-361). New York: Plenum.

Polaschek, D. (1999). *A descriptive model of the offense chain for rapists.* Ph.D. thesis, Victoria University of Wellington.

Prochaska, J. O., & DiClemente, C. C. (1986). Toward a comprehensive model of change. In W. R. Miller & N. Heather (Eds.), *Treating addictive behaviors: Processes of change* (pp. 3-27). New York: Plenum.

Proulx, J., Perreault, C., & Ouimet, M. (1999). Pathways in the offending process of extrafamilial sexual child molesters. *Sexual Abuse: A Journal of Research and Treatment, 11,* 117-129.

Proulx, J., Tardif, M., Lamoureux, B., & Lussier, P. (2000). How does recidivism risk assessment predict survival? In D. R. Laws, S. M. Hudson, & T. Ward (Eds.), *Remaking relapse prevention with sex offenders: A sourcebook* (pp. 466-484). Thousand Oaks, CA: Sage.

Quinsey, V. L. (1998). Comment on Marshall's "Monster, victim, or everyman." *Sexual Abuse: A Journal of Research and Treatment, 10,* 65-69.

Quinsey, V. L., Harris, G. T., Rice, M. E., & Lalumière, M. L. (1993). Assessing treatment efficacy in outcome studies of sex offenders. *Journal of Interpersonal Violence, 8,* 512-523.

Thornton, D. (1997, October). *Is relapse prevention really necessary?* A paper presented at the 16th Annual Research and Treatment Conference of the Association for the Treatment of Sexual Abusers, Arlington, VA.

Ward, T. (in press). Sexual offenders' cognitive distortions as implicit theories. *Aggression and Violent Behavior.*

Ward, T., & Hudson, S. M. (1996). Relapse prevention: A critical analysis. *Sexual Abuse: A Journal of Research and Treatment, 8,* 177-200.

Ward, T., & Hudson, S. M. (1998a). The construction and development of theory in the sexual offending area: A meta-theoretical framework. *Sexual Abuse: A Journal of Research and Treatment, 10,* 47-63.

Ward, T., & Hudson, S. M. (1998b). A model of the relapse process in sexual offenders. *Journal of Interpersonal Violence, 13,* 700-725.

Ward, T., & Hudson, S. M. (2000). A self-regulation model of relapse prevention. In D. R. Laws, S. M. Hudson, & T. Ward (Eds.), *Remaking relapse prevention with sex offenders: A sourcebook* (pp. 79-107). Thousand Oaks, CA: Sage.

Ward, T., Hudson, S. M., & Marshall, W. L. (1995). Cognitive distortions and affective deficits in sex offenders: A cognitive deconstructionist interpretation. *Sexual Abuse: A Journal of Research and Treatment, 7,* 67-84.

Ward, T., Hudson, S. M., & Marshall, W. L. (1996). Attachment style in sex offenders: A preliminary study. *Journal of Sex Research, 33,* 17-26.

Ward, T., Hudson, S. M., Marshall, W. L., & Siegert, R. J. (1995). Attachment and intimacy deficits in child molesters: A theoretical framework. *Sexual Abuse: A Journal of Research and Treatment, 7,* 317-334.

Ward, T., Hudson, S. M., & Siegert, R. J. (1995). A critical comment on Pithers' relapse prevention model. *Sexual Abuse: A Journal of Research and Treatment, 2,* 167-175.

Ward, T., Louden, K., Hudson, S. M., & Marshall, W. L. (1995). A descriptive model of the offense chain for child molesters. *Journal of Interpersonal Violence, 10,* 452-472.

Ward, T., McCormack, J., & Hudson, S. M. (1997). Sexual offenders' perceptions of their intimate relationships. *Sexual Abuse: A Journal of Research and Treatment, 9,* 57-74.

Ward, T., Nathan, P., Drake, C. R., Lee, J. K. P., & Pathé, M. (1999). *The role of formulation based treatment in sexual offenders.* Paper submitted for publication.

Index

About the Editors

D. Richard Laws was most recently a psychologist with Adult Forensic Psychiatric Community Services in Victoria, British Columbia and coordinator of the Victoria Adult Sex Offender Management Program. He is now retired and self-employed as South Island Consulting. He received his Ph.D. from Southern Illinois University in 1969. While completing his doctorate, he was employed as a medical research associate at the Behavior Research Laboratory, Anna, Illinois. After graduating, he moved to Atascadero State Hospital in California, where he was an experimental psychologist and director of the Sexual Behavior Laboratory from 1970 to 1985. On receipt of a grant from the National Institute of Mental Health, he moved to the University of South Florida, where he was a professor in the Florida Mental Health Institute and director of an outpatient treatment program for child molesters from 1985 to 1989. He is well known in the field of sexual deviation as an innovator in the development of assessment procedures and in program development and evaluation. He is the author of 50 articles and book chapters and an equal number of professional presentations. He currently serves on the editorial boards of the *Journal of Interpersonal Violence, Sexual Abuse: A Journal of Research and Treatment, Trauma, Violence, and Abuse,* and *The Journal of Sexual Aggression.* He is adjunct faculty in the Department of Psychology, University of Victoria, and Associate Member, Mental Health, Law, and Policy Institute, Simon Fraser University. He is a past president of the Association for the Treatment of Sexual Abusers (ATSA) and served on its executive board from 1991 to 1998. He is the editor of *Relapse Prevention With Sex Offenders* (1989), coeditor with W. L. Marshall and H. E. Barbaree of *Handbook of Sexual Assault* (1990), and coeditor with W. T. O'Donohue of *Sexual Deviance: Theory, Assessment, and Treatment* (1997).

Stephen M. Hudson, Ph.D., Dip. Clin. Psyc., is an associate professor in Clinical Psychology and Director of Clinical Training at the University of Canterbury, Christchurch, New Zealand, and a consultant to both the Kia Marama Sex Offender Treatment Program at Rolleston Prison, Department of Corrections and the New Zealand Police. He has worked as a clinical psychologist in both mental health and forensic settings since 1974. His clinical and research interests include social competency deficits in offending and offense processes, as well as issues in health psychology. He currently serves on the editorial board of the journal *Sexual Abuse: A Journal of Research and Treatment.* He is also a member of both the International Sex Offender Treatment Programme Accreditation Panel for H. M. Prison Service, London, England, and the Accreditation Panel: Sex Offender Treatment, Correctional Services Canada. He has published more than 75 articles and book chapters. His coedited books are *The Juvenile Sex Offender* (1993; with Barbaree and Marshall) and *Sourcebook of Treatment Programs for Sexual Offenders* (1998; with Marshall, Ward, and Fernandez).

Tony Ward, Ph.D., is currently Coordinator of the Forensic Psychology Doctoral Program at the University of Melbourne. His research interests include the area of attachment and intimacy deficits in sexual offenders, cognitive distortions, sexual offending theory, and relapse prevention treatment models. He has presented at many international conferences, run workshops, and has approximately 80 publications. He is a coeditor (with W. L. Marshall, Y. M. Fernandez, and S. M. Hudson) of *Sourcebook of Treatment Programs for Sexual Offenders.*

About the Contributors

Jan-Marie Alarcon is a clinical psychologist at Atascadero State Hospital. She received a master's degree in Marriage and Family Counseling in 1985 from Azusa Pacific University, a master's in psychology in 1988, and her Ph.D. in psychology in 1991 from the Rosemead School of Psychology, Biola University. She completed her clinical internship at Patton State Hospital, a forensic mental health hospital, and has worked as a clinical psychologist at Atascadero State Hospital since 1992. She was the treating psychologist for the Sex Offender Treatment and Evaluation Project (SOTEP) from 1992 to1996. Since 1996 she has been a treating psychologist for the Sex Offender Commitment Program (SOCP), under the auspices of the California Welfare and Institutions Code 6600. She has provided court testimony, supervision, and training on the treatment of sex offenders.

Dana Anderson is Clinical Director of the Sexual Offenders Treatment Program at Kingston Penitentiary, a maximum-security prison. She is currently completing her doctoral thesis at Queen's University, Department of Psychology, Canada. She is an active researcher, and among her publications, she is the coauthor of a book on the treatment of sexual offenders.

Jacqueline Bedard is a therapist at the Native Clan Organization's Forensic Behavioral Management Clinic in Winnipeg, Manitoba, Canada. She is involved in the provision of institutional and community-based sexual offender treatment programs and has been particularly active in the development and delivery of culturally appropriate treatment/healing programs for Canadian Aboriginal offenders. She is also the co-editor of *Paths to Wellness: A Gathering of Communities Addressing Sexual Offending Behaviour*. In addition to her work with offenders, Jacqueline has worked with women and children survivors of sexual abuse for more than 10 years. She received her master's degree from the University of Manitoba in 1994.

Anthony Beech is Senior Lecturer in Forensic Psychology at the University of Birmingham, United Kingdom, and Research Fellow for the U.K. government-funded STEP (Sex Offender Treatment Evaluation Project) Team. After his doctorate and postdoctoral investigations into the mechanisms underlying schizophrenic symptomatology at Oxford University, he moved into sex offender research. Over the past 8 years, he has been involved in treatment evaluation and the development of systems to look at treatment need and treatment change in sex offenders. He has written papers on these and other related projects.

Kurt M. Bumby is Clinical Director for the Missouri Division of Youth Services in Jefferson City, Missouri, and serves as the Director of Sex Offender Services at Behavioral Health Concepts, Inc., in Columbia, Missouri. He is a clinical assistant professor of psychiatry, medical psychology, at the University of Missouri-Columbia School of Medicine. In addition, he is a consultant for the Center for Sex Offender Management as well as Liberty Behavioral Health Care Corporation and serves as the state public policy representative for the Association for the Treatment of Sexual Abusers (ATSA). He earned his doctorate in forensic clinical psychology at the University of Nebraska, Lincoln, specializing in the assessment and treatment of sexual offenders. He has presented at numerous conferences and has published several articles and book chapters on sex offenders and other forensic issues.

Adam J. Carter, M.Sc., is currently the Treatment Manager of the Sexual Murderers unit at HMP Brixton. He has worked with sex offenders since 1992 and regularly trains sex offender treatment providers in both the United Kingdom and Scandinavia. He is engaged in doctoral study of risk assessment and prediction of sexual murderers and has developed considerable expertise in working with this client group.

Shirl Chartrand is the Project Manager for Aboriginal Programs at Regional Headquarters, Prairie Region, for Correctional Service Canada. Prior to this she worked at Stony Mountain Institution, where she specialized in the provision of culturally appropriate healing for Canadian Aboriginal offenders. In this capacity, she worked alongside Native Spiritual Elders and was part of the Native Clan Organization's Forensic Behavioral Management Clinic's treatment team. Shirl received her bachelor of arts degree from the University of Manitoba in 1991. She is a woman of Ojibwe and French ancestry who has put to use her Traditional teachings and gifts along with her counseling skills to support the wellness of offenders.

Joanna M. Clarke , MSc., is Head of the Psychology Professional Advisory Unit at HM Prison Service Headquarters. She has worked with sex offenders for most of her career and played a central role in establishing the Sexual Murderers Unit at HMP Brixton. This unit specializes in the assessment, treatment, and research of this complex client group, and Jo Clarke has presented both nationally and internationally on the work of the unit. She is currently researching burnout in sex offender treatment providers.

Emily M. Coleman has been the Director of the Sex Offender Program at Clinical and Support Options, Inc., a community mental health center in western Massachusetts, since 1986. She also serves as a consultant to numerous agencies in New England. She has published in the field and lectures throughout North America, specializing in the assessment and treatment of intellectually disabled sexual offenders. She is on the board of the Association for the Treatment of Sexual Abusers and on the board of Stop It Now, a national organization that focuses on the primary prevention of sexual abuse. She has more than 20 years of clinical and research experience in the assessment and treatment of sexual offenders. She received her master's degree in behavior modification from Southern Illinois University in 1975.

Georgia F. Cumming has been Program Coordinator for the Vermont Department of Corrections sex offender programs since 1986. Prior to holding this position, she was a probation and parole officer for 12 years. She has been instrumental in the development of the external supervisory dimension of the relapse prevention approach to the treatment and supervision of sexual offenders. She has presented workshops extensively throughout North America on the topic of relapse prevention and supervision of sexual offenders. She has coauthored numerous journal articles and two book chapters on adapting the relapse prevention model to the supervision of sex offenders on probation and parole. She is the coauthor of *Supervision of the Sex Offender* (1996).

David M. Day has directed the evaluation component of the Sex Offender Treatment and Evaluation Project in California since the project began in 1984.

Hilary Eldridge is Director of the Lucy Faithfull Foundation, Birmingham, England, which specializes in work with sex abuse, and runs the Wolvercote Residential Clinic for adult male sex offenders. She consults on probation and prison programs and is an international conference speaker. Her publications include the *Therapist Guide for Maintaining Change* and *Maintaining Change: Relapse Prevention Manual for Adult Male Perpetrators of Child Sexual Abuse.* Over the past 8 years, she has developed a specialism in assessing and treating female sex offenders and remaking relapse prevention techniques to suit their specific needs.

Lawrence Ellerby is Clinical Director of the Native Clan Organization's Forensic Behavioral Management Clinic in Winnipeg, Manitoba, Canada. He is also the Canadian Provincial Coordinator on the Board of the Association for the Treatment of Sexual Abusers and has a private practice in which he primarily works with violent and homicide offenders. Along with Native Spiritual Elders, he has advocated for, and developed, a blended model integrating Traditional healing and contemporary treatment for Canadian Aboriginal offenders. He has published extensively in this area. His other clinical interests and publications include the importance of a therapeutic alliance in the treatment of sexual offenders, the impact of providing sexual offender treatment on clinicians, and the treatment of sadistic sexual offenders. He received his Ph.D. from the University of Manitoba in 1998.

Yolanda M. Fernandez is currently a fourth-year doctoral student in clinical/ forensic psychology at Queen's University under the supervision of Dr. Bill Marshall. She graduated with a B.A. (Hons.) in 1994 and an M.A. in 1996 from Queen's University in Kingston, Ontario. In addition to her studies, she is a therapist for the Sexual Offender Program at Bath Institution (a medium-security federal penitentiary). She is an active researcher who currently has made several presentations at international conferences and 17 publications. Her publications include one coauthored book and one coedited book.

Lane Fischer, Ph.D. completed his doctoral studies at the University of Minnesota and practiced psychology in Minneapolis/St. Paul before joining the faculty of Brigham Young University in 1993. He worked at Wilder Child Guidance Clinic in its incest treatment project. He conducted psychological assessment of children and adolescents and led children's survivor groups in conjunction with multiple family treatment of incest. His research focuses on the assessment and treatment of children and adolescents and the psychometric qualitities of instruments such as the Abel Screen and the MMPI-A.

Dawn Fisher is a Consultant Clinical Forensic Psychologist at Llanarth Court Secure Hospital in South Wales and Honorary Senior Research Fellow at the University of Birmingham, United Kingdom. She acts as a consultant on a number of treatment programs and has experience in working with a range of sex offenders, including adolescents, adults, and those who are developmentally delayed. She has written a number of papers and book chapters on sex offenders. She has recently been appointed to the U.K. government joint prison/probation panel for accrediting offender programs.

William H. George is on the faculty at the University of Washington in Seattle where he is Associate Professor of Psychology and Director of the Institute for Ethnic Studies in the United States. He received his doctoral training in clinical psychology and his postdoctoral training in addictive behaviors from the University of Washington between 1976 and 1984. He served on the Psychology faculty at the State University of New York at Buffalo before returning to Seattle in 1992.

Don Grubin is Professor of Forensic Psychiatry at the University of Newcastle and (Honorary) Consultant Forensic Psychiatrist at Newcastle City Health Trust. He received his psychiatric training at the Maudsley and Broadmoor hospitals and the Institute of Psychiatry. He has been based in Newcastle-upon-Tyne since 1994.

James L. Haaven, M.A., is Director of the Social Rehabilitation Unit at Oregon State Hospital. He has more than 20 years of experience in working with sexual offending behavior of persons with developmental disabilities. He consults and trains internationally. He received degrees from the University of Washington and Pacific Lutheran University.

R. Karl Hanson is Adjunct Research Professor in the Psychology Department at Carleton University. He conducted clinical work with sex offenders for the Ontario Ministry of Correctional Services and the Clarke Institute of Psychiatry before starting, in 1991, his current position as Senior Research Officer with the Department of the Solicitor General Canada. His contributions to the sexual offender field have included a meta-analysis of predictors of sex offense recidivism, actuarial risk scales for sex offenders (RRASOR, Static-99), and various empathy and attitude measures. He received his Ph.D. in clinical psychology from the University of Waterloo (Ontario) in 1986.

Aaron W. B. Konopasky is currently a doctoral student in philosophy at Princeton University. His research interests include philosophy of psychology, philosophy of mind, and epistemology.

Robert J. Konopasky received his M.A. from the University of Western Ontario in 1969 and his Ph.D. from the University of Windsor in 1972. Currently he is a professor at Saint Mary's University, Halifax, Nova Scotia, Canada. Working as a clinical psychologist in private practice since 1974, he is the Senior Consultant of the Center for Psychological Services Limited. Since 1989, and under contract from Correctional Service Canada, the center has assessed more than 900 sexual offenders and treated more than 300 sexual offenders in the community. Dr. Konopasky's sexual offender research interests include empathy, cognitive distortions, and PPG. He has presented at many international conferences and run workshops.

Bernadette Lamoureux, B.Sc., is a clinical criminologist. She has been involved for more than 20 years in the sexual offenders treatment program of the Institute-Philippe-Pinel-de-Montréal, a maximum-security psychiatric institution.

Calvin M. Langton is Research Associate with the Sexual Behaviours Clinic, Forensic Program, Clarke Division, Centre for Addiction and Mental Health. He is a doctoral candidate in medical science at the University of Toronto, Ontario. His research interests include cognition and affect in sexual offenders, community management strategies for forensic patients, and the development of cognitive-behavioral interventions for clients demonstrating oppositional behaviors in the treatment context.

Patrick Lussier, M.Sc., is a criminologist. He is involved in both research and clinical activities at the Institut-Philippe-Pinel-de-Montréal, a maximum-security psychiatric institution. He is a Ph.D. student in the field of criminology.

Ruth E. Mann, M.Sc., is head of the Prison Service Sex Offender Treatment Programme and is responsible for the development, implementation, monitoring, and management of all sex offender treatment within H. M. Prison Service (England and Wales). She is interested in ways of developing motivation for change and the application of motivational interviewing strategies within sex offender treatment.

Janice K. Marques is Chief of Program Development and Evaluation for the California Department of Mental Health. She has worked for more than 20 years in the field of sexual abuse as a clinician, researcher, program developer, and consultant. She trained at the University of Washington with G. Alan Marlatt and was a pioneer in adapting his Relapse Prevention model for use with sex offenders. In California, she designed and directed the Sex Offender Treatment and Evaluation Project (SOTEP), a rigorous longitudinal study of the effectiveness of intensive cognitive-behavioral treatment in reducing reoffense among rapists and child molesters. She is past president of the Association for the Treatment of Sexual Abusers (ATSA) and a recipient of that organization's Significant Achievement Award

W. L. Marshall is Professor of Psychology and Psychiatry at Queen's University and Director of the Bath Institution Sexual Offenders Program. He has been working with sexual offenders for 30 years and has published more than 230 articles, chapters, and books. He is presently president of the Association for the Treatment of Sexual Abusers and is the 1999 recipient of the Santiago Grisolia Prize for worldwide contributions to the reduction of violence.

Robert J. McGrath is Clinical Director of the Vermont Treatment Program for Sexual Aggressors, the Vermont Department of Corrections' statewide network of 2 prison and 11 outpatient treatment programs. He has provided training to corrections, mental health, and judicial groups throughout North America and has authored more than 20 journal articles, book chapters, and monographs. He serves as a regular consultant to the National Institute of Corrections and the Center for Sex Offender Management. He is former chair of the Board of Directors of the Safer Society Foundation.

Michael H. Miner is Assistant Professor and Psychologist in the Department of Family Practice and Community Health, Medical School, University of Minnesota. He received his Ph.D. in psychology from St. Louis University in 1984. He has been involved with sex offender treatment and research since 1986, first serving as the research psychologist for California's Sex Offender Treatment and Evaluation Project and then moving to the Program in Human Sexuality at the University of Minnesota in 1992. He currently directs sex offender treatment services at the University of Minnesota's Program in Human Sexuality. He has published numerous papers and book chapters on relapse prevention with sex offenders, sex offender treatment outcome, and forensic and sex offender assessment. His current research focuses on the evaluation of sex offender treatment and the empirical investigation of causal factors for child sexual abuse in adolescents and adults.

William D. Murphy is Professor in the Department of Psychiatry at the University of Tennessee, Memphis. Since 1986, he has served as Director of the University of Tennessee Professional Psychology Internship Consortium and is Director of the Special Problems Unit, a sex offender treatment program operated through the University of Tennessee, Memphis. He has presented workshops and papers at regional and national meetings and has published chapters and journal articles in the sex offender field. He received his B.A. in psychology from Southern Illinois University in 1971 and his M.S. and Ph.D. in 1974 and 1976, respectively, in clinical psychology from Ohio University.

Craig Nelson is Clinical Administrator at California's Atascadero State Hospital. He received his doctorate in clinical psychology from Kent State University in 1980. In addition to his current position, he has previously served as a staff psychologist, Coordinator of Research, Treatment Director of the Sex Offender Treatment and Evaluation Project, and Program Director at Atascadero State Hospital. He has numerous publications in the area of sex offender treatment and assessment. The 1996 recipient of the California Forensic Mental Health Association's William T. Rossiter Award for outstanding achievement in the field of forensics, he is currently a member of the Board of Directors of the Association for the Treatment of Sexual Abusers.

Michael A. O'Connell has a practice in Everett/Mill Creek, Washington, specializing in the evaluation and treatment of sexual deviancy. He earned both his Ph.D. in counseling psychology (1997) and his M.S.W. (1977) from the University of Washington. He began his work in the social service field when, as a navy officer, he was director of a naval correctional center. He has been working with sex offenders since 1981. He coauthored *Working With Sex Offenders* (1990), a guide for judges, prosecuting attorneys, probation officers, and others about whether sex offenders should remain in the community and under what conditions.

William O'Donohue is the Nicholas Cummings Professor of Organized Behavioral Health Care Delivery at the University of Nevada, Reno. He is the director of the Sexual Assault Prevention and Counseling Program and the Victims of Crime Treatment Center. He has published over 150 journal articles, book chapters, and edited books in the areas of sexual offending and victimization, sexual harassment, child memory and forensic interviewing, child custody, sexual dysfunction, behavior therapy, and the philosophy of psychology. Growing interests include managed health care initiatives and the development of a new cognitive behavior therapy. He received his B.S. from the University of Illinois in 1979, an M.A. from SUNY at Stony Brook in 1982, a Ph.D. in clinical psychology from SUNY at Stony Brook in 1986, and an M.A. in philosophy from Indiana University in 1988.

Erin Oksol is a doctoral student in clinical psychology at the University of Nevada, Reno. She is program coordinator and therapist for the Victims of Crime Treatment Center. She is interested in the use of the polygraph with sex offenders and the relationship of behavioral economics to a theory of sexual offending. She is additionally engaged in projects related to children's memory and sexual harassment in children. She received her B.A. from Concordia College in 1996 and an M.A. from Mankato State University in 1998.

I. Jacqueline Page is Assistant Professor in the Department of Psychiatry at the University of Tennessee, Memphis. She serves as a psychologist of the Special Problems Unit, a sex offender treatment program operated through the University of Tennessee, Memphis. She has presented workshops and papers at regional or national meetings and has published book chapters and journal articles in the sex offender field. She received her B.S. in psychology in 1979 and her M.Ed. in educational psychology in 1980 from the University of Georgia. She received her M.A. in 1981 from Middle Tennessee State University and her Psy.D. in 1988 in clinical psychology from the Florida Institute of Technology.

Tamara Penix is a doctoral student in clinical psychology at the University of Nevada, Reno. She is a program coordinator for the Victims of Crime

Treatment Center and is working as an expert therapist on a federally funded grant. She is in the process of publishing several articles and book chapters in ther areas of sexual offending and victimization, reconceptualizing attachment, functional analysis, and expert witnessing. Her interests include the development of a theory of sexual offending, sexual self-control, and the development, evaluation, and dissemination of sex offender treatment. She received a B.A. from Kent State University in 1991 and an M.A. from New York University in 1994. She will complete her Ph.D. in 2001 following an internship with Atascadero State Hospital.

Jean Proulx, Ph.D, is Associate Professor at the School of Criminology, University of Montreal. During the last 15 years he has published, in French and in English, two books and more than 50 articles or book chapters, mainly in the field of sexual aggression. As a researcher and as clinical psychologist he has been involved since 1987 in the sexual offenders treatment program of the Institut-Philippe-Pinel-de-Montréal, a maximum-security psychiatric institution.

Jacqui Saradjian is a Consultant Clinical Psychologist employed by Leeds Community Mental Health Trust within the Forensic Service. She works in association with the Lucy Faithfull Foundation. She specializes in working therapeutically with victims and perpetrators of child abuse: sexual, physical, and emotional. For the past 10 years, she has carried out extensive research into female perpetrators of child sexual abuse and into the specific effects on victims of being sexually abused by females. To date, she has interviewed more than 70 such women and is a well-known conference speaker. She is the author of *Women Who Sexually Abuse Children: From Research to Clinical Practice.*

Susan A. Stoner is a doctoral candidate in clinical psychology at the University of Washington in Seattle.

Monique Tardif, Ph.D., is a clinical psychologist. She has been involved for more than 15 years in the sexual offenders treatment program of the Institut-Philippe-Pinel-de-Montréal, a maximum-security psychiatric institution.

David Thornton, Ph.D., is head of the Offending Behaviour Progammes Unit within H. M. Prison Service (England and Wales). He is responsible for the development and implementation of all rehabilitation programs for imprisoned offenders. His research interests include risk prediction in sexual offenders and the evaluation of evidence-based treatment.